Functional Performance in Older Adults

Functional Performance in Older Adults

Bette R. Bonder, PhD, OTR/L, FAOTA
Professor and Chairperson
Department of Health Sciences
Cleveland State University

Marilyn B. Wagner, MA, PT
Assistant Professor
Department of Health Sciences
Cleveland State University

 F. A. DAVIS COMPANY • Philadelphia

F. A. Davis Company
1915 Arch Street
Philadelphia, PA 19103

Printed in the United States of America

Last digit indicates print number: 10 9 8 7 6 5 4 3 2

Publisher: Jean-François Vilain
Acquisitions Editor: Lynn Borders Caldwell
Production Editor: Arofan Gregory
Cover Design By: Donald B. Freggens, Jr.

As new scientific information becomes available through basic and clinical research, recommended treatments and drug therapies undergo changes. The authors and publisher have done everything possible to make this book accurate, up to date, and in accord with accepted standards at the time of publication. The authors, editors, and publisher are not responsible for errors or omissions or for consequences from application of the book, and make no warranty, expressed or implied, in regard to the contents of the book. Any practice described in this book should be applied by the reader in accordance with professional standards of care used in regard to the unique circumstances that may apply in each situation. The reader is advised always to check product information (package inserts) for changes and new information regarding dose and contraindications before administering any drug. Caution is especially urged when using new or infrequently ordered drugs.

Library of Congress Cataloging-in-Publication Data

Functional performance in older adults / [edited by] Bette R. Bonder,
  Marilyn B. Wagner.
     p.   cm.
  Includes bibliographical references and index.
  ISBN 0-8036-0964-7
  1. Aging—Physiological aspects. 2. Aged—Diseases. 3. Aged—Health
and hygiene. 4. Mental Disorders—in old age.   I. Bonder, Bette.
II. Wagner, Marilyn B.
  [DNLM: 1. Aging—physiology. 2. Aged—psychology. 3. Activities
of Daily Living—in old age.   WT 104 F9789 1994]
QP86.F847 1994
612.6'7—dc20
DNLM/DLC   94-1427
for Library of Congress   CIP

To my mother, Evelyn Bonder, and the memory of my father, Abe Bonder.

B.R.B.

To my husband, Mick, and my daughters, Allison and Lauren.

M.B.W.

Foreword

Functional Performance in Older Adults is a timely book on a topic of growing importance. Greater numbers of people are reaching very old age as a result of biomedical advances and improvements in lifestyle. In fact, the proportion of our population reaching the age of 80 years and beyond is growing at a faster rate than all other age groups, and is likely to increase by over 100% in the final years of this century. Death rates from many of the major diseases have declined, and mortality has been delayed. Moreover, there is growing evidence of similar patterns in the age of onset and the prevalence of various forms of morbidity. Consequently, many more people are reaching very advanced ages only to become ill or disabled by nonfatal diseases. The fact that more people are living longer appears to be normative; so also is the presence of functional dependency and disability in the final stages of life.

Using functional performance as its unifying theme, this edited book provides a collection of chapters focused on the personal, physiological, psychosocial, and environmental contexts of aging for older people. This book will help present and future health care providers assist older people maintain and improve their functional performance. The multidisciplinary perspective represented in the chapters provides a richness and breadth to the discussion of aging and functioning. One of the most appealing features of this book is the way in which various chapters integrate normal aging with the predictable decline that accompanies the degenerative processes and age-related diseases. It is increasingly important that health professionals understand the nature and characteristics of aging in our population today, and develop the skills they will need to have a positive impact on the experience of disability and health dependency in old people.

The organization and features of this book are quite good. Each chapter begins with a clear statement of objectives, which are very useful for the reader. Students will especially appreciate the comprehensive glossary, as well as summaries and review questions. Many of the chapters review some of the 'classic' literature on aging. It is important for students in the geriatric health field to have a historical perspective on contemporary aging, a perspective that requires revisiting some of the earlier sociological and anthropological writings about aging and society.

Like other books on aging, *Functional Performance in Older Adults* opens with a discussion of normal aging. However, aging here is placed in various contexts to emphasize that it is more than a biological or clinical process; that it is a transition between different points in time and place. The process of growing old occurs in many contexts, each of which plays a significant role in the outcomes of aging. The successful health care provider must understand both the processes of aging and the contexts in which people become old, characterized by an increased risk of illness and disability. Historical, cultural, social, demographic, and economic contexts are reviewed at the outset of the book, to assist the health care professional in understanding the implications of social definitions and of the individual experiences of aging. The emphasis on cultural differences is an important reminder that aging is a multicultural and global phenomenon. The number of people who are reaching old age in many of the developing countries is even more dramatic than that in the more developed regions.

Following a delineation of the contexts of aging, this book focuses more on its dominant theme: the importance of functional performance. The third chapter reviews various theories of activity and how the meaning of activity changes over the lifespan. This leads to a discussion of mobility and the changes that come with age, which affect activity and performance. The authors nicely avoid the trap of 'medicalizing' aging by focusing on the implications of normative changes on functional performance, rather than on health status, which is typical in most clinical texts. Neuromuscular, cardiopulmonary, sensory, and cognitive changes are presented with specific implications for the professional — e.g., therapeutic interventions for lessening age-related neuromusculoskeletal changes with age, and exercise interventions to maximize functional performance without increasing the risks for cardiovascular systems that may already be compromised.

Two central chapters dealing with self-care reinforce an important message found throughout the book: functional performance should be promoted and assisted by the health care professional. It is not a medical intervention or a treatment that is administered to older persons. With aging and functional decline, older people are constantly challenged in the performance of basic daily activities that are essential for maintaining their independence. Health professionals need to understand this process and how to assist older people in maximizing the abilities they have. Professionals, as well as older people themselves, need to understand how functioning can be supported by personal and psychological resources, social support, and environmental structures and design. It is also important for the health care provider to understand what motivates self-health care in old age, as well as the barriers and obstacles to such care, and to learn how the professional can enhance effective self-management of chronic illness problems by older people.

Building on the earlier discussion, the chapter on assessment focuses on skills and techniques for the evaluation of self-care performance. It describes the purpose and use of self-care assessment, its various dimensions, and the content and structure of different assessment techniques. Selected instruments are reviewed for their effectiveness in making health care management decisions. This section is 'hands-on,' a change of pace from some of the more theoretical areas of the book.

Chapters on work and leisure return to the earlier theme of aging in different contexts, and the importance of psychosocial and environmental contexts of aging. The work environment provides social identity and a "place to go." Extended leisure time in old age is largely ambiguous, requiring structure or attitudes often different from those of earlier periods in life. Changes in the work role, retirement, and the use of leisure time are potentially pivotal factors in maintaining life-satisfaction, motivation, and healthy levels of physical and social activity. Health care professionals need to be aware of their importance in the functional performance of many older people.

The second half of this book deals with functional performance issues in the later stages of the aging process. Declining capacity to perform the basic activities of daily living often leads too quickly to dependency. Older people, and even many of the professionals who deal with them, may give up when faced with limited performance abilities. The nursing home 'solution' is often applied without consideration of alternative options. The role of the health care provider is to identify those individuals at greatest risk, and provide supportive assistance and services to enable them to maintain their functioning and independence for as long as possible in the community.

Subsequent sections of this book address specific risks faced by older people, including, falls, dementia, depression, and other deficits leading to limitations in functional performance. The reader will come away with a good basic understanding of the etiology and epidemiology of those problems, and a knowledge of the conceptual basis of the health promotion techniques and interventions involved. Throughout this theoretical discussion is an emphasis on skills to help the health professional design intervention programs to assist older people in maximizing their functional performance in the presence of increasing frailty.

The focus on intervention strategies and skills carries well through the next section of the book, which deals with special circumstances in home care, nursing home settings, and rehabilitation programs. Students will gain an understanding of environmental assessment for the purpose of reducing constraints and barriers, and maximizing the physical and social setting when estabilishing program outcomes and designing effective programs.

They will also benefit from reading the section on assistive technology, which reviews a range of high- and low-tech devices to assist older people with limited capabilities. It sends an important message: the health care provider needs to stay informed about changing technology and new devices to assist frail older people.

The closing sections of this book cover three very disparate topics that are essential for geriatric health care providers:

1. The therapeutic relationship, how it is fostered and maintained among professionals, older persons, and their care givers, and how it can be structured to enhance performance outcomes
2. Health care policy and advocacy
3. The common experience of loss among older people

Although the readers of *Functional Performance in Older Adults* are not likely to become expert in three such different areas, it is important for them to understand how their intervention options—as well as their overall effectiveness—will be influenced by the therapeutic relationship they establish, by the impact of cumulative losses on the capacities of older persons and their caregivers, and by the health care reimbursement system and what interventions it is willing to support.

Increasingly, the normal experience of aging is marked by the gradual decline of functional ability. Thus, a major priority for research and practice is to make it possible for greater numbers of older people to continue to live independently in the face of increasing frailty and disability.

Tom Hickey, DrPH
School of Public Health and Institute of Gerontology
The University of Michigan

Acknowledgments

This book began as the result of an informal conversation with Anne Fisher, friend and colleague. It developed out of a lot of arm twisting from Jean-François Vilain, Allied Health Publisher at F. A. Davis, who convinced us that this book needed to be written, and that we could do the project.

As is so often the case, the endeavor was much larger than we ever could have anticipated, and would not have been successful without support, encouragement, and assistance from many people. Jean-François saw the project off to a good start, then placed it in the capable hands of Lynn Borders Caldwell. Lynn provided both substantive expertise and moral support as the work dragged on.

The chapter authors have all made thoughtful and creative contributions. The manuscript reviewers, listed below, went far beyond the usual activities required for their task. They provided numerous suggestions which significantly improved this final version of the text, and their additions are greatly appreciated.

Those who reviewed much, and in some cases, all of the manuscript:

Robert C. Atchley, PhD
  Director of Scripps Gerontology
    Center
  Distinguished Professor of
    Gerontology
  Miami University at Oxford
  Oxford, Ohio

Merlene C. Gingher, EdD, OTR
  Assistant Professor and
    Director of Graduate Studies
  Department of Occupational
    Therapy
  D'Youville College
  Buffalo, New York

Carol Leonardelli Haertlein, PhD,
    OTR, FAOTA
  Assistant Professor and
    Program Director
  Occupational Therapy Program
  University of Wisconsin at
    Milwaukee
  Milwaukee, Wisconsin

Janis McGillick, AM
  Director of Education
  St. Louis Chapter, Alzheimer's
    Association
  St. Louis, Missouri
  and
  Adjunct Clinical Instructor
  Department of Social Work
  University of Illinois at Chicago
  Chicago, Illinois

Ruth U. Mitchell, PhD, PT
  Professor
  Division of Physical Therapy
  University of North Carolina
  Chapel Hill, North Carolina

Mary Ellen Riordan, MS, PT
  Assistant Clinical Professor
  Department of Physical Therapy
  Duke University Medical Center
  Durham, North Carolina

Ronald G. Stone, MS, OTR/L
Associate Professor
Department of Occupational
Therapy
University of Puget Sound
Tacoma, Washington

Ann K. Williams, PhD, PT
Associate Professor
Department of Physical Therapy
Pacific University
Forest Grove, Oregon

Those who reviewed the proposal or individual chapters:

Lynn Arrateig, MA, OTR
Interim Chair/Program Director
Department of Occupational
Therapy
Loma Linda University
Loma Linda, California

Donna El Din, PhD, PT
Distinguished Professor
Department of Physical
Therapy
Eastern Washington University
Cheney, Washington

Anne G. Fisher, ScD, OTR,
FAOTA
Assistant Professor of
Occupational Therapy
Colorado State University
Ft. Collins, Colorado

Bette Groat, OTR
Chair/Assistant Professor
Department of Occupational
Therapy
University of Mississippi
Medical Center
Jackson, Mississippi

John Jeziorowski, PhD, PT
Associate Professor
Department of Health Science
Cleveland State University
Cleveland, Ohio

Donna Joss, EdD, OTR
Program Director
Department of Occupational
Therapy
Worcester State College
Worcester, Massachusetts

Michael R. Williams, PhD
Associate Professor
Department of Social Work
Cleveland State University
Cleveland, Ohio

Karen Bradley and Susan Stupp provided excellent secretarial assistance, and several students, including Jelinda Richer, Wendy Schmidt, and Sheryl Klein, read and commented on some chapters.

Finally, our families, Pat, Aaron and Jordan Bray, and Mick, Allison, and Lauren Wagner, were a constant source of encouragement, and tolerated the Saturdays, Sundays, and evenings spent working on the book, rather than with them. Their contribution is also greatly appreciated.

B.R.B.
M.B.W.

Contributors

Judy Bachelder, PhD, OTR
Assistant Professor
Program in Occupational Therapy
Washington University School of
  Medicine
St. Louis, Missouri

William F. Benson, PhD
Deputy Assistant Secretary for Aging
Administration on Aging
United States Department of Health
  and Human Services
Washington, DC

Rose Anne Berila, MSN, RN
Nurse Manager
Adult, Child and Adolescent
  Psychiatry
The Cleveland Clinic Foundation
Cleveland, Ohio

Bette R. Bonder, PhD, OTR/L, FAOTA
Professor and Chairperson
Department of Health Services
Cleveland State University
Cleveland, Ohio

Anita Bundy, ScD, OTR, FAOTA
Associate Professor
Department of Occupational Therapy
College of Applied Human Sciences
Colorado State University
Ft. Collins, Colorado

Jean M. Canella, EdD (Cand), MOT
Assistant Professor
Department of Occupational Therapy
College of Applied Human Sciences
Colorado State University
Ft. Collins, Colorado

Neal E. Cutler, PhD
Director
Boettner Institute of Financial
  Gerontology
University of Pennsylvania
Philadelphia, Pennsylvania

Elizabeth Dean, PhD, PT
Associate Professor
School of Rehabilitation Sciences
University of British Columbia
Vancouver, British Columbia

Janet G. Dorsett, MA, PhD
Senior Consultant
Booz, Allen & Hamilton
Bethesda, Maryland

Patricia Draper, PhD
Professor
Department of Anthropology
Pennsylvania State University
University Park, Pennsylvania

Ruth E. Dunkle, MSW, PhD
Professor
School of Social Work
University of Michigan
Ann Arbor, Michigan

Dorothy Farrar Edwards, PhD
Assistant Professor
Program in Occupational Therapy
  and Neurology
Washington University School of
  Medicine
St. Louis, Missouri

Henry Harpending, PhD
Professor
Department of Anthropology
Pennsylvania State University
University Park, Pennsylvania

Betty Risteen Hasselkus, PhD, OTR, FAOTA
Associate Professor and Coordinator
Occupational Therapy Program
Department of Kinesiology
University of Wisconsin-Madison
Madison, Wisconsin

Margo B. Holm, PhD, OTR, FAOTA
Professor of Occupational Therapy
University of Puget Sound
Tacoma, Washington
and
Adjunct Assistant Professor of
    Psychiatry
School of Medicine
University of Pittsburgh
Pittsburgh, Pennsylvania

Celia Routh Hooper, PhD, CCC-SLP
Clinical Associate Professor
Division of Speech and Hearing
    Sciences
School of Medicine
University of North Carolina at
    Chapel Hill
Chapel Hill, North Carolina

Linda A. Hunt, MS, OTR
Instructor
Program in Occupational Therapy
Washington University School of
    Medicine
St. Louis, Missouri

Cary S. Kart, PhD
Professor of Sociology
Department of Sociology
The University of Toledo
Toledo, Ohio

Mary Macholl Kaufmann, MSN, RN
Associate Administrator of Resident
    Services and Director of Nursing
Margaret Wagner House of the
    Benjamin Rose Insititute
Cleveland, Ohio
and
Instructor, Gerotological Nursing
Frances Payne Bolton School of
    Nursing
Case Western Reserve University
Cleveland, Ohio

Tim Kauffman, MS, PT
Private Practice
Lancaster, Pennsylvania
and

Adjunct Assistant Professor
Department of Orthopedic Surgery
    and Rehabilitation
Programs in Physical Therapy
Hahnemann University
Philadelphia, Pennsylvania

M. Patricia Laier, PhD
Senior Consultant
Booz, Allen & Hamilton
Bethesda, Maryland

Shirley A. Lockery, PhD
Assistant Professor
School of Social Work
University of Michigan
Ann Arbor, Michigan

William C. Mann, PhD, OTR
Professor
Department of Occupational Therapy
University at Buffalo
Buffalo, New York

Kathryn Perez Riley, PhD
Associate Professor
Department of Psychiatry
Marshall University School of
    Medicine
Huntington, West Virginia

Joan C. Rogers, PhD, OTR
Professor of Occupational Therapy
School of Health and Rehabilitation
    Sciences
and
Assistant Professor of Psychiatry
School of Medicine
University of Pittsburgh
Pittsburgh, Pennsylvania

Kathleen Smyth, PhD
Director of Research Operations
Alzheimer Center
University Hospitals of Cleveland
Cleveland, Ohio
and
Assistant Professor
Department of Epidemiology and
    Biostatistics
School of Medicine
Case Western Reserve University
Cleveland, Ohio

Harvey L. Sterns, PhD
Professor of Psychology and
  Director and Senior Fellow
Institute for Life-Span Development
  and Gerontology
The University of Akron
Akron, Ohio
and
Research Professor of Gerontology
Northeastern Ohio Universities
  College of Medicine
Akron, Ohio

Rein Tideiksaar, PhD
Assistant Professor of Geriatrics
The Mount Sinai Medical Center
New York, New York
and
Director
Falls and Immobility Program
Department of Geriatric and Adult
  Development
The Jewish Home and Hospital for
  Aged
New York, New York

Contents

Introduction

*"In old age, we got a chance to find out
what a human being is, how we could be
worthy of being human. You could find in
yourself courage, and know you are vital."*
    —*Number of Days*, BARBARA MEYERHOFF

This book considers what it means to grow old. Specifically, it examines what it is that older individuals want to do, need to do, what facilitates accomplishment of those tasks, and what interferes. These are not simple matters. Philosophers and researchers have discussed these issues for centuries, and some would suggest that these discussions have yielded more heat than light.

Aging is a complex phenomenon. Among the complicating factors are history, gender, culture, and individual experience. Theory and research have historically focused primarily on describing groups, an approach that explains a great deal about aging in general while explaining little about the experience for a particular individual.

Health care providers, however, are concerned primarily with individuals. In working with the elderly, their focus is on maximizing well-being for each client.

Well-being is also a complex phenomenon. Each health profession has its own definition of the construct, although for elderly individuals the definition frequently centers around function, the ability of the individual (or some body part) to accomplish necessary or desired tasks.

In order to adequately serve the individual, health care providers must comprehend the broader context in which care is provided, and understand the service recipient from a historical, cultural, biological, and social perspective. In addition, they must understand the unique combination of these factors which make the individual what he or she is.

This book is designed to provide this background. It describes both the normal aging process and the factors that can interfere with normal aging. This material is presented from the perspective of functional performance of everyday activities, taking the stance that it is accomplishment of these activities that defines well-being and life satisfaction for elderly individuals. It is a given that an older person will experience some degree of physical or other decline, but it is not a given that this will lead to a commensurate decline in function. Further, if function does decline in a particular area, substitution of other activities may suffice to ensure a high degree of satisfaction for a particular individual.

The book is divided into two main sections. The first focuses on the normal aging process, describing both individual and more global factors that occur during the aging process. It is important to recognize that for most older individuals, normal or "well" aging is typical of most of their later years.

The second main section focuses on those events that interfere with function, the major health and social factors that are likely to occur at some point during the aging process that impede the individual's ability to do what he or she wants to do. These are the sudden events that may mark interludes of dysfunction, or may signify the beginning of the spiral of functional loss. This section also considers what it is that health care providers, particularly allied health practitioners, can do to prevent or minimize the negative effects of these events.

The first chapter is an overview of issues that are significant in understanding the performance of older adults, both what they do and how they accomplish tasks. The chapter defines old age and provides an historical accounting of how that definition has changed over the centuries. The chapter also considers cultural factors that affect how old age is viewed. These discussions are framed in terms of function, the roles and activities of older adults as they change (or remain the same) over time or across cultures.

The following 10 chapters expand on these topics, discussing the theoretical issues related to the meaning of activity, cross-cultural considerations, and our current understanding of the biological and psychosocial process of growing old. While it must be understood that there are wide individual variations, the aging process does have a somewhat predictable sequence, with some decrements in function more likely to occur earlier than others, and some functions more likely to remain intact, or even to improve over time.

Chapter 12 focuses on translating these general understandings into meaningful information about the individual. The person must be assessed in order to determine goals and desires, strengths and abilities, and areas of deficit for that person. This is crucial, for theories and research can tell only part of the story. Each individual has a past, a story to tell that contributed to what he or she is now. Each has a present, for which meaning must be made, and each must come to terms with the future, to make peace with what is to come. Those of us who work with older adults can provide support, help, encouragement, and understanding along the way, but the journey is an individual one.

The second part of the book considers the ways in which the aging process can, at some point almost certainly will, lead to dysfunction. Most older people experience periodic abrupt or severe personal, social, or environmental losses. Physical illness, for example, can lead to sudden major performance decrements. Loss of a spouse can precipitate a debilitating depression which might interfere with accomplishment or even identification of desired activities. Ice on the sidewalk can have devastating effects for an older adult if it leads to a fall.

The roles of allied health care providers in maintaining function and remediating deficits are considered. Since care is no longer provided primarily in in-patient acute care hospitals, discussion includes a variety of health care settings.

Finally, a number of special issues are presented. These include the role of the family in dealing with elderly individuals, the ways in which professionals interact, and the impact of emerging technologies on functional performance for older adults. A discussion of public policy focuses on ways in which therapists may support performance for large numbers of elders through efforts to influence policies that have broad impact.

More and more individuals are spending longer and longer periods in the late stages of life. For these individuals, quality of life and functional ability are crucial considerations. It is in all our best interests to understand the process and develop effective mechanisms for maximizing well-being. It must be recognized that this understanding is a "work in progress." As the elderly population increases, more attention is being paid to its situation. New information emerges daily that increases our ability to provide high-quality service. It is our hope that this volume will generate new questions, the answers to which may further enhance our ability to assist older adults in leading meaningful and satisfying lives.

NORMAL AGING

The data about the aging of the population are clear and are reported in some detail in the pages of this volume. Life expectancy has increased dramatically in the United States since the beginning of the century. In part this is the result of reductions in deaths from infectious diseases such as polio and measles. In part it is due to improved health practices including more healthful eating patterns, reductions in smoking, and the use of seatbelts.

It is also clear that the vast majority of older adults live in the community and adapt well to the changes that are an inevitable part of the aging process. Many of these changes are gradual, giving individuals an opportunity to learn to compensate for any abilities lost. Further, changes are both positive and negative. Individuals may have to adjust to reduced vision or hearing, but they will also have increased life experience and knowledge, which may assist them in coping. For example, as noted in this book, while older adults may learn best in ways different from younger people, they are still quite capable of acquiring new skills and abilities and may offer valuable insights and observations to younger people, as well.

Part I of this book provides an overview of the normal aging process, insofar as it is now understood. The first three chapters offer a context in which the experience of growing old can be placed, outlining the many factors that affect that experience and the importance of activity in making later life meaningful. The following four chapters review the normal aging process as it affects various components of performance. Normal changes in neuromuscular, cardiopulmonary, cognitive, and sensory abilities are considered.

These abilities must be considered in the context of the roles and activities that are important to the individual. Reductions in various capacities may or may not have an impact on actual performance. Chapters 8 through 11 consider the areas from which most individuals choose to construct their constellation of activity.

   This book is written for health care professionals; thus it must include discussion of the ways in which health care providers can assess abilities prior to intervention for the support of performance. Thus, Chapter 12 deals with functional assessment. Although its primary focus is on self-care, the issues raised apply equally to assessment of work and leisure activities.

   In order to provide the best care, providers must understand the individual, his or her history, needs, and wishes. It is essential to think of the person, not just the "disease" or "condition" with which the individual presents for services. Part I of the book is designed to offer that understanding.

INTRODUCTION AND OVERVIEW

A society's quality and durability can best be measured by the respect and care given to its elderly citizens.

—ARNOLD TOYNBEE, *Life after Death*, McGraw-Hill, New York, 1976.

Chapter

Growing Old in the United States

BETTE R. BONDER

OBJECTIVES

By the end of this chapter the reader will be able to:

1 Discuss the problems in defining old age and provide a current definition.

2 Describe historical definitions of aging and identify reasons for increased longevity in modern times.

3 Identify demographic characteristics that affect the circumstances of older adults.

4 Compare attitudes about older adults, and their roles, in Far Eastern, Hispanic, and African-American cultures.

5 Analyze the effect of place of residence on the experience of aging.

6 Identify the impact of cohort effects and individual differences on the experience of aging.

7 Discuss the ways in which cultural, economic, demographic, economic, gender, and individual personality all contribute to the individual's experience of aging.

8 Discuss the importance of these factors to the health care provider working with older adults.

Methuselah lived 969 years (Genesis 5:27). So goes the story in the Old Testament. Everyone would agree that 969 is old. This is one of the few certainties in discussions of old age, however. In some cultures, and at some times in history, individuals who survived to age 40 were considered old, while more recently longevity has increased so that the age at which one is viewed as "elderly" is considerably later in life (though no one in recent times has made it to 969).

This chapter provides an overview of some of the many factors that affect an individual's experience of growing old. The first section focuses on historical perspectives on aging, including the impact of socioeconomic and gender differences on the experience of growing old. A current definition of aging is provided. Then the effect of culture and acculturation is considered. Finally, the import of this information to health care providers is discussed. Place of residence and cohort and individual history are then considered. Finally, the implications of these interrelated factors for care providers are discussed.

Factors such as gender, cultural

background, economic situation, and societal perceptions affect the health care provider's beliefs and actions, as well as those of the client. The provider must understand his or her own beliefs about aging and about the client being served in order to assure that personal biases do not negatively impact on care for the client.

Changing definitions of aging, and differing perceptions of the aging process contribute to confusion about appropriate performance or expected roles and activities of older adults. The evolution of the United States from a primarily agricultural society to a primarily industrial society and now to a technological society has changed the experience of aging. Retirement is a recent development; in earlier times, people rarely lived long enough to retire, and those who lived to old age often had ongoing responsibilities. An historical and cultural context for understanding the aging process is important because, as Achenbaum and Sterns note, "We cannot discuss old age without some sense of trend, of where we are coming from and where we are heading."[1]

HISTORICAL DEFINITIONS OF AGING

What do we mean by old age? Who is elderly? The definition of old age has not been static over time. First of all, there is the basic issue of longevity. In very early civilizations, average life expectancy was 25.[2] This is somewhat misleading because mortality was extremely high during the first year of life. Those who survived that year might hope to reach 30 or so. As time went on, life expectancy soared to 40. This figure remained stable until about 8000 years ago.[2] In ancient Greece, Rome, and Egypt, those males who reached the age of 25 could expect to live to 48 or so. In the Middle Ages, life expectancy was roughly 33 to 35 years, although those in the upper classes might survive to age 50. By the end of the Renaissance, it was increasingly common to find individuals living as long as 70 years. At present, life expectancy is 79 for white women, 74 for African-American women, 73 for white men, and 68 for African-American men.[3]

Impact of Economic Circumstances and Gender

Economic circumstances had an effect on longevity, with nobles surviving longer than their peasant counterparts. Although we no longer identify individuals as peasants or nobles, economic factors continue to have an effect on both longevity and on the experience of aging. Individuals with more money have access to better medical care and information about lifestyle factors (e.g., diet) which contribute to longevity. They also have greater ability to act on that information by, for example, purchasing healthy food.

Gender is also related to longevity. While women generally were thought to reach old age well before men,[2,4] they also lived longer. Thus, at least in terms of perception, women have traditionally spent a much greater proportion of their lives being old than have men.[5] Throughout history, women's life expectancy has been longer than men's,[9] a situation that persists to the present day.

Until recently, old age for women was defined by loss of procreative ability, and for men, by loss of work role.[4] As a precursor of modern circumstances during later life, women had greater difficulty with old age because they were poorly prepared and did not have adequate support, either financial or societal.[5] Older men seemed to retain some prestige through their moral leadership, but women enjoyed no such advantage. Once their husbands died, most were left without financial support since it was males who were employed in paying jobs. Even after pensions were introduced as a benefit of employment, they often stopped at the husband's (probably earlier) death. At present, older women are far more likely than older men to live in poverty.[6] While this may change as more women who have held paying jobs reach old age, the economic situation continues to be bleak for many older women.

However, there were ways in certain societies in which women aged more satisfactorily than men, primarily because of ongoing responsibility for households and for grandparenting activities. These defined roles were a continuation of those women filled earlier in life, minimizing the transition to old age. It may also have been more comfortable, or at least more socially acceptable, for women to accept dependence.[5]

Attitudes about Aging from a Historical Perspective

Ambiguity of attitudes about aging is not new.[1,2] "Perceptions of the aged's worth, as well as their demographic and socioeconomic status have varied enormously according to historical time and societal context."[1]

The Old Testament suggests that older adults should be revered for their wisdom, and the ancient Hebrews believed that long life was accorded to good people. The Greeks, in contrast, believed that aging was unpleasant, as did the Romans. Historically, individuals who might now be considered middle class seem to have had the best experience both in terms of resources and respect.[5]

Historical Roles of Older Adults

Expectations about appropriate or expected functions for older people have varied over time.[4] In ancient and medieval society, contemplation was considered the appropriate use of old age.[7] It was thought of as a time to review life and seek spiritual insights. Other activities, including work, sex, and military activities were not considered appropriate. Particularly for women, marriage was unacceptable in later life.[4]

For years, conventional wisdom sug-

gested that older adults did well in agrarian societies where their supportive efforts were a vital part of the culture.[2] This assumption has been questioned. It seems that although some elderly individuals did have clearly defined roles, care of grandchildren, for example, there was, even then, a perception of them as being too weak or frail to contribute adequately to society. In addition, even in agrarian cultures, individuals who did not live on farms or with extended families were denied these roles.[8]

It is also not entirely clear that older adults in industrial settings have always been denigrated.[2] In some specific areas, including politics, religion, and academe, elderly people have been valued for their experience and wisdom.

CURRENT DEFINITIONS

Current definitions of old age relate to the rapid increase in life expectancy and the growing numbers of individuals who live to reach late adulthood. According to the 1990 U.S. Census, there are now 33 million people aged 65 or over. The elderly population continues to grow, both in absolute numbers and as a percentage of the population, both in the United States and elsewhere in the world.[6]

Neugarten[9,10] identified two groups of older adults, the "young-old," those from 55 to 75 years, and "old-old," those 76 and over. She notes that these chronological definitions are only rough categories, which are an imperfect reflection of individual circumstances and abilities. Where categorization seems necessary, as in public policy, her definitions are increasingly accepted. Some definitions go further to describe a group of "oldest-old" who are 85 or over.

CULTURAL FACTORS IN THE UNITED STATES

Historical and demographic trends are important to understand, but they are not consistent for all cultures. Thus, those who wish to understand the experience of aging must also examine cultural factors.

Demographic trends are a good indicator of some important cultural and societal differences. For example, while the over-80 age group will be 2.5 percent of the population in North America by the year 2000,[11] it will be only 0.3 percent of the African population. This is a 113 percent increase in the number of individuals over 80 in Africa during a 30-year period. In absolute numbers, however, older adults will still be a small group in that society, so that some of the concerns associated with large numbers of older adults will not be pronounced in Africa. In Sweden, 17.4 percent of the population was over 65 in 1990.[12] Sweden is now dealing with the impact on society of this large group of elderly individuals, something the United States will have to address by the turn of the century, and African countries much later.

Perceptions of Aging across Cultures

Perceptions of aging and societal expectations of older adults also vary from culture to culture. The next chapter examines this issue in detail,[13] based on a case example of two African cultures. The example demonstrates the similarities and differences in roles and functions of older individuals, as well as their perceptions of themselves and the perceptions of younger individuals. In a multicultural society, such as the United States, "the failure to attend to . . . variability among and within racial ethnic minority populations in conceptualization . . . may result in biased and distorted perspectives on the racial ethnic minority aging experience."[14]

Nydegger[15] notes that in the United States there are a number of myths about the experience of aging in other societies or at other times. She labels these the "golden age," the "golden

isles," and the "rosy family." The *golden age* refers to the tendency to believe that at some time in the past, older adults were more respected and valued than they are now. The myth includes the notion that older individuals had a place in the family, a role that constituted an important contribution. She cites considerable evidence that this is, indeed, a myth. For example, one common belief is that in preindustrial, agricultural societies, older adults were important as babysitters and homemakers. These roles have never had high status; thus they probably did not confer great importance on those who filled them. Further, in all times and in all societies, the ability to function is vital, and elderly individuals who lost function have almost always been devalued.[16]

The *golden isles myth* reflects the notion that elsewhere in the world older adults are respected and valued and have an important place in society. Most typically, this belief is held about the Far East. While cultural values about aging do vary,[13] it may not be true that there is another place in which being old is generally a positively regarded state. Some examples are provided below.

The *rosy family* refers to a belief that in some cultures, families incorporate the elderly in important and valued positions. This picture of the large, interrelated, and (presumably) happy family may hold for some specific families, and it is more prevalent in some cultures than in others. However, its existence as a cultural phenomenon has been questioned, as can be seen from the following discussion of Oriental cultures.

Aging in Far Eastern Cultures and the Impact of Acculturation on Asian Elderly

Japan is thought of as a country that has special reverence for older adults.[17] There is evidence that this has been true, although not to the extent that some authors have suggested.[18] There is also evidence that respect for elderly individuals has declined as the country has modernized. Fewer elderly Japanese now live with their families,[19] and fewer have clearly defined roles. In addition, dependence of older adults on families and society, which was traditionally viewed as acceptable, is increasingly disparaged. The golden isles and rosy family myths would seem to be only partially true in Japan.

Transplanting Asian culture to the United States changes the situation of older adults more than modernization in their own countries, particularly since the position of elderly individuals is so dependent on the presence of an extended family.[20] Early immigration policies prevented Chinese men from bringing their wives to the United States, and women immigrated alone much less frequently. As a result, many men did not marry or remained alone in the United States, and many did not have offspring to look after and revere them in their old age. This led to increasing acceptance of American views of aging, which were more disparaging.

Acculturation has also had an impact on elderly Japanese-American individuals,[20] again largely because of changing family patterns. The attitude of adult children toward their parents reflects the Asian value of independence, is more pronounced in the United States, given the strong bias in that direction in U.S. culture. The carefully defined responsibilities of children to their parents have, to a large extent, been lost in the transition to North American culture. Even so, some characteristics of Japanese culture are still evident among Japanese-American individuals. It is interesting to note, among other things, that Japanese males living in Hawaii have the longest life expectancy of males anywhere.[21] While genetics and environment probably play a role in this, culture may also have an impact.

Among Vietnamese immigrants, family patterns typical of Asian culture are more likely to be intact.[22] This may be due to their relatively recent arrival in the United States. At present, 75 percent of elderly Vietnamese live with their extended families, and most report positive family relationships. The family appears to provide the primary support; many do not draw on community resources services such as food stamps and subsidized housing. Religious institutions were not mentioned by these individuals as a significant source of instrumental support, although they report that the church is important for other reasons, particularly as a mechanism for expression of older adults' increasing interest in spiritual matters.

Hispanic Cultures

Other cultures also have norms about strong family ties and reverence for the elderly. Most Hispanic cultures reflect these values.[23,24] As in Asian cultures, older adults have specific roles based on their knowledge and wisdom, and children have defined responsibilities related to their parents. However, immigration to the United States disrupts these roles. The move robs older adults of much of the value of their accumulated wisdom. The young may see them as a burden as they struggle to make their way in a new country, and conflict may emerge. This is significant particularly because 55 percent of elderly Hispanic individuals are immigrants,[25] meaning that a large percentage have had no time to learn about their new society.

Positive as well as negative cultural effects of immigration have been identified for elderly Hispanic individuals in several areas. Markides and Lee[26] found that fewer Mexican-Americans than whites experience psychological distress in their later years. Maldonado[24] found that as individuals adjust to the culture of the United States, they may preserve some of their own cultural norms or may internalize U.S. values related to independence and that many experience considerable pride in their children's success.[24] There is evidence that family solidarity continues to be greater in Mexican-American families than in others.[28]

African-Americans

Two somewhat conflicting pictures of older African-Americans emerge from the literature. One is the image of the elderly black person who continues to experience the effects of economic disadvantage evident earlier in life.[29,30] On average, black people of all ages have higher poverty rates than white people, with accompanying poor housing, poor diet, and, ultimately, worse health.[31] Factors that further affect this situation are similar to those for other population groups, for example, married black individuals cope with aging better than those who are widowed, better-educated black individuals better than those less well educated. As a group, however, regardless of other variables, black people are disadvantaged relative to white people.[32]

Many elderly black people find that they must continue to work.[30] Their work is often in the same low-pay, low-status jobs they held earlier in their lives. Those who do not work receive lower social security benefits, on average, than other elderly Americans because they were likely to have had poorer-paying jobs when they did work.

Not all portrayals of aging among African-Americans are as bleak. Coke[33] notes that African-Americans have extensive kin networks and that their survival under difficult circumstances may give them more adequate coping skills than other groups (Fig. 1 – 1). Further, it is clear that older African-Americans have well-identified roles in family, church, and community, which may be a source of great satisfaction.

Interacting Demographic Factors

It should also be noted that many factors are involved in identified cultural differences, and it is not always clear what is cause and what is effect.[34] Nu-

Figure 1 – 1 Intergenerational support influences the aging experience. (From: Memory and Aging. The Alzheimer's Association, Chicago, 1991, with permission.)

merous methodological problems plague research: differences in education, income, and social network patterns may be the variables that really contribute to differing situations. Markides and Lee[26] found that education was a good predictor of well-being for older adults regardless of cultural background. McCallum and Shadbolt[34] note that elderly Mexican-Americans seem to rely primarily on families for support, and white individuals, on friends. Differences in support networks may be the result of cultural differences, or may be the result of other factors, such as immigrant status. It is unclear whether cultural differences persist into old age, or whether the experience of aging serves as, in

McCallum and Shadbolt's words, "the great leveler." Because aging leads to greater individual differences, cultural and societal factors may diminish in importance.

Cultural Determinants of Service Use

The use of formal support services differs considerably among ethnic groups. Recent Russian immigrants are likely to use formal services as their primary support mechanism,[22] while recent Vietnamese immigrants do not. African-Americans are less likely than other groups to use formal services.[35] Mayerhoff[27] presents a moving description of elderly Russian immigrants whose primary source of support is a senior center. In this case, the individuals lived at great distance from their families and felt somewhat abandoned by them. While it is not clear from her study how common this is, it is obviously one way in which cultural changes from one generation to the next, and from one society to another, may be manifested.

Some "cultural" differences are reflected in the kinds of health conditions that are seen by care providers. For example, African-American individuals have a lower life expectancy than white individuals until they reach age 75. At that point, their life expectancy is greater than for any other group.[36] They have greater bone density than white people, possibly reducing risk of injury secondary to osteoporosis. However, they have higher rates of some cancers, diabetes, and cardiovascular disease (until the white population catches up at age 70). Asian individuals have lower risk of some cancers and cardiovascular disease. These differences may be biological rather than cultural, meaning that greater attention to differences among ethnic groups may yield important information about disease prevention.

As can be seen, differences in the experience of growing old are culturally mediated, although it is also clear that cultural factors are not static, and that culture is only one consideration in understanding a particular individual's situation.

PLACE OF RESIDENCE

Another important factor in understanding the experience of an aging individual is the geographic location in which he or she resides. As Rowles[37] notes, place is of crucial importance to older adults. There appear to be significant differences in supports systems and service use among elderly individuals living in rural, suburban, and urban settings.

In rural environments, older adults form strong informal support networks.[37,38] The grocery store, post office, bank, and so on are important sources of socialization and support, and informal networks are effective for both maintaining health and providing care for those who are ill. A clear set of social norms and social supports appear to emerge over time.[37]

While this is true in small towns, those older adults who live at a distance from town may have more difficulty obtaining needed assistance.[39] Rural populations are quite diverse, and distance in and of itself can be a problem.

For suburban elderly individuals, transportation is frequently a problem.[40] They tend to have the greatest financial resources but fewer community resources. This is in part the result of an assumption by service providers that they are more affluent and that income shields them from problems confronted by those with fewer economic resources. Activity patterns, however, are often dictated by access to facilities.

The experience of the urban elderly population is unique in some respects from that of their rural and suburban counterparts, however, and should be considered separately. The urban elderly tend to have greatest access to transportation and services[41] but to have low incomes and inadequate housing. There also tends to be greater ethnic diversity among urban older adults, requiring that the aging process be understood in the context of both cultural and environmental factors.

INDIVIDUAL HISTORY

Personal history and cohort experiences also affect the ways in which individuals respond to growing old. Haan, Millsap, and Hartka[42] indicate that personalities are adaptive and that personal experience influences both feelings about aging and the activities that an individual undertakes.

Some older adults seem to age with grace and to identify old age as a time of special fulfillment.[43] Others seem pessimistic and dour. It may be that personal health is an important factor or that personality factors impact on attitudes about aging. In any event, it is likely that individual personality factors persist in old age, possibly diminishing or increasing somewhat, but rarely altering entirely. These factors will be discussed in greater detail in later chapters in this book.

Cohort effects are also important.[44] A *cohort*, as defined by social scientists, is a group of individuals of the same age who have shared similar life experiences. For example, the Great Depression and World War II affected an entire generation, which is now elderly. For some of these individuals, the result of these experiences has been great bitterness, while others developed increased coping mechanisms that appear to stand them in good stead as they age. Many of these elderly individuals refer frequently to these events and describe them as having a major impact on their lives. Others engage in particular behaviors, exercising extreme caution with money, for example, without necessarily identifying the historical event that shaped the behavior. Other generations have other markers, the Vietnam War, the Reagan era, and so on, which will impact on their beliefs and behavior.

SUMMARY AND IMPLICATIONS FOR SERVICE PROVIDERS

What does all this mean for health care professionals? First, in a multicultural society like the United States, there is no unitary description of old age that adequately conveys the roles and circumstances of all older adults. Individual differences are great, as are cultural differences. Further, roles and circumstances change over time. What is true today may not be tomorrow, and predictions based on current situations may or may not turn out to be accurate. For example, in another chapter in this volume, Sterns, Laier, and Dorsett[45] describe current trends in retirement in the United States, primarily in terms of earlier departure from the work force, followed by reentry into part-time jobs. If labor shortages emerge in this country, public policy would shift to encourage employees to remain in the work force longer; if unemployment rises, incentives to retire might increase. There are changes in cognitive, physical, sensory, and psychosocial performance that occur to some degree in all elderly individuals, as will be discussed in the chapters that follow. Individual differences exist within the broad parameters of these predictable changes. Social and environmental events are also at least somewhat predictable. For example, whether married, single, or divorced, whether from a large or small family, older individuals will experience losses of significant others.

We know that functional limitations increase as individuals age; the largest number occur in the old-old age group.[46] However, statistics reflect averages and do not give any definitive information about individuals.

The challenge for the health care provider is to understand not only the general patterns but also the factors that mold the individual experience of growing older. Every client must be regarded as a unique individual with special interests, abilities, and needs. This is as true for elderly individuals as for those who are younger. However, the common realities of the aging process must also be understood, in order to help the individual prepare for probable changes that will occur.

Health care for older adults is often provided in settings other than traditional hospitals and clinics. Relationships among professionals may be affected by this, as in the case of a home health situation where not all services can be provided. In these situations, it is essential for all health providers to understand the complexity of the situation and the range of possible interventions that may be employed.

Situations that impact on the performance of the older adult are highly complex, including the preceding factors, the normal biological, social, and psychological changes that accompany aging, and the likelihood that a person will have two to three chronic conditions. All health care providers must be sensitive to the myriad interacting considerations that affect function.

Attitudes toward older adults, regardless of historical or cultural context, have always been somewhat ambivalent.[47] Even in those cultures where elders are revered, some ambivalence toward aging is evident. In Japan, where older adults are presumably held in high regard, legislation is necessary to ensure that they are treated with the respect which, culturally, should be theirs by right.[48] As Glascock and Feinman[16] note, ability to function is critical for the elderly in all cultures. "Nowhere is decrepitude valued."[15]

Hendricks and Hendricks[2] indicate that "it is only when mankind is not preoccupied with the necessities of survival that a humane treatment of nonproductive members can be realized." In the United States, most older adults are at that point, although some continue to be primarily preoccupied with survival. In determining what constitutes humane treatment, it is important to note that there is no single group that can be called "the old." In addition, the productivity that characterizes much of this population must be better described and acknowledged. As with other segments of the population, diversity is great. An individual must be considered in the context of personal history, ethnic background, and environment. Without adequate attention to each of these factors, generalizations will fail to reflect personal realities.

This chapter has discussed the historical and societal factors that affect the individual's experience of growing old. The following chapters discuss the normal aging process, the roles and activities that are important to many older adults, and the ways in which health care providers can intervene to maximize function during the later years of life.

As health care professionals, we must focus on well-being rather than on physical health alone. As John Kennedy[48] said, "Our senior citizens present this Nation with increasing opportunity to draw upon their skill and sagacity and the opportunity to provide the respect and recognition they have earned. It is not enough for a great nation merely to have added new years to life — our objective must also be to add new life to those years."

REVIEW QUESTIONS

1. *How have definitions of old age changed over time? What factors have affected these definitions, and how are these factors likely to change definitions in the future?*

2. *How do cultural factors related to roles of the elderly change as immigrant groups are assimilated into mainstream culture in the United States? In what ways are these changes positive, and in what ways negative?*

3. *What factors related to place of residence can health care providers capitalize on to maximize function? What factors should health care providers attempt to minimize?*

4. *In approaching an individual client, what historical factors should be considered? What personal factors? How do these relate to intervention?*

5. Discuss factors that you feel may have particular cohort effects for your generation.

REFERENCES

1. Achenbaum, WA and Sterns, PN: Essay: Old age and modernization. Gerontologist 18:307, 1978.
2. Hendricks, J and Hendricks, CD: The age old question of old age: Was it really so much better back when? Journal of Aging and Human Development 8:139, 1977.
3. US Bureau of Census: Statistical Abstract of the United States 1991, ed 111: US Government Printing Office, Washington, DC, 1991.
4. Covey, HC: Old age portrayed by the ages-of-life models from the middle ages to the 16th century. Gerontologist 29:692, 1989.
5. Sterns, PN: Old women: Some historical observations. Journal of Family History 5:44, 1980.
6. US Bureau of Census: Statistical Abstract of the United States 1991, ed 111: US Government Printing Office, Washington, DC, 1991.
7. Moody, H: The meaning of life and the meaning of old age. In Cole, TR and Gadow, S (eds): What Does It Mean To Grow Old? Duke University Press, Durham, 1986.
8. Hagestad, GO: The aging society as a context for family life. Daedalus 115:119, 1986.
9. Neugarten, B: Adaptation and the life cycle. Counseling-Psychologist 6:16, 1976.
10. Neugarten, B: The rise of the young-old. In Gross, R, Goss, B and Seidman, S (eds): The New Old: Struggling for a Decent Aging. Doubleday Anchor, Garden City, 1978, p 47.
11. Devos, S: Deography: A source of knowledge for gerontology. In Borgatta, E and Montgomery, R (eds): Critical Issues in Aging Policy. Sage, Beverly Hills, CA, 1987, pp 30–52.
12. Swedish Institute: The Care of the Elderly in Sweden. Stockholm, 1992.
13. Draper, P and Harpending, H: Work and Aging In Two African Societies: !Kung and Herero. In Bonder, B and Wagner, M (eds): Functional Performance in the Elderly. FA Davis, Philadelphia, 1992.
14. Jackson, JJ: Guest editorial: Race, ethnicity, and psychological theory and research. Journal of Gerontology: Psychological Sciences 44:1, 1989.
15. Nydegger, CN: Family ties of the aged in cross-cultural perspective. Gerontologist 23:26, 1983.
16. Glascock, T and Feinman, S: A holocultural analysis of old age. Comparative Social Research 3:311, 1980.
17. Palmore, E and Maeda, D: The Honorable Elders Revisited. Duke University Press, Durham, 1985.
18. Tobin, JJ: The American idealization of old age in Japan. Gerontologist 27:53, 1987.
19. Tsuya, NO and Martin, LG: Living arrangements of elderly Japanese and attitudes toward inheritance. Journal of Gerontology: Social Sciences 47:S45–54, 1992.
20. Kalish, R and Yuen, S: Americans of Eastern Asian ancestry: Aging and the aged. Gerontologist 11:36, 1971.
21. Curb, JD, et al: Health status and life style in elderly Japanese men with a long life expectancy. Journal of Gerontology: Social Science (Suppl) 45:206, 1990.
22. Die, AH and Seelbach, WC: Problems, sources of assistance, and knowledge of services among elderly Vietnamese immigrants. Gerontologist 28:448, 1988.
23. Gelfand, DE: Immigration, aging and intergenerational relationships. Gerontologist 29:366, 1989.
24. Maldonado, D Jr: The Chicano aged. Social Work 20:213, 1975.
25. Biafora, FA and Longino, CF Jr: Elderly Hispanic migration in the United States. Journal of Gerontology: Social Sciences (Suppl) 45:206, 1990.
26. Markides, KS and Lee, DJ: Predictors of well-being and functioning in older Mexican Americans and Anglos: An eight-year follow-up. Journal of Gerontology: Social Sciences (Suppl) 45:69, 1990.
27. Mayerhoff, B: Number Our Days. Dutton, New York, 1978.
28. Lawrence, RE, Bennett, JM and Markides, KS: Perceived intergenerational solidarity and psychological distress among older Mexican Americans. Journal of Gerontology: Social Sciences (Suppl) 47:55, 1990.
29. Taylor, RJ and Chatters, LM: Correlates of education, income, and poverty among aged blacks. Gerontologist 28:435, 1988.
30. Gibson, RC: Reconceptualizing retirement for black Americans. Gerontologist 27:691, 1987.
31. Gohmann, SF: Retirement differences among the respondents to the retirement history survey. Journal of Gerontology: Social Sciences (Suppl) 45:120, 1990.
32. Ford, AB, et al: Race-related differences among elderly urban residents: A cohort study, 1975–1984. Journal of Gerontology: Social Sciences (Suppl) 45:163, 1990.
33. Coke, M: Correlates of life satisfaction among elderly African Americans. Journal of Gerontology: Psychological Sciences 47:316, 1992.
34. McCallum, J and Shadbolt, B: Ethnicity and stress among older Australians. Journal of Gerontology: Social Sciences (Suppl) 44:89, 1989.
35. Richardson, J: Aging and Health: Black American Elders. Stanford Geriatric Education Center, Stanford, 1990.
36. Anderson, NB and Cohen, HJ: Editorial: Health status of aged minorities: Directions for clinical research. Journal of Gerontology: Medical Science 44:1, 1989.
37. Rowles, GD: Beyond performance: Being in place as a component of occupational therapy. Am J Occup Th 45:265, 1991.
38. Windley, PG and Scheidt, RJ: Service utilization and activity participation among psycho-

logically vulnerable and well elderly in rural small towns. Gerontologist 23:283, 1983.

39. Coward, RT: Planning community services for the rural elderly: Implications from research. Gerontologist 19:275, 1979.

40. Logan, JR and Spitze, G: Suburbanization and public services for the aging. Gerontologist 28:644, 1988.

41. Cutler, SJ and Coward, RT: Availability of personal transportation in households of elders: Age, gender and residence differences. Gerontologist 32:77, 1992.

42. Haan, N, Millsap, R and Hartka, E: As time goes by: Change and stability in personality over fifty years. Psychol Aging 1:220, 1986.

43. Shneidman, E: The indian summer of life: A preliminary study of septuagenarians. Am Psych 44:684, 1989.

44. Caspi, A and Elder, GH: Life satisfaction in old age: Linking social psychology and history. Journal of Psychology and Aging 1:18, 1986.

45. Sterns, HL, Laier, MP and Dorsett, JG: Enhancing the work and retirement experience of older adults. In Bonder, B and Wagner, M (eds): Functional Performance in Older Adults. FA Davis, Philadelphia, 1994.

46. Katz, S, et al: Active life expectancy. N Engl J Med 309:1218, 1983.

47. Kastenbaum, R and Ross, B: Historical Perspectives on Care. Modern Perspectives in the Psychiatry of Old Age. Brunner/Mazel, New York, 1975, p 421.

48. Kennedy, JF: Elderly Citizens of Our Nation, 88th congress, 1st session, House of Representatives. In Document No. 72. Government Printing Office, Washington, DC, 1963, p 10.

*The idea that one might fear or resent
growing up or old does not evidently
occur in traditional preliterate,
preindustrial societies.* —M. FORTES[1]

*Life is good when you are a young adult.
In middle age you have heavy
responsibilities and you lose your energy
and ambition. Then when you are old you
just lay in the hut, cry for food, and think
about death.* —AN OLD HERERO INFORMANT

Chapter

2

Cultural Considerations in the Experience of Aging: Two African Cultures

PATRICIA DRAPER
HENRY HARPENDING

OBJECTIVES

By the end of this chapter, readers will be able to:

1 Identify the important cultural factors that affect the experience of aging.

2 Compare the roles and activities and the attitudes about aging in two African cultures.

3 Describe the relevance of findings in those cultures to the understanding of aging in other cultures.

4 Discuss ways in which cultural factors relate to the provision of health care services.

In recent years anthropologists have become increasingly interested in aging in different cultures.[2,3] The literature addresses a number of questions about aging and society. How and why does the meaning of aging vary from one society to the next? Do societal complexity and scale predict regular outcomes for elders?[4] Do elders usually fare well in simple, traditional societies where the experience of old people is valued?[5] What effects do culture change and economic development have on older adults?[6,7] As field studies of aging in non-Western societies emerge, scholars realize that attitudes and roles about aging are influenced by myriad cultural factors. No single set of predictors of graceful versus stressful aging are likely to emerge.

Understanding of cultural factors is vital to effective intervention with clients. Culture shapes attitudes and actions, requiring understanding of roles and activities of older adults in a particular culture, attitudes about aging, and the way in which older individuals are valued by the culture. These factors are mediated by:

- The sophistication of the culture
- Changes in a culture over time
- Economic status of the culture
- The degree to which the culture is settled in a specific place
- Demographic factors such as the proportion of older versus younger individuals

However, some beliefs about effects of these mediating variables may not be accurate.

For example, Simmons[8] theorized that in traditional societies the numbers of elders would be few and they would be held in high esteem because of their rarity and accumulation of knowledge. A closer look at older adults in a wide range of societies reveals that economy, material wealth, and settlement pattern are important intervening variables.[9] In societies with a secure economic base and permanent settlements, adults are able to care for elders while maintaining themselves and children. On the other hand, people in more simple societies, such as those of the hunter-gatherers and pastoral nomads, were more likely to practice senilicide or other forms of death hastening.[10] Such treatment, while harsh, was judged by members of these cultures, including the old themselves, to be necessary for the welfare of others.

Perhaps the most persistent theme in studies of aging in non-Western societies is the finding that people are more likely to age well in durable social contexts.[11,12] They age in familiar communities and among the same people they have known throughout their lives, con-

ditions that permit continuity. Another finding has to do with continuity in work roles. Productive work in traditional societies is often minimally differentiated except by sex and only broadly by age. Adult work roles emerge in late childhood or adolescence and are carried out more or less continuously thereafter. Retirement from productive roles is not clearly marked. Instead, people gradually relinquish the more demanding physical tasks as their capabilities wane.

The proportion of the population that is "old" is determined by the birth rate in a population. High levels of fertility lead to broad-based age-sex pyramids of which the old are a small proportion, while low-fertility populations are characterized by columnar age-sex pyramids with high ratios of the old to the not-yet-old. Paradoxically, mortality rates and life expectancy have little effect on the proportion of old people in a population.[13] This is because changes in longevity are reflective of reductions in early mortality due to infectious disease. *Life span*, the hypothesized maximum number of years that humans can survive (assuming the best possible set of genes and most supportive possible environment), is constant at approximately 120 years.

The relative numbers of older adults could conceivably work either for or against their well-being. Large numbers of elderly individuals could be politically visible and active, as is the case at present in the United States. On the other hand, when older people require care, it should be more readily available if there are more children and adults. In cultures where there are fewer older individuals, they might be more highly valued because they represent rare repositories of history and wisdom.

These expectations shape beliefs that influence both policy and intervention for older individuals. There is concern, for example, about changing demographics in the United States as having the potential to create an "excess" of elderly individuals, and an accompanying devaluing or resentment. Similarly, there is increasing attention to the possibility of altering policies about retirement to encourage more gradual reduction in work roles (an emerging trend even without policy incentives).

The case study here discusses the process of aging and the cultural context in which it occurs in two societies in Botswana, Africa: the !Kung Bushmen and the Herero (Fig. 2–1). These studies were carried out as part of a multicultural study of aging in five different cultures around the world.* Several special features of the study make it particularly valuable:

- The !Kung and the Herero inhabit the same regions in Botswana, yet they contrast markedly. Physically, culturally, economically, and linguistically the two groups are dissimilar. Until recently some !Kung have lived as mobile hunter-gatherers. The Herero, much more affluent than the !Kung, have a long historical tradition of pastoralism. These two adjacent groups offer many opportunities for observing the importance of cultural and eco-

---

*This project involved seven investigators in two sites in North America, two sites in Ireland, one in Hong Kong, and the two African sites that we describe in this paper. The overall project was directed by Jennie Keith and Christine Fry.

nomic factors in shaping the aging process.

- Unlike many non-Western populations, older people are not rare among the !Kung and the Herero. People over 60 years constitute about 14 percent of the total population in both groups, a figure similar to percentages of elders in modern Westernized countries. This is unlike Botswana as a whole, where people over 60 comprise 6 percent of the population.[14]
- Although the economic basis of life for the two groups is different, they share very simple levels of technology. With few labor-saving devices, the physical demands of daily life are substantial, posing real challenges for older people.
- The social structures of the two groups are very different. The differing institutional contexts have important implications for the quality of life of older adults.
- Despite marked differences in social institutions, the !Kung and Herero are unanimous in their negative evaluations of aging. Young and old in both groups agree that getting older has no redeeming value. This last finding is especially significant for it illustrates an important lesson for all who learn about another culture. Outsiders with a "view from without" may conclude, given knowledge of certain social norms, values, and institutions in a particular society, that the lives of elders must be good or bad, as the case may be. In fact, the view from without may not be supported by those who have a "view from within."

This study underscores the need for health care practitioners to analyze the cultural factors that may affect clients' expectations about what old age will be like, their plans and goals for this period of their lives, their values and attitudes about being older, and their motivations for engaging in or withdrawing from activity. It also underscores the need to set aside beliefs based on a view from without, possibly the view held by the health care practitioner, and to take the time to

Figure 2–1 Location of !Kung and Herero tribes.

really understand the perspective of those within.

What follows is an ethnographic summary of the !Kung and Herero. We discuss the significance of demography and the demographic structures of our two populations for the work roles of older individuals. We describe the requirements for everyday living for elders and the nature of the work contributions made by them. We detail certain social institutions and customs that have a significant impact on their quality of life. Finally, we report the evaluations by elders themselves of their functional abilities and provide anecdotal accounts of how old people view their own circumstances.

ETHNOGRAPHY OF TWO AFRICAN SOCIETIES

The !Kung

The !Kung of today live by a combination of food producing and food gathering-hunting techniques. They keep small stock, a few cattle, and they tend gardens while continuing to obtain a substantial portion of their livelihood from hunting and gathering. !Kung are extremely poor. Many people own no stock, others own only a few cattle and goats. Without a government-instituted program of food relief, the !Kung would have faced real hunger during the last decade of severe drought in the region. They have a subsistence-level economy, that is, they work directly to feed themselves. Cash has little relevance for them. For further information about the !Kung, see Lee and DeVore,[15] Draper,[16] Howell,[17] Marshall,[18] or Draper and Cashdan.[19]

The residential unit is a village composed of a group of people, ordinarily about 30 individuals, related to each other by kinship and marriage ties with both parents. Most !Kung are monogamous, and marriages tend to be durable. The relationship a person has with his or her spouse is an important source of economic support and companionship.

The Herero

The Herero are pastoralists who live in Namibia and Botswana. They live in homesteads, each owned by a senior male, and manage large herds of cattle, goats, and occasionally sheep. In some areas they have large fields, tended by women and old men. They maintain both patrilineages and matrilineages, that is, they have double unilineal descent. This means that family lines are understood both through the paternal set of relatives and the maternal set, although the matrilineages seem to be more salient.

The Herero in Botswana are descendants of refugees from a German war of extermination begun in 1904 in (the then) South West Africa. In three generations they have changed from impoverished refugees to one of the most prosperous tribes in the region. In the face of this rapid change, they maintain a committed ethnicity: The women all wear Victorian dresses and a unique bonnet, senior male lineage members (men related through specific male lines of descent) maintain ancestral fires that are the center of religious observances and family ceremonies, and there is little marriage outside the tribe.

Marriage is often polygynous, and it is not durable. There is much divorce and even more formal abandonment of marriages, especially when the wife passes the age of childbearing. Many children are born outside of marriage, and there is no stigma attached to unmarried childbearing. Many women, especially from prosperous families, prefer not to marry. Children of unmarried women may remain with the mother's family or move to the biological father's family upon payment of a fee.

The bases of subsistence are milk and occasional meat from the cattle, goats, and sheep, along with the maize meal, sugar, and tea purchased with the proceeds of the sale of livestock. Men are responsible for the management of cattle, while women are responsible for milking the cattle, churning the milk in gourds, and so on. House building and maintenance are stereotyped as the

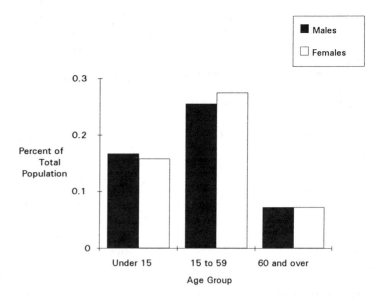

Figure 2–2 Age distribution of !Kung.

work of women, but men are often observed helping with the heavier parts of this task. Excellent descriptions of Herero can be found in papers by Gibson[20,21,22] and Vivelo.[23]

Demography

Both the !Kung and Herero have had low to moderate fertility, and older adults are not scarce. The child-elder ratio is 1.2 for !Kung and 1.1 for the Herero (Figs. 2–2 and 2–3). Despite close similarity in the numbers of available children, the two societies make very different use of the potential labor pool represented by children. The work performance of old people in the two societies varies accordingly.

The demography of the !Kung is described by Nancy Howell.[24] In our census data, 14.3 percent (142 out of 991) of the living population is over 60 years of age. Every seventh person is, by our criterion, old. Old people are promi-

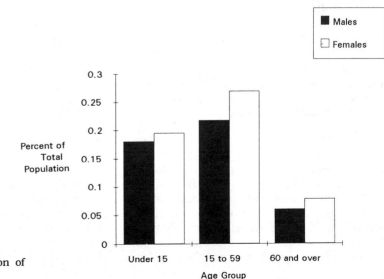

Figure 2–3 Age distribution of Herero.

nent in the daily life of !Kung villages, and the aged nature of this population is immediately apparent to a casual observer.

There are relatively few children; the price of a low birthrate is a scarcity of helpers for the dependent old. It is tempting to draw a parallel between the plight of the !Kung and that of Americans contemplating shortfalls in the social security system because there are not enough younger people paying in.

The proportion of people older than age 60 among the Herero is 14.0 percent (350 out of 2636). The high proportion of older individuals in both societies reflects the low fertility rates of these populations in the past.

Birth rates in both groups continue to increase, so that the proportion of old people is declining. The Herero are recovering from a historical infertility which, in the past meant that the *mean generation time* — roughly the average age difference between mothers and their children — changed from 22 years to almost 30 years.[25] Children of very old women today are also themselves old (a situation that is emerging in the United States at present), while in coming years very old women will have younger adult children to help with their care.

THE DEMANDS OF EVERYDAY LIFE AND AGING

Although the social environment of aging in simple societies may be desirable and generally superior to that of aging in complex industrial societies, the physical environment does not permit older adults to cushion themselves against the physical losses of aging. There are no toilets, no running water, no electricity, no analgesics, no dental prostheses, and few eyeglasses. Furniture is, by Western standards, scarce. Old people do not have soft mattresses, nor do they all have enough blankets to keep warm. The differences between !Kung and Herero are evident with respect to these factors. Many Herero are much more affluent than even the most prosperous !Kung; they have more clothing, more blankets, more substantial housing, and, as we discuss in a later section, more services from junior kin.

!Kung Society

With the exception of the periodic government distribution of maize meal, !Kung work directly to feed themselves. Water is carried from wells as much as 3 km distant from villages. All fuel for cooking or warmth is gathered in the form of firewood, which tends to be scarce near villages. Women, the chief firewood collectors, must walk several kilometers to collect enough firewood for cooking and warmth during the cold season. Not all !Kung clear and cultivate gardens, but those who do have an arduous task felling trees, clearing grass, and fencing against cattle. The work of lifting bucket after bucket of water from wells 30 to 50 feet in depth falls to men of all ages, though women assist in this work when the men are unavailable. Stock must be hand watered for at least 6 months of the year, which is a substantial task.

Everyone who is neither very young nor very old performs the same chores, though with varying degrees of vigor depending upon age and health, and, to some extent, sex. The !Kung have only recently given up their nomadic hunting and gathering lifestyle, with its extremely rudimentary division of labor, and have so far made few concessions to dividing labor more efficiently.

Older people are ambivalent about their declining ability to work. People of all ages value physical vigor and old !Kung are no exception. Physical decline leads to a high level of complaint about aches and pains and the insensitivity of kin in not doing more for them.[26] On the other hand, old people remain physically active as long as possible. They derive self-esteem from the belief that because they are still able to do some things, they are therefore "able to take care of themselves." People in their sixties and seventies make occasional gathering trips to the bush, though always accompanied by younger people. Unless they are quite decrepit, they collect their own firewood and water, gather their own grasses for roof repairs, and collect bush food. Although it takes older people longer to do these things, they are primary providers for themselves and their spouses. House building and maintenance are tasks for which most older people require help. The labor involved is onerous because raw materials must be gathered by hand at a distance and physically transported to the construction site. A major complaint from older people is that their housing is substandard, and, in truth, many older people live in houses that are more dilapidated than the huts of younger, able-bodied people. A few elders continue to live in grass huts of the sort constructed by !Kung when they were living in the bush. These grass huts are simpler for older people to construct and maintain themselves. They complain about their leaky roofs and crumbling walls and may get help from their children. However, when rain or cold sets in, elders whose housing is too shoddy move in for the night with their adult children and grandchildren.

Marriages are much more durable among !Kung than among Herero. Older couples spend a great deal of time together and cooperate in many tasks. !Kung marriage rates among older men and older women are not very different, unlike most other societies where older women are much more likely to be without a spouse. Among men over the age of 60 years, 80 percent are married, while 69 percent of women of the same age are married. Women continue to marry in their late forties and fifties. Some of this is because of the companionship nature of !Kung marriage; many !Kung reported that they like having a spouse, that living by oneself was not good. The scarcity of material goods also encourages remarriage to enable sharing of blankets, utensils, and housing.

Herero Society

There is marked sexual division of labor in Herero homesteads. Women are responsible for building and maintaining the houses and for milking the cattle of the homestead. Houses must be continually replastered, and the roof thatching must be repaired. The difficult job of repairing the houses is made easier because of availability of oxen, sledges, and yokes. Houses are large and substantial. Even women in their sixties and seventies undertake lighter construction tasks, but with age more of the work is accomplished with the help of others, especially children, help which the !Kung cannot count on.

Men manage the cattle. During the hot dry season, water must be lifted by hand from wells dug in limestone, and this involves hours in the hot sun lifting buckets of water several meters or more. The *kraals* (corrals) are constructed of large thornbrush that is cut, dragged in, and piled and that must be replaced frequently. This is heavy work that consumes many days each year. Although typically done by younger men, those in their sixties and seventies were observed dragging heavy thorn trees. Rather than retire, older people gradually relinquish more physically taxing activities to younger people.

Visiting is an important activity for pleasure, business, ritual, and social purposes. Upon the death of a relative, for example, people go immediately to the place of death and remain for as much as a year. Herero families are wealthy enough to entertain visitors for several weeks or months. Middle-aged and old people are frequently away from home on important social or ritual business while younger people remain behind to manage the village. Visiting is a means by which older people maintain control of their social environment; someone too old to travel is too old to be an effective social manager. With their donkeys and horses and high-quality tack, Herero routinely travel hundreds of kilometers even in their late seventies.

While people in their sixties and seventies are relieved of some of the very heavy tasks of daily life, those even older become increasingly dependent upon others for simple care—fetching coals from the fire to light tobacco, boiling water to make tea, fetching firewood and water. Primary caretakers are children, who are trained to obey adults and to have great deference and respect for the elderly. Many children are fostered to others among the Herero, and older people in need of care are often given children who will provide these services.

Among Herero there is an extreme disparity between marriage rates of older men and women: 77 percent of Herero men over age 60 are married, yet only 17 percent of older women are married.

SOCIAL STRUCTURAL CONTEXT OF AGING

In a comparison of !Kung and Herero, outward signs of the value of old people are most prominent among the Herero, but even among the !Kung the old are given respect and support. Different institutions of kinship have significant implications for the social and economic roles played by elderly individuals. As discussed earlier, in Herero culture people act jointly for a variety of purposes (funeral ceremonies, cattle inheritance, marriage arrangements) and make decisions about what individual or family should provide care and housing for a given elder, should that person lack close kin. Herero elders can assume that material and social resources will be provided, regardless of the precise nature and quality of the dyadic relationships that exist.

In !Kung culture, on the other hand, every individual has a different set of family members, and no culturally designated group identity emerges. Each person in !Kung society has kin, but a person's relations with various kin must be personally negotiated and cultivated over a period of years during which a history of reciprocity and "kin feeling" can be generated. For a !Kung,

merely having relatives does not guarantee support, even though there are norms about the ideal behaviors that ought to exist between particular kinsmen. Among the Herero, equipped with unilineal kinship, corporate groups assume responsibilities. The matrilineal group is called *eanda*, and *eanda* identity is important in the life of a person.

!Kung Norms

Among the !Kung, older people enjoy no special status, privileges, or authority as a matter of custom. Some elders are well provided for, but when this occurs, it is the result of having successful adult children with whom the elder is on good terms rather than a sense of obligation to elders.

!Kung children are not trained to show obedience and respect toward adults. They are cooperative but not quick to respond to adult commands and do not maintain respectful silence in the presence of adults.[27] Children are highly valued and are treated permissively by adults who watch them with benign resignation waiting for them to grow up and behave responsibly.[28] Thus, older people assume responsibility for younger, rather than the reverse.

As !Kung adapt more fully to the requirements of a food-producing, rather than a food-collecting, economy it is certain that children will receive more pressure from adults to be responsible and perform chores. Whether or not old people will benefit from these changes remains to be seen.

Unlike many African peoples such as the Herero, the !Kung do not foster their children to wealthier families or those in need of helpers. As a consequence of this and other features of !Kung life—the minimal division of labor, the absence of a hierarchy that obligates younger people to care for elders, and the scarcity of material resources—aging !Kung must continue to fend for themselves. This is accepted matter-of-factly. !Kung report two things that contribute to a good quality of life for an older person: first, having the physical stamina to do for one's self and second, having adult children to provide food when one is too old or infirm to find food for one's self.

Herero Norms

The Herero are proud of their care of older adults in the same way that North Americans are proud of their care and rearing of children. This care is often mentioned as a significant life achievement. One woman described 30 years of care of her father with great satisfaction, while mentioning neither marriage nor children until specifically prompted.

Having children is critical to good quality of life in the later years. They prefer to have children of both sexes: sons to control the cattle that provide food and income and daughters to provide physical care, grooming, laundry, and house maintenance. One 95-year-old woman was identified as someone having difficulty because she had no daughters. She lived in the village of the son of her (deceased) cowife, and this man's wife was the only adult female in the village. She was, however, well groomed, and she said that she received excellent support even though none of the villagers were especially close kin to her.

Approximately 40 percent of children in this society are fostered to others to be raised, or "given" to old people with the expectation that they will later provide routine help and services. Elderly individuals often ask their relatives for children, and as these fostered children leave the village for school, a new child may be given to take up the duties. School-age children spend the week at boarding schools. The resulting absence of children in the villages has made life more difficult for the old.

The way that the ethic of care of older adults mirrors North American values about care of children is striking. Many North Americans believe that care of their children is their primary social responsibility, and they are proud of the achievements of their children. Herero believe that care of the old is their pri-

mary responsibility, and they speak proudly of the services they provide to them.

THE VIEW FROM WITHIN: WHAT PEOPLE SAY

People of all ages were interviewed about their perceptions of the life course. We asked in detail about stages, about transitions from one stage to another, and about the advantages and disadvantages of each stage. In these societies there are no clearly defined stages or celebrations of transitions: no graduation, no puberty ceremony, no job promotion, and no retirement. Even marriage and divorce did not signify much. Herero who could tell us the years of birth and death of all their grandparents did not remember the years in which their own marriages and divorces occurred.

We asked our informants to rate the overall quality of their lives at present, using a digit scale of 1 to 5. A rating of 5 (the thumb) indicated an old person in good health, well cared for, and with adequate resources to ensure food, tobacco, comfortable housing, and so on. A rating of 1 (the little finger) represented someone in poor health with no kin and few resources.

We used the same scheme to obtain ratings of various aspects of function. We asked people to rate themselves on ability to carry out common tasks of daily life like gathering firewood, cooking, and fetching water. We also asked about basic biological functions like vision, hearing, chewing, and picking things up as well as about social tasks like visiting.

For both !Kung and Herero, the single dominant component closely related to age was the ability to do physical work.[29] In other words, the perceived decline in functionality suffered by aging !Kung and Herero is a decline in muscular strength, coordination, and endurance. We did not, to our surprise, find that functions like vision, chewing, hearing, or digestion contributed to the self-perceived age effects.

!Kung Attitudes about Aging

People of all ages regarded old age as a blight. !Kung were unguardedly frank in their disparagement of old age. When asked our standard questions, "What is it like to be old?" or "What are the things that old people do?" younger individuals' responses were immediate and negative even if old people were present. Common responses were: "All you can do is sit and think about death." "When you are old, all of your strength is gone. You can't do anything for yourself." Elderly !Kung were equally negative about their old age. Themes of loss of physical vitality and loss of the capacity to do useful work were most frequently mentioned.

In the five-digit rating scheme, older !Kung consistently rated themselves a 2 or 3 on activities calling for strength and energy such as riding a donkey, walking to another village, carrying firewood, and gathering food. Old women were more likely to rate themselves low across all these tasks than were men.

On overall quality of their lives, !Kung rated themselves higher than we expected. Old men and women both rated themselves on quality of life at 3.5 out of 5, only slightly lower than the 4 that middle-aged people rated themselves. Young people rated themselves as 5. When we asked elderly !Kung to explain why they had given themselves the quality-of-life ratings they did, we received responses like: "Well, I'm still here. I'm old, but I'm not dead. I can still do things for myself." We found these responses surprising given the overwhelmingly negative stereotype of aging. !Kung elders must derive satisfaction from some factors in their lives such as their close relations with their spouses. Those who have living children reside close to at least one of them. Eighty-four percent of men over the age of 60 and 77 percent of women of the same age live within a half-hour's walk of a child if they have at least one child alive.

Herero Attitudes about Aging

The favorable view of the life of older adults, apparent to us as outside observers, was most emphatically not shared by elders themselves. Almost every old person said that old age was the worst and most unpleasant part of the life cycle. Their feelings about old age were almost bitter—they felt that young adulthood was best and that everything that followed was downhill. This evaluation was surprising, given the excellent care and the high social status of old people, and it refutes suggestions that aging is more pleasant in rural African societies than it is in European societies where the aged do not enjoy such high status.[30] Part of this evaluation must reflect the discomforts of the physical environment and lack of basic medical care available to elders in Western society.

The average self-rating on quality of life by old Herero was approximately 2. This pessimistic evaluation was the lowest of the seven sites studied by others doing similar research in North America, Ireland, and Hong Kong; in North America, for example, older people rated their overall well-being as greater than that of younger people, while the Herero perceived that well-being declined with age, far lower than perceived by the !Kung.

Informal reports were similarly pessimistic. For example, a Herero man in his late seventies rated his own well-being as very low, 1.5. He had a beautiful homestead, two loving wives, and large herds of cattle and goats, and he was a local spiritual leader. When we challenged his self-rating, he said:

> Yesterday I walked to the well in the morning [where the cattle are watered, about 2 km from his village] and I saw that the gate post to my well was rotten. I cut a tree, took off the branches, dug up my gate post, and replaced it with the new one. Then last night I was awake half the night with pains in my shoulders, and today I am stiff and sore. I see that I am incapable of useful work any more. I am no good to anyone. I might as well give up and die.

SUMMARY

We have three general conclusions to emphasize as well as an observation about aging in these societies that we believe deserves elaboration:

1. Old people are treated well in both these groups but not because they are scarce. Both the !Kung and the Herero are low-fertility populations so the proportion of the total population that is old is high in both groups.
2. Old people do not appreciate what appears to be the good (!Kung) and superb (Herero) social support that they receive. They have nothing good to say about being old. While we perceived very positive aspects of aging in these societies, members of these societies do not share our perceptions.
3. The social support that old people receive in these societies does not begin to compensate for the absence of comforts routinely available in highly developed societies such as furniture, running water, central heat, antibiotics, analgesics, eyeglasses, and dental prostheses. Old people were, by our standards, remarkably fit, active, and involved. However, they had no choice; they could not withdraw in the way that older people in wealthy industrial societies can.

Compulsory and Voluntary Activity

We were impressed by the extent to which older people in !Kung and Herero society remained integrated into the lives around them and continued to play meaningful social roles. We do not mean to imply that all elders or even most elders are content. However, older people, including the frail elderly, were unfailingly knowledgeable about local events and sensitive to the opinions and attitudes of people with whom they were in daily contact. These elderly can best be described as "involuntarily active."

They lead full and complex lives because people and circumstances do not leave them alone. Until they are very old and near death, they are connected to many people in multiple ways. Not only is there no vocational retirement, there is neither social nor spatial retirement. People cannot choose to become less public and less accessible to the demands of others. Old people are not shielded by money or private housing from involvement in the society. Consequently they are immersed in the everyday wear and tear of living. These experiences are undoubtedly psychologically and physically exhausting at times and may well contribute to morbidity and death among the elderly. On the other hand, the high rates of compulsory participation keep old people challenged by novel events.

IMPLICATIONS FOR HEALTH CARE PROVIDERS

This study of two cultures identifies a number of factors that must be understood in order to evaluate the impact of culture on the experience of aging for any adult. They include:

- The nature of the culture, its economy, family structure, and place and types of residences
- Demographic factors such as birth rate, mortality, marriage and divorce rates
- The demands of life, both in terms of physical and social environment
- Cultural institutions like religion and government; cultural rituals
- Work and leisure roles and the value placed on each
- The degree of choice of activity available to the individual

Interventions planned without attention to these factors risk being irrelevant to the individual. For example, plans to return an individual to his home, with an assumption that adult children will provide support services, work only when there is a cultural expectation that adult children will do so.

Expecting individuals to shift interests from productive to leisure activities will work only when cultural values encourage (or at least do not discourage) this shift.

Clearly, factors other than culture enter into decisions about intervention. Individual differences are discussed in greater detail in the following chapters. Further, culture is not static, so understanding of a culture at a particular point in time will not suffice. Life is changing for the !Kung and Herero and is also changing in the United States. Cultures may overlap to create hybrids, as with Italian-Americans, Chinese-Americans, and other groups. The therapist must be sensitive to these issues both in gathering information and in providing interventions for clients.

Health care providers must understand their own culturally mediated beliefs and examine for each client the degree to which their beliefs match those of the client. For example, a therapist from a cultural background that stresses independence and individualism may have difficulty relating to an older client from a cultural background in which elders are expected to rely on family members and the community to take care of them. This difference in perspectives must be understood and accepted before realistic goals can be set for the individual. Further, the therapist must understand that neither perspective is "right." They are simply differing world views that are both "right" in a particular context.

Thus, in order to interact effectively with clients, the therapist must understand his or her own cultural beliefs and those of the client. While new ideas can be introduced to the client, goals set must reflect his or her wishes and desires based both on individual and cultural differences.

REVIEW QUESTIONS

1. *Describe the ways in which commonly held beliefs about mediating cultural factors may be inaccurate.*

2. *What factors make the external re-*

alities (view from without) of aging more pleasant for the Herero than the !Kung?

3. *Discuss the view-from-within evaluations of the aging experience for !Kung and Herero and some possible explanations for the differences.*

4. *What are the advantages and disadvantages of compulsory and voluntary activities for the elderly?*

5. *Discuss the implications of cultural factors for health care providers.*

REFERENCES

1. Fortes, M: Age, generation, and social structure. In Kertzer, DI and Keith, J (eds): Age and Anthropological Theory. Cornell University Press, Ithaca, 1984, p 99.
2. Fry, C (ed): Aging in Culture and Society. Bergin and Garvey, New York, 1980.
3. Keith, J and Kertzer, D: Introduction. In Kertzer, DI and Keith, J (eds): Age and Anthropological Theory. Cornell University Press, Ithaca, 1984, p 19.
4. Halperin, R: Age in cross-cultural perspective: An evolutionary approach. In Silverman, P (ed): The Elderly As Modern Pioneers. Indiana University Press, Bloomington, 1987, p 283.
5. Cowgill, DO and Holmes, LD: Aging and Modernization. Appleton-Century-Crofts, New York, 1972.
6. Hendricks, J: The elderly in society: Beyond modernization. Social Science History 6:321, 1982.
7. Palmore, ED and Manton, K: Modernization and the status of the aged: International correlations. Journal of Gerontology 29:205, 1974.
8. Simmons, L: The Role of the Aged in Primitive Society. Yale University Press, New Haven, 1945.
9. Press, I and McKoll, M: Social structure and status of the aged: Toward some valid cross cultural generalizations. Aging and Human Development 3:297, 1972.
10. Glascock, AP and Feinman, SL: Toward a comparative framework: Propositions concerning the treatment of the aged in non-industrial societies. In Fry, CL (ed): Dimensions: Aging, Culture, and Health. Praeger, New York, 1981, p 13.
11. Foner, N: Ages in Conflict: A Cross Cultural Perspective on Inequality Between Old and Young. Columbia University Press, New York, 1984.
12. Draper, P: Social and economic constraints on !Kung childhood. In Lee, RB and DeVore, BI (eds): Kalahari Hunter Gatherers. Harvard University Press, Cambridge, 1976, p 200.

13. Newell, C: Methods and Models in Demography. Guilford, New York, 1988.
14. Central Statistics Office: Census Administrative/Technical Report and National Statistical Tables. Government Printer, Gaborone, Botswana, 1983.
15. Lee, RB and DeVore, BI (eds): Kalahari Hunter Gatherers. Harvard University Press, Cambridge, 1976.
16. Draper, P: Cultural Pressure on Sex Differences. Amer Ethnol 2:602, 1975.
17. Howell, N: The Demography of the Dobe !Kung. Harvard University Press, Cambridge, 1979.
18. Marshall, L: The !Kung of Nyae. Harvard University Press, Cambridge, 1976.
19. Draper, P and Cashdan, E: Technological change and child behavior among the !Kung. Ethnol 27:339, 1988.
20. Gibson, GD: Double descent and its correlates among the Herero of Ngamiland. Amer Anthrop 58:109, 1956.
21. Gibson, GD: Herero marriage. Rhodes-Livingston Journal 24:1, 1959.
22. Gibson, GD: Bridewealth and other forms of exchange among the Herero. In Bohannon, P and Dalton, G (eds): Markets in Africa. Northwestern University Press, Evanston, 1962.
23. Vivelo, F: The Herero of Western Botswana. West, St. Paul, 1977.
24. Howell, N: The Demography of the Dobe !Kung. Harvard University Press, Cambridge, 1979.
25. Pennington, R: Unpublished material, 1990.
26. Rosenberg, H: Complaint discourse, aging, and caregiving among the !Kung San of Botswana. In Sokolovsky, J (ed): The Cultural Context of Aging. Bergin and Garvey, New York, 1990.
27. Draper, P and Cashdan, E: Technological change and child behavior among the !Kung. Ethnol 27:339, 1988.
28. Draper, P: Social and economic constraints on !Kung childhood. In Lee, RB and DeVore, BI (eds): Kalahari Hunter Gatherers. Harvard University Press, Cambridge, 1976, p 200.
29. Draper, P, et al: Unpublished material, 1990.
30. Fortes, M: Age, generation, and social structure. In Kertzer, DI and Keith, J (eds): Age and Anthropological Theory. Cornell University Press, Ithaca, 1984, p 99.

Man is an animal suspended in webs of significance he himself has spun.

—CLIFFORD GEERTZ, *Interpretation of Culture: Selected Essays*, Basic Books, New York, 1973.

Chapter

The Psychosocial Meaning of Activity

BETTE R. BONDER

OBJECTIVES

By the end of this chapter, readers will be able to:

1 Describe the process by which a person identifies and labels meaning in specific activities.

2 Describe major theories of activity choice for the elderly.

3 Describe a model for understanding the interrelations among factors contributing to the meaning of activities for an individual.

4 Discuss the ways in which this model might guide intervention.

In *Man's Search for Meaning*, Victor Frankel[1] concluded that those who survive are those who make meaning from their situations, who find activities that give purpose even in the most hopeless circumstances. He emphasized the necessity of finding meaning in life no matter what that life involves. He later[2] described this as a "will to meaning," identifying it as a central human motive.

This chapter examines the factors that contribute to the creation of meaning by an individual. While an activity might be similar for many people, the meaning of the activity varies based on individual characteristics, background, and circumstances. The chapter discusses theories about how meaning is constructed, and then presents and critiques several theories about activity patterns in older adults. Finally, an integrated theory of construction of meaning for older adults is presented as a possible model for health care providers to use in conceptualizing the ways in which older adults construct their activity patterns to address their "will to meaning."[2]

The theme of meaning is prevalent in the literature on the aging process.[3] Society provides less guidance for older individuals than for those who are younger relative to expected and valued roles. "We have not, as a nation, channeled equal energy into defining the nature of those added years or creating positive roles or meaningful institutions through which they may be enjoyed".[3] Thus, for older adults, the search for meaning is highly individual and begins with few reference points.

All individuals strive to find meaning in their lives.[4] They ascribe meaning to their environment, objects around them, social relationships, and to what they do with their time. A vast literature, for example, considers the meaning of work to adults, in terms of social position, life satisfaction, self-concept, and other factors. As is described in a later chapter in this volume,[5] research is under way to develop a model for the meaning of work (or, more broadly, productivity) for older adults. Similar attempts have been made to examine other kinds of activity and to apply what is learned to elderly individuals. For example, researchers have attempted to explain leisure in terms of degree of social interactions or the required level of physical activity.[6,7,8] To date, however, models that describe activity patterns and meanings are not entirely satisfactory, particularly as they apply to an individual's entire constellation of activities.

DEVELOPING MEANING

Meaning is developed through a process of "naming" and "framing," action, and evaluation as described by Schön.[9] The naming and framing process involves examination (explicit or implied) of values, cultural attitudes, and standards. Action and judgment (evaluation) follow from the frame. This process is typically a conscious one and appears to explain the mechanism by which activities are selected and valued. Although Schön focused on the ways in which health care providers make clinical decisions, the model can apply equally well to the ways in which individuals select and value activity.

An example may clarify this process. An individual who engages in an activity will apply a specific *name*, chosen on the basis of social convention and personal values. The activity might be called "word processing." This carries a different connotation than "fooling around on the computer" and will in all likelihood be *framed* as "work." The "work" label carries social meaning as productive, probably paid, and, perhaps, as something done for survival rather than for pure enjoyment. It also carries personal meaning, as a means of identifying social status, personal value as a person skilled in the activity, and so on. *Action*, in this scheme, implies the fact that having labeled "word processing" and identified it as work that carries desired meaning, the individual will engage in the activity. Finally, the individual undertakes an *evaluation* of the activity, deciding whether it indeed meets the expectations of the frame. Should the evaluation be negative, in the sense that "word processing" no longer meets some of the criteria for satisfaction as a "work" activity, the individual might opt for a change. Positive evaluation will encourage continuation of the activity.

Impact of the Environment

Rubinstein[4] describes the manner in which individuals make meaning from their environments. His findings support Schön's[9] contention that individual interpretations are related to the importance placed on environmental conditions, for example, the importance of knick-knacks or the scope of the environment. The work environment in the preceding example is an important component of naming and framing, carrying some values and expectations about the situation in which one should work. Word processing in a large room with many other people, the "secretarial pool," is a very different experience from word processing in one's private study.

Context

Context is also a critical consideration in understanding what an activity will mean to an individual.[4] Lawton noted that "the context in which older people behave is a significant determinant of how they perform."[10] Context includes environment, social or physical circumstances, and history of the individual. Activities change meaning, and meaning changes activities. For example, as people become less able or as their roles change, the meaning of specific activities may alter. Work may become less valued as physical decline occurs or as grandchildren arrive and alter priorities.

Context includes the societal events that are occurring at a given point in time. For example, new attention is being given to the "able elderly"[11,12] because people now live longer and in better health than at any time in history. Retirement is a recent phenomenon but has changed even in the few decades during which it has become common. Individuals spend a much greater proportion of their lives engaged in activities not defined as work as they live longer and choose to leave paid employment earlier in their lives than at any time in the past.

Outcomes

The consequences of an activity are important to the individual's construction of a meaning for that activity.[13] Psychological outcomes, such as a sense of satisfaction in providing service to others, can be essential to self-esteem.[19]

However, pragmatic outcomes are also important.[14] "Getting the job done" matters, in some situations as much as any altruistic motive. Meaning probably involves some interplay of pragmatic and altruistic motives. Outcomes are evaluated by the degree to which they meet both psychological and instrumental needs.

MEANING OF ACTIVITIES: THEORIES

A variety of theories have been proposed to explain activity for older adults. Several of the most prominent will be described here in order of their emergence. Strengths and limitations of each will be considered. Table 3–1 provides a summary of the theories discussed here.

Disengagement Theory

One explanation of activity choice and meaning for older adults is disengagement theory.[15] This theory holds that as people approach old age, they gradually withdraw from those occupations that had previously been important to them and that the level of involvement with ongoing activities is reduced. This occurs, according to theory, both in terms of actual participation and in terms of psychological participation. In other words, older adults do less, and they become less invested in those activities in which they had previously been quite invested. Furthermore, the theory proposes, disengagement is a desirable process. To some extent it can be thought of as preparatory to death, the ultimate disengagement. This "trajectory paradigm" seems to suggest that aging means decline, loss, and withdrawal, with no accompanying gain.[3]

Disengagement theory has been criticized more than supported through the years. Theoreticians and researchers have found a number of factors on which to refute disengagement. These are well documented by Youmans.[16] Among the criticisms on theoretical grounds, the fact that differing types of

TABLE 3-1	**Summary of Theories of Activity of Older Adults**	
Theory	**Theorists**	**Constructs**
Disengagement	Cummings and Henry[15]	1. Elderly withdraw from activity. 2. Elderly disengage emotionally from people and events.
Activity	Havighurst[19]	1. Elderly strive to maintain activity. 2. High levels of activity correlate with well-being.
Continuity	Atchley[33]	1. Elderly attempt to continue activities that were always important to them. 2. Elderly perceive activities as continuous. 3. Elderly adapt activity to compensate for change. 4. Successful aging is characterized by degree of continuity achieved.
Life span	Neugarten[38] Levinson, et al.[39] Erikson[41]	1. Old age is continuation of developmental process, representing new development stage. 2. Tasks specific to the stage can be identified. 3. Successful aging results from accomplishing tasks.
Model of human occupation	Kielhofner[47]	1. Individual is open system. 2. Subsystems are: volition, habituation, performance. 3. Effectiveness of development of each subsystem reflects successful performance.

activities were not considered independently has been cited. For example, the theory does not distinguish between work and social activity, nor does it consider that older adults might respond in different ways to these two types of activity. The theory also does not examine the opportunity older adults have to engage in various activities. The effects of mandatory retirement are not factored into the equation. Nor are individual differences taken into account, so that personal factors that might accelerate or delay disengagement — physical disability, for instance — are not addressed.

Research also offers little support of disengagement theory. While older adults do appear to lose or change some roles, such as paid worker, most of the evidence suggests that these roles are either replaced or modified.[16] A wide variety of studies report little change in number of activities or intensity of participation. It may be, however, that outcome must be carefully specified in order to determine whether disengagement applies to particular components of activity. For example, Lewinsohn and MacPhillamy[17] found that number of activities did diminish but that pleasure in activities did not. Because role loss that

does occur may be welcome or forced,[18] individual response to the loss may be variable. In addition, personality factors intervene, both in perceived loss and in personal choice to withdraw from specific activities.

Activity Theory

Activity theory had its beginnings in the work of Havighurst.[19] This theory proposes that greater activity leads to greater life satisfaction in aging individuals, making activity an end in itself. It suggests that older adults live longer and have more satisfactory adjustment to old age when they maintain the activity levels that characterized their middle years and add new activities to substitute for any lost. There is somewhat more support for this theory than for disengagement. A number of studies have found a relationship between health, both physical and mental, life satisfaction, and activity level.[20-22] In particular, social activity seems strongly correlated with morale in older adults.[23,24] Duellman, Barris, and Kielhofner[25] found that nursing home residents were more satisfied when the facility provided large numbers of activities. Activity theory has also been criticized, however. Some of the criticisms are methodological.[26] For example, almost all the research that examines its characteristics is cross-sectional, making generalization difficult. In addition, definitions of activity have varied across studies, and measures of morale, life satisfaction, happiness, and self-esteem have all been used as outcome measures. The assumption has been that these are all measures of similar attributes, in spite of an absence of supporting data.

The precise kinds of activities in which older adults actually participate are not well understood.[27] Research has repeatedly emphasized work and various kinds of social activity (usually defined in terms of formal or informal status, or in terms of relationships with friends versus family), but it has ignored the probable breadth of activity in which the elders engage or the individual activity patterns.

Methodology aside, the existing data are equivocal. Hoyt and colleagues[28] found that role loss did not diminish life satisfaction. Reich and colleagues assert that "when we encourage people to be active, we cannot automatically assume that all event transactions involved in the activity will have favorable consequences."[29]

A more serious criticism has been raised by those who believe that activity theory is more a reflection of cultural bias than it is of the experience of aging.[30] The work ethic is powerful in Western civilization, and this is reflected in a common belief that the elderly should stay active. This recasting of activity theory as a "busy ethic"[30] provides a different view of activity. It suggests that retirement is justified or validated as a state by continued high levels of activity. It also suggests that health and vigor are maintained by activity and, finally, that only by developing a cultural value that permits retirement can individuals develop true leisure activities. Thus, the busy ethic reinforces both the cultural emphasis on the work and the emphasis on health and well-being. However, Ekerdt argues, reported activity is not the same as actual behavior. Older adults may report themselves as busy in order to put a culturally acceptable face on retirement at the same time that they actually reduce their involvement.

In addition, the elderly may relish the opportunity to "take it easy," to reflect on their lives, and integrate meaning. Life review is an important activity in the later years.[31] The diary of Florida Scott-Maxwell[32] provides a compelling example of the importance of contemplation. She notes that "one has ample time to face everything one has had, been, done; gather them all in: the things that came from outside, and those from inside. We have time at last to make them truly ours."[32] In order to do this, she chose to rely on recordings in a journal, which she describes as "my dear companion."[32]

A problem with both activity and disengagement theory is the relatively narrow scope of each. Both consider largely the pattern and amount of activity. They are not concerned with personal differences, outcome of activity, with role, with meaning, or with context, either cultural or situational. Given the need to develop a comprehensive picture of activity in the elderly, both are inadequately developed.

Continuity Theory

Continuity theory[33,34] proposes that activity patterns in older adults are quite similar to those they had when younger. Individuals who were relatively inactive earlier in life will continue to be so, and those who were more active will continue to find ways to be active. In addition, the types of activities chosen will be similar. Recognizing that abilities change as individuals age, Atchley suggests that "in making adaptive choices, middle-aged and older adults attempt to preserve and maintain existing internal and external structures and . . . they prefer to accomplish this objective by using continuity."[34]

It has been suggested that because of this trend toward continuity, late life development is subtle.[35] Atchley[34] notes that even when retirement of institutionalization occurs, identity crisis is rare. Individuals describe and remember experiences in ways that provide meaning,[3] so that their interpretations of activity will contribute to continuity even if abilities or situations change. Thus, according to continuity theory, change in activity does occur, with substitution to meet ongoing and relatively stable psychological needs. This differs from activity theory, which is a more homeostatic model. Activity theory suggests that substitution is a process of recreating the previous situation, rather than a developmental process.

Society does little to support continuity.[36] Such roles as have been defined for older adults seem to be abruptly different from what they have done before. Work is traded for retirement, parenting for grandparenting, productivity for leisure. None of these new roles has a very well defined set of activities or expectations. Further, demands may be contradictory. Individuals may be encouraged to develop leisure interests but then find their activity disparaged for being unproductive.

Continuity theory has yet to be subjected to much empirical testing. Criticisms focus on the vague language and the difficulties in measuring concepts that are so hard to operationalize.[30] However, this theory does take into account the complicated interactions among factors both external to the person and inherent in personality and beliefs.

One concern raised about continuity theory is the apparent inadequacy of its discussion about change. Interactionists have long asserted that change is inherent in the process of human development.[3] They believe that self-concept is the direct result of interactions with others and that it changes on the basis of those interactions. Kaufman[3] suggests that perhaps both disengagement and continuity theories contribute to an understanding of development, that both reflect a piece of reality. Self-concept, for example, may be influenced by changing interactions with the environment but may also have a stable core component. Similarly, activity may change in some respects while remaining constant in others.

Life-Span Theories

A number of human development theories have also been proposed to explain the activities of older adults.[16] As explained by Youmans, these conceptual models recognize that the experience of aging has changed from generation to generation as new medical advances and differing environmental and societal circumstances have occurred. They also recognize that, like childhood or adolescence, growing old is part of the normal course of life. Simpson[37] suggested that retirement be considered a developmental stage, although demographic changes in recent years suggest that this would be an inadequate framing of old age. Increased longevity, improved health, later childbearing, and so on all affect developmental patterns.

Neugarten[38] identified specific developmental tasks associated with old age, which include acceptance of imminent death, coping with increasing infirmity, dealing with care decisions, and maintaining social ties. Levinson[39] described two stages for older adults. The first is a transition stage, during which tasks involved coping with physical decline and moving from formal authority to more informal life structure. The second, in late adulthood, is characterized by decreasing concern with formal authority, status, and formal rewards, forming a broader life perspective and greater inner resources, and contributing to the wisdom of others.

Some existing research supports the idea that events associated with aging may be normal developmental tasks rather than crises. Ekerdt[40] for instance, reviews the research literature about retirement and concludes that this event does not result in any of the dire consequences that are typically believed to occur. Retired individuals are not more likely to have health problems, die early, or have poor life satisfaction than those who continue to work. Thus, retirement may be a normal life event to which older adults adapt well.

Erikson[4] identifies life stages by presenting conflicts that individuals strive to resolve at various points. During late adulthood, the conflicts he identifies are:

- Generativity (productivity and creativity) versus stagnation
- Ego integrity versus despair

In essence, these conflicts reflect the need to continue to find meaning in the fact of the potential for loss of hope. Individual responses to these conflicts vary and reflect personality, personal circumstances and experiences, societal factors, health, and so on.

While developmental theories hold a great deal of appeal, tasks are not well defined for the later end of the age spectrum. Early childhood development is much better understood, with tasks much more clearly specified and developmental milestones much clearer. Furthermore, even the developmental tasks described appear to ignore the trend toward longer life and greater vigor among the current population of elderly individuals. Levinson's[39] last stage, for example, begins at age 65, although considerable current research focuses on the so called old-old aged 76 and older. This is the fastest-growing segment of the population, with needs that clearly differ from the young-old.[42] Neugarten[43] has gone so far as to say that age is not a useful variable because of the interactive effects of stress, cohort, individual differences, and other factors. If this is so, developmental theories must begin to examine these different phases and distinguish between them.

Model of Human Occupation

Based on early philosophical work by Meyer[44] and Slagle,[45] and later work by Reilly,[46] this theory views activity in terms of general systems theory. The individual is conceptualized as an open,

and therefore changing, system, with a number of subsystems that are directly relevant to activity. These subsystems include volition, habituation, and performance.

The volition subsystem encompasses personal causation, values, and interests.[47,48] According to Kielhofner,[47] "One of the first discoveries of life is the connection between personal intention, action, and its consequences." The individual must identify those actions that are important and that he or she wishes to pursue.

Desire to act is insufficient to ensure ability to act, however. Roles must be identified and habits developed. These processes constitute the habituation subsystem. In many ways, roles dictate activity patterns. For example, the role of mother involves such activities as dressing children, cooking, and talking with teachers. Roles alone, however, are not sufficient to fully explain activity. Mothers differ greatly in the specific types of activities they undertake in that role, selecting from the many activities that comprise the role. One mother might take her children to see her office, while another sews elaborate Halloween costumes.

Even when values, goals, and roles have been identified, ability to perform impacts on activity. Skills must be developed that permit the mother to cook, to talk with her children, and so on. Skills include the ability to perceive and respond, to process information, and to communicate.

In viewing the meaning of activity to older adults in this framework, each of the subsystems must be considered.[29] A problem that becomes immediately obvious is the absence of well-explained roles for older adults, lack of information about values, habits, and, to some extent, even skills.

TOWARD AN INTEGRATED MODEL

A problem with all the theories described to this point is the failure to examine the true complexity of activity and its meaning. The more complex the model, the more difficult it is to validate. However, without further elaboration, each of the preceding theories is incomplete, and one has the feeling of being a blind person examining the proverbial elephant. Table 3–1 shows the major characteristics of the theories discussed.

What follows is a proposed model of the process by which meaning is constructed by an individual and translated into a set of roles and activities. It is an effort to account for a wide array of factors, some of which have been identified in the theories just discussed, others of which remain to be developed. A comprehensive model should take into account the following:

- Factors leading to activity choice, including environmental and individual sources of meaning
- The internal processes that lead to activity choice, specifically, naming and framing
- Selection of roles and activities (including type of activity, the situational context in which it is undertaken, activity pattern, and affect associated with the activity)
- Evaluation of outcomes of the activity

Figure 3–1 shows the relationships among these factors.

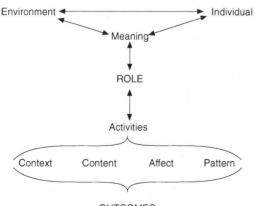

Figure 3–1 How meaning is constructed for activities.

Factors Leading to Activity Choice

Environmental context includes social and cultural factors. The work ethic[3] is an example of a cultural value that affects personal choice. Historical, that is, cohort, factors also fit this category. Thus, living through the Great Depression or the "Great War" might be expected to influence perceptions.

Individual needs and perceptions also affect activity choice. As Kaufman has said, "People are not passive observers and reactors to their surroundings; rather they actively participate in their environment, creating social reality and sense of self as they engage in community life and as they interpret and evaluate the meaning of their interactions with others."[3] Psychological factors such as motivation, self-concept, and coping strategies are among those that influence activities. Needs may be instrumental (hunger or pain) or psychological (e.g., the need for approval or a wish to help others).

Internal Processing

Schön[9] has called this process "naming and framing." Whatever the label, this is the process by which environmental and individual influences are integrated into a set of actions. Kaufman[3] suggests that this occurs through identification of important themes. She has found several themes that are fairly consistent in stories told by older adults. Among them are:

- Affective ties
- Work
- Personal achievement and social status

"Affective ties" refers to the social constellation described by the individual. "Work" includes those activities defined as "productive," including volunteer work and homemaking activities. "Personal achievement and social status" are self-evaluations that are tied to activity, both promoting specific choices and reflecting assessment once the activity is done.

Choosing Actions

Based on the factors above, individuals select a set of roles that reflect environmental imperatives, as well as individual and cohort experiences. While one's roles are not entirely open to choice, the interpretation of their meaning is, to a large extent, within the control of the individual. For example, one cannot choose to be a son or daughter but can define the meaning of the role and its expression. One may need to work for reasons of survival, but the nature of the worker role is internally mediated.

Thus, once a role has been identified, a set of activities must be chosen to express it, based on situational context, content of the activity, affect associated with the activity, and activity pattern. The activities that constitute a role may vary widely depending on these factors. *Situational context* refers to the specific conditions of the individual. This might include living arrangement, economic resources, or responsibility to others. *Content of the activity* refers to the nature of the specific activity chosen, the physical, cognitive, and psychosocial characteristics needed to undertake the activity as well as the characteristics of the activity (e.g., social versus solitary, formal versus informal). *Affect* refers to the feelings that accompany the activity, for example, pleasure or frustration. Finally, *pattern* refers to the configuration of activities undertaken by the individual. All these factors are evident in the activity choice of the individual and contribute to the final factor in activity choice, that is, the outcome. The worker role may be one that is essential, but the choice of type of work, work location, and demands of the job are largely mediated by the naming and framing process that creates the picture of a "worker" for a specific individual.

Outcome and Evaluation

Evaluation of action is of primary importance in analyzing activity and meaning. It is through the outcomes, satisfying and unsatisfying, that meaning can be inferred. This evaluative component of activity choice is the process by which a person determines whether to continue a particular activity or select new activities. Outcomes that have been identified in the literature include:

- Subjective well-being
- Productivity
- Health
- Self-maintenance

Activities that lead to negative outcomes, as evaluated by the individual, are more likely to be discontinued, while those that lead to positive outcomes are likely to be continued. The woman shown in Fig. 3–2 derived great satisfaction by combining her love of music with her need to remember her heritage and was, therefore eager to seek opportunities to enjoy playing the piano.

Figure 3–2 Playing traditional songs on the piano helps this woman maintain emotional ties with her ethnic heritage. (Courtesy of Menorah Park Nursing Home, Cleveland, Ohio.)

Much of the existing literature that examines roles and activities of older adults has concentrated on examination of outcomes. Subjective well-being in particular has been an area of research for many investigators, typically as an outcome of specific activities. For example, Medley[49] found that family life was related to life satisfaction. Bengston, Lemon, and Peterson[50] examined formal, informal, and solitary activities and found that informal and formal activities both contributed to life satisfaction. Longino and Kart[51] classified activity on axes of formal-informal and social-solitary and found that informal social activities were most likely to enhance life satisfaction. Numerous researchers have examined similar types of outcomes.[26,52]

Lachman and McArthur[53] examined well-being as related to a more comprehensive model of activity. Their findings suggest that social activity with friends contributes to satisfaction with leisure and to happiness, while social interaction with family contributes more to well-being and to self-maintenance.

Personal activity patterns and meanings are complex, deriving from many sources and contributing to a variety of outcomes. As Caspi and Elder[54] have indicated, "activity patterns depend on a host of environmental and personal factors." Older adults are quite adaptive.[3] "Old people are willing and able to reinterpret their experience so that old values take on new meaning appropriate to present circumstances."[3] However, meaningful roles must be clearly identified through examination of both personal and cultural imperatives.

How does this process translate into an individual life? Mrs. A is a 72-year-old widow who has been working full-time for the past 30 years. However, her hearing is worsening, making it difficult to continue her job as a social worker. Her daughter has recently divorced and is now a single parent to two young children. These individual and environmental conditions constituted the impetus to reexamine and reconstruct a new role and activity pattern based on changing situation and meanings.

The process by which Mrs. A made her decision about changing her activity constellation, the naming and framing process, had to do with her beliefs about her declining functional ability and its relationship to the aging process, her perceptions of the worker role, and her values about being a parent and grandparent.

Based on this internal reexamination, Mrs. A decided to retire and to assume a substantial role in the care of her grandchildren. The specific constellation of activities that constituted the roles of "retiree" and "grandparent" for Mrs. A included spending days with her grandchildren, arriving early enough that her daughter could get to work on time, taking them to school, or, on days when they had no school, to "enriching activities" like touring the art museum and baking cookies.

Unfortunately, as much as she loved her grandchildren, Mrs. A did not like baking cookies and felt personally unfulfilled in the new roles she had identified. She was frustrated by what she perceived as a lack of productivity. Clearly, the evaluation of outcomes from her choices was a negative one.

This led to a new set of choices. One possibility was to redefine "retiree" and "grandparent" to more adequately reflect her personal values and beliefs. This would include identifying some activities that Mrs. A perceived as productive, since this is an important value for her. She might volunteer at a hospital while her grandchildren are in school or give guest lectures at the local school of social work. She might involve her grandchildren in more "productive" kinds of activities as well. Another choice would be to reevaluate her decision. Perhaps the worker role was too important to relinquish, and she might consider returning to work. If she is then faced with a conflict between her need to help her daughter and her need to work, alternatives such as part-time employment or providing financial assistance to her daughter might resolve the dilemma. If she is concerned about her decreasing ability to work effectively, she might choose a job in which she could function in spite of any decline in abilities. Finally, she might reframe her current activities, relabeling grandparenting as a kind of childcare "work" that might make it more acceptable to her.

This model represents a preliminary attempt to integrate a wide variety of factors into a comprehensive description of individual creation of meaning. It remains to be tested, and testing will be challenging because of its complexity. Nonetheless, it may be helpful to health care practitioners in considering the individuals with whom they are working.

IMPLICATIONS FOR HEALTH CARE PROVIDERS

The preceding model, and the example, provide a framework for understanding how older adults establish meaningful patterns of activity. Assessment of the individual's situation and personal values is essential, and must be comprehensive. Ideally, such an assessment would be undertaken by an interdisciplinary team, with the physical therapist examining physical capacity, the psychologist and social worker considering social situation and personality factors, the occupational therapist assessing activity configurating, and the client's evaluation of those activities.

All the factors that impact on construction of an activity constellation which will be satisfying must be taken into account. Outcomes of current activities should be carefully considered, as changes in status will affect evaluation. Mrs. A was not as satisfied as she once had been with her worker role because of changes in her abilities. However, she felt strongly about the importance of working, and her chosen alternative did not have the same meaning for her.

As is clear in the example of Mrs. A, intervention is not straightforward. Simple developing a list of activities to undertake is inadequate, as the nature of the activity, the context in which it

occurs, and individual personality factors and beliefs are essential factors to consider. Because roles can be expressed in many way, the job of the health care team is to help the individual examine not only the roles but also the ways in which that individual has constructed those roles. The next step for the team is to facilitate the accomplishment of valued roles and activities through interventions that support function. A variety of methods for accomplishing these goals will be presented in the chapters that follow. It is clearly crucial to integrate the findings from a variety of assessments, in order to understand and contribute to the individual's sense of well-being and life satisfaction.

As Swensen[55] noted, "People live as long as they have something to do that needs to be done."[3] Health care providers and policy planners and older adults must develop a clear understanding of what it means, both to the individual and to society, to have something that needs to be done.

REVIEW QUESTIONS

1. *Define* naming, framing, action, *and* evaluation.

2. *Discuss the importance of environment and context to meaning.*

3. *Describe the characteristics of disengagement, activity, continuity, life-span theories, and the model of human occupation.*

4. *What research findings support or refute each of these theories?*

5. *Discuss the major characteristics of an integrated model of meaning and activity.*

6. *Describe how this integrated model might be applied to intervention with a particular client.*

REFERENCES

1. Frankel, VE: Man's Search for Meaning. Touchstone, New York, 1962.

2. Frankel, VE: The Unheard Cry For Meaning: Psychotherapy and Humanism. Simon & Schuster, New York, 1978.

3. Kaufman, SR: The Ageless Self: Sources of Meaning in Later Life. University of Wisconsin Press, Madison, 1986, p 4.

4. Rubinstein, RL: The home environment of older people: A description of the psychosocial processes linking person to place. Journal of Gerontology: Social Sciences 44:45, 1989.

5. Sterns, HL, Laier, MP and Dorsett, JG: Enhancing the Work and Retirement Experience of Older Adults. In Bonder, BR and Wagner, M: Functional Performance in Older Adults. Philadelphia, FA Davis, 1994.

6. Okun, MS, et al: The social activity/subjective well-being relation: A quantitative synthesis. Research on Aging 6:45, 1984.

7. Altergott, K: Social action and interaction in later life: Aging in the United States. In Altergott, K (ed): Daily Life In Later Life: Comparative Perspectives. Sage, Newbury Park, 1988, p 117.

8. Berkman, LF: Assessing the physical health effects of social networks and social support. Annu Rev Public Health 5:413, 1984.

9. Schön, DA: The Reflective Practitioner. Basic Books, New York, 1983.

10. Lawton, MP: Social ecology and the health of older people. Social Ecology and Health 64:257, 1974.

11. Bass, SA: Introduction. Symposium on tomorrow's able elderly: Implications for policy and practice. Gerontologist 27:403, 1987.

12. Chen, YP: Making assets out of tomorrow's elderly. Gerontologist 27:410, 1987.

13. Hatter, JK and Nelson, DL: Altruism and task participation in the elderly. Am J Occup Th 41:379, 1987.

14. Hasselkus, BR: The meaning of daily activity in family caregiving for the elderly. Am J Occup Th 43:649, 1989.

15. Cummings, EM and Henry, WE: Growing Old: The Process of Disengagement. Basic Books, New York, 1961.

16. Youmans, EG: Some perspectives on disengagement theory. Gerontologist 9:254, 1969.

17. Lewinsohn, PM and MacPhillamy, DJ: The relationship between age and engagement in pleasant activities. Journal of Gerontology 29:2909, 1974.

18. Jackoway, S, Rogers, JC and Snow, TL: The role change assessment: An interview tool for evaluating older adults. Occup Ther Mental Health 7:17, 1987.

19. Havighurst, RJ: Successful aging. In Williams, RH, Tibbitts, C and Donahue, W (eds): Processes of Aging, vol 1. Atherton, New York, 1963.

20. Palmore, E: Predictors of successful aging. Gerontologist 19:427, 1979.

21. DeCarlo, TJ: Recreation participation patterns and successful aging. Journal of Gerontology 29:416, 1974.

22. Markides, KS and Martin, HW: A causal model of life satisfaction among the elderly. Journal of Gerontology 34:86, 1979.

23. Mutran, E and Reitzes, D: Retirement, identity and well-being: Realignment of role relationships. Journal of Gerontology 36:733, 1981.

24. Graney, MJ: Happiness and social participation in aging. Journal of Gerontology 30:701, 1975.

25. Duellman, MK, Barris, R and Kielhofner, G: Organized activity and the adaptive status of nursing home residents. Am J Occup Th 40:618, 1986.

26. Burrus-Bammel, LL and Bammel, G: Leisure and recreation. In Birren, JE and Schaie, KW (eds): Handbook of the Psychology of Aging. Van Nostrand Reinhold, New York, 1985.

27. Morgan, LA: Social roles in later life: Some recent research trends. In Eisdorfer, C (ed): Annual Review of Gerontology and Geriatrics, vol. 3. Springer, New York, 1982, p 55.

28. Hoyt, DR, et al: Life satisfaction and activity theory: A multidimensional approach. Journal of Gerontology 35:935, 1980, p 37.

29. Reich, JW, Zautra, AJ, and Hill, J: Activity, event transactions and quality of life in older adults. Psychol Aging 2:116, 1987.

30. Ekerdt, DJ: The busy ethic: Moral continuity between work and retirement. Gerontologist 27:454, 1986.

31. Wallace, JB: Reconsidering the life review: The social construction of talk about the past. Gerontologist 32:120, 1992.

32. Scott-Maxwell, Florida: The Measure of My Days. AA Knopf, New York, 1968.

33. Atchley, RC: Orientation toward the job and retirement adjustment among women. In Gubrim, JF (ed): Time, Roles, and Self in Old Age. New York: Human Sciences Press, 1976.

34. Atchley, RC: Continuity theory of normal aging. Gerontologist 29:183, 1989.

35. Gutmann, D: Reclaiming Powers: Toward a New Psychology of Men and Women In Later Life. Basic Books, New York, 1987.

36. Clark, M and Anderson, M: Culture and Aging. Charles C Thomas, Springfield, 1967.

37. Simpson, IH: Problems of the aging in work and retirement. In Boyd, RR (ed): Older Americans: Social Participants. Converse College, Spartanburg, 1968.

38. Neugarten, BL: Middle Age and Aging. University of Chicago Press, Chicago, 1975.

39. Levinson, DL et al: The Seasons of a Man's Life. AA Knopf, New York, 1978.

40. Ekerdt, DJ: Why the notion persists that retirement harms health. Gerontologist 27:454, 1987.

41. Erikson, EH: Childhood and Society. WW Norton, New York, 1963.

42. Longino, CF: Who are the oldest Americans? Gerontologist 28:515, 1988.

43. Neugarten, BL: Policy for the 1980's: Age or need entitlement? Age or Need in Public Policies For Older People. Sage, Beverly Hills, 1982.

44. Meyer, A: The philosophy of occupational therapy. Am J Occup Th 31:639, 1977.

45. Slagle, EC: Habit Training. Syllabus for

Training of Nurses In Occupational Therapy, ed 2. State Hospital Press, Utica, 1933.

46. Reilly, M: Play as Exploratory Learning. Sage, Beverly Hills, 1974.

47. Kielhofner, G: Components and determinants of human occupation. In Kielhofner, G (ed): A Model of Human Occupation: Theory and Applications. Williams & Wilkins, Baltimore, 1985.

48. Rogers, JC and Snow, TL: Later adulthood. In Kielhofner, G (ed): A Model of Human Occupation: Theory and Application. Williams & Wilkins, Baltimore, 1985.

49. Medley, ML: Satisfaction with life among persons sixty-five years and older. Journal of Gerontology 31:448, 1976.

50. Lemon, BW, Bengston, VL and Peterson, JA: An exploration of the activity theory of aging: Activity types and life satisfaction among in-movers to a retirement community. Journal of Gerontology 27:511–523, 1974.

51. Longino, CF and Kart, C: Explicating activity theory: A formal replication. Journal of Gerontology 37:713, 1982.

52. Smith, NR, Kielhofner, G and Watts, JH: The relationships between volition, activity pattern, and life satisfaction in the elderly. Am J Occ Th 40:278, 1986.

53. Lachman, ME and McArthur, LZ: Adulthood age differences in causal attributions for cognitive, physical, and social performance. Psychol Aging 1:127, 1986.

54. Caspi, A and Elder, GH: Life satisfaction in old age: Linking social psychology and history. Psychol Aging 1:18, 1986.

55. Swensen, CH: A respectable old age. Am Psych 9:254 and 332, 1983.

Section

THE AGING PROCESS

Chapter

Mobility

TIM KAUFFMANN

OBJECTIVES

Fy the end of the chapter, the reader will be able
.o:

1 Describe the age-related structural changes that
affect functional abilities that occur in the muscular
system, the skeletal system, and the nervous system.

2 Discuss the changes that occur with aging in
muscle strength, posture, balance, coordination, and
gait.

3 Specify the procedures used for strength, posture,
and balance assessments and describe any
modifications of these standard techniques necessary
for assessment of the older adult

4 Describe the types of muscle training programs
that have been used to increase strength in the older
adult.

5 Discuss the relationship between muscle strength,
posture, balance, and coordination with function in
older adults.

6 Identify therapeutic interventions that may be
used to prevent or lessen age-related
neuromusculoskeletal changes in older adults.

In the biological study of living orga-
nisms, a fundamental difference between plants and animals is that animals move. The basis of movement is
the organization of the neuromuscular
systems as they relate to the skeleton.
The importance of movement from an
evolutionary perspective is clear, as it
seems likely that food gathering encouraged bipedal posture in *Homo sapiens*.[1]
This in turn affected thermoregulation
and may have influenced brain size.[2]
Over time, independent human movement has become a basic requirement
for life.

The neuromuscular aging process
varies greatly from one person to another. In 1985, Johnson conceptualized
aging as an accumulation of microin-
sults that lead to change or damage in
tissue and eventually to diminution of
physiological systems, culminating in
death.[3] These changes in tissues affect
older adults' mobility and ability to interact with the environment.

It is clear that alterations in the neuromuscular and skeletal systems occur
with the passage of time. These changes
in neuromusculoskeletal function include:

- Declines in muscle strength

- Decreases in mean muscle mass
- Change of postural alignment
- Impairments of balance, coordination, and gait
- Decreases in the speed of movement and in the initiation of responses to stimuli
- Increases in the threshold for vibration sensation and decreased proprioception

These age-related changes in combination affect the muscle strength, posture, balance, coordination, and gait of the older adult. This chapter discusses:

- The possible structural sources of these changes
- The methods used to assess the neuromusculoskeletal systems in the older adult
- Implications that these age-related changes have on functional performance
- Various interventions that can be used with the older adult if these age-related alterations occur

MUSCLE STRENGTH AND AGING

Muscle Structure

There are various changes in skeletal muscle structure with aging[4,5,6] (Table 4-1). The most notable of these changes in muscle that may affect the functional abilities of the older adult are the loss of both number and size of mus-

---

TABLE 4-1 Age-Related Changes in Muscle Morphology

1. Loss of muscle fibers
2. Atrophy of some fibers, hypertrophy of other fibers
3. Loss of muscle mass
4. Increased lipofusion
5. Increased fatty and connective tissue
6. Ringbinden found
7. Cytoplasmic bodies found
8. Myofibrillar degeneration
9. Streaming of Z lines

---

cle fibers and increase in connective tissue and fat within the muscles. These changes are likely to have negative effects on

- Strength
- Flexibility
- Reaction time
- Functional performance

Muscle mass declines with age. This loss of muscle bulk is clearly evident when comparing the muscles of a typical 60-year-old to those of a 93-year-old[7] (Figs. 4-1 and 4-2).

Histochemical changes include loss of type II or fast twitch muscle fibers, especially the IIB or fatigable–limited oxidative capacity fibers.[5] Type II fibers can rapidly develop high tension but only for short periods of time. These muscle fibers are mainly responsible for phasic activity and consist mostly of anaerobic metabolic pathways.

An increase in fatty and connective tissue has been found in senile muscle, and occasional cytoplasmic bodies and ringbinden have been reported in the muscles of older adults. These latter two findings are important because they may disrupt the normal orientation of the myofilaments. These changes along with the loss of muscle fibers reduce the tension generated by the contracting muscle, which is manifested clinically as weakness and possibly contribute to slowness and incoordination of muscle contractions.

Not all muscles demonstrate the same degree of decline with aging.[4-6,8] Muscles of an older adult show different degrees of changes as far as reduction in the numbers of fibers, appearance of ringbinden or lipofuscin, and increased connective tissue.

Strength Assessment in the Older Adult

Conflicting reports exist in the literature concerning the age when the decline of muscle strength begins. Some researchers[9-11] have reported that strength peaks during the third decade

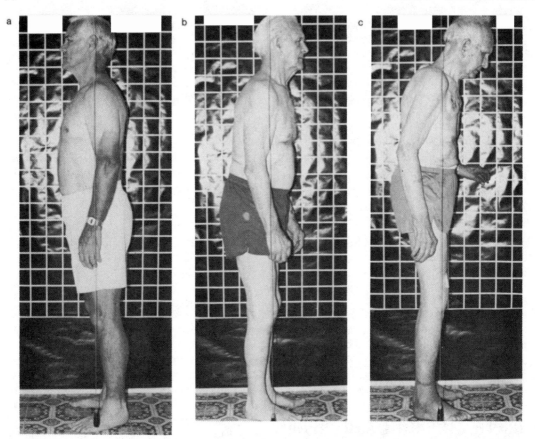

Figure 4–1 Lateral posture of (a) a 60-year old man, (b) a 78-year-old man and (c) a 93-year-old man. (Reprinted from: Topics in Geriatric Rehabilitation, Vol. 2, No. 4, with permission of Aspen Publishers, Inc. Copyright 1987)

of life and declines thereafter while others[12,13] have found that strength is maintained up to at least 60 to 70 years of age. Fisher and Birren reviewed data from 18 different reports dating back to 1835 and found that strength peaks during the third decade of life and declines thereafter.[9] In contrast, Shock and Norris did not find any decline in shoulder strength until after the seventh decade of life. They did report that muscle strength, when measured as a power output on a cranking device, declined by age 40 years.[14] Shock and Norris noted that the important difference between these two conclusions is that one test was a simple measurement of muscle strength around a single joint whereas the cranking measurement required the integration of many muscle

groups working in conjunction with the cardiopulmonary system. This suggests that actions requiring combination of multiple actions or systems are more affected by age-related changes.[15] For a more comprehensive review concerning muscle strength loss with aging, see Grimby[5] and Knortz.[16]

Muscle performance can be assessed in clinical settings using:

- Manual techniques
- Any of a variety of instruments
- Indirectly through functional activity

With some older adults it may be necessary to modify the methods that are commonly used when performing these procedures because of pain, joint defor-

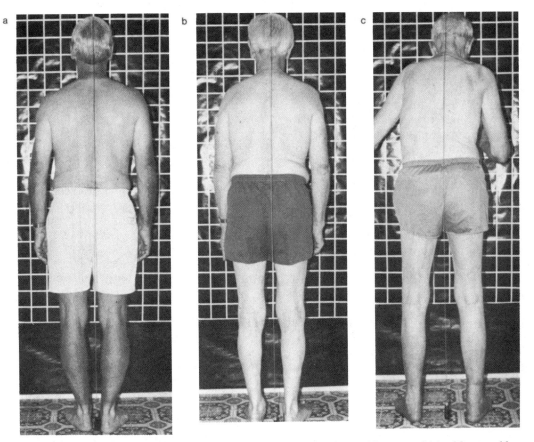

Figure 4-2 Posterior posture of (a) a 60-year-old man, (b) a 78-year-old man and (c) a 93-year-old man. (Reprinted from: Topics in Geriatric Rehabilitation, Vol. 2, No. 4, with permission of Aspen Publishers, Inc. Copyright 1987)

mities, or limitations in endurance and flexibility.

One of the most commonly used assessments of strength is the *manual muscle test* (MMT).[17] This test does not require sophisticated equipment and can be performed quickly in a clinical setting. Manual muscle testing yields an ordinal measurement of either 0, trace, poor, fair, good, or normal, or uses a scale 0 to 5, depending upon the grading method used. With the MMT the evaluator applies an opposing force to the contracting muscle as the subject moves the extremity throughout the range of motion. An alternate method of strength assessment known as the *breaktest* may be necessary for older adults who have impaired flexibility or pain. This method can be used in a pain-free range or at the end range by asking the subject to resist or to hold against the evaluator's force. The strength is determined by the amount of force needed to overcome (to break) the subject's resistance. It is rated on the same ordinal scale of 0 to normal and represents a maximal isometric contraction. With all strength assessments of older persons, the evaluator must be cautious because of osteoporosis, a common problem with aging, and the Valsalva maneuver, which may negatively affect hemodynamics.

Dynamometers may be used to measure both static and dynamic strength. Hand-held dynamometers may be used in conjunction with the manual muscle test in order to quantify the tension that is generated. More sophisticated and expensive dynamometers that measure isokinetic torques also have their place in testing the force of muscles with older adults. Not all frail individuals may be safely tested through isokinetic evaluation since upper-extremity isokinetic evaluations can cause significant increases in blood pressure. Also, the isokinetic dynamometer is not transportable, necessitating that another method of muscle testing be used to reach the large home health community.

Rating an older adult's performance of a functional activity is used by some practitioners as an alternative to traditional strength testing. For example, a functional test might indicate that the individual is able to ascend 6 steps without assistance but needs minimal assistance to complete a total of 12 steps. For older adults, this kind of assessment is most relevant since it is function, rather than absolute strength, that is at issue. It is not unusual for an older adult to be more functional than might be expected on the basis of MMT or dynamometer testing, as motivation and other factors work in combination with muscle strength to produce movement.

Strength Training

It is well documented that systematic training programs can be used with the purpose of improving strength in the older adult. A number of training methods have been used with varying degrees of success to accomplish this goal in older persons.

Hettinger used one daily maximal isometric contraction as the method for strengthening elbow flexor and extensor muscles. This author exercised both young and older men and women and found that the younger males gained the most strength.[18] The older men and women gained less than 40 percent and 30 percent, respectively, of the strength gained by younger males.

Isometric and isotonic training routines were compared by Perkins and Kaiser in 15 females and 5 males ages 62 to 84 years, mean age of 73.6 years, as methods of improving strength in the healthy, older adult. The researchers used three repetitions of maximal isometric strength and three repetitions of one-half maximal isometric strength as a basis for their training programs using a weight machine.[19] The isotonic exercise group employed the deLorme 10 *repetitions maximum* (RM) technique. The subjects participated in the training sessions three times a week for 6 weeks. The composite strength increases for the isotonic group were nearly 57 percent, and for the isometric group, 46 percent. Strength increases plateaued after 6 weeks of exercise for both groups. Five months after the end of the supervised program, gains of nearly 31 percent for the isometric group and 43 percent for the isotonic group remained.

Kauffman used a more intensive training regimen, two sets of 10 maximal isometric contractions, to test healthy, young and older women. He found that the young women (mean age of 22.6 years) gained 95 percent strength, and older women (mean age of 69.2 years), 72 percent.[13] The difference in gain in strength between the two age groups was not statistically significant.

Moritani and deVries found strength gains of 29.5 percent and 22.6 percent with five young males and five older males, respectively, when the training stimulus was 10 dynamic repetitions done twice daily, three times a week, for eight weeks.[20] The training program used the two-thirds of progressive resistive exercise principle, and the outcome measure was isometric strength. Using electromyography and skin-fold measurements, these investigators calculated the percentage of strength improvements that were due to muscle hypertrophy and those due to neural factors. The cross-sectional area of the studied muscle increased by 9 percent in the young subjects and 1 percent in the old.

Similarly, Aniansson and Gustafsson trained 12 older men, three times weekly for 12 weeks using a variety of static and dynamic exercises with only body weight for resistance.[21] They found significant increases for knee extension in isometric torque and isokinetic torque at speeds of 30, 60, 120, and 180 degrees per second. Additionally, they found a significant increase in type IIA fiber area.

Fiatarone and associates studied the effects of a training program of eight weeks' duration of high-intensity, resistive training in 10 frail institutionalized individuals aged 86 to 96 years, with a mean age of 90 years.[22] Muscle strength of the quadriceps was measured using the standard weight-and-pulley system with the one repetition maximal method of resistance. Strength gains were statistically significant. Seven of the 10 subjects had CAT scan measurements before and after training. The CAT scan showed that the muscle area increased by approximately 9 percent.

In summary, these past studies have suggested that isometric methods, isotonic programs, and simple active exercise using body weight as resistance are successful at increasing strength in well older men and women. There is some evidence to show that isotonic exercise programs can improve muscle strength in the frail older adult. Studies indicate that the strength gains accomplished in the healthy, older adult are maintained for at least short periods after the formal exercise program is discontinued. Structural changes of the muscles, that is, increases in cross-sectional type IIB fiber areas, have also been documented following formal exercise programs in older individuals.

Function and Muscle Strength Changes

Various authors have attempted to relate functional mobility problems with muscle weaknesses common to the older adult. Fiatarone and colleagues examined the relationship of muscle strength and functional abilities in a population of institutionalized older adults.[22] Persons with stronger quadri-

ceps muscles were able to stand up from a chair faster and walk a 6-meter timed walk faster.

A number of functional mobility problems have been associated with muscle weakness in the older individual. Hip abduction weakness may reduce the ability to balance on one leg and to recover from postural perturbation.[23] Hip extension strength has been related to independence in the sit-to-stand movement.[24] Weakness in ankle dorsiflexion and knee extension has been statistically associated with falls, with the greatest loss of strength found in high-velocity muscle contractions.[25] The loss of fast twitch type II muscle fibers may increase the risk of falling because of the slowness to respond to a loss of balance.

Muscle weakness, particularly stretch weakness as defined by Kendall and McCreary,[26] can be a factor in the older adult. The postural changes, flattened lower back or forward head and rounded shoulders,[7] commonly seen in this population can result in chronically stretched, weakened trunk, and neck musculature. Stretch weakness may also occur in the quadriceps muscle. Persons who sit with their knees flexed for extended periods may develop terminal knee extension lag or the inability to straighten their knee completely against gravity. Also, older adults who lie in bed or sit with a lower extremity in an adducted position, lengthen the hip abductors, which can result in weakness of this muscle group.

In summary, data that allow for the prediction of function from strength values are not presently available, but a few studies have been published that investigate the relationship between functional activities and muscle strength. These studies suggest that there are important reasons to maintain or to increase muscle strength within the aging population. The potential to increase strength in normal aged muscle has been demonstrated. A summary of points that should be considered when helping an older person with a strengthening program are shown in Table 4–2.

TABLE 4–2 **Clinical Implications and Recommendations When Strength Training Geriatric Patients**

1. Simple directions, gestures, PROM.
2. May gain strength slowly.
3. May gain less absolute strength.
4. May have less adaptability to stress. More injuries? Increased cramps?
5. Decreased oxygen consumption; perhaps may fatigue easily.
6. Short and graded exercise bouts, but apply the overload principle.
7. Use a variety of muscle contractions: isometric, isotonic, isokinetic, concentric, and/or eccentric.
8. Monitor skin, respiration, and pulse rate in response to exercise.
9. *The talk test:* Do not overexercise the aged person so that he/she cannot talk during the exercises.

THE SKELETAL SYSTEM IN THE OLDER ADULT

Posture

Posture is the alignment of body parts in relation to one another at any given moment. Posture is viewed usually as a static process, but gravity and neural control mechanisms constantly affect subtle shifts in weight and body alignment, which necessitate a dynamic type of postural control. The small oscillating movements of the body during standing is referred to as *postural sway*. Postural sway increases with age[27] and may be associated with greater risks for falling.

Wyke postulated that senile disequilibrium is influenced by progressive degeneration of mechanoreceptors of the spinal apophyseal joints.[28] He suggested that inflammatory degeneration or traumatic injuries to the spine will reduce the crucial afferent feedback to the central nervous system for postural stability.

Numerous changes have been described in the aging spine[29,30]; more specifically, cervical spondylosis has been reported in over 80 percent of persons after age 55 years.[28] This has the effect of reducing postural stability and flexibility.

The most common age-related changes in the axial skeleton are:

- The head forward position
- Increased dorsal kyphosis
- Flattened lumbar spine (see Figs. 4–1 and 4–2)

The head forward position is often considered to be abnormal, but to some degree it may be a normal compensation necessitated by other postural changes, such as age-related flattening of the lumbar spine. Scoliotic curvatures occur in the old and may be due to spinal or appendicular changes.[7]

In the extremities, the most common postural variations in aged adults are rounded shoulders with protracted scapula and slightly flexed elbows, hips, and knees. In addition, changes in the articular surfaces and joint capsules often cause varus or valgus deformities at the hips, knees, or ankles.

As described above, numerous changes occur with aging in the nervous and skeletal system that may diminish control of static posture. Additionally, changes in muscle, connective tissue, and skin alter posture with aging. Idiosyncratic trauma, lifestyle, or habits such as prolonged wearing of high heels, also contribute to postural changes with aging.

Assessment of Static Posture

Static posture is usually assessed from the front, rear, and side views as described by Kendall and McCreary.[26] A plumb line may be of benefit as a reference point. In the older adult the plumb line frequently causes the postural sway to be more apparent to the evaluator and may increase the difficulty of the postural assessment.

Treatment of Skeletal Deformities and Postural Problems

Scoliosis[31] and leg length discrepancy[32] have been associated with increased postural sway in the older adult and may be corrected simply by adding a heel lift. Other common postural problems in older persons may result from the age-related changes in the muscles and may respond to an exercise program designed to increase both flexibility and strength. Educating the older adult in correct body posture while reading or watching television and in the practice of proper body mechanics during activities can be helpful in alleviating some of the problems that can occur with postural changes in the older adult.

BALANCE, COORDINATION, AND MOVEMENT AND AGING

The ability to perform balanced and coordinated movement requires the integration of multiple muscle groups and involves afferent as well as efferent pathways. An intact neuromuscular system is necessary to produce movements that are smooth and accurate (see Fig. 4–3). Functional activities that require either gross or fine motor responses or a combination of both, such

Figure 4–3 This woman continues to be vigorous and active, in spite of age associated changes in neuromuscular functioning. (Courtesy of the Menorah Park Nursing Home, Cleveland, Ohio.)

as walking, getting out of bed, or buttoning and zipping clothing, require coordinated movements. Timing and force of muscle contractions and joint motions are crucial for controlled movements.

Age-Related Nervous System Changes

Numerous morphological and biochemical changes in the nervous system occur with aging and may impact on functional abilities. Each individual responds to the changes in the neuromuscular system in a unique manner. For some individuals profound structural changes can occur without inhibiting functional abilities, whereas in other older adults seemingly insignificant changes can cause serious functional impairments.

Examples of identified alterations in the nervous system of the older adult include:

- Gross morphological changes reflective of specific neuronal loss and decreased dendritic branching and the accumulation of lipofuscin granules
- Lewy bodies
- Plaques
- Fibrillary tangles in selective brain regions[33-37]

In addition, age-related changes in neurotransmitter mechanisms include selectively reduced activities in dopaminergic, cholinergic, and noradrenergic system.[38,39] The changes that occur in the nervous system of older adults are summarized in Table 4–3.

While alterations in specific morphological and biochemical parameters have not always been directly correlated with behavioral changes, there are indications of differences in the electrical activity of the nervous system of older adults as compared to young adults. Decreased electrical activity with aging has been reflected in electroencephalograms[40] and nerve conduction velocity studies in healthy adults.[41,42] Changes in neural activity in sensory and motor neural systems are likely to be reflected

TABLE 4–3 **Age-Related Changes of the Nervous System**

1. Cerebral atrophy
2. Increased cerebrospinal fluid space
3. Neuronal loss
4. Reduced dendritic branching
5. Increased lipofuscin granules
6. Decreased effectiveness of neurotransmitter systems
7. Reduced cerebral blood flow
8. Diminished glucose utilization
9. Alterations in electroencephalogram
10. Loss of motor nerve fibers
11. Slowing of nerve conduction velocities

in age-related alterations in adaptive motor responses.

Reaction-time tasks are good measurements of neuromuscular function because they require afferent impulses, central processing, and efferent impulses to effect a response. Potvin and colleagues report that reaction time increases with age.[8] In contrast, Spirduso showed very little decline in reaction-time tasks in older persons who were active in racket sports compared to young physically active persons.[43] The old, physically inactive persons showed the more typical age-related slowing on this test. Sherwood and Selder demonstrated similar results in a group of physically active joggers through age 50 to 59.[44]

Sudarsky and Ronthal studied the CAT scans of 50 adults, mean age 79.5 years, with undiagnosed gait disorders.[45] Various pathological changes of the nervous system were found in this sample of community-dwelling older adults. Persons with hemiparesis or major motor deficit from stroke were excluded from the study. Evidence of multiple cerebral infarcts were found in 8 (16 percent) of the cases of which only 4 had clear evidence of dementia. Hydrocephalus was found in 2 persons. For those 2 individuals, the integrative centers for locomotion located in the frontal lobe may have been compromised by ventricular expansion. Cerebellar atrophy, truncal ataxia, and peripheral neuropathy were found in 4 subjects, while another 9 showed signs of multiple sensory disorders including decrements in visual, vestibular, and/or proprioceptive afferent responses. Like the group with cerebellar atrophy, all of these persons also had evidence of peripheral neuropathy. Seven persons had essential or idiopathic gait disorders based on the stigmata of equivocal test results and clinical findings of a wide-based gait with short strides and easy posterior displacement. The CAT scans of 30 of these subjects were compared with 28 control subjects. Individuals with gait disorders had greater ventricular measurements. There was no significant difference between the groups as far as cortical atrophy.

None of the subjects in Sudarsky and Ronthal's study had been diagnosed as having gait disorders, suggesting that they were able to accomplish the activities that were important to them in spite of the obvious clinical findings. This finding is typical of a variety of "disabilities" or "problems" in the older adult, in that clinicians identify deficits that, at the time, have no functional implications for the individual. Autopsy findings on many highly functional, cognitively intact older adults, for example, demonstrate substantial cortical thinning and expansion of the ventricular spaces, consistent with findings in brains of individuals diagnosed with dementia.

Using computed tomography, Masdeu and colleagues compared 20 known fallers with 20 nonfallers, mean age of 83.3 years.[46] These authors found that white matter hypodensity was associated with poor gait and balance scores but not with cognition. The fallers scored significantly worse on these tests and had significantly greater white matter hypodensity. These investigators, like Sudarsky and Ronthal, found no significant differences between the two groups in cerebellar or cortical atrophy; but unlike the earlier report, these investigators did not find significant differences in ventricular enlargement.

Assessment of Balance and Coordination

STATIC BALANCE

Static balance is frequently assessed clinically by measuring the length of stance time on one leg. As Potvin reported, the decline in ability to perform this test from 20 years to 80 years of age was 32 percent for one-legged stance with eyes open and 100 percent with eyes closed.[8] The ability to maintain one-legged stance is important when functional activities are of concern since walking and stair climbing require balancing on one leg.

Various authors have suggested other methods that can be used to assess static balance. Shumway-Cook and Horak have described a method of assessing timed balance and sway in the bipedal position by varying sensory input.[47] The individual is tested under the following six conditions:

1. Without visual restrictions
2. With a blindfold
3. With a visual conflict dome
4. Without visual restrictions but with a foam pad to control proprioceptive sensory input
5. With a blindfold, but with a foam pad to control proprioceptive sensory input
6. With a visual conflict dome and a foam pad to control proprioceptive sensory output

These investigators suggested that these test conditions can also be used as a therapeutic intervention to improve balance.

The sharpened Romberg test, performed by placing the dominant foot behind the nondominant in a heel-to-toe fashion, is also suggested as a test of static balance.[48] The length of time the person is able to stand is then recorded. Often this test is done with the eyes open and with the eyes closed.

Moveable foot platforms have been advocated as a sophisticated method for measuring postural sway and the ability to recover from postural perturbation.[49] The expense of this method has limited its clinical application.

Recognizing the importance of weight shift and the dynamic component of postural control, a number of investigators have described clinical measurements of weight shift from foot to foot to stimulate the initiation of gait[50] and a forward reach.[51] Duncan and associates placed their subjects in a static stance and recorded balance as the greatest distance the person was able to reach forward on to a yardstick, which was at shoulder height.[51]

Wolfson and associates describe the postural stress test.[52] With the feet apart and eyes open, a belt is attached to a subject's waist, which is connected to a standard wall pulley. Specific weights of 1.5 percent, 3 percent, and 4 percent of the person's body weight were raised 2 feet from the floor. These weights as part of the wall pulley system were dropped enough distance to cause a postural displacement of the subject's body mass. These researchers developed a balance strategy score based on the postural response to this perturbation. They found their test effective in separating a group of fallers from nonfallers.

COORDINATION

When testing for coordination, other factors besides ability to perform tasks or the speed required to complete a task must be considered. Movement should be smooth and accurate with appropriate direction, timing, balance, and muscle tension.

Schmitz suggests that clinical tests of coordination can be divided into tasks that do not and those that do require equilibrium.[53] Nonequilibrium coordination tasks such as finger to nose, finger to examiner's finger, hand tapping, toe tapping, heel to shin, and circle drawing with hand and foot may be graded on a scale of 1 to 5 (Table 4–4). A grading scale of 1 to 4 was suggested for equilibrium tests of coordination such as standing normal, standing feet together, and one-legged stance and walking in a straight line, sideward, backward, on heels, on toes, and in a circle (Table 4–5). Additionally, Schmitz listed a number of commercially available tests that

TABLE 4–4 **Sample Coordination Assessment Form**

Name: _____

Examiner: _____ Date _____

PART I NONEQUILIBRIUM TESTS

Key to Grading

5. Normal performance.

4. Minimal impairment: able to accomplish activity with slightly less than normal speed and skill.

3. Moderate impairment: able to accomplish activity, but coordination deficits very noticeable; movements are slow, awkward, and unsteady.

2. Severe impairment: able only to initiate activity without completion.

1. Activity impossible.

Grade: Left	Coordination Test	Grade: Right	Comments
	Finger to nose		
	Finger to therapist's finger		
	Finger to finger		
	Alternate nose to finger		
	Finger opposition		
	Mass grasp		
	Pronation/supination		
	Rebound test of Holmes		
	Tapping (hand)		
	Tapping (foot)		
	Pointing and past pointing		
	Alternate heel to knee; heel to toe		
	Toe to examiner's finger		
	Heel on shin		
	Drawing a circle (hand)		
	Drawing a circle (foot)		
	Fixation/position holding (upper extremity)		
	Fixation/position holding (lower extremity)		

Additional comments:

From O'Sullivan and Schmitz: Physical Rehabilitation, ed. 2. F.A. Davis, Philadelphia, 1988.

TABLE 4–5 Equilibrium Tests

Key to Grading

4. Able to accomplish activity.

3. Can complete activity; minor physical contact guarding required to maintain balance.

2. Can complete activity; significant (moderate to maximal) contact guarding required to maintain balance.

1. Activity impossible.

Grade	Coordination Test	Comments
	Standing: normal comfortable posture	
	Standing: normal comfortable posture with vision occluded	
	Standing: feet together	
	Standing on one foot	seconds L( ); R( )
	Standing: forward trunk flexion and return to neutral	
	Standing: lateral trunk flexion	
	Walk: place heel of one foot in front of toe of the opposite foot	
	Walk: along a straight line	
	Walk: place feet on floor markers	
	Walk: sideways	
	Walk: backward	
	Walk: in a circle	
	Walk: on heels	
	Walk: on toes	

Additional comments:

NOTE: Notations should be made under comments section if:

1. Lack of visual input renders activity impossible or alters quality of performance.

2. Verbal cuing is required to accomplish activity.

3. Alterations in speed affect quality of performance.

4. An excessive amount of time is required to complete activity.

5. Changes in arm position influence equilibrium tests.

6. Any extraneous movements, unsteadiness, or oscillations are noted in head, neck, or trunk.

7. Fatigue alters consistency of response.

From O'Sullivan and Schmitz: Physical Rehabilitation, ed. 2. F.A. Davis, Philadelphia, 1988.

may be used to assess fine motor adaptive skills.[53]

DYNAMIC BALANCE

A mobility test combining balance and gait maneuvers was developed by Tinetti, Williams, and Mayewski in order to develop a falls risk index.[54] The balance evaluation included static sitting and standing, standing balance with eyes closed, rising from a seated position, immediate standing balance, reaction to a nudge on the chest, cervical spine range of motion, turning in a 360-degree circle, one-legged stance, and sitting down. The gait observations included:

- The initiation of gait
- The step length
- The step height
- The step continuity
- Step symmetry
- Walking stance
- Amount of trunk sway
- Path deviation

A similar test was described by Mathias, Nayak, and Isaacs as the "get-up-and-go" test.[55] Lichtenstein and associates found that area of sway, measured on a foot platform, was associated with performance on the Tinetti mobility index.[56]

Kauffman and associates have described a balance beam test as a simple screening device for potential balance dysfunction.[57] The balance beam, a simple 2×6-inch piece of wood, measures 7 feet in length. A subject walks across the balance beam five times. The speed of walking across the beam and the number of falls were recorded. A fall was described as any time the subject's foot reached the floor, a subject reached for a wall for support, or the evaluator needed to intervene. The researchers found that the people who fell traversed the balance beam with less speed. This corresponds to reports that known fallers or people with gait dysfunction have less velocity and greater availability in foot placement.[58,59]

Balance and Coordination Treatment Considerations

BALANCE DYSFUNCTION

Therapeutic intervention for balance dysfunction in the older adult should be specific to the cause or causes of the problem and the impact on function. Sometimes, simply changing shoes, altering the lighting or other environmental influences, applying a properly fitting brace or orthosis, or using an assistive device may be all that is necessary. For other older adults improving lower-extremity strength and range of motion may improve balance, as was noted in some of the research cited earlier.[7,22,23,25]

In other cases, the factors that contribute to balance dysfunction may be less specific or undiagnosed; thus the overall balance control mechanism must be "exercised." Crutchfield, Shumway-Cook, and Horak have stated that the nervous system uses three sensory inputs for automatic postural stabilization:

1. Vision for object orientation
2. Vestibular input for self-to-earth orientation
3. Somatosensory input from proprioception for self-to-self orientation and from extroception for self-to-object orientation[60]

The use of a visual conflict dome, blindfold, and a foam pad may be helpful not only in evaluation for balance deficits as previously described but also for training and documenting improvements.

IMPAIRED COORDINATION

Treatment of incoordination must take into consideration the cause. As suggested by Jette, Branch, and Berlin, musculoskeletal dysfunctions, such as pain, inflexibility, and muscle weakness, can result in loss of independence and ability to perform activities of daily living especially in the older adult.[61] The use of various physical therapeutic modalities may be of benefit in alleviating the musculoskeletal problems and therefore improving coordination. Direct practice of functional activities or environmental modification to reduce performance deficits may help to reduce incoordination. Various neurophysiological exercise approaches as developed by Rood,[62] Bobath,[63] Knott and Voss,[64] Ayres,[65] and Feldenkrais[66] may be helpful, especially for persons with central nervous system dysfunction.

GAIT DISTURBANCES

Kauffman and associates used a progressive program aimed at increasing strength, coordination, balance, and ability to recover from near loss of balance. Static exercises for hip flexion and hip abduction were employed to increase the one-legged stance time. Sit-to-stand movement, cervical spine range of motion, and scapular activities were utilized. Practice in balance and gait also included a series of dynamic activities such as side steps, cross-over steps, walking forward and backward, high steps, heel-to-toe walking, side glide and hop, and jumping in place. Static bipedal toe raises and toe tapping for dorsiflexion were included in the program (see appendix). After using this program and retesting on the balance beam, improvements were found in the velocity of traversing the balance beam and/or in the decreased number of falls in over 90 percent of the retirement community of volunteers and in clinical cases of gait disturbance in community-living medicare beneficiaries.[57,67]

Balance and Coordination Changes Related to Function

Many authors have studied balance and coordination by examining different activities. One such research project was a large epidemiological study, published by the National Institute on Aging, that investigated many sociomedical factors including some fine and gross motor coordination for *activities of daily living* (ADL).[68] A portion of the data from the East Boston sample for males, ages 65 to 69, 75 to 79, and 85+ years is presented in Table 4–6. The data provide some evidence of a decline in coordinated motor skills over 2 decades in late life. Particularly noteworthy were the age-related changes in late life. Particularly noteworthy were the age-related changes in the subjects' ability to independently hold small objects or write (91 to 68 percent) and walk across a small room (93 to 74 percent). Other data sets showed similar, but not identical, results.

Other investigators have reported declines in performance of upper-extremity functional tests, such as removing or inserting an electrical plug into a socket.[69] In 70-year-old women, 8.9 percent could not perform this task, and 6.9 percent could do so only with difficulty. The subjects who had difficulty removing or inserting an electrical plug were found to be significantly weaker on a key grip test than the persons who were independent with the task. These same subjects were tested on their ability to open a clothespin and to place the pin into a hole. The researchers reported that this task required a force of 16 N. The 70-year-old subjects needed 40 percent more time to complete the task than the younger group, ages 20 to 30 years.[70]

Potvin and associates studied 61 males between the ages of 20 and 80 years.[8] They calculated the difference in performance between the age groups. In the activities of living test, based mostly on speed of completion, the decline between age groups was 30 percent with the biggest difficulty of putting on a shirt and cutting with a knife. Some of the other large declines in fine motor coordination tests of neurological function were:

- 63 percent in hand steadiness
- 28 percent in simple reaction time
- 23 percent in hand tapping speed
- 27 percent in finger grasping of pegs on the right
- 25 percent on the left

The same investigators reported large declines in vibratory sense at the:

TABLE 4-6	**Selected Measurements of ADL Independence in East Boston Sample**		
	(% No assistance needed)		
Activities	**Age 65-69**	**Age 75-79**	**Age 85+**
Pressing	92.6	92.5	82.1
Putting on shirt, shoes			
Zipping			
Buttoning			
Personal grooming	98.2	96.4	89.3
Brushing hair			
Brushing teeth			
Washing face			
Eating	97.7	96.8	92.0
Holding fork			
Cutting foot			
Drinking from glass			
Holding or handling small objects	90.6	84.2	67.7
Writing			
Transfers bed to chair	96.1	94.4	86.6
Walking across a small room	93.0	90.5	74.1

- Wrist (64 percent)
- Elbow (52 percent)
- Shoulder (58 percent)
- Rib (68 percent)
- Clavicle (56 percent)

Gait changes are predominant[71] in the older adult and the most common of all functional activities researched. The most typical gait changes with aging are:

- Decreased step length[72]
- Decreased stride length[73]
- Slower walking velocity[73]
- Decreased ankle range of motion[73]
- Decreased push-off with the toes,[74]
- Increased double-stance time[74]

These changes are not found in all healthy older adults,[75] but they are more predominant in persons with gait disturbances or problems of falls.[58,71]

SUMMARY

Clearly, changes occur in the neuromusculoskeletal systems with aging. There is no clear line between what is part of "normal" aging and what constitutes "disease" or "dysfunction." Most older adults manage their daily tasks quite well until some specific event, for example, a fall or an acute illness, changes their physical status or until an accumulation of small decrements reaches some breakpoint at which a particular activity or set of activities becomes impossible.

Factors other than neuromuscular integrity, such as arthritis, impaired vision, and changes in cognition, may cause a decline in functional abilities. Jette, Branch, and Berlin suggested that declining musculoskeletal integrity was a major factor associated with the loss of independence in activities of daily living.[61]

This chapter discusses the normally expected age-related changes in the neuromusculoskeletal systems and the resulting impact on functional performance. It is important to recognize that these generalizations about change reflect an "average" and that individual variability is great.

Because some of these changes cause major problems for the individual, such as balance dysfunction, falls, and loss of motor control, a variety of assessment methods and intervention techniques have been presented. If the goal of care is to return or to maintain the older adult to his or her highest functional level, it is paramount for health care providers to view each aging person as having unique life experiences.

REVIEW QUESTIONS

1. *What are the most profound structural changes in the aging neuromusculoskeletal systems? What are the functional implications of these changes in the everyday lives of older adults?*

2. *Your client is a 73-year-old woman without chronic illness. How would you expect her muscular system to differ from that of a 35-year-old? Be sure to include both structural and histochemical aspects.*

3. *Compare three different strength assessment procedures that are commonly used with the aged individual. Under what circumstances should they be used?*

4. *Muscle strengthening programs in the older adult have been successful. Describe any special considerations that should be adhered to during strength training of an older adult.*

5. *What are the expected age-related changes in posture, balance, and coordination?*

6. *Define: postural sway, dynamic postural control, static posture, static balance, and dynamic balance. How are each of these measured? Why are they important?*

7. *What practical, therapeutic suggestions can be given to a person with balance and coordination dysfunctions?*

REFERENCES

1. Leakey, R: Origins of mankind. Presentation at Pucillo Gymnasium, Millersville University, November 1987.
2. Bortz, W: Physical exercise as an evolutionary force. J Hum Evol 14:145, 1985.
3. Johnson, H: Is aging physiological or pathological? In Johnson, HA (ed): Relations Between Normal Aging and Disease. Raven Press, New York, 1985.
4. Shafiq, F, et al: Electron microscopic study of skeletal muscle in elderly subjects. In Kaldor, G and DiBattista, WJ (eds): Textbook of Aging, Vol 6, Aging and Muscle. Raven Press, New York, 1978.
5. Grimby, G: Muscle changes and trainability in the elderly. Topics in Geriatric Rehabilitation 5:54, 1990.
6. Frolkis, V, et al: Aging of the neuromuscular apparatus. Geron 22:244, 1976.
7. Kauffman, T: Posture and age. Topics in Geriatric Rehabilitation 2:13, 1987.
8. Potvin, A: Human neurologic function and the aging process. J Amer Ger Soc 28:1.
9. Fisher, M and Birren, J: Age and strength. J Appl Psychol 31:490, 1947.
10. Burke, W, et al: The relation of grip strength and grip strength endurance to age. J Appl Physiol 5:628, 1953.
11. Asmussen, E, et al: A follow-up longitudinal study of selected physiologic functions in former physical education students after forty years. J Am Ger Soc, 23:442, 1975.
12. Petrofsky, J and Lind, A: Aging, isometric strength and endurance, and cardiovascular responses to static effort. J Appl Physiol 38:91, 1975.
13. Kauffman, T: Strength training effect in young and aged women. Arch Phys Med Rehabil 66:223, 1985.
14. Shock, N and Norris, A: Neuromuscular coordination as a factor in age changes in musculature exercise. Med and Sport 4:92, 1970.
15. Shock, N: Systems integration. In Finch, C and Hayflick (eds): Handbook of the Biology of Aging. Van Nostrand Reinhold, New York, 1977.
16. Knortz, K: Muscle physiology applied to geriatric rehabilitation. Topics of Geriatr Rehab 2:1, 1987.
17. Daniels, L, Williams, M and Worthington, C: Muscle Testing. WB Saunders, Philadelphia, 1956.

18. Hettinger T: die Trainierbarkeit menschlicher Muskeln in Abhangigkeit vom Alter und Geschlect. Int Z Angew Physiol einschl Arbveitsphysiol 17:377, 1958.

19. Perkins, L and Kaiser, H: Results of short term isotonic and isometric exercise programs in persons over sixty. Phys Ther Rev 41:633, 1961.

20. Moritani, T and deVries, H: Neural factors versus hypertrophy in time course of muscle strength gain. Am J Phys Med 58:115, 1979.

21. Aniansson A, Grimby G, Hedberg M, et al: Muscle morphology enzyme activity and muscle strength in elderly men and women. Clin Physiol 1:73, 1981.

22. Fiatarone, M, et al: High intensity strength training in nonagenarians. JAMA 263:3029, 1990

23. Probst, C: The Influence of Hip Abduction Strength on Postural Sway in Elderly Females, thesis. University of Pittsburgh, 1989.

24. Kauffman, T: Association between hip extension strength and standup ability in geriatric patients. Physical and Occupational Therap in Geriatrics 1:39, 1982.

25. Whipple, R, Wolfson, L and Amerman, P: The relationship of knee and ankle weakness to falls in nursing home residents: An isokinetic study. J Am Ger Soc 35:13, 1987.

26. Kendall, F and McCreary, E: Muscles: Testing and Function. Williams & Wilkins, Baltimore, 1983.

27. Sheldon, J: The effect of age on the control of sway. Gerontol Clin 5:129, 1963.

28. Wyke, B: Conference on the aging brain. Age and Aging, 8:251, 1979.

29. Fielding, JW: The cervical spine. In Sculco, TP (ed): Orthopedic Care of the Geriatric Patient. Mosby, St. Louis, 1985.

30. Sculco, TP: The lumbar spine. In Sculco, TP (ed): Orthopedic Care of the Geriatric Patient. Mosby, St. Louis, 1985.

31. Brocklehurst, JC, Robertson, D and James-Groom, P: Skeletal deformities in the elderly and their effect on postural sway. J Am Ger Soc 30:534, 1982.

32. Mahar, R, Kirby RL and McLeon, DA: Simulated leg-length discrepancy: Its effect on mean center-of-pressure position and postural sway. Arch Phys Med Rehabil 5:691, 1985.

33. Rossor, M: The central nervous system-neurochemistry of the aging brain and dementia. In Brocklehurst, JD (ed): Textbook of Geriatric Medicine and Gerontology, ed 3. Churchill Livingstone, London, 1985.

34. Dayan, A and Lewis, P: The central nervous system-neuropathology of aging. In Brocklehurst, JD (ed): Textbook of Geriatric Medicine and Gerontology, ed 3. Churchill Livingstone, London, 1985.

35. Henderson, G, Timlinson, B and Gibson, P: Cell counts in human cerebral cortex in normal adults throughout life using an image analyzing computer. Journal of the Neurological Sciences 46:113, 1980.

36. Dayan, A: Quantitative histological studies on the aged human brain. I. Senile plaques and neurofibrillary tangles in "normal" patients. Acta Neuropath 16:85, 1970.

37. Dayan, A: Quantitative histological studies on the aged human brain. II. Senile plaques and neurofibrillary tangles in senile dementia. Acta Neuropath 16:95, 1970.

38. Brizzee, K: Neuron aging and neuron pathology. Relations Between Normal Aging and Disease. Raven Press, New York, 1985, p 191.

39. Hoyer, S: Brain glucose and energy metabolism during normal aging. Aging 2:245, 1990.

40. Keller, W, et al: Physiology of the aging brain: Normal and abnormal states. Relations Between Normal Aging and Disease. Raven Press, New York, 1985, p 165.

41. Swallow, M: Fibre size and content of the anterior tibial nerve of the foot. J Neurol Neurosurg Psychiat 29:205, 1966.

42. O'Sullivan, D and Swallow, M: Fibre size and content of the radial and sural nerves. J Neurol Neurosurg Psychiat 31:464, 1968.

43. Spirduso, W: Reaction and movement time as a function of age and physical activity level. Journal of Gerontology 30:435, 1975.

44. Sherwood, D and Selder, D: Cardiorespiratory health, reaction time, and aging. Med Sci Sports 11:186, 1979.

45. Sudarsky L and Ronthal M: Gait disorders among elderly patients: A survey of 50 patients. Arch Neurol 40:740–743, 1983.

46. Masdeu, J, et al: Brain white-matter changes in the elderly prone to falling. Arch Neurol 46:1292, 1989.

47. Shumway-Cook, A and Horak, F: Assessing the influence of sensory interaction on balance. Phys Ther 66:1548, 1986.

48. Brigg, R, Gogsman, M, Birch, R, et al: Balance performance among noninstitutionalized elderly women. Phys Ther 69:748, 1989.

49. Woollacott, MH, Shumway-Cooke, A and Nashner, L: Postural reflexes and aging. Adv Neurogerontol 98, 1982.

50. Goldie, P, Matyas, T, Spencer, K, et al: Postural control in standing following stroke: Test-retest reliability of some quantitative clinical tests. Phys Ther 70:234, 1990.

51. Duncan, P, Weiner, D, Chindler, J, et al: Functional reach: A new clinical measure of balance. Journal of Gerontology 45:M192, 1990.

52. Wolfson, L, Whipple, R, Amerman, P, et al: Stressing the postural response: A quantitative method for testing balance. J Am Ger Soc 34:850, 1986.

53. Schmitz, T: Coordination assessment. In O'Sullivan, S and Schmitz (eds): Physical Rehabilitation: Assessment and Treatment, ed 2. FA Davis, Philadelphia, 1988.

54. Tinetti, M, Williams, T and Mayewski, R: Fall risk index for elderly patients based on number of chronic disabilities. Am J Med 80:429, 1986.

55. Mathias, S, Nayak, U and Isaacs B: Balance and elderly patients: The "get up and go" test. Arch Phys Med Rehabil 67:387, 1986.

56. Lichtenstein, M, Burger, M, Shields, S, et al:

Comparison of biomechanics platform measures of balance and videotaped measures of gait with a clinical mobility scale in elderly women. Journal of Gerontology 45:M49, 1990.

57. Kauffman, T, Gamber, W, Anderl, B, et al: Assessment of dynamic balance. Presented and published in Proceedings World Confederation Physical Therapy Conference, London, 1991.

58. Koller, W, Glatt, S and Fox, J: Senile gait: A distinct neurologic entity. Clin Geriatr Med from Symposium and Falls in the Elderly: Biologic and Behavioral Aspects. WB Saunders, Philadelphia, 1985.

59. Wolfson, L, Whipple, R, et al: Gait assessment in the elderly: A gait abnormality rating scale and its relation to falls. Journal of Gerontology 45:M12, 1990.

60. Crutchfield, C, Shumway-Cook, A and Horak, F: Balance and coordination training. In Scully, R and Barnes, M (eds): Physical Therapy. Lippincott, Philadelphia, 1989.

61. Jette, A, Branch, L and Berlin, J: Musculoskeletal impairments and physical disablement among the aged. Journal of Gerontology 45:M203, 1990.

62. Stockmeyer, S: An interpretation of the approach of Rood to the treatment of neuromuscular dysfunction. Am J Phys Med 46:900, 1967.

63. Bobath, B: Abnormal Postural Reflex Activity Caused by Brain Lesions, ed 2. William Heinaman Medical Books, London, 1971.

64. Knott, M and Voss, D: Proprioceptive Neuromuscular Facilitation Patterns and Techniques, ed 2. Harper & Row, New York, 1968.

65. Ayres, J: The development of perceptual-motor abilities: A theoretical basis for treatment for dysfunction. Amer J Occup Th 17:221, 1963.

66. Feldenkrais, M: Awareness Through Movement. Harper & Row, New York, 1978.

67. Kauffman, T: Impact of age-related musculoskeletal and postural changes on falls. Topics of Geriatric Rehabilitation 5:34, 1990.

68. Cornoni-Huntley, J, et al (eds): Established Populations for Epidemiologic Studies of the Elderly. US Department of Health and Human Services, NIH Publication, 86-2443.

69. Aniansson, A, Rudgren, A and Sperling, L: Evaluation of functional capacity and activities of daily living in 70 year old men and women. Scand J Rehab Med 12:145, 1980.

70. Sperling, L: Evaluations of upper extremity function in 70 year old men and women. Scand J Rehab Med 12:139, 1980

71. Wolfson, L, Whipple, R and Amerman, P, et al: Gait and balance in the elderly: Two functional capacities that link sensory and motor abilities to falls. Clin Geriatr Med 1:649, 1985.

72. Gabell, A and Nayak, U: The effect of age in variability in gait. Journal of Gerontology 39:662, 1984.

73. Hageman, P and Blanke, D: Comparison of gait in young women and elderly women. Phys Ther 66:1382, 1986.

74. Winter, D, Patla, A, Frank, J, et al: Biomechanical walking pattern changes in the fit and healthy elderly. Phys Ther 70:340, 1990.

75. Blanke, D and Hageman, P: Comparison of gait of young men and elderly men. Phys Ther 69:144, 1989.

APPENDIX 4-1: EXERCISES FOR PERSONS 55 YEARS OLD AND OLDER

These exercises are to be started gradually. Work at your own pace and level of ability. Start with 5 or 10 repetitions, and do fewer or more if you must or can. Slowly increase by adding 2 to 4, or more, repetitions every 5 to 10 days. Progress until you can do approximately 15 to 25 repetitions of each exercise. Do these exercises at least three times weekly.

1. High step

Hold on to chair for balance; stand up straight. Raise one foot off the floor so that your knee is as high as your hip. Reverse legs. Try not to lean on the chair too much. As you get stronger, you may be able to raise your leg higher, hold for count of 5 (less if necessary), and decrease amount of leaning on chair.

Purpose: To increase hip and leg strength and balance.

2. Side step

Hold on to chair for balance, stand up straight. Move one leg out to your side and hold it in the air. Don't bend at the waist. Hold leg for 5 seconds, or less if necessary. Reverse legs. At first, you may be unable to hold your leg in the air. If so, simply move your foot out to the side.

Purpose: To increase hip and leg strength and balance.

3. Stand up-sit down

This is the key to being independent. Simply stand up, then sit down. To do this, you must get your feet under the front of the chair. Move your center of gravity forward and then up. If necessary use the chair's arm rest. As you get stronger, decrease the amount of push that you need from your arms (see illustration below).

Purpose: To improve strength, balance, coordination, and joint motion.

4. Shoulder shrug

Sit up or stand up straight. Shrug your shoulders up high and release. Pull your shoulders back. You should feel your shoulder blades pull together. Purpose: To strengthen back, stretch chest muscles, and improve posture.

5. Cervical range of motion

Sit up or stand up, head erect but not forward.
a. Turn your chin to your left shoulder and reverse to the right.
b. Lean your ear to your left shoulder and reverse to the right.
c. Lightly place your finger on your chin and push your chin backward. *Do not* roll your head backward as if looking up at the ceiling.
Purpose: To improve posture, balance, and range of motion.

6. Walk, walk, walk

Walk at whatever level of ability you have. If you can walk only 50 feet, start at that level and try to increase the distance and improve your gait speed. Avoid stops and starts. If you are walking longer distances, such as a half-mile or longer in 5 to 10 minutes, do a little stretching before starting. When finishing your walk, cool down by simply walking slowly, stretching, and doing a few of these exercises or your favorite ones.
Purpose: To enhance overall health of muscles, bones, joints, circulation, heart, lungs, digestion, bowels, and mind.

If you need help getting started or if you have any concerns about your health, show these exercises to your physician.

The weakest and oldest among us can become some kind of athlete, but only the strongest can survive as spectators, only the hardiest can withstand the perils of inertia, inactivity, and immobility.

—J. H. BLAND AND S. M. COOPER, Musculoskeletal System. In Leon Sokolof: *The Musculoskeletal System*, Williams & Wilkins, Baltimore, 1975.

Chapter

Cardiopulmonary Development

ELIZABETH DEAN

OBJECTIVES

In relation to a specific case history, readers will be able to:

1 Describe the age-related changes that are expected in cardiopulmonary and cardiovascular function.

2 Describe the impact of disease on any changes in cardiopulmonary and cardiovascular function secondary to primary or secondary disease.

3 Describe the impact of inactivity on any changes in cardiopulmonary and cardiovascular function secondary to recumbency and inactivity.

4 Describe any changes in cardiopulmonary and cardiovascular function secondary to extrinsic factors, that is, to medical interventions, drugs, and so forth.

5 Describe any changes in cardiopulmonary and cardiovascular function secondary to intrinsic factors, that is, to the individual's characteristics, lifestyle, long-term occupation, coexistent morbidity, and so forth.

6 Based on the changes identified in objectives 1 through 5, describe and prioritize the goals of treatment.

7 Based on the changes identified in objectives 1

through 5, describe the focus of the assessment and the measures that would be most relevant to record.

8 Based on the changes identified in objectives 1 through 5, describe the treatment plan vis-à-vis prescribing training for functional performance, that is, ADL, functional capacity, or both.

9 Describe the precautions that you would take in assessing and prescribing ADL and/or exercise.

10 Given that a maximum exercise test was not feasible:
(a) describe the rationale for the short- and long-term responses that you would expect to your treatment plan, and
(b) describe what adverse responses this individual could exhibit in response to your treatment plan.

Human beings are designed to be bipedal, upright, and moving in a gravitational field, but they tend to spend less time upright and moving against gravity as they progress over the life cycle. This factor, combined with physiologic decline, contributes to overall losses in functional performance, ability to accomplish *activities of daily living* (ADL), and functional capacity, that is, aerobic capacity. As a result, an older person is more susceptible to debility and illness; even minor infections and afflictions can be a threat to life in an older recumbent, inactive person.

The primary goal of rehabilitation for older persons is to maximize function. Cardiopulmonary and cardiovascular capacity are significant determinants of functional abilities. There are two components of function that need to be addressed during rehabilitation. The first one is to maximize the person's physiologic capacity to adapt to the upright position and move against gravity, which are central components of functional performance. Secondly, an older person's cardiopulmonary and cardiovascular reserve capacity must be maximized to exceed his or her critical functional performance threshold.

A person's ability to perform functional activities is primarily dependent on the integrity of the cardiopulmonary and cardiovascular systems and their combined ability to effect oxygen transport and tissue oxygenation. Functional performance reflects the integrated action of multiple systems. (See Chapters 4, 6, and 7 in this text.)

Over the life cycle, the changes in the cardiopulmonary and cardiovascular systems have significant functional consequences (Tables 5–1 and 5–2). These effects are compounded by several other factors in older populations including the effects of cardiopulmonary and cardiovascular disease, the effects of recumbency and immobility, extrinsic factors related to medical care the person may be receiving, and intrinsic factors related to his or her unique characteristics, lifestyle, and coexistent morbidity.

The purposes of this chapter are to:

- Describe age-related changes in the cardiopulmonary and cardiovascular systems and their function
- Characterize other age-related factors that affect cardiopulmonary

and cardiovascular function in the older adult
- Analyze the functional consequences of age-related changes in the cardiopulmonary and cardiovascular systems
- Describe the implications of age-related changes for management of older persons with respect to maintaining or improving functional performance
- Examine means of optimizing an older person's ability to perform functional activities.

AGE-RELATED ANATOMIC CHANGES IN THE CARDIOPULMONARY SYSTEM AND ITS FUNCTION

Aging has a direct effect on each component of the cardiopulmonary system including the airways, lung parenchyma and its interface with the circulation (the alveolar capillary membrane), chest wall, and respiratory muscles. Ventilation of the alveoli and oxygenation of venous blood depends on the anatomic and physiologic integrity of these components.[1]

Airways

As in other systems, aging leads to a decrease in the amount of elastic tissue and an increase in fibrous tissue. Since the large airways are predominantly rigid connective tissue, few changes with aging are reported. Because the medium and small airways are composed of less connective tissue and more smooth muscle, a decrease in the elasticity of these structures occurs with aging, resulting in reduced structural integrity of the tissue and increased compliance.[2]

Lung Parenchyma

The lung parenchyma is composed of spongy alveolar tissue that is designed

TABLE 5-1 **Age-Related Changes in the Cardiopulmonary System and Its Function**

Morphological and Structural Changes	Functional Significance
Thorax	
Calcification of bronchial and costal cartilage	↑ Resistance to deformation of chest wall
↑ Stiffness of costovertebral joints	↓ Effective use of accessory respiratory muscles
↑ Anteroposterior diameter	↓ Tidal volume
↑ Wasting of respiratory muscles	↑ Exercise-induced hyperpnea
	↓ Maximal voluntary ventilation
	↓ Force of cough
	↑ Risk of aspiration or choking
Lung	
↑ Size of alveolar ducts	↓ Surface area for gas exchange
↓ Supporting duct framework	↑ Physiologic dead space
↑ Size of alveoli	↓ Elastic recoil
↑ Mucous glands	↓ Vital capacity
↑ Alveolar compliance	↓ Inspiratory reserve volume
	↑ Expiratory reserve volume
	↑ Functional residual volume and residual volume
	↓ Ventilatory flow rates
	↓ Distribution of ventilation
	↑ Closure of dependent airways
	↑ Arterial desaturation
	↑ Resistance to airflow in small airways
	↓ Pulmonary capillary network
	↓ Distribution of perfusion
	↑ Impaired diffusion capacity
	↑ Fibrosis of pulmonary capillary intima
	↓ Ventilation to perfusion matching

Source: Adapted from Reddan[1] and Bates.[4]

to be ventilated and provide an interface with the pulmonary blood through the alveolar capillary membrane, which has a large surface area to promote the oxygenation of blood. Age-related increases in connective tissue and elastin disintegration reduce elastic recoil, the principal mechanism of normal expiration. The loss of normal recoil contributes to uneven distribution of ventilation, airway closure, air trapping, and impaired gas exchange. The net result of these changes is a decrease in alveolar surface area.[3]

Alveolar Capillary Membrane

The alveolar capillary membrane is uniquely designed to optimize the diffusion of gases between the alveolar air and the pulmonary circulation. The diffusing capacity, that is, the ability of oxygen to diffuse from the aveolar airspaces into the pulmonary capillary, progressively declines with age and has been attributed to reduced alveolar surface area, alveolar volume, and pulmonary capillary bed.[4]

Chapter 5 • Cardiopulmonary Development
65

TABLE 5–2 **Age-Related Changes in the Cardiovascular System and Its Function**

Morphological and Structural Changes	Functional Significance
Heart	
↑ Fat constituents	↓ Excitability
↑ Fibrous constituents	↓ Cardiac output
↑ Mass and volume	↓ Venous return
↑ Lipofuscin (byproduct of glycogen metabolism)	↑ Cardiac dysrhythmias
↑ Amyloid content	
↓ Specialized nerve conduction tissue	
↓ Intrinsic and extrinsic innervation	
↑ Connective tissue and elastin	
↑ Calcification	
Blood Vessels	
↑ Loss of normal proportion of smooth muscle to connective tissue and elastin constituents	↓ Blood flow to oxygenate tissues
	↓ Blood flow and risk of clots in venous circulation
↑ Rigidity of large arteries	↓ Cardiac output
↑ Atheroma arterial circulation	↓ Venous return
↑ Calcification	
↑ Dilation and tortuosity of veins	

Source: Adapted from Higginbotham, Morris, and Williams,[7] Kantrowitz et al,[12] and Campbell, Caird, and Jackson.[15]

Chest Wall

The chest wall is composed of the structures separating the thorax from the head and neck, the diaphragm separating the thorax from the abdomen, the rib cage, the intercostal muscles, and the spinal column. With age, the joints of the thorax become more rigid, and cartilage becomes calcified; hence the chest wall becomes less compliant. The chest wall becomes barrel-shaped, the anteroposterior diameter increases, and the normal three-dimensional motion of the chest wall during the respiratory cycle is diminished.[5]

Respiratory Muscles

The diaphragm, the principal muscle of respiration, tends to flatten with age-related hyperinflation of the chest wall, reduced lung compliance and air trapping in the lungs, and possibly secondary to reduced muscle mass. Loss of res-piratory muscle mass parallels the age-related reduction in skeletal muscle mass in general.[6] Loss of abdominal muscle strength reduces the force of coughing, which can contribute to aspiration.

Net Effect of Age-Related Cardiopulmonary Changes

These anatomic changes give rise to predictable physiologic or functional changes in pulmonary function after the pulmonary system has matured (Table 5–1). Respiratory mechanics that largely reflect the resistance to airflow and the compliance of the chest wall and lung parenchyma are altered. Specifically, both airflow resistance and lung compliance increase. With respect to pulmonary function, forced expiratory volumes and flows and inspiratory and expiratory pressures are reduced.[7,8] Functional residual capacity and residual volume are increased. These effects are further accentuated in recumbent positions. Arterial oxygen tension and saturation are also reduced linearly with age.[9] Thus, progressively over the life cycle, the lung becomes a less efficient gas exchanger.

AGE-RELATED CHANGES IN THE CARDIOVASCULAR SYSTEM AND ITS FUNCTION

The cardiovascular system is composed of the heart and vasculature. Loss of efficiency of the cardiovascular system occurs with age.

Heart

ELECTRICAL BEHAVIOR

With aging, the heart's conduction system changes such that the frequency and regularity of cardiac impulses may become abnormal secondary to fibrotic changes in the specialized nerve conduction system of the heart and musculature.[10] In cases where the electrical activity of the heart cannot be stabilized or regulated with medications, artificial pacemakers are often implanted.

MECHANICAL BEHAVIOR

The heart pumps less effectively with age as a result of changes in the mechanical properties of the cardiac muscle, which alter the length-tension and force-velocity relationships. Additionally, changes with age in both the integrity of the valves—those between the atria and ventricles and those between the ventricles—and variations in the aging pulmonary and systemic circulations result in less efficient pumping action of the heart.[11]

Histologically, the heart tissue becomes fattier, and both heart mass and volume increase. *Amyloidosis*, a histologic feature of aging observed in many organs including the heart and vasculature, is characterized by the progressive deposition of amyloid protein.[12] This waxy protein infiltrates tissue, rendering it dysfunctional.

In general, the walls of the heart become more compliant with age. The myocardial fibers no longer contract at optimal points on the length-tension or force-velocity curves, which reduces the efficiency of myocardial contraction.

Blood Vessels

Blood vessels require varying degrees of distensibility or compliance depending on their specific function. The forward motion of blood on the arterial side of the circulation is a function of the elastic recoil of the vessel walls and the progressive loss of pressure energy down the vascular tree. The decrease of elasticity of the arterial vessels with aging may result in chronic or residual increases in vessel diameter and vessel wall rigidity, which impair the function of the vessel.

The reservoir function of the venous circulation is dependent on its being highly compliant to accommodate the greatest proportion of the blood volume at rest. Although the mechanical characteristics of venous smooth muscle have been less well studied compared with arterial smooth muscle, the efficiency of its contractile behavior can be expected to be reduced with aging. Further, its electrical excitability and responsiveness to neurohumoral transmitters tends to be less rapid and less pronounced.

BLOOD

A discussion of the effects of aging on the cardiopulmonary and cardiovascular systems would not be complete without reference to the blood—the medium that it moves—and the ability of the heart and vasculature to move blood. The ability of the vasculature to move blood through the vascular system and shift volumes of blood between vascular beds depending on need is diminished with aging, and the rapidity with which these changes can be effected is correspondingly reduced.[13] The ability to effect these vascular adjustments in response to gravity and exercise are tantamount to effective physical functioning.

Net Effects of Age-Related Cardiovascular Changes

The age-related anatomical and physiological changes of the heart and blood vessels result in reduced capacity for oxygen transport at rest and in particular, in response to situations imposing an increase in metabolic demand for oxygen[14] (Table 5–2). Therefore, activities associated with a relatively low metabolic demand are perceived by older persons as physically demanding. Certain activities may no longer be able to be performed whereas others may require rest periods in between.

Fifty percent of older persons have been reported to have electrical conduction abnormalities at rest, which has considerable implications for the mechanical behavior of the heart and the regulation of cardiac output, particularly when stressed during activity and exercise.[15] A high proportion of conduction irregularities occurs in the absence of clinical heart disease.[16]

OTHER FACTORS THAT AFFECT CARDIOPULMONARY AND CARDIOVASCULAR FUNCTION

Numerous factors contribute to impaired oxygen transport in older persons and are summarized in Table 5–3. Establishing the relative contribution of these factors is central to defining treatment goals and treatment parameters. (See "Implications for the Management of Older Persons" later in this chapter.)

Pathophysiology

Cardiopulmonary disease is prevalent in older age groups.[17] Chronic airflow limitation is most frequently manifested as chronic bronchitis and emphysema. Asthma, characterized by hyperexcitability of bronchial smooth muscle, may occur on its own or as a component of chronic airflow limitation. Although less common, restrictive lung disease is also prevalent in older age groups and results from prolonged exposure to a variety of pulmonary irritants[18] (Table 5–4).

Depending on the severity of the disease, individuals may report shortness of breath on exertion or at rest. In chronic airflow limitation, the person presents with a barrel chest. Loss of the elastic recoil of the lungs results in hyperinflation of the chest wall, flattening of the hemidiaphragms, and air trapping. Although total lung capacity is unchanged, these changes impair the efficiency of respiratory mechanics, resulting in inefficient ventilation, impaired gas mixing, and impaired ventilation and perfusion matching.[19] These individuals tend to adopt a breathing pattern characterized by prolonged expiration to help promote gas exchange in the lungs. The metabolic cost of breathing is also increased. Individuals with restrictive lung disease tend to have fibrotic, stiff lungs which have reduced compliance and thus are more difficult to expand and ventilate with normal ventilatory efforts. The work of breathing needed to inflate the lungs and counter the greater proportion of dead space particularly during exercise is disproportionate. To reduce the work of breathing, individuals with restrictive disease adopt rapid shallow breathing patterns.

Both types of lung pathology, airflow limitation and restriction, can lead to impaired oxygen tension in the blood during exercise and in severe cases even at rest. The additional metabolic cost of breathing in individuals with moderate to severe disease of either type contributes significantly to the overall metabolic cost of a given activity or exercise. These individuals are in danger of significantly desaturating their blood during increased workloads; thus monitoring vital signs, arterial saturation, and subjective response during prescribed activities or exercise is essential.

Cardiovascular abnormalities are

TABLE 5–3 **Factors Contributing to Cardiopulmonary and Cardiovascular Dysfunction and Impaired Oxygen Transport in Older People**

I. AGE-RELATED CHANGES
  Cardiopulmonary system
  Cardiovascular system
  Hematologic factors

II. CARDIOPULMONARY AND CARDIOVASCULAR DISEASE
  Acute
  Chronic
  Acute and chronic

III. BEDREST OR RECUMBENCY AND IMMOBILITY
  Removal of gravitational stress
  Removal of exercise stress

IV. EXTRINSIC FACTORS, I.E., THOSE IMPOSED BY MEDICAL OR SURGICAL CARE
  Hospitalization
  Fever
  Malaise
  Reduced arousal
  Surgery, e.g., type, positioning, type and depth of sedatives and anesthesia, incisions, duration, blood and fluid administration, use of bypass machine, intraoperative complications
  Dressings and bindings
  Casts or splinting devices, traction
  Incisions
  Invasive lines, catheter, or chest tubes
  Monitoring equipment (invasive and noninvasive)
  Medications
  Portable equipment, e.g., IVs, O_2 tanks
  Intubation
  Mechanical ventilation
  Suctioning
  Pain
  Multisystem complications

V. INTRINSIC FACTORS, I.E., THOSE IMPOSED BY THE INDIVIDUAL'S CHARACTERISTICS, LIFESTYLE, AND MEDICAL AND SURGICAL HISTORIES
  Gender
  Ethnicity
  Sociocultural background
  Smoking history
  Occupation
  Environment, e.g., humidity, temperature, oxygen concentration, and air quality
  Quantity and quality of sleep
  Obesity
  Nutritional deficits
  Stress, anxiety, and depression
  Deformity
  Congenital abnormalities
  Walking aids and devices
  Habitual activity and conditioning level
  Reaction to medications
  Adherence to medication schedules
  Adherence to recommendations from health care professionals
  Immunity
  Fluid and electrolyte balance
  Anemia or polycythemia
  Thyroid and other endocrine abnormalities
  Previous medical and surgical histories

Source: Adapted from Dean and Ross[28] and Dean and Ross.[31]

TABLE 5–4 **Pulmonary Diseases and Cardiovascular Abnormalities**

Type	Presenting Symptoms and Signs	Anatomical and Physiological Changes	Impairments
Chronic airflow limitation	Barrel chest May have shortness of breath on exertion or rest Breathing pattern: Prolonged expiration	Hyperinflation of chest wall Flattening of hemidiaphragms Air trapping Increased metabolic costs of breathing	Inefficient ventilation Impaired gas mixing Impaired ventilation
Restrictive lung disease	Breathing pattern: rapid, shallow	Fibrotic stiff lungs	Reduced compliance Increased effort to inflate lungs
Atherosclerosis	High blood pressure Ischemic chest pain Myocardial infarction	Fatty atheromatous plaques within blood vessel walls Vessel wall rigidity	Stenosed arteries Increased peripheral resistance
Diabetes	Hypoglycemia with activity or exercise	Similar to atherosclerosis	Similar to atherosclerosis

common in older age groups.[19] Atherosclerosis, blood pressure abnormalities, and the vascular components from diabetes are common in the older adult. *Atherosclerosis* is a degenerative disease of the arterial vasculature, especially the large arteries. Atherosclerosis affecting the coronary arteries is termed *coronary artery disease* and is the major cause of morbidity and mortality in older persons in the Western industrialized countries.

Hypertension is the blood pressure abnormality frequently occurring in the older adult.[20] Because hypertension is not generally associated with unpleasant symptoms, the individual may be unaware of the condition and may not seek medical attention nor be inclined to take medication regularly. The consequences of high blood pressure, stroke, and heart disease are dire, and its control significantly reduces the complications, cardiovascular death, congestive heart failure, and stroke.[20] Alternatively, some older persons are prone to hypotension particularly during positional changes. A diminished responsiveness of autonomic adjustments may be responsible.

Another common disease in the older adult that has serious vascular conse-

quences is diabetes, usually of the adult-onset type.[21] Hypermetabolism associated with activity and exercise places increased demand on the energy stores and insulin requirements. Another vascular consequence of diabetes is that the rate of atherosclerosis is accelerated by a decade compared with the nondiabetic older population, and these individuals are at an additional risk during activity and exercise.

Gravitational Stress and Exercise Stress

Oxygen transport and tissue oxygenation are dependent upon the body's ability to provide an adequate cardiac output to the peripheral tissues commensurate with tissue demand. Physical factors that normally challenge the body's ability to maintain or increase cardiac output include position change, activity or exercise, and emotional stress. The older adult may be limited in ability to adjust to the gravitational and exercise stress caused by normal activities if a greater proportion of time has been spent recumbent or if activity has been limited. Reduction in gravitational stress and exercise stress contributes to physiological deterioration and susceptibility to illness.

PHYSIOLOGICAL RESPONSES TO GRAVITATIONAL STRESS

Orthostatism refers to the ability of the body to maintain normal cardiac output, in particular, cerebral perfusion, during assumption of the upright body position. On moving from the recumbent to the upright position, blood volume is displaced toward the abdominal cavity and the legs.[22,23] This blood volume displacement reduces venous return; hence, cardiac output, resulting in a compensatory increase in heart rate and peripheral vascular resistance to increased blood pressure and cardiac output. If this neurological compensation is ineffective, cerebral perfusion is compromised, and a blackout or fainting may ensue.

During recumbency, this sequence of events is reversed. The blood volume is displaced centrally toward the heart and lungs. Venous return is increased, resulting in a compensatory decrease in heart rate and peripheral vascular resistance to maintain cardiac output. The increased central blood volume leads to a compensatory diuresis within hours of assuming the recumbent position. Thus, overall blood volume is reduced, and the person is prone to orthostatic intolerance on assuming the upright position.[24] The loss of fluid volume–regulating mechanisms, rather than cardiovascular deconditioning, has been reported to be the primary factor responsible for bed rest deconditioning.[25,26] The only means of preventing orthostatic intolerance following recumbency is to assume the upright position frequently. This adaptation is further augmented if coupled with movement; however, exercise in the absence of being upright fails to counter orthostatic intolerance.[27] In addition to the primary beneficial adaptive responses that being upright and moving have on oxygen transport, virtually every other organ-system benefits when an individual is upright and moving.[28]

PHYSIOLOGICAL RESPONSES TO EXERCISE STRESS

Exercise increases the metabolic demand for oxygen and substrates. With aging, the oxygen transport system is less capable of responding to exercise stress as a consequence of the diminished efficiency of the various steps in the oxygen transport pathway.[29]

Despite the reported age-related changes, the considerable reserve capacity of the cardiopulmonary and cardiovascular systems tends to offset the potential functional consequences. The degree of this compensation, however, is highly variable among individual older persons. Although this variability reflects genetic factors to a considerable extent, fitness and lifestyle factors also have a significant role. Cardiopulmonary and cardiovascular reserve capacity are maximized with exercise irrespective of age.[30]

Extrinsic Factors

Extrinsic factors that can affect cardiopulmonary and cardiovascular function in older persons include *iatrogenic factors*, that is, secondary effects from the medical care that an individual may be receiving.[31] In the context of function in the older medically stable adult, the effects of medication and routine medical procedures are likely to be the most important extrinsic factors. It is not uncommon for older persons to be taking one or more medications. Although a medication may have a specific and beneficial effect, it may have an untoward effect elsewhere. For example, beta blockers are highly effective in improving the mechanical efficiency of the heart; however, these drugs blunt the normal hemodynamic responses to exercise, and some patients report experiencing undue fatigue when on these medications. Routine medical procedures adversely affect cardiopulmonary and cardiovascular function secondary to confinement to a body position (typically recumbent) for a prolonged period, immobility, insertion of invasive lines and leads, and associated medications and hospitalization. The morbidity and mortality associated with these routine procedures are accentuated in older persons.

Intrinsic Factors

Intrinsic factors that affect cardiopulmonary and cardiovascular function are those that are imposed by the general history, background, and characteristics of the individual.[31] For example, the effects of nonprimary cardiopulmonary and cardiovascular disease—that is, manifestations of diseases of the renal, hepatic, neurological, endocrine, gastrointestinal, immune, hematologic, and musculoskeletal systems—can have significant consequences on cardiopulmonary and cardiovascular function.[32] In addition, connective tissue disorders can have significant cardiopulmonary and cardiovascular manifestations. Although the secondary manifestations of diseases of these systems can be more obscure than manifestations of primary disease of the heart and lungs, their diagnosis is more difficult and their prognosis tends to be poorer.

Like other dynamic functions of the human body, the function of the heart and lungs is dependent on adequate nutrition and hydration. The appropriate energy sources must be available to the metabolically active tissues. Older persons may be uninformed or negligent about their nutritional and fluid needs or incapable of meeting these needs either physically or economically. On the other extreme is the problem of obesity, which has been described as being a problem of epidemic proportions in North America. With reduced muscle mass and reduced cardiopulmonary and cardiovascular reserves associated with aging, being overweight constitutes a significant additional load that can further impair heart and lung function and musculoskeletal function, and hence, threaten functional independence. In Western countries, there is a tendency to gain weight with advancing years; however, this trend reverses in the very old age groups.

Other intrinsic factors that affect cardiopulmonary and cardiovascular function include current and long-term lifestyle practices. An individual's long-term occupation and the environment in which it was carried out can have significant long-term consequences, for example, the occurrence of interstitial lung disease in workers exposed to toxic environmental agents. Also, years of active and passive smoking are well-known risk factors for chronic airflow limitation and cancer.

Reduced cardiopulmonary and cardiovascular function can result from factors other than dysfunction of the primary organ systems that are directly responsible for effecting functional activity. For example, sleep deprivation, nutritional deficits, or impaired cognition have obvious ramifications on function and independence. Some older persons may experience stress, anxiety and depression, which contribute to low energy, fatigue, withdrawal, and social isolation.[33] Impaired cognitive ability or dementia[34] may significantly restrict an older person's activity level because of the need for supervision.

FUNCTIONAL CONSEQUENCES OF AGE-RELATED CARDIOPULMONARY AND CARDIOVASCULAR CHANGES

Function can be categorized as ADL, exercise, or general activity. The focus of this chapter is on ADL and exercise. ADL includes self-care activities, sexual activity, and home and family management and work. Exercise encompasses those activities that require some degree of endurance, demanding the maintenance of increased oxygen transport and tissue oxygenation. Although other types of "activity," such as card playing, require an increase in metabolic demand greater than at rest, the increased metabolic demand is not usually sustained. In addition, this chapter distinguishes between functional performance and functional capacity. *Functional performance* pertains to task completion required in ADL that impose stress on the oxygen transport system above that imposed by resting metabolic demand. *Functional capacity* refers to the capacity of the cardiovascular system to transport oxygen.

Different types of exercise tests are used to assess functional performance and functional capacity. In both cases, appropriate standards, procedures and monitoring are essential to ensure the tests are valid and reliable and are performed with maximal safety. Tests of ADL assess functional performance whereas conventional exercise tests are designed to measure functional capacity. The results of both types of tests yield important, but different, types of information about an individual's level of functioning.

The Functional Performance Threshold

The ability to perform ADL to a criterion compatible with personal care and independent living can be thought of as a functional performance threshold.[35] Young people have considerable physiological capacity and reserve that enable them to perform activities and exercise well in excess of the metabolic and physical demands required by routine daily activities. With aging, however, changes to the various organ systems, particularly the lungs, heart, nervous system, endocrine system and musculature, reduce physiological capacity and reserve. If physical decline results in a functional capacity below the functional performance threshold, that individual will be unable to meet the minimum criterion for self-care and independent living. Falling below this threshold can result from progressive age-related changes or an extended period of immobility or illness sufficient to lower an individual's already minimal reserves (Fig. 5–1).

The rate of decline in functional capacity with age and the decline in functional performance are qualitatively different. Although functional capacity deteriorates linearly with advancing age, the decrease in functional performance declines in a curvilinear manner. Thus, an individual can lose significant capacity yet retain considerable function over the years (Fig. 5–2).

A rational objective of rehabilitation for older persons is to maintain physiological capacity and reserve well above the functional performance threshold. The basis for this objective is threefold. First, the individual will be able to perform self-care and be functionally independent. Second, this level of physical performance will avoid the negative consequences of immobility and is consistent with health promotion. Third, should the individual be exposed to a period of relative inactivity or become ill, a greater initial functional capacity provides a greater margin of safety. Detraining effects will be minimized, and faster recovery will be likely. Research is needed to determine precisely the level of functional performance that is needed in older persons to minimize morbidity and mortality, and the optimal parameters of an exercise prescription that would best achieve this result.

Metabolic Demand of Activities of Daily Living and Exercise

The metabolic demand of an activity can be defined by the unit called the *metabolic equivalent* (MET). One MET is equal to 3.5 mL O_2/kg of body weight per minute, the normal basal metabolic demand for oxygen.[36,37] By convention, the metabolic demands of different activities are expressed as multiples of the basal metabolic rate[38] (Table 5–5). Theoretically, the metabolic demand for a given activity does not vary. Even though an individual is deconditioned or older and perceives an activity as more physiologically demanding, the metabolic demand of activities does not change.[39] The effect of skill level and

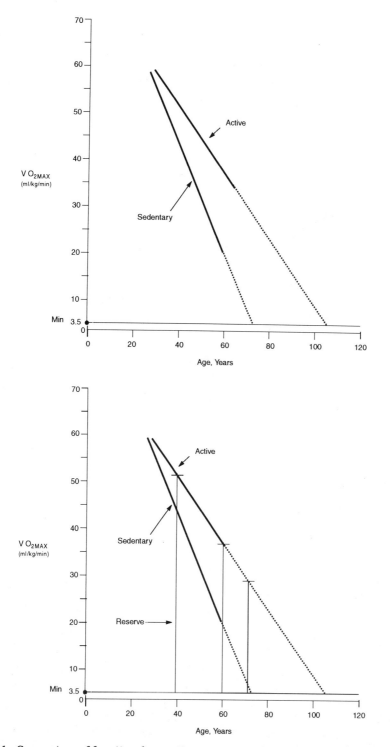

Figure 5–1 Comparison of functional capacity reserve in sedentary and active men across the life cycle. The upper graph illustrates that the rate of decline in functional aerobic capacity is less in active than sedentary men. The lower graph illustrates that functional capacity is increased disproportionately with aging in active versus sedentary individuals. Min VO_2 refers to basal metabolic rate (i.e., 3.5 ml O_2/kg of body weight/min). (Adapted from Davies.[14])

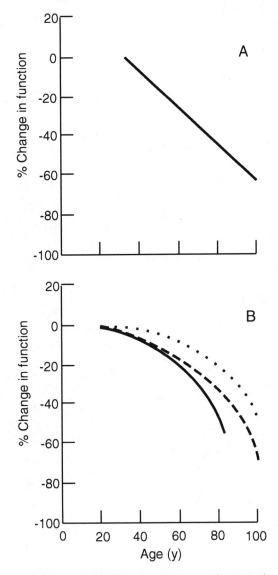

Figure 5–2 Comparison of changes in functional capacity and functional performance over the life cycle. Graph *A* illustrates the linear decline of the percent change in functional capacity with increasing age. Graph *B* illustrates the curvilinear decline in the percent change in functional performance with increasing age. After the ages of 70 to 80, the decline in percent change in functional capacity and performance tend to parallel each other. (Adapted from Convertino et al[25], Luce et al[6] and Vandervoort et al.[84])

biomechanical efficiency on metabolic cost of common activities is generally small. Research is needed, however, to examine the effect of aging on metabolic cost of activity. The effect of changes in stature over the life cycle and altered center of gravity on the metabolic cost of physical activities as well as gender differences need to be studied.

The metabolic costs of sexual activity and the capacity to work has been relatively neglected in the literature particularly with respect to older persons. The American Heart Association[40] recommends that sexual activity can be tolerated if the individual can maintain steady-state exercise of 6 to 8 cal/min on the treadmill or 600 klb/m on the cycle

	TABLE 5–5 **Metabolic Demands of Activity and Exercise**		
Intensity, 70-kg person	**Endurance Promoting**	**Occupational**	**Recreational**
1½–2 MET 4–7 mL/kg/min 2–2½ kcal/min	Too low in energy level.	Deskwork, driving auto, electric calculating machine operation, light housework, polishing furniture, washing clothes	Standing, strolling (1 mi/h), flying, motorcycling, playing cards, sewing, knitting
2–3 MET 7–11 mL/kg/min 2½–4 kcal/min	Too low in energy level unless capacity is very low.	Auto repair, radio and television repair, janitorial work, bartending, riding lawn mower, light woodworking	Level walking (2 mi/h), level bicycling (5 mi/h), billiards, bowling, skeet shooting, shuffleboard, powerboat driving, golfing with power cart, canoeing, horseback riding at a walk
3–4 MET 11–14 mL/kg/min 4–5 kcal/min	Yes, if continuous and if target heart rate is reached.	Brick laying, plastering, wheelbarrow (100-lb load), machine assembly, welding (moderate load), cleaning windows, mopping floors, vacuuming, pushing light power mower	Walking (3 mi/h), bicycling (6 mi/h), horseshoe pitching, volleyball (6-person, noncompetitive), golfing (pulling bag cart), archery, sailing (handling small boat), fly fishing (standing in waders), horseback riding (trotting), badminton (social doubles)
4–5 MET 14–18 mL/kg/min	Recreational activities promote endurance. Occupational activities must be continuous, lasting longer than 2 min.	Painting, masonry, paperhanging, light carpentry, scrubbing floors, raking leaves, hoeing	Walking (3½ mi/h), bicycling (8 mi/h), table tennis, golfing (carrying clubs), dancing (foxtrot), badminton (singles), tennis (doubles), many calisthenics, ballet
5–6 MET 18–21 mL/kg/min	Yes	Digging garden, shoveling light earth	Walking (4 mi/h), bicycling (10 mi/h), canoeing (4 mi/h), horseback riding (posting to trotting), stream fishing (walking in light current in waders), ice or roller skating (9 mi/h)
6–7 MET 21–25 mL/kg/min 7–8 kcal/min	Yes	Shoveling 10 times/min (4½ kg or 10 lb), splitting wood, snow shoveling, hand lawn mowing	Walking (5 mi/h), bicycling (11 mi/h), competitive badminton, tennis (singles), folk and square dancing, light downhill skiing, ski touring (2½ mi/h), water skiing, swimming (20 yard/min)

continued

TABLE 5–5 **Metabolic Demands of Activity and Exercise (Continued)**

Intensity, 70-kg person	Endurance Promoting	Occupational	Recreational
7–8 MET 25–28 mL/kg/min 8–10 kcal/min	Yes	Digging ditches, carrying 36 kg or 80 lb, sawing hardwood	Jogging (5 mi/h), bicycling (12 mi/h), horseback riding (gallop), vigorous downhill skiing, basketball, mountain climbing, ice hockey, canoeing (5 mi/h), touch football, paddleball
8–9 MET 28–32 mL/kg/min 10–11 kcal/min	Yes	Shoveling 10 times/min (5½ kg or 14 lb)	Running (5½ mi/h), bicycling (13 mi/h), ski touring (4 mi/h), squash (social), handball (social), fencing, basketball (vigorous), swimming (30 yard/min), rope skipping
10+ MET 32+ mL/kg/min 11+ kcal/min	Yes	Shoveling 10 times/min (7½ kg or 16 lb)	Running (6 mi/h = 10 MET, 7 mi/h = 11½ MET. 8 mi/h = 13½ MET, 9 mi/h = 15 MET, 10 mi/h = 17 MET), ski touring (5+ mi/h), handball (competitive), squash (competitive), swimming (greater than 40 yard/min)

Source: From Fox et al,[38] with permission.

ergometer. If aerobically conditioned, an older person can perform physical activity such as sexual intercourse with reduced heart rate and blood pressure and overall exertion.[41] To further minimize the metabolic demand and exercise stress, sexual encounters can be timed with medications and with energy peaks during the day. Body positions during intercourse can be modified; upright positions will likely be better tolerated than recumbency.

Increased longevity and nonmandatory retirement has raised interest in vocational assessment for older persons. The ability to perform a certain type of work can be predicted on the basis of an exercise test. If a given occupation exceeds 40 percent of an individual's peak oxygen consumption in an exercise test, the American Thoracic So-

ciety has advocated that the individual would not be able to tolerate working at that occupation for prolonged periods.[42] Research is needed to refine and extend guidelines for older persons who are considering changing occupations or reentering the labor force.

Progressive changes in the cardiopulmonary and cardiovascular systems in conjunction with changes in the capacity for oxygen and substrate utilization in the musculature results in less efficient oxygen transport in the older adult. With activity and exercise, the increased metabolic demand for oxygen and substrate require a commensurate increase in ventilation and cardiac output. Both maximal ventilation and cardiac output decline linearly with age, and maximal oxygen consumption is correspondingly reduced. The extraction of oxygen at the tissue level, however, which is measured by the arteriovenous oxygen difference, does not change significantly with age.

The degree of endurance needed to perform ADL varies depending upon the task. Those ADL that are primarily skill-based, such as dressing, toileting, grooming, shaving, bathing, and feeding, are associated with low metabolic demand and generally require little endurance. Restriction of skill-based ADL in older persons tends to reflect musculoskeletal or neuromuscular deficits rather than difficulties with oxygen transport or gas exchange. However, other ADL, including ambulation, climbing stairs and hills, yardwork, housework, shopping, gardening, sexual activity, volunteer work, gainful employment, managing transportation, and social activities outside the home are associated with higher metabolic demand, require greater endurance, and tend to reflect the status of the cardiopulmonary and cardiovascular systems.

Whether an active lifestyle contributes to or results from cardiopulmonary and cardiovascular conditioning warrants discussion. The question can best be addressed by examining the elements of aerobic conditioning. To elicit an aerobic training response, the stimulus must be of sufficient intensity, frequency, and duration and carried out over a sufficiently long period of time. The critical parameters of the prescription needed to effect an aerobic training response are the performance of aerobic exercise for 20 to 30 minutes, at 60 to 70 percent of the maximum oxygen consumption that is associated with a heart rate between 70 to 80 percent of the maximum heart rate, for a minimum of 3 days a week for 3 to 6 months.[36] The physiological adaptations that result reflect an increased ability to transport oxygen and to utilize oxygen and metabolic substrates at the tissue level.

Depending on an individual's age, most ADL and habitual activity are not performed at a sufficient intensity, or duration, frequency or over a sufficient time period to effect long-term aerobic adaptations. However, habitual activity does maintain sufficient physiological adaptation to perform tasks associated with low metabolic demand.[43] Given that maximal heart rate and aerobic capacity diminish with age, even skill-based ADL can become aerobically demanding. Routine walks down hospital corridors, for example, can be associated with an intensity of exercise that exceeds acceptable limits in some older individuals using walkers.[44] This scenario is one in which individuals are frequently not monitored. Thus, routine tasks and activities not considered to be metabolically demanding must be analyzed at two levels: their relative physiologic demand on a given individual and the individual's capacity to meet that metabolic demand such that the adaptation that is elicited is both therapeutic and safe.

Assessing Functional Performance

The objective of the assessment of functional performance is to determine the individual's ability to perform ADL. Numerous performance tests have been described previously in the literature.[45-50] Such tests must be performed according to standardized criteria to ensure their validity and reliability. A major liability of these tests, however, is that patient monitoring is seldom considered an integral component of the test. Although not associated with large metabolic demands, ADL are often experienced as physically demanding by older persons. With cardiopulmonary dysfunction superimposed, monitoring an older person's responses to normal ADL and exercise are critical components of assessment. Without appropriate monitoring, the rehabilitation specialist may underestimate the physiological demand placed on the patient.

Although fundamental to normal function, movement constitutes a physiological stressor, thus is inherently risky, particularly in older persons.[51] Possible adverse effects include abnormal heart rate, blood pressure, and breathing frequency; cardiac dysrhythmias; altered intraabdominal and thoracic pressures; and reduced venous return, stroke volume, and cardiac output. In turn, the work of breathing and of the heart may be excessive, which adds further to the overall metabolic cost of the activity.

Assessing the ability to perform an ADL should be viewed as a unique form of exercise test. Base-line measures including heart rate and rhythm, breathing frequency, systolic and diastolic blood pressure, rate pressure product (the product of heart rate and systolic blood pressure, which is highly correlated with myocardial oxygen consumption and the work of the heart), and perceived exertion provide valuable information about an individual's ability to perform an activity.

The rehabilitation specialist needs a thorough understanding of the physiological demands of the activity or exercise that the person is performing so that the person is performing so that the exercise response can be anticipated and is appropriate. For example, aerobic activities with incremental work rates, preferably involving the legs, will result in a commensurate increase in heart rate, blood pressure, breathing depth and rate, and increased perceived exertion.[52] Activities involving primarily the arms, such as hair combing or snow shoveling, result in a disproportionate increase in blood pressure and work of the heart compared with dynamic exercise, and should be monitored carefully in the older person.[53]

Many ADL require a change in body position, such as getting out of bed, the tub, or a chair or picking up something off the floor. Although these may not be metabolically demanding, such activities lead to significant fluid shifts secondary to the effect of gravity and have profound hemodynamic consequences. Because the fluid volume–regulating mechanisms in older persons may be blunted, dizziness, blackouts, or fainting can result. Thus, the hemodynamic status of these individuals needs to be monitored until the rehabilitation spe-

cialist has confidence that these activities can be safely performed.

Activities such as getting out of bed, the tub, or a chair or getting off the toilet may appear comparable; however, the mechanisms of orthostatic intolerance associated with each can differ. Getting out of bed in the morning may be accompanied by morning stiffness, imbalance, slowed vital signs, slowed autonomic responsiveness, and reduced muscle pump activity in the legs. Getting out of the tub is associated with significant peripheral vasodilation from having been in warm water for a period of time. Thus, adaptation of the normal fluid shifts will be poorer on assuming the standing position. Getting off the toilet may follow a period of autonomic changes and physical straining, hence reduced venous return. Orthostatic intolerance associated with getting out of a chair may reflect fluid shifts and pooling of blood in the abdomen and legs during sitting. Finally, orthostatic intolerance associated with picking an item off the floor may reflect reduced cerebral blood flow secondary to the sudden movement to the erect position and the lack of the normal rapid compensatory response. Observing and monitoring each individual's objective and subjective responses to changes in body position enables the rehabilitation specialist to make specific recommendations aimed at reducing the risk of blackouts, fainting, and falling.

Another critical factor that may have significant effects on an older person's ability to perform an activity or exercise is impaired thermoregulation. Older people have a reduced capacity to thermoregulate. A significant proportion suffer from hypothermia,[54] and others may have an impaired ability to lose exercise-induced body heat. The increase in peripheral blood flow to dissipate heat during activity, especially in a warm ambient environment, may compromise cardiac output and blood flow to the working muscles. Failure of blood pressure–regulating mechanisms may be responsible.[55] Activity in warm environments taxes the individual to an even greater extent and may exacerbate congestive heart failure and dehydration. The individual may show signs of lightheadedness, disorientation, instability, fainting, and heart irregularities.

Functional Capacity

Functional capacity refers to the capacity to respond to an exercise stimulus, maintain the physiological adjustments necessary to sustain aerobic exercise for a period of time, and then recover appropriately from that stimulus on cessation of exercise. Although this capacity declines with increasing age, individual differences in older people are considerably greater than for young people. Formal exercise in the older adult accrues the same physiological benefits as in younger people with respect to enhanced oxygen transport.[56-58]

Assessing Functional Capacity

Assessing functional capacity involves determining an individual's peak aerobic power or ability to sustain aerobic exercise over time. These assessments are typically based on the results of a peak exercise test or endurance test. Although exercise testing is a well-established practice for patients with cardiopulmonary and cardiovascular dysfunction as well as for healthy people, exercise testing and training in older age groups is not as advanced. This may reflect the inherent challenges of dealing with older age groups related to the prevalence of multisystem complications such as arthritis, cardiopulmonary and cardiovascular dysfunction, hypertension, obesity, diabetes, thyroid problems, depression, and cognitive impairment. Although peak aerobic power may be of physiological interest in older people, endurance is likely to have greater practical value with respect to functional capacity overall.

To assess functional capacity in young people, maximum exercise testing is considered the gold standard. The results of a maximum exercise test provide a profile of the individual's capacity to transport oxygen during progressive increments in work rates and the upper limit of oxygen consumption for that individual.

Although maximum tests have a role in assessing older athletes, they are of less value in assessing older people in general. Maximum exercise tests are neither feasible nor safe for most nonathletic older people, and the criterion for defining the test as a true maximum test is unlikely to be achieved in this population. Instead, peak or submaximal exercise tests are used in older people as they provide practical information regarding an individual's functional capacity and endurance. In a maximum exercise test, the individual undergoes an incremental protocol until the maximum oxygen consumption is reached. Submaximal testing is associated with less risk, is more pleasant to perform, and can be readily administered by a knowledgeable rehabilitation specialist.

Principles for selecting and administering submaximal exercise tests have been described in detail in the literature previously[28]; the clinical decision-making process is summarized in Table 5–6. The goal of the test needs to be determined and a decision made as to whether a symptom and/or sign limited test or a steady-state exercise test is indicated. Endurance can be tested either with a continuous steady-state test or a test involving an interrupted protocol for individuals with very low functional work capacity.

Considerable research is needed to maximize the validity and reliability of submaximal exercise testing procedures and thereby increase the diagnostic and clinical value of performing these tests in populations where maximum testing has fewer indications. Despite their limitations, if carefully administered and the procedures appropriately documented, submaximal exercise testing can provide a basis for prescribing activity and exercise that is both therapeutic and safe for older people.[59]

TABLE 5-6	**Clinical Decision-Making Process: Principles for Selecting and Administering Submaximal Exercise Tests**

PRESESSION PATIENT CHECK
Appropriateness of time of day for activity or exercise for individual
Quality of night's sleep
Activity prior to the session, e.g., visitors, tests, agitations or irritations
Discomfort or pain
Competing demands
Timing with respect to medications
Types of changes in medications
Lability of vital signs or hemodynamic instability
General well-being
Interest and motivation

ESTIMATE FUNCTIONAL CAPACITY
Estimate based on history and assessment
Possible outcomes: High, intermediate or low

IF THE ESTIMATED FUNCTIONAL CAPACITY IS HIGH*:

Test Options
Peak exercise test
Continuous incremental protocol on treadmill or ergometer
Maximal exercise test
Continuous incremental protocol on treadmill or ergometer

Note: Depending on the individual's age, history, and assessment, either type of test may require a
physician present.

Activities of daily living
High metabolic demand

Test End Points
Based on the history and assessment, determine relative and absolute end points that indicate the
discontinuation of ADL or exercise

IF THE ESTIMATED FUNCTIONAL CAPACITY IS INTERMEDIATE:

Test Options
Submaximal exercise test
Continuous incremental or steady-state protocol on modality or 6- or 12-min walk test
Activities of daily living
Intermediate metabolic demand

Test End Points
As above

IF THE ESTIMATED FUNCTIONAL CAPACITY IS LOW:

Test Options
Submaximal exercise test
Interrupted protocol on modality or 3- or 6-min walk test
Activities of daily living
Low metabolic demand either interrupted or uninterrupted

Test End Points
As above

MONITORING
Level of monitoring before, during, and after testing determined by history and assessment

Basic
Heart rate
Systolic and diastolic blood pressure
Rate pressure product (product of heart rate and systolic blood pressure provides an index of myocardial
oxygen consumption and work of the heart)
Breathing frequency
Chest or breathing discomfort
Perceived exertion
Breathlessness
Fatigue
General discomfort or pain

continued

TABLE 5-6 **Clinical Decision-Making Process: Principles for Selecting and Administering Submaximal Exercise Tests (Continued)**

Other parameters: Color, perspiration, orientation, coordination, stability, facial expression, comfort, and ability to talk

Advanced
  EKG
  Arterial saturation (noninvasive pulse oximeter)
  Respiratory gas analysis,† i.e., oxygen uptake, minute ventilation, tidal volume, etc.
  Cardiac output (can be determined noninvasively)
  Serum enzymes and lactate (require blood work)

*Estimated high functional work capacity: approximately equal to or greater than that of a healthy normal sedentary person

†Oxygen consumption studies can provide detailed profile of respiratory, hemodynamic, and metabolic responses to incremental or steady-state exercise; this information is used to aid diagnosis of the mechanisms of exercise limitation and define the parameters of the exercise prescription.

FUNCTIONAL CONSEQUENCES OF FITNESS IN OLDER PEOPLE

Deconditioning

The effects of deconditioning following immobility have been well documented over the past 50 years. Other than respiratory muscle strength and endurance, most of the effects of immobility on the cardiopulmonary system have been those associated with recumbency, that is, reduced lung volumes and capacities with the exception of closing volume of the airways which increases.[60-63] The alveolar-oxygen difference and arterial oxygen tension are reduced. In the cardiovascular system, resting and submaximal heart rates and blood pressure increase,[64] and maximal oxygen consumption is reduced.[65] Total blood volume and plasma volume are reduced,[64,66] and blood viscosity is increased along with the risk of thromboembolism.[67,68] The rate of deconditioning has been reported to exceed that of conditioning, which has particular consequences in the older individual with less physiologic reserve.[68,69] The effects of deconditioning are accentuated in older people.

Conditioning

Exercise training elicits the same physiologic benefits in older persons with respect to oxygen transport and oxygen and substrate utilization as in younger people. Adaptation to exercise training in older people results in increases of 10 to 20 percent in aerobic power and strength, which is comparable to the magnitude of change observed in younger people.[30] Submaximal heart rates, blood pressure, and ventilatory rates are reduced. Stroke volume increases, and oxygen extraction at the tissue level is also increased. These improvements translate into increasing functional capacity over and above the critical functional performance threshold.[43,56,58,70-72]

Even though the absolute metabolic cost is constant, older people experience a given activity as more physiologically demanding than younger people because of the reduced capacity of their oxygen transport systems and their musculature to respond to the physical demand. Thus, even fit older people report that activities such as walking, climbing stairs, and carrying objects are demanding. With increasing age, these seemingly innocuous activities can be the equivalent of a maximal effort and may increase an older individual's heart rate, blood pressure, and oxygen consumption to maximal values.

The prescription parameters of an exercise program are based on the results of an exercise test. The clinical decision-making process involved in defining the parameters of an exercise program has been described in detail in the literature previously[28] and is summarized in Table 5-7. However, there are two additional principles of exercise

TABLE 5-7 **Clinical Decision-Making Process: Principles for Prescribing Activities of Daily Living and an Exercise Program**

PRESESSION PATIENT CHECK
  Appropriateness of time of day for activity or exercise for individual
  Quality of night's sleep
  Activity prior to the session, e.g., visitors, tests, agitations or irritations
  Discomfort or pain
  Competing demands
  Timing with respect to medications
  Types or changes in medications
  Lability of vital signs or hemodynamic instability
  General well-being
  Interest and motivation

PRESCRIPTION OF ACTIVITIES OF DAILY LIVING

OBJECT: To maximize functional performance by promoting the appropriate physiologic adaptation and
  task endurance, with maximum movement economy, comfort, and least risk

PARAMETERS:

Type
  Based on individual's needs; prioritize

Intensity
  Activity Phases:
  If feasible, tailor a specific ADL or sequential ADL into:
    Warm-up (up to 75% of the intensity for the steady state)
    Steady state (performed within target range based on predetermined levels of physiologic or subjective
      variables)
    Warm-down
    Recovery (monitored until within 10% of base-line values and individual appears to have returned to
      base line)
  Lower Target Limit: None other than pathologically low values for physiologic variables, e.g., consistent
    with a hypotensive episode
  Upper Target Limit: Physiologic variables not to exceed a predetermined level of physiologic variable,
    e.g., heart rate, blood pressure, exertion level, or subjective experience of exertion, breathlessness,
    discomfort or pain, fatigue, chest pain

Duration
  If recovery less than 30 min, can likely tolerate an increase in duration
  If recovery between 30 min and 3 h, duration probably optimal
  If recovery longer than 3 h, duration is likely too long
  (This recovery excludes the anticipated cumulative fatigue over the course of the day.)

Frequency
  If recovery within 30 min, likely too infrequent
  If recovery between 30 min to 3 h, optimal frequency
  If recovery longer than 3 h, likely too frequent

Time Course
  Based on adaptation to performance criterion, optimal movement economy, sufficient
    cardiopulmonary-cardiovascular conditioning, velocity, and safety

Progression
  Reduce demands of activity if individual consistently in the upper limit of target range; individual can
    tolerate higher-demand activities if the physiologic responses are not consistently reaching the
    target therapeutic range.
  If low functional work capacity, performance and adaptation are enhanced with lighter-intensity,
    shorter, more frequent sessions

EXERCISE PRESCRIPTION

OBJECT: To maximize functional capacity by promoting physiologic adaptation to an exercise stimulus,
  with maximum movement economy, comfort, and safety, and thereby increase functional capacity
  reserve above the functional performance threshold commensurate with the individual's needs.

IF THE ESTIMATED FUNCTIONAL CAPACITY IS HIGH:

Type
  Based on goals and results of the exercise test

TABLE 5-7 **Clinical Decision-Making Process: Principles for Prescribing Activities of Daily Living and an Exercise Program (Continued)**

Intensity
  If normal exercise response and adaptation can be expected, then steady-state exercise at 70 to 85% of peak physiologic parameters on peak test, e.g., heart rate, blood pressure, perceived exertion

  If abnormal aerobic responses and adaptation to exercise are expected, e.g., chronic airflow limitation, restrictive lung disease or heart disease, define target training range on basis of breathlessness scale, exertion or chest pain provided that physiologic parameters remain within acceptable limits

Duration
  20 to 40 min per session

Frequency
  3 to 5 times per week

Time Course
  In health, 3 to 6 months; but in sedentary persons, change can be observed in 4 to 8 weeks

Progression
  With adaptation, target range is no longer maintained, i.e., heart rate, blood pressure, and exertion levels consistently below selected range based on initial exercise test; progression based on a repeated exercise test to redefine exercise prescription parameters

IF ESTIMATED FUNCTIONAL CAPACITY IS INTERMEDIATE:

PARAMETERS: Set between those for high and low.

Type
  E.g., treadmill, ergometer, walking, swimming, water exercises

Intensity
  60 to 75% of peak work rate achieved on exercise test

Duration
  20 min or less

Frequency
  1 to 2X per day

Time Course
  With pathology, can expect prolonged course

Progression
  Maintain exercise parameters: if exceeding values, cut back; if consistently below, can increase the duration and/or frequency

IF ESTIMATED FUNCTIONAL CAPACITY IS LOW:

Type
  E.g., walking, water exercise, and general light activity or exercise

Intensity
  Based on heart rate: lower limit = resting heart rate + 0.60 (peak heart rate from the exercise test —resting heart rate)
  Upper limit = resting heart rate + 0.75 (peak heart rate from the exercise test—resting heart rate)

  If heart rate inappropriate or invalid measure of exercise intensity, blood pressure, perceived exertion, or the talk test

  Can be used to define the target training range

Duration
  Maximize tolerance by maintaining power output constant and velocity changes to maintain perceived exertion constant

  Emphasis on prolonging duration by using an interrupted regimen of alternating higher- and lower-demand work, or low-demand work with rest

Frequency
  Several times daily guided by pre-exercise-session check

Time Course
  If reduced functional capacity due to deconditioning, adaptation will be observed daily and weekly

  If reduced functional capacity due to physical limitations, weeks to months for central and/or peripheral adaptation to occur

continued

TABLE 5–7   Clinical Decision-Making Process: Principles for Prescribing Activities of Daily Living and an Exercise Program (Continued)

Progression
   Exercise progressed as soon as the target training parameters are no longer consistently reached in the exercise session

MONITORING
   Refer to guidelines in Table 5–5
   Essential to guide exercise prescription, training, and for general safety

---

Note: Supplemental oxygen may be a component of the ADL or exercise training session.

---

physiology that have particular relevance in prescribing therapeutic activity and exercise for older people, namely, the principles of training specificity and reversibility. The human body is extremely efficient in that physiological adaptation to exercise stress is unique to a specific activity or exercise. Thus, to improve an individual's ability to perform an activity, that activity should be the primary object of training. The lower the initial functional capacity, the more significant is the principle of specificity. Also, once training has been discontinued, the training effect does not carry over and deconditioning begins immediately. Thus, to maintain a given level of activity or exercise, the training stimulus must be presented at the required intensity, duration, and frequency and over the requisite period of time that is consistent with eliciting physiological adaptation.[36,37]

IMPLICATIONS FOR THE MANAGEMENT OF OLDER PEOPLE

Goals

The primary goal of rehabilitation for older people is maximizing function of which cardiopulmonary and cardiovascular capacity is a significant determinant. The two principal subgoals are (1) to maximize the cardiopulmonary and cardiovascular reserve capacity such that this capacity exceeds an individual's critical functional performance threshold and (2) to maximize an individual's ability to perform ADL. The latter largely requires the physiological capacity to adapt to the upright position and to move against gravity; these are both central components of functional performance. Whether the focus is directed toward functional performance, functional capacity or both, rehabilitation is based on a detailed analysis of these factors that contribute to functional impairment of that individual.

The rationale for improving an individual's ability to perform ADL and functional capacity appears inherently reasonable. However, the goal of enhancing functional capacity in an individual with cardiopulmonary or cardiovascular dysfunction may appear paradoxical and warrants some discussion. Given that the purposes of the cardiopulmonary and cardiovascular systems are oxygen transport and gas exchange and that these are effected through an integrated system of steps along the oxygen transport pathway, it becomes clear that augmenting the function and efficiency of the steps in the pathway can enhance oxygen transport overall. Although there may be weak links in the pathway due to disease, these can be compensated for by improved efficiency of other steps in the pathway.[31,52,73] The net result of improved efficiency of various steps in the pathway is improved maximum functional capacity.

Individuals with severe cardiopulmonary and cardiovascular disease who cannot achieve an intensity of exercise that is sufficient to stimulate improved aerobic capacity can improve their functional capacity via other mechanisms, including desensitization to shortness of breath, increased motivation, and improved movement efficiency.[74,75]

With respect to optimizing function in the older person, endurance is a primary objective. Although muscle strength, balance, coordination, and so forth are also central to function, these can frequently be optimized commensurate with endurance activities and exercise. The principle of exercise specificity indicates that optimal adaptation results if the target activity serves as the training stimulus. Although commonly practiced, the precise relationship between strength training, for example, and functional activity and its efficacy in relation to function has not been studied in detail.

Assessment

In order to prescribe ADL or exercise for older people, the mechanisms contributing to impaired function must be analyzed in detail. Prescribing activity and exercise for older people is as exacting as drug prescription in that exercise is inherently risky particularly in older age groups and needs to be prescribed based on clear indications. Exercise is also associated with side-effects and contraindications. Maximizing therapeutic gain and minimizing risk is the objective and may be achieved with the application of a 6-point system of analysis of function (Table 5–8). Collectively,

the contribution of these six factors is established so that the mechanisms of functional impairment are understood and ADL and exercise can be prescribed appropriately by directing the intervention at specific causes of functional impairment and within an individual's capacity. The exercise or activity prescription can maximize oxygen transport and hence function in the long term.

The object of the assessment is to determine the individual's ability to meet the metabolic demands of the activities or exercise of interest. Common parameters that are measured during exercise include heart rate, systolic and diastolic blood pressure, rate pressure product, and breathing frequency. Oxygen consumption can be measured using a metabolic measurement cart; however, this measure is not routinely performed. Rather, oxygen consumption is estimated based on tables, provided that the work rate or work performed can be accurately determined. Other responses that need to be monitored will depend on the specific individual and the particular factors that contribute to functional deficit. For example, cardiopulmonary disease would require continuous arterial saturation monitoring. Although the availability and sophistication of monitoring equipment has increased, the rehabilitation specialist needs to determine what measures are of particular interest, clinically relevant, and meet the requirements of being valid and reliable.

Because exercise testing is an exacting procedure and must be methodically executed to be meaningful, the rehabilitation specialist must standardize and appropriately record the pretest, testing, and posttest conditions of the exercise test. The details of the specific protocol must be established and the times of work rate changes and measurement recording clearly noted so that the test can be performed in precisely the same way on another occasion or by another person if necessary. There is greater potential for variability in performing tests of ADL than standardized exercise tests; thus such tests need to be strictly stan-

---

TABLE 5–8 Exercise Requirements for Analysis of Function and Prescribing Activity in the Older Adult

1. Know effects of normal aging on all organ systems.
2. Understand normal exercise responses and effects of position stress in combination with exercise stress.
3. Determine contribution of cardiopulmonary or cardiovascular dysfunction to functional impairment.
4. Establish impact of recumbency and immobility to functional impairment.
5. Verify effect of extrinsic factors, such as medications or medical procedures, on function.
6. Consider intrinsic factors related to specific characteristics of individual and lifestyle.

dardized to maintain quality control, validity, and reproducibility.

Prescription of Activities of Daily Living and Exercise

The rehabilitation specialist must consider several factors when prescribing ADL or exercise for a given individual. First, the object of the prescription needs to be defined, that is, to enhance functional performance, functional capacity or both. If the object is to enhance functional performance of an ADL, then activity is the focus of training. The activity must analyzed in terms of its cardiopulmonary and cardiovascular demands in addition to whether the individual is capable of performing the activity from a neuromuscular and musculoskeletal perspective. The body position assumed in performing an activity and the use of any assistive device can alter the metabolic demand.

Although some degree of aerobic fitness is desirable in the older adult, maximal aerobic fitness is not needed to perform ADL and live independently. Rather, activity performance, velocity, and safety are the primary considerations. Assessment of an individual's functional capacity should be based on the demands expected in the individual's living environment. For example, an individual who is to be ambulatory in the community will need to be able to walk 332 m at 50 percent normal velocity (greater than 40 m/min) and be able to negotiate three steps and a 3 percent ramp with rails and a curb.[76]

An individual's ability to perform an ADL or exercise will also depend on such factors as the time of day, whether the individual has eaten recently, what medications the individual may be receiving, and general well-being on a given day. Also, how rested and energetic the individual feels will influence the ability to perform the activity or exercise. A low-demand activity that needs to be performed once is less demanding overall than the same or more demanding activity that has to be performed multiple times. High-demand ac-

tivities can be effectively interspersed with rest periods. Even in healthy young people, this type of interval training can significantly increase the overall amount of work performed.

Two concepts that are applied nonspecifically in the clinic are energy conservation and pacing. Although conserving energy may be a goal, energy sparing needs to be balanced with energy expenditure to avoid the deleterious effects of inactivity and deconditioning. The pace of an activity or exercise affects the overall metabolic cost. Performing an activity too slowly as well as too fast can increase metabolic cost; therefore, the pace at which optimal efficiency is achieved needs to be included as a component of the prescription.[77] Research is needed to examine the concepts of energy conservation and activity pacing so that these concepts can be prescribed on a rational basis and exploited therapeutically.

The assessment identifies ADL deficits and the type of exercise program that will improve function. The capacity of the individual to meet the metabolic demand, however, must also be evaluated. An exercise stimulus, whether prescribed to promote adaptation to ADL or exercise should involve no more than 60 to 70 percent of peak effort and be tolerated without undue fatigue or distress.

Metabolism for daily activities requires the interplay of anaerobic and aerobic metabolic processes. Sprint-type activities demand rapid release from sources of oxygen; thus, the anaerobic system of metabolism is stimulated. Light activities and activities demanding more prolonged submaximal endurance are affected by aerobic metabolism. A physiological steady state is achieved during aerobic exercise and is more functional than anaerobic training. Aerobic adaptation can be achieved with a maximum training intensity of 40 percent of the maximum heart rate in older persons,[78] whereas in young people a minimum training intensity of 60 percent of the maximum heart rate is required. Anaerobic activities or exercise are seldom indicated for older people as these can be excessively demanding physiologically and are associated with greater risk. In addition, high levels of anaerobic capacity are not as essential in daily living compared with aerobic capacity.

The parameters of activity or exercise prescription include a warm-up, a steady state, warm-down, and recovery period.[36] Even in prescribing ADL, these components are essential if maximal benefit is to be derived with the least risk. The warm-up and warm-down are critical in priming the cardiopulmonary, cardiovascular, and musculoskeletal systems for work and recovery, respectively. An appropriate warm-up will improve the efficiency during the steady-state portion of the prescription. Monitoring during all portions of the prescription is important including the warm-down and recovery. These components are needed to ensure that the physiological adjustments needed to perform work have returned to base-line conditions, for example, the degradation of lactate and circulating catecholamines. Also, adequate warm-down and recovery reduces late-onset fatigue and soreness.

Older people, particularly those with low functional capacities, can perform large amounts of work in an interval exercise program. Interval training, analogous to "fartlek" training in the athlete, involves either alternating relatively high and low metabolically demanding activity or low metabolically demanding activity and rest periods.[79,80] Cumulatively, an individual can perform an overall amount of work that would not be achievable if attempted all at once. In addition, such a schedule is considerably safer and subjectively tolerated better. Interval training regimens need to be exploited in a systematic manner in therapeutic programs for older people by rehabilitation specialists.

A balance of activity and rest can also be incorporated over the course of a day to maximize function.[81] Theoretically, judicious rest periods contribute to physiological restoration, enabling the individual to perform more work and activity over time. The prescription of rest

periods warrants as much attention as exercise, given that the negative effects of excessive rest as well as exercise are particularly hazardous in the older person. Rest needs to be viewed as a therapeutic intervention, and similarly the appropriate parameters need to be selected to optimize function. Considerable research is needed to improve the prescription of rest in conjunction with activity and exercise so that its inclusion will maximize work output and minimize deleterious effects of inactivity.

Monitoring

Although they may appear to be performing activities associated with low metabolic demand, many individuals will be working at loads that would be unacceptable in young people, or that alternatively are not within the therapeutic threshold to elicit the maximal benefit. Given that exercise constitutes a risk and that to be therapeutic its intensity needs to be gauged, objective as well as subjective monitoring should be a standard component of assessment and therapeutic interventions. All too often, however, stringent monitoring is neglected in medically stable older people.

The inherent risk of exercise is accentuated in older people[82] for several reasons that add further to the need to monitor these individuals. There are many conditions associated with aging that require special attention. For example, individuals with a history of cardiopulmonary or cardiovascular disease should be monitored closely during activity or exercise. Some people may have no cardiac history but report ischemic leg pain at rest or during exercise. These individuals have a high probability of having cardiac involvement and require cardiac and blood pressure monitoring. Older people are prone to high blood pressure and, in general, are more apt to experience blood pressure irregularities during exercise than young people. Alternatively, some older people are prone to hypotensive episodes. Thus, judicious blood pressure monitoring is essential. Although many individuals will be on medications for heart disease and hypertension, monitoring hemodynamic status is still essential. Individuals with heart disease who are on drugs such as nitrates for coronary artery dilatation should not be treated unless monitoring devices are readily available. The rehabilitation specialist needs to be very familiar with how these and other medications will affect exercise response. Some medications interfere with normal hemodynamic responses to exercise, in which case other parameters need to be used. Special provision needs to be made for diabetic patients, and a sugar source must be available in the event of a hypoglycemic episode associated with increased activity or exercise.

Safety

Safety issues are a foremost concern when testing and prescribing ADL and exercise.[83] An activity or exercise is prescribed within the anticipated upper limit of an individual's physiological capacity, yet above the lower limit of the therapeutic threshold range, and appropriate monitoring is conducted to verify this. A thorough knowledge of signs and symptoms of distress during exercise is essential, and these need to be anticipated for each individual and taught to an older person when self-monitoring is appropriate. Rehabilitation specialists involved with prescribing activity or formal exercise for any population must have current certification in cardiopulmonary resuscitation. Rehabilitation departments and clinics should have facilities in the case of an emergency and a procedure outlined in the event of a cardiac arrest. All members of the department need to be reappraised of emergency procedures on a regular basis.

CUSTOMIZING THE ENVIRONMENT TO MAXIMIZE FUNCTION

An astronaut living and working in space is not considered disabled. Modifications ranging from breathing, toileting, washing, exercising, and working have been made to enable the astronaut to survive and be functionally independent in space. Hence, an individual is only as restricted as the surrounding environment is restrictive. The physical environment of older people requires constant surveillance to optimize this environment and promote function and independence as the individual continues to age. Mobility aids and assistive devices within and outside the home need to be reevaluated. In this way, independent living is promoted, the amount of time the individual is upright and moving is maximized, and the risk of morbidity, falls, and injury is reduced.

SUMMARY

The principal goals of rehabilitation in the management of the older person are to improve the ability to perform activities of daily living and to enhance functional capacity, the reserve of the cardiopulmonary and cardiovascular systems, and the efficiency of oxygen transport overall. Such an approach raises the individual's functional capacity above the critical functional performance threshold so that with progressive aging and in the event of illness or immobility, the individual has sufficient reserve to minimize functional deterioration and dependency.

The rehabilitation specialist must have a high level of expertise in the assessment and prescription of activities of daily living and exercise. Such expertise is based on a knowledge base encompassing the following areas:

- Normal age-related changes in the cardiopulmonary and cardiovascular systems in addition to multiple other systems that work in an integrated manner to effect functional performance and enhance functional capacity with training.
- Primary and secondary pathophysiologic changes resulting in cardiopulmonary and cardiovascular dysfunction and the implications of these changes on functional performance and capacity.

- Effects of gravitational stress and acute exercise stress on the cardiopulmonary and cardiovascular systems.
- Effects of extrinsic factors related to the individual's medical care. For example, in the medically stable individual, these include medications and medical procedures.
- Effects of intrinsic factors related to the general history and characteristics of the individual as well as the individual's occupations and lifestyle of the life cycle.
- Knowledge of exercise physiology in health and disease, the principles of adaptation to activity and exercise in older people, and the basis for activity-exercise prescription in this population where multiple factors (the first five listed here) contribute to functional deficits.

Rehabilitation specialists are in a unique position to maximize functional performance and functional capacity in the older adult based on the scientific literature and to identify areas that warrant further study. Moreover, based on a thorough knowledge of exercise physiology in health and disease, these specialists have a responsibility to advise other health care professionals in the promotion of activity and exercise in the older population from both a therapeutic and lifestyle perspective.

REVIEW QUESTIONS

In relation to the *specific case histories* that follow, address each of the questions posed in the objectives:

1. Describe the age-related changes that are expected in cardiopulmonary and cardiovascular function.
2. Describe the impact of disease on any changes in cardiopulmonary and cardiovascular function secondary to primary or secondary disease.
3. Describe the impact of inactivity on any changes in cardiopulmonary and cardiovascular function secondary to recumbency and inactivity.
4. Describe any changes in cardiopulmonary and cardiovascular function secondary to extrinsic factors, that is, to medical interventions, drugs, and so forth.
5. Describe any changes in cardiopulmonary and cardiovascular function secondary to intrinsic factors, that is, to the individual's characteristics, lifestyle, long-term occupation, coexistent morbidity, and so forth.
6. Based on the changes identified in objectives 1 through 5, describe and prioritize the goals of treatment.
7. Based on the changes identified in objectives 1 through 5, describe the focus of the assessment and the measures that would be most relevant to record.
8. Based on the changes identified in objectives 1 through 5, describe the treatment plan vis-à-vis prescribing training for functional performance, that is, ADL, functional capacity, or both.
9. Describe the precautions that you would take in assessing and prescribing ADL and/or exercise.
10. Given that a maximum exercise test was not feasible:
    (a) describe the rationale for the short- and long-term responses that you would expect to your treatment plan, and
    (b) describe what adverse responses this individual could exhibit in response to your treatment plan.

Case History 1.

Ms. BH, 85 years of age, underwent total hip replacement surgery 1 week ago. She had fallen in her two-story home 10 days ago after getting up in the night because she does not sleep well. She was found by a neighbor who helps with her bath and breakfast each day. On admission to the hospital, she was mildly dehydrated; her blood work indicated that she was moderately anemic. Ms. BH's height and weight were 154 cm and 40.5 kg, respectively. She lived and worked on a farm most of her life. She has a long history of bronchial asthma. She reports being frequently short of breath during the day, although she claims to use her inhaler faithfully every morning. She has never smoked.

Case History 2.

Mr. WT, 69 years of age, is attending day hospital for regulation of his insulin. His height and weight are 169 cm and 70 kg, respectively. He has a right below-knee amputation and walks with a prosthesis and cane. Mr. WT was a three-pack-a-day smoker for 50 years but quit a year ago due to a cancer scare. Mr. WT lives with his son's family, but relations have been strained because he has become increasingly short of breath and unable to perform some light household chores that he is responsible for.

Case History 3.

Ms. MP, 76 years of age, has been transferred from the intensive care unit to the ward. She had triple-vessel bypass surgery and developed some cardiac dysrhythmias that were refractory to treatment. These complications delayed her transfer to the ward by several days. She had poliomyelitis in her teens. Although she has no visible residual of the disease, over the past 3 years she has been experiencing new problems with fatigue and weakness. She quit smoking 2 years ago because she was experiencing shortness of breath with activity; she had previously smoked 15 to 20 cigarettes a day since she was 25 years of age. Her height and weight are 165 cm and 61.5 kg, respectively. Ms. MP lives in an apartment with her husband who is a low-level paraplegic from an injury sustained 32 years ago. A homemaker has been coming in two mornings a week.

Case History 4.

Mr. PR, 73 years of age, continues to work out of his townhome in his financial consultation practice. He has had a 15-year history of moderately severe osteoarthritis in his left hip and knees. His height and weight are 170 cm and 86 kg, respectively. He has been minimally active over the past 8 years following a heart attack. He takes nitroglycerin for chest pain which he experiences on moderate exertion. Mr. PR has never smoked. He lives alone. He has trouble getting on the bus because of pain in his knees and hip, so he has relied on walking to a shopping center four blocks from home. Although this aggravates his joint discomfort, his walking tolerance is limited primarily by exertion and frequent chest pain. He relies on at least one cane most of the time.

REFERENCES

1. Reddan, WG: Respiratory system and aging. In Smith, EL and Serfass, RC (eds): Exercise and Aging. Enslow, Hillside, NJ, 1981.
2. Turner, JM, Mead, J and Wohl, ME: Elasticity of human lungs in relation to age. J Appl Physiol 25:64–671, 1968.
3. Thurlbeck, WM and Angus, GE: Growth and aging of normal lung. Chest 67:3s–7s, 1975.
4. Bates, DV: Altered physiologic states and associated syndromes. In Respiratory Function in Disease, ed 3. WB Saunders, Philadelphia, 1989, pp 81–105.
5. Pump, KK: The aged lung. Chest 60:571–577, 1971.
6. Luce, JM and Culver, BH: Respiratory muscle function in health and disease. Chest 81:82–90, 1982.
7. Kent, S: Decline in pulmonary function. Geriatrics 33:100–111, 1978.
8. Mahler, DA, Rosiello, RA and Loke, J: The aging lung. Geriatr Clin North Am 2:215–225, 1986.
9. Davies, C, Campbell, EJM, Openshaw, P, Pride, NB and Woodruff, G: Importance of airway closure in limiting maximal expiration in normal man. J Appl Physiol 48:695–701, 1980.
10. Tammaro, AE, Calabrese, G and Forin, G: Intraventricular blocks in the elderly. In Platt, D (ed): Cardiology and Aging. Schattauer, Stuttgart, New York, 1983.
11. Higginbotham, MB, Morris, KG and Williams, RS: Physiologic basis for the age-related decline in aerobic work capacity. Am J Cardiol 57:1374–1379, 1986.
12. Kantrowitz, FG, Munoz, G, Roberts, N, Schatten, S and Stern, S: Rheumatology in geriatrics. In Gambert, SR (ed): Contemporary Geriatric Medicine, Vol 2. Plenum Medical Books, New York, 1986, pp 197–200.
13. Timiras, PS: Aging of the skeleton, joints and muscles. In Timiras, PS (ed): Physiological Basis of Geriatrics. Macmillan, New York, 1988, pp 349–370.
14. Davies, CTM: The oxygen-transporting system in relation to age. Clin Sci 42:1–13, 1972.

15. Campbell, A, Caird, FI and Jackson, TF: Prevalence of abnormalities of electrocardiogram in old people. Br Heart J 36:1005–1011, 1974.
16. Davies, MJ and Pomerance, A: Quantitative study of aging changes in the sinoatrial and internodal tracts. Brit Heart J 34:150–155, 1972.
17. Snider, GL: Symposium on Emphysema. Clinics in Medicine, WB Saunders, Philadelphia, 1983.
18. Chung, F and Dean, E: Pathophysiology and cardiorespiratory consequences of interstitial lung disease—review and clinical implications. Phys Ther 69:956–966, 1989.
19. Strasser, T: Cardiovascular Care of the Elderly. World Health Organization, Geneva, 1987.
20. The Working Group on Hypertension in the Elderly. Statement on hypertension in the elderly. JAMA 256:70–74, 1986.
21. Harris, MI, Hadden, WC and Knowler, WC: International criteria for the diagnosis of diabetes and impaired glucose tolerance Diabetic Care 8:562–567, 1985.
22. Blomqvist, CG and Stone, HL: Cardiovascular adjustments to gravitational stress. In Shepherd, JT and Abboud, FM (eds): Handbook of Physiology. Sec 2: Circulation, Vol 2. Bethesda, MD, American Physiological Society, 1983, pp 1025–1063.
23. Wenger, NK: Early ambulation: The physiologic basis revisited. Advances in Cardiology 31:138–141, 1982.
24. Sandler, H: Cardiovascular effects of inactivity. In Sandler, H and Vernikos, J (eds): Inactivity Physiological Effects. Academic, New York, 1986, pp 11–47.
25. Convertino, VA, Hung, J, Goldwater, D and DeBusk, RF: Cardiovascular responses to exercise in middle-aged men after 10 days of bedrest. Circulation 65:134–140, 1982.
26. Hahn Winslow, E: Cardiovascular consequences of bed rest. Heart and Lung 14:236–246, 1985.
27. Chase, GA, Grave, C and Rowell, LB: Independence of changes in functional and performance capacities attending prolonged bed rest. Aerospace Medicine 37:1232–1237, 1966.
28. Dean, E and Ross, J: Mobilization and body conditioning. In Zadai, C (ed): Pulmonary Management in Physical Therapy. Churchill Livingstone, New York, 1992.
29. Astrand, PO and Rodahl, K: Body dimensions and muscular exercise. In Textbook of Work Physiology. Physiological Bases of Exercise. McGraw-Hill, New York, 1986, pp 391–411.
30. Shephard, RJ: Physical training for the elderly. Clin Sports Med 5:515–533, 1986.
31. Dean, E and Ross, J: Oxygen transport: The basis for contemporary cardiopulmonary physical therapy and its optimization with body positioning and mobilization. Physical Therapy Practice 4(1):34–44, 1992.
32. Skerrett, SJ, Niederman, MS and Fein, AM: Respiratory infections and acute lung injury in systemic illness. Clin Chest Med 10:469–502, 1989.
33. Fry, PS: Functional disorders in the elderly: Description, assessment, and management considerations. In Depression, Stress, and Adaptations in the Elderly. Aspen, Rockville, MD, 1986, pp 205–254.
34. American Psychiatric Association: Diagnostic and Statistical Manual of Mental Disorders, ed 3 (DSM-III R). American Psychiatric Association, Washington, DC, 1987.
35. Young, A: Exercise physiology in geriatric practice. Acta Med Scand 711(Suppl):227–232, 1986.
36. American College of Sports Medicine. Guidelines for Exercise Testing and Prescription, ed 4. Lea & Febiger, Philadelphia, 1991.
37. Blair, SN, Painter, P, Pate, RR, Smith, LK and Taylor, CB: Resource Manual for Guidelines for Exercise Testing and Prescription, Lea & Febiger, Philadelphia, 1988.
38. Fox, SM, Naughton, JP and Gorman, PA: Physical activity and cardiovascular health. III. The exercise prescription; frequency and type of activity. Modern Concepts of Cardiovascular Disease 41:25–30, 1972.
39. Shephard, RJ: Limitations upon the rate of working. In Physiology and Biochemistry of Exercise. Praeger, New York, 1985, pp 47–94.
40. American Heart Association, Committee on Exercise: Recommendations concerning sexual activity in post-coronary patients. In Exercise Testing and Training of Individuals with Heart Disease or at High Risk for its Development: A Handbook for Physicians, 1975, pp 57–58.
41. Stein, RA: The effect of exercise training on heart rate during coitus in the post-myocardial patient. Circulation 55:738–740, 1977.
42. American Thoracic Society: Evaluation of impairment/disability secondary to respiratory disorders. Am Rev Respir Dis 130:1205–1209, 1987.
43. de Vries, HA: Physiological effects of an exercise training regimen upon men aged 52 to 88. Journal of Gerontology 25:325–336, 1970.
44. Baruch, IM and Mossberg, KA: Heart-rate response of elderly women to nonweight-bearing ambulation with a walker. Phys Ther 63:1782–1787, 1983.
45. Kuriansky, JB and Gurland, BJ: Performance test of activities of daily living. Int J Aging Hum Dev 7:343–352, 1976.
46. Katz, S, Ford, AB and Moskowitz, RW: Studies of illness in the aged: The Index of ADL: A standard measure of biologic and psychosocial function. JAMA 185:914–919, 1963.
47. Mahoney, FI and Barthel, DW: Functional evaluation: The Barthel index. Maryland State Med J 14:61–65, 1965.
48. MacKenzie, R, Charlson, ME and DiGioia, D: A patient-specific measure of change in maximal function. Arch Int Med 146:1325–1329, 1986.
49. Carey, RG and Posavic, EJ: Rehabilitation program evaluation using the revised Level of

Rehabilitation Scale (LORS-II). Arch Phys Med Rehabil 69:337–343, 1988.

50. Linn, MW and Linn, BS: The Rapid Disability Rating Scale-2. J Am Geriatr Soc 30:378–382, 1982.

51. Vuori, I: The cardiovascular risks of physical activity. Acta Med Scand 711(Suppl):205–214, 1986.

52. Wasserman, K and Whipp, BJ: Exercise physiology in health and disease. Am Rev Respir Dis 112:219–249, 1975.

53. Petrofsky, JS and Phillips, CA: The physiology of static exercise. Ex Sport Sci Rev 14:1–44, 1986.

54. Martyn, JW: Diagnosing and treating hypothermia. Can Med Assoc J 125:1089–1096, 1981.

55. Weisfeldt, ML (ed): The Aging Heart—Its Function and Response to Stress. Raven Press, New York, 1980.

56. Adams, GM and de Vries, HA: Physiological effects of an exercise training regimen upon women aged 52 to 79. Journal of Gerontology 28:50–55, 1973.

57. Kasch, FW, Wallace, JP, Van Camp, SP and Verity, L: A longitudinal study of cardiovascular stability in active men aged 45 to 65 years. The Physician and Sportsmedicine 16:117–124, 1988.

58. Thomas, SG, Cunningham, DA, Rechnitzer, PA, Donner, AP and Howard, JH: Determinants of the training response in elderly men. Med Sci Sports Ex 17:667–672, 1985.

59. Shephard, RJ, Allen, C, Benade, AJS, Davies, CTM, di Prampero, PEW, Hedman, R, Merriman, JE, Myhre, K and Simmons, R: Standardization of submaximal exercise test. Bulletin of the World Health Organization, 38:765–775, 1968.

60. Craig, DB, Wahba, WM and Don, H: 'Closing volume' and its relationship to gas exchange in the seated and supine positions. J Appl Physiol 31:717–721, 1971.

61. Svanberg, L: Influence of position on the lung volumes, ventilation and circulation in normals. Scan J Clin Lab Invest 25(Suppl):7–175, 1959.

62. Clauss, BA, Scalabrini, BY and Ray JF: Effects of changing body positions upon improved ventilation-perfusion relationships. Circulation 37(Suppl):214–218, 1968.

63. Ray, JF, Yost, L, Moallem, S, Sanoudos, GM, Villamena, P and Paredes, RM: Immobility, hypoxemia, and pulmonary arteriovenous shunting. Arch Surg 109:537–541, 1974.

64. Deitrick, JE, Whedon, GD and Shorr, E: Effects of immobilization upon various metabolic and physiologic functions of normal men. Am J Med 4:3–36, 1948.

65. Convertino, VA, Goldwater, DJ and Sandler, H: Bedrest-induced peak VO2 reduction associated with age, gender, and aerobic capacity. Aviation, Space and Environmental Medicine 57:17–22, 1986.

66. Saltin, B, Blomqvist, G, Mitchell, JH, Johnson, RL, Wildenthal, K and Chapman, CB: Response to exercise after bed rest and after training. Circulation 38 (Suppl 7):1–78, 1968.

67. Lentz, M: Selected aspects of deconditioning secondary to immobilization. Nurs Clin North Am 16:729–737, 1981.

68. Sandler, H, Popp, RL and Harrison, DC: The hemodynamic effects of repeated bed rest exposure. Aerospace Med 59:1047–1054, 1988.

69. Harper, CM and Lyles, YM: Physiology and complications of bed rest. J Am Geriatr Soc 36:1047–1054, 1988.

70. Aniansson, A, Grimby, G, Rundgren, A, Svanborg, A and Orlander, J: Physical training in older men. Age Ageing 9:186–197, 1980.

71. Clark, BA, Wade, MG, Massey, BH and Van Dyke, R: Response of institutionalized geriatric mental patients to a twelve-week program of regular physical activity. Journal of Gerontology 30:565–573, 1975.

72. Stamford, BA: Physiological effects of training upon institutionalized geriatric men. Journal of Gerontology 27:451–455, 1972.

73. Dean, E and Ross, J: Integrating current literature in the management of cystic fibrosis: A rejoinder. Physiother Can 41:46–47, 1989.

74. Belman, MJ and Kendregan, BA: Exercise training fails to increase skeletal muscle enzymes in patients with chronic obstructive pulmonary disease. Am Rev Respir Dis 123:256–261, 1981.

75. Belman, MJ and Kendregan, BA: Physical training fails to improve ventilatory muscle endurance in patients with chronic obstructive pulmonary disease. Chest 81:440–443, 1982.

76. Cohen, JJ, Sven, JD and Walker, JM: Establishing the criteria for community ambulation. Top Geriatr Rehabil 3:71–77, 1987.

77. Asmussen, E: Positive and negative work. Acta Physiol Scand 28:364–382, 1953.

78. de Vries, HA: Exercise intensity threshold for improvement of cardiovascular-respiratory function in older men. Geriatrics 26:94–101, 1971.

79. Sheffield, LT and Roitman, D: Stress testing methodology. In Sonnenblick, EH and Lesch, M (eds): Exercise and Heart Disease. Grune and Stratton, Orlando, FL, 1977.

80. Astrand, PO: Aerobic work capacity in men and women with special reference to age. Acta Physiol Scand (Suppl 169):S1, 1960.

81. Dean, E: Clinical decision making in the management of the late sequaelae of poliomyelitis. Phys Ther 71:752–761, 1991.

82. Koplan, JP, Siscovick, DS and Goldbaum, GM: Risks of exercise: Public health view of injuries and hazards. Public Health Rep 100:189–194, 1985.

83. Shephard, RJ: Safety of exercise testing—the role of the paramedical exercise specialist. Clin J Sport Med 1:8–11, 1991.

84. Vandervoort, AA and McComas, AJ: Contractile changes in opposing muscles of the human ankle joint with aging. J Appl Physiol 61:361–367, 1986.

All quotations were taken from current patients in response to the question, "What advice do you have for health care professionals working with older adults?"

Patient 1: *"Tell those young folks to shave off their mustaches. I can't hear a word they're saying with all that hair."*

Patient 2: *"Tell 'em to go slow when explainin' what's wrong with me. . . . I don't listen quite as fast as I used to."*

Patient 3: *"I cain't hear so good and I cain't see so good, but thank God I can still talk."*

Chapter

Sensory and Sensory Integrative Development

CELIA ROUTH HOOPER

OBJECTIVES

By the end of this chapter, readers will be able to:

1 Understand sensory changes in aging as a reflection of physical and behavioral compensation in different body systems.

2 Discuss the age-related changes of the eye, its support structures, and the visual pathway of the nervous system.

3 Describe the changes associated with aging in the auditory system, particularly in the reception of speech sounds.

4 Identify common changes that occur in taste, smell, and touch.

5 Relate the common sensory deficits in older adults to functional performance and lifestyle issues.

6 Discover recurrent themes in changes in sensory systems, and learn that some behavior may be automatic even in the presence of sensory decline.

SENSATION AND PERCEPTION

Our bodies receive information about the physical world through specialized sensory receptors, part of our complex nervous system. These receptors, which make possible the process of sensation, begin working in most cases even before birth but start a slow, progressive decline by the second decade.[1,2]

The "senses" or systems of sensation send information via a *modality*, or sensory channel, in the peripheral nervous system to the central nervous system where the information is comprehended. This middle ground between sensation and comprehension is *perception*, a process that enables the organism to receive and perceive that a stimulus has occurred.

Investigators are unsure of the exact anatomy and physiology of perception. This theoretical construct, *to perceive* means that the sensory message has traveled beyond the end receptors, but no one is quite sure when or where reception ends and perception begins. Our perceptions are changed with experience as we learn the likely meaning of signals. Some learned perceptions may aid us as our sensory receptors begin to decline. Other chapters in this text discuss *central nervous system* (CNS) changes with age, but it is important to note in this chapter that the parieto-temporal-occipital areas of the cerebral cortex are important sensory areas. These areas are responsible for the *integration*, or association of information regarding sensory modalities.[3] Sensory information does not travel through a direct route of monosynaptic connections to the CNS from receptor cells. Somatosensory input has fiber tracts that travel through several relay stations, or integrating centers, in the brain stem and the thalamus. Any neuronal degeneration in these sensory integrative and relay structures reduces the quality of information received at the CNS level.[4] The information contained in this chapter must be viewed in the context of the many changes that take place in the normal aging nervous system. Sensory and sensory integrative changes are a reflection of those systemic changes.

This chapter will include a discussion of the age-related changes in the five senses:

- Vision
- Hearing
- Taste
- Smell
- Superficial touch

The changes in each of the systems of sensation will be related to the older adult's ability to function. A summary of these changes can be found in Table 6–1.

VISION AND FUNCTIONAL PERFORMANCE

According to the National Center of Health Statistics and the National Society for the Prevention of Blindness, visual acuity declines and the prevalence of eye diseases increases with age.[5,6] Around the age of 40 near vision begins a gradual deterioration in everyone.[7,8,9] The decline in acuity is referred to as *presbyopia* meaning "old vision."

Visual problems are of great significance for many older adults. There are estimates that there are 5.5 million visually impaired adults in the United States.[10] More than a million people are totally blind, and 70 percent of those people are 65 years of age or older.[11]

Terminology in Vision Research

Terminology in a discussion of vision is important. The term *low vision* describes a serious visual loss uncorrectable by medical or surgical intervention or with eyeglasses.[12] It is a term used to describe the person's problem, not the underlying pathology or etiology. The term *low vision*, along with *visually impaired, visually handicapped*, and *partially sighted*, implies that an individual has some vision remaining. A separate term, *legally blind*, was developed in the 1930s by the U.S. federal

TABLE 6-1 **Summary of Effects of Age-Related Sensory Changes on Functional Activities**

Sensation	Primary Aging Changes	Functional Results
Vision	Loss of subcutaneous fat around the eye Decreased tissue elasticity and tone Decreased strength of the eye muscles Decreased corneal transparency Degeneration of sclera, pupil, and iris Increase in density and rigidity of lens Increased frequency of disease processes Slowing of CNS information processing	Decreased near vision Poor eye coordination Distortion of images Blurred vision Compromised night vision Loss of color sensitivity, especially green, blue, and violet shades Difficulty with recognition of moving objects, items with a complex figure, or items that appear in and out of light quickly.
Hearing	Loss or damage to sensory hair cells of cochlea and the lower basal turn of the inner ear Nerve cell diminution of coclear ganglia Degeneration in central auditory pathways Loss of neurotransmitters	Difficulty in hearing higher frequencies Diminished ability for pitch discrimination Reduced speech recognition and reception Loss of speech discrimination
Taste	Decrease in taste buds Varicose enlargement	Higher thresholds for identification of substances
Smell	Degeneration of sensory cells of nasal mucosa	Decline in suprathreshold sensitivity for odors
Superficial sensation	Slower nerve conduction velocities	Decreased response to tactile stimuli Alterations in perception of pain Adversely affected by thermal extremes

government to qualify people for certain benefits; 85 percent of those legally blind have low vision rather than total blindness.[12]

Peripheral and Central Changes

There are changes that occur with age in the support structures of the eye, the eye itself, and the visual pathway. Changes in the support structures include loss of subcutaneous fat and decreased tissue elasticity and tone, all of which may make the eyes appear sunken.[13] Additionally, the levator palpebrae superioris eye muscle has decreased strength, and the older adult has problems with upward gaze and convergence.[14] This difficulty results in poor eye coordination and focusing.

Changes in the eye begin with the cornea, where light first enters. (See Fig. 6-1 for an illustration of a normal eye.) A ring of opaqueness forms in the cornea of some individuals, and a deposit of pigment occurs in most corneas.[15] These changes result in a reduced corneal transparency that limits the amount of light reaching the retina. The cornea also flattens after age 60 to 65, causing or increasing astigmatism. Images are distorted or blurred.

The sclera, pupil, and iris of the eyes also have degenerative changes. The scleral tissue loses water and increases its fatty deposits, causing a yellow cast and decreased opacity.[14] The pupil decreases in size, and the iris decreases in dilation ability, which is diminished due to several processes, including an increase of connective tissue, sclerosis of

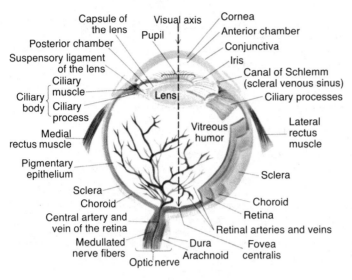

Figure 6–1 Horizontal section of the eye. (From: Miller–Keane Encyclopedia and Dictionary of Medicine, Nursing and Allied Health, 5th ed. W.B. Saunders, Philadelphia, 1992, with permission.)

the blood supply, and muscle weakness.[16,17] The light and dark adaptation is compromised, particularly for night vision. Many adults notice that as they age, more time is needed for their eyes to adjust upon entering or leaving a dark room.

The lens of the older adult's eye changes, resulting in a decrease in ability to transmit and focus light.[14] Cellular change cause an increase in density and rigidity of the lens, which may compromise both near and far vision.

Lenticular opacities, called *cataracts*, add to reduced light transmission. The eye appears cloudy and, in a small percentage of adults, may need surgical treatment.[7] These changes in the lens of the eye may also contribute to filtering of the color spectrum, resulting in a loss of color sensitivity across the total spectrum but especially for green, blue, and violet shades.[18] Loss of color sensitivity results in reduced visual acuity for subtle differences in color shadings. Improvement in vision will result if there is contrast between colors and between an object and its background and if illumination is increased.[19]

Recently an intraocular implant or artificial lens has become a common treatment of cataracts for those who can tolerate the surgical procedure. Most older adults, however, function with mild cat-

aracts and do not require surgical treatment.

All of the previously discussed changes result in less light reaching the retina, a part of the central visual nervous system which remains relatively free from normal aging changes.[20] Although age-related changes in the retina are not usual, changes in the retina can occur in response to common disease processes that present in the aged adult. Diabetic retinopathy, although it can affect all ages, often causes changes in the retina of the older adult.[11] *Age-related macular degeneration* (ARMD), a degeneration of an area 3 mm temporal to the optic disc, results in deterioration of the retina and supportive structures in as many as 30 percent of the population between ages 75 and 81.[21] ARMD is a painless, gradual loss of central vision. It is more common in whites than blacks, those with a blue iris, long-term hypertension, and those who smoke. A very few, one out of 2000 people over 65, would benefit from laser beam therapy in the early stages of the disease.[7] Victims of ARMD cannot see items in their central visual field and compensate by rotating the head or trunk in such a way as to see the missing information.

Similar to the retina, the optic nerve does not commonly change in normal, healthy aging; however, a group of diseases, collectively called the *glaucomas*, cause optic nerve damage in the older adult. Glaucoma causes a resistance to the fluid that normally leaves the eye, resulting in increased intraocular pressure.[11] If left untreated, the optic nerve can be damaged with resulting loss of peripheral vision. The visual deficit is referred to as *tunnel vision*. Although most people with glaucoma are asymptomatic for quite a while, eye examinations can detect the disease. The glaucomas result in a problem somewhat opposite of ARMD; the peripheral visual field, rather than the central part of the visual field, is missing. The adaptations used by persons with this type of visual field loss is similar to that practiced by those with ARMD in that the person must increase head or trunk rotation to see missing information.

Evidence suggests that not all age-related visual problems result from peripheral changes or disease processes. Some visual perception changes may occur along the optic pathway, resulting in a slowing of information processing and an increasing perceptual inflexibility that affects image judgment.[22] Slower information processing is characterized by research in target recognition,[23] complex recognition,[24] and off-on flicker recognition (*critical flicker fusion*).[25,26] This translates into more difficulty with recognition of moving objects, items with a complex figure or ground, and items that appear in and out of light quickly. Such activities as walking, television viewing, and driving depend on such recognition.

Functional and Behavioral Adaptations

What do these visual changes mean for functional performance of the older adult? As mentioned previously, safe mobility can be threatened because of visual problems. Besides obvious acuity problems during reading, practical day-to-day tasks, such as housekeeping, shopping, and clothing selection, can be quite frustrating. Color discrimination of critical items. such as food and medication, can be challenging. Common leisure activities such as card playing, sports requiring eye-hand coordination, television viewing, and needlepoint can become uncompromised for the older adult with age-related visual changes. Hearing loss cannot be compensated for by lip reading in the visually impaired.[14] Glare and sudden illumination contrasts can compromise vision because of slower adaptation. Night vision may be very poor, curtailing many activities including driving. Dim lighting in restaurants and other public places may contribute to trips and falls.

The older adult's emotional reaction to loss of vision varies with personality, timing, and degree of loss and use of compensatory strategies. Rehabilitation is covered elsewhere in this text, but it is important to note that sensitivity of others as well as a barrier-free environment go a long way toward helping the older adult face visual impairments without undue despair. Charness and Bosman have excellent guidelines for designing the visual environment to reduce the deleterious effects of changes in vision that occur with normal aging.[27]

They suggest:

- Proper illumination levels
- Glare control
- Color contrasts
- Large print size

HEARING AND FUNCTIONAL PERFORMANCE

Vision and hearing along with speech contribute the most to human communication, the sending and receiving of messages. Somewhat like the visual system, the auditory system likely undergoes as many central as peripheral changes with age.[28] This fact becomes critical when we consider the importance of hearing for speech in the life of an older adult.

Since the 1940s and 1950s, there has been a growing body of data on *air con-*

duction hearing, or hearing tested with tones of various *pitches* (frequencies) through binaural headphones. Through World Fair screening, public health studies, and clinical screening records, hearing loss with age is well documented, particularly in the higher frequencies.[29,30] There is some controversy over whether this hearing loss is actually *presbycusis,* the term for old-age hearing loss, or hearing loss from other causes, such as noise exposure, ototoxic drugs, or disease.[31,32,33] The conclusion from various avenues of research indicate that the age effects in hearing are the result of slow, progressive changes in the auditory system independent of other factors.[34,35]

Terminology in Auditory Research

Discussions of hearing loss in old age is problematic because levels of "normal hearing" for the older adult have never been clearly defined.[36] For younger people normal hearing is reflected by a standard decibel level (*loudness*) at selected frequencies (*pitch*) based upon published normative data. Normative data do not exist for the older adult. Instead, researchers and clinicians use either a comparison to published *audiograms* of older adults (charts of hearing values)[37,38] or some unspecified judgment of functional normalcy for age (such as subject report)[39,40] to determine hearing problems. Having one's hearing termed "normal for your age" offers little consolation to the older person who cannot hear the water running or the speech sounds of grandchildren.

Audiologists, those professionals who test hearing and treat hearing loss, usually divide hearing loss into conductive, sensorineural, and mixed loss. Collectively, the prevalence of hearing loss increases from 25 percent at ages 65 to 74 to 40 percent for those over 75. Surveys of older and less healthy groups such as nursing home residents indicate that 85 to 90 percent of these adults have serious hearing impairments,[41,42] that is, impairments that limit function.

Conductive Hearing Loss and Aging

Conductive hearing loss, or block of acoustic energy, may occur because of problems in the external or middle ear. (See Fig. 6–2 for illustrations of external, middle, and inner ear.) Too much *cerumen* (wax) may build up in the external canal, causing blockage of sound. The middle ear may be filled with fluid from eustachian tube dysfunction or upper respiratory disease, preventing the three bones of the middle ear from conducting sound efficiently past the eardrum. Diseases of the middle ear that affect bone movement, such as tumors, will affect this mechanical transmission of energy.[41,43] These conductive problems can often be corrected by cleaning of the ear, medication, or surgery. Unfortunately, conduction loss is not the primary cause of hearing loss in the elderly.

Sensorineural Hearing Loss and Aging

Sensorineural hearing loss results from loss or damage to the sensory hair

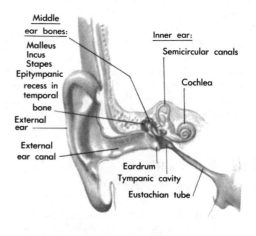

THE ORGAN OF HEARING

Figure 6–2 The organ of hearing. (From: Miller–Keane Encyclopedia and Dictionary of Medicine, Nursing and Allied Health, 4th ed. W.B. Saunders, Philadelphia, 1987, Plate 15, with permission.)

cells of the *cochlea*, or inner ear, or to the nerve cells of the cochlear ganglion, brain stem tracts, or cortex, or a combination of any of these. At the current time sensorineural loss is not correctable. Figure 6–3 shows these structures.

The hair cells of the cochlea are slowly lost and may be associated with the progressive high-frequency hearing loss of old age.[44] Damage to the hair cells can occur from exposure to a variety of drugs or noise. Although technically damage to the hair cells is not age-related, as a person ages, there is increased opportunity for exposure to these noxious factors.[41]

Some investigators have found that the cochlear or spiral ganglion has cell loss,[45,46] but more recent work has indicated that most sensorineural changes seem to occur in the hair cell loss of the lower basal turn of the inner ear.[45] Investigation of the auditory system of aged monkeys, a system much like that of humans, shows these minimal changes rather than broad nervous system otopathology. Hawkins and Johnsson compare the degenerative changes in the *organ of Corti*, the band containing hair cells, with those changes seen in age-related macular degeneration discussed earlier in this chapter.[45]

Age-related changes beyond the cochlea, those that would occur in the brain stem tracts and cortical or central auditory pathways in the temporal lobe, have been very hard to document from histological studies.[46,47,48] There may be loss of neurons in parts of the auditory pathway[46] or a decrease in the number of myelinated axons.[48] Some studies have found degeneration of white matter in the brain stem and hearing centers centrally.[47] There appears to be bilateral cell loss in the temporal lobe[47] as well as vascular changes throughout the aging auditory system.[49] The confusing results from these studies of age-related changes in the central auditory pathway may be due to the small number of subjects studied and varied investigational methods.[50,51]

A new, promising line of research in neural auditory problems is related to studies of neurotransmitter changes with aging.[52] Just as other parts of the central and peripheral nervous system, the auditory nervous system appears to have synaptic areas that suffer from loss of specific neurotransmitters.

Effects of Hearing Loss and Aging

The effects of conductive hearing loss are easy to understand. Sound is not conducted or is conducted through an obstruction (fluid or wax); thus its intensity or loudness is reduced. If sound is amplified loudly enough to reach the inner ear, it can then travel up to the

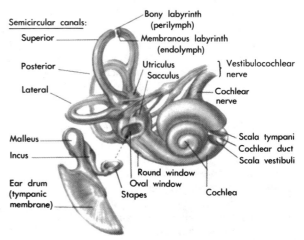

Figure 6–3 The middle ear and inner ear. (From: Miller–Keane Encyclopedia and Dictionary of Medicine, Nursing and Allied Health, 4th ed. W.B. Saunders, Philadelphia, 1987, Plate 15, with permission.)

auditory pathway in a normal fashion. In other words, make it louder, and the listener can hear you.

Unfortunately too many people, both young and old, have the misconception that all hearing loss is conductive loss. As stated previously, very few older adults suffer primarily, if at all, from conductive hearing loss. The majority suffer from sensorineural alone or in combination with conductive loss (mixed loss). The sensorineural component affects both hearing sensitivity as well as speech understanding in very complex ways.

Hearing sensitivity appears to change with age. Lebo and Reddell examined results from eight previous studies that attempted to specify normal threshold measures for individuals of increasing age (excluding noise-exposed subjects).[53] Their results indicate that after about age 32 for men and age 37 for women, there is nearly always some increase in hearing level or poorer hearing. As age increases, hearing level increases with the most dramatic difficulty being experienced in hearing the higher frequencies (pitches), such as those above 400 Hz. A big difference in hearing level for older men and women probably does not occur when the variable of noise exposure is controlled. Racial differences in hearing level with age probably do not occur.[54] Beard, in interviewing 270 centenarians, learned that hearing loss is much more gradual than loss of vision; however, the older adults had more trouble adjusting to the changes in hearing.[55]

In addition to age-related changes in threshold sensitivity, there appear to be changes in pitch discrimination and auditory reaction time. The older adult's ability to detect small changes in pitch, a skill important for the understanding of both music and speech, may begin to diminish as early as the fourth decade.[56] Beyond age 55 the ability to detect small pitch changes decreases as a linear function of age and becomes more problematic in the higher frequencies. The mechanism or site of lesion(s) for these changes is not known.

Like pitch discrimination, auditory re-

action time changes with age. Early studies of *dichotic listening*, or simultaneous presentation of different material to each ear, were intended to investigate short-term memory and aging.[57] Later researchers criticized these investigations and pointed out that they were more likely studies of reduced information input and changes in decision making for output responses.[58] Since older adults are more cautious in responding to auditory stimuli, several researchers have urged that both changes in pitch discrimination and auditory reaction time be evaluated as part of broader changes in perception and cognition that affect behavioral responses.[54,59]

Speech Understanding and Aging

One of the most critical effects of hearing loss and aging is that of poorer speech understanding. This very complex skill is related to several abilities: speech reception, speech discrimination, and speech understanding in stressful situations. Investigators are challenged to determine if changes in speech understanding are related to peripheral or central changes in the auditory nervous system or to a combination of changes throughout the auditory system. In any case, a reduction or inability to understand speech is the most common complaint among elderly hearing-impaired individuals presenting themselves to an audiology clinic.

Speech reception and recognition, typically measured as the loudness (intensity) level required to produce 50 percent correct responses for a standard list of words, has been shown to be reduced with age and often correlates with a reduction in hearing sensitivity.[60] Pestalozza and Shire found many older adults had poor speech recognition even with mild hearing loss.[61] They agreed with Gaeth's earlier work in this area and his concept of "phonemic regression," which is a description of an individual's poorer understanding of *phonemes*, speech sounds, with age.[62] Many other investigators have reached the same conclusions while matching subjects for hearing sensitivity, not age.[63,64,65]

A closely related auditory skill is speech discrimination. Speech discrimination is measured clinically by administering a test of phonetically balanced monosyllabic words. The loudness of the words is increased during the test. Corso[54] found that his young subjects were relatively stable in this skill as did Feldman and Reger[66]; however, by age 80 there was some loss of discrimination. This poor discrimination acuity can affect speech understanding of older adults and can restrict their speech intelligibility input to a more narrow intensive range.

Personal and Interpersonal Behavior and Hearing Loss

Speech understanding during stressful listening conditions is probably the most common and most troublesome for the average older adult. Stressful listening conditions exist daily and everywhere, such as in the automobile, a room with background noise, or a group speaking situation. Researchers have tried to duplicate these conditions experimentally by altering the acoustic signal, presenting competing noise, or altering the listening environment. Although speech understanding in the elderly is markedly decreased in the presence of these stressful listening conditions, it should be noted that variability exists among elderly individuals. Each difficult listening condition does not result in the same degree of perceptual difficulty in every older person. Thus it is difficult to translate speech perception research into a prognosis for any given elderly individual.

The cumulative effects of these hearing problems have been shown to affect interpersonal behavior in the older adults. At a basic level, the older adults may no longer have access to familiar sounds in the environment, which produces one more strain on an organism already adjusting to so many changes. Social interactions may decrease, and

paranoid tendencies may increase.[67,68] In people with already existing mental health and behavioral problems, such as Alzheimer's disease or depression, the existence of a hearing loss may result in excess disability.[69]

Treating the hearing loss can result in significant clinical improvement in the older person's functioning, particularly in an improved ability to attend to, understand, and respond to speech. It is particularly critical for older adults who may need the help of a mental health professional, one of the "talking professions," to be able to hear speech.[70,71]

Several excellent attitude or perceptions scales exist for use with older adults with hearing loss. One excellent scale is the Hearing Handicap Inventory for the Elderly, which translates the hearing difficulties presented here into activities of daily living,[72] such as time spent in conversation, reluctance to talk on the phone or in face-to-face conversations, and self and others' perceptions of the hearing loss. These instruments are typically administered by an audiologist.

TASTE AND SMELL: PHYSICAL CHANGES AND FUNCTIONAL PERFORMANCE

Although taste and smell are quite different mechanisms anatomically, they are considered together because of their sometimes functionally shared purpose. The senses of taste and smell change with age but are very sensitive to environmental effects such as smoking odors. Research in these two areas is just beginning with the establishment of a few research centers for the study of chemosensory disorders.[73] Current research indicates that taste changes relatively little with age, while smell has more significant change.

Changes in taste, or *gustation*, have been noted by researchers who have examined the basic tastes of sweet, salty, bitter, and sour substances. Typically, subjects sip the substance in a liquid and identify it or differentiate it from water. The threshold for recognition of sweet taste is higher in men than women of any age. Many investigators have found higher thresholds for identification of substances in older adults, but have not found a sex difference. Surprisingly, no differences have been found in smokers and nonsmokers, but this variable has not been well controlled in terms of equal numbers of subjects in each category or length of time since onset of tobacco use. Some investigators have found that older subjects confuse tastes, which may be attributed to the presence of fungus in the mouth, the wearing of dentures, or the commonly found changes in the mouth tissue of older adults.[74] All of these causes of taste changes are treatable.

Taste changes are not surprising due to the fact that the mucosa of the tongue undergoes degenerative alterations with age. Many researchers have noted a decrease in taste buds with age, some reporting as many as two-thirds lost or atrophic.[75] Varicose enlargement of the superficial veins under the surface of the tongue is common and called *caviar tongue*.[76] These structural changes have not been correlated with functional change, and it is likely that taste changes in adults without disease rarely occur until after age 60, if at all.[51]

Age-related changes in *olfaction*, or smell, have been researched less than taste. For many years investigators have known that changes in the olfactory tract and bulb are similar to changes in the central nervous system. A generalized atrophy with a loss of neurons is present. Degeneration of the sensory cells of the nasal mucosa has been noted. In subjects with severe degeneration of this system, there was not a generalized nervous system degeneration. The localized degeneration was thought to be due possibly to environmental effect. Currently, there is much research underway on the effects of smoking and olfaction, and the age effects of smoking and olfaction. An age-related decline in suprathreshold sensitivity for odors is also documented and probably affects enjoyment of food and other smells.[77]

Taste and smell changes with age may be functionally important for the individual. For example, some older people report that eating is less pleasurable, a problem that may be compounded by the need to reduce salt intake in people with high blood pressure. There is insufficient evidence that there are dramatic structural or physiological changes in people who have no disease affecting the primary sensory cells. Changes in hearing, taste, and smell have a common factor in the neuronal degeneration of the lower part of the post-central gyrus where these sensations are "appreciated."[78] If this is the case, there would not be a sensory change per se but a change in sensory integration or sensory comprehension.

SOMESTHESIS AND TOUCH: PHYSICAL CHANGES AND FUNCTIONAL PERFORMANCE

Somesthesis is often studied as one sense, rather than as just the sense of touch. *Somesthesis* includes the sensations that arise from light and deep touch of the skin and the viscera, vibration, pain, and temperature, as well as *kinesthesis*, the sensation and awareness of active or passive movement. Like research in other areas of sensation, research in somesthesis demonstrates change with advancing age, but environmental effects cannot be ruled out. Neuropathies and skin disease make age-related changes almost impossible to detect in the purest sense.

In this chapter, only the age-related changes in the superficial sensations, pain, temperature and light touch, will be reviewed. Chapter 20 will provide the reader with a summary of the changes in the proprioceptive and cortical sensations.

Decreased response to tactile stimuli and minimal alterations in the perception of pain are common sensory disturbances linked to advancing age.[78] Investigators have many explanations for these changes, most of which are incomplete. Some possible explanations include a lower concentration of touch corpuscles, diminished circulation, slower nerve conduction velocities due to irregularities in nerve fibers, and dietary deficiencies.[79,80]

Pain and temperature sensitivity involves much more than touch in terms of nervous system involvement and psychological factors. Experiments can be biased due to either the subject's fear of the experiment or the instructions given to subjects, or both.[81] It is likely that there is a sensory loss of pain perception in later years, but, as with auditory research, there is a conservative response in reporting that pain is present.[82] Temperature changes with age are anecdotally known, even by heating and air-conditioning repair persons but are not documented in research.[83] Research reports on hot or cold comfort levels do not document an age difference, but research on thermal extremes does show changes with aging.[84] Older adults are more adversely affected by extremes of hot or cold, prompting many social service agencies to have special programs for the elderly during the very hot or cold times of the year.

SENSORY INTEGRATION: A CONCLUSION

Changes in sensation and perception in the sensory systems of older persons, previously discussed (Table 6–1), have a recurrent theme:

1. Sensitivity may be decreased.
2. Perceptual changes may be general nervous system changes, not specifically due to changes of the sensory modality.
3. Reaction in an experimental condition may be conservative and reflective of general slower CNS information processing.
4. Perception over a lifetime may become learned and automatic, with a maintenance of functional skills even in the presence of sensory decline.

There are both positive and negative aspects to the learned sensory and per-

ceptual patterns one adopts over a life span. On the one hand, the elderly adult can "fill in" missing information based on remembered events and learned contexts. On the other hand, life can be dangerous if sounds, sights, and other sensory events are misperceived and erroneously interpreted. One may answer a question incorrectly, fail to see an unsafe situation, or touch something dangerous. One might lose enjoyment from previous pleasurable sensory events, such as movies, religious events, conversations, and music.

There are those who think changes in sensory and perceptual information affect cognitive function rather than changes in cognition affecting adaptation to the physical environment. In other words, research in age-related cognitive change (covered elsewhere in this text) may be biased by sensory and perceptual abilities of older subjects. Of course, there is much more to cognition, but the role of sensory sensitivity diminution must be taken into account. One example of this is hearing sensitivity. Researchers have known that there is a negative correlation between hearing sensitivity and scores on intelligence or memory tasks.[84,85] Two important and interesting facts about the sensory perceptual systems and their neural pathways are:

1. They are associated at a higher cortical level, the "association cortex" described by Geschwind.[3]
2. It is likely that sensory and perceptual losses share a common component of degeneration, such as neurotransmitter change or effects on basic cell action.

These common connections and common associations may have functional effects. Just as the older adult "can't hear without my glasses on," he or she may find one sensory pathway aiding another as sensitivity decreases. Although, unlike a young adult who can compensate well if one sensory system suffers, the older adult may be compensating or adapting to sensory or perceptual losses with systems that are likewise impaired. Perhaps learned patterns and memory of sensory stimuli play a greater role than compensation for some events. This is an area that is yet to be examined.

REVIEW QUESTIONS

1. *What general sensory changes occur with aging in all sensory organs or systems?*

2. *How might changes in all sensory systems affect the older adult's behavior? Are any changes generally more devastating than others, or is this an individual occurrence?*

3. *How might an older adult change his or her daily activities as a result of visual changes? Auditory changes?*

4. *How might social life change for an older adult who cannot understand speech sounds normally?*

5. *What dangers might an older adult face with changes in taste, smell, or superficial sensations? Based upon known physiological changes, are any of these dangers more likely to occur than others in the vast majority of older adults?*

6. *Imagine that you are designing a retirement or life care center, or group home, for normal older adults. Taking the research about sensory and sensory integrative changes into account, what are a few important steps you would take to ensure that sensory stimuli are received optimally by all residents of your facility? Try to go beyond state and federal legislation or regulations relating to health and safety. You may decide the role that financial constraints may play, or you may design both the ideal and the practical facility!*

7. *Identify interventions commonly employed with older adults to compensate for sensory deficits in vision, hearing, taste, touch, and smell.*

REFERENCES

1. Kennedy, RA: The Physiology of Aging. Year Book Medical Publishers, Chicago, 1982, pp 72–76.
2. Kennedy, RA: The Physiology of Aging. Williams & Wilkins, Baltimore, 1988, pp 67–70.
3. Geschwind, N: Disconnection syndromes in animals and man. I and II. Brain 88:237, 1965.
4. Ayres, AJ: Developmental dyspraxia and adult-onset apraxia. Paper presented at Sensory Integration International, Torrance, CA, July 1985.
5. Harris, CS: Fact Book on Aging: A Profile of America's Population. National Council on the Aging, Washington, DC, 1978, pp 100–111.
6. National Society to Prevent Blindness: Vision Problems in the US: Data Analysis. National Society to Prevent Blindness, 1980.
7. Thornton, HA: A Medical Handbook for Senior Citizens and Their Families. Auburn House Publishing, Dover, MA, 1989, pp 125–129.
8. Anderson, B and Palmore, E: Longitudinal evaluation of ocular function. In Palmore, E (ed): Normal Aging II: Reports from the Duke Longitudinal Studies. Duke University Press, Durham, 1974, pp 24–32.
9. Verner, C and Davidson, C: Physiological Factors in Adult Learning and Instruction. Research Information Processing Center, Tallahassee, FL, 1971.
10. Crews, JE, Frey, WD and Peterson, PE: Independent living for the handicapped elderly community: A national view. J of Visual Impairment and Blindness, 81:305–308.
11. Weinreb, RN, Freeman, WR and Selezinka, W: Vision Impairment in Geriatrics. In Kemp, B, Brummel-Smith, K and Ramsdell, JW (eds): Geriatric Rehabilitation. Little, Brown, Boston, 1990, pp 223–225.
12. Faye, E: Clinical Low Vision, ed 2. Little, Brown, Boston, 1984, pp 1–3.
13. Andrew, W: The Anatomy of Aging in Man and Animals. Grune and Stratton, New York, 1971, pp 206–216.
14. Sullivan, N: Vision in the Elderly. In Stilwell, EM (ed): Handbook of Patient Care for Gerontological Nurses, Journal of Gerontological Nursing. Slack Incorporated, Thorofare, NJ, 1984, pp 1–9.
15. Leslie, WJ: Senescent changes of the cornea. J Am Optom Assoc 49:774, 1978.
16. Kasper, RL: Eye Problems of the Aged. In Reichel, W (ed): Clinical Aspects of Aging. Williams & Wilkins, Baltimore, 1978, pp 383–402.
17. Schaefer, WD and Weale, RA: The influence of age and retinal illumination on the pupillary near reflex. Vision Res 10:179, 1970.
18. Dye, CJ: Sensory Changes in Aging. In Ernst, NS and Glazer-Waldman, HR (eds): The Aged Patient. Year Book Medical Publishers, Chicago, 1983.
19. Weale, RA: The Aging Eye. HK Lewis, London, 1963.

20. Corso, JF: Sensory Processes and Age Effects in Normal Adults. Journal of Gerontology 26:90, 1971.
21. Leibowitz, HM, et al: The Framingham eye study monograph. Surv Ophthalmol (Suppl) 24:335, 1980.
22. Bergman, M: Aging and the Perception of speech. University Park Press, Baltimore, 1980, pp 14–17.
23. Fozard, JL, et al: Visual Perception and Communication. In Birren, JE and Schaie, KW (eds): Handbook of the Psychology of Aging. Van Nostrand Reinhold, New York, 1977, pp 517–519.
24. Surwillo, WW: Timing of Behavior in Senescence and the Role of the Nervous System. In Talland, GA (ed): Human Aging and Behavior. Academic Press, New York, 1968, pp 1–36.
25. Woodruff, DS: A Physiological Perspective of the Psychology of Aging. In Woodruff, DS and Birren, JE (eds): Aging: Scientific Perspectives and Social Issues. Van Nostrand Reinhold, New York, 1975.
26. Fozard, JL: Vision and Hearing in Aging. In Birren, JE and Schaie, KW (eds): Handbook of the Psychology of Aging, ed 3. Academic Press, San Diego, 1990.
27. Charness, N and Bosman, E: Human Factors and Design for Older Adults. In Birren, JE and Schaire, KW (eds): Handbook of the Psychology of Aging, ed 3. Academic Press, San Diego, 1990.
28. Bergman, M: Hearing and aging: An introduction and overview. In Roush, J (ed): Seminars in Hearing: Aging and Hearing Impairment. Thieme-Stratton, New York, 1985, pp 99–114.
29. Glorig, A, et al: 1954 Wisconsin State for Hearing Survey. Subcommittee on Noise in Industry. American Academy of Ophthalmology and Otolaryngology, 1957.
30. Montgomery, HC: Analysis of World's Fairs' Hearing Tests. Bell Laboratory Record 18:98, 1939.
31. Rosen, S, et al: Presbycusis study of a relatively noise-free population in the Sudan. Annals of Otology, Rhinology and Laryngology 71:727, 1962.
32. Weston, TET: Presbycusis. J of Laryngology and Otology 78:273, 1964.
33. Lowell, SH and Paparella, MM: Presbycusis: What is it? Laryngoscope 87:1710, 1977.
34. Glorig, A and Nixon, J: Hearing loss as a function of age. Laryngoscope 72:1596, 1962.
35. Robinson, DW and Sutton, GJ: Age effect in hearing—A comparative analysis of published threshold data. Audiology 18:320, 1979.
36. Gelfand, SA and Silman, S: Future perspectives in hearing and aging: Clinical and research needs. In Roush, J (ed): Seminars in Hearing: Future Perspective in Hearing and Aging: Clinical and Research Needs. Thieme-Stratton, New York, 1985, pp 207–219.
37. Konkle, DF, Beasley, DS and Bess, FH: Intelligibility of time-altered speech in relation to chronological age. JSHR 20:108, 1977.
38. Newman, CS and Spitzer, JC: Prolonged auditory processing time in the elderly: Evidence from a backward recognition-masking paradigm. Audiology 22:241, 1983.
39. Rowe, MJ: Normal variability of the brainstem auditory evoked response in young and old subjects. Electroencephalography and Clinical Neurophysiology 44:459, 1978.
40. Bosatra, A and Russolo, M: Comparison between central tonal tests in elderly subjects. Audiology 21:334, 1982.
41. Glass, LE: Hearing impairment in geriatrics. In Kemp, B, et al: Geriatric Rehabilitation. College-Hill, Boston, 1990, pp 235–251.
42. American Speech and Hearing Association: The epidemiology of hearing loss: Incidence and prevalence. In Williams, PS, et al (eds): Management of Hearing Impairment in Older Adults. ASHA, Rockville, MD, 1984, pp 10–25.
43. Davis, H: Acoustics and psychoacoustics. In Davis, H and Silverman, SR (eds): Hearing and Deafness. Holt, Rinehart and Winston, New York, 1978, pp 8–45.
44. Schuknecht, HF: Further observations on the pathology of presbycusis. Arch Otolaryngology 80:369, 1964.
45. Hawkins, JE and Johnsson, L: Otopathological changes associated with presbyacusis. In Roush, J (ed): Seminars in Hearing: Aging and Hearing Impairment. Thieme-Stratton, New York, 1985, pp 115–133.
46. Kirikae, I, Sato, T and Shitara, T: A study of hearing in advanced age. Laryngoscope 74:205.
47. Hansen, CC and Reske-Nielsen, E: Pathological studies in presbycusis. Arch Otolaryngol 82:115, 1965.
48. Konigsmark, BW and Murphy, EA: Volume of ventral cochlear nucleus in man: Its relationship to neuronal population and age. J Neuropath Exp Neurol, 31:304, 1970.
49. Corso, JF: Auditory Perception and Communication. In Birren, JE and Schaie, KW (eds): Handbook of the Psychology of Aging. Van Nostrand, Reinhold New York, 1977, pp 535–553.
50. Ferraro, JA and Minckler, J: The human lateral lemniscus and its nuclei. Brain and Language 4:277, 1977.
51. Corso, JF: Sensory process and age effects in normal adults. Journal of Gerontology 26:90, 1971.
52. Musiek, F: Update on audiology research. Paper presented at the 50th anniversary alumni conference, Department of Communication Sciences and Disorders, Case Western Reserve University, Cleveland, OH, 1990.
53. Lebo, CP and Reddell, RC: The presbycusis component in occupational hearing loss. Laryngoscope 82:1399–1409, 1972.
54. Corso, JF: Confirmation of normal discrimination loss for speech on CID Auditory Test W-22. Laryngoscope 67:365–370, 1957.

55. Beard, BB: Sensory decline in very old age. Gerontol Clin 11:149–158, 1969.

56. Koenig, E: Pitch discrimination and age. Acta Oto-Laryngol 48:475–489, 1957.

57. Ingles, J: Effects of age on responses to dichotic stimulation. Nature 194:1101, 1962.

58. Clark, LE and Knowles, JB: Age differences in dichotic listening. Journal of Gerontol 28:173–178, 1973.

59. Craik, FIM: The effects of aging on the detection of faint auditory signals. Proceedings of the 7th International Congress of Gerontology, vol 6, Vienna, 1966.

60. Jerger, J: Audiological findings in aging. Adv Otorhinolaryngol 20:115–124, 1973.

61. Pestalozza, G and Shore, I: Clinical evaluation of presbycusis on basis of different tests of auditory function. Laryngoscope 65:1136–1163, 1955.

62. Gaeth, J: A study of phonemic regression in relation to hearing loss. PhD dissertation. Northwestern University, Evanston, IL, 1948.

63. Jerger, J: Audiological findings in aging. Paper presented at the International Oto-Physiology Symposium, Ann Arbor, MI, 1971.

64. Luterman, DM, Welsh, OL and Melrose, J: Responses of aged males to time-altered speech stimuli. Journal Speech Hearing Research, 9:226–230, 1966.

65. Kasden, SD: Speech discrimination in two age groups matched for hearing loss. J Aud Res 10:210–212, 1970.

66. Feldman, RM and Reger, SN: Relations among hearing, reaction time, and age. J Speech Hearing Res 10:479–495, 1967.

67. Knapp, PH: Emotional aspects of hearing loss. Psychosomat Med 10:203–222, 1948.

68. Hyams, DE: Psychological factors in rehabilitation of the elderly. Geront Clin 11:129–134, 1982.

69. Cohen, GD: Psychology and mental health in the mature and elderly adult. In Birren, JE and Schaie, KW (eds): Handbook of the Psychology of Aging, ed 3. Academic Press, San Diego, 1990, pp 359–371.

70. Dunkle, RE and Hooper, CR: Using language to help depressed elderly aphasic persons. Social Casework 64:539–545.

71. Hooper, CR and Johnson, AF: Assessment and intervention. In Ripich, D (ed): Handbook of Geriatric Communication Disorders. Pro-Ed, Austin, TX, 1992.

72. Ventry, I and Weinstein, B: The hearing handicap inventory for the elderly: A new tool. Ear and Hearing 3:128–134, 1982.

73. Bartoshuk, LM and Weiffenback, JM: Chemical Senses and Aging. In Birren, JE and Schaie, KW: Handbook of the Psychology of Aging, ed 3. Academic Press, San Diego, 1990, pp 429–443.

74. Balogh, K and Lelkes, K: The tongue in old age. Gerontologia Clinica 3:38, 1961.

75. Kocsard, E, Ofner, F and D'Abrera, V St E: The histopathology of caviar tongue. Dermatologica 140:318, 1970.

76. Liss, L and Gomez, F: The nature of senile changes of the human olfactory bulb and tract. Archives of Otolaryngology 67:167, 1958.

77. Murphy, C: Age-related effects on the threshold, psychophysical function, and pleasantness of menthol. Journal of Gerontology 38:217–222, 1983.

78. Kenney, RA: Physiology of Aging. Year Book Medical Publishers, Chicago, 1982, pp 71–79.

79. Lascelles, RG and Thomas, PK: Changes due to age in internodal length in the sural nerve in man. J Neurol Neurosurg Psychiat 29:40–44, 1966.

80. Horwitt, MK, et al: Studies of vitamin deficiency. Science 104:407–408, 1946.

81. Gelfand, S: The relationship of experimental pain tolerance to pain threshold. Can J Psych 18:36–42, 1964.

82. Clark, WC and Mehl, L: Thermal pain: A sensory decision theory analysis of the effect of age and sex on d', various response criteria, and 50 percent pain threshold. J Abnorm Psychol 78:202–212, 1971.

83. Kenshalo, DR: Age changes in touch, vibration, temperature, kinesthesis and pain sensitivity. In Birren, JE and Schaie, KW (eds): Handbook of the Psychology of Aging. Van Nostrand Reinhold, New York, 1977, pp 562–579.

84. Granick, S, Kleban, MH and Weiss, AD: Relationships between hearing loss and cognition in normally hearing aged persons. Journal of Gerontology 31:434–448, 1976.

85. Thomas PD, Hunt, WC, Garry PJ, et al: Hearing acuity in healthy elderly population: Effects on emotional, cognitive and social status. Journal of Gerontology 38:321–325, 1983.

Life has changed me greatly, it has improved me greatly, but it has also left me practically the same.

—FLORIDA SCOTT MAXWELL, *The Measure of My Days*, Penguin Books, New York, 1968, p. 17.

Cognitive Development

KATHRYN PEREZ RILEY

OBJECTIVES

By the end of this chapter, readers will be able to:

1 Explain the results of research in cognition and aging, identifying the methodology. Describe the inherent strengths and limitations of the design.

2 Discuss the changes in intellectual abilities using the model of crystallized and fluid intelligence.

3 Describe the changes that occur in problem solving, abstract reasoning, memory, and attention with normal aging.

4 Discuss the effect normal age-related cognitive change has on occupational performance, leisure activities, and activities of daily living.

5 Identify practical methods that can be taught to the older adult to permit job maintenance and enhance performance and satisfaction in leisure and daily life activities.

Does the aging process bring on inevitable and inexorable waning of intellect, memory, and reason? Is the aging adult forced to give up work, play, and independence because of this loss of cognitive ability? Those who have grown old or who have studied or worked with others who have grown old can answer both questions with a resounding *no!* Yet there are documented changes and losses that may require adaptation on the part of aging adults as they seek balance in lifestyle, occupation, and daily activities.

This chapter will address the issue of normal age-related changes in cognitive abilities as related to functional performance in older adults. First, the nature of these cognitive changes will be reviewed, which will be followed by a discussion of the relationship between cognition, activities, and occupational performance.

COGNITIVE CHANGES IN NORMAL AGING

Researchers first began investigating and documenting the changes in cognition that accompany the aging process in the 1920s and 1930s, not long after the use of standardized intelligence tests became common. The early literature focused on performance on intelligence tests and gradually branched out into the study of other forms of cognitive activity, including problem solving, memory, attention, and language.[1,2] The following sections will discuss these areas of cognition, serving as an abbreviated summary of a voluminous body of literature. The reader should not be tempted to extrapolate from the generalized research findings reported here to an individual's experience with cognitive changes during the aging process. While it will be seen that changes and declines do occur in older adults as a population and while older adults tend to perform more poorly on many laboratory tasks than do younger people, the *individual* older adult may:

- Never experience these changes
- May objectively experience a decline that is never subjectively felt

Thus when one is working with an older adult in any applied or real-life setting, any assumptions made about intellectual functioning are less likely to be accurate than an actual assessment of that person's ability.

Methodological Considerations

To understand past and present research results in the area of cognition and aging, it is necessary to recall the basic methodologies employed in these investigations. The cross-sectional design is by far the most common approach used to study age differences in any number of factors. In this design, one essentially compares two or more age groups at one point in time. Thus it is quite common to see studies that have examined cognitive test performance in 20-, 40-, 60-, and 80-year-olds. While these studies yield information about differences between age groups, they cannot address the issue of actual maturational changes — that is, changes that accompany the aging process within an individual. A longitudinal design is required to address this question, involving the repeated testing of a group of individuals over an extended period of time.

An additional variable that is of relevance to both methods of investigation is the cohort effect. A *cohort* is generally defined as a group of individuals born within a certain time frame, for example, a 5- or 10-year period. The differential effects of one's birth year upon one's cognitive abilities or test performance can be great, in light of the importance of educational opportunities, life experience, access to medical care, and occupational opportunities.

Cross-sectional studies are limited in that they show differences between current cohorts of adults, but they cannot predict the patterns of differences between future cohorts. These studies cannot report with any certainty that the older cohorts studied have actually declined (or improved) in any area of cognitive ability.

Longitudinal studies can better answer the question of maturational change, but they are able to address the issue of change only in the limited number of cohorts included in their sample. Past and future cohorts' experiences with intellectual change cannot reliably be predicted using longitudinal results.[3,4] This method is further complicated by dropout rates resulting in bias.

A partial solution to the limitations of these two methods of research is the cross-sequential design developed by Schaie, Baltes, and colleagues as cited in Woods and Britton,[2] in which different age groups are tested at repeated intervals over a fairly extended period of time. In some cases, both new and old samples of subjects from the same pool are included in the retest samplings. Cross-sequential designs, then, can yield information about age differences and age changes, both within individuals and between cohorts. Unfortunately, the complexity of this design makes it difficult to carry out, and it is not without methodological problems. Thus the bulk of available literature on cognitive changes in aging is based primarily on cross-sectional designs and secondarily on longitudinal studies.

Intelligence

The very early data on IQ test performance among older adults were based almost entirely on cross-sectional studies. These early findings, comparing young adults in their twenties to older persons aged 60 and above, generally showed very large differences between young and old on tests such as the Army Alpha Test and later on the Wechsler Adult Intelligence Scale (WAIS and WAIS-Revised).[2,5] In general, these early data were interpreted as showing a rather precipitous decline in intelligence beginning at about age 25 and continuing into the seventh and eighth decades.

More recent research has resulted in a major change in thinking about declines in intellectual abilities. Cross-sectional studies now indicate declines beginning at about age 60, while longitudinal research results show declines beginning in the late 60s. Both methods of research indicated fairly significant changes occurring by the mid to late 70s.[3,5]

While general declines in the full-scale WAIS scores and other general measures of intelligence have been documented in the advanced years, it is important to note the differential rates of decline and stability seen in the various subtests or categories of intellectual ability. The most prominent of these is the verbal performance split seen on these two scales of the WAIS. Specifically, the performance scale that measures speed and accuracy in problem solving and psychomotor and perceptual abilities shows earlier and more significant decline than does the verbal scale, which measures abilities and knowledge acquired over a lifetime, including vocabulary skills, a general fund of information, and verbal comprehension and reasoning. Cattell[7] and Horn and Cattell[6] have explained this differential decline using the model of crystallized and fluid intelligence. *Fluid intelligence*, which involves the ability to adapt to and use new information in reasoning, solving, and integrating problems or novel information, corresponds to the subtests of the WAIS performance scale. *Crystallized abilities*, corresponding to the verbal scale, reflects the accumulated, practical skills and knowledge of the individual. The decline in fluid intelligence has been postulated as being due to biological changes in the central nervous system and to a decline in speed of information processing and psychomotor output.[2,4] While none of these models or explanatory devices has been accepted as complete or definitive, it is clear that normative samples of older adults consistently show the verbal performance split in both longitudinal and cross-sectional studies, making it reasonable to accept lowered performance scaled scores in aged adults as normal and expected. Significant declines or impairment in the verbal scales in people under the age of 80, however, would not be expected and may be an indication of a pathological process such as dementing illness or other central nervous system dysfunction that may require professional intervention.

SPEED OF INFORMATION PROCESSING

Of special relevance to this chapter is the finding that speed of information processing has been shown to decline with advancing age. Although extraneous variables such as motivation, ecological validity of the tests used, depression, cautiousness, and motor skills all complicate the issue of measuring pure central processing speed, the idea that a generalized cognitive slowing occurs with advancing age remains as a dominant concept in the literature.[14] This slowing has been postulated as accounting for the age-related decline seen in the (timed) performance subtests of the WAIS; yet when older adults are given more time on these tests, their improved scores generally still fail to reach the level of younger adults.[15] The relevance of these empirical findings to the older adults' daily functioning will be discussed later in this chapter, as these changes in speed of information processing may in fact be perceived as troublesome by the older individual in his or her daily activities and vocational performance.

Other Cognitive Abilities

PROBLEM SOLVING

Designing research to examine the problem-solving abilities of older adults is a complex matter, given that factors such as speed of information processing, intelligence, memory, and relevance of test items all affect one's problem-solving skills. In general, studies that have taken these factors into account using cross-sequential methodological approaches[8] indicate that there is a decline in the speed and efficiency of problem solving associated with the aging process.[2,9] The selection of inappropriate strategies, information overload, and poor organizational processes all may contribute to the observed declines in performance. Since problem-solving skills have received relatively little systematic attention in the literature, many questions concerning the reasons and implications of these changes remain unanswered. Difficulties in the area of problem solving are certainly not cited by older adults as being of major concern, and it remains unclear whether laboratory-based tests designed to measure problem solving do in fact approximate real-life decision making to an adequate degree.

ABSTRACT REASONING

Closely related to problem-solving skills is the ability to abstract. This ability is most often assessed through the use of tests of concept formation such as the similarities subtest of the WAIS and the Halstead-Reitan battery's category test. Reasonably significant and consistent age differences have been found on these types of tests, suggesting that older adults are less proficient at abstract reasoning tasks than are young adults.[10] Once again, the tasks used to evaluate this skill must be evaluated in terms of the amount of variance in performance that is accounted for by factors such as memory, attention, and lack of ecological validity. Mental flexibility, or set shifting in reasoning tasks, also has been shown to decline somewhat with advanced age even when memory demands are minimal.[11]

Memory and Attention

Of all the cognitive abilities, memory is the most discussed, studied, and evaluated by researchers and laypersons alike. Changes in memory functioning with advancing age are expected, feared, and exaggerated in common folklore, and it is fair to say that similar biases occur in empirical investigations. It is in the area of memory research that the cross-sectional design has been predominant, with relatively little data coming from either longitudinal or cross-sequential studies.

Before one can meaningfully discuss memory, the role of attention must be considered. Hasher and Zacks[12] have reviewed much of the relevant literature on attention in elderly adults.[22] Attention may be divided into sustained attention, attentional capacity, and selective attention. For the most part, the available literature would suggest that little significant decline is found in the older adult's sustained and selective attention abilities. Older adults seem just as able as the young to perform well on tasks involving, for example, the ability to ignore distracting or irrelevant information while attending to target stimuli.[13] Digit span and continuous performance tasks also reveal stability throughout the life span.[10] However, the results of investigations into the attentional capacity of older adults are less clear, with some studies indicating decline and others finding no age-related deficits.[14] It may be, then, that while older adults are unlikely to experience declines in the ability to attend to material that falls within the normal span of immediate memory (5 ± 2 items) or in the capacity to select relevant material from the irrelevant, there may be a decrease in the maximum amount of attentional resources available.[10]

MEMORY PROCESS

It has been stated that the attentional abilities of older adults are, for the most part, essentially intact. This is important to the consideration of normal changes in memory functions, since without attention there can be no memory. There are a variety of theoretical models of memory functioning, some of which focus on the contents of the memory stores[14] and others that focus on the process and nature of the storage system.[10,15] The accumulation of research evidence into age changes and age differences in memory has led to a generally accepted understanding of the memory skills of older adults. First, it is fairly clear that there is little if any decline seen in the earliest stage of memory, the sensory stage. Similarly, short-term or primary memory is not thought to be deficient later in life. Thus one can expect that older adults will be able to perceive, attend to, and hold on to information within the normal span of 5 ± 2 items without noticeable difficulty.[2,16]

Secondary Memory and Encoding Strategies

It is in the area of *secondary* (long-term) *memory* that the largest and most consistent age differences are found. This memory store is generally viewed as containing an unlimited amount of information for almost any length of time. In order for data to reach secondary memory, the information must be actively processed or transferred from primary memory. Older adults have been shown to have deficits in recall of information from the secondary memory store, with the deficits being more pronounced in tests of free recall than in tests of recognition.[10] While there is little evidence for reduced capacity of the

secondary memory store in normal aging, there is strong evidence to support deficits in the encoding processes used to transfer data into this storage system. This rather large body of data[15,17,18] clearly documents the failure of older adults to spontaneously use effective strategies to encode to-be-learned material. That is, while younger adults are likely to use a variety of organizational, semantic, or "deep" processing strategies, older adults either fail to employ any such strategy or may use one that is less efficient. These deficits in the transfer of data from one storage system to the next affect the amount of information stored and the efficiency with which it can be retrieved.

It is important to note that while older individuals may not employ encoding strategies spontaneously, when structure is imposed upon the material or when older adults are trained to use mnemonic devices, the deficits previously seen in secondary memory are diminished.[19,20] Increasing the ecological validity or meaningfulness of the materials also may minimize age-related deficits.[18] Thus while there may be some degree of absolute decline in secondary, or long-term, memory accompanying the aging process, these deficits can be alternately exaggerated or reduced, depending upon the nature of the to-be-remembered material, the instructions that accompany the learning task, and the manner in which memory is tested (i.e., free recall versus recognition). These differences in laboratory procedures also may reflect differences in daily life memory demands, and it is not unusual for older adults to report that their memory for important or personal relevant information is better than their recall for uninteresting stories or events. In addition, while they may not be able to recall the name of a new acquaintance as readily as in the past, older adults are likely to report little trouble with facial recognition or remembering the names of old friends.

Remote Memory

Another area in which laboratory data may reflect the older adult's self-report is in the area of *remote* (or very long term) *memory*. Although this aspect of memory functioning has not been studied as extensively as the other storage systems, the literature seems uniform in finding little, if any, age-related remote memory deficits in normal aging.[21] Information found in this storage system is likely to have been maintained over a period of many years and is thought to be resistant to decay even in the early stages of Alzheimer's-type dementia. These findings certainly support the common observation that older adults are more likely to remember the events of 30 years ago better than the happenings of yesterday. However, one problem with both laboratory research and self-report or casual observation is that it is difficult to develop tests of remote memory that ensure that the remembered material is accurate.[2] That is, it is not at all clear whether an individual's "memories" of his or her childhood or early days of marriage are actual factors or hazy recollections of an amalgam of one's own (and perhaps others') experiences. Empirical tests of remote memory suffer from the problem of determining whether the subjects ever knew the test material (e.g., famous faces, years when World War I was fought). These considerations must be taken into account when examining the issue of remote memory in older adults.

Everyday or Practical Memory

The preceding discussion of cognitive abilities and memory has focused on research conducted with traditional laboratory and clinical tests. In recent years, the ecological validity of some of these tests has been called into question as gerontologists began to examine the effects of the older adults' motivation and interest on test performance. Some work has been done in the area of everyday or practical intelligence,[22] and an increasing body of literature is available on the issue of everyday memory.[23,24,27] The goal of this work is to develop measures that will tap into those areas that are important in the older adult's daily life activities, including work, leisure, and interpersonal interactions.

AGE-ASSOCIATED MEMORY IMPAIRMENT

A final issue related to age-related changes in cognition is that of *age-associated memory impairment* (AAMI).[28] AAMI has replaced the older term of *benign senescent forgetfullness* and describes those changes in memory that are commonly seen in healthy, well-functioning older adults in the absence of any form of physical illness or central nervous system disease. AAMI encompasses the relatively deficient performance of older adults in secondary memory, including encoding and retrieval, in conjunction with complaints of memory impairment in everyday activities.[26,28,29] The onset of memory loss in AAMI is gradual and fairly subtle and is defined as occurring only in healthy individuals of at least average intellectual functioning. The use of the term *AAMI* has been helpful in pointing out the subjective complaints of memory deficits in the absence of objective test data may point to other conditions such as depression[18,30] or neurological disorders. Furthermore, test data that show deficits in the older adult when compared to younger persons's scores are not to be used as evidence of AAMI unless they are also accompanied by that individual's complaints of diminished performance in daily life. The definition of this condition and subsequent research on AAMI have led to remediation problems that show promise in improving the quality of life for many older adults.[24,25,28] As will be seen, this knowledge of the laboratory and everyday memory changes seen in healthy older adults can be usefully applied to considerations of the functional performance of older adults.

COGNITION AND ACTIVITIES IN NORMAL AGING

The previous discussion of normal age-related changes in cognition focused almost entirely on the performance of older adults in laboratory settings. As has been mentioned, these data indicate a substantial degree of stability in older

TABLE 7–1	Changes in Cognition with Normal Aging	
Cognitive Abilities	**Changes**
Problem solving	Delayed until late in sixth decade
	Many changes remedial through instruction and practice
Memory	
Sensory	Little if any decline
Short term	None
Long term (secondary)	Some decline; deficits in encoding processes
Very long term (remote)	Little decline
Psychomotor skills	Decline may begin in early 50s
	Not altered by intervention
Information processing	Decline may begin in early 50s
	Not altered by intervention
Verbal skills	Declines not until 80 years
Abstract reasoning	Older adults may be less proficient on laboratory tests

adults' abilities throughout the life span (Table 7–1).

The remainder of this chapter will focus on a discussion of the relevance of these cognitive changes to the older adults' occupational and daily life functioning. Of particular interest is the identification of those changes that may have a detrimental effect on functioning. In addition, the findings from cognitive aging literature will be applied to a consideration of how best to optimize the fit between older individuals and their work or leisure environment.

Health, Cognition, and Functional Performance

The term *normal aging* has been employed in this chapter as a means of distinguishing physically and mentally healthy older adults from those who suffer from conditions and diseases that are likely to affect cognitive abilities. It can be assumed that the remainder of this chapter will deal only with the occupational and daily life performance of essentially healthy older adults.

Age, Vocational Performance, and Cognitive Change

Detailed consideration of general changes in vocational performance that accompany normal aging may be found elsewhere in this volume. As has been noted by Sterns and Alexander,[32] there exists a "serious lack" of information concerning these age differences in job performance. There is even less data on the relationship between cognitive change and vocational skills, although some investigators have addressed this issue.[33,34] A literature review conducted by Rhodes[35] and a meta-analysis by Waldman and Avolio[36] examined the existing literature on the job performance of older workers. It should be noted that while most gerontological researchers use the age of 65 to define an elderly sample, the literature on older workers focus on persons *up to* the age of 60 or 65.[37] Thus it should be immediately evident that many, if not most, of the age-related changes in cognitive functioning that have been reviewed thus far will not apply to the older worker, since the declines are not likely to be seen until after retirement age. However, as some of the changes begin in the fifth and sixth decades of life and workers commonly continue in their vocations well past the age of 60, a discussion of cognitive change and job performance is possible and relevant.

In general, it may be stated that the available literature in industrial gerontology indicates little overall decline in the vocational performance of healthy older adults.[35,36,38] Increased job satisfaction, job involvement and commitment, and decreased turnover rates all have been associated with the aging worker.[35] The actual job performance of the older worker may be described as declining in a limited number of situations, specifically in jobs that are physically demanding or require extremely fast responses.[35,38,39] Waldman and

Avolio[36] have noted that while supervisors' ratings of older adults may indicate a decline in job performance, objective ratings do not. Similarly, Baugher,[33] Rebok et al.,[41] and Green[43] note the relative lack of evidence for negative changes in older workers' performance. A consistent conclusion drawn in industrial gerontology literature is that the greatest amount of age-related vocational deficits will be seen in physically challenging jobs such as manual labor and some blue-collar jobs. The least decline is to be expected in vocations that require primarily mental effort, such as teaching. Moderate levels of change might be seen in jobs that require a combination of intellectual and physical skill.[33] These data suggest that older workers are as able as younger workers to meet the demands of their work, providing they are physically able.

What, then, is the role of cognitive change in the vocational performance of older adults? While only a few studies have directly addressed this issue, inferences may be drawn between the cognitive aging literature and the work of industrial gerontologists.[32,40]

THE DISUSE THEORY, COGNITION, AND THE OLDER WORKER

It has been hypothesized that greater environmental complexity and stimulation may prevent or attenuate intellectual decline in older adults.[41] Some researchers[42] have discussed the idea that older adults (as nonstudents or nonworkers) are less likely to encounter the types of situations that require active problem solving, memory, and other intellectual skills. This lack of environmental demand has been hypothesized, with limited empirical support, to account for the declines in fluid intelligence and secondary memory seen in older adults.

This form of "use-it-or-lose-it" theorizing has been used to explain the adequate performance of older workers who remain actively engaged in their vocation[41] to account for cognitive deficits seen in laboratory tasks,[43] and as the basis for remediation efforts in intellec-

tual and memory skills.[25] This concept and what is known about the nature and timing of age-related cognitive changes combine to support the general findings that any deficits in cognitive abilities that would be significant enough to affect job performance are not likely to occur until after the age of 65 or 70, and thus, after retirement age for most people.

When Does Cognitive Decline Affect Vocational Performance?

Although the preceding discussion has focused on continuity and adequacy of vocational performance in older workers, there may be some areas in which cognitive changes will affect one's work. These changes include decline in fluid intelligence, increased cautiousness, decreased speed of information processing, and the declines in secondary memory seen in AAMI.

Rebok and associates[41] have noted that older managers may perceive declines in intellectual processing abilities. This perceived decline is likely to be related to the laboratory-based findings of declines in fluid intelligence and slower information processing and response rates. It may be that the older worker whose job requires the active processing of a great deal of information and/or fast rates of output and decision making may in fact feel less effective in his or her job. However, as Rebok and associates[41] and others[38,43] have found, this type of older worker is also likely to use a variety of intellectual and instrumental coping strategies to compensate for any declines in cognitive ability, thus leading to an intact sense of competence and self-efficacy. Baugher[33] and Haberlandt[44] have discussed the fact that the tendency of older adults to be more cautious in decision making in ambiguous situations may pose some problems for their effectiveness in job performance. However, neither author is willing to suggest that this increased cautiousness is likely to result in substantial work-related deficits, and both Haberlandt and Baugher offer suggestions for reducing cautious responses on the part of the older worker.

The normal age-related changes in memory and those deficits seen in AAMI are potential sources of decreases in the vocational performance of older persons. If one's job begins to involve a higher level of memorization than was previously required or if the need to transfer significant amounts of information into secondary memory begins to exceed the aging worker's capacity, then a decline in job capability may be seen. It is to be emphasized that most healthy older workers will not experience AAMI or other forms of memory impairment that will be severe enough to cause this kind of dysfunction. In addition, it is likely that older adults will develop or maintain those coping and information management skills necessary to counteract any reduced efficiency in their memory abilities.[33]

In summary, then, normal age-related cognitive changes are likely to have an adverse affect on vocational performance only when the amount of information exceeds the older worker's rate or capacity of processing (fluid intelligence, response speed), when quick responses are to be made in ambiguous situations (cautiousness), or when the memory demands of a particular job increase or exceed the memory capabilities of the older worker (secondary-memory deficits, AAMI). Generally, however, the stability of crystallized intelligence and advantages of years of accumulated knowledge and vocational experience,[37,45] along with job-related coping and time management skills, will result in an older worker whose competence is little diminished.

Job Training and Retraining: A Note on Cognitive Aging

One remaining area of interest to this discussion of vocational performance, cognition, and the older adult involves job training or retraining. The interested reader is referred to excellent reviews and articles by Birren, Robinson, and Livingston,[31] Sterns and Alexander,[32] and Haberlandt[44] for more in depth treatment of this issue. Briefly, it has been suggested that we apply what is known about the intellectual and memory abilities of older adults[18,25] to vocational training programs. It has been noted[38,43] that one of the first issues to address should be the motivation of the older adult to engage in such training or retraining. Deficient self-esteem, negative expectations of (younger) others, and anxiety about new learning all must be allayed if the older worker is to be successfully trained.[43] Literature on everyday memory[23,34] and ecological validity[46] of to-be-learned material indicates that the training sessions must involve information that is of relevance and interest to the older adult. Sterns and Alexander[32] add that the use of familiar material and learning methods will enhance the older worker's chance of being successfully trained. These authors also stress the importance of providing feedback on successes during the training program in order to bolster self-confidence and maintain motivation.

Additional considerations for the training or retraining of older workers are related to changes in speed of information processing and transfer of information into secondary or long-term memory. It has been recommended[38,44] that older adults be given more time to learn new skills and that a self-paced format of learning be employed whenever possible. These strategies have been shown to improve performance on laboratory tasks[31] as well as in real-life learning situations.[25,32,44] Finally, the changes in memory that accompany normal aging and that are seen in AAMI may be overcome if the older worker is instructed in or provided with organizational and other mnemonic strategies that enhance the effectiveness of encoding, transfer, storage, and retrieval of the material to be learned.[25,32,44]

One final point should be made regarding the performance of older workers and the planning of training programs for them. Before one attempts to modify the vocational environment or training procedures on behalf of an older adult in an attempt to overcome normal age-related changes in cognition, it is essential to first determine if modifications are necessary. A great deal of extra effort may be saved by discovering that the older adult in question has not experienced a significant amount of cognitive decline and thus is not in need of special treatment on the job or in the training process.

Cognitive Changes: Leisure and Daily Activities

There is little research to be found that addresses the issue of how cognitive abilities in the healthy elderly are related to leisure and daily activities. It is extremely unlikely that the cognitive changes associated with the normal aging process will bring about significant deficits in instrumental and personal activities of daily living such as shopping, cooking, managing one's finances, taking medications, or performing personal care and hygiene activities. Instead, impairment in these areas is generally considered to be indicative of physical illness, dementia, or mental illness.[47,48,49]

LEISURE ACTIVITIES

While a reasonably large body of literature on social and leisure activities in the elderly is available,[50,51] research linking cognitive abilities to these activities for healthy, community-dwelling older adults is scarce. Much of the literature deals either with leisure, life satisfaction, or retirement without reference to the role of cognitive abilities[51,52] or it is related to activities programs for the institutionalized, impaired older adult.[47,50] The pursuit of leisure activities among healthy elderly individuals, whether retired or not, is likely to involve either continued involvement in well-established hobbies and interests or the development of new activities following retirement or other lifestyle changes such as the retirement of a spouse. If one recalls the concept of crystallized intelligence,[7,53] which is a stable form of cognitive ability composed of overlearned information and

skills, then it is reasonable to assume that similar stability would be seen in the older adult's ability to pursue familiar hobbies and interests such as playing cards, doing needlepoint, or repairing machinery. These activities, in which the older person may have engaged for as many as 40 or 50 years, should not be affected by the types of normal cognitive changes we have discussed.[54] Possible exceptions to this general conclusion will be presented below.

It is not surprising to suggest stability in the pursuit of life-long hobbies and leisure activities, but what of the older adult who chooses to learn a new skill in his or her efforts to find meaningful leisure activities? While there may be little direct empirical data to answer this question, it is reasonable to apply what we know from the industrial gerontology and general cognitive aging literature to this question. Since older adults have repeatedly demonstrated the ability to be retrained in new job skills[38,43,44] and to be able to maintain high levels of performance in changing work environments,[33,55] then there is no reason to assume that older people could not learn the new skills or information necessary to engage in novel forms of entertainment or leisure activity. While some of the training principles discussed earlier may be as helpful in leisure as in work-related activities,[32,41] most healthy older adults should be able to pursue any type of recreational pastime they desire, assuming they are physically and financially able to do so, and have the requisite skills.

Exceptions to the Rule

The normal changes in cognition that may be relevant to the older adults' functional performance in leisure activities are slowed speed or information processing and changes in memory abilities. This author[25] and others[24] have reported observational or self-report data suggesting that older adults may perceive the slowing of central processing and perceptual motor response time as a reduced ability to follow news presentations, television programs, or movies; similar age-related deficits may become evident to the older adult as he or she engages in activities such as bingo or challenging card games like bridge or cribbage. Each of these leisure activities requires the kind of rapid information processing and/or decision making that has been documented to be problematic for older adults in a variety of settings.[33,34] However, these cognitive changes should not lead to the older adult's inability to enjoy movies or play bridge. Instead, they may result in a minor sense of irritation on the part of the older adult, leading to some adaptation of the activity such as making notes or relinquishing some of the details in a film or news program.

The other area in which leisure activities could be affected by cognitive change involves the deficits in secondary memory seen in many healthy elderly adults, which have been subsumed under the category of AAMI. The types of difficulties described by older adults who experience AAMI include problems remembering the names of new acquaintances, misplacing objects, forgetting newly learned telephone numbers, and difficulty remembering multiple items or tasks on a list.[28] While it is not yet clear what proportion of healthy older adults experience AAMI, it is likely that a reasonably large number of them will perceive some of these memory changes. It is easy to see how these changes could lead to frustration and reduced enjoyment of leisure activities, particularly when these activities involve the learning and memorization of large amounts of new information such as traveling with a group of new acquaintances, learning to play bridge or keeping track of a busy schedule of social engagements. It is crucial to emphasize, however, that normal age-related memory deficits should not force older adults to give up these activities, unless their level of frustration tolerance is very low and they expect perfect memory performance in every situation. It has been this author's clinical experience in the neuropsychological assessment and differential diagnosis of dementing illnesses in older adults that

when an individual does give up many previously enjoyed and well-practiced leisure (or occupational) interests, it is generally a sign of true dementia or a serious depression. The physically and emotionally healthy adult may alter activities in some way as a concession to memory, but major lifestyle changes are rarely necessary (Table 7–2).

The Use of Memory Aids and Intervention Programs

We have already discussed the application of findings from cognitive aging research to vocational issues related to job maintenance and retraining. Similar applications may be made if one desires to enhance performance and satisfaction in leisure and daily life activities of older adults. Literature on AAMI,[14,28] everyday memory,[26] and cognitive intervention programs[25] all indicate that formal and informal methods of intervention and adaptation may help the older adult compensate for the effects of age-related memory changes. It has been this author's clinical observation that many older adults are experiencing frustration in their daily lives because they refuse to use the kind of memory aids that many younger people use — and that they in fact used when they were younger. These aids are simple forms of reminders, including lists and note pads for shopping, errands, and telephone numbers or messages, a daily diary or calendar for social engagements

TABLE 7–2 **Effect on Function of Age-Related Changes in Cognition**	
Components of Cognition	**Effect on Function**
Long-term memory	Unable to recall uninteresting stories or events or newly learned facts or people
	Difficulty if job requires high level of memorization
	Misplacing objects
Information processing	Decreased ability to watch TV or movies or perform challenging games

or appointments, and various devices used for monitoring medication dosages and timing. Many older adults are afraid to use these aids because they fear that this means they are getting "senile" or are developing Alzheimer's disease. Others subscribe to the use-it-or-lose-it theory of cognitive aging and worry that if they rely on external aids, their memory will fail rapidly. It seems reasonable to encourage the active older adult, or one who takes many medications, to use concrete and simple assistive devices to help him or her remember and function well. It is helpful to remind the worried older person who avoids these aids that he or she probably used them earlier in life and that there is no reason not to use them now.

In addition to these informal and concrete memory aids, some older persons may benefit from taking a class or reading a book on memory skills enhancement. Experimental evidence shows that a variety of training methods can improve the memory performance of older adults.[56] The main problem with this kind of formal training is that motivation to continue to use the mnemonic strategies after training ends seems low.

FUTURE DIRECTIONS

As older individuals continue to live longer, healthier, and more productive lives, gerontologists will continue to study the changes and continuities in cognition, lifestyle, and occupational performance that accompany the aging process. Future research is likely to emphasize the practical importance of these issues as well as to grow more sophisticated in research design and methodology. The accumulation of data from longitudinal studies begun in recent years should provide valuable insights into the ways in which aging persons work, think, retire, and enjoy life. It is to be hoped that this kind of research, along with medical advances, will enable gerontologists to deemphasize dysfunction and disability and focus instead on health and positive functioning in older adults.

REVIEW QUESTIONS

1. *Research studies on cognitive changes with aging have been performed using cross-sectional, cross-sequential, and longitudinal designs. What are the strengths and limitations of each of these designs as related to this topic?*

2. *Differentiate between crystallized and fluid intelligence. Describe how each changes with normal aging.*

3. *List and define the three areas of attention. Which area shows decline with normal aging?*

4. *What are the five stages of memory? In which of the stages is the older adult likely to show deficiency?*

5. *How do the cognitive changes with age influence the older adult's ability to use encoding strategies?*

6. *Define age-associated memory impairment. Give an example.*

7. *How might the job performance or leisure activities of the adult decline with normal aging?*

8. *How is the disuse theory used to explain the performance of the older worker?*

9. *What issues should be considered by a person devising job training or retraining for the older adult?*

10. *How might the older adult be instructed to compensate for the effects of age-related memory changes?*

REFERENCES

1. Schaie, KW and Eisdorfer, C: Annual Review of Gerontology and Geriatrics, Vol 7. Springer, New York, 1987.
2. Woods, RT and Britton, PG: Clinical Psychology with the Elderly. Aspen Systems, Rockville, MD, 1985.
3. Cunningham, WR: Intellectual abilities and age. In Schaie, KW and Eisdorfer, C (eds): Annual Review of Gerontology and Geriatrics, Vol 7. Springer, New York, 1987, p 117.

4. Albert, MS and Moss, MB (eds): Geriatric Neuropsychology. Guilford Press, New York, 1988.
5. Albert, MS and Heaton, RK: Intelligence testing. In Albert, MS and Moss, MB: Geriatric Neuropsychology. Guilford Press, New York, 1988, p 13.
6. Horn, JL and Cattell, RB: Age differences in fluid and crystallized intelligence. Acta Psychobiologica 26:107, 1967.
7. Cattell, RB: The theory of fluid and crystalline intelligence. Journal of Educational Psychology 54:1, 1963.
8. Arenberg, D: Changes with age in problem solving. In Craik, FI and Rehub, S (eds): Aging and Cognitive Processes. Plenum Press, New York, 1982, p 221.
9. Rabbitt P: How do old people know what to do next? In Craik, FI and Trehub, S (eds): Aging and Cognitive Processes. Plenum Press, New York, 1982, p 221.
10. Albert, MS: Cognitive function. In Albert, MS and Moss, MB: Geriatric Neuropsychology. Guilford Press, New York, 1988, p 33.
11. Albert, MS, Duffy, FH and Naeser, MA: Nonlinear changes in cognition and their neurophysiologic correlates. Canadian Journal of Psychology 41:141, 1987.
12. Hasher, L and Zacks, RT: Automatic and effortful processes in memory. Journal of Experimental Psychology 108:356–388, 1979.
13. Gilmore, GC, Tobias, TR and Royer, FL: Aging and similarity grouping in visual search. Journal of Gerontology 40:586, 1985.
14. Kausler, DH: Impairment in normal memory aging: Implications of laboratory evidence. In Gilmore, GC, Whitehouse, PJ and Wykle, MR (eds): Memory, Aging and Dementia. Springer, New York, 1989, p 41.
15. Perlmutter, M, Adams, C, Berry, J, Kaplan, M. Person, D and Verdonik, F: Aging and memory. In Schaie, KW and Eisdorfer, C (eds): Annual Review of Gerontology and Geriatrics, Vol 7. Springer, New York, 1987, p 57.
16. Craik, FI: Age differences in human memory. In Buren, JE and Schaie, KW (eds): Handbook of the Psychology of Aging. Van Nostrand Reinhold, Cincinnati, 1977.
17. Poon, LW, Fozard, JL, Cermak, LS, Arenberg, D and Thompson, L (eds): New Directions in Memory and Aging. Erlbaum, Hillsdale, NJ, 1980.
18. Poon, LW, Gurland, B, Eisdorfer, C, Crook, T, Thompson, LW, Kaszniak, A and Davis, K (eds): Handbook for the Clinical Assessment of Older Adults. American Psychological Association, Washington, DC, 1986.
19. Smith, A: Age differences in encoding, storage and retrieval. In Poon, LW, Fozard, JR, Cermak, LS, et al (eds): New Directions in Memory and Aging. Erlbaum, Hillsdale, NJ, 1980, p 23.
20. Zachs, RT: Encoding strategies used by young and elderly adults in a keeping track task. Journal of Gerontology 37:203, 1982.
21. Weingartner, H and Parker, E: Memory Consolidation. Erlbaum, Hillsdale, NJ, 1984.
22. Willis, S: Cognitive training and everyday competence. In Schaie, KW and Eisdorfer, C (eds): Annual Review of Gerontology and Geriatrics, Vol 7. Springer, New York, 1987, p 159.
23. West, RL: Everyday memory and aging. Developmental Neuropsychology 2:313, 1986.
24. West, RL and Sinnott, JJ (eds): Everyday Memory and Aging: Current Research and Methodology. Springer-Verlag, New York, in press.
25. Riley, KP: Bridging the gap between researchers and clinicians: Methodological perspectives and choices. In West, RL and Sinnott, J (eds): Everyday Memory and Aging: Current Research and Methodology. Springer-Verlag, New York, in press.
26. West, R and Tomer, A: Everyday memory problems of healthy older adults: Characteristics of a successful intervention. In Gilmore, GC, Whitehouse, PJ and Wykle, ML (eds): Memory, Aging and Dementia. Springer, New York, 1989.
27. Szuchman, LT, Rothberg, ST and Erber, JT: Performance on everyday memory tasks: Patterns of prediction for young and older adults. Paper presented at Cognitive Aging Conference, Atlanta, March 1990.
28. Crook, T, Bartus, RT, Ferris, SH, Whitehouse, PJ, Cohen, GD and Gershon, S: Age associated memory impairment: Proposed diagnostic criteria and measures of clinical change—Report of a National Institute of Mental Health work group. Developmental Neuropsychology 2:261, 1986.
29. Riley, KP: Psychological interventions in Alzheimer's disease. In Gilmore, GC, Whitehouse, PJ and Wykle, MR (eds): Memory, Aging and Dementia. Springer, New York, 1989, p 199.
30. Fry, PS: Depression, Stress and Adaptations in the Elderly. Aspen, Rockville, MD, 1986.
31. Birren, JE, Robinson, PK and Livingston, JE (eds): Age, Health and Employment. Prentice-Hall, Englewood Cliffs, NJ, 1986.
32. Sterns, HL and Alexander, RA: Industrial gerontology: The aging individual and work. In Schaie, KW and Eisdorfer, C (eds): Annual Review of Gerontology and Geriatrics, Vol 7. Springer, New York, 1987, p 243.
33. Baugher, D: Is the older worker inherently incompetent? Aging and Work 1:243, 1978.
34. Salthouse, T: Effects of age and skill in typing. Journal of Experimental Psychology: General 113:345, 1984.
35. Rhodes, SR: Age related differences in work attitude and behavior: A review and conceptual analysis. Psychological Bulletin 93:328, 1983.
36. Waldman, D and Avolio, B: A meta-analysis of age differences in job performance. Journal of Applied Psychology 71:33, 1985.
37. Welford, AT: Thirty years of psychological research on age and work. Journal of Occupational Psychology 49:129, 1976.
38. Sterns, HL: Training and retraining adult and older adult workers. In Birren, JE, Robinson,

PE and Livingston, JE (eds): Age, Health and Employment. Prentice-Hall, Englewood Cliffs, NJ, 1986.

39. Yokomizo, Y: Measurement of ability in older workers. Ergonomics 28:843, 1985.

40. Avolio, BJ, Barrett, GV and Sterns, HL: Alternatives to age for assessing occupational performance capacity. Experimental Aging Research 10:101, 1984.

41. Rebok, GW, Offerman, LR, Wirtz, PW and Montaglione, CJ: Work and intellectual aging: The psychological concomitants of social organizational conditions. Educational Gerontology 12:359, 1985.

42. Salthouse, T, Kausler, D and Saults, JS: Investigation of student status, background variables, and feasibility of standard tasks in cognitive aging research. Psychology and Aging 3:29, 1988.

43. Singleton, WT: Age, skill and management. International Journal of Aging and Human Development 17:15, 1983.

43. Green, RF: Age, intelligence and learning. Industrial Gerontology 12:29, 1972.

44. Haberlandt, KF: Learning, memory and age. Industrial Gerontology 19:20, 1973.

45. Salthouse, T: Experience and cognitive aging. In Schaie, KW and Eisdorfer, C (eds): Annual Review of Gerontology and Geriatrics, Vol 7. Springer, New York, 1987, p 135.

46. Erickson, R and Scott, M: Clinical memory assessment: A review. Psychological Bulletin 84:1130, 1977.

47. Auerback, S and Katz, N: Assessment of perceptual cognitive performance. Comparison of psychiatric and brain injured adult patients. Occupational Therapy in Mental Health 54:57, 1988.

48. Katz, N, Itkovich, M, Auerbach, S and Elazar, B: Loewenstein Occupational Therapy Cognitive Assessment (LOTCA) battery for brain-injured patients: Reliabilty and validity. American Journal of Occupational Therapy 43:184, 1989.

49. Leng, NR, Taylor, SR and Hanley, O: A rating scale for assessing elderly patients. British Journal of Occupational Therapy 51:60, 1988.

50. Carstensen, LL: Age-related changes in social activity. In Carstensen, LL and Edelstein, BA: Handbook of Clinical Gerontology. Pergamon Press, New York, 1987, p 222.

51. Kaufman, JE: Leisure and anxiety: A study of retirees. Activities, Adaptation and Aging 11:1, 1988.

52. Kelly, JR and Ross, J: Later-life leisure: Beginning a new agenda. Leisure Sciences, 11:47, 1989.

53. Hayslip, B and Sterns, H: Age differences in relationships between crystallized and fluid intelligences and problem solving. Journal of Gerontology 34:404, 1979.

54. Purcell, RZ and Keller, MJ: Characteristics of leisure activities which may lead to leisure satisfaction among older adults. Activities, Adaptation and Aging 13:17, 1989.

55. Olson, SK and Robbins, SB: Guidelines for the development and evaluation of career services for the older adult. Special issue: Career counseling of older adults. Journal of Career Development 13:53, 1986.

56. Scogin, F, Storandt, M and Lott, R: Memory skills training, memory complaints and depression in older adults. Journal of Gerontology 40:562–568, 1985.

57. Sheikh, JI, Hill, RD and Yesavage, JA: Long term efficacy of cognitive training for Age-Associated Memory Impairment: A six month follow-up study. Developmental Neuropsychology 2:413–421, 1986.

58. Yesavage, JA and Jacob, R: Effects of relaxation and mnemonics on memory, attention and anxiety in the elderly. Experimental Aging Research 10:211–214, 1984.

59. Gilmore, GC, Whitehouse, PJ and Wykle, ML (eds): Memory, Aging, and Dementia: Theory, Assessment and Treatment. Springer, New York, 1989.

ACTIVITIES OF OLDER ADULTS

My kitchen linoleum is so black and shiny that I waltz while I wait for the kettle to boil. This pleasure is for the old who live alone. The others must vanish into their expected role.

—FLORIDA SCOTT-MAXWELL, *The Measure of My Days*, Penguin Books, New York, 1968, p. 28.

Chapter

Self-Care

RUTH E. DUNKLE
CARY S. KART
SHIRLEY A. LOCKERY

OBJECTIVES

By the end of this chapter, readers will be able to:

1 Discuss the ways in which physical, mental, and social health interrelate with functional ability in activities of daily living (ADL) and instrumental activities of daily living (IADL).

2 Describe five ways in which physical health can be operationalized, and indicate the limitations of each.

3 Describe the ADL abilities common to the elderly, and discuss how advancing age alters these.

4 Describe the IADL abilities common to the elderly, and discuss how advancing age alters these.

5 Define the concept of environmental demand or press.

6 Discuss the press-competence model.

7 Describe the ways in which social support, psychological resources, and environmental design support function.

All humans strive for competence across the life span whether in the area of work, family, or basic personal, emotional, and functional capacity. As described in other chapters, many older people find various aspects of their daily lives compromised with advancing age and seek ways to adapt to maximize competence.

One view of performance is that humans interact with their environment to create and maintain certain behaviors. This notion of person-environment fit, where the individual and the environment affect each other, is not one of a dichotomy but rather of confluence. Thus, it is not an issue of environmental determinism versus human adaptability but one where environments produce behavior and behavior produces environments.[1] It could be argued that certain behaviors such as breathing or athletic prowess are at an intraindividual level of competence, but many other competencies such as physical and instrumental self-maintenance are the result of an interaction between the individual and the environment.[2]

Previous chapters focused on describing functional ability and/or decrements in functioning. This chapter will deal with various aspects of maintaining health and function with age and is divided into two main sections. The first deals with the broad issues of health and function, discussing general physical health, as well as physical and instrumental activities of daily living (ADL). The second section focuses on adjustment to change in function and includes a discussion of the theoretical connection between environment and behavior with specific attention to social support mechanisms, psychological resources, and environmental design.

MAINTAINING HEALTH AND FUNCTION WITH AGING

Efforts aimed at maintaining health and functioning in old age involve the assessment of health status. This task is complex for three related reasons[3]:

1. The elderly are often subject to multiple illnesses and, thus, multiple and sometimes disparate diagnoses.
2. The physical, mental, and social health of elderly individuals are closely interrelated, and, as a result, assessment of health status must be multidimensional.
3. Measures of functioning that allow for assessment of an individual's ability to carry on activities independently, despite disease or disability, are probably the most useful indicators for practitioners.

The concept of physical health can be broken down into at least three subcategories, roughly reflecting a hierarchy[3,4]:

1. General physical health or the absence of illness
2. The ability to perform basic activities of daily living (ADL)
3. The ability to perform more complex self-care activities that allow for greater independence including what are known as *instrumental activities of daily living* (IADL), for example, cooking and budgeting.

These subcategories are thought to be hierarchical, with each level requiring a higher order of functioning than the preceding one.

The 1984 National Health Interview Survey (NHIS) and Supplement on Aging (SOA) provides information on the assessment of health and functioning of older Americans. The purpose of the SOA was to collect health and community service utilization information on the portion of the 1984 NHIS sample that was aged 55 and over. The SOA was administered to half the people in the NHIS sample who were aged 55 to 65 at the time of the interview and all those then aged 65 and over. More than 16,000 people were included in the SOA. Data are derived from individuals' reports of their health status, not from medical records. Individuals' awareness and willingness to report accurate information is taken as a given. There were no estimates of under- or overreporting. Thus, SOA data should be viewed as a social record of health, different though not necessarily inferior to, a medical or clinical record.

General Physical Health

General physical health is typically operationalized in one of five different ways. These include:

1. Number of illnesses or conditions
2. Days spent in bed
3. Self-ratings of health
4. Physician visits
5. Hospitalizations

Each has disadvantages. The number of illnesses may be an inadequate indicator of health because a single illness that is severe may be more problematic for an individual than mild cases of multiple illnesses or conditions. Days at home spent in bed can be related to psychological mechanisms including depression and hypochondria. Self-ratings of health can be subject to variation over time and distortion based on psychological or environmental factors. Physician visits may reflect accessibility of services, ability to pay, and physician-initiated referrals. Hospitalization is at best a crude indicator of general health; few aged individuals experience short-stay hospitalizations in a 12-month period.

Most health survey data show a pattern in which vigorous old age predominates,[5] but advancing age correlates with poorer functioning.[6] Manton[6] suggests that function can be maintained well into advanced old age and that people vary greatly in the rate at which functional loss occurs. The potential for rehabilitation exists even where lower functioning is the result of a currently untreatable disease.[7] An active approach to preserving function with increasing age includes changing medical and institutional responses to disability and chronic disease among elderly individuals and altering negative attitudes about normal aging, even though these attitudes are accepted by many older adults themselves.

NUMBER OF ILLNESSES OR CONDITIONS

The great majority of older Americans live in the community and are cognitively intact and fully independent in activities of daily living. Those who remain active may be individuals who exercise, eat nutritionally, and have a positive psychological view of life.[6] Still, most older Americans have had or currently have a serious illness. SOA respondents were asked if they ever had one or more of a list of 13 illnesses including osteoporosis, coronary heart disease, stroke, cancer, and Alzheimer's disease. Slightly over 43 percent reported never having had one of these illnesses, while 21 percent reported having two or more.

Table 8-1 shows the number of illnesses of the SOA respondents. Individuals aged 55 to 64 are the only demographic group in which a majority of individuals have never had one of these

serious illnesses. Those aged 75 to 84 years are twice as likely as this younger group to have two or more of these illnesses; 34.9 percent of those aged 85 years or more report having two or more illnesses.

Modest differences in number of reported illnesses also exist by gender, family income, race, and residence. In general, females, those with income below $15,000, nonwhites, and rural residents reported the greatest number of illnesses despite poorest access to diagnostic resources.

DAYS SPENT IN BED

Table 8-1 also shows the average number of days spent in bed in the past 12 months as reported by SOA respondents. A linear relationship exists between age and bed days; with age, the average number of bed days increases so that those 85 years and older spend twice as many days in bed as those 55 to 64 years. Females, those with lower income, nonwhites, and nonsuburbanites, spend the most time, on average, inactive in bed.

SELF-RATINGS OF HEALTH

Table 8-2 reports on the self-assessment of health status. About 70 percent of SOA respondents reported their health status in positive terms (excellent, very good, or good). It is important to remember that a substantial correlation exists between subjective health status and measures of functional status in aged adults[8,9] and physical examinations or physician ratings.[10,11] While almost three out of four persons 55 to 64 years assess their health in positive terms, less than two out of three of those 85 years and older do. Even among the very-old living in the community, however, only about one-third assess their health as fair or poor. Thus, although assessment of health is increasingly negative with increasing age, it is relatively positive for all elderly.

Demographic factors are also related in many instances to self-assessment.

TABLE 8-1	**Number of Illnesses and Average Number of Bed Days by Selected Characteristics**				
	Number of Illnesses			**Bed Days**	
	None, %	1, %	2+, %	*	†
Age, years					
55–64 years	53.2	33.5	13.2	9.4	32.4
66–74	42.2	36.0	21.8	10.7	40.2
75–84	34.9	37.5	27.6	14.9	52.2
85+	30.7	34.3	34.9	20.9	67.8
Gender					
Male	47.5	31.9	20.5	10.9	40.5
Female	40.2	38.2	21.6	12.4	43.4
Family Income					
Under $15,000	38.0	37.6	24.5	15.1	50.8
$15,000 or more	47.3	33.8	19.0	8.4	29.3
Race					
White	43.8	34.8	21.4	11.4	39.9
Nonwhite	38.4	43.5	18.1	16.2	63.7
Residence					
Central city	42.7	36.8	20.5	13.1	45.2
Surburban	46.2	34.1	19.8	10.6	38.1
Rural	40.7	36.2	23.1	12.0	44.3

*Average number of days per last 12 months, all cases.

†Average number of days per last 12 months, *excluding* all cases with zero days.

Source: 1984 Supplement on Aging, NHIS.

Less affluent elderly were almost twice as likely as were more affluent elderly to assess their health as fair or poor. Whites were more likely than nonwhites to assess their health positively; 45.6 percent of nonwhites and 28.7 percent of whites assessed their health as fair or poor. This differential is consistent with prior research.[12] Most nonwhites in the SOA are black. Black-white racial differences in self-assessment of health status reflect real differences in health status and health service utilization.[13] Geographic locale is also an important consideration. Elderly suburbanites assess their health more positively than do elderly residents of central city and rural areas. Gender differences in self-assessments of health status among the aged are quite modest. This is particularly interesting in light of the significant female advantage over males in mortality rates and life expectancy.[14]

PHYSICIAN VISITS

Demographic considerations are also relevant to the use of health service. Over the past 20 years researchers in different parts of the world have noted the effects of social class and income on the use of health services. Andersen, et al.,[15] in Sweden and Snider[16] in Canada have described the inverse relationship between social class or income and use: older individuals from lower socioeconomic backgrounds used more health services. In general, higher levels of annual physicians visits are related to advanced age, higher educational attainment, being female, and being married.[17,18]

HOSPITALIZATION

Although men report fewer physician visits and bed days than women, when

TABLE 8-2   **Self-Assessed Health Status by Selected Characteristics**

	Self-Assessed Health Status			
	Excellent or Very Good, %	Good, %	Fair, %	Poor, %
Age, years				
55–64	44.1	30.8	16.6	8.4
65–74	36.5	32.0	21.1	10.3
75–84	36.0	31.1	20.7	12.2
85+	35.0	28.6	23.2	13.2
Gender				
Male	39.4	30.3	19.1	11.2
Female	37.9	32.0	20.4	9.7
Family Income				
Under $15,000	30.2	30.5	24.7	14.6
$15,000 or more	46.9	31.8	15.2	6.1
Race				
White	39.5	31.8	19.1	9.6
Nonwhite	28.7	25.6	27.1	18.5
Residence				
Central city	38.0	31.1	20.6	10.3
Suburban	42.0	32.3	17.5	8.2
Rural	35.3	30.3	21.7	12.7

Source: 1984 Supplement on Aging, NHIS.

men are hospitalized, they spend more days in the hospital. Male-female differences in illness patterns may contribute to this. For example, men are more likely than women to report heart disease and stroke. Also, men may be sicker when hospitalized, regardless of illness. Those with family income below $15,000, nonwhites, and nonrural residents spend on average more days in the hospital.

About 80 percent of SOA respondents had at least one contact with a physician during the previous year. The average number of physician visits during the past year was highest among those aged 75 to 84 years. As Table 8–3 shows, when those with no physician contacts during the past 20 months are excluded, the average number of physician contacts more than doubles. Women, those with family income under $15,000, nonwhites, and central city residents average the most physician contacts.

Haug[19] has raised the question of whether health service utilization among the elderly is appropriate to the symptoms they experience. She finds that the elderly report overutilization of physicians for less serious complaints, which may occur as a result of physician advice. Others have identified the importance of physician-diagnosis and/or recommendation in health service use.[20]

Eighteen percent of SOA respondents experienced a short-stay hospitalization during the 20 months prior to being interviewed. The oldest-old remained in the hospital longer than the young-old. The average number of days spent in the hospital during the past 12 months by those aged 85 years and older was 13.7 days; those 55 to 64 years, 11.9 days.

TABLE 8-3	**Average Number of Physician Visits and Hospital Days per Year by Selected Characteristics**

	Physician Visits		Hospital Days	
	*	†	*	†
Age, years				
55–64	4.5	9.9	1.5	11.9
65–74	5.2	10.6	2.2	12.9
75–84	6.4	13.5	3.0	13.4
85+	5.5	12.4	3.4	13.7
Gender				
Male	4.8	10.6	2.5	14.3
Female	5.5	11.5	2.1	11.8
Family Income				
Under $15,00	5.8	11.6	2.7	13.5
$15,000 or more	4.8	7.5	1.8	11.6
Race				
White	5.1	10.2	2.3	12.7
Nonwhite	6.8	20.5	2.3	14.5
Residence				
Central city	6.0	13.2	2.2	13.0
Suburban	5.1	10.3	2.3	13.3
Rural	4.8	10.6	2.3	12.4

*Average visits or days per last 12 months, all cases.

†Average visits or days per last 12 months, *excluding* all cases with zero visits or days.

Source: 1984 Supplement on Aging, NHIS.

Activities of Daily Living

Physical health measures may not assess the degree of independence and functioning an individual possesses. For this reason, practitioners and researchers sought to develop measures that reflect functioning in daily life activities.

With some variation across instruments, items that measure basic self-care or ADL include:

- Bathing
- Dressing
- Going to the bathroom
- Getting in or out of a bed or chair
- Walking outside the house or apartment
- Feeding

These are typically ordered in terms of decreasing dependency and are thought by some to form a Guttman scale.[3,21] Kane and Kane[3] point out that the choice of ADL scale influences results, with different indicators being more or less sensitive to change over time.

Table 8–4 shows the proportions of those in the SOA reporting limitations in ADL by age, gender, family income, race, and residence. The oldest-old, women, individuals with family income under $15,000, nonwhites, and those residing in rural areas report the most limitations. Age and income seem the strongest predictors of ADL score. Almost 90 percent of those 55 to 64 years of age compared to about one-half of those 85 years and over report no limitations in ADL; more than one-third of the oldest-old report two or more limitations. SOA respondents with family income under $15,000 were about twice as likely as other respondents to report limitations in ADL.

TABLE 8–4 Percent with Limitations in Activities of Daily Living (ADL) and Instrumental Activities of Daily Living (LADL) by Selected Characteristics

	ADL*				LADL†			
	One, %	Two/Three, %	Four/More, %	Total, %	One, %	Two/Three, %	Four/More, %	Total, %
Age, years								
55–64	5.4	3.9	2.5	11.8	9.8	2.5	1.6	13.9
65–74	7.9	5.6	3.7	17.2	13.0	4.2	3.3	20.5
75–84	11.1	9.1	7.3	27.5	15.9	9.0	7.6	32.5
85+	12.7	17.2	19.6	49.5	14.9	14.2	30.6	59.7
Gender								
Male	7.6	4.8	3.8	16.2	7.5	2.5	3.5	13.5
Female	8.5	7.6	5.7	21.8	16.0	6.8	5.7	28.5
Family Income								
Under $15,000	10.7	8.7	6.1	25.5	16.5	7.6	5.6	29.7
$15,000 or more	5.6	4.0	3.5	13.1	9.3	2.7	3.6	15.6
Race								
White	8.0	6.3	4.7	19.0	12.5	4.9	4.6	22.0
Nonwhite	9.6	7.8	7.1	24.5	15.5	7.7	7.1	30.3
Residence								
Central city	8.5	7.1	5.1	20.7	12.7	6.6	4.6	23.9
Suburban	7.1	5.1	4.7	16.9	11.3	3.8	4.9	20.0
Rural	9.0	7.4	5.1	21.5	14.3	5.4	4.9	24.6

*ADL include bathing, dressing, going to the bathroom, getting in or out of bed or chair, walking, getting outside the apartment or house, and feeding.
†IADL include preparing meals, shopping, managing money, using telephone, doing light housework, and doing heavy housework.

Source: 1984 Supplement on Aging, NHIS.

Instrumental Activities of Daily Living

The concept of *instrumental activities of daily living* (IADL) includes basic skills reflected in ADL measures and more complex ones of commonly used IADL indicators. Shopping, for example, requires being able to get out of bed, dress, walk, and leave the house. Because the IADL tasks are more complicated and multifaceted, functional decrements are expected to show up first in IADL items and more older people to report limitations and need for assistance in carrying them out than is the case for the more basic ADL. As indicated in Table 8–4, a greater proportion of SOA respondents report limitations with IADL than ADL.

IADL included in the SOA were:

- Preparing meals
- Shopping
- Managing money
- Using the telephone
- Doing light housework
- Doing heavy housework

While the general pattern shown for IADL in Table 8–4 is similar to that reported for ADL, some differences are noteworthy. First, a significant majority of the oldest-old individuals report one or more limitations in IADL with almost one-third indicating four or more limitations. This suggests that many of the oldest-old group are housebound, in need of major assistance at home and, perhaps, are at risk for institutionalization.

Secondly, female SOA respondents are more than twice as likely as males to report IADL limitations. This is consistent with the finding that women were more likely than men to have had one or more illnesses and more physician visits. Nathanson[22] offers three possible explanations for this finding:

1. It is culturally more acceptable for women to be ill.
2. Women's social roles are more comparable with reports of illness and use of medical services than is the case for men.

3. Women's social roles are, in fact, more stressful than those of men. Consequently, they have more real illness and need more assistance and care.

The merits of these explanations continue to be debated.[23]

Kane and Kane[3] suggest that, because of the complexity and multifacetedness of IADL, respondents' reports on individual items may be biased by variations in motivation, mood, and overall emotional health. For instance, a depressed older person might be more likely to neglect IADL activities such as managing money or doing the housework than basic aspects of personal self-care such as dressing or using the toilet. For most older adults, these continue to be important activities (Fig. 8–1).

It can also be argued that social structural or environmental factors contribute to IADL limitations. A widower who never performed certain IADL tasks when his spouse was alive may report limitations because he never learned the skills, not because of an inability to perform the function. Also, an older woman may report limitations in shopping because stores are scarce in inner city neighborhoods, and she lacks

Figure 8–1 Good grooming is important to many older adults, just as it is to younger individuals. (Courtesy of Menorah Park Nursing Home, Cleveland, Ohio.)

transportation to other areas. As Lawton and Nahemow[24] reported, when the "fit" between an individual's competence and the environment in which the individual resides is good, adaptation is positive. This may be the case for the great majority of older people. When environmental demands are too great, adaptation may be poor.

ADJUSTMENT TO CHANGE IN FUNCTION: ACHIEVING COMPETENCE

Lawton and Nahemow[24] derived an ecological model of aging based on the environmental docility hypothesis[25] where behavior is viewed as a function of the competence of the individual and the demand made by the environment. Muray[26] called the environmental demand "press." These two basic concepts, competence and press, are not unidimensional even though individuals are typically categorized as having an overall degree of competence. In reality, each person has a profile of competencies that may fluctuate over time.[2] High competence is associated with less dependence on the environment, and lower competence is related to greater dependence and subsequent vulnerability to the environment.

In the press-competence model, adaptation level is incorporated as well. This takes into consideration the balance between level of external stimulation and sensitivity of the individual. As Lawton[2] states, "The hypothesis (environmental docility) suggests that lowered competence increases the proportion of behavioral variance that is associated with environmental, as compared to personal, factors" (p. 48). For example, an elder who has a hearing and vision deficit and is wheelchair bound is more dependent on the surrounding environment (whether social or physical) to maintain social, psychological, and physical functioning than is an older person who is healthy and mobile. The healthy elder can draw on personal resources to provide the stimulation to maintain well-being.

Social Support

Functional incapacity alone does not always influence the use of health and social services. Knowledge about available services and a belief that the system can help contribute to high service use.[27]

In general, aspects of social support become very important to the well-being of an older person in dealing with functional limitations. Social ties have been shown to affect the course of various diseases as well as mortality.[28,29] In examining racial differences in social support, Chatters, Taylor, and Jackson[30] suggest that informal support from family, friends, and church members is important to the health and functioning of black as well as white elders.

Social support is typically described as formal or informal. Informal support includes help from family, friends, and neighbors, while formal support involves services such as Meals on Wheels, respite care, and the like. Families provide most of the support for elders in need. In fact, 80 percent of the care is provided by family members.[31,32] Care providers are typically female with the most likely caregiver being a daughter or daughter-in-law.[33] Husbands and sons are increasingly providing care, as well.[34] Siblings are also frequent caregivers.[35]

Even though family members provide much of the needed care to older people, these relationships are not always most strongly related to the elder's well-being. In fact, research findings indicate that friendships are more closely related to well-being[36,37] for reasons that are not clearly understood. It may be that family relations are obligatory,[38,39] while friendships are not. Choice of friends may be a source of autonomy for the older person[40] and therefore, more important to their sense of well-being.

Some older people cannot rely on family. One study[41] showed that when elders had none or only one child, they were more likely to receive help from formal services than were elders who had two or more children.

While it is clear that social support affects the well-being of the elderly, the reason for this is still being debated. Cohen[42] suggests that social interaction can provide the elder with a more positive view of himself or herself, which in turn may affect feelings of mastery and competence.[43,44] Social support can be of instrumental help as well because they can be linked to services through support networks. For instance, transportation to the doctor can be provided[45] or suggestions made about what actions may be of help.[46,47]

To date, knowledge of social ties in special environments is limited but what data exist indicate that social support is affected by the environment in which it takes place. Low levels of social interaction and lack of close relationships have been documented among nursing home residents,[48,49] especially if the resident is physically or cognitively impaired.[50] This fact is particularly relevant to health care providers as they consider interventions in this setting. Low levels of interaction also occur in congregate apartments.[51] Interaction is greater among people with similar functional abilities,[52] when staffing is higher, and programming more structured.[53] In retirement communities, interaction among neighbors is high and seems to be preferred to interaction with relatives.[54]

Psychological Resources and Coping Strategies

One aspect of social support relates to psychological resources of the older person. There is an interaction between the availability of support, enabling the elder to improve his or her psychological resources, and the elder's resources that facilitate the development and enhancement of social support. Query and James[55] found that elders who were ca-

pable of communication had larger social networks than those who were not. Effective interpersonal communication that maintains social networks played an integral part in determining the life satisfaction of elders. The researchers encourage the use of support groups to enhance the psychological resources of the elder, contending that the normal losses of aging create uncertainty among older people that can adversely affect health status. Emotional support can minimize the effect of reduced mastery or control that the elder may experience.[56-58]

Other research has focused on coping strategies utilized to deal with the stressful life events, such as change in functioning, that confront older people. Coping strategies regulate stressful emotions and alter stressful person-environment relationships. Folkman, Lazarus, Dunkel-Schetter, DeLongis, and Gruen,[59] through a factor analytic procedure, identified eight coping skills that people used to deal with stressful encounters. They are:

1. Confrontive coping, that is, aggressive efforts to alter the situation
2. Distancing, that is, efforts to detach oneself
3. Self-control, regulating one's own feelings
4. Seeking social support
5. Accepting responsibility by acknowledging one's role in the problem
6. Escape-avoidance
7. Planful problem solving: deliberate problem-focused efforts to alter the situation
8. Positive appraisal through efforts to create positive meaning focused on personal growth

In attempting to discern which strategies were most effective, Folkman and associates[59] found that confrontive coping, planful problem solving, and positive reappraisal were used when people confronted situations they believed were changeable. Distancing and escape-avoidance were used when people were confronted by situations which they thought they had to accept. In some circumstances, the person needed more information before acting. Strategies used then were seeking social support, self-control, and planful problem solving. When the person believed he or he could not attain a desired outcome, strategies of confrontive coping, self-control, and escape-avoidance were used. Depending on how an elder interprets changes in health and functioning, various strategies can help maintain well-being and reduce decline.

Environmental Design

Housing is the major area is which design can be a critical feature in maintaining maximum functioning. In fact, the physical and architectural features of group-living settings can influence the well-being of elders.[60,61] For most older people, autonomy and security are of major concern.[62] When physical and instrumental functioning have not declined, elders choose ordinary housing. In fact, 85 to 88 percent of all older people live in such housing with 75 percent residing in their own homes.[63] As long as competence in IADL and ADL is not reduced, typical housing affords autonomy, as well as freedom of space, privacy, and shelter.

HOUSING MODIFICATIONS

Some people modify their housing to accommodate their limitations. Ten percent of households headed by an individual over 65 where at least one older person had health or mobility problems have been modified in some way.[64] The most common modifications are handrails, grab bars, and adaptations to accommodate wheelchair access and sensory deficits.

ALTERNATIVE HOUSING

Unfortunately, many older people find that environmental barriers posed by ordinary housing are more than they can cope with, making a move to a different kind of housing necessary. Elders who have a combination of need for security, low income, and a willingness to compromise autonomy gravitate toward alternative housing.[62] Nontraditional forms of housing include apartments that are equipped with safety features, congregate facilities, and shared housing.[65]

Continuing-Care Retirement Communities

Autonomy and security are offered in continuing-care retirement communities, facilities that offer independent housing as well as assisted-living and nursing home care. This type of housing attracts older, unmarried, childless elders who are better educated and have a higher income and in general better health. Typically, a large down payment is required along with a monthly maintenance fee.

Nursing Homes

Nursing homes can accommodate elders who are moderately to severely disabled; however, functional ability alone does not determine residency in a nursing home. For every person residing in a nursing home, there are two others in the same condition still living in the community. The differentiating features are complex, but cultural, racial, financial, and social support factors are frequent determinants. Statistics from the National Center for Health Statistics[66] show that on any given day, 1.3 million elderly live in skilled or intermediate nursing facilities, though many of these individuals will eventually return to other housing arrangements.

REASONS FOR MIGRATION

It is not clear what factors influence elders to make a move out of ordinary housing or to relocate geographically. Litwak and Longino[67] found that for those who do migrate, three moves occur. The first type of move occurs when the person retires, the second move happens when some minor disability occurs, and the third takes place when the elder suffers a major chronic disability. In the first stage, elders frequently choose to live some distance from their children. As ability wanes, the older person moves to be nearer family and institutions that can provide support, the second type of move. The third move usually occurs when kin resources are limited, and it is usually to an institutional setting.

CONCLUSION

Physical and functional decline in old age is inevitable, but it does vary. Most older people enjoy a fairly independent lifestyle until about age 80. The nature of limitations experienced by elders is affected by their social support, the psychological resources they bring to bear, and the environment in which they reside. In order to understand the health and functioning of older people and the features of their lives that help them cope with age-related changes, it is necessary to understand the interactions of this wide range of factors.

REVIEW QUESTIONS

1. *What factors interact to affect the level of independence in ADL and/ or IADL in older adults?*

2. *Describe the typical pattern of functional ability in older adults.*

3. *List five ways in which to operationalize physical health.*

4. *What is the role of gender and race in functional ability in older adults? What are some possible explanations for these factors?*

5. *Define the concept of environmental "press."*

6. *From what source do older adults obtain most of the social support needed to maintain independence?*

7. *Explain the finding that friendships may be more important than family relationships in supporting function in older adults.*

8. *What psychological factors are re-*

lated to independence in older adults and why?

9. *In what ways can the environment be structured to support performance in the elderly?*

REFERENCES

1. Ittelson, WH: As cited in Altman, I, Lawton, M and Wohlwill, JF, (eds): Elderly People and the Environment. Plenum, New York, 1984.
2. Lawton, MP: Competence, environmental press, and the adaptation of older people. In Lawton, MP, Wendley, PG and Byerts, TO (eds): Aging and the Environment: Theoretical Approaches. Springer, New York, 1982, pp 33–59.
3. Kane, RA and Kane, RL: Assessing the Elderly: A Practical Guide to Measurement. DC Heath, Lexington, MA, 1981.
4. Leering, C: A structural model of functional capacity in the aged. Journal of the American Geriatric Society 27:314–316, 1979.
5. Gilford, DM (ed): The Aging Population in the Twenty-First Century. National Academy Press, Washington, DC, 1988.
6. Manton, K: Epidemiological, demographic, and social correlates of disability among the elderly. The Milbank Quarterly 67:13–57, 1989.
7. Besdine, RW: Dementia and delirium. In Rowe, JW and Besdine, RW (eds): Geriatric Medicine. Little, Brown, Boston, 1988, pp 375–401.
8. Ferraro, KF: Self-ratings of health among the old and old-old. Journal of Health and Social Behavior 21:377–383, 1980.
9. Ferraro, KF: The effects of widowhood on the health status of older persons. International Journal of Aging and Human Development 21:9–25, 1985.
10. LaRue, A, Bank, L, Jarvik, L and Hetland, M: Health in old age: How do physicians' ratings and self-ratings compare? Journal of Gerontology 8:108–115, 1979.
11. Maddox, GL and Douglass, EB: Self-assessment of health: A longitudinal study of elderly subjects. Journal of Health and Social Behavior 14:87–93, 1973.
12. Schlesinger, M: Paying the price: Medical care, minorities, and the newly competitive health care system. Milbank Memorial Fund Quarterly (Suppl) 65:270–296, 1988.
13. Gibson, R and Jackson, J: The health, physical functioning, and informal supports of the black elderly. Milbank Memorial Fund Quarterly (Suppl), 65:421–454, 1987.
14. Zopf, P: America's older population. Cap and Gown Press, Houston, TX, 1986.
15. Andersen, R, Anderson, O and Smedby, B: Perceptions of and response to symptoms of illness in Sweden and the U.S. Medical Care 6:18–30, 1986.

16. Snider, E: Young-old versus old-old and the use of health services. Does the difference make a difference? Journal of the American Geriatrics Society 29(8):354–358, 1981.

17. Andersen, R and Aday, L: Access to medical care in the U.S.: Realized and potential. Medical Care 17:533–546, 1978.

18. Marcus, A and Siegel, J: Sex differences in the use of physician services: A preliminary test of the fixed role hypothesis. Journal of Health and Social Behavior 23:186–196, 1982.

19. Haug, M: Age and medical care utilization pattern. Journal of Gerontology 33:103–111, 1981.

20. Wilensky, G and Rossiter, L: The relative importance of physician-induced demand in the demand for medical care. Milbank Memorial Fund Quarterly, 61(2):252–277, 1983.

21. Katz, S, Ford, A, Moskowitz, R, Jackson, B and Jaffee, M: Studies of illness in the aged. The index of ADL: A standardized measure of biological and psychosocial function. Journal of the American Medical Association 1985: 914–919, 1963.

22. Nathanson, C: Illness and the feminine role: A theoretical review. Social Science and Medicine 9:57–62, 1975.

23. Verbrugge, LM: Gender and health: An update on hypotheses and evidence. Journal of Health and Social Behavior, 26:155–177, 1985.

24. Lawton, M and Nahemow, L: Ecology and the aging process. In Eisdorfer, C and Lawton, MP (eds): Psychology of Adult Development and Aging. American Psychological Association, Washington, DC, 1973.

25. Lawton, MP: Ecology and aging. In Pastalan, LA and Carson, DH (eds): The Spatial Behavior of Older People. Institute of Gerontology, University of Michigan, Ann Arbor, 1970.

26. Murray, HA: Explanations in Personality. Oxford, New York, 1938.

27. McCaslin, R: Service utilization by the elderly: The importance of orientation to the formal system. Journal of Gerontological Social Work 14(2):153–174, 1989.

28. Rowe, JW and Kahn, RL: Human aging: Usual vs. successful. Science 237:143–149, 1987.

29. House, JS, Robbins, C and Metzner, HL: The association of social relationships and activities with mortality: Prospective evidence from the Tecumseh community health study. American Journal of Epidemiology 116:123–140, 1982.

30. Chatters, LM, Taylor, RJ and Jackson, JS: Size and composition of the informal helper networks of elderly blacks. Journal of Gerontology 40(2):605–614, 1985.

31. Biaggi, M: Testimony before the select committee on aging. House of Representatives, 96th Cong, Washington, DC, 1980.

32. Brody, EM: Women in the middle and family help to older people. Gerontologist 21:470–480, 1981.

33. Brody, EM and Schoonover, CB: Patterns of parent-care when adult daughters work and when they do not. Gerontologist 26:372–381, 1986.

34. Chappell, N: Aging and social care. In Binstock, RH and George, L (eds.): Handbook of Aging and the Social Sciences. Academic Press, San Diego, 1990, pp 438–454.

35. Bengtson, V, Rosenthal, C and Berton, L: Families and aging: Diversity and heterogenity. In Benstock, RH and George, L (eds): Handbook of Aging and the Social Sciences. Academic Press, San Diego, 1990, pp 263–287.

36. Adams, R and Blieszner, R: Perspectives on Later Life Friendship. Sage, Beverly Hills, 1989.

37. Matthews, SH: Friendships through the Life Course: Oral Biographies in Old Age. Sage, Beverly Hills, CA, 1986.

38. Cicirelli, VG: A measure of filial anxiety regarding anticipated care of elderly parents. Gerontologist 28(4):478–482, 1988.

39. Troll, LE: New thoughts on old families. Gerontologist, 28(5):586–591, 1988.

40. Adams, RG: Emotional closeness and physical distance between friends: Implications for elderly women living in age-segregated and age-integrated settings. International Journal of Aging and Human Development 22:55–76, 1986.

41. Cicirelli, VG: Kin relationships of childless and one-child elderly in relation to social services. Journal of Gerontological Social Work 4(1):19–33, 1981.

42. Cohen, S: Psychosocial models of the role of social support in the etiology of physical disease. Health Psychology 7:269–297, 1988.

43. Lawton, MO, Moss, M and Kleban, MH: Psychological Well-Being, Mastery, and the Social Relationships of Older People. Submitted, 1989.

44. Sarason, IG, Sarasan, BR and Pierce, GR (eds): Social Support: An Interactional View. Wiley, New York, 1989.

45. George, LK: Easing caregiver burden: The role of informal and formal supports. In Ward, RA and Tobin, SS (eds): Health in Aging: Sociological Issues and Policy Directions. Springer, New York, 1987, pp 133–158.

46. Kasl, S: The health belief model and behavior related to chronic illness. In Becker, M (ed): The Health Belief Model and Personal Health Behavior. Slack, Thorofare, NJ, 1974, pp 106–127.

47. Caplan, G: Mastery of stress: Psychological aspects. American Journal of Psychiatry 138:413–420, 1981.

48. Noelker, LS and Poulshock, SW: Intimacy: Factor's affecting its development among members of a home for the aged. Paper presented at the annual meeting of the American Sociological Association, New York, August 1980.

49. Tesch, S and Whitbourne, S: Friendship, social interaction and subjective well-being of older men in an institutional setting. International Journal of Aging and Human Development 13:317–327, 1981.
50. Stephans, MAP, Kinney, JM and McNeer, AE: Accommodative housing: Social integration of residents with physical limitations. Gerontologist 26:176–180, 1986.
51. Kaye, LW and Monk, A: Social Network Reciprocity in Enriched Housing for the Aged. Paper presented at the annual meeting of the Gerontological Society of America, Washington, DC, November 1987.
52. Sheehan, NW: Informal support among the elderly in public senior housing. Gerontologist 26:171–175, 1986.
53. Lemke, S and Moos, RH: Personal and environmental determinants of activity involvement among elderly residents of congregate facilities. Journal of Gerontology 44:5139–5148, 1989.
54. Sullivan, DA: Informal support systems in a planned retirement community: Availability, proximity, and willingness to utilize. Research on Aging 8:249–267, 1986.
55. Query, J and James, A: The relationship between interpersonal communication competence and social support among elderly support groups in retirement communities. Health Communication 1(3):165–184, 1989.
56. Berkman, LF: The assessment of social networks and social support in the elderly. Journal of the American Geriatrics Society 31:743–749, 1983.
57. Cohen, CI, Teresi, J and Holmes, D: Social networks, stress, and physical health: A longitudinal study of an inner-city elderly population. Journal of Gerontology 40:478–486, 1985.
58. Cohen, CI, Teresi, J and Holmes, D: Assessment of stress-buffering effects of social networks on psychological symptoms in an inner-city elderly population. American Journal of Community Psychology 14:75–91, 1986.
59. Folkman, S, Lazarus, R, Dunkle-Schetter, C, Delargis, A and Gruen, R: Dynamics of a stressful encounter: Cognitive appraisal, coping, and encounter outcomes. Journal of Personality and Social Psychology 50(5):992–1003, 1986.
60. Moore, GT, Tuttle, DP and Howell, SC: Environmental Design Research Directions: Process and Prospects. Praeger, New York, 1986.
61. Moos, RH and Lemke, S: Special living environments for older people. In Birren, JE and Schare, KW (eds): Handbook of the Psychology of Aging. Van Nostrand Reinhold, New York, 1985.
62. Parmelee, P and Lawton, MP: The design of special environments for the aged. Handbook of the Psychology of Aging. Academic Press, San Diego, 1991.
63. Lawton, MP and Hoover, SL (eds): Community Housing Choices for Older Americans. Springer, New York, 1981.
64. Struyk, RJ: Housing adaptations: Needs and practices. In Regnier, V and Pynoos J (eds): Housing and Aging: Design Directives and Policy Considerations. Elsevier, New York, 1987, pp 259–276.
65. Eckert, JK and Murray, M: Alternative modes of living for the elderly. In Altman, I, Lawton, MP and Wohlvrel, J (eds): Human Behavior and the Environment: The Elderly and the Physical Environment. Plenum, New York, 1984.
66. National Center for Health Statistics: Use of nursing homes by the elderly: Preliminary data from the 1985 National Nursing Home Survey. Advance Data from Vital and Health Statistics. No 135. DHHS Pub No (PHS) 87-1250. Public Health Service, Hyattsville, MD, 1987.
67. Litwak, E and Longino, CF: Migration patterns among the elderly: A developmental perspective. Gerontologist 27:266–272, 1987.

The "Who am I?" question is answered by the self-sufficient in personal terms: "I am an individual who must make my own way through life and who, in the end, can rely on no one else to get me through difficulties."

—JR KELLY, *Peoria Winter:*
Styles and Resources in Later Life, DC Heath & Co.,
Lexington, MA, 1987, p. 81.

Chapter

Self-Health Care

CARY S. KART
RUTH E. DUNKLE
SHIRLEY A. LOCKERY

OBJECTIVES

By the end of this chapter, readers will be able to:

1 Define self-health care.

2 Describe three kinds of self-health care.

3 List five kinds of self-health care programs in the United States.

4 Describe self-medication practices typically employed by the elderly.

5 Describe the hazards of self-medication.

6 Discuss preventive self-health care methods.

7 Discuss demographic and personal factors that impact on the probability that an individual will practice self-health care.

8 Describe the obstacles to self-health care.

9 Discuss the relationships between professional and self-health care.

Self-health care among the elderly is complex; even the definition is debatable. This chapter has been divided into two parts:

1. Definitional and conceptual issues
2. An evaluation of the efficacy of self-health care

We identify practices and correlates of self-health care including self-medication and address the question of whether self-health care is a substitute, supplement, or stimulus to the use of formal health care.

DEFINITION

Professional care constitutes the minority of health care provided to people today, regardless of age. Levin[1] estimates that self-health care practices such as self-medication and wellness activities (dietary modifications, exercise, and so on) account for 85 percent of all health care in the world. Helman[2] and Blumhagen[3] report that between 70 and 90 percent of all illness episodes are managed without "expert" intervention.

Self-health care is recognized as an important part of every health care system. The World Health Organization defines self-health care as: "all the actions and decisions that an individual takes to prevent, diagnose, and treat personal ill health; all individual behaviors calculated to maintain and improve health; and decisions to access and use both informal support systems and formal medical services."[4] Dean[5] views self-health care, including the decision to take no health care action, as a major determinant of physical and psychological well-being and of functional capacity.

Self-evaluation of symptoms and self-treatment are the basic and predominant forms of primary health care.[6,7] They represent efforts on the part of people to take control of their health. As Cassedy[8] has observed, "Wherever people have been able to obtain their own medicines, or have read books about hygiene, or have had relatives, neighbors, or travellers to suggest remedies, they have been ready in large number to rely on such sources and on their own judgments rather than resort to physicians even with serious ailments."

Most symptoms do not lead to medical consultation regardless of the severity of symptoms.[9-11] Many people who do have contact with medical care providers have treated their disorders themselves first.[12] Even those who seek professional medical care and follow a prescribed treatment regimen often supplement this regimen with self-prescribed remedies.[13] Appropriate and timely self-care such as bed rest for a back injury can reduce health care costs by causing symptoms to lessen more rapidly and by lessening the demand on the health care system. Attributing illness symptoms to old age per se[14] or employing inappropriate self-health care

practice may, however, delay access to professional care and have catastrophic consequences for an elderly person.

CONCEPTUAL ISSUES

There have been several attempts to create conceptual models for self-care study. For example, Butler and his colleagues[15] conceptualized self-care in terms of three concentric circles (Fig. 9–1). Each circle reflects acts performed as part of an individual's efforts to keep healthy. The inner circle includes acts regularly performed as part of daily living:

- Good nutrition
- Routine hygiene
- Dental care
- Common first aid

The second ring of self-care encompasses activities designed to improve health knowledge and awareness. These activities include efforts at continuing preventive health education through formal education or mass media approaches. The outside, or third, ring represents those activities that have generally been in the province of formal health care providers:

- Measuring heart rate or blood pressure
- Evaluating blood-sugar levels and providing insulin injections

among many other actions formerly within the domain of professional health care.

The History of Self-Care

While self-care practice is widespread in the United States, it is not a contemporary phenomenon. Dean[6] reports that in England, as early as the seventeenth century, distinguished scientists produced formulas for self-medication that was widely distributed. William Buchan's *Domestic Medicine*, published in Edinburgh in 1769, was probably the first comprehensive medical self-care guide in English.[16]

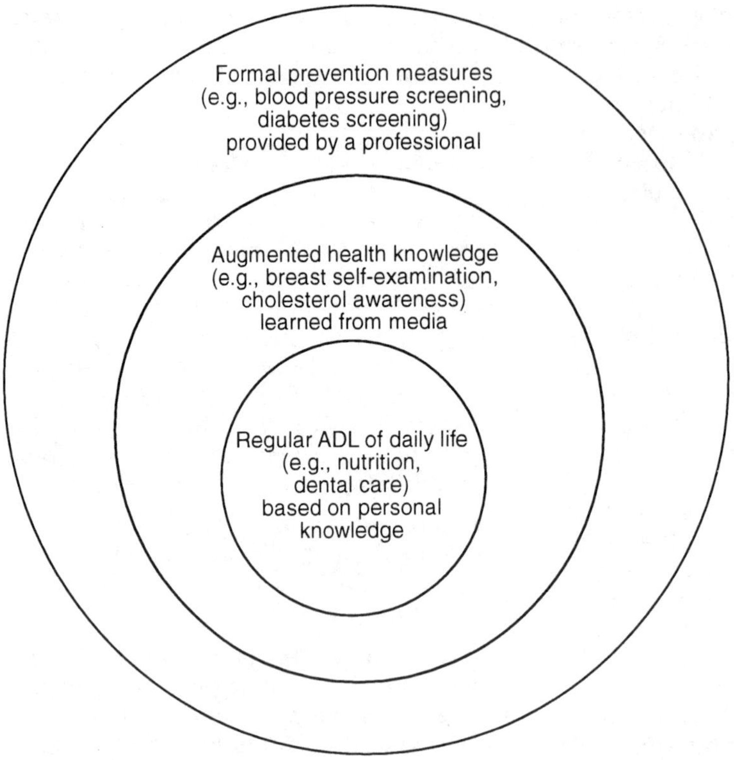

Figure 9–1 Levels of preventive health care. Adapted from: Butler, RN, Gertman, JS, Oberlander, DL, Schindler, L: Self-care, self-help and the elderly. International Journal of Aging and Human Development 10(1), 1979.

In the nineteenth century, interest in the United States in self-health care was associated with other social and political movements of the Jacksonian era.[17] Notions of self-health care reflected American values of self-reliance and individualism. During this period, both in the United States and in Europe, scientific medicine was in its infancy and medical practitioners were not held in high esteem. As a result, self-treatment was an acceptable alternative to the therapies of "bleedings, blisterings and purgings."[18]

The current debate in Europe and the United States about access to medical care and quality of health services reinforces the more recently accepted perception that health care provided by professionals and health care generally are synonymous. Yet health care includes health enhancement, disease prevention, symptom evaluation, illness treatment, and health restoration, all functions fulfilled by self-health care, sometimes more successfully than by professional health care providers.

Some argue that the professional health care system promotes self-care because its capacity to deal effectively with the chronic health problems of older adults is so questionable.[19,20] Fleming, Giachello, Anderson, and Andrade[21] report that older individuals more involved in self-care are likely to visit physicians less often and spend less time in the hospital. Haug[22,23] found those 75 years of age and older were more likely to avoid professional care in the face of certain symptoms (e.g., depression, heavy cold) than those 46 to 74 years of age. Chappell[24] reported a positive correlation between self-maintenance measures (e.g., eat a balanced diet and avoid smoking) and use of formal care services. Chappell argues that, to the extent that using the formal care system necessitates active involvement on the part of the individual, formal care service use is a type of self-health care.

Support System

The prevalence of assistance from family and friends to the elderly is now well documented. Silverstone[25] describes this support system as "a rich fabric of informal relationships which envelops the majority of elders in our society along a number of dimensions. This fabric is bonded most strongly by marriage, and adjacent generational and peer relationships and, for racial minorities, by extended kin as well." While most gerontological researchers and practitioners recognize that the needs of frail and vulnerable elderly are best met through the proper balance between formal and informal supports, with each system performing the tasks for which it is best suited,[26] little is known about the interplay of self-care with the formal and informal care systems. Evans and Northwood[27] and Schmidt[28] report that among older adults use of formal service is most often a last resort.

Health Beliefs

Health beliefs have an impact on which system of care will be selected for use: self, informal, or formal. If an individual believes a disease is incurable or that medical treatment has unknown or minimal efficacy, we might expect absence or delay in seeking medical treatment.[24] Pill and Statt[29] report that among working-class women who believe in the germ theory of disease there was an accompanying belief that there was little that could be done to prevent disease. In a sample of over 700 residents aged 45 years and older, Haug, Wykle, and Namazi[30] found that subjective assessment of good health was predictive of self-treatment for ailments viewed as minor, but that low faith in doctors was a factor in the decision to self-treat for more serious symptoms.

Self-Health Care Instruction

Self-health care has been viewed as a learned skill, much like literacy, that is useful for everyday functioning in contemporary society. It follows from this view that formal self-care instruction

can be provided to enhance the capacities of individuals in matters related to health. Selected efforts have been made to inventory self-care programs in the United States potentially useful to elderly people. Three types of programs were identified in a 1976 report to the U.S. Department of Health, Education, and Welfare[13]:

1. "Comprehensive" self-care programs teaching a wide variety of skills
2. "Focused" programs providing self-care instruction for dealing with a scientific disease or disability
3. Programs emphasizing self-screening or preventive care efforts that individuals can carry out for themselves.

DeFriese and Woomert[13] cite Tom Ferguson, who identifies the following varieties of self-care programs in the United States:

- Programs that emphasize a high level of wellness and include instruction in stress management, nutrition, fitness, and the like
- Industrial programs that emphasize health promotion and illness prevention and include health education and health risk analysis
- Programs that emphasize home health care training and include information on aging, older adult care, decision making about illnesses and injuries, and the efficacy of home remedies
- Programs emphasizing medical consumerism which include information on use of medications, health planning and insurance, and available health resources in the community
- Programs that train individuals to be more active managers of their illnesses and emphasize self-diagnosis and management of chronic illnesses such as diabetes and hypertension

Little is known about the effectiveness of such programs as virtually no formal studies have been carried out to evaluate self-care education and training.

THE EFFICACY OF SELF-CARE

The exploration of the efficacy of self-health care relies on understanding of the relationship of belief to practice, identification of the obstacles to care, and specification of the actual relationship of self-health care to the utilization of professional health services among older adults. Self-care beliefs and practices may vary by symptom and perception of symptom seriousness and may also be related to sociodemographic and health status characteristics of the individual.

Practices and Correlates of Self-Health Care

Self-health care practices include the use of *over-the-counter* (OTC) *drugs*, vitamins, minerals, and other substances, folk or home remedies, and nonmedicinal self-care (e.g., changes in dietary or exercise patterns).

SELF-MEDICATION PRACTICES

Self-medication is a common form of self-care among the aged. According to Eve,[31] self-medication involves two components: self-administration of medicines and self-treatment with medicines. *Self-administration* refers primarily to taking prescription medicines as part of a total regimen of care for an illness or condition. *Self-treatment* refers to using medicines not prescribed by a physician,[32] including prescription drugs (e.g., left over from a prior illness or obtained from a relative or friend), nonprescription medicines (e.g., OTC medications and substances), and social drugs (e.g., alcohol or caffeine).

While drugs and medical sundries account for about 7 percent of all health expenditures in the United States in 1986, older Americans consume approximately 30 percent of all prescription drugs,[33,34] in a study of Seattle elderly, 75 percent reported using a prescription drug regularly. Older adults are also significant users of OTC medications and substances such as ointments. Guttman[35] reported that 69 percent of 447 elderly residents of Albany, New York, were regular users of OTC agents. Ostrom and her colleagues[36] found that 82 percent of their sample group of older Seattle residents used a nonprescription drug regularly. In another recent study of how older people take care of everyday health problems, 50 percent of the actions involved either using a prescription medicine or an OTC medication in the home.[37]

Older women are more likely than older men to use both prescription and nonprescription drugs.[38,39] Cafferato, Kasper, and Bernstein[40] identified certain family responsibilities and structures and stressful life events as explaining gender differences in obtaining psychotropic drugs. Whites use all types of medicines more frequently than nonwhites,[41] although one study described black males in rural areas as heavy users of OTC products.[42] Poor health and reduced quality of life are also related to use of all forms of medicines.[31] Age is the best predictor of medication use; use of prescription medicines increases with age, while use of nonprescription medicines decreases.[31]

Coon, Hendricks, and Sheahan[37] have identified a number of factors implicated in the prevalence of drug self-treatment among older adults. These include:

- Increased availability of OTC drug products
- Media marketing
- Increased prevalence with age of certain chronic illnesses
- Problems of access to professional medical care as well as increased costs for that care
- Increased personal involvement in decisions about health

It is also important to note that one appeal of OTC drugs is the erroneous assumption that because they can be purchased without a prescription, they must be safe. Analgesics and vitamins are the most commonly used of the OTC products.

The dangers posed by self-medication include the risks of:

- Adverse reactions
- Drug interactions
- Drug-alcohol interactions
- Medication errors

Basen[44] identified older adults as the most likely age group to experience drug-induced illness. Twelve to 17 percent of all acute hospital admissions of patients over age 70 can be attributed to adverse drug reactions[45]; however, only 7 percent of all serious medication errors involving elderly patients were associated with self-medication.[46] Given the increase in availability of new prescription and OTC agents, perhaps it is time to study this question again.

SELF-HEALTH PERCEPTIONS AND PRACTICES

The practice of self-health care has been examined in relation to perceived symptoms. Haug, Wykle, and Namazi[30] examined self-care practices in independent-living individuals aged 45 and older. Respondents were asked if they had noted any of a list of 30 illness symptoms in the past 4 months and, if so, what action they had taken. Rates of self-care varied depending on whether symptoms were perceived as mild or serious; self-care was more likely for milder symptoms. Self-care rates did not differ by age, although older persons generally employed more home remedies. Good health was predictive of self-care treatment for minor ailments, while lack of faith in doctors was a factor in self-care in cases of more serious symptoms.

Importantly, belief may be different than actual practice by older adults confronted with a particular symptom. Holtzman, Akiyama, and Maxwell[47] studied beliefs regarding the appropriate response to a set of common symptoms as well as actual responses to these symptoms. While most symptoms were viewed as "serious" or "very seri-

ous" by 50 percent or more of the respondents, symptoms that were painful, persistent, or especially disruptive to daily routine (e.g., bleeding, frequent vomiting, chest pain) were ranked as more serious than those deemed commonplace (e.g., dry skin, forgetfulness, leg cramps). Generally, the more serious the symptom was perceived to be, the more likely that professional care was deemed the appropriate response.

However, when reporting actual symptoms and actions during the previous 12 months, subjects in this study used professional services much less than might have been predicted on the basis of their reported beliefs about use of professional care. For example, while 77.1 percent identified shortness of breath as a serious or very serious symptom and 63 percent recommended professional care as the appropriate response, only 28 percent of the 50 elderly respondents experiencing this symptom sought professional care; 46 percent did nothing, while 26 percent employed some form of self-care. Although numbers of subjects reporting them was relatively small, several very serious symptoms, including abdominal pains (60 percent), and rectal pain or bleeding (61.9 percent), were self-treated by substantial percentages of subjects experiencing them.

While self-health care is frequently discussed in relation to treatment of symptoms, it may be uniquely suited to preventive care. For example, Belloc and Breslow[48] found that life expectancy and good health are directly related to such basic health practices as regular meals, moderate exercise several times a week, regular sleep, moderate weight, no smoking, and no or minimal alcohol consumption. According to these researchers, by observing all these practices, the average healthy male could add 11 years and the average healthy female could add 7 years to life expectancy.

In a national telephone interview, Bausell[49] compared older and younger adults with regard to compliance with 20 recommended health-seeking behaviors including dietary measures, weight control, appropriate sleep, and safety precautions in the home, among other factors. Older adults reported greater compliance than the young, attributed more importance to the value of compliance, but perceived themselves as having less control over future health.

ASSESSMENT OF SELF-CARE CAPACITY

Using data from the SOA, Kart and Dunkle[50] examined factors presumed to be associated with a person's assessment of his or her capacity to provide self-care. The major dependent variable, assessment of self-health care, was measured by a single question: "How good a job do you feel you are doing in taking care of your health? Would you say excellent, very good, good, fair, or poor?" Such a question cannot elicit information on specific self-care practices or allow for testing for the multidimensionality of self-care; however, the question does make it possible to examine correlates of perceived self-care ability in this large and nationally representative sample of community-dwelling older people.

Sociodemographic variables examined in the analysis included age, sex, race, marital status, educational attainment, and family income.[50] Five measures of health and impairment were also included. Over one-half of the respondents assessed their capacity to provide self-care as excellent or very good; one in nine, as fair or poor. While age, sex, race, and marital status all had statistically significant relationships with assessment of self-health care, differences were generally less than 3 percent. Measures of socioeconomic status showed strong, positive relationships with the global assessment of self-care. The most educated were considerably more likely than the least educated to assess self-care capacity in the most positive terms. Family income shows a similar pattern; the most affluent were considerably more likely than the poor to assess self-care as excellent or very good.

The health measures had the most positive, substantive relationships with self-care. Those who reported their current health status as excellent were almost four times as likely as those who perceived their health status as poor to assess how well they were taking care of their own health as excellent. Self-care was also related to perceived changes in health status. Those reporting their health as better than a year ago were much more likely than those reporting it as worse to assess their self-care as excellent.

Individuals with no functional limitations were considerably more likely than those with five or more limitations to perceive capacity for self-care as excellent or very good. Those who perceived themselves as having a great deal of control over their health appraised their self-health care capacities as excellent or very good.

In examining interrelationships among independent variables, the strongest correlates of self-care assessment were self-reported health status (beta = .27) and perceived control of health (beta = .17). Those who perceived their health status as excellent or very good as well as those who perceived their control over health to be great were likely to assess their capacity for self-care as excellent or very good. Sociodemographic variables contributed little to explaining variation in self-care assessment.

Findings from this and other studies support the idea that self-health care is widely practiced among the aged. Self-care may be especially appropriate for less serious symptoms and potentially effective or at least benign in many cases; however, self-care responses are not always appropriate and may be dangerous in the face of symptoms of potentially life-threatening illnesses.[47]

Obstacles to Self-Care

Most older people live at home in their communities, function well, and maintain a capacity to provide care for themselves (see Chapter 13). Still, there are forces, biological and social, that act to increase the problems associated with remaining healthy and providing self-care during illness while growing older.

BIOLOGICAL CHANGES

Biological changes may occur in later adulthood that create deficits in physical ability to provide self-care. These deficits may produce feelings of lack of control or helplessness which may limit actions the older person will undertake.[51]

SOCIAL IMPACT

Kuypers and Bengtson[52] examined the interplay between the physical changes that accompany aging and the social meaning these changes have for the older person. The social changes that occur in the Western world as one grows older include

- Role loss
- Ambiguous norms
- Lack of reference group
- A view of aging as an irreversible decline

These social changes lead to a sense of vulnerability. Older individuals may grow more dependent on societal definition of their situation and begin to doubt that competence. With increasing health problems and/or functional limitations, doubts about competence may result in the deterioration of even well-honed self-care skills.

STEREOTYPES

Negative stereotypes about the aging process contribute to behaviors by older people that confirm these stereotypes and lead to diminished feelings of control and self-esteem.[53] Fiske[54] has related self-reported decline in memory and energy among older people to their belief in negative cultural stereotypes about aging. Bandura[55] has described older adults as at risk for underestimating their competence in a number of different life areas. He attributes this underestimation to two factors;

1. The prevalence of negative social stereotypes about the aged

2. The tendency of many older people to use younger groups rather than age peers as a basis for social comparison

OLD AGE PERCEIVED AS ILLNESS

Dean[5] argues that the medical treatment model and the resultant organization of health care services are pervasive and pernicious influences on older people. Implicit in the logic of the medical model is a biological determinism that leads professionals and laypeople alike to view old age as illness. Attributing illness to biological changes and/or "pathological aging" may direct focus of the older person and health providers away from situational and social factors that affect health, although it is clear that health status is affected by retirement, widowhood, and changing living environments, among other stressful factors.[56]

LACK OF FOCUS ON HEALTH CARE

Schwartz[57] suggests that the health care system in the United States is irrational. One manifestation of this is the incompatibility of the existing acute care capabilities of medicine with the increasingly chronic nature of illness. According to Schwartz, clinical medicine emphasizes in-hospital, high-technology "sickness care," missing the focus on "health care," thereby negating efforts to encourage individual responsibility for personal health. This obstacle to self-health care is especially salient for older people, given the existing belief that good health in old age is a matter of fate or chance[5,58] and that professional medical care will protect health.[5]

The relation between control and health may actually be greater in old age, with the outcomes either more or less positive than at younger ages.[51] Three factors may be at play:

1. Experiences related to control and health seem to increase markedly in old age. Retirement, widowhood, loss of friends and family members, for example, all challenge individual competence.

2. The association between certain indicators of health, such as immunologic function, is altered by aging.

3. Frequent medical care contacts may actually reduce opportunities for control (at any age). Professional providers seem to prefer patients who are most manageable — conforming, obedient, and deferential, that is, those most receptive to the helping efforts of others.[51]

OVERCOMING OBSTACLES

Can these obstacles be overcome? Can self-health care be taught to older people? DeFriese and Woomert[13] argue that it is very difficult to address issues of program effectiveness and efficiency because many self-care programs lack clear and precise goals. They suggest that self-health care training programs may be no more effective in "normal" health care practices in promoting good health. This suggests, however, that self-care programs may be defined as effective if some proportion of participants can be encouraged to achieve a "normal" level of engagement in health practices. Further, desired outcomes of self-health care programs need not be measured in terms of gains in physical health status but rather in terms of perceived control or life satisfaction.

As has been described previously, self-care activities are widely practiced among older adults, in the form of health promotion and illness prevention as well as dealing with illness symptoms. Much self-health care seems appropriate and effective, especially where less serious illness symptoms are involved. Some evidence suggests, however, that older people employ self-care or do nothing in the presence of potentially life-threatening illnesses. Obviously, such cases are problematic. The assumption is usually made that much pain and anguish, perhaps even a life, could have been saved if only the individual had sought appropriate professional health care. Such an assumption is simplistic because it assumes a conflict between self-care and medical care.

The fact is we know too little about the impact of self-health care on professional health services utilization among older adults.

Kart, Dunkle, and Lockery, in an unpublished work, examined relationships between self-health care assessment in the 1984 SOA (described previously) and two medical care utilization indicators in a 1986 reinterview with 5151 SOA respondents age 70 and over. This provided information about the relationship between self-care assessment at time 1 (1984) and medical service use at time 2 (1986) in a nationally representative sample of community-dwelling elderly people.

Individual assessment of self-care capacity was found to be strongly related to physician visits and number of hospital stays in the 12 months prior to reinterview. Elderly individuals assessing their self-care capacities as excellent in 1984 reported fewer physician visits and hospital stays in 1986, compared to those assessing self-care capacity as fair or poor. The only demographic variable to alter this relationship was race. Health status appeared to be particularly important for understanding the relationship between self-health care and professional medical care.

Berkanovic, Telesky, and Reeder[59] analyzed data from the Los Angeles Health Survey to identify factors that helped explain whether an individual decided to seek medical attention for illness symptoms. Need factors, including chronic health problems and the disability level accompanying illness symptoms, tended to promote the seeking of medical care. The strongest predictor of medical care service use was the subject's belief in the efficacy of curative medical care; those who believed the doctor would do them some good were most likely to seek physician care. The researchers also found that those who perceived the symptoms as more serious were likely to seek physician care, those who believed it easier to go to the doctor were more likely to go, and those who thought the symptoms would recur were also more likely to go.

After reviewing much literature on

self-care, Fleming and colleagues[21] noted that most illness symptoms experienced in the United States are handled through self-care, with formal medical care being the exception, suggesting that self-care was a substitute for formal medical care. However, they also note that much of the "self-care movement," including books and courses, is controlled by physicians and medical institutions, suggesting that self-care may act as a stimulus to greater use of formal services. Finally, these researchers reported a relative independence of utilization of medical services from knowledge about health and illness, suggesting that when people acted on self-care information, they did so as a supplement to formal medical care.

Of particular interest in this study by Fleming and her colleagues[21] is that a panel of 43 practicing community physicians was employed to establish norms of physician contacts for different illness conditions (e.g., upper respiratory infection, diabetes) in the 12 months following onset. For both self-care measures, those who practiced self-care and those who did not exceeded the norms recommended by the panel of physicians. Thus, according to these physician norms, individuals engaged in self-health care activities were using physician care no less appropriately than those who did not.

SUMMARY

This chapter has covered the broad issue of self-care among older adults. It is clear that a wide range of informal care is an option for elderly individuals. Hickey, Dean, and Holstein[60] caution against a two-tier system where elders who are healthier and better educated use self-care for purposes of health prevention and maintenance, while more dependent and less educated elderly individuals may not have this option. For them, self-health care may be the only medical care.

Further research must examine the impact of self-health care on the health and well-being of elders in various cultures. At this point, there seems to be no political or cultural boundaries on self-health care.[4] An intensification of international cooperation to further understand the impact of self-health care practices around the world over time would provide valuable information to professional health care providers and laypeople alike. Clearly, self-health care may complement professional care, and mechanisms should be sought to ensure that this occurs.

REVIEW QUESTIONS

1. *Define self-health care.*

2. *Discuss the various forms of self-health care and their prevalence.*

3. *For what reasons is self-health care common among the elderly?*

4. *What demographic and personal factors contribute to decisions about self-health care?*

5. *What are the main types of formal self-health care programs available in the United States?*

6. *What are the major risks of self-health care?*

7. *What are the major advantages of self-health care?*

8. *Describe the major factors that interfere with self-health care.*

9. *What are the best ways in which to integrate professional and self-health care?*

REFERENCES

1. Levin, L: Self-care: An international perspective. Social Policy, pp 70–75, Sept/Oct 1976.
2. Helman, C: Feed a cold, starve a fever. Culture, Medicine and Psychiatry 2:107,1978.
3. Blumhagen, D: Hyper-tension. A folk illness with a medical name. Culture, Medicine and Psychiatry 1:197–227, 1980.
4. Coppard, LC in collaboration with Riley, MW, Macfadyen, DM and Dean, K: Self/Health/Care and Older People. World Health Organization, Copenhagen, Denmark, 1984.
5. Dean, K: Self-care behavior: Implications for aging. In Dean, K, Hickey, T and Holstein, B (eds): Self-care and Health in Old Age. Croom Helm, London, 1986.

6. Dean, K: Self-care responses of illness: A selected review. Social Science and Medicine 15:673–687, 1981.

7. Scambler, G and Scambler, A: The illness iceberg and aspects of consulting behavior. In Fitzpatrick, R, Hinton, J, Newman, S, Scambler, G and Thompson, J (eds): The Experience of Illness. Tavistock, London, 1984.

8. Cassedy, JH: Why self-help? Americans alone with their diseases, 1880–1950. In Risse, G, Numbers, R and Leariff, J (eds): Medicine Without Doctors. Science History Publications, New York, 1987, p 31.

9. Epsom, J: The Mobile Health Clinic: A Report on the First Year's Work. Southwark Health Department, London, 1969. (Cited in Scambler and Scambler, 1984.)

10. Ingham, J and Miller P: Symptom prevalence and severity in a general practice. Journal of Epidemiology and Community Health 33:191–98, 1979.

11. Morrell, D and Wale, C: Symptoms perceived and recorded by patients. Journal of the Royal College of General Practitioners 26:398–403, 1976.

12. Williamson, JD and Danaher, K: Self Care in Health. Croom Helm, London, 1978.

13. DeFriese, GH and Woomert, A: Self-care among U.S. elderly: Recent developments. Research on Aging 5:2–23, 1983.

14. Kart, CS: Experiencing symptoms: Attribution and misattribution of illness among the aged. In Haug, M (ed): Elderly Patients and Their Doctors. Springer, New York, 1981.

15. Butler, RN, Gertman, JS, Oberlander, DL and Schindler, L: Self-care, self-help, and the elderly. International Journal of Aging and Human Development 10:95–117, 1979–80.

16. Blake, J: From Buchan to Fishbein: Literature of domestic medicine. In Risse, G, Numbers, R and Leariff, J (eds): Medicine Without Doctors. Science History Publications, New York, 1977.

17. Levin, L and Idler, E: Self-care in health. Annual Review of Public Health 4:181–201, 1983.

18. Numbers, R: Do-it-yourself the sectarian way. In Risse, G, Numbers, R and Leariff, J (eds): Medicine Without Doctors. Science History Publications, New York, 1977, p 49.

19. Evans, R: Strained Mercy: The Economics of Canadian Health Care. Butterworth, Toronto, Canada, 1984.

20. Chappell, N, Strain, L and Blandford, A: Aging and Health Care: A Social Perspective. Holt, Rinehart and Winston, Toronto, Canada, 1986.

21. Fleming, G, Giachello, A, Andersen, R and Andrade, P: Self care: Substitute, supplement or stimulus for formal medical care services? Medical Care 22:950–966, 1984.

22. Haug, M: Age and medical care utilization pattern. Journal of Gerontology 36:103–111, 1981.

23. Haug, M and Lavin, B: Consumerism in Medicine. Sage, Beverly Hills, CA, 1983.

24. Chappell, N: The interface among three systems of care: Self, informal and formal. In Ward, R and Tobin, S (eds): Health in Aging: Sociological Issues and Policy Directions. Springer, New York, 1987.

25. Silverstone, B: Informal social support systems for the frail elderly. In Institute of Medicine/National Research Council (ed): America's Aging: Health in an Older Society. National Academy Press, Washington, DC, p 156.

26. Litwak, E: Helping the Elderly: The Complementary Roles of Informal Networks and Formal Systems. Guilford Press, New York, 1985.

27. Evans, R and Northwood, L: The utility of natural help relationships. Social Science and Medicine 13A:789–795, 1979.

28. Schmidt, M: Personal networks: Assessment, care and repair. Journal of Gerontological Social Work e:65–76, 1981.

29. Pill, R and Statt, N: Relationships between health locus on control and belief in the relevance of lifestyle to health. Patient Counseling and Health Education 3:95–99, 1981.

30. Haug, M, Wykle, ML and Namazi, KH: Self-care among older adults. Social Science and Medicine 29:171–183, 1989.

31. Hecht, A: Medicine and the elderly. FDA Consumer, pp 20–21, Sept. 1983.

32. Eve, S: Self-medication among older adults in the United States. In Dean, K, Hickey, T and Holstein, B (eds): Self-Care and Health in Old Age. Croom Helm, London, 1986.

33. Warren, F: Self-medication problems among the elderly. In Payne, B, Peterson, D and Whittington, F (eds): Drugs and the Elderly. Charles T. Thomas, Springfield, IL, 1979.

34. Lamy, P: Geriatric drug therapy. American Family Physician 36(6):118–124, 1986.

35. Guttmann, D: Patterns of legal drug use by older Americans. Addictive Diseases 3(3): 337–356, 1978.

36. Ostrom, J, Hammarlund, E, Christensen, D, Plein, J and Kethley, A: Medication usage in an elderly population. Medical Care 23: 157–164, 1985.

37. Coons, S, Hendricks, J and Sheahan, S: Self-medication with non-prescription drugs. Generations 12(4):22–26, 1988.

38. Bush, P and Rabin, D: Who's using nonprescribed medicines? Medical Care 14(12): 1014–1023, 1976.

39. Warheit, G, Arey, S and Swanson, E: Patterns of drug use: An epidemiological review. Journal of Drug Issues 6:223–237, 1976.

40. Cafferato, GL, Kasper, J and Bernstein, A: Family roles, structure and stressors in relation to sex differences in obtaining psychotropic drugs. Journal of Health and Social Behavior 24:132–143, 1983.

41. Bush, P and Osterweis, M: Pathways to medicine use. Journal of Health and Social Behavior 19:179–189, 1978.

42. Juergens, J, Smith, M and Sharpe, T: Determinants of OTC drug use in the elderly. Journal of Geriatric Drug Therapy 1(1):31–37, 1986.

43. Hershey, L and Whitney, C: Drugs and the

elderly. In Kart, C, Metress, E and Metress, S (eds): Aging, Health and Society. Jones and Bartlett, Boston, 1988.

44. Basen, M: The elderly and drugs—problem overview and program strategy. Public Health Reports 19:43–48, 1977.

45. Problems with prescription drugs highest among the elderly. American Family Physician, Vol 28 (6), 1983.

46. Schwartz, D, Wang, M, Zeitz, L and Goss, M: Medication errors made by elderly, chronically ill patients. American Journal of Public Health 52:2018–2029, 1962.

47. Holtzman, J, Akiyama, H and Maxwell, A: Symptoms and self-care in old age. Journal of Applied Gerontology 5(2):183–200, 1986.

48. Belloc, N and Breslow, L: Relationship of physical health status and health practices. Preventive Medicine 1:409–421, 1972.

49. Bausell, R: Health-seeking behavior among the elderly. Gerontologist 26(5):556–559, 1986.

50. Kart, CS and Dunkle, RE: Assessing capacity for self-care among the aged. Journal of Aging and Health 1(4):430–450, 1989.

51. Rodin, J: Sense of control: Potentials for intervention. Annals of AAPSS 503:29–42, 1989.

52. Kuypers, J and Bengston, V: Social breakdown and competence. Human Development 16:181–201, 1973.

53. Rodin, J and Langner, E: Aging labels: The decline of control and the fall of self-esteem. Journal of Social Issues 36:12–29, 1980.

54. Fiske, M: Tasks and crises of the second half of life: The interrelationship of commitment, coping and adaptation. In Birren, J and Sloane, R (eds): Handbook of Mental Health and Aging. Prentice-Hall, Englewood Cliffs, NJ, 1980.

55. Bandura, A: Self-referent thought: A developmental analysis of self-efficacy. In Riley, J and Ross, L (eds): Social Cognitive Development: Frontiers and Possible Futures. Cambridge University Press, New York, 1981.

56. Kart, CS: The Realities of Aging, ed 3. Allyn & Bacon, Boston, 1990.

57. Schwartz, H: Irrationality as a feature of health care in the U.S. In Schwartz, H (ed): Dominant Issues in Medical Sociology, ed 2. Random House, New York, 1987.

58. Cicirelli, V: Relationship of family background variables to locus of control in the elderly. Journal of Gerontology 35:108–114, 1980.

59. Berkanovic, E, Telesky, C and Reeder, S: Structural and social psychological factors in the decision to seek medical care for symptoms. Medical Care 19(7):693–709, 1981.

60. Hickey, T, Dean, K and Holstein, B: Emerging trends in gerontology and geriatrics: Implications for the self care of the elderly. Social Science and Medicine 23(12):1363–1369, 1986.

Retire? Are you kidding? I'm having the time of my life. What would I do, go fishing? Fish don't applaud, do they?
—BOB HOPE, *from* DAVID MELTON, *Images of Greatness*, Independence Press, Independence, MO, 1977.

Chapter

Work and Retirement

HARVEY L. STERNS
M. PATRICIA LAIER
JANET G. DORSETT

OBJECTIVES

By the end of the chapter, readers will be able to:

1 Describe the characteristics of the older work force.

2 Discuss forms of employer-sponsored wellness programs for older workers and their value in enhancing work performance.

3 Discuss issues of work performance of older workers.

4 Describe characteristics that contribute to continuing competence of older workers.

5 Describe mechanisms for retraining older workers.

6 Describe issues related to decisions to retire and adjustments to retirement.

7 Discuss the development of retirement preparation programs and alternatives to retirement.

8 Discuss issues related to unemployment among older workers.

The study of aging and work, focusing on the employment and retirement issues of middle-aged and older workers, is called *industrial gerontology*.[1] The aging of the work force creates unique issues — early retirement options, staffing shortages, career patterns, training and retraining, performance, productivity, and health and disability.[2]

Whether older workers continue to occupy their present jobs or change jobs will be determined by their career choices, retraining, experience, health, and retirement preferences. Older workers will be in direct competition with younger workers. Competent, able, older workers who desire to continue to work should be competitive in the workplace of the future.

This chapter explores issues and research relevant to enhancing the work and retirement experience of older adults. Current data regarding the employment patterns of older workers are provided. The role of health as a determinant of employment and retirement and related research issues are discussed next. Interventions such as wellness programs are also described.

The chapter then turns to issues such as older worker performance, obsolescence, and competence. Training and retraining and other interventions are discussed. Retirement is considered, and the role of retirement preparation and alternative approaches to work and retirement are analyzed. In addition, the complex factors that determine vocational and retirement outcomes are examined.

THE OLDER LABOR FORCE

Over the past 30 years, there have been significant changes in the work force participation of older adults (Table 10–1).[3] The percentage of these individuals in the work force has decreased although the absolute number has increased.

Among the 3 million older adults aged 65 and over working in 1984, 1.8 million were men, half of whom worked full time, and 1.2 million women, most of whom worked part time.[4] Half of these workers were in white-collar occupations. Gender and race are also important predictors of occupation. (While the majority of white women were clerical workers and a majority of black women were in service occupations, men work in a wide range of occupations). About one-half of older white male workers were in white-collar occupations; one-quarter worked in blue-collar work.[4]

Because older women have worked primarily in clerical and service occupa-

tions, their work opportunities tend to be limited. Women over 65 represent 25 percent of all clerical workers, and 21 percent of all service workers.[5]

The labor force is projected to reach 129 million persons in 1995, up from 114 million in 1984. Blacks are expected to account for 20 percent of the future labor force growth, and women are expected to account for 60 percent of the growth.[6] Participation among people age 55 and over is expected to be only 25 percent in 1995. However, many older workers will have some sort of postcareer employment before they retire.[7] Most workers are employed in at least one lengthy job during their prime working years, and a small number are employed at a single job for the majority of their working life.[8] Retirement with ''bridge jobs'' appears to fill the period from the end of the longest job to the point of retirement.

A recurrent theme in work for the older adult is health.[9] Health, along with functional capacity, are important variables affecting the behavior of older workers.[10] It is somewhat difficult to determine the impact of age-related health changes to work because most health measures reflect poor health (presence of disease or disability) rather than good health. Functional capacity is difficult to assess, and needed databases are not available.[10] Among other concerns, older adults have greater variability in work-related functional ability than younger people. Reporting older adults as a single group distorts the reality of their functional ability, with the result that young-old people are portrayed as less functional than they actually are.[10] Research is needed to develop indexes that incorporate variables such as sickness, impairment, and limitation, as

TABLE 10-1	**Percent of Older Adults in the Work Force, 1950–1990**			
	Males		**Females**	
	55–64, %	**65 and over, %**	**55–64, %**	**65 and over, %**
1950	87	46	27	10
1990	65	14	42	7

Source: Adapted from Kutscher and Fullerton.[3]

well as functional capacity, as they relate to work.[10]

Robinson[11] suggests two pertinent questions related to the effects of age on health and job performance. First, "Is the job performance of middle-age and older workers adversely affected by age-related factors," and secondly, "if so, how can these age-related effects be minimized through work-place interventions?" As the working population ages, employers must pay attention to the relationship of aging to health and performance. Age-related health changes affecting job performance may be attributed to genetic predisposition, environmental influences, lifestyle, behavior, and stress.

Although there are some general trends, same-age people differ greatly on measures of health and functional capacity. Data from the military and Metropolitan Life Insurance Company personnel suggest that age differences in work capacity exist and that there is an increase, with age up to 65 years, of work loss days due to injury or illness. However, numerous other factors that affect job performance measures within age groups far outweigh differences between age groups, and age differences are more obvious in some occupations such as airline pilots than others such as clerical work.[11]

Health and functioning do not inevitably decline in the middle and later working years, and interventions such as reducing work hazards and promoting health-related behaviors can prevent or reduce health decrements. The workplace is a reasonable site for interventions because of the large amount of time spent at work. Workplace interventions include assessments (which may reveal reduced capabilities), workplace accommodations (such as environmental modifications), and retraining. However, these interventions may be threatening to workers concerned about revealing deficits.

Employers may fail to implement these programs because of:

- Lack of awareness of their potential benefits

- Lack of published data on health and job performance

Workplace interventions offer numerous benefits for business in terms of reducing health hazards, promoting good health, assessing change, providing alternate working arrangements, redesigning jobs, and maintaining a skilled and committed work force.[11]

WELLNESS PROGRAMS FOR OLDER ADULTS

Health promotion on the part of employers can maintain health and possibly even slow the changes associated with the aging process.[12] There are many economic and social benefits for organizations that promote wellness.

Wellness programs emphasize a holistic approach to health. Preventive efforts are directed at reducing the risk of illness through physical fitness, nutrition, weight control, stress management, hypertension control, and smoking cessation programs.[13] Studies that have empirically evaluated the effectiveness of health promotion programs have found them to be effective in increasing fitness levels, decreasing health risk factors, lowering absenteeism rates, and reducing medical costs.[14] A study of a work site health promotion program at General Mills reduced employees' smoking behaviors and absenteeism and increased their exercise levels, and their seat-belt use.[15] Interest in wellness programs appears to be increasing.[16] Employer-sponsored programs specifically designed for older workers are currently being developed but are still somewhat uncommon.[17]

Retirees are often overlooked in an organization's health promotion efforts. Deobil[18] suggests that one possible reason for the dearth of health promotion programs for retirees is the attitude, held by both employers and older employees and retirees, that it may be too late to develop preventive behaviors. Deobil[18] suggested that the scope of wellness programs be expanded to include not only prevention but maintenance and rehabilitation of *functional capacity* (the ability to carry out daily activities).

Health promotion efforts directed toward older workers and retirees are worthwhile. With the recent increases in health care costs and the increased usage of health care with age,[13,18] wellness programs are an attractive method for controlling escalating costs.[18] Wood, Olmstead, and Craig[15] found that General Mills "TriHealthalon produced paybacks of $3.10 and $3.90 for every dollar spent on the program in 1985 and 1986." The implementation of a wellness program may also enable older adults to remain functional in the work force longer. If health is maintained, with the aid of health promotion programs, employees may be able to increase their tenure at work.

Older adults, both workers and retirees, have shown a great interest in wellness programs. Areas of expressed interest include weight management, physical fitness and exercise, health after retirement, and nutrition.[19,20]

Current Approaches to Wellness Programs

Methods for providing health information include appraisals of health risk (e.g., medical screenings) written health-related information (e.g., newsletters), classes and seminars on aging-related subject matter, and modified fitness programs for older workers and retirees (e.g., senior aerobics classes).[13,18,20]

Approaches that are most likely to be successful are easily accessible, offered at no cost, promise new information, and require minimal time.[19,20] These factors and those that follow should be considered in the development of wellness programs for older adults.

Considerations for Developing Wellness Programs

When designing the wellness program's goals, the needs, desires, and health level of the participants need to be considered. Social, psychological, and physical needs must be addressed.[15,18] Three important psychological factors are motivation, safety, and confidence. Any concern about engaging in exercise may be reduced through careful instruction about monitoring intensity of exercise and making needed modifications. Positive feedback and an enjoyable atmosphere can enhance older participants' confidence and motivation to continue in the exercise program.[18]

Ethical issues must also be considered. These include the question of responsibility (who is responsible for an individual's health, the organization or the individual?), voluntary participation, and confidentiality.[14] Assurance that these factors have been addressed will reduce participant concerns about such factors as invasion of privacy.

Work site wellness programs can clearly benefit older workers and retirees. The programs have been shown to be empirically effective[21] and offer many potential benefits to older workers, retirees, and the organization.

OLDER WORKER PERFORMANCE

In view of the increasing number of age discrimination cases,[22] the elimination of mandatory retirement for most occupations, and the increasing number of older workers, there has been a burgeoning need for an understanding of the relationship between age and work performance.[23–25] However, studies of age and work performance are plagued by poor designs and inadequate analyses. They tend to ignore variations in job demands, individual experience, and measures of performance.[26] Following a qualitative review of the literature, Rhodes[26] concluded that an equal number of studies support a decline, an increase, and a stability in performance with age.

Waldman and Avolio[24] conducted a meta-analysis of 40 studies and found the relationship between age and performance to vary with the type of job performance measure. Supervisory ratings of employees' performance showed a slight decline with age. With more objective measures, employees' performance increased slightly with age. These researchers also found that one's profession may act as a moderator of the age and work performance relationship. The relationship between age and supervisor's ratings of performance was more positive in professionals than nonprofessionals. McEvoy and Cascio[27] performed a meta-analysis on 96 studies. Like Waldman and Avolio,[24] they found a slight correlation between age and work performance but did not find performance criterion and type of work to affect the relationship.

Researchers' inability to find a consistent linear relationship between age and work performance may suggest that such a relationship does not exist. Waldman and Avolio[25] developed a nonlinear model that illustrates the compounding effects of individual characteristics, such as personality, ability, and motivation, and contextual characteristics, such as organizational policies, reward systems, and job demands. These characteristics may influence a worker's professional competence and performance.[25,28]

Another reason for inconsistent findings could be the interactions between experience and age.[25] Experience has been found to be a better predictor of performance than age.[25,29] Qualitative experience, though, is rarely examined and may be as important as quantitative experience. Workers with equal number of years of experience may perform differently due to the individual and contextual experiences such as more effective supervision or more challenging work assignments.

Waldman and Avolio[25] propose that future researchers focus on life-span experiences that are both work- and nonwork-related. The life-span approach may enable us to understand individual and contextual factors that impact on continued productivity in later years.

OBSOLESCENCE VERSUS MAINTAINING COMPETENCE

A major issue for the 1990s is the question of how long a worker's skills will remain current. With rapid technological changes occurring today, workers may find it necessary to continually update their *knowledge, skill, and abilities* (KSAs) or they may become obsolete. Obsolescence occurs when the demands of a job become incongruent with a worker's KSAs.[30] There have been a variety of approaches to the study of obsolescence.[31] Recent writings on the topic have focused on the process of maintaining professional competence.[30] As Figure 10–1 demonstrates,

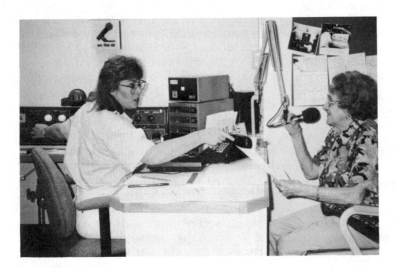

Figure 10–1 Continuation of work roles is important to many older adults. Here we see an older adult with her own radio show. (Courtesy of the Menorah Park Nursing Home, Cleveland, Ohio.)

older workers are capable of learning to use new technologies to maintain competence.

Professional competence has been defined as "the ability to function effectively in the tasks considered essential within a given profession."[30] A developmental approach suggests that maintaining professional competence through updating is a continual process, starting as soon as an individual enters the work force and continuing throughout his or her career. This approach is contrasted with a *remedial approach*, which views updating as a process done to compensate for obsolescence after it occurs.[30] The developmental perspective seems more effective as a means for avoiding obsolescence and suggests that as workers age, they must continually develop new KSAs. Aspects of both the individual (e.g., age) and the job setting (e.g., organizational climate) are related to obsolescence.

Individual Characteristics

AGE

Older workers may face a greater risk of obsolescence since they have been out of school for a longer period of time. Empirical studies of this assumption, however, have produced inconsistent results. In engineering, for example, obsolescence has been found to increase as early as the midthirties.[32,33] Willis and Tosti-Vassey found no age differences between up-to-date college professors and those less up to date.[34] This may mean that age is related to obsolescence only in specific occupations. Additionally, Shearer and Steger[33] found an increase in obsolescence with age for a civilian sample of engineers but the opposite effect in air force engineers. There was a negative relationship between age and obsolescence for the air force personnel. These results suggest that maintaining competence though updating is critical for workers of all ages.

Training and development programs may be the most common means by which individuals maintain professional competence.[35] Older workers underuse training opportunities, possibly because they have not been afforded as many opportunities as younger workers.[34] While special issues need to be considered when developing training programs for older workers,[37,38] the fact remains that older workers benefit from training. Why, then, don't they participate in as much training as younger workers?

The answer to this question may lie in the older workers themselves or in the organization where they work. Individual factors such as motivation and values impact on engagement in training or other updating such as reading and networking. Additionally, external forces (in the organization or elsewhere) can influence workers at all stages of their careers and help determine the amount of updating and other career-development activities they will participate in.[30,39]

MOTIVATION AND ABILITY

Motivation may be one of the most important determinants of whether or not someone will remain up to date at work. Motivation alone, however, does not guarantee this outcome. The worker must also possess the ability to successfully execute the behaviors necessary to remain professionally competent. Therefore, adequate ability and motivation are both critical for maintaining competence.[40]

External Factors

While the ultimate responsibility for maintaining professional competence rests on the individual employee, the organization can foster or discourage the necessary updating behaviors by providing opportunities for updating and enhancing motivation through challenging work assignments and opportunities for interaction between peers and management. An organization should remain flexible and committed to professional development.[30,39,41] As is true for all workers, these factors can influence the likelihood that an older worker will engage in various activities to update his or her skills. The issues to consider include:

- Challenging work coupled with security
- Interaction with coworkers and management
- Flexibility on the part of the organization, accompanied by an understanding that change may occur slowly
- Organization support for continued training
- An effective system of rewards, both formal and informal[41-46]

The environment and the policies of the organization can influence the likelihood that all workers, old and young alike, will take the necessary steps to maintain competence. While professionals of all ages may be threatened by obsolescence, special issues need to be considered when training older workers.

TRAINING OLDER WORKERS

While older workers may be more in need of training due to obsolescence, statistics show that they receive less training than younger workers. Lillard and Tan[36] reported that 30 percent of young men but only 10 percent of older men receive training. Cross[47] cites three barriers to older adult participation in training: situational, dispositional, and institutional.

Barriers to Training

SITUATIONAL BARRIERS

These barriers include lack of information and lack of money. Older workers may be unaware of community-based job-related training. When training is on-site, managers may fail to tell older workers about the opportunity because of stereotypes managers may have about older workers' learning abilities.[47,48] Education of management and

workers can minimize these stereotypes and increase participation in training. Paid release time from work and tuition reimbursement are powerful incentives for participation in training.[47]

DISPOSITIONAL BARRIERS

Dispositional barriers relate to self-perception. Older workers may have internalized the negative stereotype that they are too old to learn. This may be one reason why older workers are those least likely to volunteer for training.[50] Encouragement from managers can minimize this barrier.

INSTITUTIONAL BARRIERS

Institutional barriers include logistical policies and procedures such as difficult registration procedures, inaccessible sites, or inconvenient times. Training scheduled right after work or at deadline times may cause fatigue or poor attendance. Policies that do not reward older workers through benefits and incentives for acquiring skills may actually encourage retirement.[51] The upcoming work force has more formal education than the present older work force. Fear of education may also be lower among the future older workers, and managers may be better educated about the value of older workers to the company.

Designing the Training Program

As with the development of any training program, the initial step must be a needs analysis, which includes an analysis of the organization, the job, and the person.[52] In developing a training program for workers of all ages, factors to consider include motivation, structure, active participation, familiarity, organization, time, and learning strategies.[37] With older workers, special sensitivity to these dimensions may be important.

MOTIVATION

Older workers are least likely to volunteer for instruction, so trainers may need to encourage them more than others.[50] Their desire to learn may be impeded by fear of failure or feelings of inadequacy as compared to younger workers. Older workers who have had little formal schooling may have particularly low self-esteem. Belbin and Belbin[53] found that both motivation and self-concept of older workers can influence training involvement and success. Trainers can help alleviate feelings of fear or inadequacy by providing continuous positive feedback and reminders of training goals. Trainers should also ensure support is being given by managers and coworkers.

The environment also affects motivation. Lighting, noise, and temperature should be adjusted to maximize comfort. Frequent rest periods help alleviate fatigue.

STRUCTURE

The training program should be relevant to the job based on a careful job analysis. This analysis can assist in the arrangement of training sequences. Anxiety of participants can be reduced by ensuring that the trainee masters each simple component of a task before moving on.[38] This mastery also gives trainers opportunities to provide positive feedback.

ACTIVE PARTICIPATION

Active participation is desirable for older trainees, as lecture and/or rote memorization formats may cause difficulty.[37] Active participation may reduce cautiousness and hesitancy. Additionally, older workers' wealth of experience should enhance group discussions and learning.

FAMILIARITY

If possible, trainers should utilize former skills of the trainees and build upon their past knowledge, skills, and abilities. Providing relevant or generalizable examples during training may also increase participants' attention,

which would improve training effectiveness.

ORGANIZATION

Cognitive research has shown older adults have difficulty organizing information effectively.[38] As a result, trainers should organize the material being presented to help retention and comprehension[37] by placing material into meaningful groupings. Teaching older trainees organizational strategies is another effective option in training.[54]

TIME

Behavioral research consistently indicates slowing of reaction time and increases in learning time with age. Thus, slower presentation of training material and provision of longer study and test periods should aid older workers. Given sufficient time, older learners perform as well or better than younger learners.[38] Self-paced learning is optimal.[55] However, trainers should not just add more time without teaching the older adult efficient time use.[38]

STRATEGIES

Provision of learning strategies such as mnemonic techniques is the final critical component to be included in training older workers. Trainers expect trainees to learn but often fail to teach them how to learn. Older learners may never have learned strategies for retention, recall, and application, or they may have forgotten them.

Design may actually be of more importance in the success or failure of training than content.[56] A design that addresses the factors identified here will facilitate success of the older learner by enhancing motivation and self-esteem and decreasing feelings of failure and anxiety.

Some of the factors listed here stem from *andragogy*,[37] the term used to describe the instructional process for adults. Five andragogical assumptions are:

1. Adults are increasingly self-directed.
2. Adults are rich in experience.
3. Adults' choice of learning depends on the stage of development.
4. Adults are problem centered.
5. Adults are motivated internally.[57]

To apply these andragogical assumptions, Knowles[57] suggests trainers share their authority with the adults and allow the adults to be active participants in the determination of training content, method, goals, and evaluation. The result should be greater job relevance of training content and increased motivation of trainees. Participation in evaluation techniques may also reduce fear of failure. With this approach, trainers can also gain insight into the trainees' expectations, problems, functioning, and knowledge.

Knowles[57] also highlights the importance of a positive environment. Support from trainers, managers, and peers will increase self-confidence, risk taking, and participation. Knowles does add, though, that the *situation* is the best determinant of instructional techniques. *Pedagogical approaches*, that is, approaches used with children, may be best if the topic is extremely technical. If the adults do not know anything about the material to be discussed, it will be difficult for them to develop training content.

Training or Retraining Applications

Numerous examples of effective training programs can be found in the literature.[58–60] In one example, researchers trained younger (18 to 28 years), middle-aged (37 to 46), and older volunteers (55 to 67) in word processing skills over a 2-week period.[55] The design of the program was chosen to be optimal for older adults; the seven $3\frac{1}{2}$-hour training sessions were self-paced, and a trainer was available at all times for assistance. Participants of all ages learned the fundamentals of word processing, but older adults took longer to complete

the subunits, evaluation protocol, and examination than the young and middle-aged groups. They also needed more trainer interventions even though they did not request them. Requesting assistance might have reduced training time for the older trainees. Among the recommendations that emerged was the strategy of comparing new methods to those familiar to the older employee.[55]

In another example, Gist, Schwoerer, and Rosen[61] conducted a 3-hour workshop to enhance the acquisition of computer skills, comparing younger (under 45 years) and older trainees (over 45 years) as well as the effects of two training conditions, tutorial and modeling. The *tutorial* was a self-paced set of spreadsheet exercises and problems, with immediate feedback on performance. The *modeling* condition had subjects observe a man demonstrate and discuss the steps involved in making a spreadsheet. After observing the model, subjects practiced the steps and were given feedback. The authors found that on the post-test the younger adults significantly outperformed the older adults. The 3-hour time constraint may have limited the performance of the older subjects. The modeling condition was found to be superior for both age groups. Gist, Schwoerer, and Rosen[61] provide two possible explanations for this finding. Realistic expectations of actions required for performing each step may have been developed, or vicarious reinforcement may have existed.

Even though no single method has been determined to be best for training older adults, the most successful programs are sensitive to older workers' needs. Training is a growing need for all workers, and added research should help improve methods.

RETIREMENT

Retirement creates many life changes for older adults. For the vast majority of people, with retirement comes an increase in free time as well as a decrease in income. Although not the only

157

changes that result from retirement, they may be the most dramatic.[11,62]

Do the changes that result from the retirement process lead to negative consequences for retirees? Research studies examining this question have reached inconsistent conclusions. Some research has found that retirement does create problems for retirees. For example, Bosse and associates[63] discovered that retired men (mean age = 66.35 years) reported a greater number of psychological symptoms than did working males (mean age = 56 years). Retirees scored significantly higher on depression, anxiety, somatization, phobic anxiety, and obsessive-compulsive scales. These differences, with the exception of the anxiety scale, held up even when health was taken into consideration. Men who were still working after the age of 65 reported the fewest symptoms. The authors suggest that loss of income, loss of friends, and marital difficulties could lead to the psychological difficulties found.

Retirement does not always lead to adverse effects on the functioning or well-being of retirees. For example, George, Fillenbaum, and Palmore[64] found no adverse effects of retirement on life satisfaction. Beehr[65] found that the mental health of retirees was similar to their mental health prior to retirement. This outcome was moderated by the amount of planning, occupational goal attainment, retirement expectations, and the propensity to work. Therefore, even if retirement does promote negative effects, these effects are influenced by characteristics of the individual.

Factors Influencing the Retirement Experience

The effects of retirement are largely determined by an individual's specific experience. One factor is whether the decision to retire is voluntary. In addition, four personal characteristics have been linked to retirement satisfaction: health, income, attitudes, and preparedness for retirement.

VOLUNTARY VERSUS NONVOLUNTARY RETIREMENT

The negative effects of retirement may be more pronounced for those who do not choose to retire. Voluntary retirees have reported higher life satisfaction, income, health, and occupational status than involuntary retirees.[66,67] Involuntary retirees, in contrast, have shown signs of poor adaptation.[68,69]

In 1986, amendments to the Age Discrimination in Employment Act eliminated mandatory retirement policies in most occupations. However, mandatory retirement legislation is only one cause of involuntary retirement; another cause is poor health.[70] Those forced to retire because of poor health are more likely to suffer negative consequences than those who retire as a consequence of mandatory retirement laws. Palmore and associates[70] analyzed data from three longitudinal studies and discovered that retiring for compulsory reasons other than health had no significant effects on life satisfaction, while health-related retirement was related to lower living standards, poorer health, and lower satisfaction (with life, leisure, activity, and retirement). Kimmel, Prince, and Walker[67] found that health and preretirement attitudes were the most significant predictors of retirement satisfaction, whether retirement was voluntary or not.

Therefore, the elimination of mandatory retirement may not greatly improve retirement satisfaction. Rather, it may be the factors that influence the retirement decision, such as health, income, and preretirement attitudes, that will determine adjustment.[65,66,72-74]

HEALTH

Health is a pervasive force that affects the experiences of older adults. Although health may not be the primary factor in the decision to retire, poor health is probably the most salient reason for poor adjustment to retirement. Healthier retirees have higher life satisfaction and an easier retirement transition than unhealthy persons.[66,67,75]

INCOME

Another personal variable that influences adjustment to retirement is income level.[75-77] The loss of money in retirement has been regarded as a primary stressor in retirement.[63] On the other hand, Maxwell[78] found that life satisfaction was related to the absolute level of retirement income, as opposed to the level of income relative to preretirement income. While the loss of money may be a stressor in retirement, what may be more important is the adequacy of the older person's present income. In order to successfully adapt to retirement, individuals need adequate financial resources, in addition to the other factors discussed.

ATTITUDES

Positive attitudes toward retirement are related to better adjustment to retirement in some samples[71,87] but have been shown to be unrelated to adjustment for women[79] or blacks.[70] Additionally, people with positive attitudes toward retirement are not always prepared for the changes that will occur with retirement. Behling and Merves[80] found that white professionals were better prepared financially for retirement than were blacks or Puerto Ricans, in spite of similar attitudes toward retirement. What may be more important than a positive attitude is a realistic appraisal of the retirement situation,[65] coupled with adequate preparation.

PREPARATION FOR RETIREMENT

People who plan for major life changes tend to be more successful in dealing with them.[81] Since retirement is a major life change, those who are prepared for retirement will be better able to adapt to the retirement process. Research suggests that this is so.[65,82,83]

Demographic characteristics influence the degree to which an individual is prepared for retirement. For example, research has indicated that people with higher incomes are better prepared and have a greater number of resources to utilize in retirement.[84] However, regardless of income, active planning for retirement can ease the transition. Planning for retirement can not only enhance financial circumstances and contribute to a healthier lifestyle but also provide an opportunity to explore new leisure activities and alternative housing.[85] So, the sooner planning is begun, the better!

Retirement Preparation Programs

Formal retirement preparation programs, provided by an employer, a nonprofit organization, a consulting firm, or an independent retirement specialist may be helpful.[86] Unfortunately, only a small percentage of workers participate in formal preretirement preparation programs, and the majority of organizations do not even offer such programs. Research at the organizational level suggests that few employers provide such programs.[87,88] Fortunately, the situation may be improving. The number of professionals who are involved in administering preretirement programs is increasing. Membership in The International Society of Pre-Retirement Planners grew from 150 in 1983 to 750 in 1988.[86] Hopefully, the increasing number of opportunities will result in better planning on the part of all workers, especially those who are approaching retirement age.

COMPREHENSIVENESS OF PROGRAMS

Preretirement programs range from single sessions with individual employees discussing benefits to several group sessions covering a broad array of topics.[89] The most common topic covered in preretirement programs is a financial planning.[90] Other topics commonly covered in comprehensive programs include health issues, leisure, housing, interpersonal relationships, legal issues, the use of time, and adjustment to changing roles.[86,89,90]

DO RETIREMENT PLANNING PROGRAMS WORK?

While there has not been a great deal of research,[91] there is some evidence that these programs do improve the retirement experience. They have been effective in improving participants' attitudes toward retirement,[92] increasing the amount of planning,[93,94] increasing retirement knowledge,[94] and enhancing satisfaction with retirement over time. The benefits of these programs, however, may not be sustained over time.[95]

INFORMAL PREPARATION

It is clear that some form of planning is essential. However, people do not have to attend formal programs to prepare for retirement. Informal methods, such as consulting with advisors and getting support from retired friends and family members, are much more common than participating in formal programs[97] and can improve satisfaction, expectations, and knowledge.[97] In fact, informal means may be more effective than formal ones.[96,98]

ALTERNATIVES TO RETIREMENT

Surveys estimating the preference for continued work after retirement suggest that more than half of retirees would like to continue some part-time work rather than retire totally.[99-101] Far fewer actually do so. There are several possible explanations for this.[102] Alternative work schedules are not readily available,[103] and individuals may be unable to find part-time work in their area of expertise. A large variety of alternative part-time options exist (Table 10–2),[104,105] and employers may retain highly skilled workers by providing one or more of these options.

Many advantages for older employees result from these options. They can continue to earn an income and remain productive. Phased or alternative work options also enable the older person to adjust psychologically to life without constant work demands, and the

TABLE 10–2 **Part-time Work Alternatives**	
Job sharing	Two or more part-time workers share hours, responsibilities, and benefits of one job.[104]
Job splitting	A single job's tasks are divided and assigned to two or more employees.[105]
Work sharing	One group of workers reduces its hours to enable employment of another group.[105]
Phased retirement	Gradual reduction in hours or extended nonwork periods of several months at a time.[104]
Job transfer	Transfer to a job with fewer responsibilities.[106]
Reemployment	Rehiring of retirees on a temporary basis.[106]
Flextime	Full-time work with flexible working hours.[106]
Variable days	A variation on flextime in which work days vary.

shorter or flexible work hours make it possible for workers to take care of personal matters more easily. The major barriers for older employees are the social security earnings test, tax penalties, and pension plans that preclude working or limit hours.[106] Additionally, job coordination may be difficult,[104] and many of these options fail to provide benefits for the older workers.

Advantages for employers include decreased absenteeism, turnover, and tardiness, increased productivity, and decreased overtime costs.[104,106] Older workers have fewer voluntary absences, less turnover, fewer accidents,[26] and can provide ideal role models to younger employees. They can also help train younger employees and may attract older consumers.[104] Disadvantages for employers include supervision and scheduling difficulties[104] and the potential for higher benefit costs.

UNEMPLOYED OLDER WORKERS

The unemployment rate of older adults 60 and over is the lowest among all age ranges.[107] These rates are often just estimates, though, because older discouraged workers may choose to retire rather than continue a frustrating job search. It takes an average of 7 weeks longer for an older worker to find employment compared to a younger worker, and if one is a black male, a male with health problems, or one with less formal education, this time is even longer.[108] When the number of discouraged workers are added into the unemployment rates, the rate becomes much higher, 2.9 to 4.8 percent.[107] These rates are closer to those of younger workers.

DISPLACED WORKERS

With the many recent company buyouts, layoffs, and closings and increases in technology, the number of displaced workers is dramatically increasing. Plant closings and layoffs together were responsible for the loss of over 11.5 million jobs between the years 1979 and 1984.[109] Job displacement has been found to be related to decreases in income and future job status, loss of pension benefits, increases in drug abuse, suicide, divorce, depression, illness, and homicide.[109,110]

In many cases, older workers are less likely to be displaced and more likely to be recalled for employment. Yet, when additional training is required due to technological changes, older workers are more likely to be displaced.[108] Federal employment and training programs are available for displaced or disadvantaged workers 14 years of age and over. The Senior Community Service Employment Program, under Title V of the Older Americans Act, is a program specially designed for older workers. Additionally, the Job Training Partnership Act allocates special funds for older unemployed adults. There is a great disparity, though, between the number of eligible older people and the number participating in such program.[108]

CONCLUSION

In the future, older workers are expected to represent a smaller proportion of the work force. At the same time, their absolute work force number will increase.

The decision to retire or continue working reflects a complex array of factors including economic well-being, personal preference, subjective health, attitudes regarding leisure, and the desire to continue work.

Contradictions in the research literature must continue to be clarified. Emphasis needs to be placed on individual differences in the nature of life and work experience. Satisfaction and ability to work reflect normative aging, generational differences, and unique life events of the older adult worker. Intervention in the workplace in such areas as wellness promotion, training and retraining, and human resources management may make work life extension a more frequent choice.

The ultimate responsibility for maintaining professional competence rests on the individual employee. At the same time, an organization can foster competence by providing updating opportunities, challenging work assignments, and interaction with coworkers and management.

Research on retirement indicates that in the 1990s we will need to carefully weigh the importance of voluntary and involuntary decisions to retire and relevant factors related to satisfaction. For over 20 years, a major emphasis has been on the positive aspects and normalcy of retirement and approaches to facilitate the transition. At the same time, the United States stands alone in its advocacy for the rights of older adult workers to continue to work if they are capable and able. A serious question for the future is what efforts will be made to make the workplace more attractive to work life extension.

REVIEW QUESTIONS

1. *In what ways are the capabilities and needs of older workers different from those of younger workers?*

2. *An employer in a midsize company is interested in retaining its older*

workers for as long as possible. She is considering implementing both wellness and retraining programs for those workers but is unsure about potential benefits and best structure for these programs. As a consultant to the company, what information would you gather, and what considerations would you advise her to review before making a decision?

3. *You are working with an older person who is trying to decide whether or not to retire. What factors would you encourage him or her to consider?*

4. *You have a client who does not want to retire but is no longer interested in working full time. What alternatives might be available?*

REFERENCES

1. Sterns, HL and Alexander, RA: Industrial gerontology: The aging individual and work. Annual Review of Gerontology and Geriatrics 7:243, 1987.
2. Sterns, HL, Matheson, NK and Schwartz, LS: Work and retirement. In Ferraro, KF (ed): Gerontology: Perspectives and Issues. Springer, New York, 1990.
3. Kutscher, RE and Fullerton, HN: The aging labor force. In Bluestone, I, Montgomery, RJV and Owen, JD (eds): The Aging of the American Work Force. Wayne State University Press, Detroit, 1990, p 37.
4. Taeuber, C: Older workers: Force of the future? In Robinson, PK, Livingston, J and Birren, JE (eds): Plenum Press, New York, 1984, p 75.
5. Berch, B: The Endless Day: The Political Economy of Women And Work. Harcourt Brace Jovanovich, San Diego, 1982.
6. Fullerton, HN: The 1995 labor force: BLS's latest projections. Monthly Labor Review, Nov 17, 1985.
7. Doeringer, PB: Economic security, labor market flexibility, and bridges to retirement. In Doeringer, PB (ed): Bridges to Retirement, ILR Press, Cornell University, Ithaca, NY, 1990.
8. Ruhn, CJ: Career jobs, bridge employment and retirement. In Doeringer, PB (ed): Bridges to Retirement. ILR Press, Cornell University, Ithaca, NY, 1990.
9. Quinn, JF and Burkhauser, RV: Work and retirement. In Binstock, RH and George, LK (ed): Handbook of Aging and the Social Sciences, ed 3. Academic Press, San Diego, 1990, p 307.
10. Newquist, DD: Toward assessing health and functional capacity for policy development on work-life extension. In Birren, J, Robinson, P and Livingston, J (eds): Age, Health and Employment. Prentice-Hall, Englewood Cliffs, NJ, 1986, p 27.
11. Robinson, PK: Age, health, and job performance. In Birren, JE, Robinson, PK and Livingston, JE (eds): Age, Health and Employment. Prentice-Hall, Englewood Cliffs, NJ, 1986.
12. LaBar, G: The 1990's: What challenges await safety and health professionals? Occupational Hazards 51:53, 1989.
13. Pfeiffer, GJ: Health promotion programs for older workers. Generations 8:28, 1989.
14. Hollander, RB and Hale, JF: Work site health promotion programs: Ethical issues. American Journal of Health Promotion 2:37, 1987.
15. Wood, EA, Olmstead, GW and Craig, JC: An evaluation of lifestyle risk factors and absenteeism after two years in a work site health promotion program. American Journal of Health Promotion 4:128, 132, 1989.
16. Pelletier, KR: Healthy people in healthy places: Health promotion programs in the work place. In Cataldo, MF and Coates, TJ (eds): Health and Industry: A Behavioral Medicine Perspective. Wiley, New York, 1986.
17. Levin, R: Wellness programs for older workers and retirees. Washington Business Group on Health, Washington, DC, 1987.
18. Deobil, SJ: Physical fitness for retirees. American Journal of Health Promotion 4:85, 1989.
19. Connell, CM, Davies, RM, Rosenberg, AM and Fisher, EB: Retirees; perceived incentives and barriers to participation in health promotion activities. Health Education Research 3:325, 1988.
20. Rakowski, W, Carl, F and Flora, JA: Health education for older workers: Interest and preferences of university employees aged 55 and over. Family Community Health 11:65, 1988.
21. Fitch, VL and Slivinske, LR: Maximizing effects of wellness programs for the elderly. Health Social Work 13:61, 1988.
22. Jorgensen-Snyder, C and Barrett, GV. The Age Discrimination and Employment Act: A review of court decisions. Exp Aging Res 14:3, 1988.
23. Avolio, BJ, Waldman, DA and McDaniel, MA: Age and work performance in non-managerial jobs: The effects of experience and occupational type. Academy of Management Journal 33:407, 1990.
24. Waldman, DA and Avolio, BJ: A meta-analysis of age differences in job performance. J Appl Physiol 71:33, 1986.
25. Waldman, DA and Avolio, BJ: Aging and work performance in perspective. Unpublished manuscript, State University of New York at Binghamton, 1990.
26. Rhodes, SR: Age-related differences in work attitudes and behavior. A review and conceptual analysis. Psychol Bull 93:328, 1983.
27. McEvoy, GM and Cascio, WF: Cumulative ev-

idence of the relationship between employee age and job performance. Journal of Applied Psychology 74:11, 1989.

28. Miller, DB: Organizational, environmental, and work design strategies that foster competence. In Willis, SL and Dubin, SS (eds): Maintaining Professional Competence. Jossey-Bass, San Francisco, 1990.

29. Giniger, S, Dispenzieri, A and Eisenberg, J: Age, experience, and performance on speech and skill jobs in an applied setting. J Appl Psychol 68:469, 1983.

30. Fossum, JA, Arvey, RD, Paradise, CA and Robbins, NE: Modeling the skills obsolescence process: A psychological/economic integration. Academy of Management Review 11:363, 1986.

31. Willis, SL and Dubin, SS: Maintaining professional competence: Directions and possibilities. In Willis, SL and Dubin, SS (eds): Maintaining Professional Competence. Jossey-Bass, San Francisco, 1990.

32. Dalton, GW and Thompson, PH: Accelerating obsolescence of older engineers. Harvard Business Review 49:57, 1971.

33. Shearer, RL and Steger, JA: Manpower obsolescence: A new definition and empirical investigation of personal values. Academy of Management Journal 18:263, 1975.

34. Willis, SL and Tosti-Vassey, JL: Professional obsolescence in mid-career college faculty. Paper presented at the Eastern Psychology Association, April 19, 1986.

35. American Association of Retired Persons: The aging workforce: Managing an aging work force. Older Employees Instructional Resources for Instructors of Higher Education, 1990.

36. Lillard, LA and Tan, HW: Private sector training: Who gets it and what are its effects? Rand Corporation (for the US Department of Labor), Santa Monica, 1986.

37. Sterns, HL: Training and retraining adult and older adult workers. In Birren, JE, Robinson, PK and Livingston, JE (eds): Age, Health and Employment. Prentice-Hall, Englewood Cliffs, NJ, 1986, p 93.

38. Sterns, HL and Doverspike, D: Training and developing the older worker: Implications for human resource management. In Dennis, H (ed): Fourteen Steps to Managing an Aging Workforce. Lexington, New York, 1988.

39. Farr, JL and Middlebrooks, CL: Enhancing motivation to participate in professional development. In Willis, SL and Dubin, SS (eds): Maintaining Professional Competence. Jossey-Bass, San Francisco, 1990.

40. Kaufman, HG: Relations of ability and interest to currency of professional knowledge among engineers. J Appl Psychol 56:495, 1972.

41. Kaufman, HG: Management techniques for maintaining a competent professional workforce. In Willis, SL and Dubin, SS (eds): Maintaining Professional Competence. Jossey-Bass, San Francisco, 1990.

42. Pelz, DC and Andrews, FM: Scientist and Organizations. Wiley, New York, 1976.

43. Forisha-Kovach, B: The Flexible Organization. Prentice-Hall, Englewood Cliffs, NJ, 1984.

44. Fossum, JA and Arvey, RD: Market place and organizational factors that contribute to obsolescence. In Willis, SL and Dubin, SS (eds): Maintaining Professional Competence. Jossey-Bass, San Francisco, 1990.

45. Votruba, JC: Strengthening competence and vitality in midcareer faculty. In Willis, SL and Dubin, SS (eds): Maintaining Professional Competence. Jossey-Bass, San Francisco, 1990.

46. Lawrence, JH: Developmental needs as intrinsic incentives. In Baldwin, RG (ed): Incentives for Faculty Vitality. Jossey-Bass, San Francisco, 1985, pp 59–68.

47. Cross, KP: The missing link: Connecting adult learners to learning resources. College Entrance Examination Board, New York, 1978.

48. Peterson, DA: The older worker: Myths and realities. Andrus Gerontology Center, USC, Los Angeles, 1980.

49. Rosen, B and Jerdee, TH: Older employees: New roles for values resources. Dow-Jones-Irwin, Homewood, 1985.

50. Peterson, DA: Facilitating education for older learners. Jossey-Bass, San Francisco, 1987.

51. Cooperman, LF and Keast, FD: Adjusting to an Older Workforce. Van Nostrand Reinhold, New York, 1983.

52. Wexley, KN and Latnam, GP: Developing and Training Human Resources in Organizations. Scott, Foresman, Glenview, IL, 1981.

53. Belbin, E and Belbin, RI: Problems in Adult Retraining. Heineman Publishing, London, 1972.

54. Treat, NJ and Reese, HW: Age imagery and pacing in paired-associate learning. Developmental Psychology 12:119, 1976.

55. Elias, PK, Elias, MF, Robbins, MA and Gage, PL: Acquisition of work processing skills by younger, middle-aged, and older adults. Psychology and Aging 2:340, 1987.

56. Valasek, DL and Sterns, HL: Task analysis and training: Applications from lab to field. Paper presented as part of the "Symposium on Industrial Gerontological Psychology: Why Survive?" 34th Annual Meeting of the Gerontological Society of America, November, Toronto, Ontario, 1981.

57. Knowles, MS: The Modern Practice of Adult Education. Association Press, Chicago, 1989.

58. Sterns, HL and Doverspike, D: Aging and the training and learning process. In Goldstein, I and Associates (eds): Training and Development in Organizations. Jossey-Bass, San Francisco, 1989, p 299.

59. Belbin, E and Downs, SM: Activity learning and the older worker. Ergonomics 7:429, 1964.

60. Belbin, RM: The discovery methods in train-

ing older workers. In Sheppard, HL (ed): Toward an Industrial Gerontology. Schenkman, Cambridge, 1970, p 56.

61. Gist, M, Schwoerer, C and Rosen, B: The influence of training methods and trainee age on the acquisition of computer skills. Personnel Psychology 41:255, 1988.

62. Johnson, ES and Williamson, JB: Retirement in the United States. In Markides, KS and Cooper, CI (eds): Retirement in Industrial Societies. Wiley, New York, 1987.

63. Bosse, R, Aldwin, CM, Levenson, MR and Ekerdt, DJ: Mental health differences among retirees and workers: Findings from the Normative Age Study. Psychology and Aging 2:383, 1987.

64. George, LK, Fillenbaum, GG and Palmore, E: Sex differences in the antecedents and consequences of retirement: Journal of Gerontology 39:644, 1984.

65. Beehr, TA: The process of retirement: A review and recommendations for future investigation. Personnel Psychology 39:31, 1986.

66. Howard, JH, Marshall, J, Rechnitzer, PA, Cunningham, DA and Donner, A: Adapting to retirement. J Am Geriatr Soc 30:488, 1982.

67. Kimmel, DC, Prince, KF and Walker, JW: Retirement choice and retirement satisfaction. J Am Gerontol 33:575, 1978.

68. Markides, KS: Reasons for retirement and adaptation to retirement by elderly Mexican Americans. In Standford, EP (ed): Retirement: Concepts and Realities of Ethnic Minority Elders. San Diego State University, University Center on Aging, San Diego, 1978.

69. Peretti, PO and Wilson, C: Voluntary and involuntary retirement of aged males and their effect on emotional satisfaction, usefulness, self-image, emotional stability, and interpersonal relationships. Int J Aging Hum Dev 6:1311, 1975.

70. Palmore, EB, Burchett, BM, Fillenbaum, GG, George, LK and Wallman, LM: Retirement: Causes and Consequences. Springer, New York, 1985.

71. Beck, SH: Position in the economic structure and unexpected retirement. Res Aging 5: 197, 1983.

72. Hayslip, B and Panek, PE: Adult development and aging. Harper and Row, New York, 1989.

73. Palmore, E, George, LK and Fillenbaum, GG: Predictors of retirement. Journal of Gerontology 37:733, 1982.

74. Prothero, J and Beach, LR: Retirement decisions: Expectation, intention, and action. Journal of Applied Social Psychology 14:162, 1984.

75. Dorfman, LT, Kohout, FJ and Heckert, DA: Retirement satisfaction in the rural elderly. Res Aging 7:577, 1985.

76. Liebig, PS: The three legged stool of retirement income. In Dennis, H (ed): Retirement Preparation: What Retirement Specialists Need to Know. Lexington Books, Lexington, MA, 1984, p 43.

77. Riddick, CC and Daniel, SN: The relative contribution of leisure activities and other factors to the mental health of older women. Journal of Leisure Research 16:136, 1984.

78. Maxwell, N: The retirement experience: Psychological and financial linkages to the labor market. Social Science Quarterly 66:22, 1985.

79. Belgrave, LL: The effects of race differences in work history, work attitudes, economic resources, and health or women's retirement. Res Aging 10:383, 1988.

80. Behling, JH and Merves, ES: Pre-retirement attitudes and financial preparedness: A cross-cultural and gender analysis. Journal of Sociology and Social Welfare 12:113, 1985.

81. Seibert, EF and Seibert, J: Retirement: Crises or opportunity. Personal Administrator 31:43, 1986.

82. Behling, JH: Planning during pre-retirement years and differential patterns of retirement preparedness. Paper presented at the Interdisciplinary Conference on Health and Human Services, Charleston, WV, 1981.

83. Draper, JE: Work attitudes and retirement adjustment. University of Wisconsin Bureau of Business Research and Service. Madison, 1967.

84. Meier, EL: Over 65: Expectations and realities of work and retirement. Industrial Gerontology 2:95, 1975.

85. Singleton, JF: Retirement: Its effects on the individual. Adaptation and Aging 6:1, 1985.

86. Dennis, H: The current state of retirement planning. Generations 13:28, 1989.

87. Morrison, M and Jedrziewski, MK: Retirement planning: Everybody benefits. Personnel Administration 1:74–80, 1988.

88. Underwood, D: Toward self-reliance in retirement planning. Harvard Business Review 3:18, 1984.

89. Feit, MD and Tate, NP: Health and mental health issues in preretirement programs. Employee Assistance Quarterly 1:49, 1986.

90. Rowen, RB and Wilks, CS: Pre-retirement planning, a quality of life issue for retirement. Employee Assistance Quarterly 2:45, 1987.

91. Olson, SK: Current status of corporate retirement preparation programs. Aging and Work 14:175, 1981.

92. Shooksmith, G: Change in attitude to retirement following a short pre-retirement planning seminar. J Psychol 114:3, 1983.

93. Fitzpatrick, EW: Evaluating a new retirement planning program—results with hourly workers. Aging and Work 2:87, 1979.

94. Glamser, FD and Dejong, GK: The efficacy of preretirement programs for industrial workers. Journal of Gerontol 30:595, 1975.

95. Glamser, FD: Predictors of retirement attitudes. Aging and Work 4:23, 1981.

96. Evans, L, Ekerdt, DJ and Bosse, R: Proximity to retirement and anticipatory involvement: Findings from the Normative Aging Study. Journal of Gerontol 40:368, 1985.

97. Kamouri, AL and Cavanaugh, JC: Research

note: The impact of preretirement education programmes on workers' preretirement socialization. J of Occupational Behavior 7: 245, 1986.

98. Kroeger, N: Preretirement preparation: Sex differences in access, sources, and use. In Szinovacz, M (ed): Women's Retirement: Policy Implications of Recent Research. Sage, Beverly Hills, 1982.

99. Usher, CE: Alternative Work Options for Older Workers: Part I—Employees' Interest, Aging Work. Andrus Gerontology Center, Los Angeles, 1981, p 74.

100. Cooperman, LF, Keast, FD and Montgomery, DG: Older workers and part-time work schedules. Personnel Administrator 26:35, 1981.

101. Sheppard, HT and Mantovani, BE: Part Time Employment After Retirement. Travelers Insurance Companies, Hartford, 1982.

102. Parnes, HS: Postretirement employment: How much is there: How much is wanted? Generations XIII 2:29, 1989.

103. American Society for Personnel Administration and Commerce Clearing House, 1988. ASPA/CCH Survey Human Resources Management. Commerce Clearing House, Chicago, 1988, p 1.

104. Paul, CE: Implementing alternative work arrangements for older workers. In Dennis, H (ed): Fourteen Steps in Managing an Aging Work Force. Lexington Books, Lexington, MA, 1988, p 113.

105. Newstrom, JW and Pierce, JL: Alternative work schedules: The state of the art. Personnel Administrator 24:19, 1979.

106. Rosow, JM: Extending working life. In Bluestone, I, Montgomery, RJV and Owen, JD (eds): The Aging of the American Work Force. Wayne State University Press, Detroit, 1990, p 399.

107. Sandell, SH: The Problem Isn't Age: Work and Older Americans. Praeger, New York, 1987.

108. Sandell, SH and Baldwin, SE: Older workers and employment shifts. Policy responses to displacement. In Bluestone, I, Montgomery, RJV and Owen, JD (eds): The Aging of the American Work Force. Wayne State University Press, Detroit, 1990.

109. Kinicki, A, Bracker, J, Kreitner, R, Lockwood, C and Lemark, D: Socially responsible for plant closing. Personnel Administrator 32:116, 1987.

110. Frese, M and Mohr, G: Prolonged employment and depression in older workers. A longitudinal study of intervening variables. Soc Sci and Med 25:173, 1987.

*Age is opportunity no less than youth
itself, though in another dress. And as
the evening twilight fades away, the sky
is filled with stars, invisible by day.*
— H. W. LONGFELLOW, *Morituri Salutamus,*
stanza 24, 1875.

Chapter

11

Leisure

ANITA BUNDY
JEAN M. CANNELLA

OBJECTIVES

By the end of this chapter, readers will be able to:

1 Define leisure.

2 Discuss three major leisure theories: activity, stereotypes, and derivation.

3 Discuss leisure as a statement of identity.

4 Define the important characteristics of leisure: control, motivation, disengagement, and absorption.

5 Understand the importance of these characteristics in intervening with clients.

Leisure activities represent one of myriad types of activities in which older people engage.[1] Through all their activities, older individuals make important statements about who they are.[1,2] Although *leisure* typically is defined as a set of activities, it also can be defined as an experience.[1,3] When individuals experience leisure, they typically become totally absorbed[4] in activity that:

- Is freely chosen[2]
- Allows them to disengage from the concerns of ''real'' life[3]

Individuals who, because of age-related barriers or disabling conditions, lose the ability to engage in treasured leisure activities, lose an important life experience and means of self-expression.[5] Thus, there is a need for professionals who intervene with older individuals to take seriously the value and promotion of leisure.

Viewed as a statement of identity and as an experience rather than activities done in leftover time, leisure takes on tremendous importance to professionals who intervene with older adults.

This chapter is composed of five major sections:

1. We critically analyze existing leisure theories and research.
2. We discuss leisure as a statement of identity.
3. We probe four important components of leisure: control, motivation, disengagement, and the ability of the individual to become completely "absorbed."
4. We offer a tentative model of leisure designed particularly for use by service professionals (e.g., occupational, recreational, and activity therapists and social workers) who seek to assess and promote leisure with older clients.
5. We provide suggestions and examples of the use of this model.

APPLYING EXISTING LEISURE RESEARCH

Because of the paucity of research and theory-based literature in their own fields, occupational and activity therapists, and social workers who promote leisure with older clients must draw heavily on theories and research of other professionals (e.g., psychologists, sociologists). While existing psychology and sociology literature gives service providers important insights and ideas about what to expect and how to help their clients, they do not, and never were intended to, meet all the service-related needs of clinicians. Given the group designs of published studies and the tremendous amounts of variance that generally goes unexplained, the likelihood that a particular individual will not conform to the pattern of variables described in existing literature is very high.

Each publication in professional literature describes, or reflects, a particular definition of leisure and a hypothesized relationship among constructs related to leisure. To apply existing theories and experimental results to a particular in-

dividual, a professional first must understand the implicit and explicit definitions, assumptions, and relationships among constructs and limitations associated with a particular theory.

Kelly[1] described and criticized three "inadequate models of leisure" that typically underlie research and theoretical treatments of leisure. He referred to these as:

• The activity model
• The derivation model
• The stereotypes model

Kelly indicated that, while each of these three models contains useful insight and is based on some evidence, "the problem with each is that it is partial and may be misleading."

When the activity model forms the basis for research in leisure, subjects typically are asked to indicate their leisure activities, often selected from a predetermined list of activities (e.g., gardening, playing cards), and to describe the frequency with which they engage in those activities. Kelly[1] indicated that "from this perspective leisure has often been viewed as activity that fills time and substitutes for lost relationships and investments" rather than as "freedom for intrinsic satisfaction, development, and social integration" (p. 273).

Another problem with the activity model of leisure is the narrowness of the leisure activities from which the subjects must select. Many potential leisure activities do not appear on the lists and activities that are thought of as self-care or work (e.g., bathing) are omitted even though they may be viewed as leisure activities by the respondent. Further, a particular individual may commonly engage in some listed activities (e.g., cooking) for reasons other than leisure. It is likely that many subjects respond more to the question, "In which of these activities do you engage?" than to the question, "In which of these activities do you engage for leisure?" Further, investigators using this model usually assume that the more activities in which an individual engages, the better. There is no evidence that this is true. In fact, greater intensity of involvement in fewer activities may be more desirable than less intense involvement in many activities.[1]

Allen and Chin-Sang[6] also criticized the activity approach to leisure for its lack of generalizability. The subjects for investigations based on this model typically are white North American males; the results cannot be applied readily to women or to males of other ethnic or racial origins.

When the derivation model is used to understand leisure, researchers typically use leisure as a dependent variable to be explained by work- or social-status-related factors. In this view, leisure is, at best, a secondary concern "related to recuperation from and for work, status symbolism, and the occupation of idle hours. The intense personal engagement of some individuals [is] seen as an anomaly or as the result of some kind of alienation from primary roles."[1]

Leisure clearly is more than time left over from work and self-care. Thus, professionals attempting to apply research based on the derivation model of understanding must take care not to minimize the importance of leisure. Further, because we view leisure as experience (rather than as activity) and as an important influence on and reflection of self-identity, we seek to promote older individuals' involvement in leisure that meets their self-defined needs. Intense involvement is an important part of our model of leisure.

When the stereotypes model is used to understand leisure, attempts are made to categorize leisure activities and to predict which segments of the population are most likely to participate in activity from these categories. Generally, this is accomplished by factor-and-cluster analysis procedures.

Literature based on the assumptions of the stereotypes model provides some important insights to professionals intervening with older adults. As Kelly indicated[1]:

> Leisure choices are made in situations with an interplay of influences, opportunities, and aims. Further, socialization factors, access to environments, and identity-development tasks change through the life course. [However,] if we are to grasp the meanings and functions of leisure in later life, it is necessary to go beyond oversimplistic models to approaches that encompass the complexity of both leisure and its contexts. (p. 278)

Clear-cut stereotypes of leisure participation are not supported in the literature. Age, sex, race, and social position, even when considered collectively, account for very little (less than 15 percent) of the variance to be explained.[1] Further, when leisure activities are categorized statistically[1]:

> Activities with the most widespread participation do not appear in the factors at all, presumably because they [do] not differentiate groups of participants. Such activities as informal family interaction, reading, watching television, listening to the radio or records or tapes, walking and hiking, and spending a social evening with relatives are absent from the factors. Rather than differentiate groups, they are common to the adult population. (p. 278)

Thus, when service professionals attempt to apply research based on the stereotypes model to a particular individual, they must consider the full range of leisure possibilities. They should not overemphasize participation in certain "leisure" pursuits or be too quick to develop stereotypical leisure programs. Leisure is a highly individualized experience. If we wish to learn about and promote leisure with particular individuals, we must tailor our assessments and interventions to those people. We must take care not to fall into the trap of stereotyping.

Professionals who intervene with older adults have a need and a responsibility to develop applied theories of leisure and to examine those theories through research. Because of clinicians' concerns with individuals, rather than with generalizations, those theories must be based on the broadest possible definition of leisure. According to Kelly[1]:

> The first requirement of any useful definition of leisure is that it be adequately inclusive. Leisure may include activity of low intensity, such as television watching,

as well as the higher intensity of the final rehearsal of a string quartet. It includes activity that is solitary as well as social, spontaneous as well as scheduled, and disciplined as well as relaxing. Leisure may take place at home as well as in special environments, be highly ritualized as well as processual, and take place entirely in the imagination as well as incorporate the full resources of mind and body. (p. 269)

In our model, we seek to apply this broad-based definition of leisure and leisure activities.

LEISURE AS A STATEMENT OF IDENTITY

We are what we do.[7] That is, our actions shape our selves. Each activity we perform is associated with a self-specific experience of that activity. The same activity is experienced very differently by different people. It is likely that the experience associated with any activity is more important than the activity itself in contributing to development.

Conversely, we do what we are.[7] That is, our actions reflect our selves; they are outward manifestations or statements of who we are. Through our actions, we tell others, and ourselves, about ourselves.

Each activity in which we engage reflects one or more life roles or identities.[1,8] Further, leisure roles and identities seem more important:

- To some people than others
- In certain periods of life than in others[1]

However, because leisure experiences are freely chosen, they seem to make a very special and important statement of who we are.[1,2]

It is common to decorate our homes with mementos of leisure experiences and pictures or other reminders of individuals with whom we commonly engage in leisure.[9,10] Older people, in particular, enjoy displaying those objects and reminiscing with other people about

events associated with them. In so doing, individuals make statements about their accomplishments, and perhaps more importantly, their identities.

Leisure identities and activities, perhaps in part because of their significant relationship with the perceived self, also seem to be particularly vulnerable to age-related barriers and disability. "If I can't do it the way (often translated 'as well as') I used to, I don't want to do it at all," is a comment frequently made by older people who no longer engage in particular leisure pursuits.

Rockwell-Dylla[10] related the story of Stan, a 62-year-old white male who had been an avid golfer prior to suffering a stroke. Following the stroke, he was unwilling even to hit whiffle balls in the yard, despite the urgings of his wife. Rockwell-Dylla wrote:

Stan didn't take [his wife] up on her suggestions because he knew he wouldn't be able to hold the golf club like he used to do with ease. He wasn't afraid of having to learn to do something in a new way, but what did concern him was how he appeared in front of other people. Stan shared with me how he thought the neighbors would make comments like "what's he trying to do, he's a disabled person, we don't want anything to do with him." (pp. 85–86)

Golfing once made a statement about Stan's physical prowess; however, following his stroke, he perceived that golfing would make a statement about his physical disability. Stan seemed to worry about looking foolish. Perhaps he feared that his neighbors would generalize his physical disability to a cognitive or mental impairment. He seemed to fear that his neighbors' memories of Stan, the athlete, would be replaced by visions of Stan the "cripple," or Stan "the fool." Stan could no longer make desirable statements about himself through golf, so he gave it up. Perhaps he would have benefited from having someone help him "change the frame" around golf. Rather than a statement of his incapacity, he might have been helped to transform golf into a statement of "triumph over adversity."

ELEMENTS OF LEISURE

Leisure both contributes to, and reflects, identity. Further, leisure, as was previously mentioned, is more aptly characterized as experience rather than activity. However, the experience of leisure generally occurs in the context of activity. Thus, in order to promote leisure, it is necessary to be able to separate leisure from nonleisure activities and experiences. It is possible to extract from that literature factors that contribute to and define leisure. We propose that four factors are particularly important. These are control, motivation, disengagement, and absorption. Each factor represents a complex interaction between an individual, his or her life experiences, and the environment. Thus each requires further discussion.

Control

Control is a complex phenomenon. When one is in control during an activity or event, he or she is free to choose what to do and with whom.[11] *Being in control* also refers to the ability to determine the outcome of an activity. In this section, we discuss multiple aspects of control as they apply to the determination of a leisure experience.

Freedom of Choice

Freedom of choice typically is the most important determinant of whether or not an activity is experienced as leisure.[2,12] Generally, if individuals must, or feel they must, perform a task or an activity, it is not leisure.[2] By this criterion, all activities can be leisure under certain circumstances. What may be among the most mundane of tasks for some people, for example, bathing, can become leisure for the individual who chooses to "steal" some time away from the concerns of daily life for a long, restful bubble bath.

Freedom of choice seems a fairly simple criterion for distinguishing leisure from nonleisure pursuits; however, the very simplicity of freedom of choice may make it confusing when trying to analyze the leisure value of complex activities for particular individuals. For example, is the grandmother who offers freely to care for her grandchildren, even though her son and daughter-in-law had no previous plans, experiencing leisure? Using the criterion of free choice alone, she is. It is likely that she actually does experience leisure during some, or even most, moments of the weekend; however, it is equally likely that there will be moments in that weekend when what the woman experiences is far from leisure, even though she has freely chosen to care for her grandchildren. Control entails more than making an initial decision to engage in an activity. In the course of that activity, one must also feel in control of its various aspects and components.

Control is not an all-or-none phenomenon. Rarely is a person in total control of any activity or event; in fact, total control may not be desirable. What is desirable is that the individual feel that his or her skills and abilities are matched to the challenges of the activity.[4,13] Many things contribute to feelings of control or lack of control; these include such dimensions as complexity of the activity, number of other people involved, and duration of the activity. In general, the more complex the activity, the more other people are involved, and the longer the duration, the less likely a person is to feel in control, and hence, to experience leisure.

Because control is such a complex issue, a freely chosen activity often is not determined to be a leisure experience until it has been completed. That is, until the individual can reflect on the experience and weigh the relative amount of control experienced, the determination of whether or not leisure was experienced cannot be made definitely. Sometimes, based on past experience or anticipation of relative lack of control, an individual may decide not to engage in a particular activity, or to alter it significantly, in order to increase the chances that leisure will be experienced.

For example, consider Barbara, a 60-year-old black woman who lives alone in a high-rise apartment in Chicago (Fig. 11–1). She has three daughters and several grandchildren who live locally and visit frequently. While she enjoys their company, she often wishes she could get away from their demands. Recently, Barbara received two plane tickets as a gift, enabling her to make two trips anywhere in the country or to take a companion with her on a single trip. As Barbara made plans to travel to Houston to visit a cousin for the Christmas holidays, she entertained the notion of taking Cherie, one of her older grandchildren, with her. In the end, however, she decided to take two trips by herself. In her words, "For a minute, I lost my mind. I thought it would be fun to take Cherie, but then I started thinking, 'I'm doing this for me. How much fun will I have if I take an 8-year-old along?' I'll go by myself to Houston. And I made a reservation to go to Atlanta for Thanksgiving. I have another cousin in Atlanta. She has a house there. I always have fun in Atlanta."

Barbara opted to use her tickets in a way that she perceived increased the chances she would experience leisure. She saw that if she traveled with an 8-year-old, she might have fewer opportunities to do what she wanted to do. Barbara might have experienced just as much leisure had she taken Cherie with her, but her past experiences suggested that having the responsibility for an 8-year-old significantly reduced her choices; thus, the chance for a leisure experience was also reduced.

Determination of Outcomes

For some leisure experiences, being in control extends to determining the outcome of an activity.[11] This is particularly true for creative endeavors; however, the need to determine the outcome of an activity is not always a part of the leisure experience. In fact, certain leisure activities are selected particularly for their lack of predictability. Many games fall under this rubric.[14] Bingo and card games often are listed by older adults as favorite leisure activities.[15–17] Yet when the players are certain of the

Figure 11–1 Barbara enjoys spending time with her grandchildren. (Photo courtesy of Anita Bundy, used with permission.)

outcome of the game (i.e., the winner), they throw in the chips or the hand; they either quit or begin a new game, thereby reintroducing the unpredictability.[14]

Even within games and other activities where lack of predictability is a part of the appeal, a certain amount of control must be present if the experience is to be leisure. The individual must feel in control of the necessary materials (e.g., cards, bingo chips) and other aspects of the situation (e.g., able to hear the bid of a partner or the bingo caller). In creative endeavors such as knitting, woodworking, and cooking, control includes the ability to manage materials in such a way as to construct a pleasing product. Activities vary widely in their demand for skill. The degree to which activities are experienced as leisure depends, in part, on the individual's physical skills and abilities (e.g., dexterity, strength); however, even the most physically skilled individual may lack the aesthetic sense to combine colors, shapes, or spices into a pleasing product; thus, physical skill alone does not ensure that an individual will have sufficient control in an activity to experience leisure.

Matching Challenges to Skill

With regard to control, what all the aforementioned activities have in common when they are experienced as leisure is that the challenges presented match the skills of the individual.[4,13] If that is not the case, no matter what the activity, the person engaging in it cannot be experiencing leisure. The grandmother caring for her grandchildren must feel that she can skillfully manage the range of events that she might encounter while babysitting. The older man who experiences leisure in woodworking must feel that he can manage the materials he will need to create a visually pleasing and, perhaps, utilitarian object. This may entail more than using tools and managing wood; it also may mean visualizing an object in a block of wood or creating jigs for completing some aspect of the project. Simi-

larly, the older woman knitting an afghan or a sweater for her husband and herself must be able to control the needles and the yarn and, perhaps, follow a pattern easily.

Optimal Levels of Choice

To be experienced as leisure, any activity must contain an optimal level of choice. Optimal choice is determined by the individual and is a function of that person's level of skill and experience in that activity. For example, the inexperienced painter, or the painter who perceives himself or herself as lacking certain skills or abilities, may be more likely to experience leisure with a paint-by-number picture than with a blank easel. On the other hand, the established artist probably would be bored with a paint-by-number picture.

Motivation

Motivation, the reason one chooses to engage in any activity, also is a variable typically discussed as a determinant of leisure. According to some leisure theories, motivation must be intrinsic; that is, the activity is done only for its own sake, for the pleasurable experience associated with it, and not for any long-term gains by the individual, payment, or the benefit of someone else.[2,4,13,18]

While motivation clearly is an important factor in the determination of leisure, the degree to which motivation must be intrinsic is not clear. What is clear is that the activity must have an *autotelic aspect*. That is, the individual must experience most or all of the various aspects of the activity as pleasurable, whether or not the activity was originally undertaken for its intrinsic value.[4]

This lack of clarity about whether or not the motivation for leisure activities is always intrinsic can be seen throughout the leisure-related literature. Many authors[3,6,15,16,18–21] have examined and discussed older individuals' motivations for leisure in general or for specific leisure activities. Typically, many motivations are listed. Havighurst's list is representative; he and his colleagues included the following as motivations typically associated with leisure activities:

- Just for the pleasure of it
- Welcome change from work
- New experience
- Contact with friends
- Chance to achieve something
- Make time pass
- Allows creativity
- Benefit to society
- Helps financially
- Promotes self-respect
- Gives me more standing with others
- Makes me popular

Further, Havighurst[15,16] and his colleagues[20,21] have indicated, not surprisingly, that certain motives are more commonly associated with certain leisure activities than with others and that certain individuals experience different motivations for the same activity. Havighurst and his colleagues are among the few researchers[6,22] who have attempted to examine individual differences in activity-specific motivations. These researchers have provided significant insight to professionals seeking to promote leisure with elderly clients.[1]

Clearly, not all the motivations for leisure activities listed by Havighurst[15,16] and his colleagues[20,21] can be considered intrinsic; however, there is no indication that the subjects of these investigations:

- Did not also experience intrinsic reward in their activities
- Found their activities to be less rewarding because of the relatively extrinsic character of the motivations associated with them

In fact, Mannell, Zuzanek, and Larson[18] found that elderly people experienced greater "flow" in activities they performed for their own long-term gain or for another's benefit; however, when the subjects indicated that they primarily performed particular leisure activities for extrinsic motivations, they may have been responding as much to perceived social acceptability as to their true motivations. The notion of justifying one's pleasure by the long-term gains associated with an activity or by the possibility of another's gain has been suggested by Ekerdt[23] in his discussion of the "busy ethic" and by Cohen[24] in his descriptions of adults playing with children.

Complexity of Motivation

The motivation to engage in a particular activity clearly is a complex phenomenon. As Havighurst[15,16] noted, the experience of leisure is strongly associated with one's personality. Individuals are of many different personality types; what "drives" one individual is very different from what drives another. Some individuals are clearly more people oriented than others.[25] Thus, some people perceive service to others as an important motivation for leisure[15,16,20,21] and derive meaning from it.[6,22] There is ample evidence this is true for both men and women.

Havighurst's[15,16,20,21] statements that leisure activities are associated with different motives for different people suggest a certain degree of complexity in the relationship between leisure and motivation. There may be many more motivations associated with a particular activity than are immediately apparent, and many powerful motivations may not appear on lists such as those developed by Havighurst. Uncovering an individual's motivation for a leisure activity is particularly important when the need arises to substitute one activity for another.

Ron is a 72-year-old white man; he is a retired engineer. As long as anyone can remember, Ron has built things. He spends a significant amount of time creating small pieces of furniture and repairing objects in his home. He enjoys these activities thoroughly; he expressed pleasure both in the completed project and with all steps of the process. He particularly enjoys figuring out how to do a project and creating the necessary jigs and devices needed for the project.

Several years ago, Ron experienced an illness that was exacerbated by the dust and chemical fumes associated with his woodworking. He was urged by his physician to give up woodworking and to replace it with another activity. Ron chose painting as an alternative since it seemed to offer many of the same benefits he derived from woodworking but without the negative consequences. That is, painting allowed him to be creative and to work with his hands.

For approximately 1 year, Ron painted instead of doing woodworking; he became a good painter. However, he also became increasingly disenchanted with his new leisure activity. Painting, while capturing some of the same benefits of woodworking, apparently was not a suitable substitute. After that year, Ron put away his paints permanently and, once again, took out his woodworking tools. "If I'm going to die," he expressed, "I'm going to die happy."

Clearly, the motivations for woodworking most salient to Ron were not captured in painting. Perhaps if Ron had worked with a professional trained to help him examine his motivations and recapture them in a suitable substitute, he might have been able to adopt a leisure activity that did not have the negative consequences associated with woodworking. Unfortunately, that did not happen.

Certainly, it sometimes is possible to capture the most salient motivations for one activity in another and thus to help a person substitute a new leisure activity for one in which he or she can no longer engage. Rockwell-Dylla[10] related the story of Les, a 90-year-old white man who had survived two strokes and a bout with cancer. Les was the retired owner of a paint company. Prior to his illnesses, he spent much of his leisure time decorating the interior of his home (which he had built). As a result of both his age and his disability, Les was no longer able to move furniture and perform other activities required for interior decorating. While he might have elected to direct others in the interior

decoration, this apparently did not hold the same motivation for Les (or perhaps for the others in his life). At the suggestion of an occupational therapist, Les got involved in decoupage. He created dishes and other decorative objects, mixing and matching colors and patterns as he desired. This substitution of decoupage for home decorating was highly successful with Les. Although many of the most obvious traits of home decoration were not present, apparently the motivation most important to Les was "playing" with colors; that could be recaptured in decoupage.

Disengagement

Kleiber[3] defined *disengagement* as "the creating of a space/time context through the removal or relinquishing of some constraint or set of constraints" (p. 231). In the experience of leisure, disengagement from the constraints of real life is a necessary component.[3] Constraints may be real or perceived, and they take many forms (e.g., family demands, financial constraints, pain, poor health, or disability).[15,16,26,27] If an individual is to experience leisure, he or she must be able to disengage temporarily from those constraints.

As Kleiber[3] noted, disengagement alone may be sufficient to produce the leisure experience; however, many individuals find it extraordinarily difficult to maintain their disengagement from real-life concerns unless they subsequently engage in some activity in which they can become totally absorbed.

Engaging in activity that allows one to disengage from some of life's demands does not necessarily ensure that an individual will experience leisure. When individuals find that they are motivated to engage only, or primarily, in activities that depend on certain skills, abilities, or resources that are constrained, they have extraordinary difficulty experiencing leisure.

Mary is a 79-year-old white woman whose vision has become progressively more limited over the past 15 years; her visual impairments are, in part, the result of excessive drinking. Throughout her life, reading has been a primary leisure source for Mary; she often read for several hours a day. However, Mary's vision has now worsened to the point that she can no longer read even enlarged print. Mary expresses no interest in talking books, tapes, or the radio as a substitute for reading. In fact, she has been able to find no activity, except drinking, that enables her to disengage from the constraints of her life. The only activities in which she expresses interest are visually dependent. Thus, her "leisure" pursuits only serve to continually remind her of the constraints of her life that most concern her. As she attempts to disengage, she actually becomes more aware of her difficulties. Mary succeeds in disengaging by drinking, but drinking exacerbates her visual impairments and contributes to her decreased ability to seek alternative and true leisure experiences. Mary is caught in a vicious cycle. She is motivated to engage in a leisure pursuit for which she lacks a critical ability; because she has little "control" of the written word, she is unable to disengage from the constraints of her visual impairment. To succeed in developing alternative leisure options, Mary will need help to examine the benefits she once derived from reading and to devise activities that provide some of the most important benefits without depending heavily on vision. Alternatively, Mary might be helped to examine other important motivations that, if satisfied through activity, might enable disengagement and opportunities for leisure.

Absorption

Numerous authors[3,4,12,13,28] have used various terms (*flow, engagement, involvement*) to describe the total absorption in an activity that characterizes leisure. Loss of self-consciousness, the open cognitive set, and the pleasurable sensations associated with total absorption in a leisure activity are crucial to the experience of an activity as leisure.[3,4,13]

The concept of total absorption is particularly powerful in examining and seeking to promote leisure with older individuals. Asking older adults, "Tell me about the activities you do (or have done in the past) in which you become totally absorbed (forget about everything else)" has been much more successful in identifying the experience of leisure for an individual than asking people what they do in their leisure.

In response to the latter, people often indicate that they have no leisure. If they attempt to answer the question, they seem constrained by listing activities that have been socially sanctioned as leisure, for example, golf, gardening, games, or television. In contrast, when people talk about activities in which they become totally absorbed, they often relate thick narrative accounts[29] of their experiences. It is then quite easy to elicit further information from them about the benefits they derive from those pursuits. In the case of individuals who have lost the ability to engage in those absorbing activities, one also can examine whether or not it is possible, or desirable, to adapt the previously enjoyed activity or a suitable substitute.

Desiree is a 78-year-old traditional Navajo woman. In addition to all the "traditional activities" in which she has engaged since a very young age, Desiree works several hours each week as a volunteer in a day care center supported by the Navajo tribal government. When Desiree was asked (through an interpreter) what she did in her leisure, she laughed aloud. She indicated that even as a child she had not had time to play. She lived with her disabled grandmother and was responsible for all the home maintenance tasks that required mobility (including cooking and cleaning) and for tending the sheep. All her life, chores took up most of her time; there was always something that needed to be done. Play and leisure were "a waste of time"; she rarely even sat down to rest. Desiree clearly was not interested in talking about leisure. Throughout the dialogue, her tone of voice remained stern, and, at one point, she asked why the interviewer was asking such silly questions.

In contrast, when Desiree was asked what she did, now or in the past, in which she became totally absorbed, her voice took on warmth and she became involved and interested in the conversation. Desiree began to talk about weaving. She indicated that she learned to spin yarn when she was about 3 years old and to weave as soon as she was old enough. When she was engaged in spinning or weaving, she forgot everything else.

Navajo women do not weave their rugs from patterns; rather, they create the patterns they envision in their heads on the loom. Desiree recounted that as the pattern of the rug began to emerge and the rug "took on a life of its own," she became more and more involved in its creation. Csikszmentihayli[13] and his colleagues[30,31] described similar benefits when they asked adults about times they experienced total absorption in an activity.

For professionals seeking to promote leisure with older individuals, this method for examining leisure as an experience in which one becomes totally absorbed is particularly valuable.[32] Rowles[33] noted that older people respond particularly well to interview. Interview for the purposes of developing intervention is most useful when it elicits rich narrative description and the opportunity to seek additional detail as needed.

Total absorption can occur in the context of virtually any activity, as long as the person engaged in the activity feels a sense of control and is able to disengage from his or her real-life concerns[3,4,13] and when that activity is sufficiently motivating. We do not seek to help older individuals to conform to socially accepted classifications of leisure activity. Rather, we seek to enable individuals to become totally absorbed in, and reap the accompanying benefits of, self-defined leisure. In so doing, we seek to help them make the kind of statements they want to make about who they are as individuals.

A TENTATIVE MODEL

We have described four concepts related to leisure:

1. Control
2. Motivation
3. Disengagement
4. Absorption

None of these can be described as all-or-none phenomena; each is much better described with a continuum. We propose that control, motivation, and disengagement, collectively, determine whether or not a person becomes totally absorbed in an activity; that is, whether or not the person experiences leisure. The summative contributions of control, motivation, and disengagement to absorption are illustrated schematically in Figure 11–2.

The elements of leisure are mutually influencing. That is, an individual engaging in an activity in which she or he feels little control is unlikely to be able to disengage from the constraints of real life. The converse also is likely to be true. Thus, our model will require further refinement. However, we find it useful to conceptualize leisure in this way when planning intervention with older people.

The desired outcome of intervention is that people develop a repertoire of activities:

- In which they can become totally absorbed
- That allow them to make desired statements of self-identity

Consideration of the elements of leisure as a continuum enables us to:

- Reflect with individuals on their relative positions on each line in the content of a particular activity
- Determine which of the elements will yield most productively to intervention. That is, where can or should we begin in intervention to

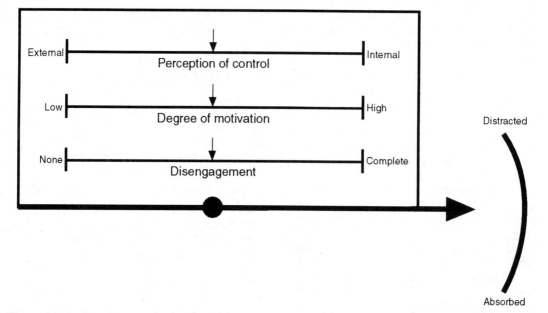

Figure 11-2 Summative contribution of the elements of leisure to total absorption in a leisure activity.

enable this person to experience leisure in his or her daily life?

PROMOTION OF LEISURE: APPLICATION OF THE MODEL

Applied models of leisure are useful only to the extent that they allow clinicians to explain relationships among constructs, make meaningful predictions, and implement successful interventions with individuals. Successful intervention depends on thorough assessment. Assessment of leisure is more likely to be thorough (i.e., to capture the most salient aspects) when it reflects an organized conceptualization of the elements of leisure.

We have suggested that leisure can be defined as the experience of total absorption in an activity. We have proposed that three elements contribute to that leisure experience: control, motivation, and the ability to disengage from the constraints of real life. Assessment based on this conceptual model of leisure entails the examination, with the individual, of each of these elements and of particular activities. There are many ways to go about gathering this

information, including checklists, but we believe that interview is an essential tool.

We recommend that clinicians assess leisure by:

- Inquiring about activities in which the individual is or was able to become totally absorbed (forgets everything else)
- Examining the individual's motivations for, degree of control in, and disengagement opportunities in each activity

Asking the individual to rate himself or herself along the continuum reflecting the leisure elements can also be helpful.

In the assessment, the clinician seeks to determine:

- Whether or not an individual experiences, or has ever experienced, leisure
- The relative presence, in the context of particular activities, of the elements contributing to the leisure experience
- The interrelationships among these elements

When this information has been gathered, it is possible to plan and evaluate the effectiveness of intervention. Intervention must be individually tailored and targeted toward promoting the leisure experience and eliminating barriers associated with it.

We will illustrate this process with two examples. Anna is an 83-year-old black woman who lives alone. She suffered a mild *cerebrovascular accident* (CVA) 6 months prior to intervention. Anna said that cooking for her family was the activity in which she became most absorbed. When she cooked big meals, she forgot everything else and became totally "caught up" in timing events and creating the perfect combination of ingredients. However, Anna complained that, since her stroke, she was no longer able to "cook like she used to." Although she still cooked, she did it only for herself, rather than for her family, and she was forced to use mixes, rather than begin from "scratch." These adaptations made cooking less enjoyable and failed to provide Anna with the same leisure experience she once enjoyed. Anna's profile for cooking is shown in Figure 11–3.

Anna was highly motivated to do a particular kind of cooking; she enjoyed the experience itself and saw it as a means of giving of herself to her family. The problem for Anna in cooking from scratch was with control. Because of mild weakness on her left side and abnormal movements in her arm, she no longer felt comfortable lifting and carrying pans. Further, her timing seemed off, and she worried about having one thing burn on the stove while she was attending to another thing at the sink. These concerns prevented her from disengaging from real life since she was continually reminded of the constraints imposed on her by her physical limitations. The combination of lack of control and inability to disengage prevented Anna from experiencing total absorption (leisure).

The occupational therapist working with Anna intervened by facilitating more normal patterns of movement in Anna's arm and helping her move more quickly. The therapist intervened in the context of complex cooking activities which Anna selected. The occupational

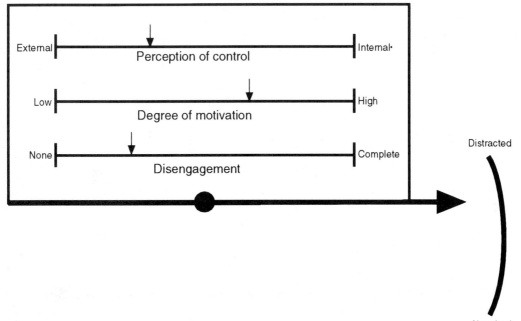

Figure 11–3 Anna's profile of the elements of leisure as they relate to cooking complex meals for her family.

therapist understood that the purpose of her intervention was to enable Anna to experience leisure by gaining greater control for cooking in a particular way. Thus, when she made decisions with regard to intervention, she framed her decisions in the context of leisure, rather than in the context of motor control.

Intervention with Anna was highly successful and took place over a reasonably short period of time (6 weeks). When the occupational therapist contacted Anna by phone several weeks after the last intervention session, Anna was too busy to talk; she was involved in preparing Thanksgiving dinner for her family.

Anna's problems with cooking related to physical limitations that reduced her feelings of control and prevented her from disengaging from the constraints of real life. Individuals like Anna typically receive intervention from occupational therapists. However, intervention often centers on gaining control of movement rather than facilitating leisure experiences. While intervention centered on motor control might have been effective with Anna, we believe that her intervention was much more meaningful (and perhaps of shorter duration) because it focused on enabling her to experience leisure.

Our second example is of a woman who also experienced difficulty with control in her leisure pursuits, but her difficulties were manifest in an entirely different way than Anna's. Thus, she required an entirely different kind of intervention.

Laura is an 84-year-old white woman living alone in a residence for senior citizens. Laura's major complaint was that she had too much time on her hands. She was bored.

When the occupational therapist inquired about activities in which Laura became totally absorbed, he was able to elicit a number of responses. However, the activity Laura described with the greatest enthusiasm was bingo. Thus, the therapist began with that activity. When she played bingo, Laura got caught up in the excitement of the game; there was always a chance she would win. Laura also enjoyed bingo because she got out of the house and had a chance to socialize with others.

Laura's profile for bingo is shown in Figure 11–4. While she experienced leisure when she played bingo, she expressed relatively little control over this activity. This lack of control puzzled the therapist as Laura possessed all the necessary skills. When the therapist asked Laura about her perceived lack of control for bingo, she indicated that she lacked a means of transportation; the

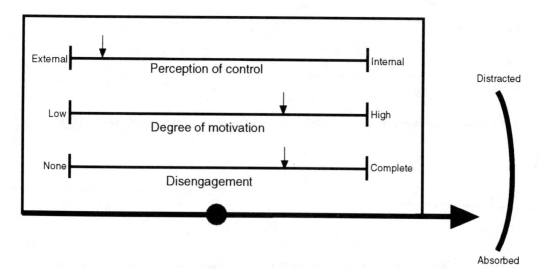

Figure 11–4 Laura's profile of the elements of leisure as they relate to bingo.

closest bingo games were played 5 miles from her home.

The therapist accepted Laura's assessment at face value. He intervened by inquiring about senior citizen travel services in her community; these were readily available. Given Laura's apparent enthusiasm for bingo and the ease with which she might have gotten there, the therapist began to wonder if, in fact, Laura's perceived lack of control for bingo was actually derived from sources that she was unwilling or unable to express. Thus, he accompanied her to a bingo game.

Upon arrival at the bingo hall, the therapist began to understand other potential sources of difficulty for Laura. Bingo games are associated with a kind of ritual; players have particular seats,[17] and there is a procedure for entering the social environment of the bingo game. Sensing Laura's reluctance to enter this complex social situation, the therapist served as a conduit for Laura, enabling her to enter the social circle more easily. He struck up conversations with "insiders" and introduced Laura into their circle. Having been given "entree," Laura engaged in bingo with the enthusiasm the therapist had expected. By the therapist's intervention, Laura gained the true source of control she sought. After two successful experiences in which the therapist accompanied her, Laura began to seek her own transportation and attended bingo regularly.

Recognizing that bingo might not satisfy all of Laura's needs for leisure experiences, the therapist also helped Laura to examine other motivations for and potential benefits from leisure. He attempted to promote Laura's sense of control in particular activities. This therapist's interventions were successful because he worked from a frame of leisure as experience that depends on control, motivation, and freedom to disengage from the constraints of real life.

SUMMARY

In this chapter, we have considered leisure to be experiences through which older people make important statements about their identities. We have proposed that leisure is experienced in the context of activities in which a person becomes totally absorbed. We have delineated three elements that contribute to the leisure experience: control, motivation, and the freedom to disengage from the constraints of real life. We have offered a methodology for examining and promoting leisure with older individuals. It is our hope that:

- Professionals who seek to promote leisure experiences with their clients will find our model useful for framing their assessments and interventions.
- This model will spark further research that will lead, in turn, to its refinement.

REVIEW QUESTIONS

1. *Define leisure.*

2. *What characteristics are most important to identifying an activity as a leisure activity?*

3. *In what ways are leisure activities important to the elderly?*

4. *In what ways does leisure represent an expression of identity?*

5. *What considerations are important in intervening to support an older person's optimal engagement in leisure?*

6. *Observe a group leisure activity in a retirement setting or nursing home. Describe participants' reactions to the event using the four factors of control, motivation, disengagement, and environment. Map these using the model described by Bundy and Canella.*

REFERENCES

1. Kelly, JR: Leisure in later life: Roles and identities. In NJ Osgood (ed): Life after Work. Praeger, New York, 1982.
2. Neulinger, J: The Psychology of Leisure: Research Approaches to the Study of Leisure. Charles C. Thomas, Springfield, IL, 1974.

3. Kleiber, DA: Motivational reorientation in adulthood and the resource of leisure. In Kleiber, DA and Maehr, ML (eds): Advances in Motivation and Achievement, Vol 4. JAI Press, Greenwich, CT, 1985, pp 217–250.

4. Csikszmentihayli, M: Beyond Boredom and Anxiety. Jossey-Bass, San Franciso, 1975.

5. Bundy, AC: Assessment of play and leisure: Delineation of the problem. American Journal of Occupational Therapy 47:217–222, 1993.

6. Allen, KR and Chin-Sang, V: A lifetime of work: The context and meanings of leisure for aging black women. The Gerontologist 30:734–740, 1990.

7. Clark, F: The occupations of Stuart (sic) Johnson. Paper presented at the Second Annual Research Colloquium of The American Occupational Therapy Foundation, Cincinnati, June 1991.

8. Kielhofner, G (ed): A Model of Human Occupation: Theory and Application. Williams & Wilkins, Baltimore, 1985.

9. Csikszmentihayli, M and Rochberg-Halton, E: The Meaning of Things. Cambridge University Press, New York, 1981.

10. Rockwell-Dylla, LA: Older adults' meaning of environment: Hospital and home. Unpublished master's thesis, University of Illinois at Chicago, 1991.

11. Newmann, EA: Elements of Play. MSS Information, New York, 1971.

12. Gunter, BG: Leisure styles: A conceptual framework for modern leisure. Sociological Quarterly 21:361–374, 1980.

13. Csikszmentihayli, M: Emergent motivation and evolution of the self. In Kleiber, DA and Maehr, ML (eds): Advances in Motivation and Achievement, Vol 4. JAI Press, Greenwich, CT, 1985, pp 93–119.

14. Caillois, R: Man, Play, and Games. Schocken Books, New York, 1979.

15. Havighurst, RJ: Leisure and aging. In Hoffman, AM (ed): The Daily Needs and Interests of Older People. Charles C. Thomas, Springfield, IL, 1976, pp 165–174.

16. Havighurst, JR: The nature and values of meaningful free-time activity. In Kleemeier, RW (ed): Aging and Leisure. Arno, New York, 1979, pp 309–345.

17. Dixey, R: It's a great feeling when you win: Women and bingo. Leisure Studies 6:199–214, 1987.

18. Mannell, RC, Zuzanek, J and Larson, R: Leisure states and "flow" experiences: Testing perceived freedom and intrinsic motivation hypotheses. Journal of Leisure Research 20:289–304, 1988.

19. Crandall, R: Motivations for leisure. Journal of Leisure Research 12:45–53, 1980.

20. Donald, MN and Havighurst, RJ: The meanings of leisure. Social Forces 37:355–360, 1959.

21. Havighurst, RJ and Feigenbaum, K. Leisure and lifestyle. In Neugarten, BL (ed): Middle Age and Aging: A Reader in Social Psychology. University of Chicago Press, Chicago, 1968.

22. Henderson, KA and Rannells, JS: Farm women and the meaning of work and leisure: An oral history perspective. Leisure Sciences 10:41–50, 1988.

23. Ekerdt, DJ: The busy ethic: Moral continuity between work and retirement. Gerontologist 26:239–244, 1986.

24. Cohen, D: The Development of Play. New York University Press, New York, 1987.

25. DeBoer, AL: The Art of Consulting. Arcturus, Chicago, 1986.

26. Burrus-Bamel, LL and Bammel, F: Leisure and recreation. In Birren, JE and Schaie, K Wa (eds): Handbook of the Psychology of Aging, ed 2. Van Nostrand Reinhold, New York, 1985, pp 848–863.

27. McAvoy, LH: The leisure preferences, problems, and needs of the elderly. Journal of Leisure Research 11:40–47, 1979.

28. Wilson, R: The courage to be leisured. Social Forces 60:282–303, 1981.

29. Geertz, C: The Interpretation of Cultures. Basic Books, New York, 1973.

30. Csikszmentihayli, M and Graef, R: The experience of freedom in daily life. American Journal of Community Psychology 8:401–414, 1980.

31. Larson, R and Csikszmentihayli, M: The experience sampling method. In Reis HT (ed): Naturalist Approaches to Studying Social Interaction. (New Directions for Methodology of Social and Behavioral Sciences, no. 15) Jossey-Bass, San Francisco, 1983, pp 41–56.

32. Krefting, K and Krefting, D: Leisure activities after a stroke: An ethnographic approach. The American Journal of Occupational Therapy 45:429–437, 1991.

33. Rowles, GD: Beyond performance: Being in place as a component of occupational therapy. American Journal of Occupational Therapy, in press.

'Th' saddest thing that's come my road,
though, is not bein' able t'do near what I
use to. I can't get about and get stuff
t'give people like I used to. . . . Can't give
away quilts now like I use to cause I can't
quilt. Can't cook'em somethin good t'eat
and give'em a good drink a'water like I
use to cause I can't hardly cook.
And there's s'many things I'd love t'be
able t'show you younguns how t'do, but I
can't now. Can't crochet any more. Can't
card and spin any more. Can't make
willer baskets and bottom chairs any
more. Can't do hardly anything I use t'do.
But I can still love.

—LINDA G. PAGE and ELIOT WIGGINGTON,
Aunt Arie: A Foxfire Portrait, EP Dutton,
New York, 1992, p. 199.

Chapter

12

Assessment of Self-Care

JOAN C. ROGERS
MARGO B. HOLM

OBJECTIVES

By the end of this chapter, readers will be able to:

1 Delineate the role self-care assessment plays in geriatric medicine.

2 Outline the purposes for conducting a self-care assessment.

3 Identify the categories of daily living activities involved in self-care assessment, and specify their distinguishing characteristics.

4 Define the dimensions used to evaluate self-care performance.

5 Identify the methods of obtaining information about self-care performance and analyze their advantages and disadvantages.

6 Apply the concepts of assessment content, dimensions, and methods to selected instruments for measuring self-care.

7 Relate information about self-care to clinical decisions.

Self-care assessment is an integral component of the health care of older adults.[1-4] While the medical assessment spans the etiology, pathology, and prognosis of disease, the self-care assessment encompasses the residual consequences of disease and trauma in daily life. The former focuses on a review of systems, the latter on a review of functions. The two assessment processes are complementary, with each contributing distinct and essential information for improving the health of older patients.

There are several reasons why self-care assessment assumes an importance in geriatric medicine that it is not accorded in adult medicine:

1. The diseases that predominate in late life are generally not curable, although they may be controllable. Diseases like cardiovascular disease, arthritis, and parkinsonism are chronic and debilitating in nature and are more likely to result in long-term difficulties in doing tasks than are acute, curable diseases. It is estimated that about 85 percent of community-dwelling, older adults have at least one chronic condition and that 42 percent are limited in function.[5]

2. Self-care assessment contributes to a better understanding of geriatric medical problems. Older adults vary considerably in the number and types of diseases they have, the severity with which disease manifests itself, and the length of time they have coped with chronic conditions. One patient may have osteoarthritis coexisting with macular degeneration, while another may have osteoarthritis, cardiopulmonary disease, and dementia. The stroke may have occurred months or years ago. Depression may reflect the recurrence of a life-long problem or an initial episode. In effect, each patient is a unique combination of health and illness. This uniqueness complicates clinical decision making. It makes it difficult to define problems clearly and hence to group patients according to similarity of medical status. Without such classification, the precise relationship between medical problem, treatment, and outcome remains obscure. The development of expert clinical judgment and geriatric medicine is thus retarded. By adding self-care data to disease data, a more adequate understanding of geriatric illness is achieved.[6] In self-care assessment, disease is measured indirectly through its impact on daily life. Self-care assessment takes into account the cumulative and interactive effects of disease and yields an index of illness severity. Since it cuts across disease categories, it provides a uniform criterion for evaluating the severity of illness.

3. Changes in self-care may be the first indication of disease progression and hence may signal a need for medical evaluation.[7-9] The frail elderly, for example, often come to their physicians with complaints about performing daily living activities, such as walking or eating, rather than with specific symptoms. These functional deficits thus serve as the focal point for tracing the underlying disorder, which if alleviated may restore function. Functional changes may also signal a need to reexamine the course of medical treatment. Some medications, for instance, may impair function by altering vision, gait, eye-hand coordination, or mental status.

4. The data generated by self-care assessment is directly relevant to long-term care needs. Self-care status is a significant predictor of admission to nursing homes,[10] use of home care,[11] use of in-home support,[8,12] and living arrangements.[13] The type and degree of self-care deficit define the kind and extent of resources patients need. Resource needs are matched with the informal and formal supports available to patients to fill identified needs. Decisions about how unmet needs are to be met in turn determine liv-

ing arrangements, including institutional care.[8]

5. Self-care assessment responds to the concerns of older patients. Older patients perceive health and quality of life in terms of their level of functioning and activity more than their medical diagnoses.[14] They want to know how to manage their lives despite chronic illness. Self-care assessment draws attention to the person experiencing a disease. Hence, it balances the disease orientation of the medical model. Often, the priorities that patients set for their functional problems assist in focusing medical treatment.

The salience of self-care assessment in geriatric medicine thus relates to the contributions it makes to detecting, diagnosing, and treating medical problems and managing disease-generated self-care problems. The optimal care plan flows from good assessment. Self-care assessment extends the database for clinical decisions beyond the medical history, physical examination, and laboratory findings to task performance characteristics. Thus, it facilitates medical decisions that promote self-sufficiency and optimize the possibility of enhancing quality of life.

PURPOSE OF SELF-CARE ASSESSMENT

The overall content to be covered in the self-care assessment as well as the specific tasks to be evaluated depend on the purpose of the assessment. Basic purposes for undertaking a self-care assessment are description, screening, assessment, monitoring, and prediction.

Description

Clinicians may be interested in describing the self-care status of the patient population they serve. Descriptive data may be used for multiple purposes. From the perspective of a particular fa-

cility, descriptive data may be used to establish functional goals for specific diagnostic groups. For example, the performance of older adults following hip replacement surgery and rehabilitation may be evaluated. Group data may then be used to set feasible rehabilitation goals for similar patients undergoing hip replacement surgery in the future. these data may also be used for program evaluation by comparing self-care outcomes to the standards set for a facility or by comparing them to data from similar facilities. From the perspective of a community, descriptive data are useful for determining the need for health and social services. Surveys documenting the disabilities of older adults living in a particular community address the need to have or develop services to respond to these needs. For example, disabilities in meal preparation or driving indicate the need for Meals on Wheels and transportation services, respectively. From a public health perspective, descriptive data provide the basis for health care policy. More theoretically, clinicians may collect descriptive data to advance understanding of self-care status. For example, data may be analyzed to determine which tasks are the hardest for patients with various diagnoses to perform.

Screening

An evaluation may also be carried out to identify older adults who have or are likely to have problems. Screening is done to separate older adults who need further, more extensive assessment, from those who do not. It is a case-finding procedure that requires sufficient sensitivity so that those who need help are not misclassified as not needing help. Ideally, screening procedures should be brief, easy to administer, and inexpensive.

Assessment

Assessment is more comprehensive and detailed than screening. It covers a broader range of tasks and evaluates disabilities in depth. The objective of assessment is to identify the range of disabilities present so that appropriate health and social services can be initiated. When rehabilitation is indicated, evidence is sought of patients' potential for improving function, hypothesized causes of task disabilities, and the remedial and compensatory interventions that are most likely to improve function. Periodic reassessment is done to measure the adequacy of the services provided or progress toward meeting rehabilitation goals. Changes are introduced in the plan of care based on the results of the reassessment.

Monitoring

Monitoring involves checking for changes in self-care status. Monitoring is often done as a follow-up to rehabilitation to estimate the extent to which the gains made during rehabilitation are maintained after discharge or the need to reinstitute care. It may also be undertaken for "untreated" disabilities to determine the natural progression of disability. The natural rate of functional change provides a baseline for evaluating the efficacy of intervention for expediting the rate of improvement or retarding the rate of deterioration.

Prediction

At times, measures of self-care may be used as markers or predictors of subsequent events. For instance, disabilities in home management are predictive of problems in personal self-care. Similarly, disabilities in personal self-care are predictive of institutionalization. Based on task performance in the hospital, clinicians are frequently asked to evaluate (i.e., predict) patients' continued capacity to live independently or the appropriate level of care if supportive assistance is needed.

WHAT IS INCLUDED IN SELF-CARE?

The self-care assessment focuses on *activities of daily living* (ADL). Theoretically, ADL encompass all tasks that individuals routinely engage in. The most valid ADL assessment would consider the broad scope of activities that older adults undertake to care for their personal needs, maintain their homes, and promote their well-being and quality of life. It would take into account the unique ways in which these activities are enacted and coordinated by each individual. The ADL for a homemaker caring for an ill spouse would be expected to differ substantively from those of a retired banker working as a volunteer in a preschool. In practice, however, ADL assessment is generally limited to three categories of everyday tasks—mobility, personal self-care, and home management.[3,15]

Mobility

Mobility tasks involve the ability to move the body from one place to another. Mobility assessment involves functional movements of the trunk and lower extremities, such as transfers and walking. Functional movements that are commonly assessed are listed in Table 12–1.

Personal Self-Care

Personal self-care involves the ability to take care of one's fundamental, personal needs, like dressing and toileting. Table 12–2 provides a more complete listing of the specific tasks generally included in this category. In addition to being able to control one's body, these tasks require one to control the objects needed to complete a task. For example, in brushing teeth, object control is reflected in getting toothpaste onto a toothbrush and in holding the toothbrush. In this task, body control sup-

---

TABLE 12-1 *Mobility:* **The Ability to Move (Control) One's Body**

Move in Bed

Transfer to and from
  Bed
  Chair
  Commode
  Bathtub
  Car

Stand

Walk
  On a level surface
  On an inclined surface
  Up and down stairs
  Up and down curbs
  Change directions (e.g., forward, backward)

---

ports object control through erect posture. The movements associated with self-care tasks are oriented toward the body. Terms often used synonymously with *personal self-care* are *ADL, basic ADL, physical ADL, basic self-maintenance, physical self-maintenance*, and *personal self-maintenance*.[16-18]

TABLE 12-2 *Personal Self-Care:* **The Ability to Take Care of Personal Needs**

Feed

Bathe

Perform Hygiene
  Comb hair
  Wash hair
  Perform oral hygiene
  Groom fingernails
  Shave, put on makeup

Dress

Toileting
  Use commode
  Bladder incontinence
  Bowel incontinence

Basic Communication (Make Needs Known)
  Verbally
  Nonverbally

Home Management

Home management involves the ability to live independently in the community. Tasks included in this category are associated with human needs for food, clothing, shelter, health care, and social interaction. There is less agreement about the specific areas and tasks that should be assessed under home management than there is about the other two categories.[18] Typical tasks included under this rubric are outlined in Table 12-3. Home management tasks involve using the body and objects to control the environment. Actions are oriented outwardly rather than toward the self. Terms used synonymously with *home management* are *independent living skills, instrumental activities of daily living* (IADL), and *extended ADL*.[17,19]

Hierarchical Nature of Daily Living Skills

The three categories of daily living tasks are generally perceived to be hierarchical, ranked on the basis of task complexity and social expectations for human performance. Mobility tasks are at the lowest end of the hierarchy because they involve a heavy motor component, focus on control of the body in space, and support both personal self-care and home management tasks. All adults are expected to be able to do mobility tasks, and an inability to perform them is perceived uniformly as a loss of function.

Personal self-care tasks are viewed as more complex than mobility tasks. Whereas in mobility tasks, gross motor actions are tested separately and in isolation from goal-oriented tasks, in personal self-care tasks, their coordinated use is tested, and testing is done in the context of real-life task performance. For example, in mobility assessment an older adult might be asked to get into and out of the bathtub to test bathtub transfers. In personal self-care assessment, the ability to complete bathtub

---

TABLE 12–3   *Home Management:* The Ability to Live Independently

---

Advanced Mobility

　Enter and exit one's own home

　Walk carrying a weight (e.g., take out the garbage, as in shopping)

　Move around the community (e.g., using car, taxi, bus)

Advanced Personal Self-Care

　Manage medication

　Communicate

　　Use telephone

　　Respond to correspondence

　　Obtain help in an emergency

Light Housekeeping

　Shop for food and clothing

　Cook or prepare meals

　Wash dishes

　Do laundry

　Clean household items (e.g., bathtub, refrigerator)

　Dust furniture

　Vacuum or sweep rugs or floor

　Make a bed

　Perform minor home repairs (e.g., fix flashlight, change light bulbs)

　Rake leaves

　Water lawn

Heavy Housekeeping

　Change bed linens

　Wash floors, windows, or walls

　Perform major home maintenance tasks or repairs (e.g., put up storm windows, paint the walls)

　Shovel snow

　Weed

Financial Management

　Manage money

　Pay bills

　Write checks

　Balance checkbook

Leisure

　Read

　Listen to radio, conversation

　Watch television

---

transfers would be tested in the context of bathing since this task incorporates transfers and object use (e.g., opening and closing faucet, handling soap, getting washcloth to feet). As with mobility tasks, the movements associated with self-care tasks have a heavy motor component; however, they also have a more substantive cognitive component. Cognition is involved in processes like initiating task performance at the appropriate time, using task objects correctly, and sequencing the steps involved in a task so that it is completed efficiently and successfully. Like mobility tasks, all humans are expected to be able to do personal self-care tasks independently, and an inability to do them is regarded as a disability. Exceptions occur for grooming hair and nails where it is socially acceptable for adults to rely on help. Similarly, if one has sufficient wealth to afford a personal valet or maid, assistance in bathing and dressing is acceptable. These dependencies would not be classified as disabilities because they would result from personal preferences, not disease or injury.

Home management tasks are at the highest end of the hierarchy. Like personal self-care tasks, home management tasks are supported by the coordinated use of functional movements. If you are going to cook, you have to be able to move to the storage cupboard, retrieve food items from the shelves, carry them to the preparation area, and prepare them for consumption. Unlike personal self-care tasks, the actions associated with home management tasks are oriented more toward the environment than toward oneself. Thus, the environment is a stronger determinant of home management tasks than of personal self-care tasks. In some home management tasks the motor component predominates (e.g., bed making, sweeping, dusting) while in others the cognitive component predominates (e.g., checkbook balancing, medication management). More complex decisions are involved in home management tasks than personal self-care tasks. In contrast to mobility and personal self-care tasks, home management tasks are more optional in nature. While they must be done to maintain independent living, they do not have to be done by each person. If older adults are unable to cook, they can have someone else cook for them by relying on a family member, going to a restaurant, or contracting for Meals on Wheels. Hence, all humans are not expected to be independent in these tasks. In fact, the majority of indoor home management tasks, especially those found on IADL instruments[1], have traditionally been done in American society by women. Many men in the present older cohort have never learned how to cook, do the laundry, or repair clothing. Similarly, many older women have not learned how to drive or manage finances. In view of the nonobligatory nature of home management tasks, an older adult's history of task performance needs to be taken when a dysfunction is identified. This assists clinicians to ascertain if the dysfunction is due to illness, a failure to ever learn how to do the task, or a personal preference.

A hierarchy of task performance is of practical value to self-care assessment. If tasks can be arranged in order of increasing difficulty, then an assessment could be terminated at the point in the hierarchy where disability is detected. It could then be assumed that a patient would be able to complete all tasks ordered lower on the hierarchy and would have difficulty with those above. The evaluation could also be concentrated on the narrow spectrum of tasks that a clinician hypothesizes to be problematic for a patient. This would further shorten testing because only those tasks perceived to be in the "critical range" would be examined. Empirically, Katz delineated a hierarchy for six mobility and personal self-care items and combined these into the Katz Index of ADL.[20] The order of tasks arranged from most to least difficult is bathing, dressing, toileting, transfer, continence, and feeding. A hierarchy of five IADL tasks was identified by Fillenbaum.[16] The rank order of tasks from most to least difficult is the ability to do housework, travel, shop, prepare meals, and handle personal finances. More research needs

to be conducted on task hierarchies before their potential for streamlining functional assessment can be realized in geriatric practice. It is likely that task difficulty emerges as an interaction between a person's competence and the specific task requirements and hence that task hierarchies will differ for patients with physical, rather than cognitive or emotional, impairments or coexisting conditions.

Self-care assessment emphasizes two aspects of task performance. In much of the geriatric literature, these are called *capacity* and *performance*. *Capacity* refers to the ability to perform a task. Synonymous terms are *competence, maximum performance capability*, and *skill*. Questions aimed at examining capacity are phrased in terms of "Can you . . . ?" "Are you able to . . . ?" "If the circumstances required, could you . . . ?" or "If your life depended on it, could you . . . ?" Capacity is observed when patients respond to requests to demonstrate task performance. *Performance* refers to routine behavior. Patients may have the capacity to dress themselves and yet fail to do this. Terms used synonymously with *performance* are *actual, usual, routine*, or *customary performance* and *habits of daily living*. Questions phrased in terms of "Do you perform . . . ?" or "Do you usually . . . ?" examine performance. To evaluate performance using observation requires observation of unprompted behavior over time.*

Typically, functional assessment instruments examine either capacity or

---

*Rehabilitation professionals often use the terms *capacity* and *performance* differently than defined here, and we need to be aware of the difference. In rehabilitation, *capacity* implies the potential to perform a task rather than the ability to do so. It may be noted, for example, that a patient has the motor and cognitive skills to feed and yet is not presently able to feed because these skills are not adequately integrated. This patient would be viewed as having the capacity to feed (i.e., ability to do this in the future) even though self-feeding is not now feasible. *Performance* as used in rehabilitation is equivalent to *capacity* as used in geriatrics and implies ability.

performance but not both aspects. This is unfortunate since they relate to different dimensions of self-care competence and each contributes unique information needed for treatment planning. Capacity defines the upper limit of performance, that is, "best" task performance. Performance defines the lower limit, that is, usual performance. If patients can do a task once, they are potentially capable of repeating that performance. Hence, the goal of treatment is to increase the frequency of task performance until it becomes routine and meets acceptable standards. Patients who can do tasks but do not do them address the need for interventions aimed at increasing endurance or improving motivation. For patients who lack the ability to perform tasks, intervention aims at teaching task performance through training or retraining. Supportive services may be used to compensate for task performance that fails to reach acceptable levels. There is a growing awareness of the need to consider simultaneously measures of capacity and performance.[21]

WHAT DO WE WANT TO KNOW ABOUT SELF-CARE?

In the clinical situation, self-care assessment is basically an evaluative and decision-making process. The categories of self-care define the content of the assessment and indicate the specific tasks that are to be evaluated. The assessment dimensions define what we want to know about the older adult's performance of self-care tasks and are reflected in the verbal and numerical descriptions that are provided about a patient's self-care status. A clinician may observe that a patient is independent in going to the toilet, feeding, and maintaining continence and dependent in bathing, dressing, and transfers (i.e., verbal description) or obtained a score of 3 on the Katz Index of ADL (i.e., numerical description). In general, the assessment dimensions may be classified as pertaining to independence, quality, or causality.

Level of Independence

Evaluations of task capability and performance yield lists of tasks that patients are able to do independently and those they are unable to do independently. We may find, for example, that a patient can independently dress and manage money but is unable to bathe or shop. A rating of independence means that patients can do a task by themselves. A rating of dependence means that assistance is needed to do a task. Independence-dependence ratings may also connote that a task is completed within reasonable or unreasonable time, or without or with technical aids, or safely or unsafely, or in a normal or abnormal manner.

When disabilities are identified, more precise measurement of task performance may be desired than that of able and unable. The degree of ability is generally rated along a continuum of independence-dependence. The yardstick or measure of ability is the amount of assistance needed to complete a task. Commonly, measurement is on an ordinal scale indicating minimal, moderate, or maximal assistance, which translate, respectively, to minimal, moderate, and severe disability. Although this is the most common method of rating ability, it is recognized that the amount of assistance given may be more than that actually needed to complete a task.

The kind of assistance needed may also enter into the rating scheme. A distinction is often made between assistance received from nonhuman and human sources. Nonhuman help includes the use of assistive devices and adaptive equipment and the presence of architectural modifications. The use of nonhuman help only generally implies greater functional independence than the use of human helpers.

The specific type of assistance received from humans may also be of interest. Human help takes into account an array of physical, verbal, and visual assists. *Physical assistance* means that physical support is required. Examples include a clinician's assisting a patient to get up from a chair and a patient's leaning on a clinician to maintain stability while walking. *Standby assistance* means being physically present to monitor tasks performance and initiate actions to prevent accidents. Examples include walking alongside a patient using a walker and overseeing a patient who is doing stovetop cooking. *Physical guidance* means physical contact with a patient to promote task initiation, continuation, or completion. Examples include manually moving a patient's arm toward a cup of water and repositioning a patient's hand on a walker. *Verbal guidance* means using words to promote task initiation, continuation, or completion. Examples include cuing patients to eat or reminding them to attend to a task. *Visual guidance* means the use of visual cues to promote task initiation, continuation, or completion. Examples include pointing to the directions on package mix and demonstrating how to execute a bathtub transfer. *Setup* means that help is needed only to provide and/or arrange the objects needed for task performance. Examples include opening milk cartons and cutting meat. Human help that is constant or that requires physical contact with patients signifies greater dependency than other types of help. In considering human help, it may be important to know who the helpers are and how much time they spend with a patient each day and week. Helpers' skills in giving the assistance that is needed as well as their willingness to provide this help should also be appraised. Care-giver burden may be reduced by providing training in caregiving skills and substituting formal for informal services.

Independence-dependence ratings may be applied to a task as a whole or to the subtasks that comprise a task. In the first scheme, a clinician would grade a patient's participation in bathing based on a qualitative judgment of the overall effort put forth by the patient and the clinician to complete a task. The *Functional Independence Measure* (FIM),[22] for example, uses a scale ranging from 100 percent independent, to 75 percent independent, to 50 percent independent, to 25 percent independent to 100 percent dependent. In the second scheme, grading is based on task analysis, that is, on the number of subtasks comprising a task that are done independently. For example, if bathing were regarded as a five-step task and a patient completed four of the five steps independently, the patient would be 80 percent independent in bathing.

Although the various types of human and nonhuman help are cumbersome to record, taken together, they define the conditions under which self-care was evaluated. Unless the evaluation conditions are replicated in real life, self-care status is likely to change accordingly. Systematically recording the conditions under which task performance occurs facilitates working toward reproducing those conditions in the postdischarge living situation. Likewise, identifying the conditions under which task performance occurs in the postdischarge setting facilitates replicating those conditions in the hospital for assessment and intervention.

A particular problem in assessing older adults emerges because of fluctuations in capability and performance. Most self-care assessment procedures assume that behavior is stable. However, dependence in a task may be intermittent, situational, or seasonal.[21] An older adult may be dependent when arthritis is exacerbated, when performing in an unfamiliar setting (e.g., moving to a senior apartment in a new neighborhood), or when snow covers the sidewalk. These disabilities are likely to be alleviated when the flareup subsides, the setting becomes familiar, and the snow melts. Fluctuations in task performance can be readily managed in descriptive reports of self-care. However, they are less easily accommodated on quantitative scales. Scales using frequency of independent performance (e.g., often, sometimes, frequently, or practically never) as assessment markers make some allowance for fluctuations in behavior.

Regardless of whether the grading criterion is the level or the frequency of independent performance, the grading categories share a common weakness: The meaning accorded the terms used for grading is open to interpretation, and the distinctions between levels of independence are unclear. One clinician's perception of "minimal assistance" or "sometimes" may match another clinician's perception of "maximal assistance" or "frequently." Thus, finer gradations of independence level may result in more confusion than clarification.

Level of Quality

The quality of a patient's task performance and of the outcomes of that performance may be as critical to assess as the level of independent performance. Cues about a patient's motivation for functional independence reside in the interest or disinterest displayed in initiating, sustaining, and completing tasks. Movement may be characterized as normal, safe, or efficient, or adaptive, unsafe, or inefficient. It may be done with difficulty or ease at a slow, normal, or hurried pace. Action may be accompanied by pain or be pain free. The outcome or product of performance may be acceptable, marginal, or unacceptable. Regardless of its objective quality, it may evoke feelings of satisfaction, dissatisfaction, pleasure, or displeasure in a patient.

An overall index of task efficiency that is receiving increased attention is timed performance, with longer time associated with increased difficulty of performance. However, timed performance may be more appropriate for rudimentary motions (e.g., Williams's[23] test of manual dexterity) than for self-care and home management tasks since accurate and acceptable behavior is of more functional interest in these tasks than speed. Furthermore, in some patients, most notably those who are impulsive or manic, speed may be at the expense of task standards. Although patients may dress quickly, the end result may be an unkempt appearance.

Etiology of Task Dependence

If a task disability is to be alleviated through the provision of a supportive service, the mere detection of a disability is sufficient for planning intervention. If an older adult is unable to dress, transfer to a personal care home that offers assistance in dressing may be indicated. For remedial interventions, however, understanding the etiology, or cause, of a disability is a prerequisite for planning intervention. A disability in dressing may occur because a patient is not motivated to dress and therefore does not (i.e., motivational impairment), because a patient is unable to perform the movements needed for dressing (i.e., physical impairment), or because a patient has forgotten how to dress (i.e., cognitive impairment). The appropriate type of intervention would differ depending on the underlying cause of the task disability. In the case of dressing disability, a motivational impairment might be approached by getting a patient involved in volunteer work and hence giving a reason to dress; a physical impairment, through muscle reeducation; and a cognitive impairment, through visual cuing.

Three strategies are used to assess the etiology of task disability:

1. Disease-specific instruments for disability assessment are designed to emphasize the tasks that are particularly problematic for persons with that disease. Thus, the direct assessment of functional status,[24] which was devised for persons with Alzheimer's disease and related disorders, has items pertaining to financial management, while the functional status index,[25] which was designed for persons with arthritis, does not. It is assumed that task disabilities are precipitated by the disease, which led to the selection of the disease-specific instrument to begin with. This strategy is less useful in geriatric medicine than it is in adult medicine because of the

multidiagnostic nature of geriatric illness.

2. Function is evaluated at the level of impairment as well as disability. An *impairment* is a loss or abnormality of psychological, physiological, or anatomical structure or function. Impairment is an organ dysfunction, while disability is a task dysfunction.[26] Impairments may be physical (e.g., decreased range of motion or muscle strength), cognitive (e.g., loss of memory or decreased attention span), or emotional (e.g., depression). Task disabilities are assumed to be caused by the impairments identified. For example, if a patient's score on the short portable mental status questionnaire[27] indicated substantive cognitive impairment, task disabilities might be attributed to cognitive deficit. If, however, the test indicated intact mental status, another impairment would be examined as the potential cause of the task dysfunction. The problem with this approach is that there is no one-to-one correspondence between impairment and disability.[28]

3. Disability and impairment are assessed simultaneously as previously, but impairment is assessed in the context of task performance rather than separately. For example, if a patient has difficulty getting out of the bathtub, a clinician would use the qualitative aspects of a patient's performance to suggest the potential cause or causes of the disability. A clinician might conclude that a patient's difficulty getting out of the bathtub was due to poor motor planning (i.e., cognitive impairment) because the patient had difficulty effectively positioning the body for standing. But once the patient was cued to "put your feet under yourself," the patient followed the cue and performed the action without difficulty.

HOW IS INFORMATION ABOUT SELF-CARE GATHERED?

Information about an older adult's self-care may be obtained through three basic methods:

1. By asking questions
2. By observing performance
3. By measuring performance[29]

Procedures like the clinical judgment of an individual clinician or a patient care team or a review of a patient's medical record rely on one or more of these basic methods. No method is intrinsically superior, and each method has its advantages and disadvantages. The decision to use one method exclusively or to combine methods depends in large part on the overall reason for conducting the self-care assessment.

Data Gathering Methods

ASKING QUESTIONS

In the *questioning method* of data collection, information is obtained by posing verbal questions usually to the patients themselves. For example, a clinician asks, "Can you dress yourself?" or "Can you do your own banking, including writing checks and balancing your checkbook?" Questions are asked because a clinician is not informed about a patient's self-care status and needs to become informed to plan intervention. In other words, questioning aims at information seeking, and a patient's responses are of direct interest. If patients are unable or unwilling to respond to questions, a proxy, who is knowledgeable about a patient's self-care, may be used instead. Questioning may be done in an oral format through an interview or a written format through a questionnaire. Questionnaires may be administered by a patient (i.e., self-administered), clinician, or trained examiner. Regardless of whether an interview or questionnaire is used, the degree of structure imposed on questioning may vary considerably.

The questions themselves may be very specific (e.g., "Can you dress? Bathe?") or very general (e.g., "Can you take care of yourself?"). They may be fixed and unalterable or mere reminders of self-care areas to be probed. Similarly, answers may be selected from a list of predetermined responses, or they may be open-ended.

OBSERVING PERFORMANCE

In the *observation method*, data are obtained by watching patients as they carry out self-care tasks. Task performance may be observed under natural or prompted conditions. Under natural conditions, task performance is rated as it occurs within the context of daily living. For example, a clinician may observe patients as they arise in the morning and bathe, groom, dress, and feed themselves. Under prompted conditions, clinicians structure the assessment so that tasks are performed expediently for the convenience of clinicians. For example, a patient scheduled for assessment at 3:00 PM may be requested to demonstrate morning care routines. Observation-based assessment may occur in a patient's actual living situation or in an experimental environment, such as an occupational therapy or physical therapy clinic. Like questions, observations may be general or specific. A clinician has the option of recording a patient's overall ability to dress or the ability to complete each step of the dressing sequence (e.g., don socks, shoes, lower-extremity garments, upper-extremity garments).

MEASURING PERFORMANCE

In the *measurement method*, numbers are assigned to indicators of task performance for the purpose of estimating self-care status. The indicators of task performance may be obtained through either questioning or observation. For example, a patient's responses to a series of questions about feeding, bathing, dressing, toileting, and grooming would be converted to a score. The

score in turn would serve as an index of the amount of personal self-care capacity possessed by the patient. The scores enable us to consider differences in the degree to which patients possess different amounts of self-care status.[29,30] In contrast to the use of questions in the questioning method where the objective is to learn about a patient's actual ability to perform specific tasks, the intent here is to use the aggregate of responses as an indicator of self-care status. Of course, by going back to the individual items (i.e., questions or observations) that comprise the measuring device, information about performance on each task can be retrieved. Measurement assumes that procedures are carried out in a standardized way, so that measurement conditions are the same for all patients.

ADVANTAGES AND DISADVANTAGES OF THE DATA COLLECTION METHODS

A major advantage of questioning compared to observing is that it provides a relatively easy, fast, and inexpensive way to collect information. These factors in large part account for its prevalence in geriatrics. The training required to administer interviews and questionnaires is less than that required to make observations. Personal contact is often not needed, and when questionnaires are used, it is possible to test older adults in groups rather than individually. Complex tasks, like meal preparation and shopping, that are difficult to observe can be easily queried.

Among the limitations of questioning is that the questions may not be clear to the respondents. For example, when Mrs. Jacks is asked if she needs help with heavy housework, she may not know the meaning of *heavy housework*. She may interpret this as "spring housecleaning," while another patient may assume that it means only vacuuming the rugs. Patients may also not be able to understand the subtle difference between questions probing capacity (i.e., "Can you . . . ?") and those probing performance (e.g., "Do you . . . ?").

Even when the meaning of questions is clear, patients may be unsure of how to respond. Unless patients have recently done a task, and hence tested their capacity, they have meager evidence for judging their capacity accurately. They may think that they can do heavy housework, climb a flight of stairs, or drive a car even though they have not done so for a number of years.

Questions are also susceptible to bias. Respondents may deliberately try to distort their responses. Patients, for example, may seek to hide their deficits, fearing that they will be institutionalized if their disabilities become known. Patients with depression typically underestimate their capabilities while those with dementia tend to exaggerate them. Care givers may seek to accentuate disabilities in the hope of receiving increased services. Research has shown systematic bias in responses to questions based on the source of information. Typically, family members rate patients' performance more negatively than nurses, and nurses more negatively than patients themselves.[31] Thus, the person used to obtain information about self-care influences the ratings of self-care, and these in turn influence the plan of care.

The most direct method of assessing self-care is observation. When observing, clinicians gather objective evidence about self-care, and hence they do not need to rely on the subjective impressions of patients or their proxies. There is less chance of introducing error than when questioning is used. Among the advantages of observation is that by watching patients perform tasks and analyzing the problems they have performing and completing them, clinicians obtain data about the causes of task disabilities that are needed to initiate rehabilitative interventions. They observe, for example, that a patient is having difficulty rising from the bottom of the bathtub because of weakness in the legs or poor motor planning. Causal data are not generally obtainable through questioning. Making causal inferences and testing them out in the

clinical situation requires professional knowledge of performance capability and of task demands that patients do not possess.

Observation may take place under conditions that are *standardized* (i.e., measurement method) or *nonstandardized* (i.e., observation method). When tasks are *standardized*, the meaning of self-care items is clearly defined and is comparable for all patients. The ambiguity that is present in questions is eliminated because tasks are defined by the instructions given and the materials and equipment available. Standardization is of concern when there is a need to compare one patient's self-care status with that of others. This might be the case when data are collected to describe a clinical population or to evaluate a program. In clinical care, however, the need is usually to identify and understand the problems involved in task performance so that appropriate therapy or supportive services can be provided to a specific patient.

To the extent that standardized tasks are relevant to the task demands that a patient encounters in daily living, they will yield a valid impression of that patient's self-care. Conversely, incongruence between standardized tasks and a patient's daily living tasks may lead to false impressions. In other words, ecological validity may suffer when standardized tasks are used because task performance is environmentally dependent. Patients are accustomed to doing tasks in their own living environments, using their own tools and equipment and in the presence of their customary helpers. Changes in environmental conditions may facilitate or impede task performance depending on whether or not they compensate for personal deficits. Under standardized testing conditions, clinicians learn less about patients' ability to function in their own homes. They have to use test performance to extrapolate how well patients have adapted to their own environments. When observation is done under *nonstandardized conditions*, allowances can be made for individual patient needs. In this situation, the meaning of self-care items is clearly defined but it is not comparable from patient to patient.

On the negative side, compared to questioning, observation is very time-consuming and labor intensive. Patients can respond to questions about their personal self-care in a few minutes, but it may take them hours to complete these same tasks. Because some tasks may be difficult for them to do, professional supervision is needed to ensure safety, reduce the risk of injury, and manage any accidents that may take place during observation. Professionals are also needed to make the causal observations that lead to appropriate interventions. Face-to-face contact is required for observation, and for standardized testing, patients must either be brought to the testing site or clinicians and test materials transported to patients' homes. Regardless of assessment method, the rapport that clinicians establish with patients influences both the willingness of patients to respond and their responses themselves. Some clinicians are more effective than others in eliciting information or action from patients. However, clinician-patient interaction is generally marked by a greater concern with observation than questioning. Observation provides a check on the validity of the data collected and hence may be more threatening to patients than questioning.

A frequently mentioned drawback of observation is that its use is restricted to mobility and personal self-care tasks. Observation of the more complex home management tasks is regarded as not feasible. This accounts for the absence of observation-based instruments for home management. This criticism is largely unfounded, however, as is evidenced in the use of work-sampling methods in vocational evaluation to test complex tasks. The value of observation rests on the direct assessment of task performance that it enables. Just as neurologists do not ask patients if they can touch their nose or walk a straight line but rather observe these behaviors, so too, clinicians profit from the opportunity to observe the qualitative aspects of task performance.[14] Currently, substantive attention is being directed to the benefits of observing as a data-gathering method in geriatrics and newly developed measures are beginning to include performance tests.[32] The Direct Assessment of Functional Status,[24] for example, includes performance measures of financial management and shopping.

Conclusions about self-care status may differ depending on how observations are made just as they differ depending on informant source. Although the meaning of a test item is the same for any test, there is no agreement between tests. For example, according to the Barthel Index,[33] patients must be able to cut up their food and spread butter to be scored as independent, although in the Katz Index of ADL[20] these aspects are excluded from the definition of feeding. Thus, patients may be dependent or independent based on how tasks are operationalized in the instrument.

If questioning and observation yielded comparable results, most clinicians would opt for the quicker method. Research results indicate, however, that data obtained through questioning and observation are not interchangeable, particularly for the more complex home management tasks. Agreement between methods varies from 5 to 95 percent depending on diagnosis, intellectual impairment, duration of disability, the specific ADL or IADL tested, and the informant source.[31,34–39]

Medical Records and Clinical Judgments

Like measurement, medical record audits and clinical judgments are also dependent on questioning and observation. The chief asset of these techniques is that they are expeditious. However, this advantage is outweighed by their disadvantages. For both techniques, little is known about the method or combination of methods used to obtain information about task performance. Making assumptions about data collection methods is hazardous. For instance, although staff nurses have the opportunity to observe patients as they carry out personal self-care tasks, they may evaluate performance based on their beliefs about patients' abilities without actually observing them. Having the opportunity to observe task performance is not the same as taking the opportunity to observe it. Or nurses may assist patients to expedite their own work and subsequently grade task performance based on the help given. Thus, record reviews and professional judgments provide little knowledge about data quality. Obtaining information from record review has the further disadvantage of being limited to the data that are already available however incomplete they may be.

SELECTED SELF-CARE INSTRUMENTS

This chapter highlights self-care assessment for clinical decisions. Data are gathered, recorded, and interpreted to maintain or improve a patient's functional independence. Instruments, or tests, can facilitate these processes. They provide a structure for questions and observations, a format for organizing data, and guidelines for interpreting their meaning.

A comprehensive discussion of self-care instruments is beyond the scope of this chapter. A list of references that provides an overview of self-care instruments may be found in the appendix at the end of the chapter. The purpose of this section is to illustrate the concepts of assessment purpose, content, dimensions, and methods in regard to selected instruments to foster a practical understanding of their application to clinical practice. Two mobility, two personal self-care, and two home management instruments will be discussed. For convenience, the scientific properties of validity and reliability are discussed for each instrument. *Reliability* is the consistency of the results of evaluation in repeated administrations of the instru-

ment in the absence of real change. *Validity* is the appropriateness of evaluation results for the purpose for which the instrument is being used. An instrument may be valid for one purpose (e.g., screening) but not for another purpose (e.g., assessment).

Performance-Oriented Assessment of Balance and Performance-Oriented Assessment of Gait[40]

PURPOSE

The Performance-Oriented Assessment of Balance and Performance-Oriented Assessment of Gait were designed to assess balance and gait characteristics, respectively, in the elderly. The intent was to create an instrument for use in prospective studies of falling that would require no equipment, would be easy to learn how to administer, would be reliable yet sensitive to significant changes, and would reflect the position changes used during normal daily activities. Clinically, the instruments can be used to identify maneuvers that patients are likely to have difficulty with in daily living activities, possible reasons for these difficulties, and potential medical, rehabilitative, or environmental interventions to improve mobility. Information pertinent for diagnosis and therapy is thus gathered concurrently.

CONTENT

Mobility is defined as the ability to get around one's environment. The balance instrument assesses 13 positions and position changes that stress stability; sitting balance, arising from a chair, immediate standing balance, standing balance, balance with eye closed, turning balance, balance with nudge on sternum, neck turning, one-leg standing balance, back extension, reaching up, bending down, and sitting down. The gait instrument rates nine components of gait: initiation of gait, step height, step length, step symmetry, step continuity, path deviation, trunk stability, walk stance, and turning while walking. Both instruments assess capacity.

ASSESSMENT DIMENSIONS

The balance maneuvers are graded as normal, adaptive, or abnormal based on correspondence with descriptive statements. Arising from a chair, for instance, is graded normal if the person is able to arise in a single movement without using the arms; adaptive if the person uses the arms (on chair or walking aid) to pull or push up and/or moves forward in the chair before attempting to arise; and abnormal if multiple attempts are required or the person is unable to arise without human assistance. The gait components are graded dichotomously as normal or abnormal based on descriptive statements. Abnormal grades on these instruments provide cues about the underlying cause of the balance and gait abnormalities.

METHOD

Both instruments use observation. Performance is initiated by requests from the examiner to perform each maneuver or walk.

VALIDITY AND RELIABILITY

Content validity and operationalization of instrument items was based on consultation from bioengineers, orthopedists, neurologists, rheumatologists, and physical therapists. Interrater reliability done on 15 subjects yielded agreement of 85 percent on individual items with the total score never differing by more than 10 percent.[40] The instruments have been found to be useful for detecting risk for falls.[41]

Barthel Index (The Maryland Disability Index)[33]

PURPOSE

The Barthel Index was designed to assess the ability of patients with neuromuscular or musculoskeletal disorders to care for themselves before and after rehabilitation. It has been used extensively in medical rehabilitation. Repeated assessment enables progress to be detected, including the specific tasks where improvement is exhibited and the overall rate of improvement.

CONTENT

The Barthel Index assesses capability. It is composed of 10 tasks: feeding, including cutting food; bed transfers; personal toilet, defined as washing the face, combing hair, shaving, and cleaning teeth; toileting including managing clothing, perineal care, and flushing; bathing; walking on a level surface (or moving wheelchair if walking is not feasible); ascending and descending stairs; dressing; bowel control; and bladder control. Thus, there are 3 mobility and 7 personal self-care items. Granger and Greer[42] expanded the instrument to 15 items: 6 mobility and 9 personal self-care.

ASSESSMENT DIMENSIONS

Each item on the Barthel Index is rated as "independent" or "with help." Ratings are based on descriptions of independent and dependent performance. *Help* is defined as the use of human help. Use of specialized equipment only is not viewed as help; however, the examiner is to make note of any equipment used. For scoring, an item is weighted based on assumptions about the time and amount of physical assistance required if patients are unable to perform an item. The maximum possible score is 100, which signifies the ability to do all tasks independently. Patients scoring 100 would not need help for personal self-care, although they may not be able to live independently. The lowest score is 0, which indicates complete dependence. A score of 60 is suggested as the pivotal point between independence and more marked dependence.[42] Adaptations in the assessment dimensions include changes in the weight given to various items as well as expansions of the dichotomous rating scale.[34,42,43]

METHOD

The instrument was designed to be rated by health care personnel (e.g., nurses, physical therapists, physicians) based on observation of performance. It has been adapted for self-report or proxy report,[44,45] telephone interview,[39] and medical records review.[43]

VALIDITY AND RELIABILITY

The Barthel index correlates highly with other measures of self-care status[43,46] as well as clinical judgments of functional level.[47] It has also been shown to predict discharge status and death.[42,47,48] Test-retest reliability was reported as .89,[43] and interobserver as .9.[34] Validity and reliability studies often used adapted versions of the Barthel Index. Collin and associates[34] obtained a significant Kendall's coefficient of concordance ($W = .93$) between ratings obtained by four different data gathering methods.

Kenny Self-Care Evaluation[49]

PURPOSE

The Kenny Self-Care Evaluation was designed to be used in setting treatment goals and in evaluating progress during rehabilitation. Aggregate data can be used for quality assurance.

CONTENT

The tasks included on the Kenny Self-Care Evaluation were considered to represent the minimum requirements for an individual to function independently in the home or other protected environment. It contains seven categories of self-care: bed activities, transfers, locomotion, dressing, personal hygiene, bowel and bladder, and feeding. Within each category, there are 1 to 4 tasks, each of which is divided into subtasks. The subtasks comprise the small steps

involved in the task; for example, "turn to right side" is one of the steps in "moving in bed." The 17 tasks are divided into 85 subtasks. Capacity is assessed.

ASSESSMENT DIMENSIONS

Each subtask is rated as totally independent, totally dependent, or anything in between complete independence and complete dependence. Each task is graded on a 5-point Likert scale, which ranges from 0 meaning all subtasks rated as dependent to 4 meaning all subtasks rated as independent. A score of 3 is given to the person who needs assistance or supervision in only 1 or 2 of the subtasks that make up the task; a score of 1 is given to the person who is dependent in all but a few of the subtasks. All other configurations of subtasks receive a 2.

METHOD

Each task must be observed by the examiner. Ratings are made following observation of each task. Self-reports of performance are not acceptable.

VALIDITY AND RELIABILITY

Comparisons between Kenny Self-Care Evaluation and Barthel Index ratings of stroke patients yielded a Kappa coefficient of .42 and a Spearman correlation of .73.[46] the reliability of the locomotor score (.46 or .42) was markedly lower than that of the other scores, which ranged from .71 to .94. Interrater reliability was calculated as between .67 to .74.

IADL Screener[16,50]

PURPOSE

The instrument is designed to identify community-resident elderly who are at risk for dependency. It is a screening instrument.

CONTENT

The tasks comprising the scale are those needed for continued community residence. The IADL screener consists of five of the seven IADL questions of the ADL section of the OARS Multidimensional Functional Assessment Questionnaire,[51] namely, the ability to do housework, travel, shop, prepare meals, and manage personal finances. The five items comprise a Guttman scale and are listed in order of most to least difficult. Capability is assessed.

ASSESSMENT DIMENSIONS

Performance on each item is scored as without help (scored 1), with some help (score 0), and not answered. A high score indicates higher functioning. The items are summed to give a total score.

METHOD

Like the OARS Multidimensional Functional Assessment Questionnaire from which it is derived, the IADL screener is administered by interview.

VALIDITY AND RELIABILITY

Validity of the ADL screener is based on correlations with physical ($r = .54$ to .55) and mental health ($r = .54$ to .60), predictions of physical ($r = .50$ to .51) and mental health ($r = .48$ to .51) as well as death, and relationships to type of in-home services.

Functional Activities Questionnaire[52]

PURPOSE

The *Functional Activities Questionnaire* (FAQ) is a screening tool for assessing the activities necessary for independent living. It was designed for use in community studies of normal older adults and those with mild senile dementia.

CONTENT

The Functional Activities Questionnaire concentrates on higher-level IADL. The 10 items making up the scale involve: personal finance (e.g., writing checks); managing forms like tax records and insurance claims (e.g., insurance, social security); shopping for groceries or clothing; playing a game of skill or working on a hobby; making tea or coffee; preparing a meal; keeping track of current events; tracking information presented orally or in writing (e.g., a television show or magazine article); remembering commitments (e.g., doctor's appointments, festivities); and traveling out of the neighborhood. The FAQ is intended to tap universal skills of older adults. Thus, performance is assessed. If older adults are not presently performing a task, their capacity to do so is queried.

ASSESSMENT DIMENSIONS

Each item is rated using a 6-point scheme. Although the response options are phrased differently for some items, they all involve performing a task without difficulty or advice, with difficulty, with frequent advice or assistance, and with substantive or total assistance. Each item is scored from 0 to 3, with 0 indicating independence and 3 dependence. For activities not normally undertaken by a person, the proxy must specify whether the person would be unable to undertake the task if required (scored 1) or could do so if required (scored 0). The total score is the sum of the individual item scores. Higher scores reflect dependency.

METHOD

The FAQ is to be completed by a spouse, relative, or close friend of the patient. It is administered in written format.

VALIDITY AND RELIABILITY

Ratings on the FAQ correlated .72 with Lawton and Brody's IADL scale[53] and differentiated between normal, depressed, and demented patients.[54] The FAQ predicted mental status and functional assessments better than the IADL scale.[53] Scores on the FAQ in a longitudinal study reflected both clinical judgments of change and cognitive status.[55] The item total correlations for all items exceeded .80.

SELF-CARE ASSESSMENT AND CLINICAL DECISION MAKING

Self-care assessment is the starting point for the clinical decision making that underlies patient care. It provides information that is useful in devising a plan of care. Patients who have difficulty doing tasks or are dependent in task performance need a mechanism for fulfilling these needs. Self-care assessment points out the kind and extent of care needed, but it does not dictate how these needs are to be filled. There is no formula for converting unmet needs to a plan of care. Matching self-care needs with health and social services is a complex decision-making process that takes into account multiple factors other than self-care status.

When it is possible, practical, and desired, the task dysfunctions identified through self-care assessment should be remediated. When remediation is viewed as not feasible, compensatory strategies are employed. In general, these aim at creating an environment that supports function. Patients differ in the resources that they can bring to bear on providing environmental supports. Some have family members or friends who are able and willing to provide the needed care, while others lack these "people" resources. Some have the financial means to provide for themselves within their own home, while others lack such economic resources. By identifying a patient's options and then weighing the risks and benefits associated with each option, an optimal decision can be made. When deliberating various alternatives, it is particularly critical to bring into focus a patient's

abilities, not just disabilities. Self-care assessment focuses on problem areas because these require attention. However, one should not lose sight of self-care competencies since these data contribute to defining the parameters of the least restrictive setting in which the older adult can function safely and productively.

Underlying each plan of care is a set of values related to how a patient's needs might best be met. Central to these values are beliefs about how much risk is acceptable for a patient, how protective the care should be, and how much money should be spent to furnish the needed care. Patients and their families may not share the same values and hence may seek different care plans. While value conflicts are not easily resolved, optimal clinical decision making about self-care cannot occur without respect for, and consideration of, fundamental differences in value orientations.

REVIEW QUESTIONS

1. *Prior to her discharge from a rehabilitation hospital following a left cerebral vascular accident, one home assessment is covered by Mrs. Tapen's insurance carrier. What level(s) of self-care performance should be given a priority during the home assessment, and why should it (they) be given a priority?*

2. *Katz and Fillenbaum have identified task hierarchies that rank order tasks from those that are most difficult to perform to those that are least difficult to perform. In your estimation, would the hierarchies hold true regardless of pathology (e.g., rheumatoid arthritis, parkinsonism, Alzheimer's disease, schizophrenia) or impairment (e.g., limited range of motion, incoordination, hearing impairment, short-term memory deficit)? How would differential pathologies and impairments reorder these task hierarchies?*

3. *What are the potential risks of not differentiating between capacity and performance when conducting a self-care assessment through self-report or proxy report?*

4. *When determining the level of independence in self-care, why is the type of assistance needed just as important, or more important, than the fact that assistance is needed?*

5. *When an interdisciplinary team approach is used, identify which data collection methods would typically be used by each professional and how multiple data points derived from different methods can impact data quality.*

6. *Propose a geriatric assessment strategy for the facility in which you work.*

REFERENCES

1. American College of Physicians, Health and Public Policy Committee: Comprehensive functional assessment for elderly patients. Annals of Internal Medicine 107:70–72, 1988.
2. Applegate, WB, Blass, JP and Williams, TF: Instruments for the functional assessment of older patients. Current Concepts in Geriatrics 322:1207–1213, 1990.
3. Katz, S: Assessing self-maintenance: Activities of daily living, mobility, and instrumental activities of daily living. Journal of the American Geriatrics Society 31:721–727, 1983.
4. Society of General Internal Medicine Task Force on Health Assessment: Health status assessment for elderly patients. Journal of the American Geriatrics Society 37:562–569, 1989.
5. US Department of Health and Human Services, National Center for Health Statistics: Current estimates from the national health interview survey, United States, 1981, Vital and Health Statistics, Series 10, no 141, DHHS publication No (PHS) 83-1569. U.S. Government Printing Office, Washington, DC, October 1982.
6. Katz, S and Stroud, MW: Functional assessment in geriatrics: A review of progress and directions. Journal of the American Geriatrics Society 37:267–271, 1989.
7. Besdine, RW: Introduction. In Abrams, WB and Berkow, R (eds): The Merck Manual of Geriatrics. Merck, Sharp, & Dohme Research Laboratories, 1990, Rahway, NJ, pp 2–4.
8. Frengley, JD, Lefton, E, Farkas, K, and Mion, L: An index of dependency that assesses assistance needs. In Maddox, GL and Busse, EW (eds): Aging: The Universal Human Experience. Springer, New York, 1987, pp 341–349.
9. Goodenough, GK and Lutz, LJ: Loss of function in the frail elderly. Postgraduate Medicine 82:75–85, 1987.
10. Hanley, R, Alecxih, L, Wiener, J and Kennell, D: Predicting Elderly Nursing Home Admissions: Results from the 1982–84 National Long-Term Care Survey. The Brookings Institute, Washington, DC, 1989.
11. Newman, S, Struyk, R, Wright, P and Rice, M: Overwhelming Odds: Caregiving and the Risk of Institutionalization. U.I. Report 3691-01. The Urban Institute, Washington, DC, November 1988.
12. Branch, LG: Functional abilities of the elderly: An update on the Massachusetts health care panel study. In Haynes, SG and Feinleib, M (eds): Second Conference on the Epidemiology of Aging. US Department of Health and Human Services, NIH Publication No 80-969, 1980, pp 237–265.
13. Bishop, C: Living arrangement choices of elderly singles. Health Care Financing Review 7:65–73, 1986.
14. Guralnik, JM, Branch, LG, Cummings, SR and Curb, JD: Physical performance measures in aging research. Journals of Gerontology: Medical Sciences 44:M141–M146, 1989.
15. Barer, D and Nouri, F: Measurement of activities of daily living. Clinical Rehabilitation 3:179–287, 1989.
16. Fillenbaum, GG: Development of a brief, internationally usable screening instrument. In Maddox, GL and Busse, EW (eds): Aging: The Universal Human Experience. New York, Springer, New York, 1987, pp 328–334.
17. Lawton, MP and Brody, EM: Assessment of older people: Self-maintaining and instrumental activities of daily living. The Gerontologist 9:179–186, 1969.
18. Lawton, MP: Behavioral and social components of functional capacity. Geriatric Assessment Methods for Clinical Decision Making. NIH Consensus Development Conference, October 19–21, 1987, pp 23–29.
19. Nouri, FM and Lincoln, NB: An extended activities of daily living scale for stroke patients. Clinical Rehabilitation 1:301–305, 1987.
20. Katz, S, Ford, AB, Moskowitz, RW, Jackson, BA and Jaffe, MW: Studies of illness in the aged. The Index of ADL: A standardized measure of biological and psychosocial function. Journal of the American Medical Association 185:914–919, 1963.
21. Branch, LG and Meyers, AR: Assessing physical function in the elderly. Clinics in Geriatric Medicine 3:29–51, 1987.
22. Granger, CV, Hamilton, BB and Sherwin, FA: Guide for Use of the Uniform Data Set for Medical Rehabilitation. Buffalo General Hospital, Buffalo, NY, 1986.
23. Williams, ME, Hadler, NM and Earp, JL: Manual ability as a marker of dependency in geriatric women. Journal of Chronic Diseases 35:115–122, 1982.

24. Lowenstein, DA, Amigo, E, Duara, R, Guterman, A, Hurwitz, D, Berkowitz, N, Wilkie, F, Weinberg, G, Black, B, Gittelman, B and Eisdorfer, C: A new scale for the assessment of functional status in Alzheimer's Disease and related disorders. Journal of Gerontology 44:P114–P121, 1989.

25. Jette, AM: Functional Status Index: Reliability of a chronic disease evaluation instrument. Archives of Physical Medicine and Rehabilitation 61:395–401, 1980.

26. World Health Organization (WHO): International Classification of Impairments, Disabilities, and Handicaps (ICIDH). World Health Organization, Geneva, 1980.

27. Pfeiffer, E: A Short Portable Mental Status Questionnaire for the assessment of organic brain deficit in elderly patients. Journal of the American Geriatrics Society 23:433–441, 1975.

28. McCue, M, Rogers, JC and Goldstein, G: Relationships between neuropsychological and functional assessment in elderly neuropsychiatric patients. Rehabilitation Psychology 35:91–99, 1990.

29. Fox, DJ: The Research Process in Education. Holt, Rinehart and Winston, New York, 1969.

30. Frey, WD: Functional outcome: Assessment and evaluation. In DeLisa, JA (ed): Rehabilitation Medicine. JB Lippincott, Philadelphia, 1989, pp 158–172.

31. Rubenstein, LZ, Schairer, C, Wieland, GD and Kane, R: Systematic biases in functional status assessment of elderly adults: Effects of different data sources. Journal of Gerontology 39:686–691, 1984.

32. Branch, LG: An alternative approach in multidimensional functional assessment. In Maddox, GL and Busse, EW (eds): Aging: The Universal Human Experience. Springer, New York, 1987, pp 335–340.

33. Mahoney, FI and Barthel, DW: Functional evaluation: The Barthel Index. Maryland State Medical Journal 14:61–65, 1965.

34. Collin, C, Wade, DT, Davis, S and Horne, V: The Barthel ADL Index: A reliability study. International Disabilities Studies 10:61–63, 1988.

35. Harris, BA, Jette, AM, Campion, EW and Cleary, PD: Validity of self-report measures of functional disability. Topics in Geriatric Rehabilitation 1:31–41, 1986.

36. Klein-Parris, C, Clermont-Michel, T and O'Neill, J: Effectiveness and efficiency of criterion testing versus interviewing for collecting functional assessment information. The American Journal of Occupational Therapy 40:486–491, 1986.

37. Kuriansky, JB, Gurland, BJ, Fleiss, JL and Cowan, D: The assessment of self-care capacity in geriatric psychiatric patients by objective and subjective methods. Journal of Clinical Psychology 32:95–102, 1976.

38. Malzer, RL: Patient performance level during inpatient physical rehabilitation: Therapist, nurse, and patient perspectives. Archives of

39. Shinar, D, Gross, CR, Bronstein, KS, Licata-Gehr, EE, Eden, DT, Cabrera, AR, Fishman, IG, Roth, AA, Barwick, JA and Kunitz, SC: Reliability of the activities of daily living scale and its use in telephone interview. Archives of Physical Medicine and Rehabilitation 68:723–728, 1987.

40. Tinetti, ME: Performance-oriented assessment of mobility problems in elderly patients. Journal of the American Geriatrics Society 34:119–126, 1986.

41. Tinetti, ME and Ginter, SF: Identifying mobility dysfunctions in elderly patients: Standard neuromuscular examination or direct assessment. Journal of the American Medical Association 259:1190–1193, 1988.

42. Granger, CV and Greer, DS: Functional status measurement and medical rehabilitation outcomes. Archives of Physical Medicine and Rehabilitation 57:103–108, 1976.

43. Granger CV, Albrecht, GL and Hamilton, BB: Outcome of comprehensive medical rehabilitation: Measurement by PULSES Profile and the Barthel Index. Archives of Physical Medicine and Rehabilitation 60:145–154, 1979.

44. Roy, CW, Togneri, J, Hay, E and Pentland, B: An inter-rater reliability study of the Barthel Index. International Journal of Rehabilitation Research 11:67–70, 1988.

45. McGinnis, GE, Marymae, BA, Seward, BA, DeJong, G and Osberg, JS: Program evaluation of physical medicine and rehabilitation departments using self-report Barthel. Archives of Physical Medicine and Rehabilitation 67:123–125, 1986.

46. Gresham, GE, Phillips, TF and Labi, MLC: ADL status in stroke: Relative merits of three standard indexes. Archives of Physical Medicine and Rehabilitation 61:355–358, 1980.

47. Wylie, CM and White, BK: A measure of disability. Archives of Environmental Health 8:834–939, 1964.

48. Granger, CV, Sherwood, CC and Greer, DS: Functional status measures in a comprehensive stroke care program. Archives of Physical Medicine and Rehabilitation 58:555–561, 1977.

49. Iversen, IA, Siberberg, NE, Stever, RC and Schoening, HA: The Revised Kenny Self-Care Evaluation: A Numerical Measure of Independence in Activities of Daily Living. Sister Kenny Institute, Minneapolis, MN, 1973.

50. Fillenbaum, GG: Screening the elderly: A brief instrumental activities of daily living measure. Journal of the American Geriatrics Society 33:698–706, 1985.

51. Fillenbaum, GG: Multidimensional Functional Assessment of Older Adults. Lawrence Erlbaum, Hillsdale, NJ, 1988.

52. McDowell I and Newell, C: Measuring Health: A Guide to Rating Scales and Questionnaires. Oxford University Press, New York, 1987.

53. Pfeffer, RI, Kurosaki, TT, Harrah, CH, Chance, JM and Filos, S: Measurement of functional activities in older adults in the

community. Journal of Gerontology 37:323–329, 1982.

54. Pfeffer, RI, Kurosaki, TT, Harrah, CH, Chance, JM, Bates, D, Detels, R, Filos, S and Butzke, C: A survey tool for senile dementia. American Journal of Epidemiology 114:515–527, 1981.

55. Pfeffer, RI, Kurosaki, TT, Chance, JM, Filos, S and Bates, D: Use of the Mental Function Index in older adults: Reliability, validity, and measurement of change over time. American Journal of Epidemiology 120:922–935, 1984.

APPENDIX 12–1

Resources for Functional Assessment Instruments

Ernst, M and Ernst, NS: Functional capacity. In Mangen, DJ and Peterson, WA (eds): Health, Program Evaluation, and Demography, Vol 3. University of Minnesota, Minneapolis, 1984.

Kane, RA and Kane, RL: Assessing the Elderly. DC Heath, Lexington, MA, 1981.

McDowell, I and Newell, C: Measuring Health: A Guide to Rating Scales and Questionnaires. Oxford University Press, New York, 1987.

Psychopharmacology Bulletin. Assessment in diagnosis and treatment of geropsychiatric patients, Vol 24, 1988.

Spilker, B: Quality of Life Assessment in Clinical Trials. Raven Press, New York, 1990.

PART

II

INTERRUPTIONS IN PERFORMANCE

Part I of this volume considered what happens during the normal aging process, both in terms of individual functioning (cognitive, psychosocial, neuromuscular, sensory, and sensory integrative) and in terms of performance of various kinds of functional activity. Part II considers common events that occur in later life which can interfere with function, and discusses what health care professionals can do to minimize the negative impact of these interruptions.

It is inevitable that at some point in the aging process, something will interfere with performance. Death comes to us all sooner or later, in spite of increases in life expectancy. This is the ultimate interruption in performance, but there is considerable potential for events prior to death that may limit the individual's ability to accomplish needed or desired activities. As has been noted in earlier chapters in this book, it is typical that an older individual will experience some loss of physiological functioning and have two to three chronic diseases as well.[1] These factors do not occur equally among all older adults, nor do they impact equally on individual function. Given demographic changes, it is not clear whether the average health status of older adults will improve or decline.[2] However, it is clear that the absolute numbers of elders with illnesses and functional decrements will increase. Davis[2] predicts that the elderly nursing home population will rise from 2.3 million in 1990 to 4.1 million by the year 2020, and elderly individuals needing home care, from 4 million to 6.3 million.

For older adults, interruptions in function may relate to individual changes, either loss of physiological function or onset of a disease process, or to the social milieu. Loss of family and friends may have as great an impact on function as loss of physical ability. To get a feel for the effect of such a loss, imagine that you do not know how to drive and that your roommate, who has always served as your chauffeur, decides to move out. If an older individual has never learned to drive, cook, or manage money, independence may be compromised by loss of important services, in addition to loss of emotional support. Environmental factors have an effect on function, as well. Supportive environments can enhance performance regardless of loss of physical ability; unsupportive environments can impair function in the most able of individuals. To experience environmental challenges personally, simply take a walk on an icy day. Now imagine that you are an older individual with some degree of osteoporosis and diminished visual acuity, and consider the additional difficulties such an individual might have taking the same walk.

The first section of Part II presents data about functional dependence of older adults,[3] indicating that absolute numbers of individuals in need of support for function will increase considerably. In the three chapters that follow, examples of events which cause interruptions in performance demonstrates some of the special characteristics of impairment in older adults. The first example is dementia. This is a cognitive disorder which is most common among older adults. Although dementing illnesses may occur as young as age 40, such illnesses are most likely to emerge after age 65 and are quite common after age 80. The second example, depression, is a psychological disorder that is common in people of any age but, as is true for many disorders, has special characteristics in elderly individuals. The third is falls, an example of a physical dysfunction caused, perhaps, by a combination of sensory integrative and environmental factors (at least, as best we understand the causes at this time).

These are by no means the only interruptions that can be encountered by older adults, but they demonstrate some of the special factors of performance interruption in elderly individuals. Among the other problems that must be considered is the long-term consequences of chronic disease. Many elderly people must contend with emerging disability caused by many years of diabetes or arthritis. In addition, a whole range of diseases increase in incidence with increasing age, most notably cancer and cardiovascular diseases such as heart disease and stroke. Sensory loss may be compounded by actual disease process such as cataracts or macular degeneration.[4,5] Older adults are not immune from such social problems as alcoholism and drug abuse.[6,7] Finally, a psychosocial interruption that is inevitable with advancing age is the issue of loss. One 95-year-old woman, who described herself as being in good health, except, of course, for macular degeneration, high blood pressure, and arthritis, complained that she had buried all her friends, and had no desire to go on. When she suffered a mild stroke, from which someone in her physical condition would most typically have recovered, she stated that she was ready to be with her friends, stopped eating, and died three weeks later. This is not the inevitable outcome of such a series of losses, and most older adults choose to find ways to cope with the inevitable losses. It is, however, an issue not to be ignored in working with older adults.

The second section of Part II considers what it is that health care providers can do to assist the older adult to maintain his or her desired level of functional performance. Each of the four chapters discusses a particular system in which health care is provided: preventive, home health, rehabilitation, and nursing home. Type and location of service (e.g., community based or institutional) must be matched to the particular need. Interventions may be targeted directly to the individual, the social system, or the environment. Thus, following careful assessment of the individual and the environment, the care provider must decide whether to develop a treatment plan for the person, to confer with informal care givers, or to consult to planners of the environment such as architects and policy makers.

Intervention with older adults has some special characteristics. All elderly people have some degree of physiological loss, for example, muscle strength, flexibility, and reaction time. At the same time, not all people experience the same kinds of loss,[8] and the extent to which the loss impacts on performance is highly variable.

In addition, most older adults have two to three chronic diseases that hover in the background, perhaps with exacerbations which intrude on day-to-day task performance.[1] These chronic diseases can pose challenges when their effects are conflicting. For example, an individual may have arthritis and osteoporosis. For osteoporosis, some form of weight-bearing exercise would typically be recommended, but such a regimen must be established with particular care in the presence arthritis, where further joint damage is cause for concern. Riley[9] notes that exercise may injure joints and muscles if not carefully planned. These types of "multiple interactions"[10] (p. 85) when added to other factors, social and environmental, create situations of considerable complexity.

Seriousness of diseases is different in older adults. Some kinds of cancer that are relatively lethal in younger people may be much less aggressive in an older person. One elderly man was diagnosed with prostatic cancer 25 years ago, on his sixty-fifth birthday. Although not disease free, he is vigorous and active, and it now appears that this cancer will not be the cause of his death. His case is not unusual. On the other hand, influenza, which is merely unpleasant for a younger person, may be lethal to an older one. Older people, require more time to return to base line following such a stress.[8]

In working with an older person, the social system and environment cannot be ignored. Many people may be involved with the elder, providing various informal (or formal) forms of functional support. Changes in their situations or needs can impact on an older adult. For example, one older woman lived with her adult daughter's family. When the daughter's husband was required to move because of a job change, the woman was faced with a choice of leaving the community in which she had lived all her life or finding a place to live outside the family support system.

Health care professionals working with the elderly are likely to find their roles somewhat blurred. In some instances, home health, for example, the provider may need to assume responsibilities more typical of another professional, simply because he or she is the only one intervening with the client. A nurse may need to complete an assessment of instrumental activities of daily living if an occupational therapist is not available to do so. In institutional settings, teams of providers often work together, and their roles in the particular facility may have idiosyncratic definitions, based on the institution and the availability of particular disciplines. Collaboration is essential.[8]

It is beyond the scope of this volume to consider in detail the specific roles of various professionals working with older adults. In fact, most care providers assert that they are concerned with function. The specific way in which they define function and the kinds of interventions they provide are significantly different. The physician is concerned with the function of organ systems, the nurse with health and with assuring that medical interventions are carried out. The social worker focuses on the environment, particularly social, and assuring that relevant resources are made available to the individual. The physical therapist emphasizes physical mobility, the occupational therapist, ability to accomplish needed or desired tasks. There are many other professionals who may be involved in care, as well, and each has a unique perspective and emphasis.

The most helpful intervention will be provided if each professional identifies and integrates his or her unique contribution into a plan that recognizes the needs of the client. Professionals should be firm in asserting that while they *could* provide a wide variety of interventions, other professionals may have greater expertise in specific areas. When this does not occur, the client's care will suffer.

The desired outcomes from intervening with an older person are function and life satisfaction rather than "health" or "wellness."[11] It is unrealistic to expect that every older adult will be "cured." It is also unnecessary since the presence of "illness" does not automatically imply impairment.

Careful consideration must be given to the wishes of the individual. The 95-year-old woman described previously lived in fear of total isolation and the possibility of being confined to a nursing home, a circumstance that was anathema to her. For her, the desirable outcome was death. This is often difficult for health care professionals to accept, as there is a strong societal bias toward preserving life at all costs. Similarly, there is an assumption that independence is always desirable. The independent living movement has contradicted that belief, holding that it is up to the individual to decide how much, and what kind, of independence is optimal. An individual might choose not to dress himself if this requires a level of energy expenditure that leaves none for other activities which he defines as more gratifying.

The third section of Part II focuses on some special issues that are of importance in working with older adults. One of these, as discussed previously, is the fact that health care providers often work with people who are dying.[12] It is incumbent on professionals to recognize when this is the case and to work effectively to make the process as satisfying as possible for the individual and family. It is also incumbent on the professional to recognize when there is hope, and when an individual is giving up prematurely, perhaps because of depression. It is not easy, but it is essential, to make this distinction and intervene effectively.

As noted, families are of particular importance in working with older adults. Even the definition of family is no longer simple,[10] as families now include multiple generations and informal social networks, all of which may be fluid over time. Relationships between professionals and families can be problematic or can enhance outcomes for the older individual.[13] Similarly, relationships among professionals can be problematic or can support desirable outcomes of service.

Technological advances have done more than prolong life. They have provided a wide range of methods for making life more satisfying and helping people accomplish what they need and want to do.[14] Some professionals are tempted to assume that older adults do not relate well to so-called high-technology interventions. While this may be true for some, it is equally true that many elderly individuals respond extremely well to new technologies and find them quite enjoyable and gratifying. In circumstances where they are not well accepted, it may be due to the manner in which they are introduced rather than the technologies themselves.

A discussion of public policy is essential to understanding the circumstances of older adults.[15] A wide range of policies affect the lives of older adults.[16] Social Security, Medicare, the Age Discrimination in Employment Act, the Older Americans Act, and the Omnibus Budget Reconciliation Act of 1986 have substantial impact on the lives and well-being of older individuals. Some policies have unplanned consequences. Social security, for example, discourages people from working between the ages of 65 and 72 by taxing benefits heavily if recipients exceed a modest earned income. Given the current state of the work force, and the dramatically increasing social security burden, this may not be desirable, and the policy may need to be reconsidered. It is incumbent on professionals to assist their clients not only by working directly with them but also by influencing policy to operate in their best interests.

In working with older adults, health care professionals must consider all the special circumstances that characterize the aging process. In doing so, they can help assure that the later stages of life are satisfying to the individual, the family, and the broader society. This is a challenge to the professional but one that carries considerable potential benefit to all.

REFERENCES

1. Albert, MS: Assessment of cognitive dysfunction. In Albert, MS and Moss, MB (eds): Geriatric Neuropsychology. Guilford Press, New York, 1989, pp 57–81.
2. Davis, K: Health in an aging America. CRS Review, Sept-Oct, 1990, pp 32–34.
3. Cutler, NE: Functional limitation and the need for personal care in the older population. In Bonder, BR and Wagner, M (eds): Functional Performance in Older Adults. FA Davis, Philadelphia, 1994.
4. Branch, LG, Horowitz, A and Carr, C: The implications for everyday life of incident self-reported visual decline among people over age 65 living in the community. Gerontologist 29:359–365, 1989.
5. Heinemann, AW, Colorez, A, Frank, S and Taylor, D: Leisure activity participation of elderly individuals with low vision. Gerontologist 28:181–184, 1988.
6. LaGreca, AJ, Akers, RL and Dwyer, JW: Life events and alcohol behavior among older adults. Gerontologist 28:552–558, 1988.
7. Alexander, F and Duff, RW: Social interaction and alcohol use in retirement communities. Gerontologist 28:632–636, 1988.
8. Seigler, IC: Developmental health psychology. In Storandt, M and VandenBos, GR (eds): The Adult Years: Continuity and Change. Ameri-

can Psychological Association, Washington, DC, 1990, pp 119–142.

9. Riley, MW: Aging in the Twenty-First Century. Boettner Lecture. Boettner Research Institute, Bryn Mawr, PA, 1990.

10. Gatz, M: Clinical psychology and aging. In Storandt, M and VandenBos, GR (eds): The Adult Years: Continuity and Change. American Psychological Association, Washington, DC, 1990, pp 83–114.

11. Rodenheaver, D: When old age became a social problem, women were left behind. Gerontologist 27:741–746, 1987.

12. Smyth, KA: Loss and activity. In Bonder, BR and Wagner, M (eds): Functional Performance in Older Adults. FA Davis, Philadelphia, 1994.

13. Hasselkus, B: Working with family caregivers: The therapeutic alliance. In Bonder, BR and Wagner, M (eds): Functional Performance in Older Adults. FA Davis, Philadelphia, 1994.

14. Mann, WC: Technology. In Bonder, BR and Wagner, M (eds): Functional Performance in Older Adults. FA Davis, Philadelphia, 1994.

15. Benson, W: Public Policy and functional performance. In Bonder, BR and Wagner, M (eds): Functional Performance in Older Adults. FA Davis, Philadelphia, 1994.

17. Neugarten, BL and Neugarten, DA: Policy issues in an aging society. In Storandt, M and VandenBos, GR (eds): The Adult Years: Continuity and Change. American Psychological Association, Washington, DC, 1990, pp 147–167.

INTRODUCTION

One of the greatest indicators of long-term institutional care of elderly people is not medical need but, rather, the lack of social support when need arises. Older people with few or limited family relationships are prime candidates for institutionalization when they become sick . . . —N. L. CHAPPELL[6]

Chapter

Functional Limitation and the Need for Personal Care

NEAL E. CUTLER

OBJECTIVES

By the end of this chapter, the reader will be able to:

1 Discuss the relationship of aging to dependence.

2 Define *care-giver ratio.*

3 Estimate the changes in need for personal health care by the year 2010.

4 Estimate the supply of personal care givers by the year 2010.

5 Describe two potential scenarios for outcomes based on estimates for care needs and care givers.

6 Discuss the policy implications of two differing scenarios for care needs and care givers.

This chapter focuses on the connections among aging, functional limitations, and personal care, with estimates of the availability of personal care for older persons over the next 20 years. It is true, of course, that an aging society does not necessarily mean a dependent society. The good news, after all, is that 95 percent of older people do not live in nursing homes and 75 percent of older people do not have functional disabilities; but it is important to identify the kinds of dependency that are likely to increase so that societal responses can be planned.

Questions of aging, dependency, and long-term care are often discussed in the context of institutional care. Yet it has become very clear that most older men and women can and do continue to live in the community and in their own homes, even if they are ill, and have some measurable level of disability.

THE CAPACITY OF OLDER PERSONS TO CONTINUE LIVING IN THE COMMUNITY

Several factors contribute to the capacity of older persons to continue to live in the community. In addition to individualized personal care provided by other people, these factors include:

- New medical procedures and services
- Sophisticated pharmaceuticals
- Innovative architectural planning and increased housing options
- Community-based nutrition and social support services such as adult day care

Such developments assist people to avoid entering a nursing home, which might have been the solution to dependency a few years ago.

THE IMPORTANCE OF PERSONAL CARE GIVING

The importance of personal care giving in an aging society is not difficult to image. Within a diverse older population some groups are increasing at a much faster rate than others.[1] Of special importance are the "oldest-old,"[2] where most of the men and women who are in need of personal care can be found.

Consider the population growth from 1980 to 2010. The total U.S. population is projected to grow by 24.5 percent, with the 65+ age group having double the growth rate, 54.1 percent. The 85+ age group, by contrast, is projected to increase by 173.0 percent in this same period. Furthermore, from the perspective of individual and societal demands for personal care, even this increase in the 85+ population, from 2.2 to 6.1 million people, may be a conservative esti-

mate. The next 2 decades are likely to see continued improvements in medical science further prolonging life and increasing the number of older-old people beyond current estimates.[3]

In the longer term, the need for personal care will be even greater. The projections of the older-old population to the year 2010 cited here do not include the future impact of the Baby Boom. In 2010 the oldest boomer will be only 64 years old and won't have her 85th birthday until the year 2031.

THE RESEARCH CHALLENGE

The challenge for research in societal and financial gerontology as well as for public policy is to identify those limitations in physical functioning that need not be responded to by the "nursing home solution." When the problem is one of the need for personal care in the home, for assistance with everyday activities of daily living, then the logical and obvious solution is to somehow provide that personal care. If all that an older women or man needs is regular help in taking a bath at home, there's no reason to send her or him to a nursing home.

PROJECTIONS OF THE CARE-RECEIVER AND CARE-GIVER POPULATIONS

In developing projections of the care-receiver and care-giver populations, 1980–2010, this chapter explores the following conceptual and empirical issues:

- The amount of dependence potentially found in the older population is defined and estimated in terms of limitations in *activities of daily living* (ADL) among older persons. In our model it represents societal demand for personal care-giving services and is estimated by applying national ADL rates to national demographic projections.

- The supply of personal care givers is similarly defined and measured. In family and societal terms substantial research documents the proposition that daughters and daughters-in-law are the primary personal care givers of elderly people. In demographic terms, consequently, our analysis focuses on middle-aged women (age 55 to 64) as the population group which, in spite of recent changes in gender roles, represents and will probably continue to represent the largest pool of informal care givers. While this is not to deny that sons are often effective care givers, most prior research suggests that national estimates should focus on middle-aged women.
- The size and health status of the older population change in response to the underlying dynamics of mortality and morbidity. A decline in old-age mortality will produce an increase in the number of frail older-old persons. In the short run, however, medical procedures, pharmaceuticals, and social services will extend the lives of older people who in previous years may well have died. By contrast, in the longer run, healthy longevity will be produced by such life-long health-span dynamics[22] as improvements in diet and smoking behavior. Until this attractive longer-range future arrives, many of the increased numbers of surviving older people will remain alive but in a more dependent and less healthy condition.[4]
- Combining the estimates of older care receivers in need of personal assistance with estimates of the supply of care givers provides the basis for calculating a population-based *care-giver ratio* (CGR), which can be projected to future years. Beyond simple projection to the near future, however, the care-giver ratio is used to stimulate how alternative future circumstances might affect the overall care-giving relationship, under circumstances of increased functional dependency (increased demand) or a reduced ability or willingness of middle-aged women to provide personal care to their parents or in-laws (reduced supply).

The years between now and 2010 reflect only the nearer future demands for personal care and is a time during which the baby boomers born in 1946 to 1964 are just moving into their middle age.[5] As these 80 million people move into old age, however, the ratio of care givers to potential care receivers will become especially acute.

MEASURING THE NEED FOR PERSONAL CARE: ACTIVITIES OF DAILY LIVING

As Kane and Kane[15] emphasize, when we talk about the need for personal care on the part of older people, we are talking about functional limitation, conceptualized in terms of a standard set of *activities of daily living* (ADL).[7] A person is considered to have some degree of functional limitation if he or she cannot perform the activities without the assistance of another person. The implied focus of most ADL research is on people living in the community who need assistance with these activities in order to stay independent, rather than on people living in nursing homes or hospitals who require much more substantial and complex personal and medical supports. The standard set of five activities of daily living are:

- Bathing
- Dressing
- Moving (from a bed or chair)
- Toileting
- Eating

Not included in this definition are personal limitations in such activities as cooking, housecleaning, and money management, referred to as *instrumental activities of daily living* (IADL), which reflect a less acute need for daily assistance. Overall estimates of the need for care would, of course, be higher if IADL and ADL were combined.

These ADL measures of functional limitation have been used in a broad array of research and have been included in major federal government surveys (such as the 1984 National Health Interview Survey, and the 1984 Survey of Income and Program Participation), the goals of which include estimation of functional limitation for the older population.[8,28] In addition, there is increasing use of ADL indicators to trigger private health and long-term care insurance benefits.[9] Analysis of ADL played a central role in a recent federal litigation over the allocation of Older Americans Act dollars.[10] Probably the most general endorsement of the widespread importance of this approach to the measurement of functional limitation for all gerontology disciplines is the inclusion of a version of the ADL scale in the 1990 census.[11]

The typical use of these five activities is to determine if the older person can perform them independently or only with the help of another individual.[12] The five activities are usually treated as of equal importance in measuring overall functional limitation. A summed ADL score is calculated, ranging from 0 to 5 limitations, representing the individual's level of dependence on the personal assistance of another person to perform the activities.

The measurement of functional capacity via large-scale survey assessment of ADL is certainly not the only way to assess the need for personal care. Clearly, continued cooperation among gerontological, demographic, and clinical researchers is necessary to:

- Refine and sharpen definitions
- Ensure that the intensity of the day-to-day experience of care giving and care receiving is reflected in this research

The connection among the ADL concept, independence, and the "nursing home solution" is fairly straightforward: Without the help of the other person to assist in the everyday personal tasks, the functionally dependent man or woman might have to be institutionalized. Economic concern as well as dignity and humanity suggest the senselessness of dispatching someone to a nursing home when the real need is simply regular personal assistance in getting dressed or eating. Dependency over time may well become too acute, too complex, or too expensive for home care. However, as suggested by Professor Chappell,[6] quoted at the beginning of this chapter, there is an identifiable range of functional limitations that does not require the nursing home solution as the first order response.

The present study uses the ADL rates produced by the Supplement on Aging of the 1984 Health Interview Survey, a nationally representative survey conducted by the U.S. National Center for Health Statistics. The Supplement on Aging included interviews with 11,497 respondents age 65 and above, representing 26,433,000 community-residing older persons in 1984.[8] As detailed below, we applied the age-sex ADL rates from the survey to the parallel age-sex U.S. Census population projections[13] in order to estimate the magnitude of the ADL dependent population over the 1980–2010 period.

Having said this, however, one important caveat is in order: Technically speaking, the 1984 Health Interview Survey is not a complete population survey. As with virtually all surveys, it sampled the population of community households and residents, excluding persons living in institutions. Normally, this is not a significant limitation since the percentage of the total population living in institutions is relatively small.

In the present context, however, this deviation from complete population sampling should be noted, even though it does not detract from the utility of the 1984 Supplement on Aging data. Among the institutions not included in the otherwise nationally representative Health Interview Survey are hospitals, nursing homes, and other residential care facilities. Older persons with the highest levels of functional limitation, that is, men and women who require institutional care, are thus not included in the sample and are not represented in national estimates of overall quantity of dependency in the older population or in care-giver ratios.[3]

On the other hand, once we acknowledge that for many older men and women personal care in the home is a feasible and desirable alternative to nursing home residence, then the following key questions should be examined:

1. Given the aging of the population and the strong correlation between older age and functional limitation, how much ADL-related personal care will U.S. society require as we enter the twenty-first century?
2. Where will this personal care come from?

NATIONAL ESTIMATES OF THE DEMAND FOR PERSONAL CARE

What, then, is the magnitude of ADL-defined functional limitation in the community-resident older population? Three points should be emphasized with respect to the national ADL rates presented in Table 13–1:

1. Each of the five daily activities is related to age; the older the man or woman, the greater the need for personal care to accomplish the activity. For example, six times as

TABLE 13–1 **ADL Rates per 1000 Persons**

Bathing	Total	Male	Female
65–74	35.2	33.4	36.7
75–84	80.9	68.2	88.8
85+	217.2	194.9	227.9

Dressing	Total	Male	Female
65–74	29.3	32.5	26.8
75–84	50.8	56.6	47.3
85+	132.3	126.5	135.7

Moving	Total	Male	Female
65–74	17.7	17.4	17.9
75–84	36.7	28.8	41.8
85+	89.6	66.7	99.1

Toileting	Total	Male	Female
65–74	12.4	13.6	11.4
75–84	29.3	22.7	33.4
85+	82.8	56.4	95.3

Eating	Total	Male	Female
65–74	6.3	8.5	4.7
75–84	15.3	17.6	13.9
85+	27.4	23.9	29.0

1+ ADL	Total	Male	Female
65–74	47.4	48.1	46.7
75–84	95.2	89.5	98.6
85+	238.8	218.8	247.7

Source: Supplement on Aging, 1984 Health Interview Survey. Sample *N* (65+) = 11,497.

many persons (217 per 1000) age 85+ as compared to those age 65 to 74 (35 per 1000) need help of another person to take a bath. On the other hand, the age relationship is not uniform, as seen in Figure 13–1 (which graphs the "total" column of Table 13–1). Eating has the lowest rate overall and the weakest connection to age; bathing, the strongest.

2. There are substantial differences in the level of limitation across the five activities (listed in Table 13–1 in decreasing order of severity). For every person age 85+ who needs help eating (27 per 1000), there are eight (217 per 1000) who need help taking a bath.

3. There are some gender differences in ADL rates. Women tend to have somewhat higher levels of functional limitation than men in each age group. The male-female rate differences are not especially large, however, and are in part a statistical reflection of greater female longevity. It is likely that within each age group the average older woman is older than the average older man. Because the ADL rates are largest precisely where the number of women and men are most different (in the 85+ age group), it is especially important to use age-sex-specific ADL rates in the projection of the future size of the care-receiver population.

Throughout this analysis we use a composite measure in which an older person is considered in need of personal care if he or she needs assistance with any one or more of these five ADL. This 1+ measure is included in both Table 13–1 and Figure 13–1 and shows the highest rate of needed assistance to carry out one or more of the five activities of daily living.

In summary, Table 13–1 suggests that the rates of ADL functional limitation increase significantly with advanced age and are slightly higher for older women than for older men. Bathing is the activity that most often triggers the need for personal assistance, followed by dressing, moving from bed to chair, toileting, and eating. Overall,

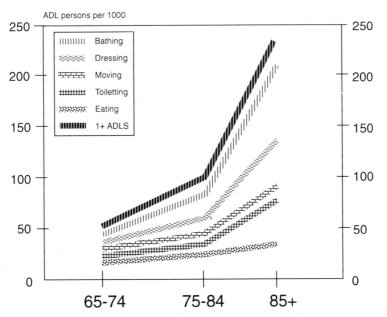

Figure 13–1   Age patterns in ADLs.

approximately 5 percent of the young-old and 24 percent of the older-old have one or more functional limitations. While the overall ADL rates suggest that the large majority of older persons have a score of 0 on the summed 0 to 5 ADL measure, a sizable minority of all older persons requires personal assistance to carry out one or more of the five activities.

ESTIMATING THE NATIONAL NEED FOR PERSONAL HEALTH CARE, 1980–2010

The national rates for older persons reporting one or more ADL limitations (listed at the bottom of Table 13–1) are used to estimate the size of this population from 1980 to 2010. The 1984 age and sex ADL rates of Table 13–1 were multiplied by the parallel age-sex Census projections to produce the projected trends reported in Table 13–2. This is done separately for men and women to account for the different sex composition of the older age groups, as well as the different ADL rates for older men and women. These separate age-sex ADL estimates are then summed into total ADL estimates for each age group. Overall, in 1980 there were 2 million older (65+) persons with one or more ADL limitations. This is estimated to increase to 3.6 million persons by 2010, an increase of 80 percent. Among older-old men and women (85+) there is

a projected 173 percent increase in the need for personal care.

A key assumption here is that the ADL rates measured by the National Health Interview Survey in 1984 can be used to describe the population over the period of 1980 to 2010. The initial assumption (modified later in this analysis) is that if in 1984, 21.9 percent of men and 24.8 percent of women (age 85+, Table 13–1) have one or more ADL limitations, these percentages will apply during the 1980 to 2010 period.

How reasonable is this assumption? Over the long run ADL rates will no doubt change. The optimistic view is that future cohorts of the elderly will be in substantially better health than today due to a lifetime of health consciousness translated into better diet, more exercise, and lower rates of smoking.[14,15] The pessimistic view is that medical technology and health care delivery will combine to keep some older persons alive who in an earlier era would have died of their illness. Furthermore, reductions in the mortality caused by such middle-age killers as heart disease and cancer will result in more older-old men and women susceptible to the longer-term debilitating effects of Alzheimer's and other degenerative diseases.[16]

In the longer run the 1984 ADL rates will become outdated, although it is not clear whether they will rise or decline. In the shorter run, however, the 1984 data represent a reasonable estimate of current rates of functional limitation

TABLE 13-2	Projected Need for Personal Care: Population Estimates of Persons with 1 or more ADL Limitation				
	1980	1990	2000	2010	% Change: 1980–2010
65–74	737,139	869,412	863,487	996,042	35.1
75–84	735,990	945,052	1,142,015	1,159,308	57.5
85+	535,386	779,486	1,106,664	1,462,926	173.2
Total	2,008,515	2,593,949	3,112,166	3,618,276	80.1
Care givers: women, age 55–64	11,551,000	11,260,000	12,601,000	18,257,000	58.1

and dependency upon personal care. The 1984 rates represent a base line from which variations can be used to examine alternative future care-giving scenarios.

ESTIMATING THE SUPPLY OF PERSONAL CARE GIVERS

In contrast to the estimation of the demand for care givers, the identification of the supply of care givers is both easier and more difficult. The task is more difficult because of the broad range of family capabilities and attitudes involved. It would be especially useful to have comprehensive national data on care-giving relationships. Because we don't have such information, our task becomes procedurally easier, and we use the Census-defined population of middle-aged women, women age 55 to 64 years old, as our operational definition of care givers.

Gerontological research has increasingly documented the proposition that the primary care givers for functionally limited older people who continue to reside at home (rather than nursing homes) are their own family members, primarily their adult daughters or daughters-in-law.[17–21]

As gerontological research and (more recently) the popular media have increasingly noted, these within-family care-giving women are a "generation in the middle." They are "the sandwich generation" because they find themselves at a time in their lives when they are caring for parents alongside continuing responsibilities for their older children. Many are new "empty-nesters" who have recently entered or reentered the paid labor force. They are women in their fifties and early sixties. Not all older persons have daughters who are available care givers, and not all daughters will in fact provide such care. The analytic task of identifying within-family care providers is a complex one. Ideally, we would have a large nationally representative survey of older parent-child dyads in order to identify all older

persons who have potential care givers in the family. Interviews with these potential care givers, no matter where they live, would measure such factors as attitudinal willingness to provide care, geographic obstacles to providing care, and the skill, energy, and financial resources to be able to provide the care.

This would be a longitudinal panel study so actual care-giving patterns at T_2 (time 2) could validate the predictive value of the variables measured at T_1 (time 1). In summary, the matter of a valid conceptual and operational definition and measurement of care-giving potential in the U.S population includes a complex set of tasks. (Positive steps in this lengthy journey are being taken in a doctoral dissertation at the University of Pennsylvania using data from the cross-sectional 1987 National Survey of Families and Households.[22])

In the absence of such large-scale national analyses of care givers, we use middle-aged women (age 55 to 64) as a demographic surrogate. The bottom row of Table 13–2 identifies this population of potential care givers. There were 11.5 million middle-aged women in 1980, projected to increase to 18.3 million by 2010. This 58 percent increase is smaller than the 80 percent increase in the overall number of older care receivers and substantially smaller than the 173 percent projected increase in the demand for care among older-old (age 85+) people. Finally, we note that these data identify only *potential* care givers since not all middle-aged women can or will provide such care, and some care will be provided by spouses, male children, siblings, and friends. This consideration is reflected in the simulation of alternative futures described below.

CARE GIVER RATIOS, 1980–2010

The preceding discussion identified the demand and supply components of the care-giving relationship. The demand component (care receivers) is defined as the number of older persons with one or more functional ADL functional limitations. The supply of care givers is defined as the number of middle-aged women. More generally, this relationship can be summarized by the care-giver ratio, which identifies the number of potential care givers per one care receiver. A number of alternative care-giver ratios can be defined and projected over the next 20 years; the alternatives are produced by changing the definition of either the care receivers or the care givers.

As a base line and first illustration of the care-giver ratio, Figure 13–2 compares two versions of the ratio, the difference being the definition of the care receivers. The top line shows a "better" set of ratios, that is, a large number of care givers for each care receiver. In this top line, the care-giver ratio uses the ADL estimates to define the need for personal care; it indicates that across the 1980 to 2010 period there are about 5 to 6 potential care givers for each care receiver. The only difference in the lower line of Figure 13–2 is that the definition of the care receivers is changed to all older-old (age 85+) men and women. The ratio drops rather no-

ticeably since the same number of care givers is now allocated to a substantially larger number of care receivers. In the first decade of the twenty-first century, this ratio declines to about three potential care givers per older-old person.

Since it is obvious that all 85+-year-olds are not in need of personal care, as documented in Table 13–1, why is the comparison in Figure 13–2 even included here? Two reasons:

1. It allows us to see that the care-giver ratio is in fact sensitive to changes in definition and trends in the population.
2. While the age 85+ version of the ratio may be unrealistic, it does define a kind of worst-case limit, that is, what could happen if increasing numbers of older persons do become dependent on personal care.

ALTERNATIVE VIEWS OF THE FUTURE

The analysis thus far has assumed that the 1984 national rates will realistically describe the older population in the near future. It has been argued,

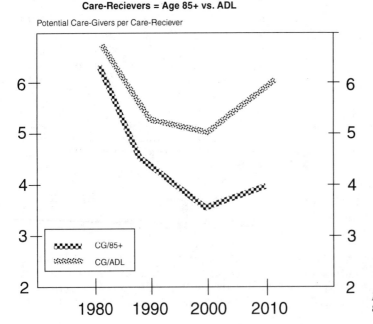

Care-Recievers = Age 85+ vs. ADL

Potential Care-Givers per Care-Reciever

CG/85+
CG/ADL

Figure 13–2 Care-receivers age 85+ versus ADLs.

however, that dependency within the older population is increasing.[3,16] As new medical procedures help keep older people alive longer, some of them will remain alive in a less healthy, more dependent condition.

In the long run we might achieve the goal of "squaring the longevity curve," the "one-horse shay" model of long life.[15] In such a future, we all remain frightfully healthy, with no functional dependence — until we succumb to total system failure, the day after Willard Scott wishes us a Happy 100th Birthday on the *Today Show*. But in the shorter term, increased longevity may well bring about increased illness and dependency.

How might these conditions affect the need for and availability of personal care? To examine such alternative futures, we reestimate the dependent population, first assuming ADL rates 25 percent higher than in 1984, and second, ADL rates 50 percent higher than in 1984. These simulated or revised rates are applied to the 1990 to 2010 U.S. Census projections, with the results in Table 13–2. Using the 25 percent rate revision, the total number of older (65+) persons with one or more

ADL limitations increases from 2 million in 1980 to 4.5 million in 2010, a 125 percent increase. When the rates are increased by 50 percent, the need for personal care increases by 170 percent overall, and by more than 300 percent among persons 85 and older.

In addition to alternative estimates of the demand side of the care-giver ratio, it is also important to consider variation on the supply side of the relationship. It is probable that not all middle-aged women are the daughters or daughters-in-law of living older persons. Many who are may be unable or unwilling to provide personal home care. As suggested earlier, many middle-aged empty-nest wives have returned to the paid labor force; others live too far away from their parents; still others may simply prefer not to engage in the activity. For these and other reasons, we include a 50 percent reduction in the number of potential care givers as part of this "alternative-futures" analysis.

Figure 13–3 presents the two extreme versions of the care-giver ratio that are produced by the combinations of simulated demand and supply. The top line, from the previous graph, uses 100 percent of the 1984 ADL rates and 100 per-

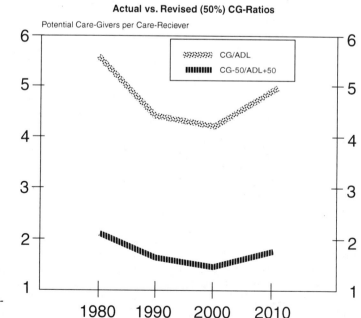

Actual vs. Revised (50%) CG-Ratios

Figure 13–3 Actual versus revised (50%) CG ratios.

cent of middle-aged women as care givers. The lower line demonstrates the impact of 50 percent higher rates of functional limitation and 50 percent fewer care givers.

As expected, the care-giver ratios in the latter scenario are noticeably worse. That is, there are substantially fewer care givers for each care receiver. The ratio declines through the year 2000 and then increases during the first decade of the next century—as the baby boomers enter middle age.

CONCLUSIONS AND IMPLICATIONS

In assessing the implications of this somewhat somber alternative future view of the care-giver ratio, we raise one final question: Is the ratio influenced more by the supply or by the demand side of the relationship? Does an increase in functional limitation or a decline in number of potential care givers have a greater impact on the blend?

The care-giver ratio and its alternative futures reflect a synthetic relationship between care givers and care receivers. Nonetheless, like other such statistical devices, it provides a kind of heuristic model of real relationships. That is, it provides a basis for examining the implications of various trends and dynamics within the social system.

Whether the need for personal care in the older population will in fact rise by 50 percent in the first years of the next century, or if only half of all daughters will actually provide such care, it is likely that the societal demand for personal care will increase. It is likely to increase somewhat in the shorter run and substantially when the baby boomers move from their care-giving middle age to care-receiving older age. Consequently, we return to analysis of the care-giver ratios a final time to explore the supply-demand question: Which of the two components of the relationship, supply or demand, appears to have greater short-term impact on the care-giver ratio? The trends in Figure 13–4 suggest that it is the supply of care givers that is the more dominant factor.

In the top set of three care-giver ratios we hold the supply factor constant at the full number of middle-aged women (CG), but vary the demand factor across three ADL care levels: the full ADL rate, ADL + 25 percent, ADL + 50 percent. The lower set of trends holds the supply factor constant at the lower level of 50 percent fewer middle-aged women care givers and again varies the need for personal care. The differences are fairly noticeable. All of the top three trend lines, which use the larger supply factor, produce higher ratios of care givers to care receivers. Alternatively stated, when the lower supply factor is used, the care-giver ratios are always lower, no matter what level of personal care demand is used.

The analysis suggests that, at least in the short run, social policy should aim to increase the supply of personal care givers. If family members are unavailable to provide personal care, then the social and economic system should provide access to such services, either as public benefit or a purchased good. While motivation, recruitment, and training are part of the story, it is also a matter of money, as any home care agency or nursing home administrator will testify. We cannot help to attract and to retain caring and sensitive people to take care of our parents and grandparents by paying the minimum wage or less.

But concern with the care receivers and their families as individuals and consumers is equally critical. If social policy is successful in producing a supply of nonfamily personal care givers, how will such care be acquired and paid for? The issue is one of both public policy and private-sector involvement. Public policies should expand home care and personal care health-related benefits alongside the community-based supportive social services now available. Medicare and Medicaid should emphasize well-compensated personal care as a matter of general health care policy; however, the catastrophic extension of

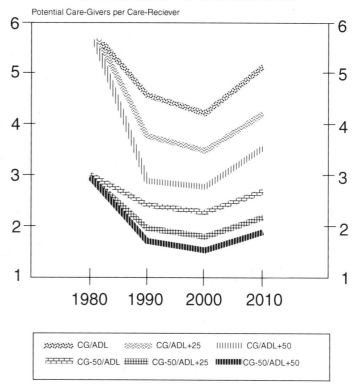

THE LARGER IMPACT OF CARE-GIVER SUPPLY

Potential Care-Givers per Care-Reciever

Legend:
- CG/ADL
- CG/ADL+25
- CG/ADL+50
- CG-50/ADL
- CG-50/ADL+25
- CG-50/ADL+50

Figure 13–4 The larger impact of care-giver supply.

Medicare was repealed, and public long-term care insurance is at best a distant goal.

Thus, attention must also be directed to private long-term care insurance. Such insurance should be encouraged to include generous home care and personal care provisions and benefits. Indeed, the more innovative long-term care policies in this new insurance market do offer home care as a benefit.[9] In both cases, private and public, the compensation and benefit structure must be one that works to attract, to compensate, and to retain quality care givers.

At the same time, the marketing of health and long-term care insurance, public or private, must be user-friendly in giving all consumers, both care givers and care receivers, sufficient price and product information to make comfortable and informed choices.[23,26] Indeed, choices concerning such insurance should not be seen simply in terms of health but as part of a family's overall "wealth-span" strategy.[5,24]

In an interesting way the attractiveness and affordability of long-term care insurance is part of a typical chicken-and-egg dilemma. Resistance to the purchase of such insurance may reflect the perception that care-giving services will not be available for purchase when needed. At the same time, the required supply of willing and able paid care givers will not develop without appropriate pay levels — which in turn are reflected in public and private compensation profiles and insurance benefit schemes.[25]

The years leading to the next century are crucial for identifying goals and making progress in the development of personal care giving and the minimization of dependence and institutionalization for elderly men and women. This is especially important now because — as has been very well documented in other research — demographic dynamics will produce a much more acute scenario in the middle years of the twenty-first century.

REVIEW QUESTIONS

1. Some researchers suggest that dependency rates are increasing in the older population, while others suggest that they are decreasing. Provide support for each point of view. Which point of view do you believe is more accurate?

2. Define dependency. What are the limitations of this concept?

3. Discuss the methodological difficulties in developing a care-giver ratio.

4. What factors will affect the availability of personal care givers?

REFERENCES

1. American Demographics: The 1990 Census questionnaire. American Demographics, April 1989, pp 24–31.
2. Beck, M: Trading places [cover story]. Newsweek, July 16, 1990, pp 48–54.
3. Brody, EM: "Women in the middle" and family help to older people. Gerontologist 21:471–480, 1981.
4. Brody, EM and Schoonover, CV: Patterns of parent-care when adult daughters work and when they do not. Gerontologist 26:372–381, 1986.
5. Cates, JL: Long term care: Past . . . Present . . . Future. Broker World, May 1990, pp 52–135.
6. Chappell, NL: Aging and social care. In Binstock, RH and George, LK (eds): Handbook of Aging and Social Sciences, ed 3. Academic Press, San Diego, 1990, pp 438–454.
7. Cutler, NE: Minority targeting in the Older Americans Act, 1978–1988. From "Greatest Economic or Social Need" to Meek v. Martinez. National Resource Center on Minority Aging Populations, San Diego State University, 1989.
8. Cutler, NE: Myths and realities of the "Mature Market." Journal of the American Society of CLU & ChFC, July, 1992.
9. Doyle, RL, Tacchino, KB, Kurlowicz, T, Cutler, NE and Schnepper, JF: Can You Afford to Retire. Probus Publishing, Chicago, 1992.
10. Employee Benefits Research Institute: Dependent Care. Employee Benefit Plan Review, May 1990, pp 12–29.
11. Fries, JF: The compression of morbidity. Milbank Memorial Fund Quarterly 61:397–419, 1983.
12. Fulton, JP, Katz, S, Jack, SS and Hendershot, GE: Physical functioning of the aged. Vital and Health Statistics, Series 10, No. 167:1–16, 1989.
13. Gregg, DW: The Human Wealth Span: A Life-Span View of Financial Well-Being. University of Pennsylvania, Boettner Institute of Financial Gerontology, Philadelphia, 1992.
14. Haan, MN, Rice, DP, Satariano, WA and Selby, JV: Introduction to: Living longer and doing worse? Present and future trends in the health of the elderly. Journal of Aging and Health 3:133–137, 1991.
15. Kane, RL and Kane, RA: Health care for older people: Organizational and policy issues. In Binstock, RH and George, LK (eds): Handbook of Aging and the Social Sciences, ed 3. Academic Press, San Diego, 1990, pp 415–437.
16. Katz, ST, Downs, TD, Cash, HR and Grotz, RC: Progress in the development of the index of ADL. Gerontologist 10:20–30, 1970.
17. Lewis, J and Meredith, B: Daughters caring for mothers: The experience of caring and its implications for professional helpers. Aging and Society 8:1–20, 1988.
18. Manton, KG: Changing concepts of morbidity and mortality in the elderly population. Milbank Memorial Fund Quarterly/Health and Society 60:183–244, 1982.
19. Marton, WP: Aging, the Family and Informal Care of the Elderly in the United States 1987–2025. University of Pennsylvania Population Studies Center (dissertation), Philadelphia, 1993.
20. McNeil, JM, Lamas, EJ and Harpine, CJ: Disability, Functional Limitation, and Health Insurance Coverage, 1984/85 US Government Printing Office, Washington, DC, 1986.
21. Rosenwaike, I and Logue, B: The Extreme Aged in America: A Portrait of an Expanding Population. Greenwood Press, Westport, CT, 1985.
22. Rowe, JW and Kahn, RL: Human aging: Usual and successful. Science 237:143–149, 1987.
23. Shanas, E: The Family as a Social Support System in Old Age. Gerontologist 19:169–174, 1979.
24. Stone, R, Cafferata, GL and Sangl, J: Caregivers of the frail elderly: A national profile. Gerontologist 27:616–626, 1987.
25. Taeuber, C: Diversity: The dramatic reality. In Bass, SA, Kutza, EA and Torres-Gil, FM (eds): Diversity in Aging. Scott, Foresman, Glenview, IL, 1990, pp 1–46.
26. Cutler, NE: The emerging dynamics of financial gerontology: Individual aging and population aging in the new century. In Cutler, NE, Gregg, DW and Lawton, MP (eds): Aging, Money, and Life Satisfaction: Aspects of Financial Gerontology. Springer Publications, New York, 1992, pp 1–21.

FACTORS CONTRIBUTING TO DYSFUNCTION IN OLDER ADULTS

This is the state of man: to-day he puts forth the tender leaves of hopes; to-morrow blossoms, And bears his blushing honours thick upon him; The third day comes a frost, a killing frost, And, when he thinks, good easy man, full surely His greatness is a-ripening, nips his root, And then he falls, as I do.
And when he falls, he falls like Lucifer, Never to hope again.

—WILLIAM SHAKESPEARE, *Henry VIII*

Chapter

Falls

REIN TIDEIKSAAR

OBJECTIVES

By the end of this chapter, readers will be able to:

1 Define falls and discuss their frequency and consequences for older adults.

2 Discuss the reasons for falls in older adults.

3 Describe the assessment of falls and falls risk.

4 Describe environmental interventions to prevent falls.

5 Discuss the fear of falling as it affects function for the elderly.

6 Discuss issues relative to the use of restraints to prevent falls and alternatives to restraints.

Falls are among the most serious health problems faced by older people. They are a major cause of premature death, physical injury, immobility, psychosocial dysfunction, and nursing home placement. The rapidly growing population of people 75 years and older are those at greatest fall risk.[1] To reduce the alarming rate of falls and related excessive mortality and morbidity, efforts to detect persons at fall risk and prevent or reduce the frequency of falls must be attempted. To facilitate such approaches, it is essential to know why (and under what conditions) older people fall or are at risk for falls. There are many interacting factors that predispose to falling, but approaches to fall prevention are not well examined.

This chapter reviews the epidemiology of falls, their complications, and the various host and environmentally related causes of falls. An approach to clinical assessment and environmental intervention in older people who fall and at fall risk is discussed. Finally, the fear of falling and alternatives to the use of physical restraints in preventing falls are highlighted.

EPIDEMIOLOGY

Approximately one-third of community-residing persons over age 65 fall each year; of these, one-half suffer multiple falls[2,3]; Falls are even more frequent in nursing homes, where up to 50 percent of older residents fall annually[4]; over 40 percent experience more than one fall.[5] Older hospital in-patients also fall frequently, averaging about 1.5 falls per bed per year.[6] The likelihood of falling increases with age.[2] Incidence begins to rise steadily after the age of 75, peaks between 80 to 84, and decreases in frequency after the age of 85.[7] This decline may represent a survival tendency by the over-85 age group or a restriction of activities that place them at fall risk. Females are reported to fall three times more frequently than males.[8,9]

The true extent of falling may be underestimated.[10] Only falls with injury requiring medical attention or causing problems with mobility are likely to be reported. Falls may not be reported if they are thought to be a consequence of "normal" aging, a reminder of increasing frailty, or due to fear that reporting will lead to restriction of activities or placement in a nursing home. Even in institutional settings, many falls are unwitnessed, and persons may fail to report them, perhaps because of an inability of persons with cognitive dysfunction to communicate or fear of being placed in physical restraints.

Complications

Falls are the leading cause of death due to "accidents" or unintentional injury in persons aged 65 years and older.[11] About 9500 deaths per year are attributable to falling.[2] Of those persons hospitalized as a result of falling, only about one-half will be alive 1 year later.[12] Mortality appears not be the direct result of the fall since the majority of fatalities occur weeks to months after the fall,[13] but rather a consequence of comorbidity (e.g., pneumonia, heart failure, and so on). The true number of fall-related deaths is probably much higher because falls are not listed consistently on death certificates.[14]

For those who survive a fall, significant morbidity is likely to follow. An estimated 5 percent of falls by both community and institutionalized older persons result in fractures, and an additional 10 percent of falls result in non-fracture injuries,[1,15,16] including head injuries, hematomas, joint dislocations, and muscle sprains. Females experience a higher rate of fracture and non-fracture injuries than males.[1]

The most common fractures associated with falls are those of the forearm and hip.[17] Distal forearm or Colles' fractures occur when an older person attempts to break a fall by extending the arms outward. The incidence of forearm fractures plateaus after the age of 65, at which time there is a steep increase in the incidence of hip fractures.[17,18] Diminished ability to exhibit the protective reflex of extending the arms is given as a reason for the decline in Colles' fractures.[19]

Approximately 200,000 hip fractures occur annually in the United States, 84 percent in persons 65 years of age and older.[20] The majority of hip fractures are the direct result of falls onto hard surfaces such as concrete, linoleum, or wood.[17,21] Some hip fractures occur spontaneously as a result of osteopenia, causing a fall.[17] For this reason, debate continues as to whether the hip fracture precedes the fall or is a consequence of the fall.[22] Evidence for the former, that fractures result in a fall, is supported by the fact that about 9 out of 10 hip fractures in older females are associated with either moderate or no evidence of trauma.[23] Probably, hip fractures occur as a result of both low bone mass and striking a hard ground surface.

The cost of hip fractures approaches $7 billion[24] and results in substantial mortality and morbidity. Up to 20 percent of older people with hip fractures are dead within the first 6 months after fracture,[25] perhaps because of the high incidence of coexisting chronic disease. After a hip fracture, many older persons never again their premorbid level of ambulation. Approximately 60 percent of persons have decreased mobility, and another 25 percent become functionally dependent in walking. This latter group requires mechanical or human assistance and nursing home care.[26]

Falls that do not result in physical injury can lead to a restriction of activities and self-imposed immobility related to fear of falling. Up to 50 percent of older people who have suffered multiple falling episodes admit to avoiding some activities because of fear of additional falls and injury.[27] If the resulting avoidance of mobility leads to prolonged immobility, a host of complications may develop, including deep venous thrombosis, decubitus ulcers, urinary tract infections, hypostatic pneumonia, muscle atrophy, joint contractures, depression, and functional dependence.[28] Falling and instability are a leading contributor of nursing home placement, a factor in 40 percent of admissions.[1]

CAUSES OF FALLING

Falls occur when an individual engages in an activity that results in a loss of balance and the body mechanisms responsible for compensation fail. In older people, falls often occur during routine activities, such as walking; descending or climbing steps; transferring on or off chairs, beds, toilets, or in or out of bathtubs; and reaching up or bending down. The fall may be a sign of an underlying problem indicative of intrinsic host factors, including age-related physiological changes, diseases, medications, or extrinsic factors or environmental hazards.[28,30]

Age-Related Physiological Changes

Normal age-related physiological changes contribute to both falling and fall risk. The most important occur in the visual, neurological, cardiovascular, and musculoskeletal systems.

Vision

One of the most important functions of the eye in mobility is detecting cues in the surrounding environment. Elements of visual function related to occurrence of falls include visual acuity, contrast sensitivity, accommodation, visual fields, visual threshold, color perception, glare recovery, and depth perception.

Balance

The body's ability to maintain balance or postural stability during standing and walking is dependent largely upon feedback received from the vestibular, visual, and proprioceptive systems. With age, postural sway tends to increase to a level of unsteadiness.[31] Older persons who fall have more sway than nonfallers,[32] and persons with multiple falls demonstrate greater sway than those with single falls.[33]

Age-related disturbances of sway or balance have been attributed to visual, vestibular, and proprioceptive loss. People with a decline in visual acuity[34] or poor proprioception[35] have increased sway.[34] A loss or proprioception is also associated with orthostatic drops in blood pressure[36] and impaired vibration sense.[37] The vestibular righting response also declines with age,[38] which can lead to a failure to maintain balance during postural displacements.

Musculoskeletal

An older person's gait and balance are affected by a number of changes in the musculoskeletal system as discussed in Chapter 6[39] of this text. These include muscular atrophy, calcification of tendons and ligaments, a flattening of the disks between the vertebrae, and increased curvature of the spine that results in kyphosis. Walking speed and step length in older people who fall is even more compromised than that of normal elderly individuals,[40] resulting in a slower walk and shorter steps.

Blood Pressure

Baroreflex activity, a mechanism of the cardiovascular system, plays a crucial role in the regulation of systemic blood pressure. With advancing age, there is a progressive decline in baroreflex sensitivity to both hypotensive and hypertensive stimuli.[41] As a result heart rate in older people often fails to increase in response to postural changes in position (e.g., moving from supine to sitting position). Also, older people have less capacity for cardioacceleration or increase in heart rate to compensate for the hypotensive effects of medications. This leads to hypoxia and accompanying falls.

DISEASES

Risk of falling increases with the number of medical conditions or intrinsic factors present. Virtually any chronic or transient medical problems that interferes with mobility may predispose an individual to falling. Visual, neurological, cardiovascular, musculoskeletal, and psychological disorders are some of the most important.

Vision

Diseases of the eye such as cataracts, macular degeneration, and glaucoma have been associated with falling.[1,27] Superimposed on age-related changes in vision, they can further impair visual function. Even without severe visual impairment, the decline in visual perception and acuity is sufficient to increase fall risk when combined with environmental factors. Objects (e.g., upended rug edges or step heights) are difficult to perceive.

Neurological

Neurological disorders such as dementia, neuropathy, stroke, cervical degeneration, and parkinsonism are particularly important in predisposing older people to falls.[1,42] Dementia, especially Alzheimer's disease, is associated with gait changes, ataxia, and altered proprioception.[42] As a consequence, people tend to walk more slowly, with shorter steps, increased double support time, and greater step-to-step variability.[43] Also, people with dementia tend to have problems with the spatial recognition of objects in the environment.[44,45] This, along with poor judgment in perceiving hazards, commonly results in trips and slips. People with neuropathy as a result of diabetes, pernicious anemia, or nutritional disorders can have lower-extremity weakness, hyperactive reflexes, and altered proprioceptive function, leading to poor balance and abnormal gait.[46] People with hemiparetic gait, especially with decreased ankle dorsiflexion, are susceptible to tripping falls. Cervical degeneration, the result of diseases such as ankylosing spondylosis and rheumatoid arthritis, is a common cause of proprioceptive dysfunction,[47] which can lead to gait abnormalities and postural instability. People with parkinsonism often display alterations of gait and postural control that contribute to balance loss and fall risk. Their gait becomes short stepped and shuffling, feet barely clearing the ground. At times gait initiation becomes difficult, and people stutter-step or take short rapid shuffling steps when they walk. Other gait changes include a "freezing walk": The feet suddenly come to a halt, but the body keeps moving forward, placing persons at risk for balance loss. This can result in *propulsion*, an uncontrolled forward motion when walking, or *retropulsion*, falling backward. Loss of automatic postural reflexes can affect ability to maintain upright posture and stability. To preserve balance, people compensate by assuming a stooped posture, with their neck, trunk, and limbs held in forward flexion with bent arms and knees.[22,46,48]

Cardiovascular

Any cardiovascular disorder that results in a reduction of cerebral perfusion can precipitate a fall. Common disorders include cardiac arrhythmias, carotid sinus node disease, and abnormalities in blood pressure regulation. *Cardiac arrhythmias* produce extremely slow or fast heart rates that can lead to cerebral hypoperfusion and dizziness. Carotid sinus node disease presents with syncope and is brought on by such common activities as turning the head to one side as if looking over one's shoulder or hyperextending the neck and head backward. This disorder is due either to carotid sinus sensitivity or a mechanical obstruction[49] that interferes with the supply of blood to the brain. *Postural*, or *orthostatic*, *hypotension* can lead to instability following changes in body position (e.g., rising from the supine or sitting position). It has several causes including autonomic dysfunction, hypovolemia, low cardiac output, parkinsonism, and medications such as diuretics. Another abnormality of blood pressure homeostasis is *postprandial hypotension*.[49] This syndrome, which leads to profound declines in blood pressure after eating, has no known cause. People who have fainting spells following a meal should be suspected of having postprandial hypotension and cautioned against sudden rising or activities after dining.

Musculoskeletal

Diseases of the bone, muscle, and joints may contribute to the risk of falling.[2] Osteoarthritis of the hip and knee joints can limit the ability to walk, climb, or descend stairs and transfer effectively. Muscle weakness resulting from thyroid disease, polymyalgia rheumatica, hypokalemia, or deconditioning may lead to gait and transfer problems. *Osteomalacia*, characterized by deficient mineralization of bone, causes proximal muscle weakness and an unstable, waddling gait.

Psychological

Older people with depression may suffer a loss of concentration, which can lead to judgment errors, a misperception of environmental hazards, and fall risk.[50] In those persons who fall frequently and have severe, prolonged depression, the falling episodes may be a sign of suicidal intent or need for attention.

Medications

While some studies have failed to demonstrate a relationship between drugs and falls,[24,51] it is generally agreed that medications increase fall risk in older people.[52] Any drug that interferes with postural control, cerebral perfusion, or cognitive function (e.g., sedatives, antipsychotics, diuretics, antihypertensives, tricyclic antidepressants, or alcohol[53,54,55] may induce a fall. Generally, fall risk is greater for drugs with extended half-lives (i.e., greater than 24 hours) and increases with the number of medications a person receives.[56,57]

Environmental Factors

The overwhelming majority of falls experienced by community-residing older people occur in the home,[28] especially the bedroom, bathroom, and stairway. In the hospital and nursing home, the bed and bathroom represent the most common locations where people fall.[28,51]

Several environmental obstacles, design factors, and host activities are associated with falling: transferring from low or high beds, chairs, or toilets; walking in poorly illuminated areas and tripping over low-lying objects or floor coverings, such as thick-pile carpets or unsecured rug edges; slipping on waxed or wet ground surfaces; and climbing or descending steps that lack handrail support or are difficult to see.[28,58]

This list is by no means exhaustive. Its importance lies in the fact that it is evidence of a causal relationship between environmental hazards and falling.

Ironically, assistive devices may contribute to falls. Bedrails may actually increase the risk as a result of attempts by the older adult to leave the bed without lowering the rails.[59] Wheelchairs contribute to falls as a result of poor transfer techniques or forgetfulness about procedures (e.g., not locking wheel brakes).[60,61] Canes and walkers can cause falls,[51,61] presumably due to improper size or application of these aids. The use of physical restraints to prevent falls may in some instances contribute to further falls.[55,59,60] The precise reason for this is unknown, but it may be due in part to improper restraint application by staff.

CLINICAL ASSESSMENT AND INTERVENTION

The goals of fall prevention in both the home-living and institutionalized population are similar. First, persons at risk must be identified, and for those with falls, the cause must be determined. Second, the risk of falling or sustaining further falls must be reduced by implementing interventions that maintain the older person's mobility.

Interaction among risk factors can increase risk of falls. Identifying those factors and defining fall etiology in persons who have fallen require a multidisciplinary approach directed toward assessing both intrinsic and extrinsic risk factors. Assessment components include a medical and medication history, physical examination, mobility evaluation, environmental assessment, and a fall history. A psychosocial assessment may uncover a history of substance abuse or related risk factors. While the approach to the assessment of fall risk and falls are similar, each is discussed separately and is followed by a consideration of potential intervention strategies.

Fall Assessment

The components of an assessment of falls in older people is shown in Figure 14–1. As a first step, persons who have fallen need to be identified. In the institutional setting, this can be done by simply recording falls on the incident report. For community-residing persons, this is best accomplished by asking during a medical visit whether they have experienced any recent falls. Discovering falls that have occurred within the past 3 months is most useful since these are most predictive of future falls. Because older people tend to underreport falls, family members living with the person should be questioned.

It is important to ask people not only about completed falls, that is, episodes in which the individuals actually come to rest on the ground, but near falls as well. These include events in which people lose their balance but manage to avert a fall by grabbing an environmental object such as a chair or bathroom towel bar for support. Near falls are as important as completed falls since, if the environmental object were not available, the person would probably have fallen.

If the person has fallen, it is important to obtain a fall history. This includes asking about the precise number of completed and near falls and, for each episode, the circumstances. A convenient acronym to help remember the components of the fall history is SPLAT: Symptoms, Previous falls, Location, Activity, and Time. Family members and other witnesses can help provide a complete fall history. In the institutional setting, documentation of circumstances should be a part of the incident report. Staff who have opportunity to observe the resident should be ques-

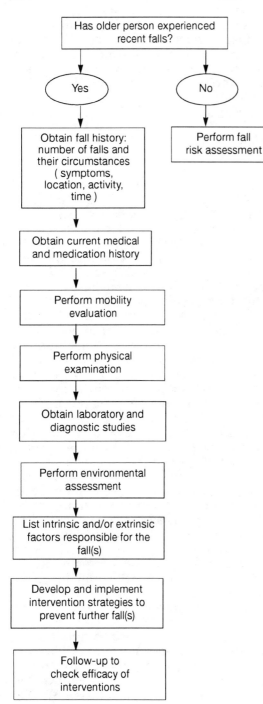

Figure 14–1   Fall assessment.

tioned, including nurses and aides, therapists, and, depending on the setting, individuals in dietary and housekeeping.

When alert individuals are unable to remember the circumstances of their falls, determining the reasons for falling is difficult. For these individuals, the use of a fall diary (Fig. 14–2) to record the circumstances of falls may provide a

FALLING DOWN IS NOT A NORMAL PART OF GROWING OLD. THERE ARE MANY CAUSES OF FALLING WHICH CAN BE TREATED. IN ORDER TO PREVENT FALLS, WE NEED TO KNOW AS MUCH ABOUT YOUR FALLS AS POSSIBLE. THIS DIARY WILL HELP YOU TO REMEMBER THE TIMES WHEN YOU FALL. EACH TIME YOU FALL, WRITE DOWN THE DATE, TIME OF DAY WHEN THE FALL OCCURRED, WHERE THE FALL OCCURRED (LOCATION), WHAT YOU WERE DOING AT THE TIME (ACTIVITY), AND HOW YOU FELT (SYMPTOMS). BELOW WE HAVE LISTED TWO EXAMPLES.

	DATE	TIME	LOCATION	ACTIVITY	SYMPTOMS
	4/8	8:00 AM	Bedroom	Getting out of bed	I felt dizzy
	5/1	10:00 PM	Bathroom	I slipped while walking	None
1.					
2.					
3.					
4.					
5.					

Figure 14–2 Fall diary.

clearer account of falls and help identify causes.

This information can point to possible causes of falling. For example, falls associated with rising from a lying or seated position and experiencing symptoms of dizziness suggest orthostatic hypotension. If no such symptoms are present, design of furniture may be a causative factor. If a person complains of tripping or slipping, a gait or balance disorder must be suspected, either by itself or in conjunction with an environmental hazard, such as an uneven or slippery floor surface or poor lighting. Other questions to ask during the history that might indicate the presence of psychosocial factors include: Does the person live alone? How long was the person on the ground after the fall(s) (i.e., postfall lie time)? Have physical injuries resulted? What effect did the fall have on the person's self-confidence? Does he or she fear further falls? Has he or she restricted activities as a result? Do family or care givers have any concerns about safety?

Next, obtain a current and comprehensive history of medical problems, complaints, and medications. In particular, the relationship between prescription and over-the-counter medications (e.g., when started, stopped, dosage changes, and compliance) and falls should be reviewed. An association may

indicate that the fall is due to an adverse medication effect.

The physical assessment of the individual includes a mobility evaluation, an assessment of gait, balance, and ability to change position (e.g., standing up or sitting down). It is particularly helpful in providing clues to underlying causes of falling, localizing the organ systems involved, isolating potential environmental problems, and designing interventions. A number of simple mobility evaluations are available that require little time, special expertise, space, or equipment. These include the "get-up-and-go test"[62] in which the person is asked to rise from a chair, stand still momentarily, walk a short distance, turn around, walk back, and sit down. The test is scored on a 5-point scale with 1 being normal and 5, severely abnormal. Another is the "Performance-Oriented Assessment of Mobility."[63] This is a scored performance of balance and gait that examines the person's ability to rise from and sit down in a chair, standing balance, and gait with respect to step initiation, height, and symmetry, walking deviation, trunk stability and turning ability.

Table 14–1 shows a mobility evaluation devised in part from existing tests. It can generally be administered in less than 5 minutes and is simple to understand, administer, and record. The eval-

TABLE 14–1 **Mobility Evaluation**

Instructions: Ask the person to perform the following maneuvers. For each, indicate whether the person's performance is normal or abnormal.

Ask Person To:	Observe:	Response:
1. Sit down in chair. Select a chair with armrests that is approximately 16 to 17 inches in seat height.	Able to sit down in one smooth, controlled movement without using armrests.	Normal
	Sitting is not a smooth movement; falls into chair or needs armrests to guide self into chair.	Abnormal
2. Rise up from chair.	Able to get up in one smooth, controlled movement without using armrests.	Normal
	Uses armrests and/or moves forward in chair to propel self up; requires several attempts to get up.	Abnormal
3. Stand after rising from chair for approximately 30 seconds in place.	Steady; able to stand without support.	Normal
	Unsteady; loses balance.	Abnormal
4. Stand with eyes closed for approximately 15 seconds in place.	Steady; able to stand without support.	Normal
	Unsteady; loses balance.	Abnormal
5. Stand with feet together push lightly on sternum 2 to 3 times.	Steady; maintains balance.	Normal
	Unsteady; loses balance.	Abnormal
6. Reach up onto tiptoes as if attempting to reach an object.	Steady, without loss of balance.	Normal
	Unsteady; loses balance.	Abnormal
7. Bend down as if attempting to obtain object from floor.	Steady, without loss of balance.	Normal
	Unsteady; loses balance.	Abnormal

Instructions: If the person uses a walking aid such as a cane or walker, the following walking maneuvers are tested separately with and without the aid. Indicate type of aid used.

Ask Person To:	Observe:	Response:
8. Walk in a straight line, in your "usual" pace (a distance approximately 15 feet); then walk back.	Gait is continuous without hesitation; walks in a straight line and both feet clear the floor.	Normal (with aid) Normal (without aid)
	Gait is noncontinuous with hesitation; deviates from straight path; feet scrape or shuffle on floor.	Abnormal (with aid) Abnormal (without aid)
9. Walk a distance of 5 feet and turn around.	Does not stagger; steps are smooth, continuous.	Normal (with aid) Normal (without aid)
	Staggers; steps are unsteady, discontinuous.	Abnormal (with aid) Abnormal (without aid)
10. Lie down on the floor and get up.	Able to rise, without loss of balance.	Normal
	Unable to rise, or loses balance in the process.	Abnormal

uation is based on the performance of 10 activities, scored as either normal or abnormal. Difficulty in performing these maneuvers may indicate underlying myopathy, arthritis, parkinsonism, postural hypotension or vestibular dysfunction, loss of proprioception, or balance problems.

The best method to assess a person's mobility is to observe the described maneuvers in his or her living environment (e.g, home or nursing home). This takes into account the relationship between performance and the environment (e.g., types of floor surface or chair design).[64] In addition, activities such as bed, toilet, and bathtub transfer and stair climbing and descending maneuvers can be assessed.

After the mobility evaluation, the next step is to conduct a physical examination and perform laboratory and diagnostic studies. Information gathered from the fall history and mobility evaluation serves as a guide to elements of the physical examination that deserve special attention. For example, if the fall history reveals that falls occur in association with dizziness during changes in position, orthostatic hypotension should be considered.

The extent of the laboratory and diagnostic studies is dictated by the information gathered from all previous evaluations. If the physical examination confirms the presence of orthostatic hypotension, blood and stool tests to evaluate volume-depletion states such as dehydration are ordered.

The next step is the environmental assessment. Under the best circumstances, all older people who have falls should have their living environment evaluated. Environmental assessment is essential for people whose fall history and mobility evaluation suggests the presence of an extrinsic cause of falling.

The goal of the environmental assessment is to determine a person's level of mobility function, that is, to identify environmental areas or design features that increase fall risk and the need for environmental modification and adaptive equipment.

In the home setting, the person should be observed walking through every room, transferring on and off beds, chairs, and toilet; getting in and out of the bathtub or shower; reaching to obtain objects from kitchen and closet shelves; bending to retrieve objects from the ground or low heights such as coffee tables; and negotiating stairs. The institutional assessment of the environment is similar; activities usually not performed independently by the person, such as stair climbing or bathtub transferring, can be omitted. Environmental obstacles that interfere with safe mobility should be noted and modifications recommended.

Once all evaluations are complete, a list of factors responsible for the person's falls can be constructed and interventions to prevent further falls designed. Follow-up should ensure that intervention strategies are effective and needed changes made.

Fall Risk Assessment

The components of an assessment program for fall risk are shown in Figure 14–3. While these factors are easy to identify, their true risk is represented by their accumulation,[56] and effects on an individual's mobility. Therefore, a mobility evaluation should be performed as a screening test. If it is normal and the routine physical examination are normal, the person is probably not at elevated fall risk. In these individuals the mobility evaluation should be repeated every 6 to 12 months. However, if an abnormality is detected, a complete fall evaluation should be performed and intervention planned to alleviate risk factors (see Fig. 14–4).

INTERVENTIONS

Intervention to reduce fall risk is based on assessment results. Interventions can be divided into those that address intrinsic and extrinsic factors.

Intrinsic interventions include the

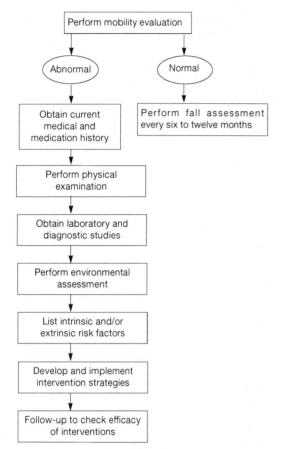

```
        Perform mobility evaluation
                    │
        ┌───────────┴───────────┐
        ▼                       ▼
    Abnormal                 Normal
        │                       │
        ▼                       ▼
  Obtain current        Perform fall assessment
    medical and         every six to twelve months
 medication history
        │
        ▼
 Perform physical
   examination
        │
        ▼
Obtain laboratory and
  diagnostic studies
        │
        ▼
Perform environmental
    assessment
        │
        ▼
 List intrinsic and/or
 extrinsic risk factors
        │
        ▼
Develop and implement
 intervention strategies
        │
        ▼
Follow-up to check efficacy
   of interventions
```

Figure 14–3 Fall risk assessment.

treatment of acute underlying disease processes, such as infections, and chronic disease, such as parkinsonism and arthritis. Medications suspected as causative of falling or placing persons at risk can either be stopped or reduced in dosage. To reduce fall risk, the number of medications, dosages, and regimens should be simplified and kept at a minimum.

Chronic neurological and musculoskeletal conditions affecting mobility may respond to exercise programs such as gait, balance, and strength training. Walking aids such as canes, walkers, and adaptive footwear may improve mobility. These aids should be tailored to the person and the environment so that the aid itself is not a risk factor for falling.

Extrinsic interventions consist of eliminating or modifying environmental conditions that interfere with safe mobility. For individuals residing in the community, health professionals can encourage elimination of hazards such as slippery floors, bathtub surfaces or rugs, and inadequate lighting. Checklists[2,64–66] can serve as a guide in helping make homes safe. At the same time people should be cautioned to avoid hazardous activities that may predispose them to falls, such as standing on chairs to reach objects from high shelves, walking across wet floors, or using stairways that are in ill repair or poorly illuminated.

This approach may not be effective, particularly for those people who have not fallen but are at risk. Older people may not be motivated or financially or physically able to correct environmental conditions[67] and may not restrict those activities that they don't perceive as being "hazardous." Those who have sustained falls, especially when associated with physical injury and decreases in function, appear to be more willing to make changes.

Figure 14–4 Careful assessment of balance and gait is important in designing falls prevention intervention. (Courtesy of the Menorah Park Nursing Home, Cleveland, Ohio.)

COMMON ENVIRONMENTAL HAZARDS

Table 14–2 identifies environmental hazards and design features of furnishings and structures in both the home and institutional setting most likely to be unsafe and addresses their modification.[28]

A major point to consider when modifying the environment is whether the suggested adaptations are acceptable to the person. Compliance is enhanced if older people understand why the adaptation is being made; if the adaptation improves mobility and reduces falls and is at the same time in keeping with the aesthetic features of the environment; and if the adaptation is affordable and easy to obtain and apply.

FEAR OF FALLING

Fear is an instinctive reaction to danger. Thus, older people with histories of falling avoid situations they perceive as dangerous, recognize their physical limitations, and adjust their activities. In this sense fear works to the person's advantage, functioning as a protective mechanism. However, fear of

TABLE 14–2	**Environmental Modifications to Reduce Risk of Falls**
Floors	1. Avoid polish or wet floors. 2. Use slip-resistant surfaces. 3. Add nonslip adhesive strips. 4. Use indoor-outdoor carpet. 5. Use slip-resistant floor wax. 6. Avoid thick or patterned carpet. 7. Use double-faced tape at carpet edges.
Walls	Add grab bars, especially in bath, hall, stairs (round, 16 to 26 inches high, color contrasted to wall, 2 to 3 inches from wall).
Lighting	1. Increase intensity by two to three times, especially in baths and stairways. 2. Use three-way bulbs and rheostats. 3. Use full-spectrum, fluorescent light. 4. Add night lights and bedside lamps with secure bases. 5. Add easy-to-find switches (accessible, contrasting color, pressure sensitive). 6. Use tinted windows, mylar shades to reduce glare. 7. Add automatic-turn-on timers.
Tables	1. Avoid unsteady tables. 2. Avoid drop-leaf or pedestal styles. 3. Use nonslip tops. 4. Avoid low-lying, glass- and mirror-top tables.
Shelves	1. Move frequently used items to middle shelves. 2. Use reachers.
Bath	1. Use grab bars, securely fastened. 2. Use adjustable toilet seat, securely fastened, with vinyl with color contrast. 3. Use nonslip strips in tub or shower. 4. Install soap dispenser. 5. Add hand-help shower hose.
Bed	1. Place at easiest transfer height. 2. If on wheels, lock and put on nonslip strips or immobilize legs.
Stairs	1. Add rails, extended 12 inches beyond stair and curved in at end. 2. Add nonslip adhesive. 3. Replace worn runners. 4. Mark edges.
Chairs	1. Tailor height to person. 2. Feet should be firmly on floor; feet at 90 degrees; seat depth 15 to 18 inches. 3. Armrests should be 7 inches above seat. 4. Use sturdy chairs.

falling can work against the best interests of an individual. Some older people become so frightened and preoccupied with fall avoidance that they limit activity unnecessarily. When asked what concerns them about falling, common responses include a fear of not being able to get up by themselves and needing assistance, having prolonged postfall lie times, feeling embarrassed about falling in public places and displaying an image of frailty, and a fear that a fall will result in a hip fracture or placement in a nursing home.[28] If the fear of falling is left untreated and unresolved, severe restriction of physical and social activities is likely to result, often with dire consequences. People residing in the community may become increasingly immobile to the point of becoming house bound, eventually requiring long-term care. Hospitalized people may avoid discharge to their home and require nursing home placement, and in the nursing home, people may end up living their lives in a wheelchair or require excessive assistance.

Several terms have been coined to describe abnormal fear of falling: *ptophobia*[68] *fallaphobia*,[28,30] and the *3-F syndrome*, that is *fear of further falls*.[69] While the true prevalence of fear of falling is not known, up to 50 percent of persons who fall admit to being afraid, and 25 percent report restricting their mobility as a result.[70] An abnormal fear of falling, or fallaphobia, is more common in persons who have a cluster of falls, increased postfall lie time,[71] fall-related injury, poor balance and gait, or live alone. Fallaphobia may be accompanied by panic attacks when attempting an activity that previously resulted in a fall. These attacks usually subside once the feared activity has either been accomplished successfully or abandoned. These persons display abnormal gaits, typified by hesitancy and irregularity of steps when walking, usually the result of an underlying balance disturbance.[71] As a consequence they ambulate by clutching or grabbing onto furniture or only attempt walking with the help of human assistance for support. They express great anxiety about their ability to walk safely.

The goal of treating fallaphobia is to help these people regain confidence in their ability to achieve safe, independent mobility. This is accomplished by a multidisciplinary program that includes reducing identifiable fall risk factors, eliminating environmental hazards, education and counseling, and behavioral modification.[28,68,72]

Behavioral modification to correct fallaphobia is most successful if the approach is started early and fully explained. The approach involves progressively increasing involvement in the feared activity, with close supervision. The supervisor should ensure the person's physical safety and provide verbal reassurance to build confidence. The person should proceed at a pace that is comfortable and non-anxiety provoking. Clearly, the professional undertaking such an approach should have a good grasp of behavior modification principles.

People who have prolonged postfall lie times or who have difficulty getting up after a fall tend to have more fear than others. An alarm device, worn around the neck as a pendant or attached to the belt, which allows the person to summon help can reduce anxiety. While these devices are generally well accepted,[73] some older people resist them because they find them inconvenient or difficult to operate,[12,74] remind them of their frailty and dependency, or are too costly to purchase.[75]

ALTERNATIVES TO PHYSICAL RESTRAINTS

Physical restraints were frequently used in hospitals and nursing homes to prevent falls. A *physical restraint* is any appliance used to inhibit independent mobility by securing a person in a bed, chair, or wheelchair. This includes such devices as posey restraints, belts, sheets, harnesses, or bed rails. As noted previously, evidence suggests that restraints do not remove such risk and may actually promote falls.[55,60]

Restraints can also contribute to a host of untoward complications such as impaired circulation of legs and arms, breathing problems, skin abrasions, decubitus ulcers, and strangulation.[28]

New federal legislation, specifically the *Omnibus Budget Reconciliation Act* (OBRA)[77] mandates the avoidance of physical restraints. Thus, both law and common sense require other approaches. A number of alternatives are available.[28] To prevent chair falls, the seat should slant down toward the back, making it difficult to rise without assistance. The use of wedge cushions can achieve this effect. Deep-seated, soft-cushioned, or bean bag chairs will prevent a person from rising unassisted.

To prevent bed falls, a water mattress filled to half capacity can minimize unassisted transfers. Bed alarm systems, which attach to the person or the bed,[78] are intended to warn nursing staff that a person who should not be leaving the bed unassisted is doing so. The efficacy of bed alarm devices is dependent on the response time of the nursing staff. Candidates for bed alarm devices are persons at risk for bed falls and restraint complications,[78] including those with multiple bed falls, those who need but do not ask for assistance in bed transfers (e.g., individuals with dementia), and persons with congestive heart failure in whom restraints will interfere with physiological compensation to clear the lungs of fluid (i.e., sitting up from the supine position).

Caution is advised in using bed alarms. Research about their effectiveness is conflicting.[79,80,81] The main objection is that they can cause false alarms (i.e., the alarm sounds when the person is not leaving the bed). Even when they sound appropriately, nurses on occasion feel that they don't have sufficient time to get to the patient.

SUMMARY

Falls are an important health problem for older people, resulting in significant mortality and morbidity. Most falls are not random "accidental" events but are the result of a cumulative effect of multiple intrinsic and extrinsic factors. Prevention requires a multifaceted and multidisciplinary approach aimed, first,

at identifying and assessing older people who have sustained falls and are at fall risk and, second, at attempting realistic interventions focused on reducing fall risk factors.

REVIEW QUESTIONS

1. *For what reasons might someone underreport falls? Why might they be overreported?*

2. *In what ways can environmental adaptations to the risk of falls be made more acceptable to the individual?*

3. *A client you are working with reports having fallen 2 weeks ago. How will you determine whether the individual is at risk of falling again?*

4. *Assuming that you determine the client's risk of falling is substantial, what strategies will you employ to help reduce the risk?*

5. *What are the potential negative outcomes if the individual does fall again?*

REFERENCES

1. Kennedy, TE and Coppard, LC (eds): The prevention of falls in later life. Dan Med Bull 34 (Suppl)4:1, 1987.
2. Tinetti, ME and Speechley, M: Prevention of falls among the elderly. N Engl J Med 320:1055, 1989.
3. Cummings, SR, et al: Epidemiology of osteoporosis and osteoporotic fractures. Epidemiol Rev 7:718, 1985.
4. Rubinstein, LZ, et al: Falls and instability in the elderly. J Am Geriatr Soc 36:266, 1988.
5. Berry, G Fisher, RH and Long, S: Detrimental incidents, including falls, in the elderly institutional population. J Am Geriatr Soc 29:322, 1981.
6. Brummel-Smith, K: Falls and instability in the older person. In Kemp, Brummel-Smith, K and Ramsdell, JW (eds): Geriatric Rehabilitation. College-Hill Press, Little, Brown, Boston, MA, 1990.
7. Prudham, D and Grimley, EJ: Factors associated with falls in the elderly: A community study. Age Ageing 10:141, 1981.
8. Campbell, AJ, et al: Falls in old age: A study of frequency and related clinical factors. Age Ageing 10:264, 1981.
9. Kalchthaler, T, Bascon, RA and Quintos, V: Falls in the institutionalized elderly. J Am Geriatr Soc 26:424, 1978.

10. Cummings, SR, Nevitt, MC and Kidd, S: Forgetting falls: The limited accuracy of recall of falls in the elderly. J Am Geriatr Soc 36:613, 1988.

11. Baker, SP, O'Neil, B and Kark, RS: The Injury Fact Book. Lexington Books, DC Heath, Lexington, MA, 1984.

12. Wild, D, Nayak, USL and Isaacs, B: How dangerous are falls in old people at home? Br Med J 282:266, 1981.

13. Morfitt, JM: Falls in old people at home: Intrinsic versus environmental factors in causation. Public Health J Lon 97:115, 1983.

14. Fife, D: Injuries and deaths among elderly persons. Am J Epidem 126:936, 1987.

15. Tinetti, ME, Speechley, M and Ginter, SE: Risk factors for falls among elderly persons living in the community. N Engl J Med 319:1701, 1988.

16. Tinetti, ME: Factors associated with serious injury during falls by ambulatory nursing home residents. J Am Geriatr Soc 35:644, 1987.

17. Melton, LJ and Riggs, BL: Risk factors for injury after a fall. Clin Geriatr Med 1:525, 1985.

18. Farmer, ME et al: Race and sex differences in hip fracture incidence. Am J Public Health 74:1374, 1987.

19. Evans, JG: Relevance of osteoporosis in women with fracture of the femoral neck. Br Med J 288:1083, 1984.

20. Haupt, BJ and Graves, E: Detailed diagnosis and surgical procedures for patients discharged from short stay hospitals: United States, 1979. DHHS Publication No (PHS) 82-1274-1. US Department of Health and Human Services, Washington, DC, 1982.

21. Evans JG: Fractured proximal femur in Newcastle upon Tyne. Age Ageing 8:16, 1979.

22. Sabin, TD: Biologic aspects of falls and mobility limitations in the elderly. J Am Geriatr Soc 30:51, 1982.

23. Alffram, PA: An epidemiologic study of cervical and trochanteric fracture of the femur in an urban population. Acta Orthop Scand 65:1, 1964.

24. Centers for Disease Control: Year 2000 health objectives for the nation: prevent and control unintentional injuries. Report of the interagency workgroup. Division of Injury Epidemiology and Control. Center for Environmental Health and Injury Control, CDC, Atlanta, GA, April 10, 1989.

25. Osteoporosis Consensus Conference. JAMA 252:799, 1984.

26. Evans, JG, Prudham, D and Wandless, I: A prospective study of fractured proximal femur: Incidence and outcome. Public Health 93:235, 1979.

27. Nevitt, MC, et al: Risk factors for recurrent nonsyncopal falls. A prospective study. JAMA 261:2663, 1989.

28. Tideiksaar, R: Falling in Old Age: Its Prevention and Treatment. Springer, New York, 1989.

29. Smallegan, M: How families decide on nursing home admission. Geriatr Consult 1:21, 1983.

30. Tideiksaar, R and Kay, AD: What causes falls? A logical diagnostic procedure. Geriatrics 41:32,1986.

31. Hasselkus, BR and Shambes, GM: Aging and postural sway in women. J Gerontol 30:661, 1975.

32. Brocklehurst, JC, Exton-Smith, AN, Lempert-Barber, SM, et al: Fracture of the femur in old age: A two centre study of associated clinical factors and the cause of the fall. Age Ageing 7:7, 1978.

33. Overstall, PW, et al: Falls in the elderly related to postural imbalance. Br Med J 1:261, 1977.

34. Doran, MB, Fernie, GR and Holliday, PJ: Visual input: Its importance in the control of postural sway. Arch Phys Med Rehabil 59: 586, 1978.

35. Era, P and Heikkinen, E: Postural sway during standing and unexpected disturbances of balance in random samples of men of different ages. J Gerontol 40:278, 1985.

36. Lichtenstein, MJ, et al: Clinical determinants of biomechanics: Platform measures of balance in aged women. J Am Geriatr Soc 36:996, 1988.

37. Brocklehurst, JC, Robertson, D and James-Groom, P: Clinical correlations of sway in old age-sensory modalities. Age Ageing 11:1, 1982.

38. Cape, R: Aging: Its Complex Management. Harper and Row, New York, 1978.

39. Kaufman, T: Mobility. In Bonder, BR and Wagner, M (eds): Functional Performance in Older Adults. FA Davis, Philadelphia, 1994.

40. Guiamares, RM and Isaacs, B: Studies of gait and balance in normal old people and in people who have fallen. Internat Rehabil Med 2:177, 1980.

41. McGarry, K, Laher, M, Fitzgerald D, et al: Baroreflex function in elderly hypertensives. Hypertension 5:763, 1983.

42. Bucher, DM and Larson, EB: Falls and fractures in patients with Alzheimer-type dementia. JAMA 257:1492, 1987.

43. Visser, H: Gait and balance in senile dementia of Alzheimer's type. Age Ageing 12:296, 1983.

44. Steffes, R and Thralow, J: Visual field limitation in the patient with dementia of the Alzheimer's type. Am J Geriatr Soc 35:189, 1987.

45. Nissen, MJ, et al: Spatial vision in Alzheimer's disease: General finding and a case report. Arch Neurol 42:6677, 1985.

46. Sudarsky, L: Geriatrics: Gait disorders in the elderly. N Engl J Med 322:1441, 1990.

47. Wyke, B: Cervical articular contributions to posture and gait: Their relation to senile disequilibrium. Age Ageing 8:251, 1979.

48. Alta, JE: Why patients with Parkinson's disease fall. JAMA 247:515, 1982.

49. Lipsitz, LA: Abnormalities in blood pressure homeostasis that contribute to falls in the elderly. Clin Geriatr Med 1:637, 1985.

50. Jacobson, SB: Accidents in age. NY State J Med 1:637, 1985.

51. Dimant, J: Accidents in the skilled nursing facility. NY State J Med 85:202, 1985.
52. Macdonald, JB: The role of drugs in falls in the elderly. Clin Geriatr Med 1:621, 1985.
53. Johnson, ET: Accidental falls among geriatric patients: Can more be prevented? J Nat Med Assoc 77:633, 1985.
54. Blumenthal, MD and Davie, MB: Dizziness and falling in the elderly psychiatric outpatients. Am J Psychiatry 137:203, 1980.
55. Feist, RR: A survey of accidental falls in a small home for the aged. J Gerontol Nurs 4:15, 1978.
56. Tinetti, ME, Williams, TF and Mayewski, R: Fall risk index for elderly patients based on number of chronic diseases. Am J Med 80:429, 1986.
57. Ray, WA, et al: Psychotropic drug use and the risk of hip fractures. N Engl J Med 316:363, 1987.
58. Archea, J: Falls in the elderly: Environmental factors associated with stair accidents by the elderly. Clin Geriatr Med 1:555, 1985.
59. Rubenstein, HS, et al: Standards of medical care based on consensus rather than evidence: The case of routine bedrail use for the elderly. Law, Medicine and Health Care 11:271, 1983.
60. Innes, EM and Turman, WG: Evaluation of patient falls. QRB 9:30, 1983.
61. Lund, CL and Sheafor, ML: Is your patient about to fall? J Gerontol Nurs 11:37, 1985.
62. Mathias, S, Nayak, USL and Isaacs, B: Balance in elderly patients: The "Get-Up and Go" test. Arch Phys Med Rehabil 67:387, 1986.
63. Tinetti, ME: A performance-oriented assessment of mobility problems in elderly patients. J Am Geriatr Soc 34:119, 1986.
64. Tideiksaar, R: Fall prevention in the home. Topic Geriatr Rehabil 3:57, 1987.
65. Tideiksaar, R: Preventing falls: Home hazard checklists to help older patients protect themselves. Geriatrics 41:26, 1986.
66. United States Consumer Product Safety Commission (USCPC). Home safety checklist for older consumers. USCPC, Washington, DC, 1986.
67. Isaacs, B: Clinical and laboratory studies of falls in old people: Prospects on prevention. Clin Geriatr Med 1:513, 1985.
68. Bhala, RP, O'Donnell, J and Thoppil, E: Ptophobia: Phobic fear of falling and its clinical management. Phys Ther 62:187, 1982.
69. Overstall, PW: Determining the causes of falls in the elderly. Geriatric Medicine Today 2:63, 1983.
70. Tinetti, ME, Speechley, M and Ginter, SF: Risk factors for falls among elderly persons living in the community. N Engl J Med 319: 1701, 1988.
71. Murphy, J and Isaacs, B: The post-fall syndrome: A study of thirty-six elderly patients. Gerontol 28:265, 1982.
72. DiScipio, WJ and Feldman, MC: Combined behavior therapy and physical therapy in the treatment of a fear of walking. J Behav Exp Psychiatr 2:151, 1971.
73. Dibner, AS, Lowey, L and Morris, JN: Usage and acceptance of an emergency alarm system by the frail elderly. Gerontol 22:538, 1982.
74. Feeney, RJ, Galer, MD and Gallagher, MM: Alarm systems for elderly and disabled people. Institute for Consumer Ergonomics Ltd. University of Technology, Loughborough, England, 1975.
75. Davies, KN: Emergency alarms. Brit Med J 300:1713, 1990.
76. Evans, LK and Strumpf, NE: Myths about elder restraint. Image: Journal of Nursing Scholarship 22:124, 1990.
77. PL 100-203: Omnibus Budget Reconciliation Act, Subtitle C, Nursing Home Reform, Government Printing Office, Washington, DC, 1987.
78. Tideiksaar, R and Osterwell, D: prevention of bed falls. Geriatric Medicine Today 8:70, 1989.
79. Widder, B: A new device to decrease falls. Geriatr Nurse 6:287, 1985.
80. Innes, E: Maintaining fall prevention. QRB 11:217, 1985.
81. McHutchion, E and Morse, JM: Releasing restraints: A nursing dilemma. J Gerontol Nur 15:16, 1989.

The once lusty man is now an old carl sitting on his dyke, having reached that terrible time . . . of knowing that he will never be allowed by his well-intentioned off-spring to do another day's work for ever and ever. Sometimes, to give him an hour's pride, they let him wheel a barrow. He will have to die gradual on a fine bed of straw, but he would rather be gotten with his hammer in his hands.

—J. M. BARRIT, *Farewell Miss Julie Logan*, Charles Scribner's Sons, New York, 1932.

Chapter

Dementia

ROSE ANNE BERILA

OBJECTIVES

By the end of this chapter, readers will be able to:

1 Define dementia.

2 List reversible and irreversible causes of dementia.

3 Discuss the differences among forms of dementia and the diagnostic process.

4 Discuss the known and hypothesized causes of dementia.

5 Discuss pathological features of dementia.

6 List risk factors for dementia.

7 Discuss symptoms of various forms of dementia.

8 Discuss the reactions of patients and families to Alzheimer's disease. How does the disease interrupt performance?

9 Describe the stages of progression of Alzheimer's disease.

10 Discuss interdisciplinary strategies for managing Alzheimer's disease and other dementias.

Dementia is defined by the American Psychiatric Association[1] as a deterioration of intellectual capacities that has a significant, negative impact on social and personal functioning. The incidence of dementia is expected to increase as the number of people living beyond the age of 65 increases. It is currently estimated that in the United States alone 2.6 million people suffer from dementia. By the year 2000, the number of people with this disorder is expected to rise to 4 million, and by the year 2040, nearly 9 million Americans will be diagnosed with dementia.[2] The financial and emotional consequences of this disorder for society, the health care system, and individuals with dementia and their families is devastating and poses a serious challenge for health care providers. In the United States the cost of providing care to people with Alzheimer's disease (AD), the most common form of dementia, has been estimated at $36 billion a year,[3] with over $25 billion going to pay for nursing home costs.[4]

Dementia is classified as either reversible or irreversible. Reversible dementias account for about 13 percent of all suspected dementias. Of the reversible dementias, 28.2 percent were associated with drug toxicity, 26.2 percent with depression, and 15.5 percent with metabolic disorders.[5] Tables 15–1 and 15–2 list some of the more common causes of reversible and irreversible dementias. Because Alzheimer's disease is the most common of all dementias, much of this chapter will be devoted to understanding this disorder.

TABLE 15–1 **Causes of Reversible Dementia**

Depression

Drug toxicity

Normal pressure hydrocephalus

Subdural hematoma

Hypothyroidism

Benign brain tumor

Vitamin B_{12} deficiency

Source: Adapted from Barry and Moskowitz,[10] p. 1915.

TABLE 15–2 **Causes of Irreversible Dementia**

Alzheimer's disease

Multi-infarcts of the brain

Huntington's chorea

Pick's disease

Parkinson's disease

Acquired immunodeficiency syndrome

Source: Adapted from Pary, Tobias, and Lippman,[9] p. 1184.

DIAGNOSTIC CRITERIA

The diagnosis of Alzheimer's disease is made primarily by ruling out other causes for the global cognitive changes that impair a person's ability to function.[6] Currently, the most commonly used criteria for identifying Alzheimer's disease in the United States are those developed by the National Institute of Neurological and Communication Disorders and Stroke-Alzheimer's Disease and Related Disorders Association (NINCDS-ADRDA) Work Group[7] and the *Diagnostic and Statistical Manual* III, Revised.[1] These criteria are:

- Global, progressive memory loss and loss of other intellectual functions in an adult who is alert
- Gradual onset of symptoms
- Progressive deterioration over time
- Exclusion of medical, neurological, and psychiatric disorders that can impair cognitive functioning[8]

NINCDS-ADRDA criteria also distinguish three levels of confidence for the diagnosis of AD:

1. Probable AD, in which the symptoms of this disorder occur alone
2. Possible AD, in which symptoms are believed to be Alzheimer's disease, but atypical features are present, or other disorders that have the potential to cause dementia are present but are not seen as contributing significantly to the cognitive decline
3. Definite AD, when the disease is confirmed by brain biopsy findings after death.[8]

Clinically, it can be difficult to distinguish Alzheimer's disease from other illnesses that cause dementia. The literature supports that the most significant indicators are gradual onset; memory loss; an insidious, progressive course of illness; difficulty in learning; compromised judgment; and problems with orientation.

There are subtle symptomatic differences among the various dementias that can assist in diagnosis. For example, subcortical dementias (Parkinson's, for example) are characterized by motor deficits such as tremor and gait disturbances. Mixed dementias are characterized by unpredictable mixtures of cortical and subcortical dementia. Multi-infarct dementia, for example, may manifest with a mixture of cortical and motor signs. Among the cortical dementias, factors such as presence of aphasia (a characteristic of Alzheimer's disease), poverty of response (characteristic of depression), and agraphia (characteristic of the familial type of Alzheimer's disease) may assist in differential diagnosis.

Since no existing medical tests confirm the diagnosis of AD while the patient is alive, diagnosis is made by exclusion. This is done using the following tests: chemistry profile, thyroid function tests, vitamin B_{12} and folate levels, serology, HIV test, *computerized tomographic* (CT) *scan* of the head, *electroencephalogram* (EEG), and an *electrocardiogram* (EKG).[9] Barry and Moskowitz[10] stress the importance of a good medical, neurological, and psychiatric exam, including some standardized mental status exam that assesses memory, judgment, and orientation.[11] Ability to perform activities of daily living and orientation to geographic location should be assessed.[12] A thorough history from the patient and the family is also critical and should include the questions found in Table 15–3.

It is also important that the mood of the patient be assessed since depression can mimic dementia. Factors that distinguish true dementia from *pseudodementia*, or depression, were identified by Wells,[13] and are summarized in

TABLE 15–3 **Questions for History Taking**
1. What types of problems have you noticed with your memory? Was the onset sudden or gradual?
2. Has there been any difficulty with finding the words you want when speaking?
3. Has there been any change in personality?
4. Has there been any difficulty in making change or handling a checkbook?
5. Has there been any difficulty in remembering such things as shopping lists or how to play a game?
6. Has there been any change in abiilty to cook, dress, bathe, or toilet?
7. What medications are being taken? (Ask specifically about over-the-counter medications, borrowed medications, old prescription medications that are still in the home, and alcohol.)
8. Is behavior consistent, or are there changes in performance and emotional tone?

Source: Adapted from Crystal,[43] p. 298.

Table 15–4. Unlike AD, depression is treatable. When it occurs, diagnosis and treatment can return the individual to his or her highest level of functioning.[14]

PATHOLOGIC FEATURES

The findings that support a diagnosis of definite AD are the presence of neuritic plaques and neurofibrillary tangles in the neocortex and hippocampus of the brain.[15] These plaques and tangles were first discovered in 1907, by Alois Alzheimer while examining the brain of a 55-year-old woman who had died after a progressive course of dementia. Despite his findings, the relationship between senile dementia in the elderly and Alzheimer's disease remained controversial until the latter half of this century.

Cell death and massive loss of neurons occur in the brain of an Alzheimer's patient, leading to cerebral atrophy. The neuritic plaques and neurofibrillary tangles are believed to contribute to neuronal loss, but it is not clear how this occurs.[4] A decrease in the enzyme choline acetyltransferase, re-

TABLE 15-4	**Distinguishing Characteristics of Dementia and Pseudodementia**
Pseudodementia	**Dementia**
Sudden onset	Gradual onset
Family and patient aware of dysfunction and severity.	Family and patient unaware of dysfunction.
Frequent, specific complaints of cognitive loss by the patient.	Few, vague complaints of cognitive loss by the patient.
Patient emphasizes disabilities.	Patient conceals disabilities.
Patient makes little effort to do tasks.	Patient struggles with tasks.
"Don't know" answers typical.	Near-miss answers typical.
Cognitive losses appear to vary with similar tasks.	Cognitive losses.

Source: Adapted from Wells,[13] p. 898.

quired for the synthesis of acetylcholine, occurs in the brains of patients with AD and is associated with cognitive impairment.[16]

Research continues to discover the relationships between the presence of neuritic plaques, neurofibrillary tangles, decreased choline acetyltransferase levels, cell death, and the cognitive losses associated with Alzheimer's disease. One promising line of research is examination of the presence of abnormal levels of a protein known as *beta amyloid* in the brains of individuals with Alzheimer's disease. The meaning of the finding is not yet known, but it may yield information about the cause of the disease and potential treatments.

RISK FACTORS

Increasing Age

Increasing age is the most significant risk factor for developing Alzheimer's disease.[15] At age 65, the prevalence of Alzheimer's disease is about 1 percent.[2] Over the age of 85, the prevalence rate ranges from 15 percent to 47 percent.[2,17] It should be noted that the disease has occurred in individuals in their forties.

Family History

Family history increases the risk of developing Alzheimer's disease in first-degree relatives (grandparents, parents, siblings), particularly when the age of onset for the disease is under 75.[18] However, studies involving identical twins underscore the importance of nongenetic risk factors since the concordance rate for developing AD in this population is only 50 percent.[19] Alzheimer's may be an *autosomal dominant trait*, meaning that the probability of transmission of the gene is 50 percent. However, since it is not expressed at a rate of 50 percent, clearly other factors must be present in order for the disease to emerge.

It is difficult to examine familial risk since many individuals die of other causes before AD has an opportunity to appear. Considerable attention has been paid to the twenty-first gene[20] because people who have Down's syndrome (trisomy 21) universally develop symptoms of AD if they live into their thirties. This fact provides support for a genetic explanation of at least some forms of AD. The familial type seems to emerge earlier, has a more severe course, and is characterized by agraphia and severe expressive aphasia.

Other Factors

Other risk factors under investigation are head trauma, particularly associated with loss of consciousness[21] and maternal age.[22] Rocca and associates[22] found that early (15 to 19 years) and late (over 40 years) maternal age may be a risk factor in developing Alzheimer's disease. The correlation of maternal age to AD is strengthened by the finding of similar neuropathologic features in persons with Down's syndrome who live past the ages of 30 to 40; advanced age is known to be a risk factor in Down's syndrome.[23]

INDIVIDUAL AND FAMILY EXPERIENCE OF ALZHEIMER'S DISEASE

Alzheimer's disease has significant impact on both the individual and the family. It is essential to understand the experience of Alzheimer's disease from the person's and the family's perspective and to know the stages of the disease and methods for managing symptoms.

Trying to understand what the individual with Alzheimer's disease experiences subjectively is difficult. A growing number of first-hand accounts of the experience are emerging, but these describe only the earlier stages of the disease. Cohen and Eisdorfer[24] report the following experience of a woman diagnosed with Alzheimer's disease:

> My memory lapses were humiliating. I couldn't depend on myself anymore. Mysteriously, I was changing. I knew about this Alzheimer's disease, how it destroys intelligent behavior in bits and pieces, but I was afraid to think that it was happening to me. When the doctor began to talk to me in the office, I began to get nervous. I wanted to run away. It may sound absurd, but I thought if I didn't hear the words then I couldn't have the disease. (p. 59)

Another such account was written, with the help of his wife, by Robert Davis, a minister. Davis[25] wrote of how Alzheimer's disease was affecting him several months after his diagnosis:

> In my present condition . . . there are times when I feel normal. At other times I cannot follow what is going on around me; as the conversation whips too fast from person to person and before I have processed one comment, the thread has moved to another person on another topic, and I am left isolated from action — alone in a crowd. If I press myself with greatest concentration to try to keep up, I feel as though something short circuits in my brain. At this point I become disoriented, . . . my speech becomes slow, or I cannot find the right words to express myself. (p. 86)

Davis draws a parallel between Alzheimer's disease and infancy, seeing the disease as a reversing of the aging process. Freedom is gradually compromised as Alzheimer's disease progresses because it requires family to supervise the person to keep him or her safe and functioning at an optimal level. This in no way is meant to imply that people with Alzheimer's disease should have their freedom usurped but rather that the family, with the assistance of health care professionals, must weigh the consequences of freedom versus dependence in making their decisions as the disease progresses. This process is just the opposite of what parents do as their children grow, and underscores the validity of Davis's insights into what having Alzheimer's disease must be like. A caution is in order here: In spite of their behavior, people with Alzheimer's disease are not children. It is important to help them maintain their dignity and sense of self for as long as possible.

When people think of the subjective experience of Alzheimer's disease, they frequently assume that the person with AD never understands or remembers what is happening. Realization of gradually losing one's sense of self is intolerable for most people to conceptualize, so it is easier to believe that the person with Alzheimer's disease never perceives this loss. However, clinical experience suggests that persons with Alzheimer's disease do perceive their losses.

For the families, the diagnosis of Alzheimer's disease is equally devastating. Davis's wife, Betty,[25] writes in her husband's book of her experience of his illness:

> Sometimes in weakness and despair I want to give voice to that primal scream starting way down in the hidden recesses of the lungs—down where the ever-present knot that lives in my stomach resides—let it whirl through that vortex that's sucking my life and being into the black hold of never-ending pain, emptiness, and loneliness—just give it voice as it rises and explodes through the top of my head—Noooooooooooo! No God, no! Not us! Not this! Not his mind! Not his personhood! Anything, God but this! . . . How do you prepare for the holocaust? How can you say goodnight to your sweetheart and wonder—will this be the night from which reason will never again waken? Will morning find that new person in my bed—the man who will not know who I am or why I am in his bed? (pp. 139–140)

Mace and Rabins[26] spell out clearly the stressors families have in dealing with the diagnosis. Changes in roles within a family occur, requiring redefinition of relationships and sense of self. Family conflicts frequently resurface at a time when members are emotionally drained. The phrase "36-hour day"[26] is no exaggeration of what a typical day feels like for the care giver.

Once the diagnosis is made, the individual and the family struggle to pull their lives together, to find meaning, to make decisions, and to go on. One of the first decisions to be faced is whether to give the diagnosis to the person with the disease. Cohen and Eisdorfer,[24] maintain that patients should be informed because honesty is essential in any relationship and to be less than honest damages relationships. Other decisions that the family and person with Alzheimer's disease face early on include arranging finances, making wills, and arranging durable powers of attorney for finances and health care. These decisions may require assistance from legal and medical professionals, as well as community agencies. Families often delay because of the pain involved in making some of these decisions, all of which reflect the gradual loss of ability of the diagnosed individual.

Families will need a strong support system, as will the person with Alzheimer's disease, if they are to cope with this illness effectively. Support groups are available in most cities through local chapters of the Alzheimer's Association. Information may be obtained by calling 1-800-621-0379. Support groups help families to manage more successfully the behavioral and physical changes seen in AD, as well as to cope with the stress of making decisions about placement and restrictions in freedom.

STAGES AND ASSESSMENT OF ALZHEIMER'S DISEASE

There are numerous ways to stage Alzheimer's disease. The staging that will be presented here is based on functional ability and behavior and was developed by Reisberg and associates.[27] Seven functional stages (*fast stages*) were described by these authors, but the first two stages represent normal aging; only fast stages 3 through 7 describe dementia. Fast stages offer a precise description of the progressive course of Alzheimer's disease. This staging system describes concrete, observable behaviors listed in the order in which they occur. This allows health care professionals to identify where a person with Alzheimer's is on a continuum in order to educate the family and patient as to what to expect next. Reisberg and associates[27] fast stages are presented in Table 15–5. Fast stages 3 and 4 are descriptive of mild, 5 and 6 of moderate, and 7 of severe Alzheimer's disease. The rate of progression in Alzheimer's disease remains uncertain. It appears that there is a relatively small initial decline in cognitive functioning, followed by a more rapid decline in the middle phase of the illness, and then by a slower progression in the later stage of the disease.[28]

Lowenstein and colleagues[29] examined AD using a functional framework.

TABLE 15–5 **Fast Stages**

Fast Stage 1

No objective or subjective changes in functional ability over time.

Fast Stage 2

Subjective changes noted in memory that do not interfere in functional ability; not noted by others.

Fast Stage 3

Objective changes that note a decline in functional abilities related to complex social or occupational tasks. Withdrawal from these situations may occur and will mask deficits.

Examples: Forgetting of important appointments.
Decreased ability to complete complex, familiar tasks.
Decreased ability to travel independently to new locale.

Fast Stage 4

Objective changes that interfere with one's ability to handle complex tasks, such as finances, without assistance.

Examples: Difficulty balancing checkbook.
Difficulty remembering items to be purchased when shopping.

Fast Stage 5

Assistance required to choose proper clothing.

Examples: Assistance needed with selection of season- or occasion-appropriate clothes.
Reminders needed to change clothes.

Fast Stage 6

Assistance required to clothe, bathe, and/or toilet self. Loss of ability to speak in complete sentences by end of this stage.

Substage 6*a*: Compromised ability to put clothing on properly.

Examples: Dresses over night clothes.
Difficulty buttoning, tying, zipping.

Substage 6*b*: Compromised ability to bathe.

Examples: Difficulty adjusting water temperature.
Difficulty entering tub, washing, drying self.

Substage 6*c*: Compromised ability to toilet self.

Examples: Forgets to flush.
Forgets to wipe.
Difficulty adjusting clothes afterward.

Substage 6*d*: Urinary incontinence.

Substage 6*e*: Fecal incontinence.

Fast Stage 7

Loss of speech and/or motor abilities.

Substage 7*a*: Vocabulary of six words or less.

Substage 7*b*: Single-word vocabulary.

Substage 7*c*: Inability to ambulate.

Substage 7*d*: Inability to sit independently.

Substage 7*e*: Inability to smile.

Substage 7*f*: Inability to hold head up independently.

Source: Adapted from Reisberg, et al.,[27] p. 1916.

They devised an assessment tool called the *direct assessment of functional status* (DAFS) scale. This tool assesses the following abilities: orientation to time, communication skills, shopping skills, financial skills, eating and dressing skills, and indirectly, driving competency. Table 15–6 describes what is assessed by the DAFS.

Spatial orientation also warrants close assessment.[30] Many patients in the early stages of Alzheimer's disease get lost. They appear to have poor spatial memory and impaired mental representation and functional spatial orientation in new environments. These functions were less impaired in familiar settings. Assessment tools that evaluate functional and spatial orientation allow health care workers to help families understand what the person with Alzheimer's disease can and cannot do, enabling them to set realistic expectations that promote safety and minimize stress while maintaining an appropriate level of freedom for the person with dementia.

Numerous other behaviors and symptoms occur associated with AD. These behaviors do not occur in a sequential order but significantly impact the person's ability to function independently. Hall[31] groups these behaviors into four clusters:

1. Intellectual losses
2. Personality losses

TABLE 15–6 **DAFS Scale**	
1. Orientation to time	Identify time on four clock settings. Identify day of week. Identify month, date, year.
2. Telephone skills	Pick up receiver, dial, hang up. Dial operator. Dial correct number from list. Dial number verbally given. Dial written number.
3. Preparing letter	Copy address on envelope. Return address. Stamp. Fold, put in envelope, seal.
4. Phone message	Write dictated phone message, including caller's name, time they will call back, caller's phone number.
5. Driving competency	Identify meaning of common road signs.
6. Money identification	Identify penny, nickel, dime, quarter, $1, $5, $10 bills.
7. Counting money	Count money. Make change. Write check.
8. Shopping skills	Correctly select 4 items on a shopping list from 16 items. After 10 minutes, remember and select 4 items verbally given from 16 items.
9. Eating skills	Pour water into glass. Drink from cup. Correctly use fork, spoon, knife.
10. Dressing/grooming skills	Take cap off toothpaste. Put toothpaste on brush. Brush teeth. Turn water on and off. Wash face. Brush hair. Put on coat. Tie, zip, button.

Source: Adapted from Lowenstein, et al.,[29] pp. 120–121.

3. Planning losses
4. Behaviors manifested when the patient's stress threshold is exceeded.

Examples of behaviors associated with each cluster are found in Table 15–7.

MANAGEMENT

The key to management of the behaviors associated with Alzheimer's disease and other dementing illnesses lies in working closely with the family or care giver. Ham[11] speaks to the role of health care professionals in the lives of patients who have Alzheimer's disease as follows:

For now our challenge is a challenge not of cure, but of treatment. . . . Much of the management and treatment relies on a family member, or some other caregiver, generally not a health professional. . . . Good management depends on that person gaining the strength, knowledge and skill necessary to anticipate, handle and minimize each effect. We should regard the informed caregiver as the "right arm" of the health professional. (p. 4)

The supportive and educative roles of health care professionals, identified by Ham, impact not only on symptom management but also on the quality of life of the care giver and the person with Alzheimer's disease. The importance of this partnership between the care giver and health professionals, as well as the importance of understanding the person with Alzheimer's disease in the context of his or her life, is all too often ignored. Respect for the caregiver and the impaired person and commitment to developing an effective partnership is the foundation for this framework. For this approach to be successful, health care professionals must deal honestly with their own feelings.

A cookbook approach to the management of symptoms may produce lists of helpful strategies but sometimes overlooks the reality that how a symptom appears in any given person is as dependent on the individual as on the disease process itself. Not all people develop all symptoms, and not all who do develop a given symptom manifest it in exactly the same way. Therefore, the overall approach to management needs to be individualized. Man-

TABLE 15–7 **Symptom Clusters in Alzheimer's Disease**
Intellectual Losses
Loss of recent memory first, then remote
Loss of sense of time
Compromised ability to make choices
Inability to abstract or apply logic
Impaired judgment
Compromised ability to identify auditory and visual stimuli
Loss of expressive and receptive language skills
Personality Losses
Flat affect
Emotional lability
Loss of tact
Difficulty controlling temper
Inability to delay gratification
Decreased concentration
Social withdrawal
Self-preoccupation
Confabulation
Perseveration
Paranoia
Delusions
Hallucinations
Planning Losses
Inability to plan activities
Inability to plan, set goals, organize
Motor apraxia
Loss of energy reserve with physical or mental exertion
Frustration
Increased concentration on function resulting in decreased performance
Behaviors Manifested When Stress Threshold Exceeded
Confusion
Agitation
Wandering
Violent outbursts
Belligerence
Loud, noisy activities
Purposelessness
Repetitiveness
Catastrophic reactions

Source: Adapted from Hall,[31] p. 33.

agement will be effective to the degree we are able to know the person with Alzheimer's disease in the context of his or her life. There are some basic strategies, however, that can guide health care workers in making decisions with the care giver and patient. These strategies, which are deliberately broad to allow for individualization, are:

- Restructuring the environment
- Establishing a routine
- Communicating effectively

When operationalizing these strategies, it is important to keep in mind that four major stressors are to be avoided:

1. Fatigue
2. Change
3. Excessive demands
4. Overstimulation[31]

Controlling these stressors will greatly reduce the chance of the patient's exceeding his or her stress threshold.[31] Hall[31] also identified a fifth stressor that can temporarily worsen the behavioral symptoms of Alzheimer's disease: physical illness or pain. The importance of this last stressor cannot be underestimated. Frequently a change in behavior is the first sign that something is physically wrong with a person who has Alzheimer's disease. Just as young children cannot tell their parents when they are not feeling well, Alzheimer's patients also have difficulty telling those around them when they are ill; thus the care giver must be attentive to unexplained rapid behavioral changes.

As each of the strategies outlined above is discussed, attention will be paid to how the stressors Hall identified can be avoided or minimized. Cognitive and sensory abilities are compromised, making it difficult for the individual to gather and interpret information from the environment.[32] As a result, behaviors might seem "purposeless and maladaptive, when, in fact, the responses are the most integrated ones he or she can make based on the inadequate or distorted information"[32] (p. 85). When restructuring the environment for the person with Alzheimer's disease, one must take into consideration the deficits

noted and try to provide additional cues. A stable environment is helpful. Promotion of independence, to the degree possible, and safety are important factors to keep in mind when restructuring the environment.

Visual Cues

Visual cues for important rooms and objects might include signs or easily recognizable pictures. Cues involving the other senses, such as dim lights at bedtime or food scented air fresheners at meal times, can provide additional information to the impaired person about the activities taking place. Cleaning drawers and closets so that only essential articles remain can facilitate dressing. Clothing and Velcro closures can also assist in meeting this goal. Reorganization of closets and drawers also makes it harder for the impaired person to successfully hide articles. Streamlining the contents of kitchen and bathroom cupboards can foster the person's function in these areas. Safety measures include removing chemicals and cleaning agents and providing nonskid rugs and grab bars.

Unnecessary Stimulation

Unnecessary stimulation in the environment should be eliminated when possible. This includes bright colors, glaring lights and surfaces, patterned wallpapers and drapes, mirrors outside the bathroom, and noise. Using music rather than television appears to promote a calm atmosphere and decrease overstimulation. A variety of technological devices can support memory and function, as discussed in Chapter 21.[33] In conclusion, the main objectives in restructuring the environment are to decrease overstimulation, make the environment and important objects knowable using sensory cues, and avoid continuous change once the initial restructuring is complete.

Wandering

Management of wandering is sometimes addressed environmentally. For example, an unlocked door may exit to a fenced path that leads back to the door. Beck and Heacock,[33] however, disagree with this approach and suggest that what is important is to understand the purpose behind the wandering and to use this knowledge in designing interventions.

Agitation

Agitation can be decreased by providing individuals with planned opportunities to engage in play in their environment.[34] Mayers and Griffin[34] found that engaging in play resulted in an increase in interest in the environment and a decrease in agitation. Objects related to tasks or hobbies the person enjoyed in the past may be a way to improve self-esteem.

Establishing a Routine

Establishing a routine can decrease overstimulation and fatigue. This helps prevent the stress associated with changes for the Alzheimer's patient. Repetition of the same routine every day allows the patient to function automatically, providing a sense of security. Rest and quiet times are important because older adults may have lower energy reserves. In people with Alzheimer's disease a great deal of energy is expended in interpreting the environment; therefore, they tend to function best early in the day.[31] Schedules should include previously enjoyed activities and socialization.

Quizzing individuals with Alzheimer's disease, on the theory that this will slow the progression of the disease, should be discouraged, as it tends to frustrate them and increases the chances of a catastrophic reaction. Withdrawal, irritability, anger, and paranoia are not unusual responses when unrealistic demands are placed on the patient.

Davis[25] speaks to the importance of an established routine:

> Leaving the routine of being around my familiar home, having more people and excitement around me than I am accustomed to, varying my ritual for taking care of my grooming and health care, being unable to lie down and nap at my usual times, all brought me to a place of being unable to make even the most basic decisions for myself, of not being aware of how to relieve my discomfort. This experience taught me that if I want to function at the top of my limited capacity, I must establish a routine and keep it. (p. 88)

Communication

To increase the effectiveness of communication with an Alzheimer's patient, it is essential to keep the message simple and to communicate in a way that validates the feelings and worth of the individual. Knowledge of the patient increases the probability of understanding what he or she is trying to communicate. Mace and Rabins[26] outlined ways to improve verbal and nonverbal communication with a person who has Alzheimer's disease. Their suggestions are outlined in Table 15–8.

Reality Orientation and Validation Therapies

Reality orientation therapy and validation therapy have both been discussed as potential interventions with people with AD[35,36] (see Figure 15–1). Reality orientation therapy may cause stress if the approach is not individualized.[35] Validation therapy substantiates the person's worth by focusing on the feelings being communicated and talking about past accomplishments and experiences. Davis[25] speaks to the positive effects validation had for him:

> Blessed is the person who can take the Alzheimer's patient back to a happier time when they were worthwhile and allow them to see the situation in which they were of some use. I have baskets of letters from these angels of mercy who have writ-

---

TABLE 15–8 **Strategies to Improve Communication**

Verbal Communication

Keep voice tone low.

Eliminate competing noise in the environment.

Use short, simple sentences.

Ask only one question at a time, avoid complex choices.

Ask person to do one task (or one step in a task) at a time.

Speak slowly, allowing person time to respond.

Do not argue. Distraction may help, for example, change in approach, change in topic, visual distraction, and leaving and returning in a short while.

Nonverbal Communication

Be aware of your emotional tone. People with Alzheimer's disease are sensitive to emotional climate.

Use touch.

Smile.

Look directly at the person when speaking.

Demonstrate what you want done as you speak.

Respond to what it feels like the person is saying, if verbal message is unclear.

Source: Adapted from Mace and Rabins,[26] pp. 28–33.

---

ten to remind me of a time that I shared God's strength with them and helped them. These have been my sustenance during these dark months of loss. (p. 103)

Another way to communicate value for the individual is by selecting activi-

Figure 15–1 A reality orientation board can help some individuals with dementia remain better oriented. (Courtesy of Menorah Park Home for the Aged, Cleveland, Ohio.)

ties that are consistent with what an individual chose previously. For example, if a man with Alzheimer's disease has valued work and helping others all his life, activities that allow him to contribute to others and framing the activities in the context of work will be far more successful and affirming then pushing him to play with a toy. This approach is also less likely to cause temporary deterioration in the person's behavior.

Watching some Alzheimer's day care centers . . . gives me the "willies." I could never bear to be talked to and treated like a child at summer camp. . . . I am repulsed by activity directors on cruise ships, much less some twenty-year-old trying to get me to play childish exercises with rock music. I'm sure I would try to get back to my room and if stopped in this attempt I would become churlish and belligerent. If the insensitive director continued to push or become condescending, . . . I would probably explode. . . . Is this a result of Alzheimer's Disease? No, this is how I would react now in my best state of mind. . . . Human dignity demands that I have the right of refusal for any difficulty, . . . that I do not perceive as entertaining. . . . A person in whatever state of dementia deserves to be treated with all dignity and respect. (p. 102)

Structured, Supportive Groups

Use of structured, supportive groups to maintain a sense of connection to others and the environment is useful.[37] Gerber and associates[38] found that daily interaction, whether structured around orientation or social events, increased Alzheimer's patients' ability to interact with others and improved their orientation. Friedman and Tappen[39] recently found that Alzheimer's patients who had daily interactions while walking showed significant improvement in communication over patients who had interactions without walking. It is unclear why walking improved communication. It may be that simultaneous stimulation of two areas of the brain may be helpful, or it may be that the quality of the interactions might have been different when they included walking.

Behaviors that particularly distress families and care givers and impede communication are:

- Paranoia
- Suspiciousness
- Hallucinations
- Delusions
- Depression

Frequently these behaviors result in hospitalization of the person with Alzheimer's disease, particularly if they are accompanied by agitation or violent behavior.

Paranoia, Suspiciousness, and Delusions

Paranoia, suspiciousness, and delusions may take the form of complaints by Alzheimer's patients that others are stealing or trying to harm them. This may be a result of the person's inability to make sense of what is occurring to them states:[25] "The loss of self, . . . the helplessness to control this insidious thief who was little by little taking away my most valued possession, my mind, had made me especially wary of the rest of my possessions in an unreasonable way" (p. 91).

Hallucinations

Hallucinations can occur in Alzheimer's disease, as can other misidentifications of reality. Misidentifications include thinking that family members living in the home are strangers or that a person on television or a reflection in a mirror, is real.[40]

Interventions have significant implications for care givers and other family members. Attention must be paid to their needs, so that they will continue to have the energy and patience to deal with the individual. Routine may be best for the patient, but the care giver may need some variety. As the patient's condition worsens, the care giver may find it difficult even to get an adequate night's sleep. An important role of the professional is to help the care giver find support services and respite and to make decisions about when care has become so burdensome that it jeopardizes others in the family.

Medications

When any disruptive behavioral symptoms cannot be managed by restructuring the environment and by educating care givers about reasonable expectations for the person, effective communication techniques, and the importance of an established routine, then medications can be helpful. Neuroleptic medications are most commonly used to treat the symptoms noted above. Their use must be judicious, as side effects are more common in older adults, particularly those who are cognitively impaired. No specific neuroleptic is more effective than others; however, it is generally believed that low doses of high-potency, low-anticholinergic medications such as Haldol are preferred.[11]

When depression accompanies Alzheimer's disease, it is essential that it be treated. Antidepressant medications are useful, particularly those that are less anti-cholinergic.[11] Teri and Gallagher-Thompson[41] have found cognitive therapy to also be effective in treating depression when it occurs in the early stage of Alzheimer's disease. Behavioral treatment involving the patient and care giver appears to be successful in working with patients in the middle or late stages of the disease.[41]

A number of drugs are currently being examined for their potential in treating Alzheimer's disease.[42] Although much remains to be done, increased understanding of the underlying mechanisms that cause Alzheimer's disease provides useful clues about what kinds of drugs may alleviate symptoms.

CONCLUSION

The most important factor in the management of people with Alzheimer's disease or other dementias is demonstrating respect for their personhood. If this respect governs the implementation of any intervention chosen, then the person and care giver will both benefit. As Ham[11] eloquently states:

> The attempt is to preserve as much function as possible, for as long as possible, and thus to maintain the person in his/her own home, in a familiar environment, the environment in which he/she will be least confused and most productive and calm, for as long as possible; in the environment which is most economical, so that as much as possible of the person's capability and person can still be enjoyed by the family members, despite the presence of this illness. One does not wish to make light of this illness and the tragedy that it represents for many of those whom it afflicts. . . . However, pleasure, joy, love, affection, and an appreciation of excitement, reminiscence and beauty . . . and many other life-enhancing qualities are still there to be enjoyed by patient and family member alike. (p. 17)

REVIEW QUESTIONS

1. *Most professionals who work with demented individuals emphasize the importance of careful diagnosis.*

Discuss the reasons that this process is essential.

2. *Describe environmental and personal management strategies which seem effective with individuals with Alzheimer's disease.*

3. *Patients and families have significant emotional reactions to the diagnosis of Alzheimer's disease. Describe some of these reactions, and discuss ways in which professionals might assist individuals to cope.*

4. *What are the hypothesized causes of Alzheimer's disease? Which of these are being studied most intensely, and which have been largely discredited?*

5. *Discuss the differences in symptoms between dementia caused by depression and that caused by Alzheimer's disease.*

6. *If an older adult came to you worried about developing Alzheimer's disease, how would you help him or her assess risk?*

REFERENCES

1. American Psychiatric Association: Diagnostic and Statistical Manual of Mental Disorders, ed 3, rev. Washington, DC, 1987.
2. Gorelick, PB and Bozzola, FG: Alzheimer's disease: Clues to the cause. Postgraduate Medicine 89(4):231–232, 237–238, 240, March 1991.
3. Schneider, EL and Guralnik, JM: The aging of America. Journal of American Medical Association 263:2335–2340, 1990.
4. Skeleton, WW and Skeleton, NK: Alzheimer's disease: Recognizing and treating a frustrating condition. Postgraduate Medicine 90(4): 33–34, 37–41, September 15, 1991.
5. Clarfield, AA: The reversible dementias: Do they reverse: Annals of Internal Medicine 109(6):476–486, September 15, 1988.
6. Schoenberg, BS, Kokmen, E and Okazaki, H: Alzheimer's disease and other dementing illnesses in a defined United States population: Incidence rates and clinical features. Annals of Neurology 22:724–729, 1987.
7. McKhann, G, Drachman, D, Folstein, M, Katzman, R, Price, D and Stadlan, EM: Clinical diagnosis of Alzheimer's disease: Report of the NINCDS-ADRDA work group under the auspices of Department of Health and Human

Services task force on Alzheimer's disease. Neurology 34(7):939–944, July 1984.

8. Morris, JC and Rubin, EH: Clinical diagnosis and course of Alzheimer's disease. Psychiatric Clinics of North America 14(2):223–236, June 1991.

9. Pary, R, Tobias, CR and Lippman, S: Dementia: What to do. Southern Medical Journal 83(10):1182–1189, October 1990.

10. Barry P and Moskowitz, M: The diagnosis of reversible dementia in the elderly. Archives of International Medicine 149:1914–1918, 1988.

11. Ham, RJ: Alzheimer's disease and the family: A challenge of the new millennium. Advances in Experimental Medicine and Biology 282:3–20, 1990.

12. Hughes, CP, Berg, L, Danziger, WL, Cohen, LA and Martin, RL: A new clinical scale for the staging of dementia. British Journal of Psychiatry 140:566–572, 1982.

13. Wells, CE: Pseudomentia. American Journal of Psychiatry, 136(7):895–900, July 1979.

14. Alexopoulos, GS and Abrams, RC: Depression in Alzheimer's disease. Psychiatric Clinics of North America 14(2):327–339, June 1991.

15. Katzman, R and Saitoh, T: Advances in Alzheimer's disease. FASEB Journal 5:278–286, March 1991.

16. Patel, S and Tariot, PN: Pharmacologic models of Alzheimer's disease. Psychiatric Clinics of North America 14(2):287–308, June 1991.

17. Evans, DA, Funkenstein, HH, Albert, MS, Scherr, PA, Cook, NR, Chown MJ, Herbert, LE, Hennekens, CH and Taylor, JO: Prevalence of Alzheimer's disease in a community population of older persons: Higher than previously reported. Journal of the American Medical Association 262(18):2551–2556, 1989.

18. Heston, LL, Mastri, AR, Anderson, VE and White J: Dementia of the Alzheimer type: Clinical genetics, natural history and associated conditions. Archives of General Psychiatry 38:1085–1090, 1981.

19. Jarvik, LF, Ruth V and Matsuyama, SS: Organic brain syndrome and aging: A six year follow-up of surviving twins. Archives of General Psychiatry 37:280–286, 1980.

20. St. George-Hyslop, PH, Tanzi, RE, Polinsky, J, Haines, L, Nee, L, Watkins, PC, Myers, RH, Fledman, RG, Pollen, D, Drachman, D, Growdon, J, Bruni, A, Foncin, J-F, Salmon, D, Frommelt, P, Amaducci, L, Sorbi, S, Piacentini, S, Stewart, GD, Hobbs, WJ, Conneally, PM, Gusella, JF: The genetic defect causing familial Alzheimer's disease maps on chromosome 21. Science 235 (4791):885–890, 1987.

21. Mortimer, JA, van Duijn, CM, Chandra, V, Fratiglioni, L, Graves, AB, Heyman, A, Jorm, AF, Kokmen, E, Kondo, K, Rocca, WA, Shalat, SL, Soinen, H and Hofman, A: Head trauma as a risk factor for Alzheimer's disease: A collaborative reanalysis of case-control studies. International Journal of Epidemiology 20(2, Suppl 2):S28–S35, 1991.

22. Rocca, WA, van Duijn, CM, Clayton, D, Chandra, V, Fratiglioni, L, Graves, AB, Heyman, A, Jorm, AF, Kokmen, E, Kondo, K, Mortimer, JA, Shalat, SL, Soinen, H and Hofman, A: Maternal age and Alzheimer's disease: A collaborative re-analysis of case-control studies. International Journal of Epidemiology 20(2, Suppl 2):S21–S27, 1991.

23. Amaducci, LA, Lippi, A and Fratiglioni, L: What risk factors are known? In Henderson, AS and Henderson, JH (eds): Etiology of Dementia of Alzheimer's Type. Wiley, New York, 1988.

24. Cohen, D and Eisdorfer, C: The loss of self: A family resource for the care of Alzheimer's disease and related disorders. WW Norton, New York, 1986.

25. Davis, R: My Journey into Alzheimer's Disease: Helpful Insights for Family and Friends. Tyndale House, Wheaton, IL, 1989.

26. Mace, N and Rabins, PV: The 36-Hour Day: A Family Guide to Caring for Persons with Alzheimer's Disease, Related Illnesses, and Memory Loss in Later Life. Warner Books, New York, 1981.

27. Reisberg, B, Ferris, SH, de Leon, MJ, Kluger, A, Franssen, E, Borenstein, J and Alba, RC: The stage of specific temporal course of Alzheimer's disease: Functional and behavioral concomitants based upon cross-sectional and longitudinal observation. Progress in Clinical and Biological Research 317:23–41, 1989.

28. Burns, A, Jacoby, R and Levy, R: Progression of cognitive impairment in Alzheimer's disease. Journal of the American Geriatrics Society 39:39–45, 1991.

29. Lowenstein, D As, Amigo, E, Duara, R, Guterman, A, Hurwitz, D, Berkowitz, N, Wilkie, F, Weinberg, G, Black, B, Gittelman, B and Eisdorfer, C: A new scale for the assessment of functional status in Alzheimer's disease and related disorders. Journal of Gerontology 44(4):114–121, 1989.

30. Liu, L, Gauthier, L and Gauthier, S: Spatial disorientation in persons with early senile dementia of the Alzheimer's type. American Journal of Occupational Therapy 45(1):67–74, January 1991.

31. Hall, RG: Care of the patient with Alzheimer's disease living at home. Nursing Clinics of North America 23(1):31–46, March, 1988.

32. Roberts, BL and Algase, DL: Victims of Alzheimer's disease and the environment. Nursing Clinics of North America 23(1):83–93, March 1988.

33. Beck, C and Heacock, P: Nursing interventions for patients with Alzheimer's disease. Nursing Clinics of North America 23(1):95–124, March 1988.

34. Mayers, K and Griffin, M: The play project: Use of stimulus objects with demented patients. Journal of Gerontological Nursing 16(1):32–37, 1990.

35. McMahon, R: The "24-hour reality orientation" type of approach to the confused elderly: A minimum standard for care. Journal of Ad-

vanced Nursing 13(6):693–700, November 1988.

36. Bleathman, C and Morton, I: Validation therapy with the demented elderly. Journal of Advanced Nursing 13(4):511–514, July 1988.

37. Domenico, RA: In Zandi, T and Ham, RJ (eds): New Directions in Understanding Dementia and Alzheimer's Disease. Plenum Press, New York, 1990.

38. Gerber, GJ, Prince, PN, Snider, HG, Atchison, K, Dubois, L, Kilgour, JA: Group activity and cognitive improvement among patients with Alzheimer's disease. Hospital and Community Psychiatry 42(8):843–845, 1991.

39. Friedman, R and Tappan, RM: The effect of planned walking on communication in Alzheimer's disease. Journal of the American Geriatrics Society 39:650–654, 1991.

40. Deutsch, LH and Rovner, BW: Agitation and other noncognitive abnormalities in Alzheimer's disease. Psychiatric Clinics of North America 14(2):341–351, June 1991.

41. Teri, L and Gallagher-Thompson, D: Cognitive-behavioral interventions for treatment of depression in Alzheimer's patients. Gerontologist 31(3):413–416, 1991.

42. Pharmaceutical Manufacturers Assoc and the Alzheimer's Association: Alzheimer's Medicines in Development. Author, Washington, DC, 1989.

43. Crystal, H: The diagnosis of Alzheimer's disease and other dementing disorders. In Aronson, MK (ed): Understanding Alzheimer's Disease: What It Is, How to Cope with It, Future Directions. Charles Scribner's Sons, New York, 1988, pp 290–318.

In the middle of the journey of our life I found myself in a dark wood, For I had lost the right path.

—DANTE ALIGHIERI, *The Divine Comedy*, Inferno, canto I, l.1, circa 1310–1320.

Chapter

Depression

KATHRYN PEREZ RILEY

OBJECTIVES

By the end of this chapter, readers will be able to:

1 Compare and contrast the symptoms and manifestations of depression in older adults, including the traditional, masked, and pseudodementia forms of depressive disorders.

2 Discuss assessment and evaluation of depressive and suicidal symptoms in older adults.

3 Discuss the relationship between depression and functional abilities in older adults.

4 Identify special factors in depression in special populations, including the physically ill, demented, care givers, and institutionalized older adults.

5 Describe the major methods of treating depression through prevention, psychotherapy, medications, and *electroconvulsive therapy* (ECT).

Depression in older adults is often seen as a normal part of aging or as a reaction to the stressors and losses that most people associate with growing old. In fact, as this chapter will show, most elderly people do not ever experience a clinically significant depression and, when they do, it is rarely a result of the normative life events encountered during aging. For those older adults who do become depressed, early diagnosis and treatment is essential. Depressive disorders are as treatable in the old as in the young, but when left undetected or untreated, they can lead to functional impairments and excess disabilities, lost jobs and relationships, institutionalization, and death.[1]

This chapter includes an overview of the prevalence, symptomatology, and detection of depressive syndromes in older adults, a discussion of the relationship between depression and social and daily function, and a review of major treatment options for depressed older adults.

OVERVIEW OF DEPRESSIVE DISORDERS IN OLDER ADULTS

The term *depressive disorders* refers to the clinical symptoms listed in most diagnostic manuals as "major depressive episode and dysthymic disorder." In addition, short-term, subclinical depressive syndromes are included here, as they are often seen in older adults and are included in many research studies.[2,3]

Depression is the most common psychiatric syndrome in older adults, both in the community and in institutions.[4] Estimates of prevalence vary.[2] However, a generally accepted figure is a rate of 15 to 20 percent for community-dwelling older adults and as many as 25 percent of institutionalized individuals over 65. These figures are based on a broad definition of depression that includes the true depressive disorders of major depression and dysthmic disorder along with less severe depressive symptom patterns. Borson and colleagues[3] estimated that 10 percent of adults over the age of 65 have a clinically significant depressive illness that would meet strict diagnostic criteria and require active treatment, although others have put this figure at about 4 percent.

There are three major ways in which depression may present itself in older adults, including two that involve patterns of symptoms and complaints that differ from the type of depressive illness that has been described in most diagnostic manuals. They are traditional, masked, and pseudodementia-cognitive deficits of depression.

Traditional Depression

Although a great deal of attention has been paid to the two typical forms of depression in older adults,[1,6] older individuals experience the traditional symptoms of depression as described in the *Diagnostic and Statistical Manual of Mental Disorders* (DSM III-R).[7] These include the following symptoms:

- Depressed or sad mood
- Decreased interest in activities
- Lack of pleasure or enjoyment
- Feelings of guilt or worthlessness
- Apathy or lack of motivation
- Change (increase or decrease) in sleep, appetite, weight, energy, sexual desire
- Decline in attention, concentration, memory
- Thoughts of death or suicide

An individual who meets all of the required criteria and has experienced symptoms for at least 2 weeks would receive the diagnosis of major depressive disorder. In many studies, this diagnosis is often referred to as a "clinically significant depressive disorder."[2] DSM-III-R also describes several subtypes of major depression, of which the most relevant to older adults is the melancholic type. This type emphasizes vegetative or somatic symptoms, including weight loss, psychomotor retardation or agitation, lack of pleasure, and good response to a somatic treatment for at least one previous depressive episode.[7]

Dysthymic disorder is a less severe form of depression which has lasted for at least 2 years. Little has been published on the epidemiology of dysthymic conditions in older adults. Related to, but less severe than dysthymic disorders, is a recurrent or transient pattern of depressive symptoms that older adults (like younger persons) may experience in response to stress, life events, loss[4] or physical illness.[8]

Bipolar disorder, characterized by at least one manic episode and preceding or following depressive episodes, tends to begin earlier in life than simple depressive disorders, although late-life onset has been reported.[4] There is increasing evidence that psychiatric patients who are elderly may have been misdiagnosed as schizophrenic when in fact they suffered from a bipolar disorder. Patients who do not respond to antidepressants or antipsychotic medications may have bipolar illness and will respond to lithium, a drug used primarily for the treatment of this disorder.

Variations in Depressive Symptoms

In older adults who experience depression in ways similar to younger adults, traditional procedures are appropriate for diagnosis.[9] In addition to the greater likelihood that the melancholic type of depression will be seen in older adults, other aspects of traditional depression may be more prominent in these individuals. For example, themes of loss and hopelessness related to perceived and real losses are commonly seen in older people. While hopelessness and perceived losses are also present among the depressive symptoms of young people, these symptoms may be more reality based in an older adult who in fact has little chance of replacing or restoring that which she has valued and lost such as a spouse of 50 years or the occupational achievements of years past.[10] Apathy, withdrawal, self-depreciating behavior, and psychomotor retardation also may be prominent features of depression in older adults.[4]

It is often difficult to determine when an older adult is suffering from a depressive disorder that should be treated, as opposed to experiencing an understandable reaction to poor health, poverty and deprivation, or other cumulative losses that can come with advancing age. There are dangers in erring in either direction: If one determines that a merely distressed or unhappy person is clinically depressed, unnecessary interventions may be instituted with accompanying side effects and negative outcomes. Well-designed assessment procedures used by trained individuals can prevent the overdiagnosis and inappropriate treatment of depression in older adults.[1] Thompson, Futterman, and Gallagher[5] reviewed the available depression scales and have offered guidelines for the appropriate use of several of the better measures with older individuals. When these measures are used in conjunction with the criteria outlined in DSM III-R, mildly unhappy or temporarily distressed older adults will not meet all of the criteria for a depressive disorder.

SUICIDE

If the depressive illness of an older adult is dismissed as a "normal" reaction to growing old, there is a risk of increased disability, desperation, and death through passive or active suicide. Untreated depression can lead to a number of negative consequences, the most serious of which is, of course, an attempted or completed suicide. The risk of suicide in older adults is estimated as being nearly three times greater than the risk in younger persons.[4] This is especially true for older males for whom the incidence of suicide peaks at the 80 to 85 age bracket. A slight decline in suicide rates is seen in women after the age of 65, although the risk remains significant. Older adults are more likely to be serious about their suicide attempts with the ratio of attempts to completed suicides as high as 2 to 1.[11] Older adults are also at risk for passive suicide. Passive suicide behavior include refusing necessary medical treatments and surgeries, failing to take medications, failing to follow prescribed diet regimens, and refusing to eat. There are a number of clues and risk factors that may identify an individual as being at relatively high risk for suicide. These include:

- A presence of depression
- Feeling of hopelessness
- Single or widowed status
- Solitary living arrangements
- Recent major loss of a loved one
- Previous psychiatric illness or alcohol or drug abuse
- Previous suicide attempts or threats
- Diagnosis of an organic mental disorder
- Diagnosis of terminal illness in self or spouse
- Chronic mental illness

A combination of these factors may lead the older adult to suicide, and all threats must be taken very seriously. Indirect references such as talk of wishing one were dead or feelings of being tired of living should also be explored as potential indicators of suicidal intent. Not all individuals who commit suicide are recognizably depressed. Their suicide attempts or actions may be a deliberate and planned response to the diagnosis of a terminal illness or to the death of a spouse. Professionals need to be alert to all of the direct and oblique warning signs and signals of suicide intent in older adults in order to provide appropriate and effective interventions.

Masked Depression

While it has been demonstrated that many depressed elderly do exhibit traditional symptoms and complaints, it also has been repeatedly observed that older individuals may present only with symptoms of physical illness, without the expected emotional, cognitive, and behavioral manifestations of depression. This type of depressive illness has been called *masked, somatic,* or *hidden depression.*[4,12] In this form of depression, the older adult is likely to complain about changes in sleep, appetite, weight, energy levels, and sexual functioning, that is, vegetative signs of depression of the melancholic subtype.[7] However, when the elderly person presents these symptoms, he or she is not likely to discuss feeling sad, blue, unhappy, or hopeless.[6] Instead, additional complaints of physical dysfunction will be listed including diffuse or localized pain, headaches, gastrointestinal upset, constipation, breathing problems, and other vague discomforts.[2,11]

This form of masked or somatic depression is most likely to be seen in individuals who have their first depressive episode after the age of 65. If detected, these late-onset depressions respond well to treatment. However, older adults are likely to seek help from a family physician rather than a mental health professional even when they are experiencing emotional difficulties. This makes diagnosis of a masked or hidden depression more difficult since the individual is presenting a medical professional with symptoms of physical illness, without any indication of psychological distress.

As a primary care physicians receive more information about mental health needs of older adults and geriatrics emerges as a medical specialty, misdiagnosis becomes less likely. Emergence of multidisciplinary geriatric assessment centers has also resulted in better evaluation and treatment of psychiatric disorders in older adults. Yet as Borson and associates[3] and others[13] have noted, the number of depressed older individuals who actually receive treatment may be as low as 1 in 10. This very low proportion of treated depression in late life points to the need for further education of professionals and laypersons alike.

In order to uncover hidden depression, the most vague and seemingly unrelated set of physical complaints should be carefully evaluated.[5,14] When medical illness has been ruled out or accounted for and it seems likely that an affective disorder underlies the somatic complaints, efforts should be made to examine emotional factors that may underlie the depression. Precipitating events such as the death or illness of a relative or close friend, retirement, change in health, living arrangements, or income level, or interpersonal difficulties should be explored.[4] Any of these, alone or in combination, may be linked to a depressive syndrome in older adults.[2,3] A skillful interview may encourage the older adult to discuss some of his or her feelings, and the disturbance in mood may well become apparent. However, some older adults do not present with complaints of sad or depressed mood because they do not experience this sadness or at least are unable to express their feelings in this way.[6] Work in the field of cognitive-behavioral theory and treatment of depression has shown that the elderly person who does not readily acknowledge the emotional components of depression may be able to recognize and discuss some of the cognitive disturbances seen in the depressive disorders.[9,15]

Pseudodementia

The second atypical form of depression in older adults is *pseudodemen-*

tia.[16] This term was developed in recognition of the fact that a significant proportion of depressed older adults complain not of sadness or other emotional disturbances, nor of physical ailments but rather of deficits in cognition and memory.[17,18] These individuals, like those with masked depression, may go to a health professional to seek help for a condition that they believe is medical rather than psychological. This can lead to an inaccurate diagnosis of a dementing illness such as Alzheimer's disease, resulting in inappropriate and ineffective interventions. Alternatively, the complaints of poor concentration, memory, and other cognitive abilities may be dismissed as a normal part of the aging process, again leaving the depressive illness undetected and untreated.[19] See Table 16–1 for the differences between depression and organic dementia.

Cognitive Deficits of Depression

Data on the differential diagnosis of depression from dementia.[17,18] show that while attention, motivation, and initial learning curves all may be impaired in depressed older adults, formal testing reveals the deficits to be limited in duration, severity, and variety when compared to the cognitive deficits seen in true dementia. The additional deficits in language, memory, perception, and problem solving seen in dementia[6] are not typically seen in depression. Furthermore, it is fairly clear that while dementia has a slow and insidious onset, the depressed person's cognitive impairments often have a sudden or easily identifiable onset. O'Boyle, Amadeo, and Self[19] have documented that while there is a strong relationship between the cognitive complaints and depression scale score of depressed elderly patients, no such relationship exists between the patients' cognitive complaints and scores on a mental status examination. A final distinction between pseudo and real dementia is the fact that while some cognitive changes do occur with depression,[6] the older individual's complaints and distress concerning these changes far outweigh the actual dysfunction seen in daily life functioning and on neuropsychological testing. In contrast, the truly demented individual is likely to minimize or be unaware of his or her cognitive deficits in spite of actual dysfunction. See Table 16–2 for the types and subtypes of depressive disorders.

The preceding discussion provided a very brief summary of a large body of literature. As has been shown, depression may be manifested in a variety of traditional atypical forms in older adults, making accurate diagnosis and treatment problematic. Additional difficulties are created by the reluctance of older adults to seek help from mental health professionals and by the older adults' unfamiliarity with or inability to recognize signs and symptoms of emotional distress. Finally, the shortage of mental health professionals who specialize in geriatrics compounds the problem of inadequate treatment of depressive disorders in older adults, although this situation is improving.

TABLE 16–1 **Differences between Depression and Organic Dementia**

Dementia	Depression
Generally a gradual onset of cognitive impairments, over a period of years.	Generally has a sudden onset that coincides with onset of depressive symptoms.
Limited awareness or complaints of memory impairment.	High level of complaints of memory impairment.
Definite and global impairments eventually seen in neuropsychological testing.	Limited or no impairment seen in testing results.
Cognitive impairments become progressively worse with time.	Complaints of cognitive impairment do not become severe and will lift when depression is treated.

TABLE 16–2	**Types and Subtypes of Depressive Disorders**

I. Major depressive disorder
  A. Traditional (including melancholic)
  B. Masked
  C. Pseudodementia and cognitive deficits of depression

II. Dysthymic disorder

III. Bipolar illness (includes manic and depressive episodes)

Depression and Functional Status: An Interactive Relationship

Depressive syndromes present a significant threat to the well-being and life satisfaction of a substantial number of older adults. Impaired social, occupational, and/or interpersonal functioning are integral components of most clinically significant depressive disorders.[7] This dysfunction in daily activities can be severe enough to result in total withdrawal, isolation, and inability to care for even the most basic of personal needs. The following sections of this chapter will examine this critical link between depression and daily functioning in several subgroups of older adults.

Research on functional status in depressed elderly has focused on ADL, social and interpersonal activities, and recreational or leisure activities.[2,8] The literature leads to two conclusions: First, there is a negative relationship between depressive symptoms and activities of almost any kind.[2,20] Second, it is not clear whether depression leads to impaired function or whether deficits in functional abilities lead to depression.

Decreases in daily activities are related to symptoms of depressed mood in older adults.[21] This may be the result of lack of access to pleasurable or instrumental activities, lack of ability to engage in these activities due to physical or mental deficits, or lack of motivation. A clearer understanding of the reasons for severe depression in older adults may result from an examination of depression in physically ill, demented, institutionalized, and other special groups of older adults.

PHYSICAL ILLNESS AND DEPRESSION

Fry[4] has noted that over 85 percent of depressed older adults have significant health problems. The kinds of activities that may be affected by depression and illness are extremely varied but can be grouped into ADL, IADL, vocational activities, and social and recreational activities. Social and recreational activities generally include hobbies, conversing with friends, participating in social gatherings or outings, gardening, reading, as well as other interests the older adult might enjoy.[22]

Berkman and her colleagues[2] examined in some detail the relationship between physical health, depressive symptoms, and functioning in the elderly. They found a strong, though not causal, relationship between functional disability and symptoms of depression, noting that it was the disability rather than the illness that was associated with higher rates of depression. Some researchers have suggested that a causal pattern may involve a medical condition leading to a depressive reaction that in turn leads to functional disability.[15] The affective illness may prevent the patients from seeking or following through on rehabilitation and other services, resulting in additional functional disability. Doan and Wadden[23] found significant levels of depression in a sample of chronic pain patients suffering from headaches, arthritis, and back pain. These authors found that symptoms of depression were related either to loss of ability or desire to participate in social and recreational abilities. Doan and Wadden[23] further reported that depression was a better predictor of functional limitations in daily activities than was the amount of perceived pain. Thus medical illness, pain, and functional disabilities are all linked to depression in what seems to be a somewhat circular and amplifying relationship. While it may be that physical illness first leads to some degree of dysfunction in the ability to carry out ADL or to participate in leisure and social activities, these limitations can then cause a depressive reaction that in turn may exacerbate the illness (or perceived impact of the illness). The depression then may result in excess disability through decreased motivation to perform or engage in activity (see Fig. 16–1).

DEPRESSION AND DEMENTIA

Depressive pseudodementia, the presence of apparent organic deficits that are actually due to depression, has been discussed as one way in which depressive symptomatology may be unique for older adults. An additional group for whom depression and illness may coincide is older adults who are demented. While the most common form of senile dementia is Alzheimer's disease, multi-infarct dementia, dementia in Parkinson's disease, and other less common forms of dementing illness all affect older adults and may lead to depressive symptoms.

While depression can cause symptoms and complaints of cognitive impairment that are not related to a true organic illness, a substantial percentage of dementia patients experience symptoms of depression.[6,24] By its very nature, dementia leads to dysfunction in daily activities, first affecting more complex and demanding activities such as occupational functioning and some

forms of leisure activities (e.g., playing bridge, golfing) and then having an impact on the more basic functions involved in IADL and ADL. Given the effects of depression on these same activities, it is likely that people who become depressed as a result of their awareness of declines in cognitive abilities will also suffer from increased functional disability.

Pearson and her colleagues[25] evaluated this potential for "double disability" in a small sample of patients with *dementia of the Alzheimer's type* (DAT). These investigators noted that IADL are most susceptible to the effects of depression since shopping, housework, and cooking all require levels of motivation and initiative that may be beyond the capability of the depressed older adult. When they compared a group of depressed DAT patients to a nondepressed dementia group, Pearson and associates[25] did in fact find that the depressed patients were more functionally impaired than the group who suffered only from dementia. While it is not clear if the depressive condition was a cause or result of decreased functional capacity, it is possible that active treatment of depression in dementia patients will prevent excess disability from occurring. Given the lack of medical interventions for Alzheimer's disease and other forms of dementia, the opportu-

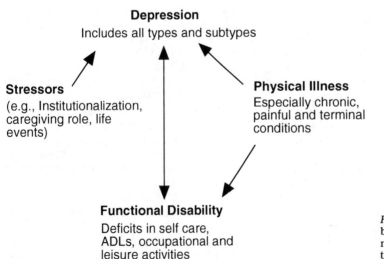

Figure 16–1 Relationships between stressors, physical illness, depression and functional disability.

nity to treat the accompanying depression may offer valuable hope and improved functioning for the dementia patient. Riley[10,26] has discussed a variety of interventions designed for dementia patients and their care givers that can help ameliorate the depressive reactions that are likely to occur in the early stages of dementing illnesses.

CARE-GIVER BURDEN, STRESS, AND DEPRESSION

Thus far, this chapter has focused on identifying and treating depression in medically ill and demented patients in order to prevent unnecessary disability and other negative outcomes. The caregiving literature also makes it very clear that this attention to mental health issues should be extended to the spouse or other individual who plays the primary care-giving role for the identified patient. The care giver has been identified as the "second victim," with depression ranking as one of the most common negative outcomes of the caregiving process.[27] In addition, much has been written in recent years about the elderly care giver's burden, with accompanying increases in stress, physical illness, and psychological distress. (The interested reader is referred to Stone, Cafferata, and Sange[28] and Zarit, Todd, and Zarit[29] for reviews on care giving.)

Care givers of demented and frail older adults are likely to be older people whose physical strength and stamina may be overburdened by the care-giving role. If this physical burden is complicated by the disabling effects of depression, then the ability to carry out daily activities and engage in social interactions will be negatively affected, and the ability to perform the care-giving role will be diminished. Interventions designed for care givers alone or in conjunction with the chronically ill older adult[26,30] can reduce the sense of perceived burden and depressive symptoms of care givers, which in turn can increase their ability to function in all of their roles.

DEPRESSION IN THE INSTITUTIONALIZED OLDER ADULT

A final group of older adults to be considered in this discussion of depression in special populations is those who are institutionalized. It has been estimated that at least one-fourth of nursing home residents over the age of 65 suffer from a depressive disorder.[4] While many people may be depressed before they enter the nursing home, the social and emotional losses brought about as a result of institutionalization are also likely to lead to depressive reactions. Furthermore, nursing home environments appear to reinforce passive, apathetic, and dependent behaviors,[31] aggravating the motivational and affective problems that characterize the depressive disorders. Learned helplessness stemming from a sense of lack of control or inadequate reinforcement for independent behaviors can add to the severity of depressive reactions in the institutionalized older adult.[32]

This high proportion of older nursing home residents who either enter the institution with a depressive disorder or who become depressed after moving to the home should be of great concern to health care professionals. Unfortunately, the lack of mental health services is even worse in institutional settings than it is in the community.[33,34] Although psychotropic medications are provided frequently to nursing home residents, the fact that only a small proportion of facilities have consulting psychiatrists or psychologists means that intervention often does not occur.

Taken in combination with the nursing home environment's emphasis on compliance and routine, the depressed elderly resident is at great risk for slipping into a withdrawn, apathetic, and even vegetative state. The lack of meaningful interpersonal relationships and daily activities exacerbates depression in elderly nursing home residents.[33] In addition to medical and psychotherapeutic interventions, treatment of depression in these residents may involve increasing their social interactions and fostering more independent behaviors to the extent possible. Although the issues of depression and dysfunction in the institutional environment are complex and defy simple solutions (see Carstensen and Fremouw[33] and Fry[32] for reviews and discussions), the basic principles of comprehensive assessment of emotional disorders followed by individualized treatment plans can prevent and diminish depressive disorders in institutionalized older adults.

TREATMENT OF DEPRESSION

It has been repeatedly noted that depression in older adults is a treatable condition, one that should not be ignored or dismissed as a normal part of aging or as a lost cause. Fist, preventive and early intervention efforts are crucial. Second, two major forms of treatment for depression — psychotherapy and antidepressant medications — are highly successful methods of intervention.[10] In addition, although less frequently used, *electroconvulsive therapy* (ECT) has been shown to be a safe and effective treatment in severely depressed older adults.[36]

Prevention and Early Intervention

In general, active, involved older adults have greater life satisfaction, higher morale, and lower incidence of depression than those who are isolated, withdrawn, and inactive (see Fry[4] for expanded discussion). While some older adults are content with solitary or inactive lifestyles, increasing the amount of meaningful activity and involvement seems to reduce depressive symptoms in many others. Ensuring that the older adult has access to and is able to participate in vocational, volunteer, or leisure activities may either prevent a depressive reaction or reduce its severity and duration. The key is for the professional, whether it be a psychologist, social worker, occupational therapist, activity therapist, or other specialist, to be certain that the activities suggested to the elderly person are interesting and meaningful to that person. Simply pushing the older person into activities without exploring their interests is not likely to yield positive results.

Next to prevention, early detection of depression in older adults is the most important function of professionals in geriatric practice. Awareness of the "triggers" of depression, risk factors, and common symptoms and manifestations of depression should help mental health and allied professionals recognize the problem in the earliest stages, leading to formal assessment, diagnosis, and development of an intervention plan.

The preceding section on physically ill older adults has important implications for health care professionals. First, both affective and medical illnesses must be evaluated in older adults who complain of one or the other of the conditions. When depressive symptoms are discovered, active intervention should be instituted in order to prevent the downward spiral of increasing functional disability, poor health, and worsening depression.[14] In addition, efforts need to be made to improve functional abilities directly, for as Umlauf and Frank[8] have found, improved functional status can lead to improvements in mood. A comprehensive approach to assessment and intervention in geriatric patients that emphasizes both emotional and physical symptoms should maximize the positive outcomes desired by elderly clients and their health care professionals.

Psychotherapy

Psychodynamic[10,37] and behavioral[38] approaches have been successful in ameliorating depression in later life; however, cognitive-behavioral therapies have received the most attention in the gerontological literature.[39] Supportive approaches emphasizing reassurance, encouragement, and direct social service interventions are also commonly used with older adults.[4] Earlier literature focused on group therapy (see Cooper[40]); recent work emphasizes individual therapy. While specific therapeutic approaches differ in style and content, some commonalities emerge. Themes of loss, illness, death, and uncontrollable change must be dealt with, regardless of theoretical orientation. An emphasis on positive coping skills and adjusting to or finding substitutes for losses is helpful to the older individual.[26,41] Short-term treatment (6 months or less) of late-life depression has been most commonly described although some long-term work also has been done.[36] Couples and family therapy are important in the treatment of the depressive disorders in older adults, and these modalities may be especially helpful when dealing with reactions to chronic medical illnesses such as cancer, Parkinson's disease, or the dementia.[26]

Consideration of psychotherapeutic interventions for older adults must also include a note on support groups. While these groups are not designed to provide formal therapy and are not generally led by professional therapists, they do provide a valuable service to many older adults who may be experiencing mild or chronic depressive reactions to loss, illness, or ongoing stress.[37] There is a large network of specialty support groups in the United States including groups for Alzheimer's disease and other care givers, cancer and other chronic illness support groups, as well as groups for the recently bereaved. These groups are often a valuable adjunct or follow-up to individual psychotherapy with the depressed elderly.

Medications and Electroconvulsive Therapy

Antidepressant medications can be safely and effectively used with older individuals if the prescribing physician is aware of the special cautions and considerations related to the older adult's reactions. There are a number of physiological changes accompanying the aging process that affect the choice and dosage of antidepressant medications. In particular, the older adult often will need only one-third to one-half the usual amount of medication in order to reach the desired therapeutic level.[37] A second issue is the fact that older adults as a group have twice the incidence of side effects and negative drug interactions as do younger people, making the prescription of psychotropic medications a job best handled by a psychiatrist who is familiar with geriatrics. See Table 16–3 for a list of common tricyclic antidepressants.

Of the major classes of antidepressant medications, the tricyclics are the most widely used, as they tend to involve few dietary restrictions and less severe side effects.[43] However, the tricyclic antidepressants are not without problems, particularly for those people who have heart conditions or who have an organic mental disorder such as Alzheimer's disease. Careful monitoring is essential. Tricyclics can increase the confusion and cognitive impairment seen in dementia patients and can also cause sleeplessness, agitation, and confused thoughts.[37] Side effects vary widely among the different medications, making careful selection vital. See Table 16–4 for a list of frequent side effects of antidepressant medications in the elderly. A final consideration of great concern when antidepressant medications are used with older people (especially women) is the fact that these drugs can cause orthostatic hypotension, leading to falls.

Used with care, antidepressants can result in dramatic recovery from the severe depressions experienced by many older adults.[4] Psychotropic medications

TABLE 16–3 **Common Tricyclic Antidepressants**	
Generic Name	**Trade Name**
Amitriptyline	Elavil, Endep
Imipramine	Tofranil, Presamine
Doxepin	Sinequan, Adapin
Nortriptyline	Pamelor, Aventyl
Despiramine	Norpramin, Pertofrane

TABLE 16–4 **Frequent Side Effects of Antidepressant Medications in the Elderly**

Confusion and disorientation

Dry mouth

Urinary retention and/or constipation

Blurred vision

Sleep disturbances and nightmares

Agitation

Cardiovascular changes including increased blood pressure or orthostatic hypotension; change in heart rate

---

may be especially helpful in recurrent depression or in suicidal and profoundly withdrawn patients. The use of both medications and psychotherapy can be a very potent treatment program for many depressed older adults who may not respond to only one of the treatment modalities. For those individuals who do not improve after medications and therapy have been tried, ECT may be the treatment of choice. There is no reason to avoid the use of this procedure in older adults, unless there are serious medical illnesses or other major contraindications.[44] The changes in the ways in which ECT is administered have made it a reasonably safe procedure. The major risk to the healthy elderly patient is probably from the anesthesia used during the treatment. Although ECT is generally considered a last-resort option, there may be some situations in which it is the first treatment of choice. These include depressed individuals who are imminently suicidal, for whom the 3- to 6-week waiting period involved in seeing the effects of antidepressant medications involves too great a risk. ECT may be particularly helpful in depressive disorders with psychotic or delusional features. Finally, when ECT has been successful in treating an elderly person's earlier episode of major depression, it may be expedient to use this treatment again.

SUMMARY AND FUTURE DIRECTIONS

This chapter has presented a brief overview of the symptomatology, assessment, daily life effects, and treatment of depressive disorders in older adults. The interactions between physical illness, dementia, life events, and emotional well-being have been discussed, and it should be clear that it is not always possible to determine the first link in the causal chain of depression and dysfunction in social, occupational, and daily activities. Work in the area of late-life depression has moved from an initial focus on the detection and assessment of the various forms and manifestations of this cluster of disorders to investigation of the most effective methods of treating depressed older adults. The next phase should involve efforts aimed at preventing depression in older adults to the extent that this is possible. The further development of second, late-life careers, voluntary work, meaningful social interactions, and community programs can all help prevent some reactive depressions. Support groups and wider availability of mental health services designed for the isolated, bereaved, ill, or disabled older adult should also result in lowered incidence or severity of late-life depression. Given the negative consequences of the depressive disorders on the independent function of the growing population of aged people, this emphasis on prevention could reduce the ultimate cost to society while enhancing the quality of life for older adults and those who care for them.

REVIEW QUESTIONS

1. *Discuss the major symptoms of depressive disorders, and describe how some of these symptoms are emphasized in the masked and pseudodementia forms of depression in older adults.*

2. *Describe some of the factors that*

may trigger a depressive or suicidal condition in the older adult, commenting on how a professional might assess these conditions in an elderly patient.

3. Explain what is meant by the "circular" relationship between depression and functional disability in older adults.

4. Describe and compare the nature of depression and functional impairment in two of the following special populations: physically ill, demented, care givers, or institutionalized elderly.

5. How might a professional work to prevent depression in older patients?

6. Discuss two different methods of treating an older adult who is depressed. Include the possible advantages and disadvantages of each method.

REFERENCES

1. Riley, KP: Interdisciplinary Geriatric Assessment: A Psychological Perspective. Western Reserve Geriatric Education Center, Cleveland, OH, 1987.
2. Berkman, LF, Berkman, CS, Kasl, S, Freeman, DH, Leo, L, Ostfield, AM, Cornono-Huntley, J and Brody, JA: Depressive symptoms in relation to physical health and functioning in the elderly. American Journal of Epidemiology 124:372–388, 1986.
3. Borson, S, Barnes, R, Kukull, W, Okimoto, J, Veith, R, Unui, T, Carter, W and Raskind, N: Symptomatic depression in elderly medical outpatients. I. Prevalence, demography and health service utilization. Journal of the American Geriatric Society 34:341–347, 1986.
4. Fry, PS: Depression, stress and adaptations in the elderly. Aspen Publishers, Rockville, MD, 1986.
5. Thompson, LW, Futterman, A and Gallagher, D. Assessment of later life depression. Psychopharm. Bull 24:577–586, 1988.
6. Thompson, LW, Gong, V, Haskins, E and Gallagher, D: Assessment of depression and dementia during the late years. Annual Review of Gerontology and Geriatrics, Vol 7. Springer, New York, 1987, pp 295–324.
7. American Psychiatric Association. Diagnostic and Statistical Manual of Mental Disorders, ed

3, rev (DSM III-R). The Association, Washington, DC, 1987. [The DSM IV will be available in Spring, 1994.—Ed.]
8. Umlauf, RL and Frank, RG: Cluster analysis, depression and ADL status. Rehabilitation Psychology 32:39–44, 1987.
9. Gallagher, D and Thompson, L: Treatment of major depressive disorders in older adult outpatients with brief psychotherapies. Psychother: Theory, Res & Pract 19:482–490, 1982.
10. Riley, KP and Carr, M: Group psychotherapy with older adults: The value of an expressive approach. Psychotherapy: Theory, Research and Practice 26:366–371, 1989.
11. Whanger, A and Myers, A: Mental health assessment and therapeutic intervention with older adults. Aspen Publications, Rockville, MD, 1984.
12. Dush, DM and Hutzell, RR: A brief MMPI depression screening scale for the elderly. Clin Gerontol 6:175–185, 1986.
13. Gaylord, S and Zung, W: Affective disorders among the aging. In Carstensen, L and Edelstein, B (eds): Handbook of Clinical Gerontology. Pergamon Press, New York, 1987, pp 76–95.
14. Towle, D, Lincoln, NB and Mayfield, L: Service provision and functional independence in depressed stroke patients and the effect of social work intervention on these. Journal of Neurology, Neurosurgery, and Psychiatry 52:519–522, 1989.
15. Brink, TL (ed): Clinical gerontology: A guide to assessment and intervention. The Haworth Press, New York, 1986.
16. Wells, CE: Pseudodementia. American Journal of Psychiatry 136:895–900, 1979.
17. Chandler, JD and Gerndt, J: Memory complaints and memory deficits in young and older psychiatric inpatients. Journal of Geriatric Psychiatry and Neurology 1:84–88, 1988.
18. Reynolds, CF, Hoch, CC, Kupfer, DJ, Buysse, PJ, Houck, PR, Stack, JA and Campbell, DW: Bedside differentiation of depressive pseudodementia from dementia. American Journal of Psychiatry 145:1099–1103, 1988.
19. O'Boyle, M, Amadeo, M and Self, D: Cognitive complaints in elderly depressed and pseudodemented patients. Psychology and Aging 5:467–468, 1990.
20. Pederson, ID: Treatment of depression in institutionalized persons. Phys & Occup Ther in Geriat 5:77–89, 1987.
21. Shoskes, J and Glenwick, DS: The relationship of the Depression Adjective Check List to positive affect and activity level in older adults. Journal of Personality Assessment 51:565–571, 1987.
22. Lomranz, J, Bergman, S, Eyal, N and Shmotkin, D: Indoor and outdoor activities of aged women and men as related to depression and well-being. International Journal of Aging and Human Development 26:303–324, 1988.
23. Doan, BD and Wadden, NP: Relationship be-

tween depressive symptoms and description of chronic pain. Pain 36:75–84, 1989.

24. Lazarus, LW, Newton, N, Cohler, B and Lesser, J: Frequency and presentation of depressive symptoms in patients with primary degenerative dementia. Am J Psychiat 144:41–45, 1987.

25. Pearson, JR, Teri, L, Reifler, BV and Raskind, MA: Functional status and cognitive impairment in Alzheimer's patients with and without depression. Journal of the American Geriatrics Society 37:1117–1121, 1989.

26. Riley, KP: Psychological interventions with Alzheimer's disease. In Gilmore, GC, Whitehouse, PJ and Wykle, M (eds): Memory Impairment and Aging: Theory, Testing and Treatment. Springer, New York, 1989.

27. Pruchno, R and Resch, NL: Husbands and wives as caregivers: Antecedents of depression and burden. Gerontologist 29:159–165, 1989.

28. Stone, R, Cafferata, G and Sangl, S: Caregivers of the frail elderly: A national profile. Gerontologist 27:616–626, 1987.

29. Zarit, S, Todd, P and Zarit, J: Subjective burden of husbands and wives as caregivers. Gerontologist 26:260–266, 1986.

30. Zarit, S, Reeves, K and Bach-Paterson, J: Relatives of impaired elderly: Correlates of feelings and burden. Gerontologist 20:649–654, 1980.

31. Kahana, E, Kahana, B and Riley, KP: Contributions of qualitative research issues to studies of institutional settings for the aged. In Rowels, GD and Reinharts, G (eds): Qualitative Gerontology. Springer, New York, 1988.

32. Fry, PS: Psychology of Helplessness and Control. North Holland, New York, 1989.

33. Goddard, P and Carstensen, LL: Behavioural treatment of chronic depression in an elderly nursing home resident. Clin Gerontol 4:13–20, 1986.

34. Kahana, E, Kahana, B and Riley, KP: Learned helplessness and dependency in the institutionalized aged. In Fry, PS (ed): Psychology of Helplessness and Control. North Holland, New York, 1989.

35. Carstensen, LL and Fremouw, WJ: The influence of anxiety and mental status on social isolation among the elderly in nursing homes. Behav Resident Treat 3:63–80, 1988.

36. Eisdorfer, C and Fann, W (eds): Treatment of Psychopathology in the Aging. Springer, New York, 1982.

37. Myers, W: Dynamic Therapy of the Older Patient. Jason Aronson, New York, 1984.

38. Vaccaro, F: Application of social skills training in a group of institutionalized aggressive elderly adults. Psychology and Aging 5:369–378, 1990.

39. Yost, EB, Beutler, LE, Corbishley, MA and Allender, JR: Group Cognitive Therapy. Pergamon Press, New York, 1986.

40. Cooper, D: Group psychotherapy with the elderly: Dealing with loss and death. Amer J Psychother 37:203–214, 1984.

41. Steuer, J, Mintz, J, Hammer, C, Hill, M, Jarvik, L, McCarley, T, Motoike, P and Rosen, R: Cognitive-behavioral and psychodynamic group psychotherapy in treatment of geriatric depression. Journal of Consulting and Clinial Psychology 52:180–189, 1984.

42. Riley, K and Yavornitzky, P: Groups for Alzheimer's caregivers: Support or psychotherapy? Paper presented at the 42nd Annual Scientific Meeting, Gerontological Society of America, Minneapolis, MN, 1989.

43. Friedel, R: The diagnosis and management of depression in the elderly patient. In Eisdorfer, C and W Fann, W (eds): Treatment of Psychopathology in the Aging. Springer, New York, 1982, pp 210–218.

44. Carstensen, LL and Edelstein, BA (eds): Handbook of Clinical Gerontology. Pergamon Press, New York, 1987.

INTERVENTION STRATEGIES

The goal of long-term care is for people to be receiving the right services, at the right time, in the most appropriate place based on their own individual strengths and needs.

—N. ENGLISH, *Long Term Care in The Community*, G. Sorensen (Ed.), *Older Persons and Service Providers*. Human Sciences Press, New York, 1981.

Chapter

Prevention of Performance Deficits

DOROTHY FARRAR EDWARDS

OBJECTIVES

By the end of this chapter, readers will be able to:

1 Define prevention, health promotion, and wellness.

2 Distinguish among primary, secondary, and tertiary prevention.

3 Distinguish between the disability and disease models.

4 Compare three theoretical models of health promotion.

5 Discuss the importance of health promotion for older adults.

6 Describe the factors that must be considered in designing health promotion programs for individuals from minority groups.

As the demographics of aging have shifted, so have the patterns of illness and disease. In the 1800s and early 1900s the health care system focused almost exclusively on the control of infectious disease. In 1900 the leading causes of death and disability were diseases such as smallpox, diphtheria, cholera, tuberculosis, typhoid fever, and measles. Prevention efforts were directed toward control of infectious disease through public health activities such as sanitation, clean water, regulation of food, and the development of immunizations.[1]

Despite a recent resurgence of infectious diseases such as tuberculosis, the problems that were prevalent in the early part of the century have disappeared from the list of leading causes of death. The major causes of morbidity and mortality in the 1980s were heart disease, cancer, stroke, diabetes, and pulmonary disease. Only one infectious disease, influenza-pneumonia, remains as a leading cause of mortality (see Table 17–1).

As the population ages, the expenditures associated with health care have risen. Approximately 30 percent of all national health care expenditures are now spent on older adults, and costs are rising rapidly. People aged 65 and older currently receive the greatest proportion of health care, and demand is projected to increase by an estimated 75 percent in the twenty-first century if current trends continue.[2] This growth challenges not only the medical care system but also the long-term care and social service systems.

Clearly, the resources required to meet this challenge are substantial. The source and nature of these resources are still unknown. Riley[3] suggests that the two critical questions about this situation remain unanswered. As the number of elderly grows, will the added years increase the proportion who are disabled or dependent, or will the majority of older people remain relatively healthy and able to function reasonably well? Cutler (Chapter 13) describes the difficulties in making this kind of projection but indicates that even in the best-case scenarios, some increase in need for services is inevitable.

DISABILITY VERSUS DISEASE MODELS

The medical system has traditionally been based on an acute care or disease model. The fundamental belief of this model is that specific biological and organismic factors determine the nature and extent of disease. This approach grew out of the "germ theories" of the 1800s,[4] which led to the control of infectious diseases and substantially increased life expectancy, providing the foundation for today's medical care and research. In this framework the ultimate goal of care is cure or elimination of the disease. This perspective does not fit the needs of people with disabilities and those at risk of disability, particularly older adults. Unlike the acute medical model, the disability perspective emphasizes the limitations of a person's ability to carry out

TABLE 17–1 **Deaths and Rates per 100,000 for Leading Causes of Death Shown by Age Groups**

Cause	Rates 65 years and over	Age Groups, No. Deaths		
		65–74	75–84	85 and Over
All causes	4,963.0	418,224	599,206	457,358
Heart disease	1,949.2	203,467	301,942	270,981
Malignant neoplasms	1,085.1	155,028	130,612	50,566
Cerebrovascular disease	408.8	26,306	50,740	49,614
Chronic obstructive pulmonary disease	225.8	27,065	30,627	12,273
Pneumonia and influenza	217.5	10,418	24,022	32,955
Diabetes mellitus	112.3	13,168	14,160	7,470
Accidents	86.6	8,812	10,256	7,764
Atherosclerosis	59.4	2,348	5,761	10,304
Nephritis and nephrosis	56.5	4,415	7,133	5,960
Septicemia	49.8	3,664	6,144	5,650

Source: Monthly Vital Statistics Report, Vol. 40, No. 8(S)2, January 7, 1992.

personal, social, and familial responsibilities as a result of health problems. Disability is defined as more than a medical issue. Rather it is viewed as a costly social public health issue and a moral issue. For example, in 1990 an estimated 35 million people, or one in every seven Americans, had a disabling condition that interfered with life activities.[5] Increased life expectancy is projected to be associated with significant limitations in activity. Given current patterns, a child born in 1987 could reasonably expect to experience 12.8 years of activity limitation in his or her 75 years of life.[6] Persons who are now approaching age 65 can expect 6.9 years of measurable limitations out of the estimated 16.9 years of remaining life expectancy.[5]

The prevalence and extent of activity limitation increases substantially with age. For example, in 1988, only 2.2 percent of children under the age of 5 were found to have activity limitations compared to 37.6 percent of adults age 70 or over. Severity of limitations also increases.[7]

The causes of activity limitations are listed in Figure 17–1.[8] While several conditions are represented on both lists, many disabling conditions (such as arthritis) are not life threatening. In fact, the increased prevalence of disability over time has been attributed directly to the decrease in mortality over the same

time period.[9] The effects of these disabling conditions vary substantially with age. Mobility impairments are the leading cause of activity limitations in all adult groups. The relative rates of these causes of activity limitations are shown by age in Figure 17–2.[8] These data demonstrate the need to shift emphasis from the acute care disease model to a more inclusive approach addressing disability prevention.

The National Institutes of Health are developing a new center specifically designed to investigate mechanisms of disability. The advisory panel has proposed the taxonomy of disability diagrammed in Figure 17–3.

Many health policy specialists have suggested that emphasis on prevention is essential to address health care related to functional disability. This recommendation is based on the premise that it is possible to prevent the development of life-threatening or disabling disease, to delay the onset of disease, and to reduce disability associated with chronic disease.[10] Such a shift requires that our views of chronic disease and disability become ''demedicalized,'' a process that would place greater emphasis on the social and personal consequences of illness.[11,12] These factors, often referred to as *quality of life*, are difficult to address in acute care, particularly for older adults, for whom preservation of life needs to be tempered with

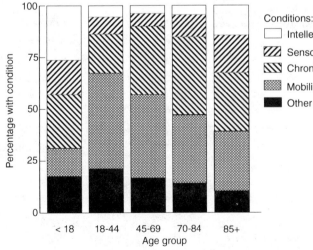

Figure 17–1 Percentage distribution of main causes of activity limitation, by age, 1983–1985. Source: Pope AM, Taylor AR (eds.): Disability in America: Toward a National Agenda for Prevention. National Academy Press, p. 3, Washington, DC, 1991. Reprinted with permission. © 1991, The National Academy of Sciences.

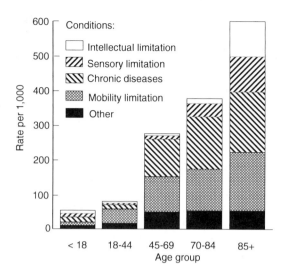

Figure 17–2 Prevalence of main causes of activity limitation, by age, 1983–1985. Source: Pope AM, Taylor AR (eds.): Disability in America: Toward a National Agenda for Prevention. National Academy Press, p. 2, Washington, DC, 1991. Reprinted with permission. © 1991, The National Academy of Sciences.

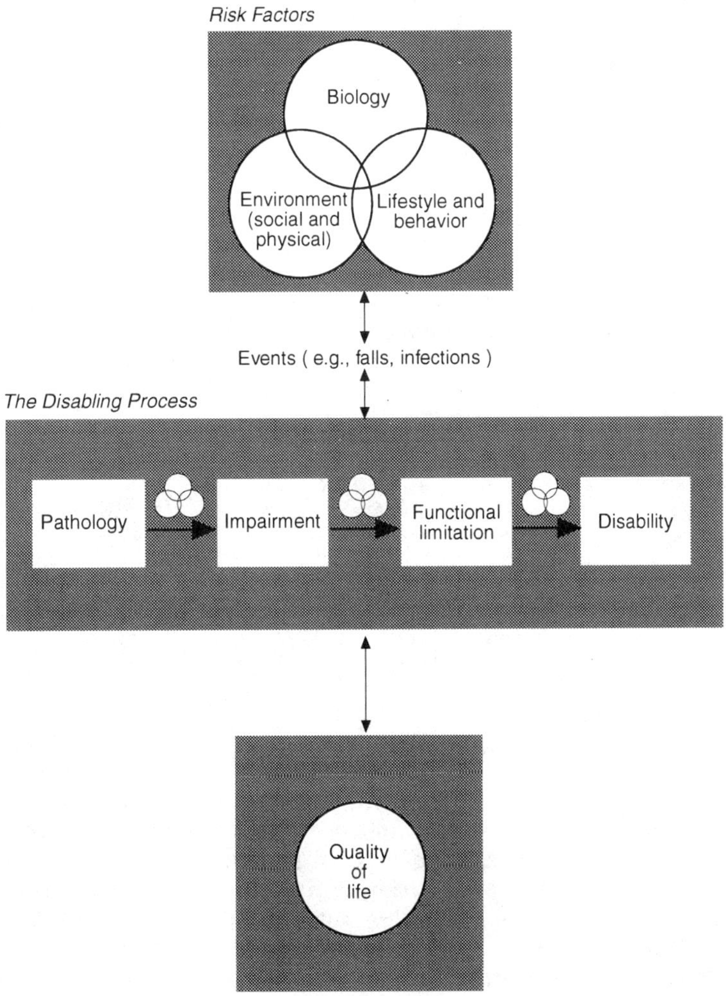

Figure 17–3 Model of disability showing the interaction among the disabling process, quality of life, and risk factors. Three types of risk factors are included: biological (e.g., Rh type); environmental (e.g., lead paint [physical environment], access to care [social environment]); and lifestyle and behavior (e.g., tobacco consumption). Bidirectional arrows indicate the potential for "feedback." The potential for additional risk factors to affect the progression toward disability is shown between the stages of the model. These additional risk factors might include diagnosis, treatment, therapy, adequacy of rehabilitation, age of onset, financial resources, expectations, and environmental barriers, depending on the stage of the model. Source: Pope AM, Taylor AR (eds.): Disability in America: Toward a National Agenda for Prevention. National Academy Press, p. 9, Washington, DC, 1991. Reprinted with permission. © 1991, The National Academy of Sciences.

Risk Factors

Biology

Environment (social and physical)

Lifestyle and behavior

Events (e.g., falls, infections)

The Disabling Process

Pathology → Impairment → Functional limitation → Disability

Quality of life

a better understanding of the effects of intervention on the autonomy and independence of the individual.

DIFFERENTIATING HEALTH PROMOTION FROM DISEASE PREVENTION

Historically, health sciences and medicine dealt with disease[13] focusing on three main questions. How to avoid it, how to cure it, or how to appease it. Public health programs were designed to address one or all of these questions. *Health* was defined as the absence of disease, and prevention efforts were fairly easy to evaluate. Critics of this approach felt that these efforts were narrow, inflexible, and often ineffective.[14] The role of the individual in this process was often ignored and the long-term effects of such interventions have been difficult to substantiate.

As attention shifted to health, as opposed to disease, health promotion programs became more popular. These programs involved not just avoidance of disease but the maintenance of positive well-being as well. Thus, while prevention focuses on minimizing disease, health promotion focuses on maximizing well-being.

Operational Definition of Health

The *World Health Organization* (WHO) has defined health as a "state of well being."[15] The utility of this type of global definition has been questioned. Antonovsky[16] has suggested that when health is defined in an all-encompassing fashion, it becomes impossible to study in any meaningful way. The WHO definition describes an abstract state in which the person experiences an ecological balance among the physical, social, and environmental determinants of well-being. There are few measures that can accurately assess the current status of a given individual or group of individuals. An even greater problem arises if it is necessary to evaluate change or the effects of intervention.

Another common strategy is to use the term *health status,* which has been defined as the individual's level of function at a given time. Ware[17] stated that function is the ability to conform to society's standards of physical and mental well-being including the performance of activities usual for a person's age and social role.

Parsons[18] defined health in the following manner: Health is that state of optimal capacity for effective performance of valued tasks. There are a number of benefits associated with viewing health in the context of performance of life roles and activities. This approach allows a move from the more reductionistic medical model to a more holistic system that incorporates the effects of the physical, social, biological, and service determinants of well-being.[19] This approach accommodates the position taken by the World Health Organization but also allows development of more precise outcome measures.

The emphasis on performance as an essential component of health is important in evaluating different approaches to health promotion. If the programs produce attitudinal change on the part of the participants but not behavioral change in terms of greater or improved performance of essential life tasks, then we may question the benefit of the program.

Historical Perspectives on Health Practices

The Surgeon General's 1979 report on health promotion and disease prevention stimulated media interest in healthy lifestyles and the growth of formal health promotion programs.[20] This report reviewed the findings of a number of epidemiological studies and concluded that 50 percent of the mortality from the 10 leading causes of death could be attributed to lifestyle. Other federal studies[21] stated that 7 of the 10 leading causes of death (heart disease, stroke, automobile accidents, diabetes, cirrhosis of the liver, and arteriosclerosis) could be reduced significantly if individuals at risk would change five behaviors:

1. Smoking
2. Alcohol abuse
3. Nutrition
4. Exercise
5. Adherence to medication for hypertension

Wearing an automobile seat belt is the only major addition to the list over the last decade.

The Alameda County study conducted by Belloc and Breslow[22] is an example of the research that identified these behaviors. Beginning in 1965, they surveyed 6928 community-residing adults aged 30 to 65 years, obtaining information on the physical health, functional disability, mental health, social well-being, demographic factors, and personal behaviors and health practices, over a nine-year period. Interim data analysis in 1972 demonstrated an association between physical health status and seven common health-related activities:

1. Physical activity
2. Cigarette smoking
3. Alcohol consumption
4. Obesity
5. Sleep habits
6. Eating breakfast daily
7. Snacking between meals

These factors were also related to mortality risk.[23] In practical terms, this study revealed that a 45 year old man observing 6 of the 7 health practices had a life expectancy of approximately 11 years more than a 45-year-old man engaging in only 3 of the practices. Subsequent statistical analyses at the end of 9 years did not support the inclusion of breakfast and snacking between meals. Of even greater interest was the finding that these practices were predictive of mortality independent of the effects of gender, socioeconomic status, age, and base-line physical health. The study also found that the strength of one's social network was associated with mortality.[24] This study provided empirical support for the development of programs designed to enhance health practices and strengthen social networks.

The authors acknowledge the difficulty of modifying these behaviors since they occurred within highly individualized social, psychological, and cultural contexts.

DEVELOPING MULTIDISCIPLINARY APPROACHES TO HEALTH PROMOTION

Over the past 30 years, health practitioners have struggled with how to increase and sustain beneficial or health protective behaviors in people at risk. Americans have responded to the data on health life-cycles (see Fig. 17–4). More people are exercising, watching their diets, and avoiding smoking. All these practices are reflected in reduced mortality. Despite these changes, there is still a lot of work to be done to increase beneficial health practices.

When specific health practices are studied, it appears that people who are at greatest risk are often the least compliant. For example, Podell[25] found that on average, only one-third of patients treated for hypertension correctly followed physician's directions. Sackett and Snow[26] reported that 50 percent of patients enrolled in a study of hypertension did not take prescribed medications in accordance with instructions. Even fewer of these patients adhered to lifestyle changes such as diet, exercise, and smoking cessation. Results such as these stimulated interest in more behavioral approaches to health promotion.

Kasl and Cobb[27] identified three major reasons for voluntary health-related behaviors:

1. To prevent illness or to detect it at an asymptomatic stage
2. In the presence of symptoms, to obtain diagnosis and to discover suitable treatment
3. In the presence of defined illness, to undertake or receive treatment aimed at restoration of health or halting disease progression

Lifestyle Behaviors and Time Period	Reduced Risk	Increased Risk
Percent of Cigarette Smokers		
Adult males, 20 years & over (1965–79)	−28%	
Adult females, 20 years & over (1965–79)	−13%	
Teenage boys, 12–18 years (1968–79)	−20%	
Teenage girls, 12–18 years (1968–79)		+51%
Per Capita Consumption of		
Tobacco (1965–79)	−16%	
Fluid milk & cream (1965–79)	−21%	
Butter (1965–79)	−28%	
Eggs (1965–79)	−10%	
Percent of adults who are heavier drinkers (1971–76)	0%	
High Serum Cholesterol (260 mg/100 ml plus)		
Adult males, 18–74 years (1960–61-1971–74)	−12%	
Adult females, 18–74 years (1960–62-1971–74)	−22%	
Untreated Hypertension		
Adults 18–74 years (1960–62-1971–74)	−10%	
Percent of adults who exercise daily (1961–80)	+92%	

Figure 17–4 Recent changes in lifestyle behaviors that affect health. Source: adapted from Harris PR: Health United States 1980. U.S. Department of Health and Human Services Pub. No. (PHS)81-1232. Washington, DC: US Government Printing Office, 1981.

This early description still provides an accurate framework for the exploration of theoretical models of health promotion.[28] *Primary prevention* refers to the modification of risk factors prior to the onset of disease. An example of this type of activity is community educational campaigns to prevent smoking. *Secondary prevention* includes strategies to slow the progression of illness early on, as in the case of dietary modification for hypertension. *Tertiary prevention* refers to rehabilitation and treatment interventions used to stop the progression of clinically manifest disease.[29]

The distinctions among these types of prevention are less clear in programs for older adults. Interventions that are classically considered secondary for one condition may simultaneously be primary prevention for another. For example, detection or treatment of hypertension is secondary prevention for hypertensive disease, whereas control of hypertension (tertiary prevention) is primary prevention for strokes.[1]

THEORETICAL MODELS

Extensive efforts have been made to understand the factors that influence preventive behaviors. The three most frequently cited models are the Health Belief Model, the Theory of Planned Behavior, and the Health Decision Model. There are many common elements in these models, but each approaches health promotion in a distinctive way.

Health Belief Model

This model was developed in the 1950s by a group of social psychologists working for the U.S. Public Health Service.[30] The two primary determinants of behavior identified in this theoretical approach are the value placed by the person on a particular goal and a person's belief that a specific action will achieve the desired goal. Other components of the model include perceived susceptibility, or the subjective assessment of risk, perceived severity, the person's estimate of the consequences of the problem, and the individual's evaluation of his or her ability to overcome barriers to effective behavior (see Fig. 17–5). This model has been applied to diverse populations, conditions, and recommended behaviors such as cigarette smoking, hypertension, cardiac rehabilitation programs, and breast

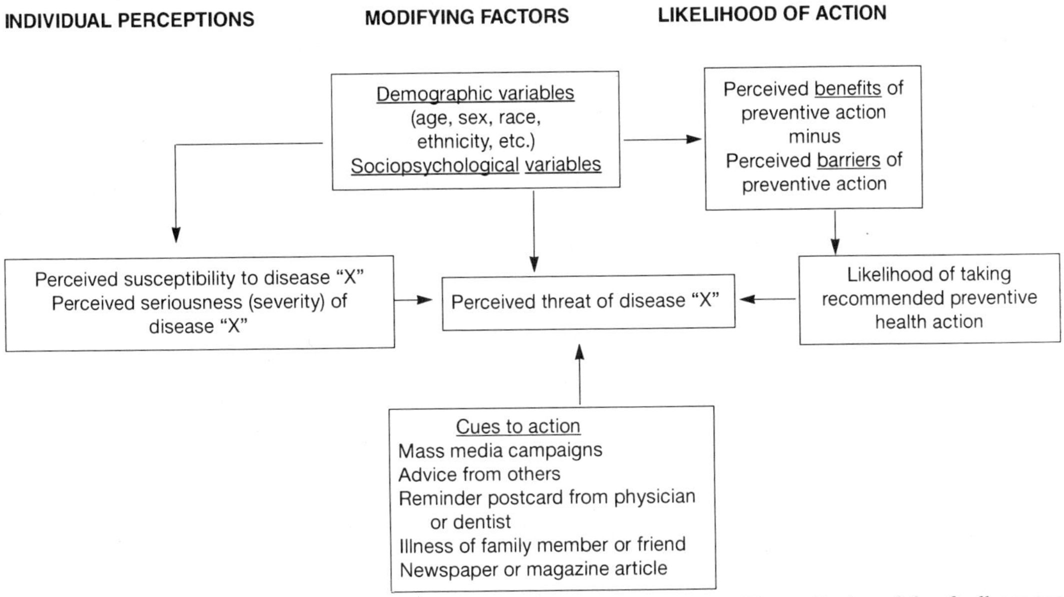

INDIVIDUAL PERCEPTIONS   MODIFYING FACTORS   LIKELIHOOD OF ACTION

Figure 17–5 The health belief model. Source: Becker MH, Marshall H: Theoretical models of adherence and strategies for improving adherence. In Shumaker SA, Schron EB, and Ockene JK (eds): The Handbook of Health Behavior Change. Springer Publishing Company, Inc., New York 10012, © 1990, pp. 5–43, used by permission.

self-examination. Few studies have supported the model in its entirety.[31] The primary criticisms are that it has poor predictive power with regard to change in health behaviors, overemphasizes psychological rather than social or cultural factors, and while it may explain phenomena retrospectively, it is not an effective model for predicting behavior.[32]

Theory of Planned Action

This theory hypothesizes that health behaviors are a function of the strength of a person's attempt to perform a behavior and the degree of perceived control over a specific action or group of actions.[33] This theory is an expansion of a previous model called the *Theory of Reasoned Action*. The approach distinguishes between intentions (i.e., I really will start a diet tomorrow) and expectations (I don't really think that I will be able to stop eating dessert altogether). These factors are influenced by variables such as past experience, confidence in one's ability to control the be-

havior, availability of a detailed plan of action, general self-knowledge, and the opinions of significant others.[34] This model has been used in studies of weight loss, smoking cessation, contraceptive usage, and Pap tests for cervical cancer. The model seems to accommodate the effects of cultural differences more effectively than other theories, but it has not been widely tested in noncollegiate adult populations. This model is presented in Fig. 17–6.

Health Decision Model

This theory represents an attempt to incorporate domains that were not well represented in early models. It quantifies the mechanisms used to make choices between benefits and risks and quantity and quality of life.[35] This model incorporates elements of the health belief model and accounts for the influence of knowledge, experience, and sociodemographic factors. It also emphasizes the effect of preexisting beliefs over statistical data in the decision-making process. This model is presented in Figure 17–7.

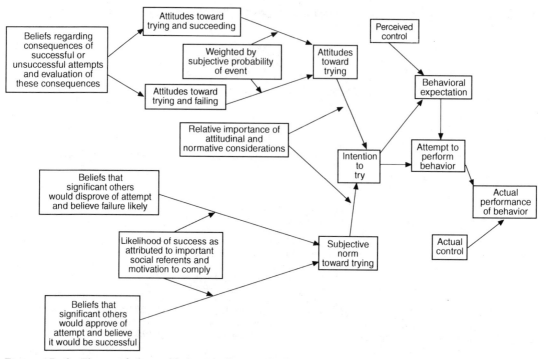

Figure 17–6   Theory of planned behavior. Source: Becker MH, Marshall H: Theoretical models of adherence and strategies for improving adherence. In Shumaker SA, Schron EB, and Ockene JK (eds): The Handbook of Health Behavior Change. Springer Publishing Company, Inc., New York 10012, © 1990, pp. 5–43, used by permission.

HEALTH PROMOTION AND AGING

The social, psychological, and biological systems that influence aging are not immutable and are subject to modification. In order to modify them, it is important to understand the relationships between health and behavior in older adults.

Health promotion activities have focused primarily on younger people. Several authors[36] suggest that health promotion programs for older adults have been limited by the belief that they represent a group that is markedly less sensitive to risk factors. These authors suggest that younger groups are more likely to show positive effects of intervention. However, the recently published report *The Second Fifty Years: Promoting Health and Preventing Disability*[37] suggests that the benefits to older individuals and to society outweigh the methodological and programmatic problems associated with implementing health promotion programs for older adults.

In working with older adults, it is essential to redefine the goals of health promotion to include disability reduction as well as disease prevention.[38] It is essential to recognize the need for quantitative as well as qualitative evidence of effectiveness,[38] to obtain better information about age-adjusted risk factors,[39] and to develop a mechanism for integrating these approaches into clinical practice.[40] The previously described theoretical models all support age-specific intervention strategies. We know, for example, that beliefs of susceptibility and efficacy are strongly age-related, as are perceived barriers to effective action. Older adults may feel that they cannot overcome the effects of an entire lifetime habit such as smoking and that they may face access problems in terms of availability of services since many preventive activities are not covered by medicare, medicaid, or private in-

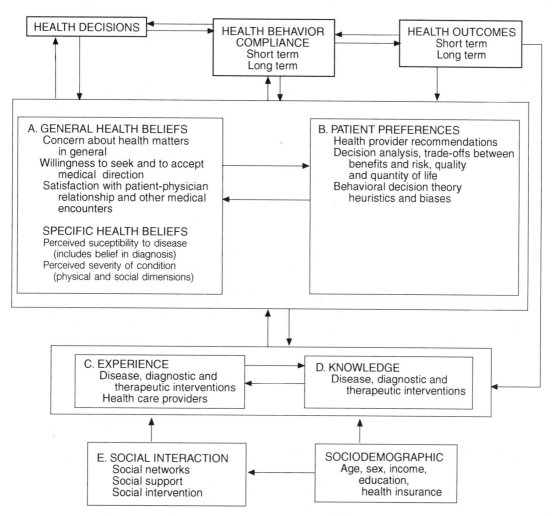

Figure 17–7 Health decision model. Source: Becker MH, Marshall H: Theoretical models of adherence and strategies for improving adherence. In Shumaker SA, Schron EB, and Ockene JK (eds): The Handbook of Health Behavior Change. Springer Publishing Company, Inc., New York 10012. © 1990, pp. 5–43, used by permission.

surers.[7] Other barriers may include a lack of support from family or friends, fear that the efforts will not produce any measurable benefit, transportation problems, and a lack of understanding of the underlying health problem. In the past 2 years, papers and reports on the effectiveness of programs on hypertension, osteoporosis, sensory loss, oral health, cancer screening, falls, and social isolation have been published. While not all of these interventions have been successful, as a group they suggest the potential benefits of health promotion in later life.

The findings from these studies suggest that older adults are motivated and capable of changing health behaviors given the right types of programs. Successful programs are those that:

- Stress that no one is too old to change.
- Offer dramatic information such as case studies.
- Promote the immediate benefits of the activity.
- Clearly establish the link between the target behavior and specific health problems.

- Give specific information about the actions required.
- Provide group support and an opportunity to rehearse or practice the behavior.
- Involve the personal physician whenever possible.
- Include older adults in the planning process.

HEALTH PROMOTION AMONG MINORITY GROUPS

Health promotion programs are particularly important for older individuals from minority groups. Statistics indicate that minorities suffer from a higher rate of disease and preventable death than white Europeans. Different ethnic groups have different risk factors and susceptibilities. Figure 17–8 illustrates these differences. Thus, while health promotion programs offer tremendous potential for improving the health status of minority elders, the focus and content must reflect the specific needs of each group.[41]

The racial and ethnic minority populations in the United States are extremely diverse. This diversity must be accommodated in the design of health promotion programs. The National Resource on Minority Aging Populations has developed a list of factors[41] that may affect the acceptance of health promotion activities by minority older adults. This list includes the following factors:

- Discrimination, oppression, and social inequalities may make it difficult for minority elders to see the value of a program and to believe that it will really work for them. For example, they may see only white models in public awareness campaigns.
- Language and comprehension barriers may reduce the effectiveness of written and presentation materials. For example, educational materials may be written at a college literacy level.
- Lack of financial resources may limit participation even when a person is highly motivated to change. For example, the cost of food may be the primary concern rather than the nutritional content.
- Different cultures have very different definitions of what is healthy. For example, some cultures associate being overweight with good health or financial security.
- Gender-related roles and activities vary by group so that program activities must be adapted to the cultural role expectations. For example, men and women may not be comfortable in a mixed-gender exercise class.

When these factors are taken into account, minority wellness programs can be very successful.[42–44]

In recognition of the need for better information and support of professionals interested in health promotion and aging, the American Association of Retired Persons has joined with the fed-

---

Hispanic American
  High Blood Pressure
  Diabetes

African American
  Heart Disease
  Stroke
  High Blood Pressure
  Diabetes
  Cancer
  Cirrhosis of the Liver

Pacific/Asian American
  High Blood Pressure
  Diabetes
  Cancer

American Indian/Alaskan Native
  Heart Disease
  Cancer
  Chronic Liver Disease
  Diabetes
  Cirrhosis of the Liver
  Pneumonia/Influenza

Figure 17–8 Differential risk for chronic disease or disability shown by ethnic or cultural group. Source: Monthly Vital Statistics Report, Vol 40, No 8, January, 1992.

eral government to establish the National Resource Center for Health Promotion and Aging. This center provides health promotion training materials, program materials, and a quarterly newsletter with an emphasis on primary prevention. The University of Missouri–Kansas City sponsors the Center on Rural Elderly. This center provides materials on the needs of rural elders and supports communication among people with particular concerns about rural elders. Professionals interested in resources on minority elders are encouraged to contact the National Resource Center for Minority Aging Populations. This center, together with the AARP, has prepared a series of materials for minority health promotion programs. In addition to this center, the Office of Minority Health Resource Center provides a bilingual, toll-free hotline and professional assistance with culturally appropriate educational materials.

A MODEL PROGRAM

Many effective programs meet a number of needs simultaneously. Perhaps one of the best known is the OASIS program.[45] This is a collaboration between a health care facility and a department store. Together, they designed a drop-in center in a shopping mall, predicated on the theory that it is important to go where the clients are and that many older adults now view malls as social centers. The facility provides an array of services, including opportunities for socialization, leisure activities, and health education brochures, pamphlets, and lectures. In addition, it offers an ideal way for health care providers to assess, in an informal way, risk factors that might put individuals in danger of developing health problems. Thus, it serves as a center for screening, information and referral, and informal activity.

SUMMARY

As the demographic and social characteristics of the United States change,

the health care system must accommodate the shift away from an acute care model to a comprehensive approach to disability prevention. This chapter has described the philosophical and theoretical foundations that influence this shift. The move away from the medical model has been reflected in the identification of risk factors and support for primary, secondary, and tertiary programs designed to improve quality of life and enhance functional independence.

Until recently, stereotypic views of the aging process and the interest and ability of older adults to participate in health promotion programs has limited health promotion activities for older adults. Health policy changes coupled with empirical data provide support for the growing interest in health promotion for older individuals.

REVIEW QUESTIONS

1. *In what ways does the disability model differ from the disease model? What factors make the disability model better suited to understanding the health problems of older adults?*

2. *How does health promotion differ from disease prevention?*

3. *Health can be defined in a number of ways. Provide three that relate to concepts of health promotion.*

4. *In what ways are the health belief model, theory of planned action, and health decision model similar? How do they differ?*

5. *You are designing a health promotion for older adults to address maintenance of functional abilities. What factors would you consider in designing the program?*

6. *How would the considerations made in question 5 differ if the population for which you were planning was composed primarily of minority individuals?*

REFERENCES

1. Reuter, J, Klebe, E and Cislowski, J: Health promotion and disease prevention for the elderly. Congressional Research Service Report, 36–40 EPW. Library of Congress, 1986.
2. Barney, K: From Ellis Island to assisted living: Meeting the needs of older adults from diverse countries. American Journal of Occupational Therapy 47:586–593, 1991.
3. Riley, M: Beyond ageism: Postponing the onset of disability. In Riley, M, Hess, B and Bond, K (eds): Aging in Society: Selected Reviews of Recent Research. Lawrence Erlbaum, Hillsdale, NJ, 1983, pp 243–252.
4. Last, JM: Scope and methods of prevention. In Last, JM and Wallace, RW (eds:) Maxey-Rosenau—Last Public Health and Preventive Medicine. Johns Hopkins Press, Baltimore, 1992, p 11.
5. LaPlante, M: Disabilities in basic life activities across the life span. Disability statistics report 1. University of California Institute for Health and Aging, San Francisco, 1989.
6. LaPlante, M: Disability risks of chronic illnesses and impairments. Disability Statistics Report 2. University of California Institute for Health and Aging, San Francisco, 1990.
7. Tarlov, A and Pope, A: Disability in America: Toward a national agenda for prevention. Institute of Medicine. National Academy Press, Washington, DC, 1991.
8. Tarlov, A and Pope, A: Disability in America: Toward a national agenda for prevention. Institute of Medicine. National Academy Press, Washington, DC, 1991.
9. Verbrugge, L: Longer life but worsening health? Trends in health and mortality of middle-aged and older persons. Millbrook Memorial Fund Quarterly 62:475–519, 1984.
10. Kasl, S and Cobb, S: Stress and health. Annual Review of Public Health 5:319–341, 1984.
11. Estes, C and Binney, E: The biomedicalization of aging: Dangers and dilemmas. Gerontologist 29:577–586, 1990.
12. Caplan, G: Loss, stress and mental health. Community Mental Health Journal 26:27–48, 1990.
13. Stachtchenko, S and Jenicek, M: Conceptual differences between prevention and health promotion: Research implications for community health programs. Canadian Journal of Public Health 81, Feb 1990.
14. Roemer, M: The value of medical care for health promotion. American Journal of Public Health 74:243–248, 1984.
15. World Health Organization. International classification of impairments, disabilities and handicaps. World Health Organization, Geneva, 1980.
16. Antonovsky, A: Editorial. Social Science and Medicine 14:187–189, 1980.
17. Ware, JE: Measures for a New Era of Health Assessment. In Stewart, AL and Ware, JE (eds): Measuring Functioning and Well Being. Duke University Press, Durham, 1993, p 3.
18. Parsons, T: The definitions of health and illness in the light of American values and social structures. In Jaco, E (ed): Patients, Physicians and Illness. Free Press, New York, 1958, pp 165–187.
19. Christiansen, C: Occupational therapy: Intervention for life performance. In Christiansen, and Baum C (eds): Occupational Therapy: Overcoming Human Performance Deficits. Slack, Thorofare, NJ, 1991, pp 3–43.
20. US Department of Health, Education and Welfare: Healthy people: The Surgeon General's report on health promotion and disease prevention. DHHS Pub No (PHS) 91-50212. US Government Printing Office, Washington, DC, 1979.
21. US Department of Health and Human Services: Promoting Health and Preventing Disease. US Government Printing Office, Washington, DC, 1978.
22. Belloc, N and Breslow, L: Health and Ways of Living: The Alameda County Study. Oxford University Press, New York, 1972.
23. Belloc, N and Breslow, L: Health and Ways of Living: The Alameda County Study. Oxford University Press, New York, 1973.
24. Berkman, L and Breslow, L: Health and Ways of Living: The Alameda County Study. Oxford University Press, New York, 1983.
25. Podell, R: Editorial: The politics of health behavior: Diet and heart disease. American Family Physician 10:16–18, 1975.
26. Sackett, D and Snow, J: The magnitude of compliance and noncompliance. In Haynes, RB, Taylor, DW and Sacketts, DL (eds): Compliance in Health Care. John Hopkins University Press, Baltimore, 1979, pp 11–22.
27. Kasl, S and Cobb, S: Health behavior, illness behavior, and sick role behavior. Archives of Environmental Health 12:246–266, 1966.
28. Shumaker, S, Schron, E and Ockene, J: The Handbook of Health Behavior Change. Springer, New York, 1990.
29. Gatchel, RJ, Baum, A and Krantz, DS: An Introduction to Health Psychology. Random House, New York, 1989.
30. Rosenstock, I: Historical origins of the health belief model. Health Education Monographs 2:328–335, 1974.
31. Wyper, M: Breast self-examination and a health belief model: Variations on a theme. Research in Nursing and Health 13:421–428, 1990.
32. Siegrist, J: Models of health behavior. European Heart Journal 9:709–714, 1988.
33. Ajzen, I: From intentions to actions: A theory of planned behavior. In Kuhl, J and Beckman, J (eds): Action Control: From Cognition to Behavior. Springer Verlag, New York, 1985.
34. Becker M: Theoretical models of adherence and strategies for improving adherence. In Shumaker, S, Schron, E and Ockene, J (eds): The Handbook of Health Behavior Change. Springer, New York, 1990.
35. McNeil, B, Keller, E and Adelstein, S: Primer on certain elements of medical decision mak-

ing. New England Journal of Medicine 293:211–215, 1975.

36. Kaplan, G and Haan, M: Is there a role for prevention among the elderly? Epidemiological evidence from the Alameda county study. In Ory, M and Bond, K (eds): Aging in Health Care. Routledge, New York, 1989.

37. Berg, R and Cassells, J (eds): The second fifty years: Promoting health and preventing disability. Institute of Medicine. National Academy Press, Washington, DC, 1991.

38. Black, J and Kapoor, W: Health promotion and disease prevention in the elderly: Our current state of ignorance. Journal of the American Geriatric Society 38:168–172, 1990.

39. Kane, R, Kane, R and Arnold, S: Prevention in the elderly: Risk factors. Paper prepared for the Conference on Health Promotion and Disease Prevention for Children and the Elderly. Founation for Health Services Research, Sept 16, 1983.

40. Larson, E: Health promotion and disease pre-

vention in the older adult. Geriatrics 43:31–39, 1988.

41. American Association of Retired Person (AARP). Perspectives on Health Promotion and Aging, National Eldercare Health Institute on Health Promotion, Washington DC, 1990.

42. Hogstell, M and Kashka, M: Staying healthy after 85. Geriatric Nursing 10:16–18, 1989.

43. Butler, R: Dispelling ageism: The cross-cutting intervention. The Annals of the American Academy of Political and Social Science 503:138–147, 1989.

44. US Department of Health and Human Services. Minority Aging: Essential Curricula Content for Selected Health and Allied Health Professions. US Government Printing Office, Washington, DC, 1990.

45. Mann, M, Edwards, D and Baum, CM: OASIS: A new concept for promoting the quality of life for older adults. American Journal of Occupational Therapy 40:784–786, 1986.

Nuns fret not at their convent's narrow
room;
And hermits are contented with their cells;
And students with their pensive citadels;
Maids at the wheel, the weaver at his loom,
Sit blithe and happy.

—WORDSWORTH, *Nuns Fret Not*, 1806.

Chapter

Home Health Care

LINDA A. HUNT

OBJECTIVES

By the end of this chapter, readers will be able to:

1 Identify the subsystems of the home environment.

2 Identify factors in the home environment that may interfere with optimal performance.

3 Evaluate strategies for adapting the home environment to promote optimal performance.

As the population of older adults grows and as health care costs escalate, the search for mechanisms for controlling those costs and for providing the most acceptable forms of care intensifies. One method for service provision that has received increasing attention is home health care. At least in theory, home health care has the potential to satisfy both concerns; it is considered desirable by care recipients as it allows them to remain in familiar surroundings and it has the potential to control costs, which are considerably higher for inpatient care.

Congress established the Medicare *Home Health Agency* (HHA) benefit as a less intensive and less costly alternative to short-stay hospital inpatient care. HHA services covered by Medicare include intermittent part-time skilled nursing care; physical, occupational, and speech therapy; part-time home health aide services; medical social services; and durable medical equipment (see Table 18–1). To be eligible for HHA

	TABLE 18-1 **Roles of the Home Health Professions**	
Profession	**Services, Treatments and Modalities That May be Covered by Medicare (Not All Inclusive)**	**Possible Exceptions to Reimbursement by Medicare**
Skilled nurse	Observation and evaluation Supervision Insertion and sterile irrigation of a catheter Teaching of administering medicine (i.e., insulin injections) Skin care	Long-term parenteral/enteral therapy
Psychiatric nurse	RN requires appropriate psychiatric accreditation Evaluation and psychotherapy	
Physical therapist	Gait training Ultrasound *Range of motion* (ROM) tests Therapeutic exercises	Reevaluation visit Postrecovery restorative therapy ROM tests to unaffected joints Reconditioning programs after surgery
Occupational therapist	Continued care only with an open plan of treatment Improve/restore functions impaired by illness/injury Restorative therapy Teaching/selecting tasks that will restore function Teaching of activities of daily living Designing/fabricating/fitting of orthotic devices Vocational/prevocational training and assessment (may be coverable when part of an overall plan to restore functions in activities of daily living; not coverable when related only to specific employment opportunities)	Patient fails to meet predetermined goals after extended therapy
Speech therapist	Restorative therapy (i.e., dysarthria, voice problems, aphasia, laryngectomy) Teaching of lip reading Maintenance therapy for a patient who has not been under a restorative speech therapy program	Maintaining therapy at restored level
Home health aide	Personal care duty	Domestic housekeeping services
Medical social services	Assessment of social/emotional factors of the patient Assessment of patient's home medical/nursing requirements Referrals to community services (i.e., food stamps, financial aid, and so on)	Psychological treatment (short-term counseling may be coverable when reasonable and necessary)

Source: A Medicare Guide to Billing for HHA's. Blue Cross/Blue Shield of Iowa, Des Moines, used with permission.

services, Medicare enrollees must be confined to home and must have a plan of treatment certified by the attending physician. Care must include part-time intermittent skilled nursing care or physical or speech therapy, and it must be provided by an agency participating in the Medicare program.

The most frequent principal diagnosis (5.7 percent) for persons using HHA services is acute, ill-defined cerebrovascular disease.[1] Other circulatory system diagnoses are heart diseases, primarily congestive heart failure (4.8 percent) and acute myocardial infarction, unspecified site (1.3 percent). Another common condition is femur neck fracture, which accounts for 2.5 percent of all persons served using HHA services. People with these cardiovascular and orthopedic conditions probably used HHA services following a hospital stay,[1] though the Omnibus Budget Reconciliation Act of 1980 eliminated the requirement for a hospital stay prior to receipt of home health care.

The National Association for Home Care (NAHC) (Washington, D.C.) predicts a future growth rate of 10 percent annually as of April 1991. The NAHC also reported a total of 12,536 home care providers, of which 5823 are Medicare certified. The noncertified agencies are made up of private-duty agencies or for-profit agencies, which are homemaker and aide service providers that would be nonreimbursable under Medicaid guidelines, and some hospice service agencies. According to NAHC, in 1987 (the latest figures) 3 million out of 26.5 million, or 11.2 percent, of all people over age 65 received home care services. As home health care increases, clinicians must understand how home care can either assist or jeopardize the treatment goals established with the patient and significant others.

This chapter will explore how some health care differs from care delivered in other treatment settings, including the importance of addressing immediate performance problems as they occur and the fact that intervention occurs in the client's real environment rather than an artificial clinical environment.

These two features require a unique conceptual approach to the older adult's treatment that avoids emphasis on isolated performance components such as range of motion, muscle strength, or self-medication. It requires that clinicians evaluate not only the immediate home surroundings but the combination of external and internal conditions that affect the performance of the older adult. In this chapter the term *home environment* refers to a complex system composed of culture, significant others, and physical attributes of the individual, all of which affect delivery of care.

DEFINING THE HOME ENVIRONMENT

Kielhofner and Burke[2] define the environment as the physical, social, and cultural setting in which a person operates. A person cannot exist without interaction with the environment, which includes external objects, people, and events that influence the person's action. Lawton[3] defines environment as a space, a physical structure, an object, an item of decor, another person, or the collective behavior of a number of people, including family, friends, or people acting as resources from the community. They indicate that person-environment congruence is important. In order to achieve this congruence, the following environmental attributes are important:

1. *Safety.* The degree to which an environment minimizes accidents and hazards and affords assistance should the need occur.
2. *Security.* The degree to which the environment provides psychological reassurance and meets other personal needs.
3. *Accessibility.* The degree to which the environment affords entry, transport, and the use of its resources. Most functional health, time use, and social behaviors are facilitated by accessibility.
4. *Legibility.* The degree to which the environment can be comprehended

by the person, whether through signs, denotative objects, or patterned stimuli. While cognitive competence is specifically enhanced by increased legibility, many other types of competent behavior are amplified by making the environment understandable and predictable.

Rowles[4] stated that the older person's residence should be viewed as a setting in which to engage in the activities of daily living. Intimate familiarity with the physical configuration of rooms, the placement of furniture, and knowledge of a place to grab hold when a dizzy spell occurs provide reassurance about the ability to maintain independence despite failing physiological and sensory capabilities, maximizing a sense of personal competence. Indeed, the individual may develop a type of automatic pilot based on an established daily routine developed over many years.[4,5] Such awareness facilitates effective functioning in a house that might otherwise impose environmental constraints beyond the competence of the older person.[4]

Understanding of the individual's relationship to the specific environment requires careful evaluation, creating the foundation for home health treatment (see Table 18–2 for summary of key concepts). Although home health is a unique treatment method, it is part of the continuum of care an elderly person may receive. Therefore, it is essential to understand how home health intervention fits in the context of other health care service settings such as acute care,

rehabilitation, and the nursing home, and how it differs.

COMPARING THE HOME ENVIRONMENT TO OTHER TREATMENT SETTINGS

Environmental factors influence the goals for therapy in different settings. For example, occupational therapy in the acute care setting, characterized by a short hospital stay, may assist patients with the following: positioning, adaptive equipment assessment and training, and home programs. In acute care, there is little opportunity to know the actual impact of these interventions in the patient's home environment. The clinician can only assume that the recommended equipment (e.g., tub bench or raised toilet seat) will fit in the patient's bathroom based on the information given by the patient and family. The clinician may not meet the care giver, in which case it cannot be established that the care giver will accurately implement the home program. Similarly, a physical therapist in an inpatient setting can observe a patient's ambulation around the ward with a walker and receive reports from nursing staff. At home, the patient may cast aside the walker when not being observed, leading to risk of injury.

In long-term rehabilitation, the clinician may work with the patient for several months. The clinician may visit the patient's home to assess equipment needs and may work with the family getting to know lifestyles and values.

TABLE 18–2 **Definition of Environment**	
Model	
Kielhofner-Burke	The physical, social, and cultural setting in which a person operates. Interaction with the environment is essential for existence.
Kielhofner	The environment is conceptualized as external objects, people and events that influence person's action.
Lawton	The space, physical structure, object, item of decor, another person, or a collective behavior of a number of people. Person-environment congruence achieved through safety, security, accessibility, and legibility.
Rowles	A setting in which to engage in the activities of daily living maximizes a sense of personal competence.

Also, the clinician may teach the family home programs to be continued once the patient leaves the long-term unit. However, the clinician often does not see the patient interacting in his or her environment. Without assessing all environmental factors, the clinician cannot predict such confounding factors as family support, motivation, excess disability,[6] and how the patient will accept equipment prescribed once it is in the home.

Sometimes during home health intervention, environmental competence gives way to environmental vulnerability.[4] The older person may realize that his or her physical condition, economic circumstances, family situation, and the inaccessibility of the home necessitate housing adjustment.[4] When home health intervention cannot address the problems, relocation to a nursing home may occur, signifying that the older adult requires an especially adapted or supervised environment.

Nursing homes are usually designed for dependent older adults. They may not promote independence in a wide range of occupational performance and may have few activities that interest the individual. Lack of opportunities to engage in preexisting interests may contribute to the apathy and inactivity that can occur in institutional settings.[7] Further, in a nursing home, it is possible that cooking or home management safety issues may not be relevant treatment goals. Treatment may be designed to work on activities that meet the demands of institutional schedules.[3] In effective nursing home settings, emphasis is on independence in activities of daily living and on engagement in meaningful and stimulating activities but not on management of instrumental activities of daily living. It should be noted that this is changing somewhat as nursing homes increasingly work with individuals who are engaged in active rehabilitation programs preparatory to returning home.

Clearly, the environments of the hospital and the nursing home differ from the home. Ideally, care in those settings lays the foundation for treatment in the home. Home health clinicians assess the older adult's personal environment using the complexities in that environment to build graded challenges that hopefully result in competent occupational performance.

SUBSYSTEMS IN THE HOME ENVIRONMENT

Cultural, social, and physical subsystems of the home are composed of their own networks of interacting elements. Culture includes attitudes, social behaviors, beliefs, and habits. Significant others may include spouse, children, other relatives, neighbors, friends, church, or other organization that provide meaningful social contact for the older adult. Finally, the physical environment includes the home itself, objects in the home, furniture and other belongings, the yard, and the surrounding neighborhood. Because these subsystems play a major role in performance and the well-being of the individual, it is important to explore their meaning and influence on home care treatment.

The Influence of Culture

The challenge of home health intervention is to improve or maintain the client's performance or health through modalities that can be put into practice only after careful assessment of environmental components. During the initial visit, the first environmental component or subsystem the clinician encounters is the client's culture.

Culture consists of particular ways of doing activities, ways of thinking and expressing thoughts, social skills, roles, values, norms, and established attitudes toward health. The particular blend of these elements determines the best methodology for service delivery.[8]

Culture can be assessed informally. Elderly people generally enjoy reminiscing about the past and talk freely about work, family, and significant life events. Often this information can be obtained while conversing during a therapeutic activity. It is this information that reveals what motivates a client, how to communicate with him or her, and the interpersonal dynamics in the environment.

If a client's culture is not known to the clinician, then the clinician may erroneously substitute her values for the client's.

CASE 1

For example, an occupational therapist who did not like housework was seeing Mrs. A in home health. Because Mrs. A had rheumatoid arthritis, she was unable to accomplish self-care, cooking, and housework all in one day. In Mrs. A's culture, homemaking was an important role for the female head of house. Unaware of this belief, the therapist focused on self-care and dressing and advised Mrs. A to hire someone to do the housework. On subsequent visits the therapist noted that Mrs. A was having her husband bathe and dress her while she struggled with household tasks. When the therapist inquired about this, Mrs. A responded that she did not want to waste her energy dressing but wanted to cook for her family and care for her home. The therapist realized that she had transferred her own bias to her intervention and revised the goals of intervention to energy conservation and joint protection for cooking and home management activities. These new goals were much more satisfactory to the client.

The preceding example illustrates how culture influences attitudes toward the importance of various tasks. Culture may also affect the older adults' willingness to accept recommendations for adaptive equipment or modifications to the home setting. In home health care, the clinician becomes a consultant, recommending changes in the environment to support performance and safety. Some older adults who have lived in their present environment for many years may view changes to the home negatively. Older adults personalize objects in their environment.[9] Objects become symbols of their lives or an extension or expression of their identity.

Generally, clinicians will not be successful in securing consent to modify the client's environment if these feelings are ignored. Changes can never be dictated or demanded. For example, a nurse may recommend a hospital bed for better positioning and ease of transfers. Yet the client remembers when her husband saved to buy the ornate bed frame that has been the focal point in their bedroom. The patient has personalized the object and rejects the idea of a hospital bed. The therapist and client then need to discuss alternatives, through the following steps:

1. Discuss options. Identify the choices and the consequences of each choice, including the option of leaving the environment unchanged.
2. Allow time for reflection and consideration of the options presented. Confusion or denial may result from a quick decision. Some older adults may want to discuss the topic with a confidant before making a decision.
3. Practice performance with a "demo" device or temporarily change the environment so that the older adult can determine if the change is helpful.
4. At a later visit, inquire if the older adult had an opportunity to make a decision. If not, the clinician may want to discuss the recommendation with the involved care giver.
5. If the equipment or modification is acceptable, then the clinician will want to order the equipment or assist with the modification.
6. After utilization of the equipment or modification, seek feedback and make adjustments as needed.
7. If the recommendation is rejected, then document the steps taken and the reason for the rejection. Recognize that clients may, indeed, know what is best for their own circumstances.

A slow demonstrative approach to environmental changes that includes the collaboration of the patient and the family may facilitate acceptance of the intervention. Every effort should be made to keep the environment intact. For example, if the patient does not want to remove her treasured bed, then perhaps the hospital bed could be set up alongside of the bed or in another room, keeping her own bed in view.

The Influence of Significant Others

Another environmental influence that affects home health treatment is the family and other social networks. Traditional family roles can be disrupted by sudden illness or chronic disease, and family dynamics may either facilitate or hinder performance.

CASE 2

Mrs. M, a 70-year-old woman, was referred by her physician to home health nursing and *occupational therapy* (OT) services following lung surgery for cancer. Her symptoms were pain, fatigue, shortness of breath, and decreased right shoulder range of motion and strength, resulting in poor endurance during ambulation and activities of daily living. Mrs. M was receiving skilled nursing care 1 day per week for wound care, blood testing, and monitoring of vital signs. Occupational therapy was ordered two times a week for energy conservation, home management, cooking, and bathroom transfers. Among the tasks emphasized in OT were cooking and home management, utilizing principles of energy conservation. Mrs. M was eventually able to prepare a meal, standing for 25 minutes without fatigue. On one visit soon after, the therapist opened Mrs. M's refrigerator to find it filled with casseroles and other prepared meals delivered by Mrs. M's daughter. With Mrs. M's permission, the therapist contacted the daughter who was surprised to learn of her mother's ability to cook independently. The daughter reported that cooking meals three times a week for her parents was overwhelming. The daughter speculated that Mrs. M received a great deal of attention by not cooking and that if Mrs. M were able, Mr. M would expect her to prepare and serve meals, and clean up. To resolve the problem, the occupational therapist met with Mrs. M, Mr. M, and the daughter. She helped them negotiate a solution that was satisfactory to all of them: Mrs. M would cook, Mr. M would serve himself and help with the cleanup, and the daughter would prepare a meal one night a week. The visiting nurse was able to monitor how Mrs. M was managing and reported later that the family successfully used the same model to negotiate solutions to other problems as they arose.

This case exemplifies how the occupational therapist and the nurse used multiple strategies to assist in the resolution of a complex problem. Intervention in the home environment made it possible to examine factors that might not have been evident in an institutional setting where the therapist might have known what Mrs. M could do but not what she did do.

The role of family and friends in health care has always been essential, as most care is provided by informal care givers. Optimizing the roles of informal social supports from family, friends, and neighbors can decrease care-giver burden while motivating the older adult to adhere to treatment regiments. Utilization of this environmental component requires the clinician to know what kind of support is provided or available (e.g., family, friends, and neighbors) and both the recipient's and the provider's assessment of the support (e.g., whether the recipient feels helped or smothered).[10]

Social network principles offer helpful insights in providing and organizing the care of older people in their home. One of these principles is the importance of quality over quantity of support.[10] Friends and family may visit the impaired older adult and never volunteer to do necessary tasks such as grocery shopping, providing transportation, taking out the trash, or installing safety rails in the bathroom. They may not know what help to offer, in which case the home health clinician can help the client organize their assistance.

Network density[11] directly relates to successful coping. High-density networks, which usually consist of family, are helpful in coping with normative life crises while low-density networks, such as friends, are helpful in coping with nonnormative life crises. Older adults turn first to their families for help, then to neighbors, and finally to the bureaucratic replacements for family such as home health agencies.[12] Care providers may want to help clients examine the degree to which each of these support systems can provide real assistance.

The following case study illustrates how a clinician respected family role delineations and used networking to solve problems of care-giver burden and the impaired elder's dependency in self-care.

CASE 3

Mr. O, a 75-year-old man, had a right cerebral vascular accident. He still had weakness in his left arm and required some assistance with bathing and dressing. Physical therapy had been prescribed to improve Mr. O's stair-climbing ability, as the bathtub and shower were on the second floor. During treatment sessions the physical therapist noted that when people called to ask how they could help, Mrs. O would respond that her daughter was there. However, Mrs. O appeared exhausted and worried and was awkward in assisting her husband with bathing and dressing. Mrs. O explained to the therapist that her daughter visited every day, confusing "visiting" with help. Mrs. O reported that Mr. O would not accept physical assistance from the daughter but that it was difficult for her to bathe and dress Mr. O and that she felt she was nagging when she asked him to do his exercises. The physical therapist worked with Mrs. O to develop options for getting help. She helped Mrs. O prepare a list of people who had offered assistance and, with Mr. O, a list of tasks with which they needed help. They then matched the two lists. The physical therapist also suggested having an occupational therapist and an aide come to the home to train and assist Mr. O in bathing and dressing until he could, if possible, perform these activities independently. The daughter agreed to take Mrs. O grocery shopping while a friend came over to visit and assist Mr. O with his home exercise program. Mr. O saw this plan as desirable because he wanted to resume his role as head of the household.

By exploring family dynamics and networking options with friends and other health care professionals, the therapist was able to reduce care-giver stress and facilitate the client's independence. By viewing her role as assisting the client and family rather than managing a case and by ensuring that treatment goals were agreeable to all concerned, she enhanced motivation and, consequently, achievement of goals.

It is important that providers enlist the services of other health professionals in this networking process when appropriate. Many times there is overlap of professional roles in the home setting. Roles are not as clearly delineated as they may be in institutional settings.

CASE 4

The following case illustrates an effective team approach in home health. Mrs. G was a 67-year-old with Parkinson's disease, referred by her physician because of frequent "freezing spells" (sudden episodes when the muscles contract and make movement impossible) and falls. The treatment plan involved a home health nurse to monitor vital signs during a change in dose of Sinemet (a drug used to reduce parkinsonian symptoms). In addition, referral was made to a physical therapist to prescribe a walking device and a home exercise program and an occupational therapist to help improve transfers and home safety. All these professionals were to monitor medication effects. Mrs. G had to take her Sinemet every $1\frac{1}{2}$ hours but had difficulty remembering to do so because the schedule was confusing to her. The nurse and occupational therapist devised a medication planner for Mrs. G and provided her with a medication timer that would beep to remind her to take her medicine. The therapist set up the system, and once a week the nurse would fill the medication planner so that all needed medicine was ready to take. After several weeks the physical therapist noted that the new medication was facilitating mobility and ambulation, enabling Mrs. G to use a cane rather than a wheeled walker. The occupational therapist then began home safety and transfer training.

Multidisciplinary services may reinforce treatments, expediting progress. This is important in a health care system which limits reimbursement for specific disciplines.

THE PHYSICAL SETTING OF HOME HEALTH INTERVENTION

The actual home setting in which the older adult resides has significant impact on performance. During the treatment process, the clinician may recommend modifications of the home environment to help the patient achieve competency. By addressing safety, security, accessibility, and legibility,[3] the clinician can help maximize a client's performance in the home. To ensure safety, clinicians recommend modifications of the environment to accommodate for decreasing abilities and prevent accidents. It is helpful, for example, to apply adhesive to scatter rugs so that they do not slip or bunch up, causing patients to lose their balance; provide safety rails in the bathroom to assist with transfers into and out of the tub, shower, or on or off the commode; and instruct care givers in sterile techniques for wound care.

To enhance a sense of security, clinicians can empower clients by maximizing their abilities. For example, a client with rheumatoid arthritis may benefit from knowledge of joint protection principles to employ while she cooks a meal and performs housework. Energy conservation techniques may enable someone with postpolio syndrome to continue to engage in lawn care. A dysphagic client may be taught to swallow in a way that reduces fear of choking. By redeveloping skills, the chronically ill elder may gain confidence that reinforces ability to live in the community.

Clinicians also may adapt the environment for accessibility. This can be as simple as removing door sills or installing a second rail on the stairway, or it can include highly sophisticated and technical equipment such as environmental controls as described in Chapter 14 in this text. Accessibility may also be achieved by prescribing an appropriate wheelchair to make rooms in the home accessible and going out into the community possible for individuals with ambulation impairments. A bedside commode provides easy access to a toilet. It is often the responsibility of the medical social worker to identify resources, to secure needed equipment, and to counsel the client and family about emotional issues related to the illness or disability. In home health, however, other professionals may have to take on these responsibilities if a social worker is not available.

Legibility is another important concern. For the cognitively impaired, modern technology such as push-button telephones, modern faucet controls at sinks, or intercom systems may be confusing and frustrating. Frustration can be reduced by installing devices familiar, such as simple posted instructions, in words or pictures. Regular telephone calls from relatives or friends may provide organization and orientation.

The home environment can be a treatment modality[13] to facilitate performance. By grading the environment to gradually increase press, the physical environment may be utilized as a treatment modality to obtain goals of performance competence in the home environment.[14] *Press* refers to the demands the environment places on the individual. Too much demand may cause stress and too little may cause boredom. Lawton and Nahemow[15] state that environmental press must be congruent with the capacities of the individual if effective behavior is to occur. Therefore, treatment in home health must utilize grading, which involves selecting activities and environments that match the abilities of the individual and change as the individual's abilities change to ensure successful outcomes.[16,17] Treatment activities must be designed to promote optimal function without anxiety, while being interesting enough to prevent boredom.[14]

THE CHALLENGE OF EXCELLENCE IN HOME CARE

Home health care clearly requires interventions that differ from those of clinical settings. Significant benefits may accrue to the client and the family if such care is provided effectively. In order to do this, a number of factors must be considered. The *American Geriatrics Society's* (AGS) position statement *Home Care and Home Care Reimbursement*[18] advocates:

- Expanded home health care benefits under medicare and public and private insurance to include coverage of chronic and continuing care and home and homemaker services.
- Clear and explicit statement by third-party payers as to which home care services will be reimbursed and the conditions to be met for reimbursement.
- Shared responsibility among health care professionals, including physicians, for the outcomes of care in the home and active involvement of physicians in the leadership and direction of home care. Home care services that the physician determines to be critical to medical care should be allowed, unless disallowed by careful, expert review.
- Encouragement of home visits by physicians. Reimbursement should be commensurate with the professional's time and skills.
- Development of quality-assurance practices, as well as processes for accreditation and certification of home care providers, to safeguard clients, and allow for flexibility and diversity of services and providers.
- Enhanced medical education and clinical research in home care.

These positions were established in hopes of assuring the quality of home health intervention as it emerges as a key component in our nations' health and social service system. The high cost of institutional care and the preference by older adults to stay in their homes,[19] may lead the older adults and their families to utilize health care services even when these services are not covered by medicare or third-party reimbursement. Families are willing to assist in care of older family members in the home,[12] but they need help to do so as the complexity of older adults' conditions increases.

Several factors require continued examination. First among these is the quality of care. Applebaum and Phil-

lips[20] describe a federally funded study designed for two regional case-management agencies operating under Ohio's medicaid waiver home care program. The project included two major components: the development of standards of care and strategies to ensure that the service delivered would be provided according to those standards. An advisory committee of professionals and consumers developed standards for each of the key services. These were then incorporated into the formal contracts with cooperating agencies.

Following development of the standards, a mechanism was developed to ensure that services were being delivered according to the standards. Quality-assurance efforts included such activities as education of clients and their families, as consumers, about the tasks to be performed by in-home workers, completion of monthly random in-home audits for a sample of clients to assess the adequacy of the services received, completion of client status reports by supervisory home care staff to provide information on client and worker progress, and the use of a feedback log completed by case managers to systematically record provider problems or strengths. To monitor quality of care, such systems are essential.

Second, before home health intervention can begin, clinicians must be trained in and familiar with appropriate assessment tools. This chapter has discussed the importance of assessing the patient's culture, social systems, and the physical environment. Davidson[21] provides an overview of assessments that are currently available that measure environmental variables. These assessments provide clinicians with a systematic and theoretical approach to assisting the cultural, social, and physical environmental components to provide the optimum person-environment fit for their clients.

Third, health care professionals working in home care must define their role in the treatment process to the client and significant others. The consumer may believe that a medicare HHA provides supportive care rather than training when in fact the goal of care is to enable the individual or an informal care giver to accomplish the task on an ongoing basis.

Fourth, home health intervention relies on the clinical insight and resourcefulness of the clinician. The clinician must be responsive to various cultures and feel secure about working in settings that are unfamiliar to him or her. Effective referral skills are essential. The clinician must work within the resources of the patient. Because older adults are usually living on fixed incomes and adaptive equipment is usually not covered by Medicare or insurance carriers, clinicians must use resources from the patients' homes or use creative funding strategies.

Finally home health clinicians must prioritize goals because the number of therapy home visits is restricted by Medicare. In particular, it may be essential to focus on diminished self-esteem and self-confidence, which often result from disability. If these factors are not addressed, the client may regress as a result of lack of sense of purpose or personal effectiveness. A vicious cycle of decreasing ability and increasing dependence then begins.[22] Clinicians need to plan for discharge from the initial visit and at subsequent visits to avoid patients and families feeling abandoned when services end. Clients may need resource information for such activities as retraining in driving a car or use of public transportation, leisure activities (e.g., day care clubs for social activities, hobbies, or exercise programs) or Meals on Wheels. Hunt[23] discusses a case study in which a community wellness program provided continuity of patient care from a home care setting to a community setting to facilitate reintegration into the community. Information on community resources and programs can encourage preventive health care and promote self-reliance.

SUMMARY

Home health intervention supports independent living. Home health profes-

sionals focus on building clients' skills in the environment where they will perform them or on modifying the environment to enhance ability. Home health providers must determine what environmental characteristics act as barriers or facilitators of performance competence. These characteristics then must be modified or enhanced in a context that is congruent with the older adult's individual history, social context, lifestyle, and values, as well as those of the family.

This chapter addressed the complexity of home health intervention. As noted, there are many factors working for and against treatment in this setting. The home environment that was once friendly to the older adult may have become hostile due to physical or mental changes. A logical approach to the complexity of the environment as a system is to break it down into subsystems: culture, significant others, and physical attributes. After these subsystems are individually assessed, their interrelationships can be examined and adapted. Next, these subsystems are integrated into the whole system, the environment. Adapting is a lifetime process. Through the process of adapting the environment, clients may overcome performance problems that could lead to dependency or institutional care.

REVIEW QUESTIONS

1. *How does the home environment influence patient performance?*

2. *Why would the approach of defining the patient's environmental subsystems and applying this information to treatment bring a more successful outcome, than merely addressing the actual deficit from injury, disease, or aging?*

3. *Why or why not is the home environment an ideal treatment setting for the elderly patient?*

4. *Describe ways to use the environment as a treatment modality.*

5. *What societal obstacles exist that*

limit the effectiveness of home health care delivery?

6. Cite barriers to utilization of home health care often mentioned by older adults. How can practitioners overcome these barriers?

REFERENCES

1. Ruther, M and Helbing, C: Use and cost of home health agency services under Medicare. Health Care Financing Review 10:105–108, 1988.
2. Kielhofner, G, Burke, JP and Igi, CH: A model of human occupation, part 4. Assessment and intervention. American Journal of Occupational Therapy 34:777–778, 1980.
3. Lawton, MP: Environment and the need satisfaction of aging. In Carstensen, LL and Edelstein, BA (eds): Handbook of Clinical Gerontology. Pergamon Press, New York, 1987, pp 33–40.
4. Rowles, GD: A place to call home. In Carstensen, LL and Edelstein, BA (eds): Handbook of Clinical Gerontology. Pergamon Press, New York, 1987, pp 335–353.
5. Seamon, D: A Geography of the Lifeworld: Movement, Rest, and Encounter. St. Martin's Press, New York, 1979.
6. Brody, EM: A longitudinal look at excess disabilities in the mentally impaired aged. Journal of Gerontology 29:79–84, 1974.
7. Barris, R: Environmental interactions: An extension of the model of human occupation. American Journal of Occupational Therapy 36:637–644, 1982.
8. Rabick, SJ: Physical Disabilities Special Interest Group Newsletter, Sept 1990. (Available from American Occupational Therapy Association, Rockville, MD.)
9. Rubinstein, RL: The significance of personal objects to older people. Journal of Aging Studies 1:225–238, 1987.
10. Antonucci, TC and Jackson, JS: Social support, interpersonal efficacy, and health: A life course perspective. In Carstensen, LL and Edelstein, BA (eds): Handbook of Clinical Gerontology. Pergamon Press, New York, 1987, pp 291–311.
11. Wilcox, BL: Social support in adjusting to marital disruption, a network analysis. In Gottlieb, BH (ed): Social Networks and Social Support. Sage, Beverly Hills, 1981, pp 97–115.
12. Shanus, E: The family as a social support system in old age. Gerontologist 19:169–174, 1979.
13. Kiernat, JM: Environment: The hidden modality. Physical & Occupational Therapy in Geriatrics 2:3–12, 1982.
14. Levine, RE and Gitlin, LN: Home adaption for persons with chronic disabilities: An educational model. American Journal of Occupational Therapy 44:923–929, 1990.
15. Lawton, ML and Nahemow, L: Ecology and the aging process. In Eisdorfer, C and Lawton, MP (eds): The Psychology of Adult Development and Aging. American Psychological Association, Washington, DC, 1973, pp 619–673.
16. Cynkin, S: Occupational Therapy: Toward Health Through Activities. Little, Brown, Boston, 1979.
17. Mosey, AC: Activities Therapy. Raven Press, New York, 1973.
18. American Geriatrics Society Public Policy Committee: Home care and home care reimbursement. Journal of the American Geriatrics Society 37:1065–1066, 1989.
19. Keenan, JM and Fanale, JE: Home care: Past and present; problems and potential. Journal of the American Geriatrics Society 37:1076–1083, 1989.
20. Applebaum, R and Phillips, P: Assuring the quality of in-home care: The "other" challenge for long-term care. Gerontologist 30:444–450, 1990.
21. Davidson, H: Assessing environmental factors. In Christiansen, C and Baum, C (eds): Occupational Therapy Overcoming Performance Deficits. Slack, Thorofare, NJ, 1990, pp 427–454.
22. Kuypers, JA and Bengston, VL: Social breakdown and competence: A model of normal aging. Human Development 16:181–201, 1973.
23. Hunt, L: Continuity of care maximizes autonomy of the elderly. American Journal of Occupational Therapy 42:391–393, 1988.

*Practitioners, trained to think of "real"
disease entities, with natural histories
and precise outcomes, find chronic
illnesses messy and threatening.*

—KLEINMAN, *The Illness Narratives*,
Basic Books, New York, 1988.

Chapter

Rehabilitation

JUDY BACHELDER

OBJECTIVES

By the end of this chapter, readers will be able to:

1 Provide examples that support the value of rehabilitation for older adults.

2 Discuss factors that affect rehabilitation of older adults, including motivation, sense of control, and differences in learning.

3 Describe the rehabilitation process for the older adult, including assessment issues, rehabilitation potential, and the risks of deconditioning.

4 Describe the health care systems in which rehabilitation is provided, including rehabilitation centers, geriatric rehabilitation units, acute care, outpatient and home health settings, and nursing facilities.

A significant proportion of older adults develop physical disabilities. As with younger people, rehabilitation should be considered for all older adults with functional losses.[1] Although similar in some respects, their treatment differs in fundamental ways from the rehabilitation of younger people. Older persons are not simply young persons who have lived longer.[2] Significant physiological, psychological, and social changes occur during the aging process. This is especially true for the oldest-old (older than 75). In addition, the older person is more likely to have multiple medical problems and chronic illnesses and can experience higher degrees of disability from the inactivity imposed by the primary conditions.

Maintenance and restoration of function are best accomplished within a biopsychosocial framework by providers with expertise in rehabilitation and geriatrics. Effective geriatric rehabilitation should be based on a holistic, functional approach that reflects understanding of aging and age-related conditions.[3] Not only is it important to add rehabilitation to the mainstream of geriatric health care but it is also important to bring geriatrics into rehabilitation.[4]

The challenge facing health care providers is an older population with a wide variation in functional abilities despite similarities in age, diagnosis, and symptoms. The older person with *simply* an amputation or stroke does not exist.[5] For example, an 80-year-old man with a recent stroke may have underlying cardiac disease, diabetes, osteoarthritis, and vision and hearing impairments as well as depression. Rehabilitation may exacerbate his cardiovascular disease and musculoskeletal pain due to increased activity. Digestive problems may develop due to pain or antidepressant medications or dietary changes. He may have insomnia and anxiety caused by the unfamiliar environment or confusion from sensory deprivation. His depression or diminished endurance may interfere with therapeutic or routine activities. Angina and cardiac arrhythmias may be exacerbated by vigorous therapy and necessitate adjustment of medications. Insulin requirements may be dramatically altered as his activity level increases. In addition to the physical response to these conditions, he may have preexisting as well as stroke-related cognitive and perceptual deficits.

Despite the fact that many older adults are less independent upon admission to rehabilitation and have multiple problems, the degree of functional improvement that can be achieved is at least as great as with younger people.[6] Regardless of the patient's age, every opportunity should be provided for the older adult to gain maximal restoration of function and to prevent secondary disabilities. Age per se is not a contraindication to treatment, nor is rehabilitation potential equated with age. As Williams,[7] former Director of the National Institute on Aging, states, "Rehabilitation is a philosophy, an approach and a set of techniques. The technology and the approach exist; what is needed is a philosophy that utilizes them."

SPECIAL ASPECTS OF REHABILITATION OF THE OLDER PERSON

There is increasing awareness of the critical interrelationships, particularly for older adults, among physical, cognitive, social, and environmental factors in functional performance. There are few norms for performance abilities of older adults but many false expectations of their inabilities. However, when some basic characteristics of the older adult are understood, therapeutic encounters can be successful.

Attitudes of Health Professionals

Attitudes influence the care of the older adult within a rehabilitation program. In spite of evidence that older people respond to treatment, studies have found that rehabilitation professionals may be resistant to working with older people or feel that they are not as susceptible to rehabilitation efforts or that they are less worthy of treatment. Therapeutic programs may be provided that ignore the older person's capacity for self-determination and foster dependency. For example, Bart-Kvitek[8] found when hypothetical client descriptions, identical except for age, were provided to physical therapists to establish treatment plans, therapists were significantly less aggressive in their goal setting for individuals who were identified as 78 as opposed to 28 years old. Treatment objectives were found to be more aggressive for the younger person in ambulation endurance, general rehabilitation potential, return-to-work, and discharge living situations. Similar findings are reported in the literature for other health professionals.

Motivation for Rehabilitation

If the older person has internalized stereotypes of aging and believes that the disabling condition is a normal part of aging, she or he may not believe it is possible to benefit from rehabilitation. This "internalized ageism" may be interpreted by practitioners as "low motivation," and the person may be deemed a poor candidate for rehabilitation.

Difficulties in motivating older people are a frequent topic of discussion in rehabilitation settings. Kemp[9,10] presents a theory of motivation for elderly people that stresses four determining factors that influence an older person's choices. These factors are illustrated by the equation: Motivation $= (W \times E \times R)/C$. To determine an older person's motivation to perform in a therapeutic program, one must know:

- What that person wants W to get from rehabilitation. For example, an 85-year-old woman with a hip fracture might want to be discharged to her daughter's home. In order to live there, she must be able to ambulate within the house. A functional goal for this woman may be independent, short-distance ambulation with the aid of a walker.
- What the individual expects E as a result of the therapeutic intervention. If a task looks too difficult, she or he will believe it cannot be done. Older people have objectively lower physical abilities than younger people. If adjustments are not made in the intensity of rehabilitation treatment procedures to compensate for the limited capabilities common to the elderly population, then the older person will not receive enough reinforcement to persevere.
- What reinforcements or rewards R are likely to be encountered. Because behavior that does not result in some form of reward is not continued, all directed and self-generated attempts at an activity should be praised. These three elements — wants W, expectations E, and reinforcements R — are affected by the physical, economical, emotional, and social costs C to the individual. Risks, price, and any negative consequence of efforts will decrease the motivation of the individual. Motivation is stronger when the purpose

of rehabilitation is important to the person, when he or she believes it is attainable, and when a modicum of success can be obtained in a reasonable period of time.

Sense of Control

Hospitalized individuals have a diminished ability to control their environment.[11] In older persons a sense of restricted control over one area of life can lead to the erroneous belief that all self-assertion is futile.

Learned helplessness is a common reaction to hospitalization and has particular relevance to the older person who has experienced a loss in physical ability. Physically impaired older people tend to become socially isolated, which can result in a vicious cycle of depression, withdrawal, and functional decline.[12,13] Unfortunately, dependency is too often fostered in acute care settings, where it is part of the staff's routine to perform most self-care tasks for the impaired person. In these acute care environments, decisions are usually made by others for those who are hospitalized rather than providing the involved individual with options and choices and allowing for independent decision making. Consequently, elderly people who have multiple or prolonged periods of hospitalizations are vulnerable to a loss of control. To minimize or reverse the negative effects of external control, each individual should be encouraged to actively participate in the decisions that are involved during rehabilitation.[11]

Differences in Learning

Rehabilitation is a learning process that involves the acquisition of motor and sensory processing skills and abilities. The ability to learn does not diminish with age, but the ability to perceive and benefit from information is different from the younger person's ability.

Older people are more likely to have a successful rehabilitation outcome when the characteristics of the older learner are incorporated into the intervention. For example, many older persons have presbycusis, which results in changes in hearing acuity. The effects of these changes can be lessened by speaking more slowly. There may be cognitive changes that result in auditory processing deficits with subsequent difficulties in comprehension. Providing diagrams with written instructions facilitates communication and comprehension in these situations. Age-related visual changes and deficits necessitate increased illumination and the use of larger print or image enhancements with all printed copy. Handouts typically provided for exercises or adaptive techniques often have lettering that is too small to read and drawings that appear cluttered to the older person. Sensory aids, for example, glasses and hearing aids, should be worn when necessary during all therapeutic activities, including self-care training.

Some guidelines to enhance learning in the older adult during rehabilitation include:

- Recognize that over arousal or anxiety should be avoided. Elderly people are more susceptible to stress and have an exaggerated and prolonged state of arousal when stressed, which interferes with learning. Eisdorfer[14] found the performance of older people in a difficult learning task increased significantly when their anxiety was reduced.[9]
- Task relevance strengthens the association of new learning to preexisting knowledge or experiences. Evidence suggests that age-related deficits in performance may be attributed to the fact that older people have problems retaining new learning because it competes with previously learned information or established habits. New learning or techniques must build on previous ways of doing things. A familiar context for material to be learned can be established with a statement such as "What I want you to do is similar to. . . ."

- Pacing of tasks is very important. Older adults do their best when tasks are not timed but rather self-paced. Sensory impairment or cautiousness may cause the older person to sacrifice speed for the sake of accuracy, that is, older adults are more concerned with being right rather than fast during a timed performance test.
- Avoid distraction or interferences such as talking to the older adult who is attempting a new task.
- Provide cues to the individual or repetition of information to improve learning of new material. For maximal effect, use auditory and visual information together.
- New learning is retained longer if immediately practiced or put to use. For example, instruction in the use of a reacher should be followed by requesting that the individual practice with the reacher during lower-extremity dressing activities.
- The evaluation of the learning that has occurred is important. This can be accomplished through the use of questions, for example, by asking "Which foot are you going to put forward first?" or by asking the person to repeat instructions in his or her own words.[15]

ASSESSMENT FOR REHABILITATION

In the rehabilitation assessment of the older adult, the therapist must analyze the impact of the most recent health problem in combination with facts concerning the preadmission physical, mental, and social status. All of the preexisting and recent factors, physical, mental, emotional, and social, may contribute individually or in combination to result in the limitation of function.[16]

Information gathered about physical functioning includes an account of the individual's level of activity and exercise tolerance prior to the most recent incident, illness, or hospitalization. This information can then be combined with the present findings to assist in goal setting. For example, a reasonable goal for an older person who has become completely dependent following an episode of pneumonia would be to regain the preillness level of function.

Assessment of premorbid mental functioning includes questions about coping style, dementia, and depression. Since early dementia may often go unnoticed or be denied by family members, specific questions should be asked about memory, language, and behavior changes that may be indicative of a dementing illness or affective disorder. Schuman and associates[17] found people with severe dementia actually did worse in traditional rehabilitation because they function best in a highly structured environment where decision making and independent activities are not expected or encouraged.

Confusion can often cause an older adult to be excluded from a rehabilitation program. A confused state in an older adult may be a result of medications or sensory deprivation rather than a dementing illness.

The practitioner in geriatrics should be aware of specific age-related physiological changes to properly understand the assessment of disease status in older adults. These primary aging changes may significantly influence not only the presentation of disease but response to treatment and potential complications that often ensue. Knowledge of common changes that occur with aging is similarly essential to understanding the underlying mechanisms of functional deterioration secondary to disease, or treatment for the disease, and to formulate effective rehabilitation approaches[13] (see Fig. 19–1).

REHABILITATION OUTCOMES

Studies of geriatric rehabilitation outcome have shown that age, by itself, is not a determinant of rehabilitation outcome.[18] There is evidence to indicate that the shorter the delay from onset of the acute event to the initiation of rehabilitation results in higher levels of

Figure 19–1 Careful seating and posture evaluation is vital to prevention of excess disability. (Courtesy of Menorah Park Home for the Aged, Cleveland, Ohio.)

function and an earlier discharge from the hospital.[19] Generally, if the person is extremely frail or if mental impairments make the benefit of intensive rehabilitation questionable, a 2-week trial period of rehabilitation is recommended.[20]

TREATMENT APPROACHES AND CONSIDERATIONS FOR THE OLDER ADULT

The therapeutic program is designed to preserve or restore the highest degree of functional ability. Rehabilitation objectives must be very specific to the necessary functional outcomes as many older adults cannot tolerate extensive, nonessential activity. Treatment focused on nonspecific tasks that do not improve function wastes an older person's energy reserves.[21]

Deconditioning is a common problem that can delay, interrupt or undermine ability to participate in rehabilitation. *Deconditioning* can be defined as multiple changes in organ systems resulting in erosions in organ reserves.[13,22] The severity and the functional consequences of deconditioning are due to complex interactions between age-related changes, premorbid activity levels, medical conditions or concurrent illnesses, and protracted bed rest associated with the onset of the primary disability.

The debilitating sequelae of inactivity and disuse occur earlier and with greater severity in older adults.[13,23] Deconditioning may go unnoticed during the acute stage of recovery from an illness since patients do not stress their cardiopulmonary or muscular system.[1, 24]

Deconditioning can be recognized by an exaggerated heart rate or blood pressure response to activity, decreased muscle power, and decreased endurance. Individuals who are encouraged to maintain activities of daily living may lose abilities less rapidly than those who are helped with all activities.[25]

Treatment for deconditioning is oriented toward preventive measures during the acute stage and, if necessary, a general conditioning program prior to the initiation of rehabilitation. The level of conditioning program is based on the expected demands in the anticipated rehabilitation program or living environment.[22] The older adult's symptoms and vital signs must be monitored during conditioning activities. In severely deconditioned older adults, the time required to recover lost strength is estimated to be three times as long as the time they were immobilized.[18]

GERIATRIC REHABILITATION DELIVERY SYSTEMS

The many possible rehabilitation settings include acute and convalescent hospitals, inpatient rehabilitation centers, in-home rehabilitation, and outpatient therapy. Due to increasing pressure to discharge patients quickly after acute hospitalization, rehabilitation that might previously have taken place in the hospital must be done in the community. The type of rehabilitation program and the setting in which it takes place must be carefully matched to the individual's needs.

Acute Care

Perhaps the greatest unmet need for rehabilitation is in the acute hospital. The potential negative effects of acute hospitalization have been well documented.[25] In acute hospitals, functional disability often goes undetected.[26] Over half of the persons within acute care facilities have difficulties with activities of daily living, and the hospital environment itself may interfere with functional recovery. Patients being treated in acute care are less medically stable and have a lower tolerance for therapy.

Patients who receive rehabilitation-oriented therapy while in acute care have a greater ability to care for themselves, maintain balance, have decreased restlessness at night, have decreased incidence of incontinence, decreased confusion, and fewer referrals to nursing homes.[27,28] A number of hospitals are developing specialized centers with the creation of geriatric units, geriatric-orthopedic units,[29,30] stroke units,[31] and geriatric assessment units.[32-35]

Rehabilitation Hospitals and Geriatric Rehabilitation Units

A regular rehabilitation unit can accept only those older adults who meet the diagnostic criteria and have the rehabilitation potential as determined by medicare guidelines. In order to receive medicare reimbursement, individuals must undergo 3 hours per day of occupational, physical, or speech therapy and must make regular progress toward specific goals. In spite of the fact that older adults may begin rehabilitation programs as more functionally dependent, with multiple chronic problems, they may show greater improvements as a result of rehabilitation in the performance of activities of daily living than persons under 65 years of age.[36]

Geriatric rehabilitation units differ in that a geriatrician (physiatrist, neurologist, orthopaedist, or any other physician with specialized training in geriatrics) coordinates the team. The emphasis is on comprehensive treatment of functional problems through careful assessment of cognitive problems, medical stability, pharmacological issues, and psychiatric and physical features that give the older adult the special consideration for maximal functional recovery and quality of life.

Outpatient Centers and Day Health Centers

Outpatient centers provide a large portion of rehabilitation services. Their advantages are:

• Their access to a wider variety of practitioners and technology
• The stimulation for the individual of being around other people
• Their ability to serve more individuals with fewer practitioners.[1]

Home Health Care

Geriatric rehabilitation is well suited to the home, where the person's ability to function can be assessed in their own environment and carry-over of techniques taught can be accurately monitored. In one study, individuals cared for at home obtained the greatest degree of functional improvement from instruction in the use of assistive devices.[37] Rehabilitation provided in the home is a viable alternative for older adults who are discharged from the hospital before they are sufficiently recovered and lack the ability to participate in an inpatient or outpatient rehabilitation program. The individualized programming and familiar setting enable patients with cognitive or affective disabilities an optimal rehabilitation opportunity.

Nursing Facilities

The nursing facility is a viable and appropriate alternative to the acute rehabilitation center for selected persons. The cost is less than for acute care or intensive rehabilitation, and the results are satisfactory.[38] Candidates for rehabilitation in a nursing facility comprise two categories: (1) individuals who have been admitted for a specific purpose but are expected to go back to independent living and (2) individuals who are permanent nursing facility residents with multiple medical problems that contribute to disability, have an impact on the quality of life, and present a burden for the care giver.[39]

The first category includes elderly people who cannot participate in the 3 hours of rehabilitation programs per day required by Medicare or who are otherwise ineligible for intense rehabilitation due to the presence of associated problems, such as depression, incontinence, or dementing disorders, which interfere with compliance during therapeutic programs. About one-fifth of individuals treated in rehabilitation-oriented nursing facilities are able to return home.[40]

The nursing facility has some advantages over acute rehabilitation for geriatric persons. The pace is slower, lasting months versus weeks, and the focus is on the individual and his or her unique requirements for participation. Geriatric rehabilitation has been found to be both cost effective and successful at improving quality of life for the older adult when the rehabilitation is provided in the setting that is most appropriately matched to the individual's level of physical, social, and emotional needs.[41-46]

CASE EXAMPLES

To clarify some of the principles just described, two case examples are included here. They are typical of the kinds of situations common among older adults, including individuals who have had a postcerebrovascular accident and who have Parkinson's disease.

CASE 1

Mr. S is a 75-year-old man with the diagnosis of right *cerebrovascular accident* (CVA). He has a history of *chronic obstructive pulmonary disease* (COPD). Following acute care in the hospital, he was transferred to a nursing care facility where he has been residing for the past 3 months. Mr. S has received physical and occupational therapy since his CVA and has made progress in many of his therapeutic activities. He still requires moderate assistance to perform most mobility and self-care activities. His rehabilitation has been complicated by depression.

The above scenario is quite familiar to the therapist who is employed at a nursing care facility. Stroke is primarily a disease of older adults with three-fourths of all strokes occurring in persons over 65.[26] The existence of multiple diagnoses that can limit participation in therapeutic activities, such as the COPD in the preceding case study, is very common in the older adult with a CVA. The Framingham study[27] found 75 percent of persons with geriatric strokes have some form of heart disease, angina, COPD, congestive heart failure, or intermittent claudication.

The slow progress in regaining functional activities is also very common. Age-associated loss of neurons may limit or slow the recovery from brain injury, which may result from neuroplasticity and adversely affect the prognosis of recovery and complicate the post-stroke course in the older adult.[28]

Older persons with CVA may have a variety of affective disorders that may compound existing cognitive deficits resulting from dementia or depression. Estimates of the prevalence of depression following stroke range from 25 to 60 percent.[29,33] Treatment of depression remains a major unmet need among older adults with CVA primarily due to the lack of detection by the rehabilitation personnel. Consequently rehabilitation efforts are often thwarted.[34]

Early rehabilitation management of the elderly stroke person is both a preventative and a therapeutic effort.[35] Initially, preventing secondary disabilities and identifying individuals who need more intense rehabilitation are the goals. Early exercise and activity are directed toward reducing the frequency and severity of joint contractures, pressure sores, orthostatic hypotension, cardiovascular deconditioning, respiratory infections, deep venous thrombosis, depression, bowel and bladder problems, maintaining activities of daily living, and preventing malnutrition due to swallowing disorders. Once the individual's medical condition is reasonably stable, intensive rehabilitation can begin. Total medical stability is often elusive in the older person, and the risks of an intervention must be weighed against the risks of waiting. For older adults with multiple conditions or severe deconditioning, inpatient rehabilitation may be too strenuous, and better results may occur with outpatient, home health, or nursing care rehabilitation. Goals, however, are similar for all older adults: to assist the patient to adapt to the new disability, to minimize the impact that the stroke exerts on the lives of the individual and his or her family, to prevent complications, and to optimize function.

The benefits of stroke rehabilitation in general have been documented.[36] Lehman and Wieland[55] found no correlation between age and the amount of improvement of function gained during rehabilitation, but negative correlations were found with discharge function. Some studies have suggested that older adults with CVA require longer lengths of stay to achieve the same functional gains as their younger counterparts.[20,38-41] Age may negatively affect the severity of the initial stroke but not the ability to benefit from rehabilitation. In concert with endogenous improvement, rehabilitation efforts following stroke in the elderly are cost effective and lead to higher functional levels.[37]

CASE 2

Mrs. K is a 70-year-old with the diagnosis of Parkinson's disease. She is living at home with her husband and is able to care for herself with his assistance. Her limited movement and mobility appears to be caused by not only the bradykinesia, tremors, and rigidity common in Parkinson's disease but also from her moderately severe osteoporosis. She has a fixed thoracic kyphosis and a past history of multiple fractures of her vertebrae.

Parkinson's disease is the most common degenerative disease in the elderly resulting in impaired mobility.[1] The peak incidence of Parkinson's diseases is between the ages of 60 and 69 years. The physical treatment of Parkinson's disease can be considered an example of "preventive" geriatric rehabilitation where the individual is trained in techniques to counter the effects of the disease. Treatment goals fall into four categories: those that counteract the effects of rigidity, others that involve preventing weakness through disuse by increasing and maintaining fine and gross motor function, those that attempt to improve speech and swallowing musculature, and those that involve maintaining or developing an environment supportive to the individual and encouraging socialization.[44]

The problems, vertebral fractures, spinal deformities and chronic pain, which this individual experienced because of osteoporosis, are common to postmenopausal women. Osteoporosis can result in decreased mobility and functional disability.[63] Programs that emphasize education, social activities, and exercise result in improved well-being, stamina, mobility, and pain tolerance.

SUMMARY AND CONCLUSIONS

Older adults in need of rehabilitation are a heterogeneous group of people with widely differing functional status, severity of illness, expectations of medical therapy, and psychosocial needs.[47] Age alone is not a barrier to successful rehabilitation, although it may alter the presentation of impairments, require modification of treatment interventions and approaches, and be delivered across a number of settings in the long-term care system. When geriatric rehabilitation is designed to enhance functional abilities and support care givers, it is cost effective and leads to fewer hospitalizations, greater levels of independence, and lower mortality.[13,48]

REVIEW QUESTIONS

1. *In which ways is rehabilitation different with older adults than with younger individuals?*

2. *What factors must be assessed in developing a rehabilitation plan for an older adult?*

3. *What is the main goal of rehabilitation with the elderly?*

4. *What factors in acute care have the potential to complicate the course of rehabilitation?*

5. *Under what conditions is medicare coverage available to elderly people for rehabilitation services?*

6. *What are the advantages of nursing facilities in providing rehabilitation for older adults?*

REFERENCES

1. Brummel-Smith, K: Rehabilitation. In Cassel, CK, et al (eds): Geriatric Medicine. Springer-Verlag, New York, 1990, p 125.
2. Kemp, B and Kleinplatz, F: Vocational rehabilitation of the older worker. American Journal of Occupational Therapy 39:322, 1985.
3. Wedgewood, J: The place of rehabilitation in geriatric medicine: An overview. Int Rehabil Med 7:107, 1985.
4. Kemp, B, Brummel-Smith, K and Ramsdell, JW (eds): Geriatric Rehabilitation. Little, Brown, Boston, 1990, p xi.
5. Brummel-Smith, K: Training health professionals. Generations 8:47, 1984.
6. Ruff, GE: R & T Center projects report preliminary results. Research and Training Center of Rehabilitation of Elderly Newsletter 3:2, 1987.
7. Williams, TF (ed): Rehabilitation in the Aging. Raven Press, New York, 1984, p 4.
8. Barta-Kvitek, SD, et al: Age bias: Physical therapists and older patients. Journal of Gerontology 41:706, 1986.
9. Kemp, B: Motivational dynamics in geriatric rehabilitation: Toward a therapeutic model. In Kemp, B, Brummel-Smith, K and Ramsdell, JW (eds): Geriatric Rehabilitation. Little, Brown, Boston, 1990, p 295.
10. Kemp, B: Psychosocial and mental health issues in rehabilitation of older persons. In

Brody, S and Ruff, G (eds): Aging and Rehabilitation. Springer, New York, 1986, p 122.

11. Aasen, N: Interventions to facilitate personal control. J Gerontolog Nurs 13:20, 1987.

12. Rodin, J and Langer, EJ: Long-term effects of a control-relevant intervention with the institutionalized aged. J Pers Soc Psychol 35:897, 1977.

13. Clark, GS and Murray, PK: Rehabilitation of the geriatric patient. In DeLisa, JA, et al. (eds): Principles and Practices of Rehabilitation Medicine. Springer, New York, 1988, p 410.

14. Eisdorfer, L: Arousal and performance: Experiments in verbal learning and a tentative theory. In Talland, GA (ed): Psychological Practices with the Physically Disabled. Columbia University Press, New York, 1962, p 362.

15. Bowling, B: Effective Patient Education Techniques for Use with the Aging Patient. Center for Learning Resources, University of Kentucky, Lexington, 1981.

16. Granger, C: The decision to rehabilitate. Generations 8:9, 1984.

17. Schuman, JE, et al: Geriatric patients with and without intellectual dysfunction: Effectiveness of a standard rehabilitation program. Arch Phys Med Rehabil 62:612, 1981.

18. Masciocchi, C, et al: Rehabilitation outcome: The age factor. Paper presented at the 110th annual Meeting of the American Public Health Association. Montreal, Canada, Nov 13–18, 1982.

19. Novack, TA, et al: Stroke onset and rehabilitation: Time lag as a factor in treatment outcome. Arch Phys Med Rehabil 65:316, 1984.

20. Steinberg, FU: Rehabilitating the older stroke patient: What's possible? Geriatrics 41:85, 1986.

21. Bottomly, JM: Maintaining strength and flexibility in elderly clients. Focus Geriatric Care Rehab 1:1, 1988.

22. Seibens, H: Deconditioning. In Kemp, B, Brummel-Smith, K and Ramsdell, JW (eds): Geriatric Rehabilitation. Little, Brown, Boston, 1990, p 177.

23. Bortz, WM: Disuse and aging. JAMA 248:1203, 1982.

24. Avorn, J and Langer, E: Induced disability in nursing home patients: A controlled trial. J Am Geriatr Soc 30:397, 1982.

25. Stell, K, et al: Iatrogenic illness on a general medicine service at a university hospital. N Engl J Med 304:638, 1981.

26. Warshaw, GA, et al: Functional disability in the hospitalized elderly. JAMA 248:847, 1982.

27. Ostrow, P, et al: Functional outcomes and rehabilitation: An acute care field study. J Rehabil Res Dev 26:17, 1989.

28. Jackson, MF: Geriatric rehabilitation on an acute-care medical unit. J Adv Nurs 9:441, 1984.

29. Sainsberg, R, et al: An orthopaedic geriatric rehabilitation unit: The first two years experience. N Engl J Med 99:583, 1986.

30. Murphy, PJ, et al: The benefits of joint orthopaedic-geriatric rehabilitation. Age Ageing 16:273, 1987.

31. Feigenson, JS, Gitlow, HS and Greenberg, SD: The disability oriented rehabilitation unit: A major factor influencing stroke outcome. Stroke 10:5, 1979.

32. Applegate, WB, et al: A geriatric rehabilitation and assessment unit in a community hospital. J Am Geriatr Soc 31:206, 1983.

33. Cardoc-Davies, TH, Dixon, GS and Campbell, AJ: Benefit from admission to geriatric assessment and rehabilitation unit. Discrepancy between health professional and client perception of improvement. J Am Geriatr Soc 37:25, 1989.

34. Rubenstein, LZ, et al: Effectiveness of a geriatric evaluation unit. N Engl J Med 311:1664, 1984.

35. Rubenstein, LZ, et al: Improved survival for frail elderly inpatients on a geriatric evaluation unit (GEU): Who benefits? J Clin Epidemiol 41:441, 1988.

36. Greant, P and Van den Brande, P: Amputation in elderly and high-risk vascular patients. Ann Vasc Surg 4:288, 1990.

37. Liang, MH, et al: Evaluation of comprehensive rehabilitation services for elderly homebound patients with arthritis and orthopedic disability. Arthritis Rheum 27:258, 1984.

38. Sutton, MA: 'Homeward bound': A minimal care rehabilitation unit. Br Med J 293:319, 1986.

39. Osterweil, D: Geriatric rehabilitation in the long-term care institutional setting. In Kemp, B, Brummel-Smith, K and Ramsdell, JW: Geriatric Rehabilitation. Little, Brown, Boston, 1990, p 347.

40. Reed, JW and Gessner, JE: Rehabilitation in the extended care facility. J Am Geriatr Soc 27:325, 1979.

41. Strax, TE and Ledebur, J: Rehabilitating the geriatric patients: Potential and limitations. Geriatrics 34:99, 1979.

42. Keith, RA, Breckenridge, K and O'Neil, WA: Rehabilitation hospital patient characteristics from the hospital utilization project system. Arch Phys Med Rehabil 58:260, 1977.

43. Liem, PH, Chernoff, R and Carter, WJ: Geriatric rehabilitation unit: A 3-year outcome. J Gerontol 41:44, 1986.

44. Adler, MK, Brown, CC and Acton, P: Stroke rehabilitation: Is age a determinant? J Am Geriatr Soc 28:499, 1980.

45. Parry, F: Physical rehabilitation of the old, old patient. J Am Geriatr Soc 31:482, 1983.

46. Kozin, F, et al: The reflex sympathetic dystrophy syndrome. Am J Med 60:321, 1976.

47. Goldberg, G: Principles of rehabilitation of the elderly stroke patient. In Dunkle, RE and Schmidley, JW (eds): Stroke in the Elderly. Springer, New York, 1987, p 103.

48. Gresham, GE, et al: Epidemiologic profile of long term stroke disability: The Framingham study. Arch Phys Med Rehabil 60:487, 1979.

Why do you stay?
My children asked;
This house is far too big;
But they don't seem to realize,
That this is where I have to be;
Each room is a reminder of the past,
When we were once a family;
Each one of you an imprint made,
Of your own personality;
So when you left to go your way,
A part of you remained;
Another house would have no warmth,
A stranger it would be;
So while I can, it's here I'll stay,
With all its memories.

—DOROTHY LAU MACHOLL[1]

Chapter

Activity-Based Intervention in Nursing Home Settings

MARY MACHOLL KAUFMANN

OBJECTIVES

By the end of this chapter, readers will be able to:

1 Describe the needs of elderly residents living in nursing homes.

2 Describe the composition and role of the interdisciplinary team.

3 Identify the types and range of activities that should comprise a nursing home activity program.

4 Describe activities that support and stimulate nursing home residents to attain, retain, or maintain their highest practical physical, mental, and psychosocial well-being.

5 Identify creative and humanistic methods to meet the needs and interests of nursing home residents through a comprehensive and diverse program of activities.

A home is far more than a roof over one's head. It is a place "profoundly connected with who one is and how one expresses this sense of self."[2] Home is also all the memories associated with self, family, and friends. A nursing home can never hope to replace the aged person's real home. It can, however, provide a "homelike" environment and caring professionals that foster growth and independence, support personal freedom and choice, and promote successful adjustment and reengagement with life for elderly people who live within its walls. Within this caring environment, pleasurable memories can be developed.

The nursing home is an essential component of the continuum of care in the United States. The comprehensive services and protective environment of the nursing home are required for many elderly people because of impaired function resulting from chronic illness and the lack of appropriate support systems in the community.[3] One service integral to quality of life for nursing home residents is an activities program. The richness and diversity of well planned and executed activities offered within this program assist the aged person to focus on living rather than surviving.

The purpose of this chapter is to describe the importance of activities in the nursing home relative to maximizing function and enhancing quality of care and life. The chapter is divided into two sections. First, the concept of a nursing home as a community within a community is presented. The physical and human components of the nursing home are discussed. In the discussion on the physical component, *nursing home* is defined and the importance of creating a homelike environment is considered. The human component includes discussions of demographic data about elderly nursing home residents and the composition, characteristics, and tasks of the interdisciplinary team often found in nursing homes. The second section focuses on the activities that should occur in the nursing home. The concept of activities is defined, the various types of activities in a comprehen-

sive and diverse program are discussed, and the implementation and evaluation of an activities program are presented. Lastly, since purposeful activities are such an important but often underappreciated function within a nursing home, the value of activities in maximizing quality of life and maintaining the nursing home resident at the highest level of function is explored.

THE NURSING HOME: A COMMUNITY WITHIN A COMMUNITY

The Physical Component

Nursing homes have become the most populated health care institutions in the United States. From 1954 to 1985, the number of nursing homes increased 111 percent, from 9000 to 19,100 facilities.[4,5] There are twice as many nursing homes as general hospitals in the United States and nearly 50 percent more nursing home beds than hospital beds.[6-8] The continued growth of nursing home care is anticipated because of population aging, federal, and state reimbursement policies, and the advent of long-term care health insurance.

DEFINITION

A *nursing home* is defined as a "residential long-term care facility that provides 24-hour care, skilled nursing care, and personal care on an inpatient basis.[4] The U.S. Department of Health and Human Services[5] defines nursing homes more specifically as facilities:

> with three or more beds that provide to adults who require it either nursing care or personal care (such as help with bathing, correspondence, walking, eating, using the toilet, or dressing) and/or supervision over such activities as money management, ambulation, and shopping. Facilities providing care solely to the mentally retarded and mentally ill are excluded. A nursing home may be either free standing or a distinct unit of a larger facility.

Since 1950, states have licensed nursing homes "under their police power to protect the health, safety, and welfare of the public." Each state determines its definition of a nursing home. In this chapter, however, a nursing home is defined as a community of frail and/or disabled individuals, many of whom are over 60 years of age, who live together within a facility because they require 24-hour care and services to attain, retain, or maintain their health and well-being.

THE NURSING HOME AS "HOME"

The nursing home is both a "home" and a treatment center. It is a challenge to create a homelike environment within which quality care can be provided to a varied group of frail and disabled individuals. One way in which this can be achieved is through creation of a physical environment that is clean and comfortable and a psychosocial environment that supports residents' dignity and self-determination, sense of well-being, and feelings of self-worth. To create such an environment, staff must encourage residents to be active in decision making, offer choices to residents in care and services, and see themselves in a supportive role.

In a homelike environment, the staff are more likely to view the resident as healthy. *Health* is defined as the ability of residents to perform at their highest functional capacity, despite the presence of age-related changes, dependency needs, and chronic illnesses.[9] Health encompasses not only physiological, psychological, and social functioning but also considers the quality of life of the residents.[10] The resident's ability to attain, retain, or maintain health is significantly influenced by the physical and psychosocial environment. There is a growing body of literature that demonstrates a strong relationship between functional ability, environment, and health.[11,12]

The Human Component

THE NURSING HOME RESIDENT

While only 5 percent of the elderly population lives in nursing homes at any one time,[5] 40 percent of the elderly population can expect to live in a nursing home at some time;[13] 25 percent of individuals who live beyond 65 will spend the last days of their lives in a nursing home.[13] The average nursing home resident in 1986 was female, 79 years of age, not married, and dependent in at least four ADL.[5]

Upon admission, nursing home residents are classified as either "short-stay" or "long-stay" residents.[4] The short-stay residents require intensive nursing care and rehabilitation therapy and are usually discharged within 3 to 6 months of admission. Long-stay residents are considered permanent residents of the facility. It is for these residents that the nursing home becomes a home and the activities program becomes an integral service to enhancing quality of life.

THE INTERDISCIPLINARY TEAM

In the nursing home, the interdisciplinary team usually includes but is not limited to the physician, registered or licensed practical nurse, nurse's aide, physical and occupational therapists and assistants, social worker, recreational therapist, dietitian, pharmacist, and administrator (Fig. 20–1).[14,15] With so many member on the team, working together can be problematic. Communication, competence, collaboration, and creativity are key ingredients to maintaining a well-functioning team.[16] The needs of the resident should determine which discipline assumes the leadership role on the team at any particular time and which disciplines will have primary involvement in care.[15] For example, a female resident, newly admitted to a nursing home following the death of her spouse and caretaker, has emotional needs surrounding bereavement, loss, relocation, and adjustment.

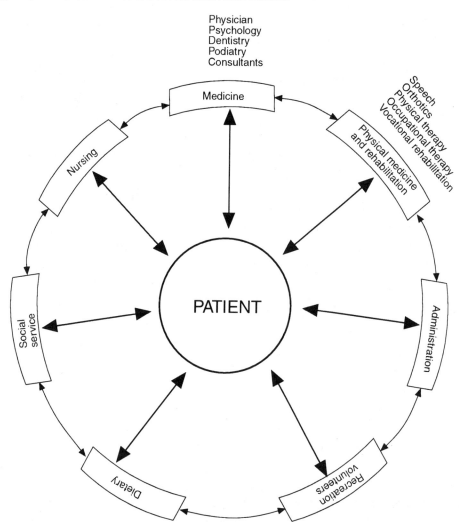

Figure 20–1 The team model. (From Lefton E and Lefton M: Health care and treatment for the chronically ill: Toward a conceptual framework. Journal of Chronic Diseases, vol 32, 1979, Pergamon Press, with permission.

In this situation, the social worker may assume the dominant role. Following adjustment to the home and resolution of loss, the resident's needs for socialization might place the recreational therapist in the dominant role. In another example, a resident with a recent *cerebrovascular accident* (CVA) has intensive physical care needs that require interventions from the physician, rehabilitation therapists (physical, occupational, and speech), and the nurse predominantly.

Most professional members of the interdisciplinary team in nursing homes are not consistently present for a variety of reasons. The physician is minimally involved in meetings with the interdisciplinary team unless the home is a nonprofit county or teaching nursing home. Nursing home regulations require that the physician only see the resident at least once every 30 days for the first 90 days after admission. Visits are then required at every 60 to 90 days thereafter. The home's medical director can represent the attending physician at interdisciplinary care planning meetings, although in practice this is rare.

Other professional team members, such as occupational therapists or social workers, may be consultants hired on a contractual basis. They may delegate major functions, such as attending interdisciplinary meetings, to less trained individuals who may or may not have the essential skills to enhance interdisciplinary care planning. For example, the *consultant occupational therapist* (OTR/L) completes the comprehensive assessment and develops the initial plan of care for a resident, while the *occupational therapy assistant* (COTA) implements the plan of care and participates at team meetings. The consultant OTR/L may be in the facility only for 1 or 2 days a week providing supervision for the COTA who is actually providing care on a daily basis.

The *Institute of Medicine* (IOM) recommends that the resident be a member of the interdisciplinary team.[4] The resident's spouse or family, guardian, friend, minister, or other interested party, such as an ombudsman, may also be part of the team. The interdisciplinary team, therefore, is best defined as a group of individuals including the resident, interested individuals from the community, and the home's health professionals (Table 20–1).

THE TASK OF THE TEAM

The team works together to develop, implement, and evaluate a plan of care that is based on the needs, strengths, and wishes of the resident. This is a complex task. In 1983, the *Health Care*

Financing Administration (HCFA) asked the IOM to conduct a 2-year study of federal regulations affecting quality of care and life for residents in nursing homes.[4] The regulatory criteria for nursing homes were revised by HCFA based on the recommendations of the IOM study.[17] In the final report from this landmark study, quality of life for residents was identified as one of the most important outcome goals for the interdisciplinary team.[4] Moreover, the report stated that the achievement of this goal was extremely complex because:

> Providing consistently high quality care in nursing homes to a varied group of frail, very old residents, many of whom have mental impairments as well as physical disabilities . . . requires that the functional, medical, social, and psychological needs of residents be individually determined and met by careful assessment and care planning—steps that require professional skill and judgment.[4]

The provision of comprehensive quality care for residents was identified as another important outcome goal for the nursing homes' interdisciplinary team by the IOM study.[4] The study emphasized that quality of life of residents is intimately related to the quality of the team. The regulatory criteria provide the interdisciplinary team with an incentive and firm foundation upon which to construct and evaluate the resident's *plan of care* (POC). A four-step process can be used in care planning. The steps are (a) assessment of resident needs, strengths, and wishes; (b) development of the POC; (c) implementation of the POC; and (d) evaluation of the POC.[18] This process is continuous; thus, the resident's plan of care is always subject to revisions based upon the team's assessment of the changing needs, strengths, and wishes of the resident.

In summary the interdisciplinary team is responsible for care planning based upon established standards. The process begins with input from the resident as an active, participating team member. The plan of care is based upon a comprehensive assessment of the functional, medical, psychological, and social needs of the resident. The out-

TABLE 20–1 **The Expanded Interdisciplinary Team in the Nursing Home Setting**		
Professional	**Individual**	**Community**
Members of the health care team of the nursing home	Resident or durable power of attorney	Spouse Family Minister Ombudsman Friend

come goals of this planning initiative for nursing home residents are improved quality of care and quality of life and enhancement of resident rights.

ACTIVITIES IN THE NURSING HOME

Even though improved quality of care and quality of life are goals addressed by all members of the team, the amount of responsibility for each goal varies by discipline. Several standards in the revised regulations for nursing homes, such as residents' rights, residents' behavior and facility practices, quality of life, and quality of care contain relevant information for development of an activity program. However, criteria specifically related to activities are found primarily in the quality-of-life standard.[17] This standard contains criteria that address:

- Respect
- Dignity
- Choice
- A comfortable, homelike environment
- The provision of opportunities for the resident to interact with the community

In this section, the definition, categories, and value of activities designed to maximize quality of life and maintain function of nursing home residents are presented. Planning, operating, and evaluating a program of activities are also discussed, as are the roles of various staff members in accomplishing these actions.

Definition of Activities

Activities, broadly defined, are all interactions in which the nursing home resident is engaged.[19,20] The *activity program*, as defined by Foster,[21] is a diverse and comprehensive collection of programming based on the interests, needs, and former lifestyles of the residents. This program is the "vehicle through which the resident can estab-

lish meaning in his life by providing opportunities for social interaction, emotional release, and mental stimulation.[21] Weiss[22] defines an activity program as a:

> written planned schedule of individual and group activities . . . staffed and equipped to provide an opportunity for the residents to engage in healthful, satisfying activity based on their individual needs and interests. The program is designed to create a stimulating living environment which will promote the highest level of function, but not necessarily to correct or remedy a disability.

McLaughlin[22] introduces the concepts of therapy, leisure, and choice into the definition of activities and further defines an activities program as a form of therapy that assists the resident to "transform endless empty hours into meaningful leisure. Therapy should be voluntary, pleasurable, experiential, and constructive for the resident.

Planning a Comprehensive, Diverse Activity Program

The philosophy of an activity program is to enhance quality of life for nursing home residents by providing opportunities for participation in healthful, satisfying activities based on the residents' backgrounds, interests, and needs. An activity program is based upon and satisfies the human needs of the residents and supports their health and function.[3,21,22] Healthy functioning is supported by an activity program if it provides opportunities for residents to engage in self-care, work, and leisure, which are the three main spheres of human activity.

The recreational therapist is responsible for planning a program of activities. The process begins with a comprehensive assessment of the nursing home residents' needs, strengths, and interests. The development of individualized activity plans of care for each resident follows. In this section, the planning of a comprehensive and diverse program is presented.

SATISFACTION OF NEEDS: WORK AND LEISURE

The needs of the resident related to work and leisure determine the content of this component of an activity program. Kaplan, as cited in Ebersole and Hess,[13] defines *leisure* "as relatively self-determined, psychologically pleasant activities experienced as leisure by participants and providing opportunities for recreation, personal growth, and service to others." *Work*, on the other hand, may be defined simply as all those activities not considered to be leisure activities for which one may receive renumeration. In a comprehensive activity program, both types of activities are available.

Residents have the right to work for the facility provided that they choose to perform the service as defined in the revised federal regulations for nursing homes.[17] Resident work includes paid work as well as voluntary services. If the resident participates in work for renumeration, compensation must be at or above prevailing rates.[24] *Prevailing rate* is defined as the "wage paid to non-disabled workers in the community surrounding the facility for essentially the same type, quality, and quantity of work requiring comparable skills.[24] In addition, the interdisciplinary team determines the medical appropriateness of the resident's desire for work.[24] Lastly, all resident work activities are documented in the resident's plan of care by the recreational therapist.

Many residents derive particular satisfaction from work activities, as the need to feel productive or to do for others may be an important value for them. Assisting with tasks around the nursing home, participating in a sheltered workshop, or making items to sell for income or to contribute to a charitable organization are all activities that can provide the resident with an opportunity to make a contribution to others or derive a sense of personal satisfaction.

Six categories of leisure activities[21] are:

1. Physical
2. Social
3. Spiritual
4. Intellectual
5. Creative
6. Recreational

Fleischmann and VanHala[25] add cultural activities as an additional category. Ebersole and Hess[13] identify and define conceptual models of leisure, namely:

- *Humanistic:* An end in itself, a celebration of life
- *Therapeutic:* An instrument of control and healing
- *Quantitative:* Free time after work is done
- *Institutional:* Compartmentalized —religious, marital, educational, or political leisure
- *Epistemologic:* Activities that provide meaning and aesthetic appreciation.

The needs of nursing home residents and their individualized activity plans determine the content of the leisure component of the activities program.

A comprehensive and diverse activity program includes a balance of activities in the following areas:

- Stimulating or restful
- Male or female
- Expressive or instrumental
- Group, one to one, or solitary
- Active or passive resident participation
- Ambulatory or wheelchair dependent
- In-facility or out-of-facility
- Introverted or extroverted
- Activities for intellectually intact or intellectually impaired residents
- Work, leisure, and self-care activities.[13,21,22]

MAINTENANCE OF FUNCTION: SELF-CARE

Foster[21] and Weiss,[22] recommend that activities be developed to assist residents to attain, retain, or maintain their highest level of function. To accomplish this objective, the recreational therapist works in concert with other members of the interdisciplinary team, such as the nurse, occupational therapist, physical therapist, and social worker. Weiss[22] identifies categories of activities to facilitate maintenance of the following functions related to self-care: memory, orientation, interaction, decision making, sensory, self-concept, and mobility. Examples of programming in the area of self-care include fitness programs[26-28]; walking programs[29-31]; wheelchair karate[32]; movement therapy[33,34]; mnemonics[37]; reminiscence activities[38]; and the provision of memory cues and sensory adjuncts to enhance learning, such as labels on drawers or pictures by objects.[39] Weiss[22] points out that the activity program must be differentiated from the rehabilitation program in which activities are designed to restore function preparatory to return to community living.

Examples of activities are provided in Table 20–2.[40-58] The reader may refer

TABLE 20–2 **Innovative Activities**	
Category of Activity	**Example of Innovative Activity**
Satisfaction of Needs	
Work or service	Resident Volunteer Program[40]
	The Good Samaritan Program[41]
Leisure	
Physical	Wheelchair Karate[32]
	Tai Chi[42]
Social	English Handbells[43]
	Adding Life to the Place[44]
Spiritual	Meditation[13,42]
	Remembrance Group[45]
Intellectual	Mental Aerobics[46]
Creative	Wheelchair Painting[47]
	Art Therapy[48]
Recreation	Outdoor Day Camp[49]
Culture	Culture Identity through Poetry Group[50]
Maintenance of Function: Self-Care	
Mobility	Rehab Lunch Program[51]
	Awards Ceremony[44]
	Movement and Drama Therapy[33,34]
Memory	Mnemonics Instruction[37]
	Reminiscence for the Alzheimer's Patient[38]
Orientation	Day Room Program[52]
	Remotivation Therapy[53]
Interaction	Intergenerational Groups[13]
	Open the Gate Ritual Ceremony[34]
Decision making	Grievance Committee[54] Resident Councils
Sensory	Eclectic Group Program[55]
	Poetry Workshops on Senses[56]
	Plush Animals[57]
	Music Therapy[58]
Self-concept	Queen for a Day[42]
	Journal Writing[42]

to the references noted in the table for further information on specific activities.

Implementing and Evaluating an Activity Program

GETTING STARTED

The heterogeneity of nursing home residents and their unique care and service needs makes it difficult to prescribe specific requirements for developing, implementing, and evaluating an activities program.[4] Nursing home administrators, however, are obligated to provide a sufficient number of activity personnel to meet the specific care and service needs of the residents as defined in the newly created standards in federal regulations: quality of life, quality of care, and residents' rights.[24] The first step in getting started with an activities program is hiring an activity director.

The Activity Director

A program of activities is planned, directed, and evaluated by the activity director. Even though this position was required in nursing homes since the early 1970s, the requirements for the activities director were minimal.[59] In 1989, however, the criteria for this position were strengthened. According to the revised federal criteria,[24] the activities program may be directed by a professional who has educational preparation specifically related to meeting residents' needs for work and leisure. An activity program, according to the revised regulations for nursing homes, must be directed by a professional who meets at least one of the following criteria:

- Is a qualified therapeutic recreation therapist
- Is a qualified occupational therapist or occupational therapy assistant
- Has 2 years of experience in a social or recreational program within the last 5 years in a patient activities program in a health care setting
- Has completed a training course approved by the state[59]

Shortly after the guidelines were published by HCFA, a recommendation was presented to HCFA to amend the regulations to include a fifth criterion for the activities program director that states: an activity program may also be directed by a qualified activity professional.[60]

The disciplines of activities and therapeutic recreation are new and evolving professions. As the need for activity professionals and therapeutic recreation specialists increases, additional educational programs leading to degrees or certificates in therapeutic and leisure activities are being developed in colleges and universities.[59] Individuals graduating from these programs possess basic knowledge and competency in the following areas: (a) conducting various activities and administrative skills in setting up and running a program of activities: (b) human relations including community, family, and volunteer relations; (c) management; and (d) normal and abnormal aging changes and the physical, mental, and psychosocial aspects of aging.[59]

In addition to the development of educational programs that prepare activity professionals, national and state organizations for activity professionals and recreational therapists have been founded to promote standards, to identify the scope and realm of the professions, and to provide support and educational opportunities.[60] The *National Association of Activity Professionals* (NAAP) is the only national organization, however, that represents activity professionals who work exclusively with the geriatric population in various settings.[60] In 1989, HCFA acknowledged the *National Certification Council for Activity Personnel* (NCCAP) as the recognized accrediting body for activity professionals.[60] In 1990, three national organizations, the *National Therapeutic Recreation Society* (NTRS), the *American Therapeutic Recreation Association* (ATRS), and NAAP began cooperative legislative efforts to enhance care and services to individuals through activities. At the state level, efforts are also underway to standardize criteria for different levels of activity personnel. In

Ohio, the *Resident Activity Personnel* (RAP) organization has developed four levels for activity personnel.[59] The *activity leader* is defined as a paraprofessional with limited experience and education in activities who works under the supervision of a professional activities person. The three professional categories of activities personnel are defined by both educational preparation and experience in conducting activities. The defined categories are as follows:

- An activity director has a minimum of an associate's degree and at least 2 years of experience.
- An activity coordinator has a bachelor's degree and at least 3 years of experience directing activities.
- An activity consultant has a bachelor's, master's, or doctoral degree in activities and at least 4 years of experience.[59]

The Activity Staff

Following the development of the activities program by the activity director, the second major step in implementing the planned program is to hire and train qualified staff and community and resident volunteers. The numbers of staff depend on the number of nursing home residents and the care and service needs of this population. In addition, the number of paid activity staff depends on the number of resident and nonresident volunteers as well as the number of interdisciplinary team members who collaborate with the activity director in conducting various activities and functions within the nursing home.

Program Evaluation

The effectiveness of a program of activities cannot be taken for granted. Systematic self-reviews, using a holistic approach to programming, should be undertaken on a regular basis by activity staff and coordinated by the activity director in order to:

- Evaluate whether or not the physical, mental, psychosocial, religious, and cultural needs of the residents are truly being met

- Determine residents' preferences for offered activities
- Review the level of participation among the residents in various activities

Structure, process, and/or outcome approaches are commonly used techniques to evaluate information on quality of care and services.[61] Outcome indicators are considered the most direct way to evaluate quality of life and quality of care provided to nursing home residents.[24] *Outcomes* are defined as measurable changes in the physical, mental, and/or psychosocial well-being of a resident that result from care and services provided by the interdisciplinary team.[24] An *indicator* is defined as a specific, measurable variable used to monitor the appropriateness of an important aspect of resident care.[62] For example, "resident satisfaction with an activity program" is an outcome indicator that can be measured for purposes of evaluation.

Outcome indicators for the services offered by the activity program can either be developed by the activity director or obtained from professional organizations, consumers, and regulatory agencies. These indicators are used by the activity director to monitor and measure the effectiveness of programming. For example, one federal regulation states that the activity program must contain at least three types of therapeutic activities:

1. Empowerment
2. Maintenance
3. Support[24]

Activity staff, therefore, annually review the specific activities of the program to ensure that empowerment, maintenance, and supportive therapeutic activities are offered. The *Joint Commission on Accreditation of Healthcare Organizations* (JCAHO) has likewise developed key indicators specific to long-term care organizations.[62] One JCAHO standard states that activity programming must provide a variety of activities that include but is not necessarily limited to:

- Exercise classes
- Recreational and social activities
- Literary and educational activities
- Community activities
- Spiritual activities
- Creative activities
- Intellectually stimulating activities
- Other programs to maintain the resident's lifestyle[62]

Annual program review ensures that the activity program provides this variety.

A systematic, self-review schedule of quality-assurance monitoring is established by the activity director. The schedule can contain weekly, monthly, quarterly, and/or annual monitoring. For example, monthly monitoring can be performed by activity personnel on:

- Program variety
- Resident participation
- Achievement of established program purposes

A sample form used to collect these data is presented in Figure 20–2. The information is analyzed to determine whether current programming is meeting the established standards of practice for the department. If the program is not meeting established standards, revisions are made. With effective monitoring in place, the activity coordinator ensures that residents always receive and participate in quality activities that meet their leisure needs.

VALUE OF ACTIVITIES IN THE NURSING HOME COMMUNITY

The meaning or value of activity for elderly people as well as a discussion on the theories of activity and aging were presented in earlier chapters in this text. In this section, the importance of activities for older adults who reside in the nursing home community is discussed.

There is a growing body of literature that supports the premise that providing a diverse and comprehensive activity program, based on the needs of the residents, is necessary for the nursing home resident to achieve quality of life and holistic health.* It is noteworthy that not only recreational therapists and occupational therapists discuss the value of activities for older adults in nursing homes but also nurses, social workers, physicians, musicians, and artists. In addition, the same diverse group of experts actually conducts these activities in nursing home settings.

Butler, a physician, noted in his 1973 classic book on aging that it would be a macabre joke if the quantity of life of people was extended without addressing the quality of this extended life.[2] Fifteen years after Butler's publication, there is solid evidence that quality-of-life issues are not being overlooked for elderly people institutionalized in nursing homes. Most recently, in the Omnibus Budget Reconciliation Act of 1987, the federal government has come forth with a dynamic statement regarding the impact of activities on the quality of life of nursing home residents. The regulations for activities are found within the newly created standard on quality of life. Each "facility must provide an ongoing program of activities designed to meet . . . the interests and the physical, mental, and psychosocial well-being of each resident."[24] The interpretive guidelines for this regulation define three categories of activities and the value for each category as it relates to quality of life.

The three categories of activities are empowerment, maintenance, and supportive.[24] Self-respect, self-expression, personal responsibility, and choice are values addressed by empowerment activities. Physical, cognitive, social, and emotional health are values enhanced by maintenance activities; whereas, stimulation and solace are values fostered by resident participation in supportive activities.

Ebersole and Hess, registered nurses, base their work with the aged on the theoretical framework of Maslow's hierarchy of needs.[13] Within this framework, higher-level needs of the nursing home resident for belonging, self-es-

---

*References 2–4, 13, 19–23, 25, 34, 63.

PURPOSE

MONTHLY ACTIVITY	Physical stimulation	Mental stimulation	Spiritual stimulation	Physical rehabilitation	Mental rehabilitation	Social	Aesthetic appreciation	Skill development	Intellectual development	Alleviate boredom	Personal satisfaction	Enjoyment	Self-worth	Therapy	Necessity	No. Participating
Discussion group		✓														11
Ceramics											✓					5
Woodcarving																0
Exercise group	✓															8
Movie program												✓				14
Residents council													✓			3
Birthday party												✓				4
Rhythm band													✓			6
Baking session						✓										6
3-D class								✓								1
Aerobics	✓															1
Scribblers		✓														3
Paint & pencil											✓					3
Art glass class								✓								2
Shopping trip															✓	3
Clothing store						✓										8
Mood music							✓									11
Shuffleboard				✓												6
Popcorn & music												✓				15
Howdy		✓														12
Prayer meeting			✓													12
Candy cart												✓				10

Figure 20–2 Example of monthly monitoring quality assurance form. (Source: Peckham CW and Peckham AB: Activities Keep Me Going. Otterbein Home, 1982, p. 20, with permission.)

teem, and self-actualization can be met through several channels, one of which is a diverse program of activities. Gwyther[64] and Mace,[65,66] a social worker and clinical psychologist, have written extensively on the special needs of individuals with Alzheimer's disease. Their work points out that activities designed around the special needs of demented residents assist this memory-impaired population to achieve higher-level needs. Profoundly regressed residents who are limited to bed rest have also achieved higher-level needs through creative activity. Research studies have supported the benefit of various types of activities for the well-being and function of long-term care residents with widely differing needs.[33,49,55,66–75]

It is also important to note here that activities can have an important role in accomplishing another OBRA (1987)[24] requirement, that is, the establishment of a restraint-free environment. Provision of meaningful activity at a level appropriate to the resident's ability can help reduce wandering and agitation, reducing the need for either physical or chemical restraints.

Residents also have indicated that they value activities when asked about quality-of-care or quality-of-life issues. In 1984 to 1985, a landmark study was conducted by the National Citizen's Coalition for Nursing Home Reform[76] to obtain the views of nursing home residents on quality of care and life. One hundred and seven of four hundred fifty-five residents rated activities fourth in order of importance after staff, food, and environment. Staff qualifications, competence, attitudes, and the quality of interactions between staff and residents were identified by the residents as most important within the general category of "staff," which includes personnel who conduct activities. In order of descending value, the residents identified five other important categories after activities: medical care, religion, resident council, resident rights, and participation in community activities. The last four areas commonly fall within the purview of the recreational therapist.

In another study of residents' views, as cited in Kolata,[77] the residents identified personal autonomy and choice as desired values. Choice in activities was identified as the fifth most important category where residents wished to have involvement. In order of descending value, the top 10 areas identified as important for residents to have a choice in were:

- Going out of the home
- Phones and mail
- Roommates
- Care
- Activities
- Food and money (tie)
- Getting up in the morning
- Going to bed at night
- Visitors

In the revised nursing home inspection guidelines mandated by the Omnibus Budget Reconciliation Act of 1987[24] and implemented on October 1, 1990, residents are interviewed by surveyors and asked their opinions regarding quality of care and quality of life in the nursing home. When residents are physically or mentally unable to communicate with the surveyor, the resident's spouse or family member is interviewed on behalf of the resident. This interview process not only encourages resident and/or family participation in the life of the nursing home but also validates that their opinions are worthwhile only if opinions are taken into account and changes, if indicated, are made. Resident and/or family involvement in nursing home inspections will be evaluated in future years as to the impact, if any, that their opinions have on improving quality of care and life in the nursing home.[78]

SUMMARY

The nursing home is one component of the continuum of care in American health care. The nursing home is more than the sum of its individual parts: physical plant, interdisciplinary team, residents, and staff. It is a community within a community—a system of individuals living, working, playing, exchanging, growing, and becoming together. It is a community of individuals bustling with activities between and among human beings, professional and nonprofessional, resident and nonresident, young and old that supports and enhances the health and well-being of its members. The goal of this community is quality of life through quality of care in an environment that enhances the rights of each individual. The recreational therapist, as a key member of the interdisciplinary team, seeks to work collaboratively, cooperatively, and assertively with other team members to create the ideal nursing home envisioned by Dr. Thelma Fogelberg, an 85-year-old resident (cited in Sandel and Johnson[34]):

> The ideal home is something that everyone from childhood to old age longs for. For the person who resides in a nursing home, the term ideal home has a special meaning. The home must be well-structured, attractive and capable of fulfilling the emotional as well as the physical needs of individuals. It must also sustain the concept of a home as the place for nurturing the growth and development of individual powers of thinking, feeling and being.

REVIEW QUESTIONS

1. *Define what quality of life means to you. To nursing home residents. Is there a difference in the two definitions?*

2. *Discuss how a program of activities enhances quality of life for nursing home residents.*

3. *What is the value of interdisciplinary teamwork toward enhancing quality of care and life of nursing home residents?*

4. *You are hired as an activity leader for a 100-bed nursing home. You are assigned to implement a planned activity program on a 20-bed Alzheimer's unit. Describe the type of activities you would expect to implement for the residents on this unit. All are female, ambulatory,*

and incontinent. Most of the residents also exhibit at least one type of behavioral problem.

5. *Describe your role and responsibility as a recreational therapist participating in an interdisciplinary care planning conference for one of your residents.*

6. *Why is it necessary to provide a diverse program of activities for an elderly person who lives in a nursing home?*

REFERENCES

1. Macholl, DL: Personal communication, Jan 1990.
2. Butler, R: Why Survive? Being Old in America. Harper and Row, New York, 1975, p. 103.
3. Ellis, NB: Nationally speaking: The challenge of nursing home care. Am J Occup Ther 40:7, 1986.
4. Committee on Nursing Home Regulation, Institute of Medicine: Improving the Quality of Care in Nursing Homes. National Academy Press, Washington, DC, 1986, pp. 10, 400.
5. Hing, E, Sekscenski, E and Strahan, G: The National Nursing Home Survey: 1985 Summary for the United States. Vital and Health Statistics. Series 13, No 97. DHHS Pub No (PHS) 89-1758. Public Health Service. US Government Printing Office, Washington, DC, 1989, pp 140, 162.
6. Rabin, DL and Stockton, P: Long-term Care for the Elderly: A Factbook. Oxford University Press, New York, 1987.
7. Rubenstein, LZ, et al (Wieland, D, Pearlman, RA, Grover P and Mabry J): Growth of the teaching nursing home. JAGS 38:73, 1990.
8. Steinberg, FU (ed): Care of the Geriatric Patient in the Tradition of EV Cowdry, ed 6. CV Mosby, St. Louis, 1983.
9. World Health Organization (WHO). The Public Health Aspect of the Aging of the Population (WHO), Copenhagen, 1959.
10. Miller, CA: Nursing Care of Older Adults: Theory and Practice. Scott, Foresman, Chicago, IL, 1990.
11. Lawton, MP: Competence, environment press, and the adaptation of older people. In Lawton, MP, Windley, PG and Byerts, TO (eds): Aging and the Environment: Theoretical Approaches. Springer, New York, 1982.
12. Kahana, E: A Congruence Model of Person-Environment Interaction. In Windley, PG, Byerts, T and Ernest, EG (eds): Theoretical Developments in Environment for Aging. Gerontological Society of America, Washington, DC, 1975.
13. Ebersole, P and Hess, P: Toward Healthy Aging: Human Needs and Nursing Response, ed 3. CV Mosby, St. Louis, 1990, p. 703.

14. Johnson, CL and Grant, LA: The Nursing Home in American Society. Johns Hopkins University Press, Baltimore, 1985.
15. Lefton, E and Lefton M: Health care and treatment for the chronically ill: Toward a conceptual framework. Journal of Chronic Diseases 32:341, 1979.
16. Osguthorpe, SG: Collaboration: A solution for the health care crises. Critical Care Nurse Currents 8:1, 1990. (A newsletter published by Ross Laboratories.)
17. US Federal Register 54:5315, Feb 2, 1989.
18. Yura, H and Walsh, M: The Nursing Process: Assessing, Planning, Implementing, Evaluating, ed 3. Appleton-Century-Crofts, New York, 1978.
19. Blinn, R: Effective one to one programming. Activities, Adaptation & Aging 7:49, 1985.
20. Hegland, A: Activities for low-functioning residents. Contemporary LTC 13:58, 1990.
21. Foster, PM: Activities: A necessity for total health care of the long-term care resident. Activities, Adaptation & Aging 3:17, 19, 1983.
22. Weiss, C: Recreation and the rules: Effective change in long term care. Aging & Leisure Living 3:7, 8, 1980.
23. McLaughlin, LT: Recreation therapy for long-term patients. Gerontion 1:14, 16, 1986.
24. The Long Term Care Survey. American Health Care Association, Washington, DC, 1990, p. 61.
25. Fleischmann, BD and VanHala, BE: It's not just bingo! Recreation in long-term care facilities. The Sounding Board, Spring 1982, p 5. (A publication of Ohio Parks Recreation and Association, Columbus, OH.)
26. Shephard, RJ: The scientific basis of exercise prescribing for the very old. JAGS 38:62, 1990.
27. Short, L and Leonardelli, CA: The effects of exercise on the elderly and implications for therapy. Physical and Occupational Therapy in Geriatrics 5:65, 1987.
28. Mullins, CS, Nelson, DL and Smith, DA: Exercise through dual-purpose activity in the institutionalized elderly. Physical and Occupational Therapy in Geriatrics 5:29, 1987.
29. Warner, DR: Walking to better health. Am J Nurs 88:64, 1988.
30. Wykle, ML and Kaufmann, MA: Teaching nursing homes test progress: Creative planning can improve practice. Provider 13:21, 1987.
31. Huey, FL: What teaching nursing homes are teaching us. Am J Nurs 85:678, 1985.
32. Portnoy, FL, Richards, C and Roberts, R: Wheelchair Karate. Geriatr Nurs 10:76, 1989.
33. Goldberg, WG and Fitzpatrick, JJ: Movement therapy with the aged. Nurs Red 29:339, 1980.
34. Sandel, SL and Johnson, DR: Waiting at the Gate: Creativity and Hope in the Nursing Home. Haworth Press, New York, 1987, p. 6.
35. Bower, ME: Self-regulation techniques in the elderly. J Gerontol Nurs 15:15, 1989.
36. Neville, K: Promoting health for seniors. Geriatr Nurs 9:42, 1988.
37. Johnston, L and Gueldner, SH: Remember when . . . ? Using mnemonics to boost memory in the elderly. J Gerontol Nurs 15:22, 1989.
38. Sheridan, C: Failure-Free Activities for the Alzheimer's Patient: A Guidebook for Caregivers. Cottage Books, Oakland, CA, 1987.
39. Davis, CM: The role of the physical and occupational therapist in caring for the victim of Alzheimer's disease. In Taira, ED (ed): Therapeutic Interventions for the Person with Dementia. Haworth Press, New York, 1986.
40. Goodwin, D: Innovative "resident volunteer" programming. In Cook, JD (ed): Innovations in Activities for the Elderly. Activities, Adaptation & Aging 6:69, 1985.
41. Seville, J: The good samaritan program: Patients as volunteers. In Cook, JD (ed): Innovations in Activities for the Elderly. Activities, Adaptation & Aging 6:73, 1985.
42. Simpler, MS: Programming in Activities for the Elderly. Activities, Adaptation & Aging 6:61, 1985.
43. Becker, M: English handbells in nursing homes. In Karras, B (ed): You Bring out the Music in Me: Music in Nursing Homes. Haworth Press, Binghamton, NY, 1987.
44. Lewallen, M: Adding life to the place: Musical activities in the nursing home. In Karras, B (ed): You Bring out the Music in Me: Music in Nursing Homes. Haworth Press, Binghamton, NY, 1987.
45. Johnson, DR: Therapeutic rituals in the nursing home. In Sandel, SL and Johnson, DR (eds): Waiting at the Gate: Creativity and Hope in the Nursing Home. Activities, Adaptation & Aging 9:151, 1987.
46. Johnson, D: Book reviews [Review of Mental Aerobics, A Resource Manual of Mentally Stimulating Group Activities]. Activities, Adaptation & Aging 13:84, 1989.
47. Berstein, M: Wheeling and dealing in art. The Plain Dealer, 11D, May 17, 1990.
48. Rugh, MM: Art therapy with the institutionalized older adult. In Cook, JD (ed): Innovations in Activities for the Elderly. Activities, Adaptation & Aging 6:105, 1985.
49. Preston, EM: Factors Affecting Nursing Home Residents' Loneliness, Leisure Satisfaction, and Leisure Activity. University of Maryland, College Park, unpublished dissertation, 1987.
50. Lyman, A and Edwards, ME: Reminiscence poetry groups: Sheepherding A Navajo cultural tie that binds. Activities, Adaptation & Aging 13:1, 1989.
50. Vogt, S: Reality therapy in the convalescent home. In Cook, JD (ed): Innovations in Activities for the Elderly. Activities, Adaptation & Aging 6:55, 1985.
52. Brunner, J: The day room program at Westmoreland Manor Nursing Home, Waukesha, Wisconsin. In Cook, JD (ed): Innovations in Activities for the Elderly. Activities, Adaptation & Aging 6:47, 1985.
53. Janssen, JA and Giberson, DL: Remotivation therapy. J Gerontol Nurs 14:31, 1988.

54. Ohio Department of Health: Nursing and Rest Home Law and Rules, 1983.

55. Maloney, CC and Daily, T: An eclectic group program for nursing home residents with dementia. In Taira, ED (ed): Therapeutic Interventions for the Person with Dementia. Physical and Occupational Therapy in Geriatrics 4:55, 1986.

56. Peck, CF: From deep within: Poetry workshops in nursing homes. Activities, Adaptation & Aging 13:19, 1989.

57. Francis, G and Baly, A: Plush animals: Do they make a difference? Geriatr Nurs 7:140, 1986.

58. Karras, B (ed): You Bring out the Music in Me: Music in Nursing Homes. Haworth Press, Binghamton, NY, 1987.

59. Peckham, CW and Peckham, AB: Activities Keep Me Going. Parthenon Press, Nashville, 1982.

60. Foster, PM: NAAP keynote address. In Foster, PM (ed): Activities in Action: Proceedings of the National Association of Activity Professionals 1990 Conference [Special Issue]. Activities, Adaptation & Aging 15:5, 1991.

61. LeSage, J and Barhyte, D: Nursing Quality Assurance in Long-Term Care. Aspen, Queenstown, MD, 1989.

62. Joint Commission on Accreditation of Healthcare Organizations (JCAHO): Long-Term Care Standards Manual. JCAHO, Chicago, 1988.

63. Blayney, JAB: Recreation — That important, but often forgotten, treatment in the total care of the long-term resident. Ala J Med Sci 12:210, 1975.

64. Gwyther, LP: Care of Alzheimer's Patients: A Manual for Nursing Home Staff. HCA and ADRDA, 1985.

65. Mace, N: Home and community services for Alzheimer's Disease. In Taira, ED (ed): Therapeutic Interventions for the Person with Dementia. Physical and Occupational Therapy in Geriatrics 4:5, 1986.

66. Mace, NL: Principles of activities with persons with dementia. Physical & Occupational Therapy in Geriatrics 5:13, 1987.

67. Forsythe, E: One-to-one therapeutic recreation activities for the bed and/or room bound. Activities, Adaptation & Aging 13:63, 1988/89.

68. Lipe, AW: The use of music therapy as an individualized activity. In Karras, B (ed): You Bring out the Music in Me: Music in Nursing Homes. Haworth Press, Binghamton, NY, 1987.

69. Sabari, J: The roles and functions of occupational therapy services for the severely disabled. Am J Occup Ther 37:811, 1983.

70. Hope, DM: The development and evaluation of recreation programs and their effect upon the morale and functioning of nursing home residents. Boston University School of Education, unpublished dissertation, 1978.

71. Bumanis, A and Yoder, JW: Music and dance: Tools for reality orientation. In Karras, B (ed): You Bring out the Music in Me: Music in Nursing Homes. Haworth Press, Binghamton, NY, 1987.

72. Kovach, CR: Promise and problems in reminiscence research. J Gerontol Nurs 16:10, 1990.

73. Kelly, GR, McNally, E and Chambliss, L: Therapeutic recreation for long-term care patients. Ther Recreation J 17:33, 1983.

74. Miller, DB and Barry, JT: The relationship of off premises activities to quality of life in nursing home residents. Gerontologist 16:61, 1976.

75. Huss, MJ, Buckwalter, KC and Stolley, J: Nursing's impact on life satisfaction. J Gerontol Nurs 14:31, 1988.

76. Spaulding, J: A consumer perspective on quality care: The residents' point of view. National Citizens' Coalition for Nursing Home Reform, Washington, DC, 1985.

77. Kolata, G: Life's basic problems are still top concern in nursing homes. The New York Times, 138:pB8(N) and pB14(L), col 2, Jan 19, 1989.

78. Jackson, LT: Leisure activities and quality of life. In Foster, PM (ed): Activities in Action: Proceedings of the National Association of Activity Professionals 1990 Conference [Special Issue]. Activities, Adaptation & Aging 15:31, 1991.

Section

VII

SPECIAL ISSUES

Old age deprives the intelligent man only
of qualities useless to wisdom.

—JOUBERT, *Pensées*, 1842

Chapter

Technology

WILLIAM C. MANN

OBJECTIVES

By the end of this chapter, readers will be able to:

1 Define and describe assistive technology.

2 Differentiate between high-tech and low-tech devices.

3 Define universal design.

4 Describe the devices used for individuals with mobility impairments, including environmental control devices and mobility aids.

5 Describe the devices that may be helpful to individuals with visual impairments.

6 Describe devices that may be helpful to individuals with hearing deficits.

7 Describe how the disability impact continuum can be helpful in determining what types of devices may be helpful to a particular individual.

8 Discuss the limitations in the usefulness of technological devices.

This chapter will provide an overview of assistive technology for increasing or maintaining functional performance in individuals with specific impairments. This will be followed by a closer examination of the Disability Impact Continuum, looking at types of assistive technology for persons falling at two different places on the scale. The chapter concludes with a brief discussion of important issues related to technology and older adults. An appendix at the end of the chapter lists resources on assistive technology for older adults.

DEFINITIONS AND CONCEPTS

With advancing age come two major challenges that impact on functional performance. The first is a gradual decline that can result in decrements in hearing, vision, and mobility. The second is the probability that one or more chronic diseases, such as arthritis, cataracts, or heart disease, will result in additional impairment. In many cases, the impact of impairment on functional performance can be overcome or reduced through the design of the places we live, work, play, and worship (environmental interventions) and through the use of assistive devices.

Assistive technology, although a relatively new term, is widely used. The Technology Related Assistance for Individuals with Disabilities Act of 1988 defines *assistive technology device* as any item, piece of equipment, or product system, whether acquired commercially off the shelf, modified or customized, that is used to increase, maintain, or improve functional capabilities of individuals with disabilities. This broad definition includes *low-tech devices*, that is, those traditionally used by therapists such as button hooks and reachers, and *high-tech devices*, which often involve microprocessors and include computers with voice output, print enlargement systems for persons with low vision, and environmental control units. The terms *assistive technology device*, *assistive technology*, and *assistive device* are used interchangeably and at times are shortened further to *technology* or *device*.

Another important concept is *universal design*. The best assistive device is one designed for all people, not just for people with impairments. Universally designed devices, such as computers, are easier to locate, lower in price, and easier to get repaired.

Universal design relates to another much simpler term, *tool*. Humans are "tool users," and with the exception of chimpanzees who use sticks to dig up insects and sea otters who use rocks to break clam shells, no other species uses objects, or tools, to enhance performance of tasks. Our tools range in complexity from spoons to space shuttles and from can openers to computers. If we view assistive devices as tools, as extensions of our selves that enhance performance, we can reduce the awe, stigma, and fear that are sometimes associated with use of assistive technology.

While assistive devices, or tools, are usually seen as objects that we hold or control, we also shape our "built" environment—buildings, side-walks, and landscaped areas—and the objects we place or include in them—cabinets, doors, and curb cuts. We can design our environments to maximize task performance, and we can build in features that make it possible for people with disabilities to use the environment in the same way as able people. We can incorporate the concept of universal design into "environmental interventions," as well as into assistive devices, and thus reduce the impact of impairments on older individuals.

AGING AND FUNCTIONAL PERFORMANCE

Demographic data about functional limitations common in the elderly have been discussed elsewhere in this volume. In addition to the rate of functional limitations, another important factor is the immediate support system of the older person.[1] While 95 percent of those over 64 live at home, nearly a third live alone. For many, there are no immediate relatives to assist. Many older adults are not aware of the availability of support services. Functional limitations are, therefore, the result of several interacting factors, making "the elderly" a very heterogeneous population.[2] Three important factors differentiate those over 64 years of age into many subgroups:

- Severity of the disease or chronic condition
- Age
- Support system available to the individual

Figure 21–1, disability impact continuum, illustrates the interaction of these three factors. Another important factor, difficult to illustrate in this three-dimensional grid, relates to intrinsic factors of the individual: motivation, experience, education, and intelligence. A highly motivated person 65 years old, with a supportive spouse, siblings, and children and one or two mild to moderate chronic conditions (person 1 in Fig. 21–1) will have very different needs

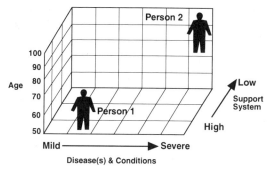

Figure 21–1 Disability Impact Continuum.

from a person 85 years old with several severe diseases and no close relatives or friends (person 2). Person 1 may require assistive devices to use at home for activities of daily living and leisure and perhaps even for employment. Person 2 is likely to be institutionalized or receiving a high level of home care support, and the assistive devices required may relate to safety, basic self-care, and, depending on mental status, environmental control or memory aids.

Many chronic diseases affect hearing and vision.[2] Cognition and mobility are also affected by some chronic diseases. Assistive technology is available for people with hearing, vision, memory, communication, and mobility impairments.

The overview of assistive technology in the next section focuses primarily on high-tech devices, assuming that the reader is familiar with the range of low-tech devices that have been available for many years. It is important to point out that *high-tech* is not synonymous with *complicated.* In fact, high-tech devices may be easier to use than traditional devices designed for the same purpose; that is, they may be "smarter" and save the user steps. A good example of this is the "intelligent" microwave oven under development at the Rehabilitation Engineering Center on Aging. This oven features a hand-held scanner that reads the bar code label on the food package and automatically sets the time and temperature controls for the correct cooking of the food product. This microwave oven includes a voice feature that tells the user the name of the product,

how long it will take to cook, and any special instructions, such as removing the lid from the food item. While the electronics for this oven are complex, the process of cooking is simplified for the user; if the user has a visual or cognitive impairment, independent cooking may be possible only with such a device. The intelligent microwave will have a much broader market than older persons with cognitive and visual impairments and could be considered a universally designed product.

ASSISTIVE TECHNOLOGY FOR OLDER ADULTS

There are over 17,000 products listed in *HyperAbleData*, a computerized database of assistive devices. In discussing products that might be useful to older adults, this section will cover the following categories of assistive devices: devices for persons with mobility and/or motor impairments (including environmental control devices and seating, walking aids, and wheelchairs) and those with vision, hearing, cognitive, and communication limitations. It is important to keep in mind that older adults often have more than one chronic condition and resultant impairments and may benefit from devices in several categories. Multiple impairments may also require modification of devices.

Devices for Persons with Mobility and/or Motor Impairments

ENVIRONMENTAL CONTROL DEVICES

Environmental control devices are designed primarily for persons with physical disabilities, although they often benefit people with cognitive or visual impairments as well. For older adults, whether living at home or in a nursing home, an environmental control device can increase ability to operate almost any device that runs on electricity: radios, computers, phone, lights, and security systems, to name just a few. Hand-held remote controls for televisions could be considered an environmental control device, one that reaches a much broader market than people with impairments. Unfortunately, universal design has not been applied yet to hand-held remotes: consider the small size of the buttons, the small print on or under each button, how close the buttons are to each other, and how complicated some of the features are. Hand-held remotes currently on the market are designed for young people with excellent fine motor control, excellent vision, and a love for "bells and whistles." A prototype hand-held remote device is under development that uses the buttons from a large-button telephone and is programmed for simplicity of use.

Haataja and Saarnio identified five components that make up an environmental control device:

1. A switch that provides the user a means to operate the device
2. A control device that provides a means for transmitting commands, through sound waves, infrared light, or hard-wired connections
3. A target device such as a lamp or radio that is actually turned on or off
4. Connections such as the sensors that pick up the infrared light signal
5. A feedback device that lets the user know the status of the system.[3]

One recent study compared two groups of nursing home patients, one of which was given hand-held environmental control devices. The group who had hand-held environmental control devices used their radios significantly more than the group who relied on nursing home staff, or themselves, to operate their radios.[4] This study used simple X-10 type hand-held remotes, available for under $35, a unit at most consumer electronics stores. This type of technology could be built into the nursing home, and therapists should consider recommending it for patients who have difficulty operating lights and radios in their room. For older persons living at home, the same is true. Of course, the therapist must consider the trade-off in

using such a device. If a person can operate the appliance without the remote, there is an element of purposeful exercise which might be eliminated if the device is used.

An X-10 environmental control device is pictured in Figure 21–2. Environmental control devices range in price from $24 to close to $10,000, and their functions vary from simple on-off of one or a few appliances to computer-based control of the total home environment, the computer itself, and telecommunications. A table listing 23 different environmental control units, a brief description of each, the manufacturer, and the cost is available from the American Occupational Therapy Association.[5] In helping a person select an environmental control device, Dickey and Shealey offer several questions to consider:

- Will the system be difficult (how difficult) to operate?
- How reliable and durable is the system?
- How will the system be installed? How easy is it to install?
- How portable is the system, especially if it will need to be moved?

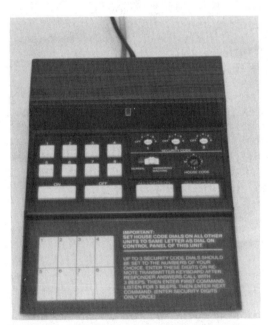

Figure 21–2 An X-10 environmental control device system.

- Who is the manufacturer, and will the manufacturer be in business when support or repair is required?
- Are the features of the device appropriate for the intended user?
- How much training will be required to ensure that the user will be successful with its operation?[6]

Environmental control devices "operate" on the electrical environment. While an environmental control device could be used to operate a mechanical device such as a lift (see Fig. 21–3), the combination of electronics and mechanical functions falls into the area of robotics. Development of useful robotic assistive devices—personal robotics—lags significantly behind industrial robotics. At the present time personal robotic devices are very expensive and of limited use.

WALKING AIDS AND WHEELCHAIRS

Walking aids are among the most common of all assistive devices. The cane, second only to eyeglasses in popularity and numbers, is also one of the oldest assistive devices. Persons experiencing some loss of balance may decide on their own to purchase a cane. For those with more serious gait impairments, perhaps as a result of stroke or Parkinson's disease, a variety of canes

and walkers are available to make mobility easier and safer. Some of the newer designs even come with a built-in seat, which allows the person to sit and rest when tired.

Wheelchairs offer another option for independent mobility, as well as making assisted mobility possible. Advances in wheelchairs have led to lighter, more comfortable designs. Depending on the needs of the person who will use the wheelchair, therapists must make recommendations involving cushions, armrests, wheels, tires, hand rims, and power. Therapists also make recommendations for wheelchair accessories including transfer boards, lapboards and trays, safety belts, clothing guards, and bags and pockets. Several references provide detailed information on wheelchairs, useful for therapists working with older adults who may need a wheelchair.[7,8]

Devices for Persons with Vision Impairments

Vision loss is very common among older persons. One out of 5 elderly persons has difficulty with reading because of visual impairment, and 1 out of 20 persons over 64 years old cannot see words or letters on a page.[9] Visual loss

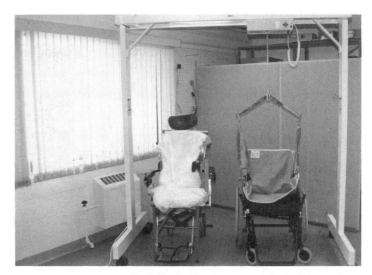

Figure 21–3 Overhead lift operated by remote control device.

may be caused by diabetic retinopathy, cataracts, and macular degeneration, as well as normal aging. A discussion of visual loss can be found in Chapter 7.

Vision loss among the elderly is associated with a decrease in outdoor mobility. A recent study determined that older and younger individuals with normal vision for their age average about 1.5 destinations outside the home each week. Older persons with visual impairments, on the other hand, average 0.5 destinations per week. Only 6 out of the 35 older blind individuals in this study reported any independent travel beyond the yard.[10]

Eyeglasses are the most common assistive device, and they are typically provided by an optometrist. For individuals who require other devices or devices that provide stronger magnification, occupational therapists often participate in providing assistive devices. The following are some basic guidelines for assisting persons with visual impairments that do not necessarily require an assistive device:

1. In speaking with a person with a visual impairment,
   - Don't increase your speaking volume unless the person also has a hearing impairment.
   - Be sure to tell the person that you are talking with him or her.
   - Tell the person when you are leaving.
2. Ask the person if assistance is needed; do not wait to be asked.
3. Allow the person to hold your arm and follow a few steps behind when guiding a person with a severe vision loss.
4. When providing assistance with setting up activities,
   - Provide larger images when possible. For example, you can set the enlargement feature on a photocopy machine to increase the size of print or pictures.
   - Position the person closer to the objects involved in the task.
   - Increase the amount and/or intensity of light, but at the same time reduce glare.

- Provide contrasting colors, for example, dark objects on a light surface. This may require placing a cloth on the table for activities.

There are a wide variety of low-cost, simple assistive devices for persons with visual impairments. These include magnifying glasses, pens that write with a bold line, and writing guides. Materials prepared in large print are available in many bookstores and libraries. Banks can print checks with large characters, and games can be bought with enlarged boards. Most electronics stores carry phones with large buttons and large numbers. Thermometers, clocks, watches, and blood sugar monitors are all available with either large-print or voice output features. Figure 21–4 pictures a thermostat with enlarged numbers and marks.

In the last decade, microprocessor and video-based technology has made it possible to develop a number of products that assist persons with visual impairments. However, the features offered by these devices make them very appropriate for older adults. These new products are categorized by the features they offer.

CHARACTER ENLARGEMENT SYSTEMS THAT ENHANCE IMAGES ON THE COMPUTER MONITOR

There are many software and hardware programs that magnify the image

Figure 21–4 Thermostat with large numbers.

on a computer screen, making it possible for a person with low vision to read what is on the screen. Prices range from under $200 to several thousand dollars. Some new graphics-based software programs, such as Microsoft Word for Windows 2.0, offer zoom features that permit character enlargement. A list of character enlargement systems is provided in the American Occupational Therapy Association text.[11] Figure 21–5 shows a computer with enlarged text.

STAND-ALONE PRINT ENLARGEMENT SYSTEMS

These devices increase the size of any written material or picture. The systems include a monitor (usually 14 to 19 inches) and a viewing table where the book or other materials is placed. Some viewing tables are automated and can be controlled with a foot pedal. For older adults with visual impairments, a print

enlargement system could make the difference in being able to read the newspaper and books that may be a major leisure activity. In fact, a recent study found that reading was one of the two activities that visually impaired older subjects most missed doing.[12] Figure 21–6 illustrates a stand-alone print enlargement system.

BRAILLE OUTPUT DEVICES

Most of us are familiar with Braille printed on heavy paper. Software is available that, together with a Braille printer, permits Braille printing of text produced on a computer with a word processor. "Refreshable Braille displays" are available on a device called the *Navigator*. Available in 20- or 40-character-long strings, tiny pins move up and down to produce the Braille characters, representing a portion of the computer screen. While a smaller percentage of visually impaired persons are now learning Braille, a significant portion of older adults who have been blind since youth are benefiting from these

Figure 21–5 Computer with software for producing enlarged text.

Figure 21–6 Print enlargement system.

computer-based Braille output devices. Figure 21–7 shows the refreshable Braille display on the Navigator.

VOICE OUTPUT SYSTEMS

A "voice" feature can be added to a computer so that words on the computer monitor are read out loud. This allows a person to write into a word processor file and then check the accuracy and content of the file contents. Existing files can be read to the visually impaired person. Together with a scanning system (described in the following section), which takes text that is already printed and converts it into a computer file, virtually any printed material becomes available to the person with a visual impairment. For older adults with severe vision loss, a talking computer may make it possible to continue work, leisure reading, and carrying out household tasks that require writing and reading.

SCANNING SYSTEMS

Scanning systems are similar to photocopy machines in that you "feed" in printed pages to a machine and get a second copy. The difference is that scanning systems, rather than produce

a second printed copy, produce a computer file, which in turn can be saved or read (with a voice system or with a character enlargement system). While a computer system with voice output and a scanner are relatively expensive, they provide virtually complete access to printed materials.

Devices for Persons with Hearing Impairments

Hearing impairment is common among older adults: One out of three persons over age 64 have some hearing impairment; this increases to almost one out of two persons over age 84.[13] Unfortunately many older adults accept hearing loss as a normal part of aging and do nothing about it. Hearing loss can impact on communication, which in turn can result in isolation and depression.[14] Hearing loss affects health and safety in other ways such as not being able to understand instructions for taking medications or not being able to hear fire alarms. Causes and types of hearing loss are discussed in Chapter 7.

The first step in addressing hearing impairment is to seek medical advice. Surgery is employed for some types of

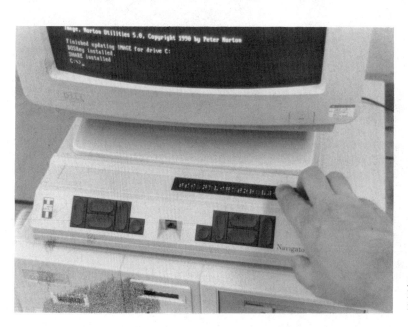

Figure 21–7 Refreshable Braille display on the navigator.

hearing loss; age should not be the determinant in considering a surgical approach. A relatively new surgical procedure, developed for profoundly deaf persons, involves implanting electrodes that bypass damaged hair cells surrounding the cochlea. While a cochlear implant can enable a person to hear sounds, the procedure has not yet been developed to the point that a person is able to discriminate speech. While cochlear implants are a promising new technology, most older adults do not have the type of profound hearing loss that would require this procedure.

Over 90 percent of persons over 64 experience tinnitus.[15] There is no cure for tinnitus, but "maskers" are sometimes used to provide a more acceptable sound than that produced by the tinnitus. Hearing aids are often used to offset the effect of the hearing loss that often accompanies tinnitus. Surgery is sometimes employed to reduce tinnitus, as are drugs, relaxation techniques, and biofeedback.

HEARING AIDS

There are many assistive devices for people with hearing impairments, the most common of which is the hearing aid, typically prescribed by an audiologist. Therapists encounter many older adults who use hearing aids but because of fine motor or vision impairment, have difficulty replacing batteries, positioning the device, or adjusting the controls. Working with older adults, the therapist often establishes a goal of improved fine motor performance that can lead to independence in use of the hearing aid. The therapist might also assist a person in finding "tools" for working the controls or replacing the batteries more easily. The tools would need to provide for a grosser grasp for manipulating the device.

ASSISTIVE LISTENING DEVICES

When hearing aids do not provide adequate sound amplification, *assistive listening devices* (ALDs) may be used. ALDs include microphones for the person(s) speaking, amplifiers to capture the sounds, and, for the person with the hearing loss, a headset. ALD systems are hard-wired or use either FM radio waves or infrared signals. More churches and theaters are installing ALD systems, usually FM and infrared systems. The hard-wired system is more often used in a home. Figure 21–8 illustrates an assistive listening device.

TELECOMMUNICATION DEVICES

Telecommunication devices (TDDs) for people who are deaf are actually small microprocessor-based devices that have a screen, keyboard, and modem. With a TDD at both ends of a telephone line, messages can be typed in and read at each end. Relay services are available in many states so that a person with a hearing impairment can type in a message to an operator, who in turn provides the final receiver with the spoken message. TDDs are now available in public places such as airports. Figure 21–9 provides a picture of a TDD.

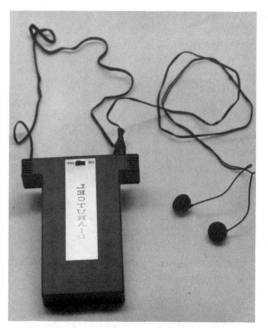

Figure 21–8 Assistive listening device.

Figure 21–9 Telecommunication device for the deaf (TDD).

AMPLIFICATION DEVICES

Electronics and phone stores carry phones that offer amplified sound and devices that can be added to an existing phone to provide amplification. Closed-captioned television provides text at the bottom of the screen on televisions equipped with a special decoding device. All new televisions now have this feature installed. Other devices include smoke detectors that provide visual alert such as a flashing light or vibration. A number of these low-cost devices can make it possible for older adults with hearing loss to continue their involvement in important life roles.

Devices for Persons with Cognitive Impairments

NOTE WRITING AND ELECTRONIC NOTEBOOKS

Memory loss can occur with a number of diseases associated with aging. One low-tech solution to memory impairment is to write a lot of notes on paper and post them in appropriate places. An alternative, high-tech solution is to use a small electronic notebook. A number of these are available for under $1000; most offer features such as a clock with an alarm. The alarm can be used to provide a reminder for taking medications. Many digital wristwatches now offer similar features. One recent study reported the effectiveness of use of an electronic memory device by persons with Alzheimer's disease. In this study, "subjects made significantly more statements of fact and fewer ambiguous utterances." In addition, subjects showed more initiative in conversations.[16] However, caution must be exercised in recommending these devices as some may be too complex for someone in even the early stages of Alzheimer's disease to operate.

OTHER DEVICES

Other helpful devices include automatic turn-off switches for stove burners, automatic timers for lights, movement-sensitive light switches that turn lamps on when a person enters a room, and security systems that can sound an alarm when someone attempts to open a secured door.

DISABILITY IMPACT CONTINUUM: DIFFERENCE IN ASSISTIVE TECHNOLOGY NEEDS

Older Adults at Lower End of Scale

Referring back to Figure 21–1, we will explore applications of technology appropriate for a person at the lower end of each scale. In assessing the advisability of providing assistive devices, the therapist should consider the individual's strengths, as well as limitations, and the acceptability of the device to the person.

Based on the disability impact continuum, person 1 has only mild impairment, as well as considerable social support. He or she may be employed. With changes in the labor markets, changes in attitudes toward aging, and changes in available assistive technology, it is not surprising that we are hearing statements like: "The private sector and government must keep workers trained in new technology to remain productive, and retirement should be restructured to encourage older individuals to work."[17]

Person 1 may drive a car. Visual problems of drivers increase with age and include difficulty with reading dim displays and road signs, reacting to unexpected vehicles, glare from oncoming headlights and from the rearview mirror, and seeing dim tail lights of other vehicles. Recognizing that some of these visual problems begin as early as age 40, it is likely that person 1 will have some difficulty with driving and may adjust his or her driving patterns accordingly, such as avoiding driving at night. Two recent issues of the journal *Human Factors* focused on "Safety and Mobility of Elderly Drivers."[18,19] With more attention to the needs of older drivers, auto makers are beginning to design features into automobiles to accommodate the needs of older drivers, such as moving traditional dashboard displays up to the windshield. This is a good example of universal design.

Leisure activities are also important for person 1. Computers offer promise for older persons for many purposes, including leisure. Computers have been marketed at younger age groups, and the images we have are based on the realities of actual use and those advertising images.[20] Therefore, many older people are reluctant to use computers. However, computers have been used successfully by older adults. In fact, a computer network, called SeniorNet, has been set up "whose purpose is to create and support an international community of computer-using seniors." A University of California at San Francisco group set up SeniorNet through which they introduced computers and computer communications to elderly people.[21] SeniorNet is used for individual communications and news and for learning other computer skills including word processing. In another related project, a group of investigators taught older adults how to use computers for communications, and they found a high rate of computer use after training.[22]

A major new concept in home building is the introduction of "Smart House." Thirty-five major corporations, working with the *National Association of Home Builders* (NAHB) have worked collaboratively in creating an "intelligent" home. The Smart House will have one cable that serves the purposes now served by power cables, doorbell wiring, thermostat wiring, cable TV, alarm system wiring, and telephone wires. There will be a single type of outlet for all devices served, and all devices in this house will be "intelligent." A central computer, working together with the home's devices and appliances, will determine how much power is needed by each device and send power as needed. Thus, there will be no "live" power in the cable, and power will pass through only when the appliance calls for it, and in the amount requested. The system will sense faulty appliances and not send power. Smart House technology is just now becoming available.

For person 1, as well as other people on the disability impact continuum, a Smart House will enhance independent functioning. Safety and security will be enhanced, and activities of daily living will become easier. Smart House will assist in tasks such as food preparation, housekeeping, home repairs, and laundry. Smart House will also enhance education and leisure activities.[23]

Older Adults at Upper End of Scale

Older adults who have a low support system and severe disabilities will employ different assistive technology—different "tools"—than person 1. Person 2 is disoriented and at risk for wandering behavior and falling. This person has significant impairments in ADL and limited ability to undertake leisure or social activities. Assistive technology requirements for person 2 are in the areas of:

- Safety
- Activities of daily living
- Mobility
- Environmental control

Wandering is a threat to safety. In nursing home settings, providing more staff may not be a realistic approach to managing wandering, and federal law now prohibits use of restraints. At a VA nursing home in Atlanta, a group of investigators studied the use of a computer-generated voice to instruct patients who had "wandered" near exits to return to their living units. There was a significant decrease in the number of "exits" with the use of this device.[24]

Falls are also a problem for older adults, as described in Chapter 14. Assistive devices to address problems of postural sway have existed for centuries and include simple canes and walkers in a wide variety of styles and features.[25] New devices may include microprocessor-based monitors that can observe gait characteristics such as postural sway and offer an "alarm"—or a voice suggestion such as, "Slow down" or "Sit down and rest"—as a way of preventing falls.[26]

Hip fractures are a major consequence of falls. In a study of 40 geriatric hip fracture patients aged 65 to 96 years, the investigators noted that prior to hospitalization all ambulated independently and three-fourths of the sample required limited or no social support. Following discharge from the hospital, after the hip fracture, none of the patients ambulated independently, and every subject required support. The investigators studied the use of assistive devices used by these hip fracture patients in their homes following discharge; the results are presented in Table 21–1.

Activities of daily living are also an important area for person 2. There are a large number of devices available that can assist a person with eating. These devices make it easier to hold utensils or prevent food from spilling off the plate or out of the cup. Dentures are used by many older persons and have obvious implications for eating. Getting dentures in or out of the mouth may be a problem for some people, and there is even an assistive device for this.[27] Tremors can also make eating very diffi-

TABLE 21–1 **Use of Assistive Devices by Hip Fracture Patients Following Discharge**[26]

Equipment	No. of Patients Using Item
Walker	36
Long-handled sponge	24
Long-handled reacher	23
Commode	23
Long-handled shoehorn	20
Raised toilet seat	19
Tub equipment	16
Stocking aid	13
Walker bag	13
Versafram	12
Dressing stick	9
Rolling cart	9
Elastic laces	5
Prosthetics	5
Cane	4
Quad cane	2
Miscellaneous	5

cult. Broadhust and Stammers developed an assistive feeding device that includes a pivoted four-bar chain mechanism, with guidance for the hand maintained by using a spring-restrained sliding handle.[28]

Toileting is another area of serious concern to many older persons. Incontinence is embarrassing and can result in social isolation. A group of researchers is working on an electronic device that will measure the decline in electromyographic activity of the muscles of the pelvic floor prior to an involuntary contraction and alert the patient to an impending bladder contraction that occurs with loss of urine.[29] At present, there are a number of companies that make adult incontinence products.

Wheelchair use is common for nursing home patients and for many older adults living at home. Poor positioning in a wheelchair can lead to radial nerve paralysis.[30] Therapists should consider this in positioning and in recommendations on length of time patients should remain in a wheelchair at one time. Safety is another consideration. Brakes must be in good working order.

The decision to use a wheelchair must include the potential user, especially if the person is cognitively alert.[31] Many nursing home patients who are physically capable of walking choose to use a wheelchair. For some, this is a result of the fear of falling; for others, multiple physical factors impact on the decisions such as pain, strength, endurance, vision, and balance.[32]

Person 2 may live in a nursing home. Nursing home patients often have little control of their environment. In fact, many older adults confined to home with severe disabilities also experience loss of control of the environment. There are many devices available that can assist an individual in turning lights on and off, control a TV, radio, or other appliance, and operate a call switch. In a recent study of nursing home patients, it was found that by providing a system that performed five functions, nursing time was saved, and patients gained an increased feeling of control over their environment.[33]

ISSUES RELATING TO USE OF ASSISTIVE TECHNOLOGY WITH OLDER ADULTS

Repair and maintenance of assistive devices is a serious concern. What are the costs, will it be available when needed, and how long will it take? Lack of repair and maintenance can be dangerous and fail to provide the optimal amount of assistance. A British study of 140 older adults, over age 75, determined that "many of the aids that the elderly had were faulty, including half of the walking aids and 15% of the hearing aids, reading spectacles, and dentures, and up to half of the aids were not used."[34] In recommending assistive devices, it is important to not only provide training in the use of the device but to leave instructions regarding repair and maintenance, either with the device user or with the care giver.

Locating service providers capable of offering quality assistive technology services is often difficult not only for the older consumer but for other service providers who make referrals. There is also some fragmentation of services as a result of specialization. Experts in vision, hearing, and cognitive disabilities may not be capable of working with the complex interweave of factors that often are present in an older person. Occupational therapists are often the most knowledgeable about assistive technology services and either make an intervention themselves or refer the client to another provider. One source of information on service providers is the lead agency in each state under the Technology Related Assistance for Individuals with Disabilities Act. The *Society for the Advancement of Rehabilitative and Assistive Technology* (RESNA) in Washington, D.C., provides technical assistance to the states and could be contacted for information on your state's lead agency.

Funding is another problem with assistive devices and the services required for successful use. While many devices are low cost and can be covered by the user, many other devices are expensive and not affordable to all who need them. The national trend is for less public funding for health care and for greater out-of-pocket funding: "The findings . . . demonstrate the startling and accelerating growth in the elderly's out-of-pocket costs for health care. In fact, the elderly's out-of-pocket health expenditures have grown much faster than Medicare and Medicaid program costs.[35] Assistive devices help people maintain or regain independence and thus, can reduce overall health care costs. However, access to assistive devices is often blocked because third-party payors do not cover them.

Acceptability of the device to the individual is a crucial factor. The person's needs and wishes must be considered. Some people may find the devices unacceptable cosmetically, and some may resist being "dependent" on these devices. Further, "high tech" is intimidating to some older adults. It may be possible to address this factor in a training program for the use of a certain device, but it is also possible that the device will still be left in a closet to collect dust or, worse, that it will get in the way and make function more difficult.

While there are problems related to assistive technology and environmental interventions, these tools offer great potential for helping older adults maintain independence. Occupational and physical therapists as well as other service providers often play an important role in identifying the appropriate technology, in training older persons in how to use it, and in providing followup support. Audiologists deal with devices related to hearing, and physical therapists, mobility devices. Opticians or optometrists may be knowledgeable about vision aides. Social workers are vital in identifying sources of financing for all these devices.

REVIEW QUESTIONS

1. What is the difference between high-tech and low-tech assistive devices?

2. What makes universal design important to "well" older adults, that is, those who have only minimal functional limitations?

3. Mrs. A is a 67-year-old widow with mild arthritis and mild presbycussis. How might environmental control devices assist her in maintaining independence in the apartment in which she lives?

4. Mr. Y is in the early stages of macular degeneration. What assistive devices might a therapist consider to help him adjust as his vision worsens?

5. A therapist has provided an environmental control device for Ms. D. On a home visit, she notes that the device is sitting on the table, collecting dust. What are the possible reasons that Ms. D might not use the device, and what could the therapist do?

REFERENCES

1. Kovar, MG: Aging in the Eighties: Preliminary Data from the Supplement on Aging to the National Health Interview Survey. Advance Data From Vital and Health Statistics, No 115 DHHS Pub No (PHS) 86-1250. National Center for Health Statistics, 1986.
2. Fowles, DG: A Profile of Older Americans 1988. American Association of Retired Persons, Washington, DC, 1988.
3. Haataja, S and Saarnio, I: An evaluation procedure for environmental control systems. Proceedings of the 13th Annual RESNA Conference, Washington, DC, 1990, pp 25–26.
4. Mann, WC: Use of environmental control devices by elderly nursing home patients. Assistive Technology 3:4, 1992.
5. Mann, WC and Lane, JP: Assistive Technology for Persons with Disabilities: The Role of Occupational Therapy. American Occupational Therapy Association, Rockville, MD, 1191, pp 42–43.
6. Dickey, R and Shealey SH: Using technology to control the environment. American Journal of Occupational Therapy 41:717–721, 1987.
7. Mann, WC and Lane, JP: Assistive Technology for Persons with Disabilities: The Role of Occupational Therapy. American Occupational Therapy Association, Rockville, MD, 1991.
8. AARP: Product Report: Wheelchair. Washing-

ton, DC, American Association of Retired Persons, 1990.

9. US Bureau of the Census: Disability, Functional Limitation, and Health Insurance Coverage: 1984/85 Current Population Reports, Series p-70, No 8, Washington, DC, US Government Printing Office, 1986.

10. Long, RG: Effects of age and visual loss on independent outdoor mobility. Rehabilitation R & D Progress Reports. VA Prosthetics Research and Development Center, Baltimore, 1989, p 364.

11. Mann, WC and Lane, JP: Assistive Technology for Persons with Disabilities: The Role of Occupational Therapy. American Occupational Therapy Association, Rockville, MD, 1991.

12. Mann, WC, Karuza, J, Hurren, D and Bentley, D: Needs of older visually impaired persons for assistive devices. Journal of Visual Impairments, in review.

13. Hotchkiss, D: The Hearing Impaired Elderly Population: Estimation, Projection, and Assessment. Monograph Series A. #1. Gallaudet Research Institute, Washington, DC, 1989.

14. Glass, LE: Rehabilitation for deaf and hearing-impaired elderly. In Brody, SJ and Ruff, GE (eds): Aging and Rehabilitation. Springer, New York, 1986, pp 218–236.

15. US Public Health Service: Prevalence of selected chronic conditions, United States, 1983–1985. Advance Data from Vital and Health Statistics, No 155 DHHS Pub No (PHS) 88-1250, Public Health Service, Hyattsville, MD, 1988.

16. Bourgeoris, MS: Enhancing conversation skills in patients with Alzheimer's disease using a prosthetic memory aid. Journal of Applied Behavior Analysis 23:1, 1990, pp 29–42.

17. Schwartz, RG: Investment for an aging population. Statistical Bulletin 70:3, 1989.

18. Human Factors Society: Special Issue: Safety and Mobility of Elderly Drivers, Part I, 33:5, 1991.

19. Human Factors Society: Special Issue: Safety and Mobility of Elderly Drivers, Part II, 34:1, 1992.

20. Eilers, LM: Older adults and computer education: Not to have the world a closed door. International Journal of Technology and Aging 2:1, 1989, p 56.

21. Furlong, MS: Creating an electronic community: The SeniorNet story. International Journal of Technology and Aging 2:2, 1989, p 125.

22. Hahn, W and Bison, T: Retirees using E-Mail and networked computers. International

Journal of Technology & Aging 2(2):113–123, 1989.

23. Lesnoff-Caravaglia, G: Smart home technology: Implications for older persons. International Journal of Technology & Aging 1:1, 1988, pp 9–10.

24. Blasch, BB, Saltzman, DM and Coombs, F: Evaluation of wandering behavior in elderly persons and interventions: A pilot study. Rehabilitation R & D Progress Reports. VA Prosthetics Research and Development Center, Baltimore, 1988, p 296.

25. Farris, DS: Dynamic postural sway measurement in elderly fallers. Rehabilitation R & D Progress Reports. VA Prosthetics, Research and Development Center, Baltimore, 1988, p 300.

26. Rosenblatt, DE, Campion, EW and Mason, M: Rehabilitation home visits. Journal of the American Geriatrics Society 34:441–447, 1986.

27. Labell, TL and Glassman, AH: An aid for swing-lock partial denture removal. Prosthetic Dentistry 59:5, 1988.

28. Broadhurst, M and Stammers, CW: A feeding mechanism for Parkinson's disease patients. Journal of Medical Engineering & Technology 12:1–6, 1988.

29. O'Donnel, PD: Electromyographic Incontinence alert device. Rehabilitation R & D Progress. VA Prosthetics Research and Development Center, Baltimore, 1989, p 352.

30. Hartigan, JD and Connolly, TJ: Is wheelchair wrist drop a new syndrome to watch for? Geriatrics 45:63–65, 1990.

31. Haworth, E, Powell, RH and Mulley, GP: Wheelchairs used by old people. British Medical Journal 28:7, 1983.

32. Pawlson, LG, Goodwin, M and Keith, K: Wheelchair use by ambulatory nursing home residents. Journal of the American Geriatrics Society 34:12, 1986.

33. Symington, DC, Lywood, DW, Lawson, JS and McLean, J: Environmental control systems in chronic care hospitals and nursing homes. Archives of Physical Medicine and Rehabilitation 67:36, 1986.

34. George, J, Binns, VE, Clayden, AD and Mulley, GP: Aids and adaptations for the elderly at home: Underprovided, underused, and undermaintained. British Medical Journal 33:3, 1988.

35. Wu, I and Sutton, DL: Escalating Out-of-Pocket Health Care Costs: A Growing Burden for the Elderly. New York State Office for the Aging, Albany, 1991, Introduction.

APPENDIX 21-1: RESOURCES

Assistive Technology for Persons with Disabilities: The Role of Occupational Therapy (1991).

Published by The American Occupational Therapy Association, Inc., Rockville, MD. This 287-page text covers assistive technology applications and assistive technology services and contains a unit on assistive technology information.

Product Reports (1990–1992).

American Association of Retired Persons (AARP), 1909 K Street, NW, Washington, DC 20049; phone (202) 434-2277. Developed for AARP members, each of these reports provides overviews of the device type and comparative information. Several reports are planned, but those currently available include "Wheelchairs," "Hearing Aids," and "Personal Alerting Devices."

Resources for Elders with Disabilities (1990).

Resources for Rehabilitation, 33 Bedford Street, Suite 19A, Lexington, MA 02173. The last chapter of this 168-page guide is titled "Aids and Devices That Make Everyday Living Easier."

The First Whole Rehab Catalog (1990).

Jay Abrams and Margaret Ann Abrams, Bettway Publications, Inc., Box 219 Crozet, VA 22932. This is a consumer-oriented publication with many pictures, detailed product descriptions, and prices.

The Lighthouse Low Vision Catalog: Optical Devices, Products, Services (1990).

The Lighthouse, 36-02 Northern Boulevard, Long Island City, NY 11101. This catalog lists low-tech products for people with visual impairments.

Technology and Aging in America (1985).

Congress of the United States, Office of Technology Transfer, for sale by: U.S. Government Printing Office, Washington, DC 20402. While somewhat dated for the rapid field of assistive technology, this 496-page book covers policy-level areas related to assistive technology and covers how technology can help in maintaining quality of life and independence.

Assistive Technology (journal).

Published by RESNA Press, 1101 Connecticut Avenue, NW Suite 700, Washington, DC 20036. This quarterly journal is the official publication of RESNA, The Society for the Advancement of Rehabilitative and Assistive Technology.

Journal of Rehabilitation Research and Development (journal).

Superintendent of Documents, U.S. Government Printing Office, Washington, DC 20402. This is a " 'scientific' engineering publication in the multidisciplinary field for disability rehabilitation." Many articles focus on assistive devices.

Technology and Disability (journal).

Andover Medical Publishers, 15 Terrace Park, Reading, MA 01867. This is a new quarterly journal, with each issue devoted to a single topic. Published topics include visual impairments, secondary and post-secondary education, and issues in credentialing service providers. An upcoming issue will focus exclusively on aging.

He was wonderful to take care of . . . and [his wife] was a wonderful care giver, which also helped. She was the kind of person that would call a lot because she needed counseling or someone to reaffirm that what she was doing was okay. But also we learned from her because she did so much above and beyond the call of duty it seemed.

—ALZHEIMER DAY CARE CENTER NURSE

Chapter

Professionals and Informal Care Givers: The Therapeutic Alliance

BETTY RISTEEN HASSELKUS

OBJECTIVES

By the end of this chapter, readers will be able to:

1 Develop an understanding of the dimensions of a therapeutic relationship, that is, responsibility for problems and solutions, power and control, and shared cultures.

2 Relate the dimensions of a therapeutic relationship to the professional–family care-giver relationship.

3 Demonstrate an understanding of techniques to promote care-giver participation, that is, ethnographic interviewing and levels of questioning.

4 Describe the four steps in the therapeutic process.

5 Describe ways to incorporate techniques to promote therapeutic relationships into educational training of professionals.

It is a myth that most frail older people are being cared for in nursing homes. More than a decade ago, Shanas[1] published research findings supporting the fact that the majority of care for older people (70 to 80 percent) was provided in the community by family members. The same year, Fengler and Goodrich[2] referred to wives of disabled men as "the hidden patients," inaugurating a rapidly growing concern among gerontologists for family care givers as a population that is susceptible to the ill effects of too much stress and strain from the care giving. Since that time, considerable research has been published on the family care giver's role—the tasks and responsibilities, the stress and burden of care giving, gender issues related to care giving, kinship bonds and care giving, care-giver support groups, parent care, respite care, and the effect of care giving on the health of the caregiver.[3-15]

It was, perhaps, natural for the professional community to first view family care givers as another group of "patients" in need of care and assistance. More recently, however, my own research[16-18,44] and that of others[19-21] has begun to reveal the family care giver more as a lay practitioner who comes to the care-giving situation with his or her own background of experience and knowledge. Care-giving concerns have begun to shift from "What does this second patient need from us as professionals" to "How can we develop a therapeutic alliance with this second *practitioner* and best provide care together?"

This chapter explores the sometimes uneasy alliance that is formed between therapists and family care givers for older people. What are the various kinds of therapeutic relationships that might be developed between therapists and family members? What seems to be the most beneficial kind of relationship in terms of facilitating functional performance and independence in the care receiver? What techniques are available to the therapist to promote the best working relationship with the family member? This chapter will include examples from field research on care giving to augment the information and discussion on this key factor in geriatric care.

THE THERAPEUTIC RELATIONSHIP REVISITED

A *relationship* is a state of being that results when a connection exists between two or more things or people. A *therapeutic relationship* is one that seeks to promote the cure or management of disease and ill health. It is axiomatic that occupational and physical therapists are expected to establish therapeutic relationships with their clients to promote optimum occupational performance in daily activities. Peloquin[22] has stated, "The therapeutic relationship promoted in occupational therapy has been an evolving blend of competence and caring" (p. 13). The concept of a therapeutic relationship is taught in academic programs, and fieldwork performance evaluations address the student's ability to form therapeutic relationships.

But what type of "connection" actually promotes optimum occupational performance? What is the precise nature of this link between therapist and client that leads to health promoting behaviors? And when this connection is formed between a therapist and a family member as they try to promote health in a third person, is the nature of this therapeutic relationship different from that between therapist and patient?

Beliefs about Problems and Solutions

A therapeutic relationship can, in fact, take many forms. Karuza and associates[23] suggest that the form of the helping relationship depends upon the participants' beliefs about who bears the responsibility for the source of the problem and for the solution. For example, according to Karuza, in the *Medical Model*, the client is not held responsible for either the cause of the problem or for the solution. In other words, clients are seen as "victims," and the medical professional is there to minister to them. This is different from the *Compensatory Model*, in which the client is not held responsible for the cause of the problem but *is* responsible for the solution. Thus, in this model, the patient is viewed as the essential agent for change and is expected to find solutions to problems by learning new skills to overcome difficulties. The professional helper in this model takes a cooperative stance. Two other models are the *Moral Model* (client is responsible for both the cause and the solution) and the *Enlightenment Model* (client is responsible for the problem but not for finding a solution).

Karuza and associates[23] hypothesize that different helping models are chosen by both the helpers and the clients to maximize their chances of bringing about what they believe to be the most desirable outcomes. Part of what determines this choice of model are stereotypes, and when working with elderly clients, the medical model is most often chosen because of often held stereotypes of the elderly population as passive, sickly, and dependent. Ironically, research findings suggest that elderly people themselves also prefer care strategies reflected by the medical model, yet at the same time a sense of personal responsibility is associated with other positive outcomes such as mood and sense of satisfaction. So questions remain about the optimum model of care for older individuals as it relates to the development of a therapeutic relationship. Karuza suggests that a formal assessment of a client's beliefs about the nature and origins of their illnesses be a part of program planning so that potential areas of conflicting beliefs between therapist and client can be identified and addressed.

A Power Continuum

From a different perspective, Arnstein[24] depicts relationships as levels of participation that are determined by a continuum of power and control. This continuum ranges from full power by the professional (*manipulation*) to full power by the client (*citizen control*). (Arnstein's arena is citizen and government control, but we may draw an apt analogy to the client and professional in health care.) In between lie intermediate categories of participation such as *informing, consultant,* and *partnership,* which represent increasing levels of citizen (client) control.

Arnstein's political and philosophical beliefs are revealed in her imagery of citizen control at the "top" of the ladder of participation, representing an ideal relationship. While we may not necessarily agree with this philosophical stance, for us as therapists it is useful to be aware of and to reflect on the power balance in our relationship to our clients. If a client's participation in therapy is limited to being informed or even being consulted, this indicates an authoritarian approach to treatment and very little power on the client's part. Is such a relationship really what we want if our ultimate goal is to foster increased independent performance in activities of daily living?

Levin,[25] in his discussion of self-care in health, stated that the authoritarian model of health care that has evolved over the past decades has led to a sense of powerlessness in health care for the layperson and a "condescending view" by the professional "that self-care is residual and supplementary" (p. 180). Levin calls for changes in medical school curriculums and in patient education to help bring about more of a balance of power in the professional-layperson relationship and growth of self-determination and self-reliance. Such statements are especially relevant to the practice of occupational and physical therapy as we profess to have as our ultimate goals the enhancement of the client's independent performance in basic living skills including self-care, instrumental activities, work skills, problem-solving and decision-making skills, and so on. Does the character of our relationships with our clients actually promote these goals?

In their discussion of power in the

medical encounter, Bloom and Speed-ling[26] state that dependence is recipro-cal to power and "the patient appears to be inherently dependent within the situ-ation of doctor-patient exchanges" (p. 158). According to Marshall,[27] issues of the power balance between client and professional may be especially impor-tant in the relationship of *older* client to professional, again, because of stereo-types of dependency in old age and older people's lifelong patterns of deference to authority figures. Occupational and physical therapists must search their own relationships to determine the ex-tent of stereotyping influences and their comfortableness with different power balances.

Shared Cultures

A third characterization of the thera-peutic relationship revolves around the concept of shared cultures. From sociol-ogy and anthropology comes a wealth of fascinating literature on illness as a cultural experience—for both the care provider and for the patient. Culture largely determines why people suffer from what they do, and why treatment follows a particular course and not another.[98]

Kleinman's concept of explanatory models[29,30] and Friedson's clash of per-spectives[31] both speak to the issue of health and health care being imbedded in social contexts and its corollary that, since the professional and the patient come from different social contexts, it follows that they also hold different explanations of the illness being ad-dressed. The two explanations or per-spectives often represent major dis-crepancies between the individuals—discrepancies in values, beliefs, and de-sired outcomes. Professionals' explana-tions tend to be derived from theoretical, scientific backgrounds, and laypeople tend to derive their explanatory models from their life experiences. Mishler[32] called these two perspectives the *life world* and the *medical world*, and he spoke to the need to strengthen the sharing of these two worlds in order for optimum health care to take place. Katz[33] further addressed the silent, un-spoken differences between profes-sional and patient perspectives and the "obligation of conversation" as a vital ingredient in a therapeutic relationship.

Occupational and physical therapists derive their illness perspectives from the theoretical and scientific knowledge base of their academic years and from their experiences in practice. Since our focus of practice is on the meaning and performance of everyday activities, it seems vital to our therapeutic relation-ships to honor the "obligation of conver-sation" by sharing meanings of the life-world and the medical world in our interactions with clients. In this way, discrepancies can be resolved and mu-tually agreed upon perspectives can be generated.

Therapeutic Relationships with Care Givers

Much of the literature cited previously addresses the concept of therapeutic re-lationships between professional and patient. How do these same character-izations translate to the arena of professional–family care-giver relation-ships?

RESPONSIBILITY FOR PROBLEMS AND SOLUTIONS

Beliefs about who is responsible for health problems and solutions can have a dramatic effect on the model of care used in the family care-giving situation. These beliefs are, after all, the source of such family care-giver attributes as a sense of commitment ("I feel like this is my responsibility"), a sense of guilt ("I should be more patient"), blame ("I think the stroke is because he smoked a lot and drank a lot of beer"), initiative ("I suggest things because the doctors don't know everything"), or resentment ("I feel forced into this, and I really re-sent it").

Therapists often transfer responsibil-ity for solutions *to* a family care giver as we teach care-giving skills and therapy techniques to be carried on at home. This transfer of responsibility is based on the assumption by the therapist that the family member also believes that he or she should be responsible for the solution. As any therapist who has worked with family members knows, this transfer process does not always go smoothly. For example, a family care giver may continue to cling to the therapist as the source of all solutions, never gaining confidence in herself or himself to assume such responsibilities:

> *Care giver:* The therapist will be through with her visits next week—I'll miss the service because then at least it [walking exercise] was done and it was done right . . . 'cuz there's lots of habits you can get into that are wrong and I wouldn't know, but she *does* know.

Or a care giver may accept responsibility from a therapist, but the end result is not entirely therapeutic. The therapist may unwittingly set up the care receiver for excessive care and dependence and the care giver for excessive self-confinement, self-blame, and fear of failure and potential guilt. In the example that follows, the therapist transferred responsibility for both a problem (falling) and solution (don't ever let him fall) to the family care giver:

> *Caregiver:* The therapist said to never let him fall, so when he gets up, I get up . . . I don't ever want him to move without me being right there. Once, when I went outside to hang up clothes, I looked back in through the window and he was trying to walk to the bathroom. So now I don't even do that. . . .

In the transfer of care-giving responsibility from therapist to family care giver, the family member emerges firmly in the role of second practitioner. It is obvious that both the relinquishing of the role of responsibility for solutions by the therapist and the acceptance of this role by the family care giver are complex processes that need to be approached thoughtfully and skillfully. In a later section of this chapter, techniques for facilitating the process will be discussed.

CONTINUUM OF POWER

Marshall[27] defines *authority* as legitimate power and believes it to be the focus of negotiation between patient and doctor. The relationship between the therapist and family care giver, too, can represent a negotiation of power and control.

Data from a study on care giving in the community[16] are replete with care-giver statements that reflect a power struggle between the care-giver and a professional:

- The doctor said there was no way that I could take care of her, but I said she's my mother and I just went there one morning and said I'm taking her home.
- I questioned the diagnosis of Alzheimer's, and the doctor hit the ceiling.
- I just dreaded the time I would have to go down to therapy with him; I'd think, "What if I really goof it up?"
- I'm not happy with what the girl [aide] did. I have powder and lotion in there, and I told her to always, always put that on him. This morning she didn't use either one.

Sometimes a care giver seemed content to let control remain with the professionals ("We just do what they tell us to"). But more often, care givers seemed to be struggling to strike a balance of control—using the professionals as a resource but critiquing and modifying their recommendations to better fit their own situations.[16]

In another interpretation of the preceding community care-giving data,[44] a model was proposed whereby the family care-givers accepted power in the professionals during the acute and/or hospitalization phase of a care receiver's illness but gradually moved toward acquiring more power for themselves during discharge planning and followup home care. Critiquing professionals' recommendations became prominent during the latter stages of care, and eventually many of the care givers strove to teach the professionals how ("I told her to always, always put that on him"). It is obvious that the sense of wanting control is closely related to a belief that one has the responsibility and expertise to provide solutions.

Partnership, a category that represents a sharing of power on Arnstein's ladder of participation, is sparsely represented in the preceding care-giving data. It was rare that a care giver described a relationship with a professional in terms of such mutuality:

> *Care giver:* She [mother-in-law] was responsible for her own medicine when she first came home, but there would be times when she would either forget to take it or would be taking it too often. So between the nurse and me talking it over, she set up four packets of pills for her to take daily. . . .

SHARING CULTURES

If, as Kleinman and others claim, illness is a cultural experience for the person who is ill, so, too, is it a cultural experience for the persons who are providing the care. Both the professional and the family care giver have explanatory models for the illness ("I questioned the diagnosis of Alzheimer's"), and these explanations may not be compatible ("and the doctor hit the ceiling"). If the therapist hopes to transfer skills and work in partnership with the family care giver to facilitate occupational performance, then perspectives must be shared to reach mutually agreeable explanations for the illness and its treatment.

One dramatic example of an absence of cultural sharing occurred between a care giver and a physical therapist. The physical therapist terminated her home visits with the husband (who was post-stroke) because of "no improvement." The care giver stated to me, "She must have been trying to do the wrong thing. She was trying to repair that left arm, and that was impossible. All that I was interested in was getting him to move easier." Whereupon, the care giver successfully attempted walking with her husband, first around the dining room table and subsequently from the wheelchair into the bathroom. Neither care

giver nor therapist had shared with each other their own perspectives of the situation. The care giver thought the therapist was trying to do something "impossible," and the therapist was unaware of the care giver's priorities of "getting him to move easier." Two very different explanatory models were never exchanged.

Nor are occupational therapists immune from such omissions. One care giver described the first days when her husband was home from the hospital as "real hard." She talked about all the different professionals who were coming in ("physical therapists, occupational therapists, visiting nurse, the woman to give him baths") and how it seemed like she "never got anything done." Then she went on to say, "And the occupational therapist, she wanted to come early and watch what I did and everything. And when they come early, it makes me so nervous and I get irritated with him. So I asked the occupational therapist not to come anymore." Again in this case two very different perspectives were never shared so that a mutually agreeable plan could be developed. (In Arnstein's terms, one might conclude that, instead of partnership, the relationship between therapist and care giver shifted to the very top of the continuum and the care giver took full control.)

TECHNIQUES FOR PRACTICE

In occupational and physical therapy, we strive for therapeutic relationships with our clients in order to best facilitate functional performance. One has only to reflect on the constraints on occupational performance present in the situation described previously of the care giver who said, "When he gets up, I get up," to realize the powerful link between a therapist's approach and a client's activity patterns. Activity of both the care giver and the patient can be dramatically affected.

How different was the occupational outcome of the example of the nurse and the care giver "talking it over" and devising together a medication-taking system that the mother-in-law could use independently. Such a system imposed a minimum of constraints on the occupational performance of both care giver and care receiver since the care giver was free from the daily routine of medication management and the care receiver was maximally responsible for her own pills. In this rare example of partnership between the family care giver and the professional, the therapeutic relationship illustrated compatible beliefs about the source of the problem and the solution, a sharing of power and control, and a sharing of perspectives. Why did the data contain so few examples of such relationships? Why was there, more often, tension and discrepancies between the professional's and the care giver's views? What can be added to practice that might better lead to therapeutic relationships with care givers?

Ethnographic Interviewing

As practitioners, what we choose to include in our interviews as we seek to gather information from the clients with whom we work should be directly related to the purpose of our clinical practice. Additionally, *how* we go about doing that interview should reflect that same purpose. According to Kleinman,[30] the purpose of medicine is "both control of disease processes and care for the illness experience" (p. 253). Kleinman further states that when working with people who are experiencing chronic illnesses, "the control of the disease is by definition limited; care for the life problems created by disorder is the chief issue. . . . *The experience and meanings of illness are at the center of clinical practice*" (p. 253, italics added).

One technique for gathering information and understanding of the illness experience of another person is *ethnographic interviewing*.[34] This is a technique, derived from anthropology, that can be adapted without difficulty for use in health care. With a family care giver, ethnographic interviewing can be used

to understand the care giver's point of view and the beliefs about the illness experience that are used to organize his or her care-giving behaviors ("When they come early like that, it makes me so nervous, . . . so I asked the occupational therapist not to come anymore"). In other words, ethnographic interviewing techniques can help the therapist understand the family care giver's explanatory model. See Table 22–1 for an overview of ethnographic interview techniques.

Ethnographic interviewing starts with very global, open-ended questions: "Can you start by telling me what your day is like?" or "Could we sit down and talk about what kinds of things you do during the day to take care of your husband?" As the therapist listens to the responses to the initial questions, he or she makes note of topics that are briefly mentioned but that probably warrant greater discussion. The therapist then begins to seek greater and greater detail about the care-giving experience, probing into topics that have been mentioned. The therapist also pays special attention to the words that the care giver uses to describe his or her situa-

---

TABLE 22–1	**Ethnographic Interview Techniques**

1. The therapist is the *learner*; the person being interviewed is the *expert*.

2. The interview is semistructured. Start with very global questions, and then probe further based on what the person starts talking about.

3. Begin to incorporate the terms used by the client as he or she talks.

4. Repeatedly express interest in what the person is saying.

5. Be careful not to slip into the authority or expert role. Express ignorance appropriately.

6. Build in opportunities for expansion and repetition.

7. The interview should be asymmetrical with the person being interviewed doing most of the talking.

Source: Hasselkus BR,[34] reprinted from OT Practice, Vol 2; No 1 with permission of Aspen Publishers, Inc. © 1990.

tion and begins to use the care giver's terms in further questions:

Interviewer: Maybe you could start by just telling me a little about how you and your husband spend a typical day.
Care giver: Well, sometimes I have to get up through the night. He kicks all the covers off, no matter how well I make the bed. That one leg is good, see, and he can kick, he can clear the bed, and he'll say "Maw," and then I have to remake the bed, sometimes two times a night. Last night it was good, he was quiet.
Interviewer: But usually you're up sometime?
Care giver: Ya, I'm mostly up sometime. And, well, on Monday and Tuesdays, he goes to the [adult day center]. I asked them to take him for two days so I could have a little time away from him, you know? . . . Then on Wednesday, I have a lady come in from the visiting nurse service, and she gives him a bath, . . . and then on other days, I come out and get dressed and brush my teeth and comb my hair and start breakfast, and then I get him up, bring him out here, wash him.
Interviewer: Okay, when you say "get him up," what does that involve?
Care giver: Well, I put his pants on laying down until I get them up to as far as I can go, and then I swing him off the bed and I put his stockings and shoes on, and then he takes a hold of the bedpost and he holds on there while I pull up the pants and zip it, and so forth. . . .

Any therapist is going to readily recognize the wonderful details of everyday functional performance that are evident in this brief excerpt from a 1-hour interview. Ethnographically, the therapist could immediately begin to identify several important domains of the care-giving experience — getting up at night, the day center, the visiting nurse who gives the bath, getting him up. The fact that the care giver started her description of the day's activities with comments about the nighttime activity might be a clue that this is an important issue in her care giving. The interviewer also successfully probed for more detail in her question, "When you say 'get him up,' what does that involve?" In asking this question, she also began to incorporate the care-giver's terms into the in-

terview. This may seem obvious and simply common sense, but we often translate our client's language into more formalized language, perhaps without even realizing it. Being "up" at night could easily be reworded into being "disturbed" or "awakened," and getting him "up" could be reworded into getting him "out of bed." A change in the words being used to describe an experience can also change the meaning of the experience. It is best to stick to the words used by the care giver. This also indirectly reassures the care giver that what they are saying and the way they are saying it is fine. Since it is the *care giver's* perspective that we hope to understand through the interview, such reassurance is vital to reaching that goal.

Kleinman,[30] too, discusses the mini-ethnography as an information gathering method by which the professional tries to understand the illness experience as it is perceived by the client. Kleinman suggests the use of an "illness problem list" (p. 235); that is, in addition to the biomedical problem list, the professional would also develop an accompanying list of problems imbedded in the illness experience. Examples from my own care-giver research would include such care-giver problems as:

- Care giver feels "like a prisoner."
- Care giver seems very upset and says she is "so ashamed" about losing her patience.
- Care giver feels it is important to devise a lap tray so her mother can do more self-feeding.

These are expressions of the care giver's illness experiences regarding the care receiver. They are obviously part of the meaning of the care-giving situation.

Further general guidelines for conducting ethnographic interviews are contained in the table. Spradley[35] has written an excellent book on ethnographic interviewing that more precisely outlines details of types of ethnographic questions and other background on ethnography.

Care-Giver Participation

Much of the literature on patient education is applicable to our work with family care givers. *Patient education* is defined as learning activities designed to assist people who are having experience with illness or disease in making changes in their behavior conducive to health.[36] DiMatteo and DiNicola[37] described the goal of patient education as "client self-sufficiency and the promotion of the practitioner-patient relationship as a partnership." Patient education, or in our case care-giver education, is thus seen as one technique by which to promote active participation of the client in the therapeutic relationship.

Techniques for patient education have been described in the literature[36] and have included special considerations for when the patient is an older person.[38-41] When the *care giver* is an older person, the same special considerations for hearing and vision losses, pacing of material, ageist attitudes ("I'm too old to learn all this"), and respect for lifelong habits and patterns of coping must be made during teaching sessions with the therapist.

Payton, Nelson, and Ozer[42] in their parent participation manual for therapists have stated, "The therapist must do everything possible to help the client assume responsibility" (p. 5), that is, to help the client take the maximum possible degree of participation in the planning, evaluation, and implementation of the therapy plan (Fig. 22–1). These authors describe interviewing techniques that parallel some of the ethnographic strategies cited previously, but they are presented within a clinical framework.

According to Payton, Nelson, and Ozer,[42] in order to encourage the greatest possible client participation, the therapist should start with open-ended questions, thereby enabling the person to function at the level of free choice (not unlike starting with global questions in the ethnographic interview). Then, as necessary, the therapist moves down a ladder of decreasing freedom for the client, switching first to questions that offer suggestions and options (multiple choice) from which the client can choose, then to questions that offer an answer or recommendation (forced choice, concurrence), and finally to *no* question but telling the client what to do (no choice, compliance or no compliance). At each shift to the lower level of questioning style, the therapist should ask the client's permission, for example, by saying, "Would it be all right if I made a recommendation?" Whenever possible, the therapist should revert back to the higher level of questioning in the in-

Figure 22–1 Clients and their caregivers should be consistently involved in design of interventions. Here a client and her daughter meet with professional members of the health care team. (Courtesy of Menorah Park Nursing Home, Cleveland, Ohio.)

terview, such as at the start of a new topic.

Payton, Nelson, and Ozer[42] claim that these questioning techniques will lead to maximum involvement of the client in the process of defining therapeutic concerns and goals. The further down the ladder the therapist moves in questioning techniques (toward less and less freedom or choice for the client), the more the goals will be therapist generated rather than client generated. As Payton states, "Each therapist must develop his or her own level of tolerance for personal anxiety before intervening by 'moving down the scale' in offering suggestions and thus taking a greater role for planning than may be necessary" (p. 20). The higher the level of participation of the client in the planning process, the greater will be the client's commitment and energy available for carrying out the plan.

Identifying and Negotiating Discrepancies

The preceding sections on ethnographic interviewing and levels of questioning describe practice techniques for the practitioner to use in gaining understanding of the care giver's perspective or explanatory model and in promoting the client's active participation in the therapeutic process. In Kleinman's[39] model, this is the first step in the therapeutic process, and it addresses questions such as "What do you think is wrong?" "What do you think has caused this?" "How has this affected your daily routine?" "What are your biggest fears?" "What do you think should be done?"

The second step in the therapeutic process is for the therapist to explain to the care giver the therapist's explanatory model. What does the therapist think is wrong? What does the therapist think is the cause? What does the therapist think should be done? This involves the often difficult translation of biomedical explanations into terms that are understandable to laypeople. The explana-

tion of the therapist's perspective, if sensitively done, can yield for the therapist the joy of "collaborating with accurately informed patients and families who can contribute to the therapeutic process. When it is poorly done, however, the stage is set for clinical communication to have serious problems, which can unsettle the therapeutic relationship and thereby undermine care" (p. 240).[30] It is the presentation of their own perspectives and subsequent comparison to the perspectives of the care-giver that enables the therapist to identify questions and discrepancies that require further understandings.

And thus the next step in this therapeutic process is to engage in negotiation with the care giver (". . . between the nurse and me talking it over"), actively seeking compromise in areas of differences and conflict. The therapist may assume responsibility for clarifying areas of conflict or discrepancies between views (based on the previous sharing of both explanatory models) and then lead the negotiation toward the resolution of these conflicts. The therapist must recognize and accept that resolution and compromise may be closer to the care giver's view or it may be closer to the therapist's view — either must be possible or it is not true negotiation.

For the therapist, there is one final step in this therapeutic process — and that is the ultimate opportunity that the therapist has for self-reflection on what has transpired, i.e., their own explanatory model, the care giver's model, the compromises, the resulting plan, the special interests and emotions that emerged along the way. As Kleinman[30] states, such self-reflection contributes not only to the development of more therapeutic relationships but also to the therapist's own personal development.

The Need for Training

It is proposed by many[30,33,42,43] that the training of health care professionals must be restructured to incorporate a philosophy of partnership and skills in reflective practice. Kleinman[30] refers to current medical school training as "deplorable" and calls for making "the patient's and the family's narrative of the illness experience more central in the educational process" (p. 255). The current biomedical emphasis on disease, diagnosis, and cure needs to shift toward the psychosocial, experiential concerns of chronic illness. Kleinman suggests that this may be accomplished partly by sending medical students out into the community to develop their skills in miniethnographic interviewing, to see patients where they actually live and work, to experience themselves the contexts of illness.

The restructuring that is proposed as needed in medical school curriculums is likely also needed in the therapy curriculums since we have long viewed the medical model as our organizing framework. Payton, Nelson, and Ozer[42] outline undergraduate coursework and in-service training for physical and occupational therapists to learn how to promote patient participation in the therapy process. The emphasis in the courses is on therapist-client problem solving, communication skills and techniques for use with clients, and psychosocial issues that influence these processes. Students view videotapes of interviews and critique questioning techniques in terms of their level of choice, appropriateness in the context, and their positive or negative contribution to the therapeutic process. Educational programs in physical and occupational therapy all incorporate practicums in their course sequences. We have ready-made opportunities to provide students with learning experiences in interviewing and questioning techniques and in developing and reflecting on their own philosophies of care. Beliefs about responsibility for health problems and solutions, about authority and control between professional and family care giver, about the role of family members in the therapist's health care experiences, and about the need for understanding the family's cultural values can all be explored and clarified in the context of the field practicums.

SUMMARY

A therapeutic alliance with a family care giver can be a rich and satisfying experience for both the therapist and the family member. The therapeutic relationship between therapist and family care giver for an older person is different from that between therapist and patient. Research findings have suggested that the family care giver tends to view himself or herself as a practitioner; it then follows that therapeutic relationships that promote partnership through sharing of control, knowledge, and cultural perspectives may best support a therapeutic alliance between therapist and family member.

The ultimate objective of occupational and physical therapy is to promote optimum performance in daily living activities. In working with family care givers for frail older people in the community, we strive to support them in their efforts to reach, in essence, the same objective for themselves and for the person receiving the care. The relationship between therapist and family member is as one between two practitioners. Our educational programs have an obligation to provide opportunities for students to experience this kind of alliance in their field practicums so they may try out techniques for interviewing and negotiating care in the real-life setting and clarify their own philosophies of care.

REVIEW QUESTIONS

1. *According to Karuza, the form of the therapeutic relationship depends upon what beliefs?*

2. *What is the medical model, and why is it often chosen when working with elderly clients?*

3. *Describe the authoritarian model of health care and give an example. What are some of its disadvantages? Does it conflict with the goals of occupational therapy?*

4. *Explain the difference between the "lifeworld" and the "medical*

world." Relate these concepts to the formation of therapeutic relationships.

5. *Relate the concept of responsibility for problems and solutions to the therapist–family care-giver relationship.*

6. *Partnership in a care-giver–therapist relationship represents a sharing of _____.*

7. *In ethnographic interviewing, the professional's use of the family care giver's terms serves what purposes?*

8. *What is the difference between an illness problem list and a medical problem list?*

9. *According to Payton, Nelson, and Ozer, what type of question represents the most free choice in a client interview?*

10. *After the client and therapist have exchanged and shared perspectives, the next step in the therapeutic process is to _____.*

11. *How would you augment academic curriculums and field practicums to incorporate skills related to establishing therapeutic relationships?*

REFERENCES

1. Shanas, E: The family as a social support system in old age. Gerontologist 19:169–174, 1979.
2. Fengler, AP and Goodrich, N: Wives of elderly disabled men: The hidden patients. Gerontologist 19:175–183, 1979.
3. Barnes, ER, Raskind, M, Scott, M and Murphy, C: Problems of families caring for Alzheimer patients: Use of a support group. Journal of the American Geriatrics Society 29:80–85, 1982.
4. Brody, EM: Parent care as a normative family stress. Gerontologist 25:19–29, 1985.
5. Cantor, M: Family and community: Changing roles in an aging society. Gerontologist 31:337–346, 1991.
6. Clark, NM and Rakowski, W: Family caregivers of older adults: Improving helpful skills. Gerontologist 23:637–642, 1983.
7. Crossman, L, London, C and Barry, C: Older women caring for disabled spouses: A model

for supportive services. Gerontologist 21:464–470, 1981.
8. Diemling, GT and Bass, DM: Symptoms of mental impairments among elderly adults and their effects on family caregivers. Journal of Gerontology 41:778–784, 1986.
9. Farran, CJ, Keane-Hagerty, E, Salloway, S, Kupferer, S and Wilken, CS: Finding meaning: An alternative paradigm for Alzheimer's disease family caregivers. Gerontologist 31:483–489, 1991.
10. George, LK and Gwyther, LP: Caregiver well-being: A multidimensional examination of family caregivers of demented adults. Gerontologist 26:253–259, 1986.
11. Hasselkus, BR and Brown, M: Respite care for community elderly. American Journal of Occupational Therapy 37:83–88, 1983.
12. Ikels, C: The process of caretaker selection. Research on Aging 5:491–509, 1983.
13. Miller, B, Glasser, M and Rubin, S: A paradox of medicalization: Physicians, families and Alzheimer's disease. Journal of Aging Studies 6:135–148, 1992.
14. Norris, VK, Stephens, MAP and Kinney, JM: The impact of family interactions on recovery from stroke: Help or hindrance. Gerontologist 30:535–542, 1990.
15. Zarit, SH, Todd, PA and Zarit, JM: Subjective burden of husbands and wives as caregivers: A longitudinal study. Gerontologist 26:260–266.
16. Hasselkus, BR: Meaning in family caregiving: Perspectives on caregiver/professional relationships. Gerontologist 28:686–691, 1988.
17. Hasselkus, BR: The meaning of daily activity in family caregiving for the elderly. American Journal of Occupational Therapy 43:649–656, 1989.
18. Hasselkus, BR: Physician and family caregiver in the medical setting: Negotiation of care? Journal of Aging Studies 6:67–80, 1992.
19. Bowers, BJ: Family perceptions of care in a nursing home. Gerontologist 28:361–368, 1988.
20. Glasser, M, Rubin, S and Dickover, M: Caregiver views of help from the physician. American Journal of Alzheimer's Care and Related Disorders & Research, July/Aug, pp 4–11.
21. Motenko, AK: Respite care and pride in caregiving: The experience of six older men caring for their disabled wives. In Reinharz, S and Rowles, G (eds): Qualitative Gerontology. Springer, New York, 1988.
22. Peloquin, SM: The patient-therapist relationship in occupational therapy: Understanding visions and images. American Journal of Occupational Therapy 44: 13–21, 1990.
23. Karuza, J, Zevon, MA, Rabinowitz, VC and Brickman, P: Attribution of responsibility by helpers and recipients. In Wils, TA (ed): Basic Processes in Helping Relationships. Academic Press, New York, 1982, pp 107–129.
24. Arnstein, SR: Eight rungs on the ladder of citizen participation. In Cahn, E and Passett, B (eds): Citizen Participation: Effecting Com-

munity Change. Praeger Publishers, New York, 1981, pp 69–91.

25. Levin, LS: Self-care in health: Potentials and pitfalls. World Health Forum 2:177–184, 1981.

26. Bloom, S and Speedling, EJ: Strategies of power and dependence in doctor patient exchanges. In Haug, M (ed): Elderly Patients and Their Doctors. Springer, New York, 1981, pp 157–170.

27. Marshall, VW: Physician characteristics and relationships with older patients. In Haug, M (ed): Elderly Patients and Their Doctors. Springer, New York, 1981, pp 94–118.

28. Logan, MH and Hunt, EE: Health and the Human Condition. Duxbury Press, North Scituate, MA, 1978, p xiii.

29. Kleinman, A: The Illness Narratives. Basic Books, New York, 1988.

30. Kleinman, A, Eisenberg, L and Good, B: Culture, illness and care. Annals of Internal Medicine 88:251–258, 1978.

31. Freidson, E: Patients' Views of Medical Practice. Russell Sage Foundation, New York, 1961, 1984.

32. Mishler, EG: The Discourse of Medicine. Ablex Publishing, Norwood, NJ, 1985.

33. Katz, J: The Silent World of Doctor and Patient. Free Press, New York, 1984.

34. Hasselkus, BR: Ethnographic interviewing: A tool for practice with family caregivers for the elderly. Occupational Therapy Practice 2:9–16, 1990.

35. Spradley, JP: The Ethnographic Interview. Holt, Rinehart and Winston, New York, 1979.

36. Squyres, WD (ed): Patient Education: An Inquiry into the State of the Art. Springer Publishing, New York, 1980.

37. DiMatteo, MR and DiNicola, DD: Achieving Patient Compliance. Pergamon Press, New York, 1982, p 66.

38. Bowling, B: Effective Communication Techniques with the Aging Patient. Center for Learning Resources, University of Kentucky, Lexington, 1981.

39. Hasselkus, BR: Patient education and the elderly. Physical and Occupational Therapy in Geriatrics 2(3):55–70, 1983.

40. Hasselkus, BR: Patient education. In Davis, L and Kirkland, M (eds): The Role of Occupational Therapy and the Elderly. American Occupational Therapy Association, 1986, pp 367–372.

41. Yoder-Wise, PS: Barriers (or enhancers) to adult patient education. Journal of Continuing Education in Nursing 10:11–16, 1979.

42. Payton, OD, Nelson, CE and Ozer, MN: Patient Participation in Program Planning: A Manual for Therapists. FA Davis, Philadelphia, 1990.

43. Schön, DA: Educating the Reflective Practitioner. Jossey-Bass, San Francisco, 1987.

44. Hasselkus, BR: Rehabilitation: The family caregiver's view. Topics in Geriatric Rehabilitation 4(1):60–70, 1988.

Chapter

Public Policy

WILLIAM F. BENSON

OBJECTIVES

By the end of this chapter, readers will be able to:

1 Describe the current state of health care policy in the United States.

2 Discuss the impact of public policy on activities and lifestyle of older adults.

3 Discuss current health care initiatives, including the Oregon Plan, Medicare, and Medicaid.

4 Describe the relevance of intergenerational conflict to health care policy.

5 Describe the process by which individuals and professional groups can influence public policy.

For the first time since the enactment of Medicare and Medicaid into law in 1965, we are on the verge of major changes in the nation's health care system, perhaps even truly historic changes. Health care reform is a significant topic of discussion among policy makers and voters. Changes are being contemplated in virtually all aspects of health care, including the delivery of health care; financing sources; constraints on the exploding costs; the services to be provided; and the extent of coverage—that is, in ensuring that all Americans have access to health care services. The call for health care reform was a major theme of Clinton's campaign for the presidency, as it was for many candidates running for Congress and others running for elected office at the state level during the early 1990s.

From the perspective of Washington, D.C. (or "inside the beltway" as the insiders' world of national policy debate is often called), it seems that virtually every person with an interest in health care policy is caught up in debating, strategizing, speculating, rumor spreading, or lobbying (or any combination of these) about health care reform. Given the magnitude of this ambitious undertaking, thousands of people are involved in the reform effort. Moreover, given the 1992 elections, it is reasonable to conclude that millions of Americans are interested in seeing comprehensive health care reform occur.

While ordinary citizens may not note or care about debates over such topics as a single-payer system, a managed competition model, employer mandates or a "play-or-pay" approach, global budgets, and so on, they do care about whether or not they or their loved ones will have health care coverage and about how much it will cost them. Further, whether they recognize the impact or not, health care and other public policy affect the everyday lives of everyone in the United States. This is certainly true for older adults, for whom life choices such as whether to continue to work or to retire, to live in the community or in a residential facility, to accept or reject various forms of health care, are all affected to some degree by public policy.

Those who earn a living in health care–related fields are vitally concerned with the current debate and are spending great amounts of time and money trying to influence the course and outcome of that debate. And they should commit considerable capital — economic, political, and personal — to doing just that, for not only is it a critical public policy endeavor but there is a great deal at stake for each of the affected parties, most notably those who receive health care. For those who believe health care is a right for all, it represents the potential dawning of a beautiful day; for those who have had the opportunity to earn high incomes largely free of government oversight, it may represent the dusk of a glorious era. In either case, it is clear that the change will be nothing short of a revolution.[1]

The effort to overhaul our health care system is receiving extraordinary atten-

tion and is the stuff of virtual daily news coverage. Public policy making that concerns health care, however, is always important news to health care professionals, for it affects their daily lives and the lives of their patients. There is an association or organization that claims to represent virtually every type of health care professional, as well as every other party affected by health care policy, including consumers. Some of these entities are clearly more influential than others. When one thinks of a powerful health care organization, the *American Medical Association* (AMA) comes to mind. Certainly, the AMA and other groups representing doctors have had tremendous clout in influencing health care policy for many years at the federal and state levels alike, but there are many other health professionals who do have a great deal to contribute to public policy and the nation's health care, including the nursing home industry, occupational and physical therapists, social workers, speech pathologists and audiologists, nurses, and the many other allied health professionals who comprise more than 60 percent of all health care providers.[2]

The importance of changes in health care policy, particularly under a comprehensive effort to reform the entire system, cannot be understated. Health care policy affects virtually every dimension of professional life:

- Whether or not occupational or physical therapy, social work, and various nursing functions are covered services and under what circumstances
- Payment structure and rates
- Administrative and regulatory — or "red-tape" — matters
- Determinations about whether service will be primarily in-hospital or at home, preventive or remedial, and incentives for and assistance with training and educational concerns
- Research

Representation by a national (or state-level) organization is an important vehicle for having a voice in health care policy, but it is not the only way. In fact, there are times when that national voice may be out of step with the rank-and-file membership. Many believe a classic and recent example of this was the fiasco over the *Medicare Catastrophic Coverage Act* (MCCA). Passed by the Congress on a bipartisan basis and signed into law by President Reagan, the MCCA was hailed as the most important improvement to the Medicare program since its enactment in 1965. The new law included coverage for prescription drugs and a respite care benefit. It also included important improvements in Medicaid, such as financial protection for spouses of those living in nursing homes. A highly controversial provision, however, was a tax on upper income–level older Americans to pay for the new benefits. In one of the most dramatic public policy reversals in recent history, the MCCA was repealed by Congress the very next year. The Congress, the Reagan administration, and many others who had supported the MCCA, were stunned by the vocal, national, and highly effective outcry from a segment of the older population and consequently swiftly moved to dump the entire act, except for the Medicaid provisions. Grassroots advocacy, or lobbying, played a large role in this reversal.

This chapter:

- Examines the ways in which policy decisions affect the lives of older adults to whom services may be provided
- Offers insights into why public policy concerning health care is important to all who have a stake in health care services
- Offers an overview of ways in which public policy can be influenced by health care providers, either individually or collectively

EFFECTS OF LEGISLATION ON FUNCTION

Many legislative initiatives affect the function of older adults in self-care, work, and leisure. Depending on the individual and the particular piece of legislation, the effects may be positive or negative. What is inescapable is that even legislation that seems rather far afield from the concerns of health care providers may have significant consequences for the kind of care which is provided.

The Social Security Act of 1935 is a good example of this concept.[3] This act, passed during the Great Depression, was designed to provide minimum support for those over 65, disabled workers, and surviving spouses and children of workers who died. As is typical with legislation, a number of changes over the years have altered the effects of this bill. For example, rules about earned income

Figure 23–1 Older adults tend to be quite involved in political action. Here, several older adults meet with their congressional representative. (Courtesy of Menorah Park Nursing Home, Cleveland, Ohio.)

have been implemented that set a ceiling on income for individuals younger than 70. Social security benefits for those between ages 65 and 69 who earn more than the ceiling are reduced by $1 for every $2 over the maximum. After age 70, an individual can earn any amount without having social security benefits reduced. Another recent change is the gradual increase of the age at which an individual can retire with full benefits, from 65 now to 67 in 2010.

These two policies work at cross purposes. The latter was passed as a way to control the rapidly expanding cost of social security at a time when the work force was shrinking. The former now serves a possibly undesirable purpose of keeping individuals out of the work force. In times of high unemployment, it may be necessary to encourage some individuals to leave the work force to provide jobs to others, but if there are not adequate numbers of workers to support the system, it is desirable to encourage people to continue to work. As now written, one social security regulation encourages individuals age 65–70 not to work, while another attempts to keep them in the labor force longer.

A second piece of legislation that has had major impact on the lives of older adults is Medicaid.[4] The primary provisions of this legislation relate to health care for indigent individuals; however, it also has provisions for funding nursing home care for older adults who have "spent down" their own resources until they are considered indigent. Like social security, specific provisions of this legislation have had "unintended effects" that are now being examined carefully. Most notably, Medicaid has not historically paid for long-term care outside of nursing homes. Medicare, the health care insurance plan for older adults, has limited provisions for community-based care, but for the most part, these costs are paid for out-of-pocket. The result may be that individuals who cannot pay for these services are forced into nursing homes, often unwillingly. Given the high cost of nursing home care, this is a highly undesirable outcome from the perspective of the government and ap-

pears to be undesirable to older adults and their families as well. Recent legislation has attempted to provide for "Medicaid waivers" to enable states to provide Medicaid funding for in-home care when the alternative is likely to be nursing home placement.[5]

The whole idea of waivers has been based on the assumption that in-home care is less expensive than nursing home care.[6] It is unfortunate, but true, that issues about quality of life and the preferences of service recipients often take a back seat to cost considerations. As data have emerged, the assumption that costs are lower is being challenged. As is often the case, cost projections are highly complex, making it extremely unclear what the reality is; reports variously suggest that in-home care is more expensive, less expensive, or equivalent to the cost of institutional care. Some researchers suggest, for example, that costs are higher because in-home care is actually being provided for individuals who would otherwise be taken care of by family members at no cost to the government. Others suggest that the cost benefit is even greater than early estimates as it is possible that reduced stress to family members results in lowered health care costs for them as well. While the debate continues, however, new legislation will continue to be drafted to address real or presumed problems with current provisions. To a large extent, it will be the influence of consumers or experts, rather than data, which will determine the outcome of this and other debates.

Clearly, both Social Security and Medicaid affect health care providers' interventions. For example, a therapist working with an older adult who wishes to return to work must, with that individual, consider the financial consequences of that decision, keeping in mind the provisions of the Social Security regulations. A therapist working with an individual who wishes to remain in his or her home must consider the availability of Medicaid waivers that may facilitate in-home care.

Appendix 23–1 lists some of the important federal legislation of the last 50 years that has significant impact on older adults. This list is only a sampling, as many pieces of human services legislation may have a direct or indirect effect on the lives of elders. For example, allocation of research funding among various agencies of the *National Institutes of Health* (NIH) may affect the likelihood that diseases or disabilities of older adults will receive adequate research attention.

THE CURRENT HEALTH CARE DEBATE

Outcomes of the current health care debate will undoubtedly have similar implications for the lives and function of older adults. This is an exciting time for those involved in or otherwise interested in health care policy in the United States. Despite the tremendous emphasis on reducing the deficit and stimulating the economy, health care reform is center stage in the Clinton administration's agenda. President Clinton made this clear in his initial State of the Union Address before the Congress and the nation on February 17, 1993.

While there is great anticipation that considerable, if not dramatic, changes will be made in the nation's health care system, there are major hurdles to overcome in achieving truly comprehensive health care reform. Not the least of these is deciding how to finance coverage for those currently without health care insurance, as well as the millions of others with inadequate coverage. Advisors to President Clinton reportedly indicated that if he were successful in achieving health care reform by the end of 1993, his first year in office, the cost would be an additional $175 billion to provide universal coverage for the 4-year period between 1994 and 1997.[7]

A number of proposals adopted as part of comprehensive health care reform are designed to generate substantial savings in current health care expenditures, estimated at well over $900 billion in 1993.[8] These savings are intended to offset some of the additional costs associated with universal coverage. Examples of areas where significant savings may be found include:

- Adopting a managed competition approach to health care delivery
- Providing scientifically established guidelines for patients and physicians on the effectiveness of various health care procedures
- Placing limits, or "caps," on national or state health care expenditures
- Reducing administrative costs
- Reducing fraud

Nonetheless, even if all of these cost-containment approaches work, there will be significant additional costs associated with providing universal health coverage for all Americans. The *Washington Post* estimated that an additional $90 billion in annual taxes will have to be raised by 1997 to pay for comprehensive health care reform.[7]

For older adults, these changes may be either positive or negative, depending on the eventual decisions made. At present, even with Medicare coverage, older adults have large out-of-pocket expenses for deductibles, prescription drugs, and so on. It is possible that some of these costs would be reduced under the proposed plan; however, choice of health care provider may be reduced, as cost-containment efforts will likely include increased reliance on health maintenance organizations. The whole issue of long-term care remains under discussion, although it seems likely that there will be an attempt to include at least some home-based care.

While there is a tremendous amount of activity at the national level regarding health care reform, there is also a great deal of work being done in many states to improve the delivery of health care and the extent of coverage for the public. For example, Hawaii, Washington, Oregon, Maryland, Texas, and California are currently vigorously debating or initiating major reforms to provide universal health care coverage or make other major changes in health care in their states.

The Oregon Plan

On March 19, 1993, the Clinton administration announced its approval of Oregon's highly controversial plan to change its Medicaid program, nearly 2 years after it was initially submitted to the federal government.[9] During a 5-year "experiment," the so-called Oregon plan will not cover certain procedures for Medicaid recipients and will use the savings from these restrictions to provide coverage for an estimated additional 120,000 low-income people in Oregon, providing access to health care for all low-income people in Oregon. This will include those ineligible for Medicaid (i.e., the "working poor").

The controversy over the Oregon proposal stems in large part from the implicit rationing of care that is built into it. Medicaid recipients would be denied treatment for some 120 procedures or conditions out of a total of 688 categories of illness and treatment established by the state. According to the *Washington Post*,[9] the list of excluded conditions and treatments includes:

- Mild forms of spinal deformities and scoliosis, although "more severe, activity-limiting forms of these conditions are above the cutoff and eligible for treatment."
- Breast reconstruction, as it "is primarily a cosmetic procedure, not a treatment for a life-threatening condition."
- Liver transplants for treatment of liver cancer because "liver cancer usually spreads quickly and recurs, and transplants are seldom successful."
- "Cancer with distant metastases, where treatment will not result in a five-year survival rate exceeding 5 percent," adding, that the "success rate of cures is very low" but noting that "comfort care is provided."

The Bush administration rejected Oregon's proposal in the summer of 1992, arguing that it violated the Americans with Disabilities Act because some of the disallowed services may adversely affect disabled individuals. More than five dozen organizations representing older adults and disabled individuals have written a letter to President Clinton arguing that the Oregon plan still violates the law.

Proponents of Oregon's plan have argued that the need for reform is so great that innovative approaches by states that provide universal coverage must be given a chance to work and that economic realities mean that public funds cannot be found to provide coverage for all forms of treatment for every health problem. Moreover, proponents point out that Oregon should be credited with choosing to restrict services that have been shown to have minimal benefit to few people rather than denying care for serious but treatable conditions for thousands of Oregonians. Oregon's plan is explicit about rationing services as opposed to the nation's current system of rationing under which there are 37 million uninsured Americans and millions more with inadequate coverage, insurance policies with restrictions on "preexisting conditions," and so on.

While the Oregon program is likely to receive considerable scrutiny and continue to be controversial, it is also likely that the underlying principles and themes, such as the limiting of certain forms of care, will be part of the broader national debate on health care reform. A major question will be whether or not such approaches will be focused only on the poor, as in Oregon, encouraging a two-tiered health care system. The Oregon Plan has special import for older individuals, since unreimbursed services may particularly affect this segment of the population. Some individuals[10] have argued that services at the end of life should be curtailed because of the high cost and perceived limited benefit of such services. This is obviously a controversial view, but it raises an issue that must addressed in decision making about implementation of a universal health care plan.

Medicare and Medicaid

Medicare is a current and visible example of how varying "interests" respond to health care programs. Since its enactment in 1965, Medicare has spawned an extraordinary amount of lobbying regarding virtually every aspect of the program. Millions of Americans depend upon the Medicare program either because it is the primary or a significant source of the health care they receive or because it provides economic benefits to them.[3] The decisions made under Medicare that affect people's lives are extensive, ranging from decisions about eligibility for coverage, the services and products that are covered (or not covered), the payment and reimbursement levels for those services and products, and the standards and mechanisms for monitoring the quality of services and the penalties for failure to meet such standards, to decisions about a wide variety of administrative matters such as billing procedures and payment mechanisms and beneficiary appeals.

The Medicaid program, enacted in 1965, has also been the subject of substantial lobbying efforts.[4] These efforts have taken place at both the federal and state levels since Medicaid is jointly administered and financed by the federal government and the states. Within federal requirements, states have considerable latitude in making decisions about most aspects of the program. Due to current pressures on state budgets, decisions about providing more funding (or continuing the same rate) or services for Medicaid create tensions on a variety of fronts. There are those who argue that money going to Medicaid needs to go elsewhere (e.g., building prisons, education, reduced taxes). Others insist that older adults receive too much of the Medicaid pie while more needs to be done for children or that too much goes to nursing home care and not enough for

alternatives to nursing home care such as home care.

Choosing between differing priorities may not be a simple or inexpensive proposition. For advocates of more primary care for children or low-income adults, or for those who want to see reinstatement of services that have been reduced or dropped from coverage, such as dental care or prescription drugs, or for those who want to see more home- and community-based long-term care services, those increases are certainly significant. The situation is the same in many states. Given the amount of money involved, the stakes are high, and therefore the various interested parties have a great deal to say about the decisions made about current or additional expenditures.

INTERGENERATIONAL CONFLICT

While these debates and the related advocacy efforts over them are an understandable, normal, and indeed, a necessary part of the public policy process, many believe that there is a disturbing and growing level of tension between advocates for children, disabled individuals, and other adults, as typified by the debate about allocation of Medicaid funds. While references to this conflict by some commentators as "intergenerational warfare" may be dismissed as overblown hyperbole or rhetorical flourish, this is, in all probability, a growing and potentially serious rift between the old and other segments of our society, which may become a deep and enduring fissure. This rift may contribute to serious public policy conflict with regard to major social programs, including health care and, of course, programs like Social Security.

For example, discussions about the United States budget deficit include consideration of taxing social security benefits[10] and reducing cost of living adjustments.[12] Older adults see these as assaults on benefits promised them by the government, while younger individuals point to the growing poverty rate among children as an example that older individuals are getting too big a percentage of federal support. Given current constraints on the federal budget, these arguments are likely to beome increasingly fierce.

PUBLIC POLICY ADVOCACY

There is nothing new or surprising about the intense lobbying efforts currently underway, and they are not limited to health care. It is almost impossible to imagine an area of concern that is not the subject of policy initiatives, and therefore lobbying efforts; these areas include the environment, education, taxation, crime, transportation, foreign affairs, defense, welfare, and so on.

The consequences of public decisions about health care are immense. Therefore, the communication of needs, expectations, and hopes about a program, service, or related matter that affects or concerns an individual is essential. In other words, our democratic society is dependent upon advocacy, the act or process of pleading the cause of another (or of one's self) or the process of defending or maintaining a cause or proposal.[13] Examples of this include advocating that a particular service be covered under Medicare (or under a new national health care system) or that the reimbursement rate for a covered service is inadequate.

For many, it seems that advocacy's "evil twin" is lobbying. They appear to find the word *advocacy* more positive or acceptable than *lobbying*, which very often is another way of saying the same thing. A definition of *lobbying* is:

> To conduct activities aimed at influencing public officials and esp. members of a legislative body on legislation. **1:** to promote (as a project) or secure the passage of (as legislation) by influencing public officials **2:** to attempt to influence or sway (as a public official) toward a desired action.[13]

Paradoxically, it seems to be a common view that when we promote or argue for something we believe to be right we are engaging in "advocacy." When another is doing the same on be-

half of an issue or cause that we do not support or feel as strongly about, they are engaging in "lobbying."

The bottom line is that advocacy or lobbying, depending upon one's preferred term, is not only part of our social fabric and a major part of our system of participatory government, it is usually what makes things happen. The coverage of occupational therapy under Part B of the Medicare program beginning in July 1987[14] was not just the product of knowledgeable and helpful members of Congress, their staff, or bureaucrats in the *Health Care Financing Administration* (HCFA). No doubt, this change in Medicare policy was the result of strong and effective advocacy by those involved with or otherwise knowledgeable about the value of occupational therapy and most likely involved a substantial degree of good old lobbying. Much of this lobbying was carried out by allied health and nursing professional organizations, acting in their own interests as health care providers and also in the interests of those who receive their care.

If we care about our work and our clients, then we must care about decisions that affect either, particularly when those decisions are in the hands of public officials. It is clear that public policy decisions have a great impact upon our personal and professional lives as well as those of the individuals we serve.

It seems then, that the important question is not whether one should express herself or himself to influence the decisions made by public policy makers; rather, the question is how to do it in a way that is consistent with one's abilities, resources (e.g., money, time), interests, knowledge, and values. The challenge to the individual is to be an effective and efficient voice on the matter(s) he or she cares about. Fortunately, in our society, there are many ways to go about that, some of which are very sophisticated and involved, and others that are very simple, as simple as making a phone call, writing a letter, or voting.

To be an effective advocate, one must recognize that elected officials are ultimately accountable to those who elect them—the voting public, which hopefully includes you the reader.

Former Speaker of the House of Representatives, Tip O'Neill, is credited with observing that "all politics are local." In other words, no matter how important or far up the ladder of public office the policy makers, or politicians, sit, whether they are members of a state legislature, U.S. senators, chairs of powerful congressional committees, or even President of the United States, they are elected by and are answerable to their constituents. Dislodging an entrenched incumbent or powerfully financed political machine can be an overwhelming, if not seemingly impossible, task, but it does happen.

Beyond being accountable to the electorate or to a boss who is accountable to the voting public, most public figures are motivated by doing what they believe is in the best interest of the public. While their perception of what is in the best interest of the public certainly will not always coincide with yours (and in some cases never will), it clearly helps to identify where your respective perceptions of the public good overlap. The public official who believes that government spends too much money on public programs, including health care, is not typically going to embrace the expansion of an existing program to include a new service or be too willing to push for higher payments to professionals, but if that official can be convinced that a particular service, such as occupational or physical therapy, or a social work or nursing intervention is cost effective and will result in fewer expenditures for more extensive and costly care, he or she may be more likely to support the expanded coverage.

Moreover, it is important to remember that public policy makers, elected and appointed, are human and want to make contributions to society in some way (the few not so inclined will want to at least look good!). They respond to arguments to support something that is consistent with most people's values, common sense, or their own personal experience. This author has observed in several elected officials a significant shift in support for public financing for home- and community-based long-term care services because of their personal experiences with family members who have become frail or suffered from Alzheimer's disease. One member of Congress was very reluctant to support the late Claude Pepper's legislation to establish comprehensive home care services for older adults because he couldn't accept the notion of public dollars paying for someone to help with housework for a frail or disabled individual, believing that if they were that incapacitated, they should be in a nursing home. A short while later, after a personal experience with a relative in a nursing home, he became convinced that remaining at home was highly desirable. This particular politician became a stalwart supporter of the Pepper legislation. It does not always take an experience with a family member to bring a public official around, as observations or personal appeals from constituents can have an equally significant effect.

Once the aspiring advocate accepts that the policy maker can be educated or otherwise convinced to do the "right thing" (from the advocate's perspective, of course) or, failing that, can be turned out of office, then it is time to consider the myriad ways in which to carry out the advocacy effort. What follows are suggestions for engaging in the process of advocacy.

The beginning point is to understand the issue about which you care or are concerned. Let's say you believe that people should have easier access to the services of an occupational therapist—in other words, to your services if you are an OT (or to the services of a physical therapist, art or dance therapist, geriatrician, midwife, social worker, and so on, depending upon what program is being promoted). Then you should understand your profession or issue well.

In this example, the basic facts are evident. Without health coverage, getting occupational therapy will be difficult. Even with health care coverage, the services of an OT may not be covered. While occupational therapy services are available under Medicare's home health care benefit, they are more difficult to obtain than certain other skilled services. OT services can be obtained only after the beneficiary has qualified for Medicare's home health care benefit. In contrast, the need for intermittent skilled nursing care or physical or speech therapy are qualifying criteria for the home health care benefit. Another barrier to access to occupational therapy may be the Medicare provision limiting annual reimbursement to independently practicing occupational therapists (and physical therapists) to $750 per beneficiary. Other potential impediments to access may be based upon local availability or distance, lack of transportation, or burdensome cost-sharing requirements (e.g., copayments). According to a recent report, "A major concern continues to be OT's difficulty in meeting the demand for qualified practitioners."[14] A 1990 report to Congress by the DHHS cited the IOM finding that there is "a need for decision makers to improve the workings of the market so that 'severe imbalances' in supply and demand may be prevented in the field of radiologic technology and occupational therapy."[15]

Resolution of any of these potential barriers to access to OT have significant public policy implications. The individual who wishes to improve access to occupational therapy needs to know what the barriers are. An argument that Medicare coverage is inadequate is likely to be more effective if the related facts are well understood. Very often the underlying reason for a limit is a plan to limit utilization and to restrain expenditures. It is helpful to be able to demonstrate that this is true, so a first step in advocacy may be gathering relevant cost-benefit information by identifying, or even undertaking, research that supports this contention.

Professional or trade associations can provide background and can represent your profession on related matters. Most professions are represented by a national organization, such as the *American Occupational Therapy Association* (AOTA) or *American Physical Therapy Association* (APTA), *National Association of Social Workers* (NASW), or *American Nurses Association* (ANA), and often there are state and local affiliates, all of which may have information about policy issues. Another source of information is associations or organizations that represent subjects or concerns that are related to your work. For health care professionals who work primarily with older patients, membership in such organizations as the *American Geriatric Society* (AGS) and the *Gerontological Society of America* (GSA) may be useful. For those who have a particular interest in research related to older individuals, the *Alliance for Aging Research* (AAR) may be another source of information, while educators may turn to the *Association of Gerontology in Higher Education* (AGHE). Consumer or public groups such as the *American Association of Retired People* (AARP) or the Grey Panthers are yet another source of information and another avenue for active involvement. Appendix 23–2 lists telephone numbers for these organizations.

Individuals may choose to be involved in advocacy through participation in these organizations, by joining committees, assisting in fund-raising efforts, or responding to letter-writing campaigns. Individual advocacy can also be of value, particularly face-to-face interaction with elected officials or their staff matters. Elected officials are interested in knowing what their constituents think about issues. Well-written letters that provide background and explain the importance of particular positions may inform a politician who might otherwise know little about an issue.

The essential point is that the daily lives of care recipients are affected in many ways by public policy. Their ability to remain at work, in their homes, involved in activities that they value depends on a wide variety of policies. Health care providers must assist to ensure that policies reflect the needs of their clients, and their professions.

SUMMARY

This chapter provides a discussion and several examples of the ways in which public policy affects the function of older adults. It considers the current debate about health care reform and the potential impact of those reforms on consumers and professionals. Finally, it describes the need for advocacy and the process by which health care providers can become involved in this process. To ensure access for our clients to the best possible care and to ensure that policy supports their needs and wishes relative to the activities they undertake in their daily lives, it is essential that care providers understand the importance of advocacy and assume responsibility for influencing public policy.

REVIEW QUESTIONS

1. *Describe the current status of health care insurance in the United States.*

2. *In what ways does public policy affect the function of older adults? Give federal, state, and local examples.*

3. *Compare the provisions of Medicare and Medicaid for older adults. What affect will the Oregon plan have on these provisions?*

4. *It has been noted that intergenerational conflict is increasing. Why is this so, and what might be done to remedy the problem?*

5. *In reading about a new health care bill, you find a provision you feel would be particularly beneficial for the type of clients you see. How would you go about expressing your views and encouraging passage of that provision?*

6. *What key provision would you include in a comprehensive health care reform package? Discuss the impact of this provision on the functional performance of older adults.*

REFERENCES

1. Johnson, EA and Johnson, RL: Hospitals Under Fire: Strategies for Survival. Aspen, Rockville, MD, 1986, pp. 437–443.
2. Shugars, DA, O'Neil, EH, and Bader, JD (eds): Healthy America: Practitioners for 2005: An Agenda for Action for U.S. Health Professional Schools. The Pew Health Professions Commission, Durham, NC, 1991.
3. Koitz, D: The Financial Outlook for Social Security and Medicare. Congressional Research Service, Washington, DC, 92-608 EPW, 1992.
4. Price, R: Health Care Fact Sheet: Long-Term Care for the Elderly—Financing Issues. Congressional Research Service, Washington, DC, 92–973 EPW, 1992.
5. O'Shaughnessy, C and Price, R: Medicaid "2176" Waivers for Home and Community Based Care. Congressional Research Service, Washington, DC, 85–817 EPW, 1985.
6. Schillmoeller, S: Adult Day Care: Background, Funding, Cost-Effectiveness Issues, and Recent Legislation. Congressional Research Service, Washington, DC, 86–121 EPW, 1986.
7. Washington Post, February 22, 1993.
8. Washington Post, February 19, 1992.
9. Washington Post, March 20, 1993.
10. Callahan, D: Setting Limits: Medical Goals in an Aging Society. Simon & Schuster, New York, 1987.
11. Kollman, G: Taxing Social Security Benefits: A Fact Sheet. Congressional Research Service, Washington, DC, 93–336 EPW, 1993.
12. Koitz, D and Kollmann, G: Social Security: The Cost-of-Living Adjustment. Congressional Research Service, Washington, DC, 92–796 EPW, 1992.
13. Webster's Ninth New Collegiate Dictionary. Merriam-Webster, Springfield, MA, 1990, pp. 59–60.
14. Institute of Medicine: Allied Health Services: Avoiding Crisis. Report of the Committee to Study the Role of Allied Health Personnel. National Academy Press, Washington, DC, 1989, p. 124.
15. Department of Health and Human Services: Seventh Report to the President and the Congress on the Status of Health Personnel. Washington, DC, DHHS publication No. HRS-P-OD-90-1, March, 1990, p. X–3.

APPENDIX 23–1: SELECTED FEDERAL LEGISLATION AFFECTING OLDER ADULTS

Listed here are some of the most significant pieces of federal legislation that affect the function of older adults. This is by no means an exhaustive list, nor does it outline all the provisions of all the bills listed. There is often considerable overlap among bills, and provisions that affect older individuals may be found in bills that are not specifically labeled as such (e.g., the Omnibus Budget Reconciliation Acts). Much legislation must be reenacted periodically, and provisions may change in the new bills. Information about pending legislation can often be obtained from organizations such as those listed in Appendix 23–2.

Older Americans Act (1965)

Title I	Broad policy objectives directed toward improving the lives of older adults.
Title II	Establishes the Administration on Aging (AOA).
Title III	Provides funds for adult day care and nutrition programs.
Title IV	Provides funding for training, research, and demonstration projects including community-based long-term care, intergenerational programs, and health promotion.
Title V	Provides funds for employment of older adults.
Title VI	Authorizes special programs for Native Americans and Native Hawaiians.
PL 90–459	1. Reauthorizes act. 2. Emphasizes services to low-income minority older adults. 3. Creates Title VII for health education and training.

	4. Special consideration established for Alzheimer's disease.
PL 100–175	Older Americans Act Amendments of 1987: 1. Reauthorizes act for 4 years. 2. Emphasizes outreach services for frail elderly living at home, and for victims of elder abuse.
PL 102–375	Reauthorizes bill through 1995. Adds Title VII to expand activities in establishing the rights of older adults. Establishes an office in AOA for the Long-term Care Ombudsman Program and the National Center on the National Center on Elder Abuse.

Social Security (1935)

PL 98–21	1. Raises the retirement age to age 67 by 2010. 2. Increases the amount of benefits taxed for certain individuals.
PL 92–603	Social Security Act Amendments of 1972. Creates funding for community-service demonstration projects.
Title XX	Social Service Block Grant (SSBG). Funds adult day care services.

Medicaid

Title XIX of the Social Security Act. Includes provisions for coverage of nursing home care for indigent older adults.

Medicare

Title XVIII of the Social Security Act:

Part A outlines hospital coverage.
Part B outlines physician, outpatient,

PL 98–21   Creates diagnosis
               related groups
               (DRGs) as a method
               to control medical
               costs.

Older American Volunteer Program (OAVP) (Retired Senior Volunteer Program, Foster Grandparent Program, and Senior Companion Program)

PL 98–288   Extends OAVP for 3
               years.
PL 101–204   Extends act through
               1993.

Age Discrimination in Employment Act (1967)

Prohibits discrimination in employment because of age.

PL 99–592   Eliminates the upper
               age limit of 70 for
               protection under the
               law

Housing and Urban-Rural Recovery Act (1984)

PL 98–181   Creates affordable
               housing for older
               adults.

Housing and Community Development Act (1987)

Authorizes housing for the elderly and handicapped.

Home and Community-Based Waiver Program

PL 97–35   Expands community-
               based services
               through Medicaid
               funding.

Omnibus Budget Reconciliation Act (OBRA) (1981)

PL 97–35   States may obtain
               waivers for
               community-based
               services through
               Medicaid.

Omnibus Budget Reconciliation Act (OBRA) (1987)

PL 100–203   1. Sets standards for
                  nursing home
                  personnel.
               2. Sets standards for
                  rights of nursing
                  home residents.
               3. Sets standards for
                  home health
                  agencies.

APPENDIX 23–2: PROFESSIONAL AND ADVOCACY ORGANIZATIONS

Alliance for Aging Research: (202)
293–2856

American Association of Retired Persons: (202) 434–2277

American Geriatrics Society: (212)
308–1414

American Nurses Association: (202)
554–4444

American Occupational Therapy Association: (301) 948–9626

American Physical Therapy Association: (703) 684–2782

Association of Gerontology in Higher Education: (202) 429–9277

Gerontological Society of America: (202) 842–1275

Grey Panthers: (215) 545–6555

National Association of Social Workers: (301) 565–0333

Chapter

Activity and Loss

KATHLEEN SMYTH

OBJECTIVES

By the end of the chapter, readers will be able to:

1 Describe the nature and scope of losses encountered by older adults; the cognitive, affective, behavioral, and somatic reactions of the elderly to loss; and the ways in which the elderly may adjust to loss.

2 Explore the relationship between activity and loss in later life.

3 Describe the role of activity in helping with older adults dealing with loss.

The losses experienced by older adults have wide-ranging and serious implications for their performance. This chapter reviews the various losses commonly experienced in old age, describes the ways in which older adults react and adjust to losses, and discusses the role of activity-focused interventions in helping older adults deal with loss.

LOSSES IN OLD AGE

Losses in old age are typically thought of in terms of the death of a spouse, siblings, and close friends. Focus on these losses is understandable since the loss of multiple significant people can isolate an older person and deplete the will to live.[1] These deaths also eliminate roles (e.g., spouse, sister or brother, confidante) that the elderly person held as a result of a relationship with the deceased. The social self is a product of relationships with others, so the death of someone close can compromise identity.[2]

While adjustment to the loss of persons may be particularly difficult, older people experience many other losses as well. These include the loss of important possessions, physical abilities, occupations or careers, financial resources, group memberships, pets, homes, and neighborhoods. More difficult to quantify, but none the less significant, is the loss of future plans and dreams in the light of the increasing limitations associated with aging.[3] At the same time, the elderly person is unavoidably confronted with evidence of his or her own mortality and thus must add loss of self to the list of losses to be faced. Raphael, cited in Kalish,[3] notes:

> The griefs of growing old begin with the first realization that one cannot do, with ease, something that one had previously been able to accomplish without thought; that one will not, now, achieve the fullness of one's hopes and dreams; that one's life is not limitless, but finite, and the time remaining is not great. (p. 33)

While the challenge of facing multiple losses is not limited to older adults, they are at increased risk for these experiences.[3] Among bereaved spouses studied by Herth,[4] for example, 90 percent reported that at least one other important loss had occurred concurrently with the loss of a spouse, and 67 percent reported more than three simultaneous losses. These losses may provoke more fear and anxiety than the thought of their own deaths.[1] As elders lose their roles in the family and community, their lives may begin to be perceived as less important, both to themselves and others.[5] As Kastenbaum notes,[6] the personal, social, and economic losses endured by older adults can be thought of as partial deaths.

Loss of a Spouse

The death of a spouse may have significant impact, resulting in the simultaneous loss of a friend, lover, and helpmate.[3] One consequence may be a tremendous decrease in the amount of stimulation in an elder's life.[7] Widowhood also has effects on other family relationships. If a couple has children, for example, the remaining spouse has to assume both parental roles.[8]

Women whose husbands die are especially vulnerable to multiple losses since the loss of a husband may result in change of residence (often to smaller or less desirable living space), as well as movement away from friends, lower income, loss of transportation, and loss of social identity.[1,3] Further, while the majority of widowers remarry within a year or two after their wife's death, most widows do not.[8] Brink[7] reports that overall, two-thirds of older men are married, while only one-third of older women are.

Widowhood also has some positive consequences. Housework demands are reduced, and more time may be available for travel and the pursuit of new interests. Widowhood presents options for choosing new roles and friendships.[8] For both husbands and wives, developing new social roles is essential to effective adjustment.[3]

Loss of an Adult Child

Because individuals are living longer, the likelihood is growing that they will experience the death of one or more middle-aged children. At least 1 in 10 older parents has lost one or more children.[9]

The loss of a child may mean the simultaneous loss of a care giver,[10] requiring elderly parents to take on tasks once performed by the child, such as managing finances, caring for younger children, providing transportation, housing, and home maintenance, and arranging social activities.[3,9] This may cause loss of independence and reduced sense of autonomy.[11] The death of a grandchild or the divorce of a son or daughter may have similar consequences.[3,12]

Loss of Possessions

Loss of one's home, whether owned or rented, is also disproportionately experienced by older adults. The loss is often compounded by the separation from neighbors and neighborhood that relocation often implies.[13] Institutionalization represents an extreme in the disruption of established patterns of social and familial interaction—the loss of an entire lifestyle.[7]

The loss of a pet can also be a significant event in the life of an elderly person. Older adults may have had lengthy and devoted relationships with their pets and may experience a severe sense of loss when a pet dies or can no longer be kept. This can be exacerbated because the loss of a pet is often not recognized as significant by others.[14]

Loss of Physical Abilities

Most older adults must deal with chronic diseases, as well as sensory decline and decreased physical capacity. Chronic physical disabilities make it more difficult for them to participate in activities[7] and may affect self-esteem.

Loss of Occupational Role

In modern societies, loss of one's occupation in old age through retirement or disability can be particularly devastating. These societies value people in terms of the functions they currently perform and what they will be able to do in the future. To the extent that individuals no longer perform occupational roles, they can lose power, influence, status, and sense of purpose.[15] Retirement also involves loss of job-related social contacts.

Loss of Self

Aging itself is a process, while being elderly is a social status or position.[16] Our society has no clear norms governing whether aging or being old is to be determined chronologically, in terms of ability to perform social roles, or on the basis of attitudes, physical appearance, or health; however, it is likely that being identified as old will result in some loss

of status, with accompanying change in self-concept.

ACCEPTING THE INEVITABILITY OF DEATH

At some point in their lives, often around 40 years of age people begin to measure life in terms of how many years of life remain, rather than in terms of how many years have passed. Fear of death can be intense at this time but has been found to diminish as people age.[8] An older adult's feelings about death are subject to numerous influences including culture, education, family and other social supports, negative and positive life experiences, and personality.[8,17]

Cohorts of elderly adults are likely to have similar views of death and exhibit similar behavioral patterns in dealing with death and dying.[18] Although generalizations must be made carefully, it appears that older adults tend to think about death more but to fear it less than younger individuals,[16] and those who do express fear about dying are more likely to be concerned about the process of dying than being dead.[8] As Kalish[16] puts it: "It isn't that they want to die, but that they are ready to die."

Older adults may see death as acceptable, given the number of years they have had to live[16]; however, it is all too easy to move from this observation to the expectation that the elderly *should* accept death and that they should be less angry or frustrated about the prospect than younger people.[8] By this measure, an acceptable death becomes one that can be accepted or tolerated by the survivors.[19] Kalish[5] suggests that generally, the death of an elderly person is less disturbing than that of a younger person since the aged are not especially valued in our society.

EXPERIENCING DYING

One's own death represents the ultimate loss, removing control over one's self and future. The process of dying involves multiple physical and mental changes, which may include loss of bodily functions, sense of hopelessness and diminished purpose, and the prospect of relinquishing current projects and plans for the future. This last change can be particularly painful, in that often people wait until their later years to pursue their non-work-related goals. As dying consumes more and more aspects of the person, identity is threatened.[16,18]

It is widely held that many people know when they are about to die,[20] and it is generally acknowledged that people can shorten or prolong their lives as a function of their thoughts, feelings, or desires.[8] For example, *parasympathetic death*, or giving up, is thought to result from feelings of helplessness and hopelessness.[8]

Generally, older adults die of chronic diseases, and their dying involves a relatively slow decline. This means that the early parts of their dying experience may be much like their normal lives and that they have time to think about their coming death. On the positive side, this trajectory allows them to review their lives, perhaps visiting old friends or familiar places, and to make decisions involving their current and future care and the disposition of their possessions and other assets. However, there are also negative implications of a prolonged dying period; for example, the costs incurred during the process are generally higher than for those who die young. Further, older adults are more likely to lack a spouse, sibling, or other relative to help with care and to die in institutions.[16]

Loss in Old Age and Activity

Kielhofner and Burke[21] point out:

Occupational behavior is an activity in which persons engage during most of their waking time; it includes activities that are playful, restful, serious and productive. These work, play and daily living activities are carried out by individuals in their own unique ways based on their beliefs and preferences, the kinds of experiences they have had, their environments and the specific patterns of behaviors that they acquire over time. (p. 12)

This perspective is important in the assessment of the meaning of loss as people grow older. Multiple losses experienced during aging affect the structure of daily living activities created over a lifetime. Losses of persons, possessions, places, and plans remove the underpinnings of occupational life, and in contrast to its well-developed norms regarding activity during young adulthood and middle age, our society is nearly devoid of expectations regarding how older people are to engage in occupational behavior.

REACTION TO LOSS

By definition, anyone suffering a loss is in the status of bereavement. Whether and how the bereaved individual *suffers grief* (an affective response or emotional reaction to being bereaved) or *mourns* (engages in particular behaviors in response to bereavement) depend on a wide variety of factors.[3] Social system, income, and health status all have been found to influence outcomes associated with bereavement.[4,13] Conway[13] notes that the type of loss, the relationship of the person to what was lost, how the loss was discovered, whether or not the loss was sudden, and whether it occurred at an expected point in the life span all affect to what extent grief will be experienced.

Some researchers have suggested that older adults may experience less severe distress in response to bereavement than the middle-aged.[22,23] Others have noted that grieving may be more difficult later in life because fewer resources are available to substitute for those lost.[24] The major difference between older adults and other bereaved individuals may not be in response to the bereavement per se but in the frequency with which the elderly experience loss and grief.[3]

Types of Reaction

Most of what we know about reaction to losses among older adults is based on studies of those who have lost a significant person such as a spouse or an adult child. These studies have documented that reactions to bereavement may be cognitive, affective, behavioral, and somatic. Some characteristic reactions in each of these categories are described below.

COGNITIVE

Disbelief, confusion, and preoccupation with and attempts to make sense of the loss are among the cognitive reactions to bereavement.[25] These expressions by an elderly person may be difficult to interpret, particularly if the individual has previously exhibited other cognitive problems. It is important to distinguish reactions to bereavement from progressive irreversible decline and to examine carefully how the behaviors may be related to the individual's abilities to function independently.[3]

AFFECTIVE

Grief is not the only emotion experienced by the bereaved. Anger, anxiety, guilt, and other emotions are common. Bereavement may also result in regression, hallucinations, obsessional review, and overidentification with and idealization of the deceased. Worden[25] points out that in terms of the hierarchy of human needs proposed by Maslow, satisfaction of physiological, safety, esteem, love, and self-actualization needs are all affected by bereavement.

Grief over the loss of a spouse may be particularly intense and persistent because of the emotional importance of marital bonds and the centrality of marital status to identity in this culture. Loss of a spouse can result in social marginality and reduced self-confidence. Aiken[8] suggests that increased mortality after loss of spouse, found especially among men, is due to the stress of widowhood rather than bereavement per se.

Osterweis, Solomon, and Green[10] report that from 10 to 20 percent of the bereaved who exhibit depressive symptoms are still depressed a year later. Bereaved individuals had slightly lower life satisfaction, but only in the first month after bereavement. Thompson and associates[26] found that in general, distress levels of the bereaved were considerably reduced over time.

Bereavement is statistically associated with increased mortality in men under age 75.[10] Increased suicide in the first year of bereavement is especially common among older widowers and single men, particularly if they lack other social attachments.[27]

The death of an adult child may elicit a number of powerful emotional reactions. Since the death of a child is an "out-of-time loss,"[13] elderly parents may feel guilty that they have survived their child[10] and may be disappointed that their hopes for their son or daughter were not fulfilled.[11] The older parent may feel (often correctly) that the child is irreplaceable and may develop an extreme sense of isolation.[11]

BEHAVIORAL

Increased smoking and use of alcohol, tranquilizers, or hypnotic medications are associated with bereavement,[27] although bereavement alone is probably not sufficient to produce such behaviors.[28] The basic patterns of alcohol use may not be different between old and young[29]; however, reduced support and changing social routines in bereavement may result in a decreased sense of social control. In a genetically predisposed individual, this may lead to alcoholism.[28]

Widowed elders may continue their care for their deceased spouse by maintaining involvement in pursuits of the spouse, or by carrying on his or her work.[30] Other behavioral manifestations of bereavement may be crying and insomnia[25]; slow movement and longer reaction time[22]; wearing the clothing of the deceased, talking to the deceased, or attachment to the deceased's belongings; and emotional and social withdrawal.[1,31]

SOMATIC

Bereavement is associated with emergence of new illnesses as well as with the worsening of preexisting conditions, and increased use of medication. Although the bereaved do not have more physician visits or hospitalizations than others, they rate their overall health as poorer than the nonbereaved.[32] Some studies suggest that the bereaved are at increased risk for specific health problems such as heart disease and infections, although this is not well documented.[27]

Some research indicates that bereaved older adults are more likely to exhibit physical manifestations of grief such as a hollow feeling in stomach, tight feeling in chest, breathlessness, weakness, and dry mouth.[1,25,33]

MULTIPLE LOSSES

The experience of multiple losses can lead to "bereavement overload," an experience of overwhelming grief brought on by many losses in a short period, with little time for grieving over each loss.[34] Wan[35] found that loss of occupation through retirement did not influence subject's assessment of health status or functional abilities; however, the coincidences of multiple stressful life events such as retirement, widowhood, and other role changes was associated with health decline.

The following conclusions can be made regarding the impact and course of bereavement[36]: Nearly every aspect of a person's life can be affected. Loneliness and problems dealing with activities of daily living are two of the most common and difficult adjustments for older bereaved spouses. Although bereavement is highly stressful, its effects on physical and mental health are often not devastating, and many older spouses recover well. Generally, bereavement is most difficult in the first several months but gradually becomes easier over time. There is considerable diversity in how older bereaved adults adjust to a spouse's death, and it is common for them to have both positive and negative feelings during the bereavement process.

Activity and Reaction to Loss

Although losses are accompanied by many activity-related changes, few studies have focused on the relationship between these changes and bereavement outcomes. An exception is the study of bereaved widows performed by Kitson and Roach.[37] They found that social adjustment (functioning adequately in role responsibilities of daily life such as home, family, work, and leisure time) was central to bereavement reactions. The greater number of difficulties widows reported in performing social roles, the less independent they felt and the higher their scores were on scales of psychological symptoms. The researchers concluded that interventions for widows should focus on helping them learn about unfamiliar tasks or roles that they feel uncertain about performing. This advice would seem to apply as well to assisting older adults with bereavement generally, regardless of its cause.

ADJUSTING TO LOSS

The bereaved face formidable obstacles to moving beyond their grief. Among these are the need to:

- Accept loss
- Overcome feelings of sadness and despair
- Resolve interpersonal conflicts
- Gain insight into the meaning and value of their lives
- Reconstruct a sense of continuity
- Strengthen self-identity and sense of individuality

These obstacles may be particularly daunting for older adults because their level of social activity may have decreased for other reasons.[17]

Duration of Grief

It is difficult to predict the length of time needed to adjust to losses, and in spite of common beliefs, a year is probably not enough time for many people.[13] In their review, Wass and Myers[38] found studies that reported periods of grief response ranging from 8 to 10 weeks to 3 to 4 years; they note that several authors question whether a significant loss can ever be fully resolved.

As Conway[13] points out, moving past grief or continuing life despite grieving are important steps on the way to recovery. She reminds us that "rather than undergoing a loss, grieving, and returning to their former level of functioning, people move to a new level of functioning that incorporates the loss and grieving experience."

Factors Affecting Adjustment to Loss

Successful recovery from bereavement is influenced by many factors. There is some evidence that the stronger the emotional bond between bereaved and deceased, the more difficult the recovery process will be.[8] Further, people who felt they were under more stress providing care prior to the death of a family member are more likely to report more strain associated with adjustment.[39] Individuals who were in poor physical or mental health prior to bereavement, who suffered from alcoholism or other substance abuse or who felt social support was absent or insufficient are at increased risk for poor outcome following bereavement.[27] Conversely, adequate perceived support and remarriage appear to protect against the deleterious effects of bereavement,[27] although overinvolvement of immediate family during bereavement may actually inhibit adjustment of a bereaved spouse.[40] Finally, the degree of control one has over losses such as retirement, death of a loved one, or institutionalization affects ability to cope.[8]

While anticipatory grieving can be helpful to adjustment, a prolonged period of grieving prior to death leads to poorer recovery after the death.[8] The funeral can be an opportunity for the bereaved to work through their feelings connected with the death.[40] It is also important in promoting a sense of solidarity among the survivors, reassuring them of the validity of their shared ideals and principles, and fostering a positive relationship between the bereaved family and the wider community.[41]

Perceived Competence and the Mourning Process

Lund, Caserta, and Dimond[42] note that the life of a surviving spouse may differ drastically from that which had been developed over a long-term marriage. Some spouses develop skills in certain areas of daily living while virtually neglecting skills in other areas, a circumstance that may force them to learn new skills following a loss.

There are many important reasons to focus on *competency*, that is, the social skills, knowledge, experience, and specific instrumental behavioral skills necessary to perform daily activities that permit a person to manage, control, or meet the demands of a changing environment:

1. Competent people have a greater variety of coping responses. Perceived competence and self-esteem are likely to be correlated, and self-esteem has a positive effect on bereavement.
2. Lund, Caserta, and Dimond[43] found that problems related to activities of daily living were second only to loneliness among problems cited by bereaved respondents. Thus competence in these areas can reduce the negative impact of a loss.
3. It may be that competence reduces fatigue resulting from worries about tasks and allows the bereaved more energy for emotional expression of grief. Bereaved elderly individuals themselves advise others to take one day at a time and keep busy, and others have pointed out the therapeutic value

of meaningful activity and task accomplishment.

4. Competence includes knowledge of and ability to access services, so that improved competence should result in more appropriate use of formal and informal supports.

Activity and Adjustment to Loss

Barclay and McDougall[44] pose this question about older workers: "If we are what we do, what happens to our identity when we don't do that anymore?" Most discussions of successful coping with loss emphasize the central role of activity. Pollock, cited in Aiken,[8] notes that in the great majority of cases, grief is resolved as the bereaved person finds a new direction for life or becomes involved in a creative endeavor of some kind. Peterson and Briley, cited in Aiken,[8] suggest that recovery can be aided by focusing on future-oriented religious or philosophical beliefs, and Ball[8] suggests intensifying old social relationships, forming new ones, or becoming actively involved with children, work, or other activities. Many people, however, require special assistance in coping with grief.[8] Although professionals are convinced of the value of bereavement counseling or related therapies, many elderly are not receptive to this type of intervention. Indirect services, such as encouraging the bereaved to contact friends and family members and teaching them creative uses of time, are effective in promoting adjustment.[38] Reinvestment in new relationships, development of new interests, and revival of old friendships and interests are signs of grief resolution.[1] Redefinition of roles is one of the main tasks of the bereavement process for the widowed[10] since death of a spouse almost always requires reallocation of some tasks.[3]

Faletti and associates[45] found a strong relationship between vocational status (working, retired, or seeking work) and adjustment to bereavement. His findings support the notion that engagement in activity promotes adaptation, perhaps because working requires attention focused on something other than loss. Wan[35] proposes that planning for the health or well-being of the elderly should focus on the development of social activities to reinforce positive feelings about functional capacities (see Fig. 24–1).

Little is known about how persons who are facing loss of self simulta-

Figure 24–1 This woman enjoyed needlework, and made whimsical figures that she left to staff in her residential facility, as well as her family prior to her death. Staff report thinking of her every time they pass one of these figures. (Courtesy of Menorah Park Nursing Home, Cleveland, Ohio.)

neously manage other roles, including family membership, community involvement, and work,[18] or how maintaining associated activities affects well-being. Although there have been anecdotal reports of positive effects resulting from the dying individual's ability to maintain activities,[46,47] there have been no systematic studies of this topic.

ACTIVITY-FOCUSED INTERVENTIONS

It is clear that activity is significantly affected by loss and that it is also an important part of adaptive responses to loss. As a result, it is natural to assume that interventions that are activity focused would be helpful to the bereaved.

Pizzi[48] suggests that intervention should enhance occupational performance and roles in lifestyle areas that are important to the individual, within limitations of the individual's biomedical status. This helps the person draw upon his or her intrinsic motivation to resume roles for both personal and social benefit.

Clearly, death threatens the life goals of the terminally ill person and his or her significant others.[48] Goals must be realigned, and new goals established and prioritized. The terminal patient must be helped to set priorities and maximize occupational roles and to problem-solve for this novel and never-before-explored situation. Pizzi[48] observes:

> Occupational therapists can emphasize that the dying are still living persons, with feelings, abilities, hopes and dreams. Our professional calling is to promote maximal adaptation and to maximize occupational roles in accordance with the needs and desires of our terminal patients.

In this context the role of the therapist is to encourage family to continue, to the extent possible, their normal activities. Intervention should be based on a clear understanding of the client's lifestyle before illness, including psychological resources, ability to manage time, attitudes toward control over temporal issues, roles played, and ways in which

the client felt useful or worthwhile. The assessment must also include a determination of family and social problems and of current limitations and precautionary measures that must be taken.[48,49] The goal is to develop a plan of care "in which the patient can accept the illness and death, yet remain as independent as possible.[49]

Oelrich[49] notes that generally suitable tasks or work can promote feeling of usefulness, although tasks may have to be limited to only familiar ones as ability to assimilate unfamiliar activities declines. Activities that structure the day for the client give it continuity. Whatever the activities, they should emphasize pleasurable experiences for the client and family and acknowledge the humorous side of everyday events.[49]

Gammage, McMahon, and Shanahan[50] suggest that learning to work with terminally ill clients involves the ability to elicit, confront, explore, and resolve one's own feelings about death; identify and understand the role of occupational therapist in this treatment; and design treatment interventions. They stress that learning should involve a staff group so that training moves beyond only "supportive" interventions that can "just as easily be done by any number of health professionals." Each health care professional must think through his or her unique contributions. The physical therapist, for example, may focus on decreasing pain and increasing mobility, enabling the occupational therapist to focus on assisting the client to use that mobility to accomplish desired activities, perhaps with the use of environmental modifications. Meanwhile, the social worker may talk with the client and family about their experiences and locate funding sources for the environmental modifications recommended by the occupational therapist.

Hospice Care

Marshall and Levy[18] suggest that the "dying career" does not begin with a diagnosis of terminal illness is made but when the person with the terminal illness recognizes that his or her life is finite and begins to estimate the amount of time left before death. With this awareness, often aided by reminiscence, can come a desire to plan for the remaining days and a more accepting orientation toward impending death. In hospice care, these goals are more explicit.

Hospice seeks to help people with life-threatening diseases adapt to changing life situations and to promote a caring community and therapeutic milieu for the ill and their care givers. In this setting, as in others, occupational therapy promotes involvement in daily life tasks and roles in work, leisure, and self-care, helping patients and families deal with problems related to loss of control, loss of role, loss of dignity, and feelings of isolation and withdrawal. After the patient's death, the therapist can provide support for the bereaved family and assist them in resuming old roles and assuming new roles necessitated by their loss.[51] At the same time, social workers, physical therapists, and nurses must remain involved to ensure that emotional, physical, and medical needs are addressed for the terminally ill patient, and that family concerns are addressed, as well.

Picard and Magno[52] explain that the hospice is concerned with adding life to the patient's remaining days, not adding days to the patient's remaining life. Once pain and other symptoms of terminal illness are controlled, the real problems of living arise, and they suggest that therapy:

> is about realizing that a person's integrity, equality, purpose, self-esteem, mastery and adaptation rest in his ability to be purposefully engaged in regular and familiar life experiences, whether he has terminal cancer or any other problem.

The dying person may ask: "What shall I do tomorrow while I'm waiting to die?" "How can I maintain as much independence as possible even while my body grows weaker each day?"[49] Working together, health care providers can help clients address these questions.

In a study of 50 people over 2 years in England and the United States, Tigges and Sherman[47] found that 40 of them identified their greatest need as being independent in self-care. Forty-six stated that their second most important need was to resume their occupational role as spouse, parent, and/or other worker. Based on these findings, they suggest that in the hospice setting, intervention should concentrate on making the most of the patient's capacity and independence in self-care, work, and play within constraints of physical limitations.

Locus of control varies from person to person and should be considered in intervention. For people who have always been dependent, controlling the dying process may not be an important goal, but for others maintaining independence and control in self-care, work, and play may be essential to the quality of their lives. The hospice philosophy mirrors this notion in that it emphasizes that the areas where control should be improved or maintained should be determined by the individual.[48]

Working with Families

Families of dying patients may need help in adapting to role changes, new schedules, alternate financial resources, child care, meals, and household chores. Health care providers can facilitate adjustment of the family to these new roles and act as a resource to facilitate the family's search for new vocational, intellectual, and social pursuits.[50] Ideally, this will be done prior to the death since it is helpful if occupational roles can be gradually relinquished in lieu of accepting the personal-social role of the dying person.

In both hospice settings and in working with the bereaved, interdisciplinary intervention is most likely to be effective. Physical therapists can assist in maximizing mobility in the terminally ill patient, providing both real and perceived maximization of activity-related physical capacity. Social workers are essential links to the array of social services that may be helpful to the individual. Further, they often have the kind of background that makes them most effective in working with families to deal with the emotions surrounding loss. Nurses can monitor physical status and ensure that the client is kept as comfortable as possible. All health care professionals must be sensitive to the need of the individual to recognize and deal with loss.

SUMMARY

Work with the dying and their families can be depressing and sometimes frustrating for health care professionals. It can also be a source of great satisfaction, as it provides an opportunity to change an experience from one of fear and sadness to one of acceptance and fulfillment. It is a great gift to clients and their families to enhance their experiences during their final days together.

REVIEW QUESTIONS

1. *In what ways do the losses experienced by the elderly differ from those experienced by younger people?*

2. *How are activity and the experience of loss related in the lives of older adults?*

3. *What is the role of activity in adjustment to loss?*

4. *What unique contributions can activity-based interventions make to a plan of care for an elderly person who has experienced the loss of a spouse or adult child? For an elderly person with a terminal illness?*

5. *There has been little exploration of the role of activity in dealing with loss outside the areas of death and dying. With what other losses occurring in later life could activity-focused therapy provide management assistance?*

REFERENCES

1. Garrett, JD: Multiple losses in older adults. Journal of Gerontological Nursing 13(8):8–12, 1987.
2. Jackson, CO: Introduction. In Jackson, CO, (ed): Passing the Vision of Death in America. Greenwood Press, Westport, CT, 1977, pp 3–6.
3. Kalish, RA: Older people and grief. Generations 2(spring):33–38, 1987.
4. Herth, K: Relationship of hope, coping styles, concurrent losses, and setting to grief resolution in the elderly widow(er). Research in Nursing and Health 13:109–117, 1990.
5. Kalish, RA: The effects of death upon the family. In Pearson, L (ed): Death and Dying. Press of Case Western Reserve University, Cleveland, 1969, pp 76–107.
6. Kastenbaum, R: Dying they live: St. Christopher's hospice. In Feilfel, H (ed): New Meanings of Death. McGraw-Hill, New York, 1977, p 177.
7. Brink, TL: The grieving patient in later life. Psychotherapy-Patient 2(1):117–127, 1985.
8. Aiken, LR: Dying, Death, and Bereavement. Allyn and Bacon, Boston, 1985.
9. Lesher, EL and Bergey, KJ: Bereaved elderly mothers: Changes in health, functional activities, family cohesion, and psychological well-being. International Journal of Aging and Human Development 26(2):81–90, 1988.
10. Osterweis, M, Solomon, F and Green, M (eds): Bereavement: Reactions, Consequences, and Care. National Academy Press, Washington, DC, 1984.
11. Brubaker, E: Older parents' reactions to the death of adult children: Implications for practice. Journal of Gerontological Social Work 9(1):35–48, 1985.
12. Kalish, RA and Visher, E: Grandparents of divorce. Journal of Divorce 5:127–140, 1985.
13. Conway, P: Losses and grief in old age. Social Casework: The Journal of Contemporary Social Work 69(9):541–549, Nov 1988.
14. Stewart, CS, Thrush, JC, Paulus, GS and Hafner, P; The elderly adjustment to the loss of a companion animal: People-pet dependency. Death Studies 9:383–393, 1985.
15. Blauner, R: Death and social structure. In Jackson, CO (ed): Passing the Vision of Death in America. Greenwood Press, Westport, CT, 1977, pp 174–209.
16. Kalish, RA: Death and dying. In Silverman, P (ed): The Elderly As Modern Pioneers. Indiana University Press, Bloomington, 1987, pp 389–405.
17. Wass, H and Myers, JE: Psychosocial aspects of death among the elderly: A review of the literature. Personnel and Guidance Journal 61(3):131–137, Nov 1982.
18. Marshall, VW and levy, JA: Aging and dying. In George, LK and Binstock, RH (eds): Handbook of Aging and the Social Sciences, ed 3. Academic Press, San Diego, 1990, pp 245–260.
19. Aries, P: Forbidden death. In Jackson, CO (ed): Passing the Vision of Death in America. Greenwood Press, Westport, CT, 1977, pp 148–152.
20. Kalish, RA and Reynolds, DK: Death and Ethnicity: A Psychocultural Study. Baywood, Farmingdale, NY, 1981.

21. Kielhofner, G and Burke, JP: Components and determinants of human occupation. In Kielhofner, G (ed): A Model of Human Occupation: Theory and Application. Baltimore, Williams & Wilkins, 1985, pp 12–36.

22. Breckenridge, JN, Gallagher, D, Thompson, LW and Peter, J: Characteristic depressive symptoms of bereaved elders. Journal of Gerontology 41(2):163–68, 1986.

23. Balkwell, C: Transition to widowhood: A review of the literature. Family Relations 30:117–27, 1981.

24. Richter, JM: Crisis of mate loss in the elderly. Advances in Nursing Science 6(4):45–54, July 1984.

25. Worden, JW: Grief Counseling and Grief Therapy. Springer, New York, 1982.

26. Thompson, LW, Gallagher, D, Cover, H, Gilewski, M and Peterson, J: Effects of bereavement on symptoms of psychopathology in older men and women. In Lund, DA (ed): Older Bereaved Spouses: Research with Practical Applications. Hemisphere Publishing, New York, 1989, pp 17–24.

27. Osterweis, M: Bereavement and the elderly. Aging 348:8–13 and 41, 1985.

28. Moos, RH and Finney, JW: A systems perspective on problem drinking among older adults. In Maddox, G, Robins, LN and Rosenberg, N (eds): Nature and Extent of Alcohol Problems among the Elderly. Springer, New York, 1986, pp 151–172.

29. Holzer, CE, III, Robins, LN, Myers, JK, Weissman, MN, Tischler, GL, Leaf, PJ, Anthony, J and Bednarski, PB: Antecedents and correlates of alcohol abuse and dependence in the elderly. In Maddox, G, Robins, LN, and Rosenberg, N (eds): Nature and Extent of Alcohol Problems among the Elderly. Springer, New York, 1986, pp 217–244.

30. Moss, MS and Moss, SZ: Some aspects of the elderly widow(er)'s persistent tie with the deceased spouse. OMEGA—Journal of Death and Dying 15(3):195–206, 1984–1985.

31. Kastenbaum, R: Death, Society and Human Experiences. CV Mosby, St. Louis, 1977.

32. Thompson, LW, Breckenridge, JN, Gallagher, D and Peterson, J: Effects of bereavement on self-perceptions of physical health in elderly widows and widowers. Journal of Gerontology 39(3):309–314, 1984.

33. Gramlich, E: Recognition and management of grief in elderly patients. Geriatrics 23(7):87–92, 1978.

34. Kastenbaum, R: Death and bereavement in later life. In Kutscher, AH (ed): Death and Bereavement. Charles C. Thomas, Springfield, IL, 1969.

35. Wan, T: Well-Being for the Elderly. Lexington Books, DC Heath, Lexington, MA, 1985.

36. Lund, DA: Conclusions about bereavement in later life and implications for interventions and future research. In Lund, DA (ed): Older Bereaved Spouses: Research with Practical Applications. Hemisphere, New York, 1989, pp 217–231.

37. Kitson, GC and Roach, MJ: Independence and social and psychological adjustment in widowhood and divorce. In Lund, DA (ed): Older Bereaved Spouses: Research with Practical Applications. Hemisphere, New York, 1989, pp 167–183.

38. Wass, H and Myers, JE: Death and dying: Issues for educational gerontologists. Educational Gerontology 10:65–81, 1984.

39. Bass, DM and Bowman, K: The transition from caregiving to bereavement: The relationship of care-related strain and adjustment to death. GSA Presentation. San Francisco, Nov 1988.

40. Bass, DM, Bowman, K and Noelker, LS: The influence of caregiving and bereavement support on adjusting to an older relative's death. Gerontologist 31(1):32–42, 1991.

41. Bowman, L: The effects of city civilization. In Jackson, CO (ed): Passing the Vision of Death in America. Greenwood Press, Westport, CT, 1977, pp 153–173.

42. Lund, DA, Caserta, MS and Dimond, MF: Impact of spousal bereavement on the subjective well-being of older adults. In Lund, DA (ed): Older Bereaved Spouses: Research with Practical Applications. Hemisphere, New York, 1989, pp 9–15.

43. Lund, DA, Caserta, MS and Dimond, MF: Gender differences through two years of bereavement among the elderly. Gerontologist 26:314–320, 1986.

44. Barclay, T and McDougall, M: Older-worker programs. Generations 14(1):53–54, 1990.

45. Faletti, MV, Gibbs, JM, Clark, MC, Pruchno, RA and Berman, EA: Longitudinal course of bereavement in older adults. In Lund, DA (ed): Older Bereaved Spouses: Research with Practical Applications. Hemisphere, New York, 1989, pp 37–51.

46. Folts, D, Tigges, K and Weisman, T: Occupational therapy in hospice home care: A student tutorial. The American Journal of Occupational Therapy 40(9):623–628, 1986.

47. Tigges, KN and Sherman, LM: The treatment of the hospice patient: From occupational history to occupational role. American Journal of Occupational Therapy 37(4):235–238, 1983.

48. Pizzi, MA: Occupational therapy in hospice care. American Journal of Occupational Therapy 38(4):252–257, 1984.

49. Oelrich, M: The patient with a fatal illness. American Journal of Occupational Therapy 28(7):429–432, 1974.

50. Gammage, SL, McMahon, PS and Shanahan, PM: The occupational therapist and terminal illness: Learning to cope with death. American Journal of Occupational Therapy 30(5):294–299, 1976.

51. Commission on Practice and the Hospice Task Force of the American Occupational Therapy Association: Occupational therapy and hospice. American Journal of Occupational Therapy 40(12):839–840, 1986.

52. Picard, HB and Magno, JB: The role of occupational therapy in hospice care. American Journal of Occupational Therapy 36(9):597–598, 1982.

Glossary

Absorption: The degree to which an activity causes an individual to become totally focused.

Accessibility: Ability to make use of something; enter, approach or communicate.

Acculturation: A process by which individuals increasingly adopt values, beliefs, attitudes, and behaviors that characterize a culture different from the culture of their birth, typically as a result of immigration or increasing contact with the new culture.

Activities of Daily Living (ADL): Basic activities that support survival, including eating, bathing, toileting, and hygiene and grooming.

Activity Consultant: A professional who has a minimum of a bachelor's, master's, or doctoral degree in therapeutic recreation and leisure activities or related field; and who is licensed or registered, if applicable, in the state in which he or she practices; and is eligible for certification as an activity professional by a recognized accrediting body or eligible for registration as a therapeutic recreational therapist by the National Therapeutic Recreation Society (NTRS); and has at least 4 years of experience in a patient activities program in a health care setting.

Activity Coordinator: A professional who has a minimum of a bachelor's degree in therapeutic recreation and leisure activities or related field; and who is licensed or registered, if applicable, in the state in which he or she practices; and is eligible for certification as an activity professional by a recognized accrediting body or eligible for registration as a therapeutic recreational therapist by the National Therapeutic Recreation Society (NTRS); and has at least 3 years of experience directing a social or recreational program in a patient activities program in a health care setting.

Activity Director: A professional who has a minimum of an associate's degree in therapeutic recreation and leisure activities or related field and has 2 years of experience in a social or recreational program in a patient activities program in a health care setting.

Activity/Exercise Prescription: Prescription based on the specific type of activity/exercise, its intensity, frequency, duration, and course of training.

Adaptation: Adjustment to environmental conditions. When used to describe visual behavior, adaptation is the ability of the eye to adjust to increases and decreases in the amount of illumination in the environment.

Aerobic Conditioning or Adaptation: Improved aerobic capacity or endurance secondary to lower resting and submaximal heart rate, blood pressure, rate pressure product, perceived exertion, cardiac output and overall cardiac work, and increased stroke volume, as well as an increased number of oxidative enzymes within the tissue that promotes oxygen extraction.

Aerobic Metabolism: Metabolic processes requiring oxygen as in periods of physiological steady-state exercise.

Affective: Pertaining to a feeling or mental state.

Affective Illness: A general psychiatric term for the mood disorder, including the depressive and bipolar syndromes.

Afferent Nerve: Nerves that transmit impulses from the periphery toward the central nervous system.

Age-Associated Memory Impairment (AAMI): Those changes in memory that are commonly seen in healthy, well-functioning older adults in the absence of any form of physical illness or central nervous system disease.

Age Related Macular Degeneration (ARMD): A degeneration of an area 3 mm temporal to the optic disc, resulting in the deterioration of the retina and supportive structures in as many as 30 percent of the population between the ages of 75 and 81 years.

Alzheimer's Disease: The main cause of dementia, a disease of unknown etiology characterized by neurofibrillary plaques and tangles, and the presence of excess amounts of beta amyloid protein in the brain.

Anaerobic Conditioning or Adaptation: Those physiologic adaptations that increase anaerobic performance, i.e., capacity to tolerate oxygen debt and high circulating lactate levels.

Anaerobic Metabolism: Metabolic processes not requiring oxygen as in short periods of strenuous sprint-type exercise.

Anticipatory Grieving: Experience of emotional distress in response to an expected loss that has not yet occurred.

Apophyseal Joints: Facet joints.

Assessment: An evaluative process intended to identify and describe self-care problems.

Assistive Device: Used interchangeably with *assistive technology.*

Assistive Technology: Any item, piece of equipment, or product system, whether acquired commercially off the shelf, customized, or modified, that is used to increase, maintain, or improve functional capabilities of individuals with disabilities.

Assistive Technology Device: Used interchangeably with *assistive technology.*

Astigmatism: An error of refraction in which a ray of light is not sharply focused on the retina.

Astrocytes: A star-shaped neuroglia cell possessing many branching processes.

Ataxia: A general term, used to describe uncoordinated movement, which may influence gait, posture, and patterns of movement.

Atrophy: Decrease in size of a normally developed organ or tissue.

Auditory Processing Deficits: A disorder characterized by difficulty interpreting auditory input at the central nervous system level.

Baroreflex Activity: A physiological mechanism by which blood pressure is regulated.

Bed-Fast: A condition in which one is confined to bed and not able to walk, sit, or move about independently.

Behavioral: Of or related to the actions of individuals or groups in response to stimuli.

Bereavement: The state or fact of being deprived by loss.

Biopsychosocial: Characterized by biological, psychological, and social factors that interact with each other.

Bipolar Illness: A psychiatric disorder characterized by the presence of at least one manic episode and generally at least one episode of depression.

Bradykinesia: Abnormally slow movement.

Capacity: The ability to perform a task, in contrast to the performance of a task.

Caregiver: The professional or family member who provides care for a patient or client.

Cataracts: Opacity of the lens of the eye, its capsule, or both.

Cerebellum: A portion of the brain forming the largest part of the rhombencephalon. Its function appears to be to blend and coordinate motion of the various muscles in voluntary movement.

Chemosensory: Detection of a chemical by sensory means.

Cholinergic: An agent producing effects resembling those of stimulation of the para-sympathetic nerve supply of a part; nerve endings that liberate acetylcholine.

Chorea: A nervous condition producing ceaseless, rapid, and jerky involuntary movements.

Choroid Plexus: Vascular fringelike folds in the pia mater in the third, fourth, and lateral ventricles of the brain, concerned with formation of cerebrospinal fluid.

Chronic: Marked by long duration or frequent recurrence.

Cochlea: The inner ear, a portion of the temporal bone which houses the membranous and bony labyrinths and includes the essential organs of hearing and balance.

Cognition: All of the mental processes involved in perception, recognition, comprehension, and reasoning.

Cognitive: Of, relating to, or involving the act or process of knowing, including perceiving, thinking, and remembering.

Cohort: A group of persons sharing a particular statistical or demographic characteristic, such as being born within a certain time period.

Cohort Effect: Common historical events experienced by a generation that shape beliefs and/or behaviors.

Comprehension: A behavior that represents the ability to understand a stimulus presented through one of the sensory organs. Comprehension is preceded by reception and perception.

Compulsory Activity: An activity that must be accomplished to ensure survival.

Concentric Muscle Contraction: An overall shortening of the muscle as it generates tension and contracts.

Conductive Hearing Loss: A hearing loss caused by disease, defect of the external or middle ear, or both. It is frequently caused by a lesion to the tympanic membrane (ear drum) or ossicle (three bones of the middle ear). The auditory system has trouble conducting sound as a result of this disorder.

Control: The ability to choose activities and determine outcome.

Coping: A person's cognitive and behavioral efforts to manage specific demands.*

Cross-Sectional Design: A research strategy in which individuals of different ages are compared at one point in time.

Cross-Sequential Design: A research strategy in which different age groups are tested at repeated intervals over an extended period of time.

Crystallized Intelligence: A form of intelligence resulting from the accumulation of knowledge and information.

Culture (1): A system of beliefs, knowledge, and patterns of customary behavior.

Culture (2): A way of doing activities, ways of thinking, expressing thoughts, social skills, roles, and values.

Cytoplasm: The protoplasm of a cell surrounding the nucleus.

Decibel: A unit used to measure the intensity, or loudness, of sound, commonly the intensity above the threshold of normal hearing.

Deconditioning: A consequence of inactivity, causing reductions in endurance and strength.

Dementia: A deterioration in intellectual capacities that has a significant negative impact on functioning.

Dendrite: A branched protoplasmic process of a neuron that conducts impulses to the cell body. There are usually several to a cell forming synaptic connections with other neurons.

---

*Folkman, S: Personal control and stress and coping processes: A theoretical analysis. Journal of Personality and Social Psychology 46:839–852, 1984.

Diabetic Retinopathy: Changes in the retina due to diabetes mellitus, characterized by small aneurysms, hemorrhages, and yellowish exudates. Dilation of the retinal veins may also occur.

Disability: A model of dysfunction that emphasizes the limitations of a person's ability to carry out personal, social, and familial responsibilities caused by health problems.

Disability Impact Continuum: A visual representation of the effects of disability in a range from totally functional to totally dysfunctional.

Disease Model: A model of disease based on the idea that specific biological and organismic factors determine the nature and extent of disease.

Disease Prevention: A set of activities designed to minimize the development of illness or disease.

Disengagement: The degree to which an activity enables an individual to lose awareness of everyday concerns.

Domain: A symbolic unit of culture.

Dopaminergic: Pertains to tissues or organs accepted by dopamine, a neurotransmitter in the central nervous system.

Dysthymic Disorder: A less severe but longer lasting form of depression, in which the individual is mildly depressed but generally able to function, for at least a period of 2 years.

Eanda: The Herero name for a king group identified by its relationships through the maternal line.

Eccentric Muscle Contraction: An overall lengthening of the muscle as it develops tension and contracts to control motion performed by an outside force.

Ecological Validity: The meaningfulness of materials.

Efferent Nerve: Any nerve that carries impulses from the central nervous system or toward the periphery; a motor nerve is an example.

Electroconvulsive Therapy (ECT): A form of treatment for severe depression in which electrical current is passed through the patient's head.

Encoding Process: The taking in of information into the memory system and the translation of it into usable form.

Environmental Control Devices: Devices designed primarily for the disabled, which enable the individual to operate any appliance that runs on electricity, including radios, televisions, computers, telephones, etc.

Environmental Docility Hypothesis: The theory that elderly individuals are primarily responsive to the demands of the environment, rather than active in changing the environment to meet their needs.

Electroencephalography (EEG): The recording and study of the electrical impulses of the brain.

Electromyography (EMG): The recording and study of the electrical activities of muscle.

Environmental Fit: The degree to which the demands of the environment match the abilities of the individual.

Environmental Interventions: Interventions that modify the environment to make it easier to manage.

Environmental Press: The demand of the environment; the degree to which the environment requires certain abilities on the part of the individual.

Equilibrium: A state of balance between opposing forces or influences. Physical equilibrium is the state of balance required for walking, standing, or sitting.

Ethnography (1): The systematic search for the parts of a culture and their relationships as conceptualized by informants.

Ethnography (2): A qualitative study of a culture, typically involving observation and interview to obtain a comprehensive view of the culture's activities, structure, values, and beliefs.

Excess Disability: A condition in which an individual is functionally impaired beyond the extent predicted by the severity of his or her illness.

Exteroceptor: Sense organ adapted for the reception of stimuli from outside the body.

Extrapyramidal Motor System: Outside the pyramidal tracts of the central nervous system. The system is important in maintenance of balance and muscle tone.

Fall: An episode in which an individual loses upright position unexpectedly and makes contact with the ground.

Fear of Falling (Ptophobia, Fallaphobia, 3-F Syndrome): A syndrome characterized by activity restrictions based on concern that the activity might lead to a fall.

Fibrillary Tangles: Abnormal neurofibers.

Fluid Intelligence: A form of intelligence that is related to the use and manipulation of new information and problem solving.

Framing: Developing a personal context for identified beliefs and actions.

Functional Capacity: Capacity to perform aerobic work; maximal aerobic power defined by maximum oxygen consumption.

Functional Capacity Reserve: Aerobic capacity in excess of that required for functional performance.

Functional Dependence: The inability to attend to one's own needs, including the basic activities of daily living.

Functional Performance: Ability to perform functional activities, i.e., activities of daily living.

Functional Performance Threshold: That level of physiologic adaptation required to perform one's activities of daily living.

Glaucomas: A group of diseases of the eye characterized by increased intraocular pressure.

Glia: The non-nerve, or supporting, tissue of the brain and spinal cord.

Grading: An activity chosen that matches the capabilities of the individual. As the individual masters an activity, then a slightly more difficult activity is introduced.

Grief: Feelings in response to bereavement.

Guttman Scale: A hierarchical scale on which an individual who can accomplish one item can, by definition, accomplish all items that fall before (or below) it on the scale.

Gyrus (*pl.* Gyri): One of the convolutions of the cerebral hemispheres of the brain.

Gyrus Rectus: A cerebral convolution in the orbital aspect of the frontal lobe.

Halstead-Reitan Test: A group of tests used in the neuropsychological assessment of cognitive functions.

Health: A state of well being; optimal capacity for effective performance of valued tasks.

Health Promotion: A set of activities designed to maximize wellness or function.

High-Density Network: A support system consisting of family members, helpful in coping with normative life crises.

High Tech: Devices that often contain micro-processors, including computers, print enlargement systems, and environmental control units.

Home Management: Higher order skills involved in the ability to live independently in the community, including cooking and money management; also called instrumental activities of daily living (IADL).

Home Management Tasks: Those tasks that are associated with human needs for food, clothing, shelter, health care, and social.

Hospice: A model of care for the terminally ill emphasizing control of pain and other disease symptoms, emotional support, and the involvement of an interdisciplinary team which includes physicians, nurses, psychologists, social workers, allied health professionals, and lay volunteers.

Hydrocephalus: A condition characterized by enlargement of the cranium caused by abnormal accumulation of cerebrospinal fluid within the cerebral ventricular system; also called *water on the brain*.

Hypertrophy: Increase in volume of a tissue or organ produced entirely by enlargement of existing cells.

Hypokinesis: Abnormally diminished motor activity to a stimulus.

Idiopathic: A primary disease that occurs without a known cause.

Industrial Gerontology: The study of older adults as workers.

Instrumental Activities of Daily Living (IADL): Higher order activities which support independence, including housekeeping, shopping, and budgeting and money management.

Intelligence: A complex concept that includes verbal ability, problem-solving skills, and the ability to learn from and adapt to the experiences of everyday life.

Interrupted Exercise Test or Training Protocol: Protocol designed for an individual with low functional work capacity; high and low demand work rates are alternated, or low demand work rates are alternated with rest periods. The net result is an increase in the cumulative amount of work performed compared with a single uninterrupted exercise test or training protocol.

Isokinetic Exercise: Contraction of a muscle during which the force exerted while the muscle shortens is maximal.

Isometric Exercise: Active exercise performed against stable resistance without change in the length of the muscle.

Isotonic Exercise: Active exercise with appreciable change in the force of the muscular contraction; shortening of the muscle occurs.

Key Indicators: Measures of quality of care and quality of life which focus on care given to residents, the results (outcome) of such care, and the manner (process) in which the care is given, i.e., use of certain drugs, and incidence of infections and decubiti.

Kinesthesis: Also called *kinesthesia*; the proprioceptive sense of the perception of movement, weight, resistance and position of the body in space.

Kyphosis: Exaggeration or angulation of the normal posterior curve of the thoracic spine, also called *hunchback*.

Learned Helplessness: A condition, often linked to depression, in which an individual experiences decreased motivation, apathy, and withdrawal as a result of an unresponsive environment.

Leisure: Experiences characterized by choice on the part of the individual, personal control, internal motivation, disengagement from the stresses of everyday life, and total absorption.

Lifeworld: The everyday context of people's lives.

Lipofuscin Granules: A yellow-to-brown pigment found particularly in muscle, heart, liver and nerve cells; it is the product of cellular wear and tear and accumulates in lysosomes with age.

Locus Ceruleus: A pigmented eminence in the superior angle of the floor of the fourth ventricle of the brain.

Longitudinal Design: Research strategy in which the same individuals are studied over a period of time, usually several years or more.

Low-Density Network: Friends that are helpful with non-normative life crises.

Low Tech: Devices traditionally used, which do not have electronic components, including button hooks, reachers, etc.

Low Vision: A term describing a serious visual loss, uncorrectable with medical or surgical intervention, or with eyeglasses. This term is used to describe a person's problem, not the underlying pathology or etiology.

Masked Depression: The form of depression in older adults in which the emotional symptoms are "masked" or hidden by complaints of physical illness or discomfort.

Matrilineage: Kin relationships which follow through the maternal line.

Maximum Exercise Test: An exercise test that increases in work rate over time. The end point is the maintenance or decrement of maximum oxygen consumption with progressive increases in work rate.

Measurement: A method of collecting data that uses questioning and observing and assigns numerical values to the indicators of task performance yielded by these methods for the purpose of estimating self-care status.

Mechanoreceptor: A nerve ending sensitive to mechanical pressure or distortions, as those responding to touch and muscle contraction.

Medical World: The technical-scientific assumptions of medical practice.

Memory: The retention of information over time.

Metabolic Equivalent for Oxygen (MET): 1 MET is equal to the resting oxygen requirement of 3.5 ml O_2/kg of body weight/min; by convention, activities and different exercise work rates are expressed as multiples of resting oxygen requirement.

Mnemonics: Techniques designed to make memory more efficient.

Mobility Tasks: Those that involve moving the body from one position or place to another.

Monitoring: The systematic and ongoing collection and organization of data related to the indicators of the quality and appropriateness of important aspects of care and the comparison of the level of performance with thresholds for evaluation to determine the need for evaluation.

Mourning: Behaviors in response to bereavement.

Myofibril: One of the slender threads of a muscle fiber that may be the contractile element. It is composed of numerous myofilaments.

Myofilament: Any of the ultramicroscopic thread-like structures composing the myofibrils of striated muscle fibers.

Naming: The process of labeling particular attitudes and actions.

Near Fall: An episode in which an individual loses upright position, but avoids making contact with the ground by grabbing an object, or using other avoidance techniques.

Neuroplasticity: The ability of the nervous system to change or adapt.

Neurotransmitter: A substance that is released from the axon terminal of a presynaptic neuron on excitation; it travels across the synaptic cleft to either excite or inhibit the target cell.

Norms: Rules defining expected, required, or acceptable behavior in particular circumstances.

Observation: A method of collecting data that relies on watching patients perform tasks under natural or prompted conditions.

Occupational: An activity in which one engages.

Old-Old: Individuals who are 76 years of age or older.

Ombudsman: A state representative or a representative of a public agency or a private nonprofit organization (which is not responsible for licensing or certifying long-term care services) who (1) investigates and resolves complaints made by or on behalf of older individuals who are residents of long-term-care facilities; (2) monitors the development and implementation laws, regulations, and policies; and (3) provides information as appropriate to public agencies regarding the problems of older individuals residing in long-term-care facilities, etc.

Ordinal Scale: Classification scheme that rates observations in terms of relationships between items.

Orthosis: An orthopedic appliance or apparatus used to support, align, prevent, or correct deformities or to improve function of moveable parts of the body.

Orthostatic Hypotension: The failure of blood pressure to increase in response to changes in posture.

Ototoxic: The property of a substance, including medication, which may cause damage to the auditory system.

Outcome Measurement: Examination of the results of a service in order to determine the quality of the service provided.

Oxygen Transport Pathway: The pathway consisting of multiple steps that is responsible for the movement of oxygen from the atmosphere to the working tissues to effect tissue oxygenation.

Paralysis Agitans: A disease of middle and late life marked by weakness, delay of voluntary motion, a peculiar festinating gait, and muscular contraction, causing unusual but characteristic positions of the limbs and head.

Passive Suicide: Behaviors that will, over a period of time, result in premature death, such as refusing to take necessary medications, failure to follow a prescribed diet, or refusing to eat.

Pastoralism: A life style that involves herding and farming as the primary means of providing food.

Patient Education: Learning activities designed to assist people who are having experience with illness or disease in making changes in their behavior conducive to health.

Patrilineage: Kin relationships which follow through the paternal lines.

Peak Exercise Test: An exercise test that is terminated when the individual can go no farther or is terminated by the tester in the event of chest pain, cardiac irregularities, etc. This test does not meet the criterion of a maximum exercise test.

Perception: The complex process by which an organism interprets sensory input so that it acquires meaning.

Perceptual Abilities: The selection, integration, and interpretation of sensory stimuli from the body and the surrounding environment.

Performance: Routine task behavior, in contrast to capacity which is the ability to perform a task.

Personal Self-Care Tasks: Those that involve taking care of bodily-oriented, fundamental, personal needs, like feeding and toileting.

Phonemic Regression: Commonly found in older adults, this is the term used to describe an individual's poorer understanding of phonemes, or speech sounds, in the presence of better understanding of nonspeech sounds. The auditory system, in phonemic regression, appears to be selectively damaged for speech sounds.

Physiatrist: A physician who specializes in physical medicine and rehabilitation.

Physical Assistance: Provision of physical support in accomplishing an activity.

Physical Guidance: Physical contact with an individual to encourage one component of the activity.

Postcentral Gyrus: The gyrus immediately posterior to the central sulcus of the cerebrum. It contains most of the general sensory area of the brain.

Postural Sway: The extent to which an individual moves anteroposteriorally or laterally while maintaining upright posture. Also, small oscillating movements of the body over the feet during bipedal standing.

Precentral Gyrus: The gyrus immediately anterior to the central sulcus of the cerebrum. It contains the pyramidal areas.

Presbycusis: Progressive perceptive hearing loss occurring with age.

Presbyopia: Defect of vision in advancing age involving loss of accommodation of the lens of the eye usually resulting in hyperopia or farsightedness.

Press: Demands placed on the individual by the environment.

Process Management: Administration of a program based on examination of process as well as outcomes.

Process Measurement: The examination of methods of providing a service in order to evaluate the quality of the service provided.

Productivity: Activities which are recognized by society as making an economic contribution. May include paid employment, volunteer work, or homemaking or caregiving activities to which a monetary value can be fixed.

Proprioception: Sensation and awareness of body positions and movements.

Proprioceptors: Sensory receptors responsible for deep sensations. They occur chiefly in muscles, tendons, ligaments, joints, fascia, and the labyrinth.

Pseudodementia: A term used to describe a form of depression in which the presenting symptoms focus almost entirely on signs of cognitive impairment, including poor memory and decreased attention and concentration. This term has generally been replaced by the phrase *cognitive deficits of depression.*

Psychomotor: A response involving both psychological and motor components.

Psychomotor Retardation: A symptom of depression in which the individual's thought and speech processes, along with movements, are markedly slowed.

Psychotropic: The property in a medication of having an effect on psychological functioning.

Purkinje's Cells: Large, branched cells of the middle layer of the brain.

Quality of Life: Includes meeting the needs of physical well being (material comforts, health and hygiene, and security); interpersonal relations (relationships with relatives, intimate relationships and community involvement); personal development (intellectual development, self-expression, gainful activity and self-awareness); recreation (socializing, passive recreation and active recreation); spirituality (self-understanding and symbolic).

Questioning: A method of collecting data that relies on asking questions of patients or their proxies, verbally or in writing.

Rehabilitation: A process of intervening to assist an individual to regain previous function lost as a result of an illness or injury.

Rehabilitation Specialist: An occupational or physical therapist specialized in the application of exercise physiological principles in the prevention and remediation of physiological dysfunction.

Rigidity: Increase in muscle tone that results in greater resistance to passive movement.

Role: Set of expectations governing the behavior of persons holding a particular position in society.

Scoliosis: Lateral curvature of the spine; it may or may not include rotation or deformity of the vertebrae.

Screening: An evaluative process intended to differentiate those people who have or potentially have problems in self-care performance from those who do not.

Self-Health Care: Any form of health care, including prevention, evaluation, and treatment, which is undertaken by a lay person without professional intervention.

Senilicide: Killing of older individuals, sometimes a culturally prescribed effort to maximize resources to enable younger individuals to survive.

Sensation: The behavioral ability of an end organ, or sense organ, such as the ear or eye, to receive an external stimuli and send this information, via specialized sensory cells and sensory nerve fibers, from the peripheral nervous system to the central nervous system. At the level of sensation, a peripheral nervous system behavior, the organism is not yet "aware" that a signal has been received.

Sensorineural Hearing Loss: Hearing loss due to damage or disease in the cochlea or auditory nervous system pathway beyond the cochlea. This is the most common type of hearing loss in the elderly.

Set Shifting: The ability to alternate between two or more tasks or concepts.

Skin-Fold Measurements: Measurements obtained through the use of calibrated calipers to evaluate nutritional status by estimating the amount of subcutaneous fat.

Social Network: The system of informal support by family, friends and neighbors.

Somatic: Pertaining to or characterizing the body as distinguished from the mind.

Somesthesis: Also called *somesthesia*. The awareness of bodily sensations, or consciousness of the body.

Spondylosis: Ankylosis of a vertebral joint; a general term for degenerative changes in the spin.

Standby Assistance: Provision of supervision as a precautionary measure.

Stretch Reflexes: The contraction of a muscle as a result of a pull exerted upon the tendon of the responding muscle; they are important for maintenance of posture.

Substantia Nigra: The layer of gray substance separating the tegmentum of the midbrain from the crus cerebri.

Subsystem: A network of interrelated elements that are part of a system.

Synapse: The point of junction between two neurons in a neural pathway, where the termination of the axon of one neuron comes into close proximity with the cell body or dendrites of another. At this point, where the relationship of the two neurons is one of contact only, the impulse traveling in the first neuron initiates an impulse in the second neuron.

System: A collective entity bound by a group of interrelated elements.

Target or Therapeutic Range: A range of values of different physiological parameters, frequently including heart rate, blood pressure, and rating of exertion that define the level of the exercise stimulus and is consistent with eliciting the therapeutic response of interest, i.e., maximizes the therapeutic benefit and minimizes the risk.

Temporal Gyri: Three gyri (superior, middle, and inferior) located on the lateral surface of the temporal lobe of the brain.

Therapeutic Relationship: A relationship that seeks to promote the cure or management of disease and ill health.

Threshold Sensitivity: The lowest level of sensitivity capable of producing a response or making a physical impression.

Torque: A force producing rotary motion.

Transferring Activities: A transfer is the shifting of an individual from one surface to another or from one object to another by means of a specified pattern of movements that are safe and efficient.

Tremor: An involuntary trembling of the body or limbs resulting from alternate contractions of opposing muscles.

Tricyclic Antidepressant: A class of medications widely used in the treatment of the depressive disorders.

Universal Design: The design of a device intended to make function easier for all individuals, not just those with handicaps, including "smart houses" and remote controls.

Valgus: A deformity of a body part in which the angulation is away from the midline of the body.

Varus: A deformity of a body part in which the angulation of the part is toward the midline of the body.

Vibratory Sense: The ability to perceive vibrations transmitted through the skin to deep tissues; usually tested by placing a vibrating fork over bony prominences.

Verbal Guidance: Verbal instructions that assist in the accomplishment of a task.

Vocational: Pertaining to a skill or trade to be pursued as a career.

Wechsler Adult Intelligence Scale (WAIS) and Wechsler Adult Intelligence Scale Revised (WAIS-R): Intelligence tests that emphasize performance and verbal skills and give separate scores for subtests in vocabulary, arithmetic, memory span, assembly of objects, and other abilities.

Young-Old: Individuals who are 55 to 75 years of age.

Index

A "t" following a page number indicates a table; an "f" indicates a figure.